Marketing Analytics

Data-Driven Techniques with Microsoft® Excel®

Wayne L. Winston

Marketing Analytics: Data-Driven Techniques with Microsoft® Excel®

Published by
John Wiley & Sons, Inc.
10475 Crosspoint Boulevard
Indianapolis, IN 46256
www.wiley.com

Copyright © 2014 by Wayne L. Winston

Published by John Wiley & Sons, Inc., Indianapolis, Indiana

Published simultaneously in Canada

ISBN: 978-1-118-37343-9
ISBN: 978-1-118-43935-7 (ebk)
ISBN: 978-1-118-41730-0 (ebk)

Manufactured in the United States of America

SKY10063058_122023

For general information on our other products and services please contact our Customer Care Department within the United States at (877) 762-2974, outside the United States at (317) 572-3993 or fax (317) 572-4002.

Wiley publishes in a variety of print and electronic formats and by print-on-demand. Some material included with standard print versions of this book may not be included in e-books or in print-on-demand. If this book refers to media such as a CD or DVD that is not included in the version you purchased, you may download this material at http://booksupport.wiley.com. For more information about Wiley products, visit www.wiley.com.

Library of Congress Control Number: 2013954089

To my wonderful family: Gregory, Jennifer, and Vivian

Credits

Executive Editor
Robert Elliott

Project Editor
Victoria Swider

Technical Editor
Lopo Rego

Production Editor
Daniel Scribner

Copy Editor
San Dee Phillips

Editorial Manager
Mary Beth Wakefield

Freelancer Editorial Manager
Rosemarie Graham

Associate Director of Marketing
David Mayhew

Marketing Manager
Ashley Zurcher

Business Manager
Amy Knies

Vice President and Executive Group Publisher
Richard Swadley

Associate Publisher
Jim Minatel

Project Coordinator, Cover
Katie Crocker

Proofreaders
Josh Chase, Word One
Louise Watson, Word One

Indexer
Ron Strauss

Cover Image
Wiley

Cover Designer
Ryan Sneed

About the Author

Wayne Winston is Professor Emeritus at the Indiana University Kelley School of Business and is currently a Visiting Professor at the University of Houston Bauer College of Business. Wayne has won more than 45 teaching awards at Indiana University. These awards include six school-wide MBA teaching awards. He has authored 25 reference journal articles and a dozen books including, *Operations Research: Applications and Algorithms* (Cengage, 1987), *Practical Management Science* (Cengage, 2011), *Data Analysis and Decision-Making* (Cengage, 2013), *Simulation Modeling with @RISK* (Cengage, 2004), *Mathletics* (Princeton, 2009), and *Excel 2013 Data Analysis and Business Modeling* (O'Reilly, 2014). Wayne has also developed two online courses for Harvard Business School: Spreadsheet Modeling, and Mathematics for Management. He has taught Excel modeling and consulted for many organizations including the U.S. Army, the U.S. Navy, Broadcom, Cisco, Intel, Pfizer, Eli Lilly, Ford, GM, PWC, Microsoft, IAC, Deloitte Consulting, Booz Allen Hamilton, QAS, eBay, the Dallas Mavericks, and the New York Knicks. Lastly, Wayne is a two-time *Jeopardy!* champion.

About the Technical Editor

Lopo Rego joined the Kelley School of Business at Indiana University in 2011 as an Associate Professor of Marketing. Trained in Economics, he "converted to the dark side" during his MBA and has since been interested in understanding the association between marketing strategy and firm performance. This proved to be a life-long quest, leading him to Ann Arbor where he eventually earned his Ph.D. in Marketing at the University of Michigan's Ross School of Business. Not surprisingly, his research interests focus primarily in understanding how marketing decisions, strategies, and investments translate into firm performance, be it at the product-marketplace level, financial-accounting level or shareholder wealth level. Additionally, Lopo is interested in marketing analytics, namely in developing and analyzing marketing metrics that drive firm performance. His research has been published in such outlets as the *Journal of Marketing, Marketing Science, European Journal of Marketing, Journal of Empirical Generalisations in Marketing, Harvard Business Review, Journal of Research in Marketing,* and *Marketing Science Institute Working Paper Series.*

Acknowledgments

O f all my books, this one was probably the hardest to write. Thanks to my wonderful wife Vivian who was so nice to me when I got frustrated during the authoring process. Wiley acquisitions editor Robert Elliott was always encouraging and his input was a great help in shaping the final product. Wiley project editor Victoria Swider did a great job in pushing me to become a better writer.

Lastly, I must give a special note of thanks to my technical editor, Associate Professor of Marketing at the Kelly School of Business, Lopo Rego. Lopo did an amazing job of suggesting alternative wording and catching errors. He went above and beyond his role as technical editor, and I am truly indebted to him for his Herculean efforts.

Contents

Introduction xxiii

I Using Excel to Summarize Marketing Data 1

1 Slicing and Dicing Marketing Data with PivotTables 3

2 Using Excel Charts to Summarize Marketing Data 29

3 Using Excel Functions to Summarize Marketing Data 59

II Pricing 83

4 Estimating Demand Curves and Using
Solver to Optimize Price 85

5 Price Bundling 107

6 Nonlinear Pricing 123

7 Price Skimming and Sales 135

8 Revenue Management 143

III Forecasting 159

9 Simple Linear Regression and Correlation 161

10 Using Multiple Regression to Forecast Sales 177

11 Forecasting in the Presence of Special Events 213

12 Modeling Trend and Seasonality 225

13 Ratio to Moving Average Forecasting Method 235

14 Winter's Method 241

15 Using Neural Networks to Forecast Sales 249

IV What do Customers Want? 261

16 Conjoint Analysis. 263

17 Logistic Regression 285

18 Discrete Choice Analysis 303

V Customer Value 325

19 Calculating Lifetime Customer Value 327

20 Using Customer Value to Value a Business 339

21 Customer Value, Monte Carlo Simulation, and
Marketing Decision Making 347

22 Allocating Marketing Resources between
Customer Acquisition and Retention 365

VI Market Segmentation 375

23 Cluster Analysis 377

24 Collaborative Filtering 393

25 Using Classification Trees for Segmentation 403

VII Forecasting New Product Sales 413

26 Using S Curves to Forecast Sales of a New Product 415

27 The Bass Diffusion Model 427

28 Using the Copernican Principle to Predict Duration
of Future Sales. 439

VIII Retailing. 443

29 Market Basket Analysis and Lift 445

30 RFM Analysis and Optimizing Direct Mail Campaigns 459

31 Using the SCAN*PRO Model and Its Variants. 471

32 Allocating Retail Space and Sales Resources 483

33 Forecasting Sales from Few Data Points 495

IX Advertising 503

34 Measuring the Effectiveness of Advertising 505

35 Media Selection Models 517

36 Pay per Click (PPC) Online Advertising 529

X Marketing Research Tools 539

37 Principal Components Analysis (PCA) 541

38 Multidimensional Scaling (MDS) 559

39 Classification Algorithms: Naive Bayes
Classifier and Discriminant Analysis 577

40 Analysis of Variance: One-way ANOVA. 595

41 Analysis of Variance: Two-way ANOVA. 607

XI Internet and Social Marketing 619

42 Networks 621

43 The Mathematics Behind *The Tipping Point* 641

44 Viral Marketing 653

45 Text Mining. 663

Index 673

Contents

Introduction xxiii

I   Using Excel to Summarize Marketing Data 1

1   Slicing and Dicing Marketing Data with PivotTables 3

   Analyzing Sales at True Colors Hardware 3

   Analyzing Sales at La Petit Bakery 14

   Analyzing How Demographics Affect Sales 21

   Pulling Data from a PivotTable with the GETPIVOTDATA Function . . 25

   Summary 27

   Exercises 27

2   Using Excel Charts to Summarize Marketing Data 29

   Combination Charts 29

   Using a PivotChart to Summarize
   Market Research Surveys 36

   Ensuring Charts Update Automatically
   When New Data is Added 39

   Making Chart Labels Dynamic 40

   Summarizing Monthly Sales-Force Rankings 43

   Using Check Boxes to Control Data in a Chart 45

   Using Sparklines to Summarize Multiple Data Series 48

   Using GETPIVOTDATA to Create the
   End-of-Week Sales Report 52

   Summary 55

   Exercises 55

3   Using Excel Functions to Summarize Marketing Data 59

   Summarizing Data with a Histogram 59

   Using Statistical Functions to Summarize Marketing Data 64

   Summary 79

   Exercises 80

II Pricing. 83

4 Estimating Demand Curves and Using
Solver to Optimize Price 85

Estimating Linear and Power Demand Curves 85

Using the Excel Solver to Optimize Price. 90

Pricing Using Subjectively Estimated Demand Curves. 96

Using SolverTable to Price Multiple Products 99

Summary 103

Exercises. 104

5 Price Bundling. 107

Why Bundle? 107

Using Evolutionary Solver to Find Optimal Bundle Prices 111

Summary 119

Exercises. 119

6 Nonlinear Pricing 123

Demand Curves and Willingness to Pay 124

Profit Maximizing with Nonlinear Pricing Strategies 125

Summary 131

Exercises. 132

7 Price Skimming and Sales 135

Dropping Prices Over Time 135

Why Have Sales?. 138

Summary 142

Exercises. 142

8 Revenue Management. 143

Estimating Demand for the Bates Motel and
Segmenting Customers 144

Handling Uncertainty. 150

Markdown Pricing 153

Summary 156

Exercises. 156

III Forecasting 159

9 Simple Linear Regression and Correlation 161

Simple Linear Regression 161

Using Correlations to Summarize Linear Relationships 170

Summary 174

Exercises. 175

10 Using Multiple Regression to Forecast Sales 177

Introducing Multiple Linear Regression. 178

Running a Regression with the Data Analysis Add-In 179

Interpreting the Regression Output 182

Using Qualitative Independent Variables in Regression. 186

Modeling Interactions and Nonlinearities. 192

Testing Validity of Regression Assumptions. 195

Multicollinearity 204

Validation of a Regression. 207

Summary 209

Exercises. 210

11 Forecasting in the Presence of Special Events. 213

Building the Basic Model 213

Summary 222

Exercises. 222

12 Modeling Trend and Seasonality 225

Using Moving Averages to Smooth Data and
Eliminate Seasonality 225

An Additive Model with Trends and Seasonality 228

A Multiplicative Model with Trend and Seasonality. 231

Summary 234

Exercises. 234

13 Ratio to Moving Average Forecasting Method 235

Using the Ratio to Moving Average Method 235

Applying the Ratio to Moving Average Method to
Monthly Data 238

Summary 238

Exercises 239

14 Winter's Method 241

Parameter Definitions for Winter's Method 241

Initializing Winter's Method 243

Estimating the Smoothing Constants 244

Forecasting Future Months 246

Mean Absolute Percentage Error (MAPE) 247

Summary 248

Exercises 248

15 Using Neural Networks to Forecast Sales 249

Regression and Neural Nets 249

Using Neural Networks 250

Using NeuralTools to Predict Sales 253

Using NeuralTools to Forecast Airline Miles 258

Summary 259

Exercises 259

IV What do Customers Want? 261

16 Conjoint Analysis 263

Products, Attributes, and Levels 263

Full Profile Conjoint Analysis 265

Using Evolutionary Solver to Generate
Product Profiles 272

Developing a Conjoint Simulator 277

Examining Other Forms of Conjoint Analysis 279

Summary 281

Exercises 281

17 Logistic Regression 285

Why Logistic Regression Is Necessary 286

Logistic Regression Model 289

Maximum Likelihood Estimate of Logistic Regression Model 290

Using StatTools to Estimate and Test Logistic
Regression Hypotheses. 293

Performing a Logistic Regression with Count Data 298

Summary 300

Exercises. 300

18 Discrete Choice Analysis 303

Random Utility Theory 303

Discrete Choice Analysis of Chocolate Preferences 305

Incorporating Price and Brand Equity into
Discrete Choice Analysis 309

Dynamic Discrete Choice 315

Independence of Irrelevant Alternatives (IIA) Assumption 316

Discrete Choice and Price Elasticity. 317

Summary 318

Exercises. 319

V Customer Value 325

19 Calculating Lifetime Customer Value 327

Basic Customer Value Template 328

Measuring Sensitivity Analysis with Two-way Tables 330

An Explicit Formula for the Multiplier 331

Varying Margins. 331

DIRECTV, Customer Value, and *Friday Night Lights (FNL)* 333

Estimating the Chance a Customer Is Still Active 334

Going Beyond the Basic Customer Lifetime Value Model 335

Summary 336

Exercises. 336

20 Using Customer Value to Value a Business 339

A Primer on Valuation. 339

Using Customer Value to Value a Business 340

Measuring Sensitivity Analysis with a One-way Table 343

Using Customer Value to Estimate a Firm's Market Value 344

Summary 344

Exercises. 345

21 Customer Value, Monte Carlo Simulation, and
Marketing Decision Making 347

A Markov Chain Model of Customer Value 347

Using Monte Carlo Simulation to Predict Success of
a Marketing Initiative 353

Summary 359

Exercises. 360

22 Allocating Marketing Resources between
Customer Acquisition and Retention 347

Modeling the Relationship between Spending and
Customer Acquisition and Retention 365

Basic Model for Optimizing Retention and Acquisition Spending . . 368

An Improvement in the Basic Model. 371

Summary 373

Exercises. 374

VI Market Segmentation. 375

23 Cluster Analysis 377

Clustering U.S. Cities 378

Using Conjoint Analysis to Segment a Market 386

Summary 391

Exercises. 391

24 Collaborative Filtering 393

User-Based Collaborative Filtering. 393

Item-Based Filtering 398

Comparing Item- and User-Based Collaborative Filtering 400

The Netflix Competition. 401

Summary 401

Exercises. 402

25 Using Classification Trees for Segmentation 403

Introducing Decision Trees 403

Constructing a Decision Tree 404

Pruning Trees and CART. 409

Summary 410

Exercises. 410

VII Forecasting New Product Sales. 413

26 Using S Curves to Forecast Sales of a New Product 415

Examining S Curves 415

Fitting the Pearl or Logistic Curve. 418

Fitting an S Curve with Seasonality. 420

Fitting the Gompertz Curve 422

Pearl Curve versus Gompertz Curve 425

Summary 425

Exercises. 425

27 The Bass Diffusion Model 427

Introducing the Bass Model 427

Estimating the Bass Model 428

Using the Bass Model to Forecast New Product Sales 431

Deflating Intentions Data 434

Using the Bass Model to Simulate Sales of a New Product 435

Modifications of the Bass Model. 437

Summary 438

Exercises. 438

28 Using the Copernican Principle to Predict Duration
of Future Sales. 439

   Using the Copernican Principle. 439

   Simulating Remaining Life of Product. 440

   Summary 441

   Exercises. 441

VIII Retailing 443

29 Market Basket Analysis and Lift 445

   Computing Lift for Two Products 445

   Computing Three-Way Lifts 449

   A Data Mining Legend Debunked! 453

   Using Lift to Optimize Store Layout 454

   Summary 456

   Exercises. 456

30 RFM Analysis and Optimizing Direct Mail Campaigns 459

   RFM Analysis 459

   An RFM Success Story. 465

   Using the Evolutionary Solver to Optimize
   a Direct Mail Campaign 465

   Summary 468

   Exercises. 468

31 Using the SCAN*PRO Model and Its Variants. 471

   Introducing the SCAN*PRO Model. 471

   Modeling Sales of Snickers Bars 472

   Forecasting Software Sales. 475

   Summary 480

   Exercises. 480

32 Allocating Retail Space and Sales Resources 483

   Identifying the Sales to Marketing Effort Relationship. 483

   Modeling the Marketing Response to Sales Force Effort 484

Optimizing Allocation of Sales Effort 489

Using the Gompertz Curve to Allocate
Supermarket Shelf Space 492

Summary 492

Exercises. 493

33 Forecasting Sales from Few Data Points 495

Predicting Movie Revenues 495

Modifying the Model to Improve Forecast Accuracy. 498

Using 3 Weeks of Revenue to Forecast Movie Revenues 499

Summary 501

Exercises. 501

IX Advertising 503

34 Measuring the Effectiveness of Advertising 505

The Adstock Model 505

Another Model for Estimating Ad Effectiveness 509

Optimizing Advertising: Pulsing versus Continuous Spending. 511

Summary 514

Exercises. 515

35 Media Selection Models 517

A Linear Media Allocation Model 517

Quantity Discounts. 520

A Monte Carlo Media Allocation Simulation 522

Summary 527

Exercises. 527

36 Pay per Click (PPC) Online Advertising 529

Defining Pay per Click Advertising 529

Profitability Model for PPC Advertising. 531

Google AdWords Auction 533

Using Bid Simulator to Optimize Your Bid. 536

Summary 537

Exercises. 537

X Marketing Research Tools. 539

37 Principal Components Analysis (PCA) 541

Defining PCA 541

Linear Combinations, Variances, and Covariances. 542

Diving into Principal Components Analysis. 548

Other Applications of PCA 556

Summary 557

Exercises. 558

38 Multidimensional Scaling (MDS) 559

Similarity Data 559

MDS Analysis of U.S. City Distances 560

MDS Analysis of Breakfast Foods. 566

Finding a Consumer's Ideal Point 570

Summary 574

Exercises. 574

39 Classification Algorithms: Naive Bayes
Classifier and Discriminant Analysis 577

Conditional Probability. 578

Bayes' Theorem 579

Naive Bayes Classifier 581

Linear Discriminant Analysis 586

Model Validation 591

The Surprising Virtues of Naive Bayes. 592

Summary 592

Exercises. 593

40 Analysis of Variance: One-way ANOVA. 595

Testing Whether Group Means Are Different 595

Example of One-way ANOVA 596

The Role of Variance in ANOVA 598

Forecasting with One-way ANOVA. 599

Contrasts 601

Summary 603

Exercises. 604

41 Analysis of Variance: Two-way ANOVA 607

Introducing Two-way ANOVA. 607

Two-way ANOVA without Replication. 608

Two-way ANOVA with Replication 611

Summary 616

Exercises. 617

XI Internet and Social Marketing 619

42 Networks 621

Measuring the Importance of a Node. 621

Measuring the Importance of a Link. 626

Summarizing Network Structure 628

Random and Regular Networks 631

The Rich Get Richer 634

Klout Score. 636

Summary 637

Exercises. 638

43 The Mathematics Behind *The Tipping Point* 641

Network Contagion 641

A Bass Version of the Tipping Point 646

Summary 650

Exercises. 650

44 Viral Marketing 653

Watts' Model 654

A More Complex Viral Marketing Model 655

Summary 660

Exercises. 661

45 Text Mining. 663

Text Mining Definitions 664

Giving Structure to Unstructured Text 664

Applying Text Mining in Real Life Scenarios 668

Summary 671

Exercises. 671

Index 673

Introduction

In the last 20 years, the use of analytic techniques in marketing has greatly increased. In April 2013, *Forbes* magazine reported a 67-percent growth in marketing-related analytics hires during the previous year and an amazing 136-percent growth during the previous 3 years.

Given this growth of interest in marketing analytics and my love of Excel modeling, I decided in 2004 to create a 7-week MBA elective in marketing analytics (K509) at the Indiana University Kelley School of Business. Although there are several excellent advanced marketing analytics books. (I am partial to *Database Marketing* by Robert Blattberg, Byung-Do Kim, and Scott Neslin (Springer, 2008).) I could not find an Excel-based book that provided a how-to-do-it approach suitable for an MBA elective or an advanced undergraduate course. With no suitable book in hand, I wrote up course notes that I used in classes for 10 years. The course has been wildly successful with nearly 65 percent of all MBA's at the Kelley School taking the class. In May 2013, I was honored to receive the Eli Lilly MBA teaching award as the best teacher in the MBA program, primarily for teaching K509. In November 2011, Robert Elliott of Wiley Publishing approached me about turning my notes into a book, and this book is the result. In addition to being utilized in K509, portions of the book have been used to teach marketing analytics to senior managers at Deloitte consulting, Booz Allen Hamilton consulting, and 3M marketing analysts.

How This Book Is Organized

Since I started using Excel in classes in 1992, I have become a total convert to teaching by example. This book is no exception. Virtually every chapter's primary focus is to teach you the concepts through how-to examples. Each example has the following components:

- Step-by-step instructions
- A downloadable Excel file containing data and solutions
- Screenshots of various steps and sections of the Excel file for clarity

The downloadable Excel files provide complete solutions to the examples, but the instructions encourage you to follow along and work through them on your own. If you follow along using the provided Excel files, you can work in empty cells alongside the completed solution and compare your result with the provided solution to ensure your success.

The book has been organized around 11 topical areas.

Part I: Using Excel to Summarize Marketing Data

This part of the book introduces the marketing analyst to many Excel tools that can be used to analyze marketing problems: PivotTables (Chapter 1), charting (Chapter 2), and Excel statistical functions (Chapter 3), including the incredibly useful COUNTIF, COUNTIFS, SUMIF, SUMIFS, AVERAGEIF, and AVERAGEIFS functions.

Part II: Pricing

The determination of a profit maximizing pricing strategy is always difficult. In this section you learn how to quickly estimate demand curves and use the Excel Solver (Chapter 4) to determine profit maximizing prices. The Excel Solver is then used to optimize price bundling (Chapter 5), nonlinear pricing strategies (Chapter 6), and price-skimming strategies (Chapter 7). A brief introduction to revenue management, also known as yield management (Chapter 8), is also included.

Part III: Forecasting

Businesses need accurate forecasts of future sales. Sales forecasts drive decisions involving production schedules, inventory management, manpower planning, and many other parts of the business. In this section you first learn about two of the most used forecasting tools: simple linear (Chapter 9) and simple multiple regression (Chapters 10 and 11). Then you learn how to estimate the trend and seasonal aspects of sales (Chapter 12) and generate forecasts using two common extrapolation forecasting methods: the Ratio to Moving Average method (Chapter 13), and Winter's Method for exponential smoothing (Chapter 14) with trend and seasonality. Then you learn about neural networks (Chapter 15), a form of artificial intelligence whose role in marketing forecasting is rapidly growing.

Part IV: What Do Customers Want?

Every brand manager wants to know how various product attributes drive the sales of a product. For example, what is most important in a consumer's choice of car: price, brand, engine horsepower, styling, or fuel economy? In this section you learn how conjoint analysis (Chapter 16) and discrete choice (Chapter 18) can be used to rank the importance of product attributes and also rank levels of product attributes. For example, what type of styling on an SUV is most preferred? You also learn about the widely used tool of logistic regression (Chapter 17), which is used to estimate probabilities involving situations in which two, or binary, outcomes must be forecasted. For example, how a person's demographic information can be used to predict the chance that he will subscribe to a magazine.

Part V: Customer Value

Companies cannot make intelligent decisions on how to spend money acquiring customers unless they understand the value of their customers. After all, spending $400 to acquire a customer who will generate $300 in long-term profits is a sure recipe for going out of business. In this section you learn how to measure customer value (Chapter 19), value companies based on the customer value concept (Chapter 20), incorporate uncertainty in customer value models (Chapter 21), and use your understanding of customer value to optimally allocate resources (Chapter 22) between acquisition and retention of customers.

Part VI: Market Segmentation

No matter what product you sell, your market consists of different market segments. For example, in Chapter 23 you will use cluster analysis to show that that every U.S. city can be classified into one of four demographic segments. In Chapter 25 you will learn how classification trees can be used to segment a market. You are also introduced to the exciting concepts behind collaborative filtering (Chapter 24), which is the basis for Amazon.com and Netflix recommendations.

Part VII: Forecasting New Product Sales

With little or no history about sales of a product, it is difficult to predict future product sales. Given a few data points, S curves (Chapter 26) can be used to predict future product sales. The famous Bass diffusion model (Chapter 27) explains how sales of products evolve over time and can be used to predict product sales even before a product comes to the market. The little-known Copernican Principle (Chapter 28) enables you to predict the remaining time for which a product will be sold.

Part VIII: Retailing

Analytic techniques can help retailers deal with many important issues. The concepts of market basket analysis and lift (Chapter 29) help retailers derive a store layout that maximizes sales from complementary products. Recency, frequency, and monetary value analysis (Chapter 30) helps direct mailers maximize profit from their mailings. The widely known SCAN*PRO (Chapter 31) model helps retailers determine how factors such as seasonality, price, and promotions influence product sales. In Chapter 32 you learn how to use analytic techniques to determine optimal allocation of store space between products and also optimize the use of a corporate sales force. Finally in Chapter 33 you learn how to forecast total sales of a product from a few data points.

Part IX: Advertising

Department store owner John Wanamaker said, "Half the money I spend on advertising is wasted; the trouble is I don't know which half." In Chapter 34 you learn how John Wanamaker could have used the ADSTOCK model to measure the effectiveness of his advertising expenditures. In Chapter 35 you learn how to allocate ads between the available media outlets to maximize the effectiveness of ads. Chapter 36 deals with the math behind online ad auctions.

Part X: Marketing Research Tools

Often the marketing analyst must deal with data sets involving many variables. Principal components (Chapter 37) and Multidimensional Scaling (Chapter 38) enable the marketing analysts to reduce data sets involving many variables to a few easily understood variables. Often the marketing analyst must classify objects into one of several groups. Naive Bayes and discriminant analysis (Chapter 39) are great tools for developing classification rules. When the marketing analyst wants to determine if a single factor or a pair of factors has a significant effect on product sales, ANOVA (Chapter 40 and Chapter 41) is a useful tool.

Part XI: The Internet and Social Marketing

In the last 20 years, the Internet has turned our world upside down, and marketing is no exception. Social media such as Facebook and Twitter create many interesting opportunities for the marketer, which require careful analysis. In Chapter 42 you learn how the theory of networks sheds light on how you can identify people who are the key to spreading the word about your product. Chapter 43 discusses the math behind Malcom Gladwell's bestselling book *The Tipping Point* (*Back Bay Books*, 2002). Chapter 44 discusses the math behind videos (such as the notorious "Gangnam Style") going viral. Finally, in Chapter 45 you learn how text mining can be used to glean useful insight from Twitter, blogs, and Facebook posts.

Who Should Read This Book

There is plenty of material in this book for a one-semester course on marketing analytics at the advanced undergraduate or MBA level. I also believe the book can be useful to any corporate marketing analyst. With regard to prerequisites for the book, I assume you understand the Copy command in Excel. That is, you know when and where to put dollars signs in a formula. If you work hard, that's about all the prior knowledge needed to get a lot out of the book.

I always try to write my books in a modular fashion, so you can skip around and read about what interests you. If you don't want to read the book from start to finish, the following table should help you navigate the book.

Chapters	Chapter Prerequisites
Chapter 1: Slicing and Dicing Marketing Data with PivotTables	None
Chapter 2: Using Excel Charts to Summarize Marketing Data	1
Chapter 3: Using Excel Functions to Summarize Marketing Data	2
Chapter 4: Estimating Demand Curves and Using Solver to Optimize Price	None
Chapter 5: Price Bundling	4
Chapter 6: Nonlinear Pricing	5
Chapter 7: Price Skimming and Sales	5
Chapter 8: Revenue Management	4
Chapter 9: Simple Linear Regression and Correlation	3
Chapter 10: Using Multiple Regression to Forecast Sales	9
Chapter 11: Forecasting in the Presence of Special Events	10
Chapter 12: Modeling Trend and Seasonality	5 and 11
Chapter 13: Ratio to Moving Average Forecasting Method	3 and 12
Chapter 14: Winter's Method	12
Chapter 15: Using Neural Networks to Forecast Sales	10
Chapter 16: Conjoint Analysis	10

Continues

(continued)

Chapters	Chapter Prerequisites
Chapter 17: Logistic Regression	16
Chapter 18: Discrete Choice Analysis	17
Chapter 19: Calculating Lifetime Customer Value	3
Chapter 20: Using Customer Value to Value a Business	19
Chapter 21: Customer Value, Monte Carlo Simulation, and Marketing Decision Making	19
Chapter 22: Allocating Marketing Resources between Customer Acquisition and Retention	4 and 19
Chapter 23: Cluster Analysis	5
Chapter 24: Collaborative Filtering	23
Chapter 25: Using Classification Trees for Segmentation	24
Chapter 26: Using S Curves to Forecast Sales of a New Product	5 and 12
Chapter 27: The Bass Diffusion Model	26
Chapter 28: Using the Copernican Principle to Predict Duration of Future Sales	None
Chapter 29: Market Basket Analysis and Lift	19
Chapter 30: RFM Analysis and Optimizing Direct Mail Campaigns	29
Chapter 31: Using the SCAN*PRO Model and Its Variants	12
Chapter 32: Allocating Retail Space and Sales Resources	5
Chapter 33: Forecasting Sales from Few Data Points	31
Chapter 34: Measuring the Effectiveness of Advertising	31
Chapter 35: Media Selection Models	4, 21, and 34
Chapter 36: Pay Per Click (PPC) Online Advertising	None
Chapter 37: Principal Component Analysis (PCA)	10 and 23
Chapter 38: Multidimensional Scaling (MDS)	37
Chapter 39: Classification Algorithms: Naive Bayes Classifier and Discriminant Analysis	37 and 38

Chapters	Chapter Prerequisites
Chapter 40: Analysis of Variance: One-way ANOVA	10
Chapter 41: Analysis of Variance: Two-way ANOVA	40
Chapter 42: Networks	None
Chapter 43: The Mathematics Behind *The Tipping Point*	42
Chapter 44: Viral Marketing	10, 15, and 39
Chapter 45: Text Mining	3

For example, before reading Chapter 5 you need to have read Chapter 4; before reading Chapter 34 you need to have read Chapter 31, and so on.

Tools You Need

To work through the vast majority of the book, all you need is Excel 2007, 2010, or 2013. Chapters 15, 21, and 35 require use of the Palisade.com Decision Tools Suite. You can download a 15-day trial version of the suite from www.Palisade.com.

What's on the Website

From the book website (www.wiley.com/go/marketinganalytics) you can download all Excel files used in the book as well as answers to all of the Exercises at the end of each chapter.

Errata

We make every effort to ensure that there are no errors in the text or in the code. However, no one is perfect, and mistakes do occur. If you find an error in this book, like a spelling mistake or a calculation error, we would be very grateful for your feedback. By sending in errata you may save another reader hours of frustration and at the same time you will be helping us provide even higher quality information.

To submit errata for this book go to http://support.wiley.com and complete the form on the Ask a Question tab there to send us the error you have found. We'll check the information and, if appropriate, post a message to the book's errata page and fix the problem in subsequent editions of the book.

Summary

A famous Chinese proverb (popularized by the late management guru Stephen Covey) states, "If you give a man a fish you feed him for a day. If you teach a man to fish you feed him for a lifetime." Hopefully this book will teach you enough about marketing analytics so you will be well equipped to develop your own quantitative marketing models for most problems that come your way. Happy modeling!

Using Excel to Summarize Marketing Data

Chapter 1: Slicing and Dicing Marketing Data with PivotTables

Chapter 2: Using Excel Charts to Summarize Marketing Data

Chapter 3: Using Excel Functions to Summarize Marketing Data

1

Slicing and Dicing Marketing Data with PivotTables

In many marketing situations you need to analyze, or "slice and dice," your data to gain important marketing insights. Excel PivotTables enable you to quickly summarize and describe your data in many different ways. In this chapter you learn how to use PivotTables to perform the following:

- Examine sales volume and percentage by store, month and product type.
- Analyze the influence of weekday, seasonality, and the overall trend on sales at your favorite bakery.
- Investigate the effect of marketing promotions on sales at your favorite bakery.
- Determine the influence that demographics such as age, income, gender and geographic location have on the likelihood that a person will subscribe to *ESPN: The Magazine*.

Analyzing Sales at True Colors Hardware

To start analyzing sales you first need some data to work with. The `data` worksheet from the `PARETO.xlsx` file (available for download on the companion website) contains sales data from two local hardware stores (uptown store owned by Billy Joel and downtown store owned by Petula Clark). Each store sells 10 types of tape, 10 types of adhesive, and 10 types of safety equipment. Figure 1-1 shows a sample of this data.

Throughout this section you will learn to analyze this data using Excel PivotTables to answer the following questions:

- What percentage of sales occurs at each store?
- What percentage of sales occurs during each month?
- How much revenue does each product generate?
- Which products generate 80 percent of the revenue?

	Y	Z	AA	AB
7	Product	Month	Store	Price
8	Tape 10	April	downtown	$2.50
9	Safety 8	August	uptown	$10.00
10	Safety 2	February	uptown	$10.00
11	Safety 8	Novembe	uptown	$10.00
12	Tape 10	October	uptown	$2.50
13	Safety 8	January	uptown	$10.00
14	Safety 8	Decembe	downtown	$10.00
15	Safety 1	Septembe	downtown	$12.00
16	Safety 2	May	uptown	$10.00
17	Adhesive	July	uptown	$7.00
18	Adhesive	March	uptown	$7.00
19	Safety 8	August	downtown	$10.00
20	Safety 8	October	downtown	$10.00
21	Tape 10	July	downtown	$2.50
22	Safety 2	February	downtown	$10.00

Figure 1-1: Hardware store data

Calculating the Percentage of Sales at Each Store

The first step in creating a PivotTable is ensuring you have headings in the first row of your data. Notice that Row 7 of the example data in the data worksheet has the headings Product, Month, Store, and Price. Because these are in place, you can begin creating your PivotTable. To do so, perform the following steps:

1. Place your cursor anywhere in the data cells on the data worksheet, and then click PivotTable in the Tables group on the Insert tab. Excel opens the Create PivotTable dialog box, as shown in Figure 1-2, and correctly guesses that the data is included in the range Y7:AB1333.

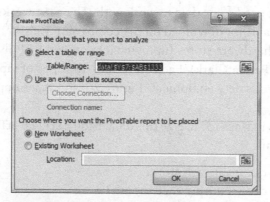

Figure 1-2: PivotTable Dialog Box

NOTE   If you select Use an External Data Source here, you could also refer to a database as a source for a PivotTable. In Exercise 14 at the end of the chapter you can practice creating PivotTables from data in different worksheets or even different workbooks.

2. Click OK and you see the PivotTable Field List, as shown in Figure 1-3.

Figure 1-3: PivotTable Field List

3. Fill in the PivotTable Field List by dragging the PivotTable headings or *fields* into the boxes or *zones*. You can choose from the following four zones:

    ■ **Row Labels:** Fields dragged here are listed on the left side of the table in the order in which they are added to the box. In the current example, the Store field should be dragged to the Row Labels box so that data can be summarized by store.

- **Column Labels:** Fields dragged here have their values listed across the top row of the PivotTable. In the current example no fields exist in the Column Labels zone.
- **Values:** Fields dragged here are summarized mathematically in the PivotTable. The Price field should be dragged to this zone. Excel tries to guess the type of calculation you want to perform on a field. In this example Excel guesses that you want all Prices to be summed. Because you want to compute total revenue, this is correct. If you want to change the method of calculation for a data field to an average, a count, or something else, simply double-click the data field or choose Value Field Settings. You learn how to use the Value Fields Setting command later in this section.
- **Report Filter:** Beginning in Excel 2007, *Report Filter* is the new name for the Page Field area. For fields dragged to the Report Filter zone, you can easily pick any subset of the field values so that the PivotTable shows calculations based only on that subset. In Excel 2010 or Excel 2013 you can use the exciting *Slicers* to select the subset of fields used in PivotTable calculations. The use of the Report Filter and Slicers is shown in the "Report Filter and Slicers" section of this chapter.

NOTE   To see the field list, you need to be in a field in the PivotTable. If you do not see the field list, right-click any cell in the PivotTable, and select Show Field List.

Figure 1-4 shows the completed PivotTable Field List and the resulting PivotTable is shown in Figure 1-5 as well as on the FirstorePT worksheet.

Figure 1-5 shows the downtown store sold $4,985.50 worth of goods, and the uptown store sold $4,606.50 of goods. The total sales are $9592.

If you want a percentage breakdown of the sales by store, you need to change the way Excel displays data in the Values zone. To do this, perform these steps:

1. Right-click in the summarized data in the FirstStorePT worksheet and select Value Field Settings.
2. Select Show Values As and click the drop-down arrow on the right side of the dialog box.
3. Select the % of Column Total option, as shown in Figure 1-6.

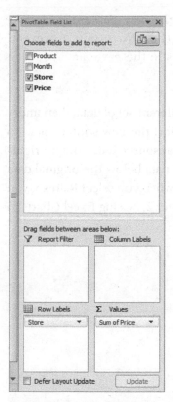

Figure 1-4: Completed PivotTable Field List

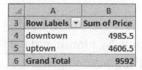

Figure 1-5: Completed PivotTable

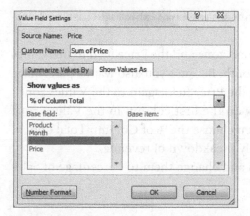

Figure 1-6: Obtaining percentage breakdown by Store

Figure 1-7 shows the resulting PivotTable with the new percentage break-down by Store with 52 percent of the sales in the downtown store and 48 percent in the uptown store. You can also see this in the `revenue by store` worksheet of the `PARETO.xlsx` file.

NOTE   If you want a PivotTable to incorporate a different set of data, then under Options, you can select Change Data Source and select the new source data. To have a PivotTable incorporate changes in the original source data, simply right-click and select Refresh. If you are going to add new data below the original data and you want the PivotTable to include the new data when you select Refresh, you should use the Excel Table feature discussed in Chapter 2, "Using Excel Charts to Summarize Marketing Data."

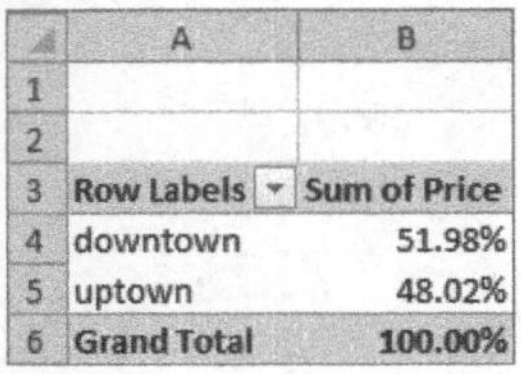

◢	A	B
1		
2		
3	Row Labels ▾	Sum of Price
4	downtown	51.98%
5	uptown	48.02%
6	Grand Total	100.00%

Figure 1-7: Percentage breakdown by Store

Summarizing Revenue by Month

You can also use a PivotTable to break down the total revenue by month and cal-culate the percentage of sales that occur during each month. To accomplish this, perform the following steps:

1. Return to the `data` worksheet and bring up the PivotTable Field List by choos-ing Insert PivotTable.
2. Drag the Month field to the Row Labels zone and the Price field to the Values zone. This gives the total sales by month. Because you also want a percentage breakdown of sales by month, drag the Price field again to the Values zone.
3. As shown in Figure 1-8, right-click on the first column in the Values zone and choose Value Field Settings; then choose the % of Column Total option. You now see the percentage monthly breakdown of revenue.
4. Double-click the Column headings and change them to Percentage of Sales by Month and Total Revenue.

5. Finally, double-click again the Total Revenue Column; select Number Format, and choose the Currency option so the revenue is formatted in dollars.

	A	B	C
1			
2			
3	Row Labels ▼	Percentage of Sales by Month	Total Revenue
4	January	8.81%	$845.00
5	February	8.55%	$820.00
6	March	6.58%	$631.00
7	April	8.10%	$776.50
8	May	8.48%	$813.00
9	June	8.87%	$850.50
10	July	8.77%	$841.00
11	August	7.13%	$684.00
12	September	8.71%	$835.50
13	October	7.85%	$753.00
14	November	9.11%	$873.50
15	December	9.06%	$869.00
16	Grand Total	100.00%	$9,592.00

Figure 1-8: Monthly percentage breakdown of Revenue

You can see that $845 worth of goods was sold in January and 8.81 percent of the sales were in January. Because the percentage of sales in each month is approximately 1/12 (8.33 percent), the stores exhibit little seasonality. Part III, "Forecasting Sales of Existing Products," includes an extensive discussion of how to estimate seasonality and the importance of seasonality in marketing analytics.

Calculating Revenue for Each Product

Another important part of analyzing data includes determining the revenue generated by each product. To determine this for the example data, perform the following steps:

1. Return to the data worksheet and drag the Product field to the Row Labels zone and the Price field to the Values zone.

2. Double-click on the Price column, change the name of the Price column to Revenue, and then reformat the Revenue Column as Currency.

3. Click the drop-down arrow in cell A3 and select Sort A to Z so you can alphabetize the product list and obtain the PivotTable in the products worksheet, as shown in Figure 1-9.

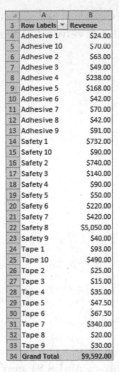

Row Labels	Revenue
Adhesive 1	$24.00
Adhesive 10	$70.00
Adhesive 2	$63.00
Adhesive 3	$49.00
Adhesive 4	$238.00
Adhesive 5	$168.00
Adhesive 6	$42.00
Adhesive 7	$70.00
Adhesive 8	$42.00
Adhesive 9	$91.00
Safety 1	$732.00
Safety 10	$90.00
Safety 2	$740.00
Safety 3	$140.00
Safety 4	$90.00
Safety 5	$50.00
Safety 6	$220.00
Safety 7	$420.00
Safety 8	$5,050.00
Safety 9	$40.00
Tape 1	$93.00
Tape 10	$490.00
Tape 2	$25.00
Tape 3	$15.00
Tape 4	$35.00
Tape 5	$47.50
Tape 6	$67.50
Tape 7	$340.00
Tape 8	$20.00
Tape 9	$30.00
Grand Total	**$9,592.00**

Figure 1-9: Sales by Product

You can now see the revenue that each product generated individually. For example, Adhesive 1 generated $24 worth of revenue.

The Pareto 80–20 Principle

When slicing and dicing data you may encounter a situation in which you want to find which set of products generates a certain percentage of total sales. The well-known *Pareto 80–20 Principle* states that for most companies 20 percent of their products generate around 80 percent of their sales. Other examples of the Pareto Principle include the following:

- Twenty percent of the population has 80 percent of income.
- Of all possible problems customers can have, 20 percent of the problems cause 80 percent of all complaints.

To determine a percentage breakdown of sales by product, perform the following steps:

1. Begin with the PivotTable in the products worksheet and click the drop-down arrow in cell A3.

2. Select Value Filters; then choose Top 10...
3. Change the settings, as shown in Figure 1-10, to choose the products generating 80 percent of the revenue.

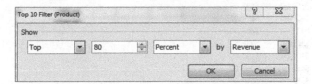

Figure 1-10: Using Value Filters to select products generating 80% of sales

The resulting PivotTable appears in the `Top 80%` worksheet (see Figure 1-11) and shows that the six products displayed in Figure 1-11 are the smallest set of products generating at least 80 percent of the revenue. Therefore only 20 percent of the products (6 out of 30) are needed to generate 80 percent of the sales.

NOTE   By clicking the funnel you may clear our filters, if desired.

	A	B
3	Row Labels 🔽	Revenue
4	Safety 8	$5,050.00
5	Safety 2	$740.00
6	Safety 1	$732.00
7	Tape 10	$490.00
8	Safety 7	$420.00
9	Tape 7	$340.00
10	Grand Total	$7,772.00

Figure 1-11: 6 Products Generate 80% of Revenue

The Report Filter and Slicers

One helpful tool for analyzing data is the Report Filter and the exciting Excel 2010 and 2013 Slicers Feature. Suppose you want to break down sales from the example data by month and store, but you feel showing the list of products in the Row or Column Labels zones would clutter the PivotTable. Instead, you can drag the Month field to the Row Labels zone, the Store field to the Column Labels zone, the Price field to the Value zone, and the Product field to the Report Filter zone. This yields the PivotTable in worksheet `Report filter unfiltered`, as shown in Figure 1-12.

	A	B	C	D
1	Product	(All)		
2				
3	Sum of Price	Column Labels		
4	Row Labels	downtown	uptown	Grand Total
5	January	$482.00	$363.00	$845.00
6	February	$363.00	$457.00	$820.00
7	March	$299.00	$332.00	$631.00
8	April	$407.00	$369.50	$776.50
9	May	$408.50	$404.50	$813.00
10	June	$400.50	$450.00	$850.50
11	July	$446.00	$395.00	$841.00
12	August	$372.50	$311.50	$684.00
13	September	$446.50	$389.00	$835.50
14	October	$394.00	$359.00	$753.00
15	November	$503.50	$370.00	$873.50
16	December	$463.00	$406.00	$869.00
17	Grand Total	4985.5	4606.5	9592

Figure 1-12: PivotTable used to illustrate Slicers

By clicking the drop-down arrow in the Report Filter, you can display the total revenue by Store and Month for any subset of products. For example, if you select products Safety 1, Safety 7, and Adhesive 8, you can obtain the PivotTable in the `Filtered with a slicer` worksheet, as shown in Figure 1-13. You see here that during May, sales of these products downtown are $10.00 and uptown are $34.00.

	A	B	C	D
1	Product	(Multiple Items)		
2				
3	Sum of Price	Column Labels		
4	Row Labels	downtown	uptown	Grand Total
5	January	$46.00	$22.00	$68.00
6	February	$44.00	$68.00	$112.00
7	March	$51.00	$63.00	$114.00
8	April	$44.00	$44.00	$88.00
9	May	$10.00	$34.00	$44.00
10	June	$89.00	$56.00	$145.00
11	July	$49.00		$49.00
12	August	$10.00	$36.00	$46.00
13	September	$88.00	$44.00	$132.00
14	October	$102.00	$87.00	$189.00
15	November	$56.00	$70.00	$126.00
16	December	$32.00	$49.00	$81.00
17	Grand Total	621	573	1194

Figure 1-13: PivotTable showing sales for Safety 1, Safety 7 and Adhesive 8

As you can see from Figure 1-13, it is difficult to know which products were used in the PivotTable calculations. The new Slicer feature in Excel 2010 and 2013 (see the Filtered with a slicer worksheet) remedies this problem. To use this tool perform the following steps:

1. Put your cursor in the PivotTable in the Filtered with a Slicer worksheet and select Slicer from the Insert tab.
2. Select Products from the dialog box that appears and you see a Slicer that enables you to select any subset of products (select a product and then hold down the Control Key to select another product) from a single column.
3. Click inside the Slicer and you will see Slicer Tools on the ribbon. After selecting the Buttons section from Slicer Tools change Columns to 5. Now the products show up in five columns (see Figure 1-14).

Product				
Adhesive 1	Adhesive 10	Adhesive 2	Adhesive 3	Adhesive 4
Adhesive 5	Adhesive 6	Adhesive 7	Adhesive 8	Adhesive 9
Safety 1	Safety 10	Safety 2	Safety 3	Safety 4
Safety 5	Safety 6	Safety 7	Safety 8	Safety 9
Tape 1	Tape 10	Tape 2	Tape 3	Tape 4
Tape 5	Tape 6	Tape 7	Tape 8	Tape 9

Figure 1-14: Slicer selection for sales of Safety 1, Safety 7 and Adhesive 8.

A Slicer provides sort of a "dashboard" to filter on subsets of items drawn from a PivotTable field(s). The Slicer in the Filtered with a slicer worksheet makes it obvious that the calculations refer to Safety 1, Safety 7, and Adhesive 8. If you hold down the Control key, you can easily resize a Slicer.

NOTE   If you double-click in a cell in a PivotTable, Excel drills down to the source data used for that cell's calculations and places the source data in a separate sheet. For example, if in the Report filtered unfiltered worksheet you double-click in the January downtown cell, you can obtain the source data in the worksheet January downtown, as shown in Figure 1-15.

You have learned how PivotTables can be used to slice and dice sales data. Judicious use of the Value Fields Settings capability is often the key to performing the needed calculations.

	A	B	C	D
1	Product	Month	Store	Price
2	Safety 7	January	downtowi	10
3	Safety 1	January	downtowi	12
4	Safety 1	January	downtowi	12
5	Safety 1	January	downtowi	12

Figure 1-15: Drilling down on January Downtown Sales

Analyzing Sales at La Petit Bakery

La Petit Bakery sells cakes, pies, cookies, coffee, and smoothies. The owner has hired you to analyze factors affecting sales of these products. With a PivotTable and all the analysis skills you now have, you can quickly describe the important factors affecting sales. This example paves the way for a more detailed analysis in Part III of this book.

The file `BakeryData.xlsx` contains the data for this example and the file `LaPetitBakery.xlsx` contains all the completed PivotTables. In the `Bakerydata .xlsx` workbook you can see the underlying daily sales data recorded for the years 2013–2015. Figure 1-16 shows a subset of this data.

	A	B	C	D	E	F	G	H	I	J	K	L	M
4					daywk	weekday	Date	Cakes	Pies	Cookies	Smoothies	Coffee	promotion
5					Tuesday	2	1/1/2013	79	46	518	60	233	none
6		1 Monday			Wednesd	3	1/2/2013	91	50	539	161	427	none
7		2 Tuesday			Thursday	4	1/3/2013	47	60	222	166	347	none
8		3 Wednesday			Friday	5	1/4/2013	89	64	734	153	358	none
9		4 Thursday			Saturday	6	1/5/2013	112	73	764	240	392	none
10		5 Friday			Sunday	7	1/6/2013	89	57	922	259	510	none
11		6 Saturday			Monday	1	1/7/2013	70	50	476	120	334	none
12		7 Sunday			Tuesday	2	1/8/2013	70	48	496	222	316	none
13					Wednesd	3	1/9/2013	59	37	587	181	156	none
14					Thursday	4	1/10/2013	71	36	488	178	298	none
15					Friday	5	1/11/2013	74	50	645	100	490	none
16					Saturday	6	1/12/2013	119	71	438	162	416	none
17					Sunday	7	1/13/2013	90	51	568	137	434	none
18					Monday	1	1/14/2013	96	48	585	194	573	promotion

Figure 1-16: Data for La Petit Bakery

A 1 in the weekday column indicates the day was Monday, a 2 indicates Tuesday, and so on. You can obtain these days of the week by entering the formula = `WEEKDAY(G5,2)` in cell F5 and copying this formula from F5 to the range

F6:F1099. The second argument of 2 in the formula ensures that a Monday is recorded as 1, a Tuesday as 2, and so on. In cell E5 you can enter the formula =VLOOKUP(F5,lookday,2) to transform the 1 in the weekday column to the actual word Monday, the 2 to Tuesday, and so on. The second argument lookday in the formula refers to the cell range A6:B12.

NOTE To name this range lookday simply select the range and type lookday in the Name box (the box directly to the left of the Function Wizard) and press Enter. Naming a range ensures that Excel knows to use the range lookday in any function or formula containing lookday.

The VLOOKUP function finds the value in cell F5 (2) in the first column of the lookday range and replaces it with the value in the same row and second column of the lookday range (Tuesday.) Copying the formula =VLOOKUP(F5,lookday,2) from E5 to E6:E1099 gives you the day of the week for each observation. For example, on Friday, January 11, 2013, there was no promotion and 74 cakes, 50 pies, 645 cookies, 100 smoothies, and 490 cups of coffee were sold.

Now you will learn how to use PivotTables to summarize how La Petit Bakery's sales are affected by the following:

- Day of the week
- Month of the year
- An upward (or downward!) trend over time in sales
- Promotions such as price cuts

Summarizing the Effect of the Day of the Week on Bakery Sales

La Petit Bakery wants to know how sales of their products vary with the day of the week. This will help them better plan production of their products.

In the day of week worksheet you can create a PivotTable that summarizes the average daily number of each product sold on each day of the week (see Figure 1-17). To create this PivotTable, perform the following steps:

1. Drag the daywk field to the Row Labels zone and drag each product to the Values zone.
2. Double-click each product, and change the summary measure to Average. You'll see, for example, that an average of 96.5 cakes was sold on Sunday.

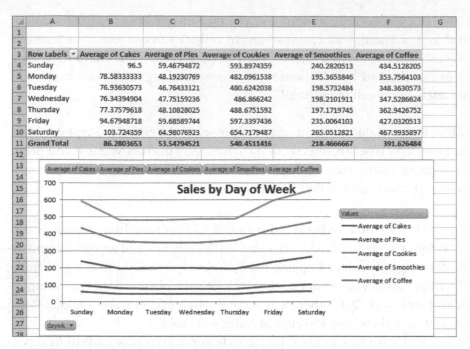

Row Labels	Average of Cakes	Average of Pies	Average of Cookies	Average of Smoothies	Average of Coffee
Sunday	96.5	59.46794872	593.8974359	240.2820513	434.5128205
Monday	78.58333333	48.19230769	482.0961538	195.3653846	353.7564103
Tuesday	76.93630573	46.76433121	480.6242038	198.5732484	348.3630573
Wednesday	76.34394904	47.75159236	486.866242	198.2101911	347.5286624
Thursday	77.37579618	48.10828025	488.6751592	197.1719745	362.9426752
Friday	94.67948718	59.68589744	597.3397436	235.0064103	427.0320513
Saturday	103.724359	64.98076923	654.7179487	265.0512821	467.9935897
Grand Total	86.2803653	53.54794521	540.4511416	218.4666667	391.626484

Figure 1-17: Daily breakdown of Product Sales

As the saying (originally attributed to Confucius) goes, "A picture is worth a thousand words." If you click in a PivotTable and go up to the Options tab and select PivotChart, you can choose any of Excel's chart options to summarize the data (Chapter 2, "Using Excel Charts to Summarize Marketing Data," discusses Excel charting further). Figure 1-17 (see the `Daily Breakdown` worksheet) shows the first Line option chart type. To change this, right-click any series in a chart. The example chart here shows that all products sell more on the weekend than during the week. In the lower left corner of the chart, you can filter to show data for any subset of weekdays you want.

Analyzing Product Seasonality

If product sales are approximately the same during each month, they do not exhibit seasonality. If, however, product sales are noticeably higher (or lower) than average during certain quarters, the product exhibits seasonality. From a marketing standpoint, you must determine the presence and magnitude of seasonality to more efficiently plan advertising, promotions, and manufacturing decisions and investments. Some real-life illustrations of seasonality include the following:

- Amazon's fourth quarter revenues are approximately 33 percent higher than an average quarter. This is because of a spike in sales during Christmas.
- Tech companies such as Microsoft and Cisco invariably have higher sales during the last month of each quarter and reach maximum sales during the last month of the fiscal year. This is because the sales force doesn't get its bonuses unless it meets quarterly or end of year quotas.

To determine if La Petit Bakery products exhibit seasonality, you can perform the following steps:

1. Begin with your cursor anywhere in the data in the BakeryData.xlsx workbook. From the Insert tab select PivotTable and the PivotTable Field List will appear. Drag the Date field to the Row Labels zone and as before, drag each product to the Values zone and again change the entries in the Values zone to average sales for each product.

2. At first you see sales for every day, but you actually want to group sales by month. To do this, put the cursor on any date, right-click, and choose Group.

3. To group the daily sales into monthly buckets, choose Months from the dialog box, as shown in Figure 1-18.

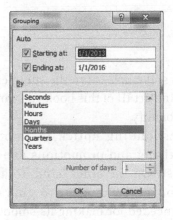

Figure 1-18: Grouping data by Month

4. Now select PivotChart from the Options tab. After selecting the first Line chart option you obtain the PivotChart and PivotTable, as shown in the monthly breakdown worksheet of the LaPetitBakery.xlsx file (see Figure 1-19).

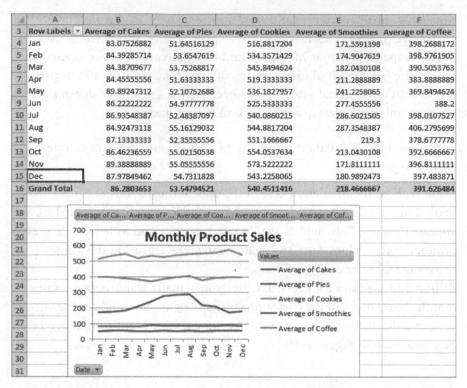

	A	B	C	D	E	F
3	Row Labels ▼	Average of Cakes	Average of Pies	Average of Cookies	Average of Smoothies	Average of Coffee
4	Jan	83.07526882	51.64516129	516.8817204	171.5591398	398.2688172
5	Feb	84.39285714	53.6547619	534.3571429	174.9047619	398.9761905
6	Mar	84.38709677	53.75268817	545.8494624	182.0430108	390.5053763
7	Apr	84.45555556	51.63333333	519.3333333	211.2888889	383.8888889
8	May	89.89247312	52.10752688	536.1827957	241.2258065	369.8494624
9	Jun	86.22222222	54.97777778	525.5333333	277.4555556	388.2
10	Jul	86.93548387	52.48387097	540.0860215	286.6021505	398.0107527
11	Aug	84.92473118	55.16129032	544.8817204	287.3548387	406.2795699
12	Sep	87.13333333	52.35555556	551.1666667	219.3	378.6777778
13	Oct	86.46236559	55.02150538	554.0537634	213.0430108	392.6666667
14	Nov	89.38888889	55.05555556	573.5222222	171.8111111	396.8111111
15	Dec	87.97849462	54.7311828	543.2258065	180.9892473	397.483871
16	Grand Total	86.2803653	53.54794521	540.4511416	218.4666667	391.626484

Figure 1-19: Monthly breakdown of Bakery Sales

This chart makes it clear that smoothie sales spike upward in the summer, but sales of other products exhibit little seasonality. In Part III of this book you can find an extensive discussion of how to estimate seasonality.

Given the strong seasonality and corresponding uptick in smoothie sales, the bakery can probably "trim" advertising and promotions expenditures for smoothies between April and August. On the other hand, to match the increased demand for smoothies, the bakery may want to guarantee the availability and delivery of the ingredients needed for making its smoothies. Similarly, if the increased demand places stress on the bakery's capability to serve its customers, it may consider hiring extra workers during the summer months.

NOTE   If you right-click any month and select Ungroup, you can undo the grouping and return to a display of the daily sales data.

Analyzing the Trend in Bakery Sales

The owners of La Petit Bakery want to know if sales are improving. Looking at a graph of each product's sales by month will not answer this question if seasonality is present. For example, Amazon.com has lower sales every January than the previous month due to Christmas. A better way to analyze this type of trend is to compute and chart average daily sales for each year. To perform this analysis, complete the following steps:

1. Put your cursor inside the data in the Data worksheet of the BakeryData .xlsx file, create a PivotTable, and drag each product to the Values zone and again change the method of summary from Sum to Average.

2. Then drag the Date field to the Row Labels zone, place the cursor on any date, and right-click Group and choose Years. You see a monthly summary of average daily sales for each Month and Year.

3. Drag the Date field away from the Row Labels zone and you are left with the summary of product sales by year, as shown in Figure 1-20 (see the work in worksheet by Year).

4. As you did before, create a Line PivotChart. The chart shows sales for each product are trending upward, which is good news for the client.

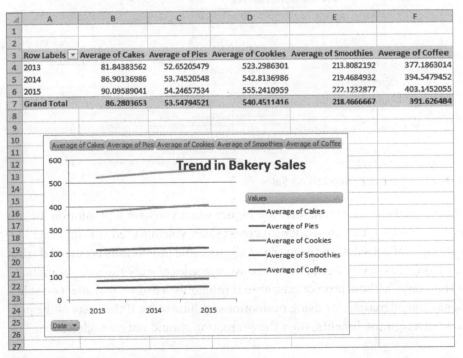

Figure 1-20: Summary of Sales by Year

The annual growth rates for products vary between 1.5 percent and 4.9 percent. Cake sales have grown at the fastest rate, but represent a small part of overall sales. Cookies and coffee sales have grown more slowly, but represent a much larger percentage of revenues.

Analyzing the Effect of Promotions on Sales

To get a quick idea of how promotions affect sales, you can determine average sales for each product on the days you have promotions and compare the average on days with promotions to the days without promotions. To perform these computations keep the same fields in the Value zone as before, and drag the Promotion field to the Row Labels zone. After creating a line PivotChart, you can obtain the results, as shown in Figure 1-21 (see the `promotion` worksheet).

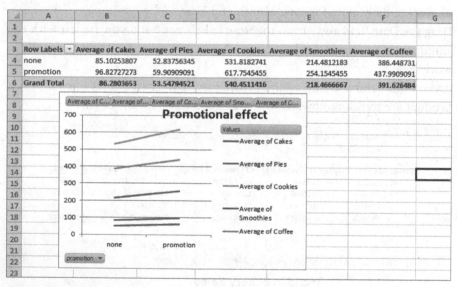

	A	B	C	D	E	F	G
3	Row Labels	Average of Cakes	Average of Pies	Average of Cookies	Average of Smoothies	Average of Coffee	
4	none	85.10253807	52.83756345	531.8182741	214.4812183	386.448731	
5	promotion	96.82727273	59.90909091	617.7545455	254.1545455	437.9909091	
6	Grand Total	86.2803653	53.54794521	540.4511416	218.4666667	391.626484	

Figure 1-21: Effect of Promotion on Sales

The chart makes it clear that sales are higher when you have a promotion. Before concluding, however, that promotions increase sales, you must "adjust" for other factors that might affect sales. For example, if all smoothie promotions occurred during summer days, seasonality would make the average sales of smoothies on promotions higher than days without promotions, even if promotions had no real effect on sales. Additional considerations for using promotions include costs; if the costs of the promotions outweigh the benefits, then the promotion should not be undertaken. The marketing analyst must be careful in computing the benefits of a promotion. If the promotion yields new customers, then the long-run value of the new customers (see Part V) should be included in the benefit of the promotion. In Parts VIII and IX of this book you can learn how to perform more rigorous analysis to determine how marketing decisions such as promotions, price changes, and advertising influence product sales.

Analyzing How Demographics Affect Sales

Before the marketing analyst recommends where to advertise a product (see Part IX), she needs to understand the type of person who is likely to purchase the product. For example, a heavy metal fan magazine is unlikely to appeal to retirees, so advertising this product on a television show that appeals to retirees (such as *Golden Girls*) would be an inefficient use of the advertising budget. In this section you will learn how to use PivotTables to describe the demographic of people who purchase a product.

Take a look at the data worksheet in the espn.xlsx file. This has demographic information on a randomly chosen sample of 1,024 subscribers to *ESPN: The Magazine*. Figure 1-22 shows a sample of this data. For example, the first listed subscriber is a 72-year-old male living in a rural location with an annual family income of $72,000.

Analyzing the Age of Subscribers

One of the most useful pieces of demographic information is age. To describe the age of subscribers, you can perform the following steps:

1. Create a PivotTable by dragging the Age field to the Row Labels zone and the Age field to the Values zone.
2. Unfortunately, Excel assumes that you want to calculate the Sum of Ages. Double-click the Sum of Ages heading, and change this to Count of Age.
3. Use Value Field settings with the % of Column Total setting to show a percentage breakdown by age.
4. Finally, right-click on any listed age in the PivotTable and select Group. This enables you to group ages in 10-year increments. You can also use the PivotChart feature using the first Column chart option to create a column

chart (see Figure 1-23 and the `age` worksheet) to summarize the age distribution of subscribers.

	G	H	I	J
3	Age	Gender	Income	Location
4	72	m	72	rural
5	29	m	68	suburban
6	33	m	57	suburban
7	25	m	62	suburban
8	38	m	164	urban
9	33	m	44	urban
10	18	f	62	rural
11	17	m	68	urban
12	32	f	53	urban
13	24	f	92	urban
14	26	f	54	suburban
15	40	m	88	urban
16	26	f	46	rural
17	21	m	83	suburban
18	29	m	144	rural
19	51	f	30	suburban
20	17	m	47	urban
21	29	m	61	urban
22	92	m	123	urban
23	20	m	76	suburban
24	20	f	57	rural
25	65	m	104	urban
26	26	m	46	urban
27	74	m	113	urban
28	37	f	109	rural

Figure 1-22: Demographic data for *ESPN*: *The Magazine*

You find that most of the magazine's subscribers are in the 18–37 age group. This knowledge can help ESPN find TV shows to advertise that target the right age demographic.

Analyzing the Gender of Subscribers

You can also analyze the gender demographics of *ESPN*: *The Magazine* subscribers. This will help the analyst to efficiently spend available ad dollars. After all, if all subscribers are male, you probably do not want to place an ad on *Project Runway*.

1. In the `data` worksheet, drag the Gender field to the Column Labels zone and the Gender field to the Values zone.
2. Right-click the data and use Value Field Settings to change the calculations to Show Value As % of Row Total; this enables you to obtain the PivotTable shown in the `gender` worksheet (see Figure 1-24.)

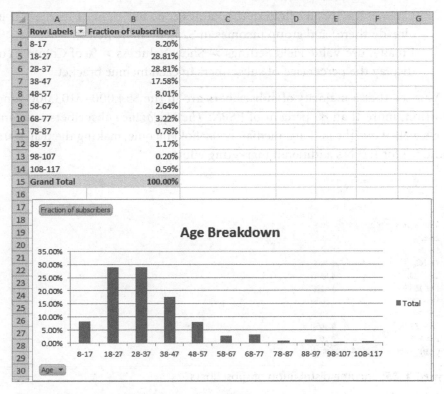

	A	B	C	D	E	F	G
3	Row Labels ▾	Fraction of subscribers					
4	8-17	8.20%					
5	18-27	28.81%					
6	28-37	28.81%					
7	38-47	17.58%					
8	48-57	8.01%					
9	58-67	2.64%					
10	68-77	3.22%					
11	78-87	0.78%					
12	88-97	1.17%					
13	98-107	0.20%					
14	108-117	0.59%					
15	Grand Total	100.00%					

Figure 1-23: Age distribution of subscribers

	A	B	C	D
1				
2				
3		Column Labels ▾		
4		f	m	Grand Total
5	Count of Gender	20.31%	79.69%	100.00%

Figure 1-24: Gender breakdown of subscribers

You find that approximately 80 percent of subscribers are men, so ESPN may not want to advertise on *The View*!

Describing the Income Distribution of Subscribers

In the Income worksheet (see Figure 1-25) you see a breakdown of the percentage of subscribers in each income group. This can be determined by performing the following steps:

1. In the data worksheet drag the Income field to the Row Labels zone and the Income field to the Values zone.

2. Change the Income field in the Values zone to Count of Income (if it isn't already there) and group incomes in $25,000 increments.
3. Finally, use Value Field Settings ➤ Show Value As ➤ % of Column Total to display the percentage of subscribers in each income bracket.

You see that a majority of subscribers are in the $54,000–$103,000 range. In addition, more than 85 percent of *ESPN: The Magazine* subscribers have income levels well above the national median household income, making them an attractive audience for ESPN's additional marketing efforts.

	A	B
1		
2		
3	Row Labels ▾	Count of Income
4	29-53	13.18%
5	54-78	35.06%
6	79-103	29.20%
7	104-128	14.55%
8	129-153	5.66%
9	154-178	1.56%
10	179-203	0.59%
11	229-253	0.10%
12	254-278	0.10%
13	Grand Total	100.00%

Figure 1-25: Income distribution of subscribers

Describing Subscriber Location

Next you will determine the breakdown of *ESPN: The Magazine* subscribers between suburbs, urban, and rural areas. This will help the analyst recommend the TV stations where ads should be placed.

1. Put your cursor inside the data from the data worksheet and drag the Location field to the Column Labels zone and Value zone.
2. Apply Value Field Settings and choose Show Value As ➤ % of Row Total to obtain the PivotTable, as shown in the Location worksheet and Figure 1-26. You find that 46 percent of subscribers live in the suburbs; 40 percent live in urban areas and 15 percent live in rural areas.

	A	B	C	D	E
1					
2					
3		Column Labels ▾			
4		rural	suburban	urban	Grand Total
5	Count of Location	14.55%	45.70%	39.75%	100.00%

Figure 1-26: Breakdown of Subscriber Location

Constructing a Crosstabs Analysis of Age and Income

Often marketers break down customer demographics simultaneously on two attributes. Such an analysis is called a *crosstabs* analysis. In the `data` worksheet you can perform a crosstabs analysis on Age and Income. To do so, perform the following steps:

1. Begin by dragging the Age field to the Column Labels zone and the Income field to the Row Labels and Value Labels zones.
2. Next group ages in 10-year increments and income in $25,000 increments.
3. Finally, use Value Field Settings to change the method of calculation to Show Value As ➤ % of Row Total. The `Income and Age` worksheet (shown in Figure 1-27) shows the resulting PivotTable, which indicates that 28.13 percent of subscribers in the $54,000 to $78,000 bracket are in the 28–37 age group.

Crosstabs analyses enable companies to identify specific combinations of customer demographics that can be used for a more precise allocation of their marketing investments, such as advertising and promotions expenditures. Crosstabs analyses are also useful to determine where firms *should not* make investments. For instance, there are hardly any subscribers to *ESPN: The Magazine* that are 78 or older, or with household incomes above $229,000, so placing ads on TV shows that are heavily watched by wealthy retiree is not recommended.

	A	B	C	D	E	F	G	H	I	J	K	L	M
1													
2													
3	Count of Income	Column Labels											
4	Row Labels	8-17	18-27	28-37	38-47	48-57	58-67	68-77	78-87	88-97	98-107	108-117	Grand Total
5	29-53	11.11%	31.85%	25.19%	15.56%	8.15%	3.70%	0.74%	0.74%	0.74%	0.74%	1.48%	100.00%
6	54-78	8.08%	27.86%	28.13%	17.27%	9.47%	2.51%	3.62%	1.11%	1.39%	0.28%	0.28%	100.00%
7	79-103	7.69%	28.43%	29.43%	18.73%	7.02%	3.34%	3.01%	1.00%	1.00%	0.00%	0.33%	100.00%
8	104-128	9.40%	25.50%	34.90%	15.44%	8.72%	1.34%	2.68%	0.00%	1.34%	0.00%	0.67%	100.00%
9	129-153	1.72%	37.93%	29.31%	18.97%	3.45%	1.72%	6.90%	0.00%	0.00%	0.00%	0.00%	100.00%
10	154-178	12.50%	37.50%	12.50%	25.00%	0.00%	0.00%	6.25%	0.00%	6.25%	0.00%	0.00%	100.00%
11	179-203	0.00%	0.00%	0.00%	50.00%	16.67%	0.00%	16.67%	0.00%	0.00%	0.00%	16.67%	100.00%
12	229-253	0.00%	100.00%	0.00%	0.00%	0.00%	0.00%	0.00%	0.00%	0.00%	0.00%	0.00%	100.00%
13	254-278	0.00%	0.00%	100.00%	0.00%	0.00%	0.00%	0.00%	0.00%	0.00%	0.00%	0.00%	100.00%
14	Grand Total	8.20%	28.81%	28.81%	17.58%	8.01%	2.64%	3.22%	0.78%	1.17%	0.20%	0.59%	100.00%

Figure 1-27: Crosstabs Analysis of subscribers

Pulling Data from a PivotTable with the GETPIVOTDATA Function

Often a marketing analyst wants to pull data from a PivotTable to use as source information for a chart or other analyses. You can achieve this by using the `GETPIVOTDATA` function. To illustrate the use of the `GETPIVOTDATA` function, take a second look at the True Colors hardware store data in the `products` worksheet from the `PARETO`.`xlsx` file.

1. With the cursor in any blank cell, type an = sign and point to the cell (B12) containing Adhesive 8 sales.

2. You will now see in the formerly blank cell the formula `=GETPIVOTDATA`(`"Price",$A$3,"Product","Adhesive 8"`). Check your result against cell E10. This pulls the sales of Adhesive 8 ($42.00) from the PivotTable into cell E10.

This formula always picks out Adhesive 8 sales from the Price field in the PivotTable whose upper left corner is cell A3. Even if the set of products sold changes, this function still pulls Adhesive 8 sales.

In Excel 2010 or 2013 if you want to be able to click in a PivotTable and return a cell reference rather than a `GETPIVOTTABLE` function, simply choose File ➤ Options, and from the Formulas dialog box uncheck the `Use GetPivotData` functions for the PivotTable References option (see Figure 1-28).

	A	B	C	D	E	F	G	H	I
1									
2									
3	Row Labels ▼	Revenue							
4	Adhesive 1	$24.00							
5	Adhesive 10	$70.00							
6	Adhesive 2	$63.00							
7	Adhesive 3	$49.00							
8	Adhesive 4	$238.00							
9	Adhesive 5	$168.00							
10	Adhesive 6	$42.00			42				
11	Adhesive 7	$70.00			GETPIVOTDATA("Price",$A$3,"Product","Adhesive 8")				
12	Adhesive 8	$42.00							
13	Adhesive 9	$91.00							
14	Safety 1	$732.00							
15	Safety 10	$90.00							
16	Safety 2	$740.00							
17	Safety 3	$140.00							
18	Safety 4	$90.00							
19	Safety 5	$50.00							
20	Safety 6	$220.00							
21	Safety 7	$420.00							
22	Safety 8	$5,050.00							
23	Safety 9	$40.00							
24	Tape 1	$93.00							
25	Tape 10	$490.00							
26	Tape 2	$25.00							
27	Tape 3	$15.00							
28	Tape 4	$35.00							
29	Tape 5	$47.50							
30	Tape 6	$67.50							
31	Tape 7	$340.00							
32	Tape 8	$20.00							
33	Tape 9	$30.00							
34	Grand Total	$9,592.00							

Figure 1-28: Example of GETPIVOTDATA function

This function is widely used in the corporate world and people who do not know it are at a severe disadvantage in making best use of PivotTables. Chapter 2 covers this topic in greater detail.

Summary

In this chapter you learned the following:

- Sketch out in your mind how you want the PivotTable to look before you fill in the Field List.
- Use Value Field Settings to change the way the data is displayed or the type of calculation (Sum, Average, Count, etc.) used for a Value Field.
- A PivotChart can often clarify the meaning of a PivotTable.
- Double-click in a cell to drill down to the source data that was used in the cell's calculation.
- The `GETPIVOTDATA` function can be used to pull data from a PivotTable.

Exercises

1. The `Makeup2007.xlsx` file (available for download on the companion website) gives sales data for a small makeup company. Each row lists the salesperson, product sold, location of the sale, units sold, and revenue generated. Use this file to perform the following exercises:

   a. Summarize the total revenue and units sold by each person of each product.

   b. Summarize the percentage of each person's sales that came from each location. Create a PivotChart to summarize this information.

   c. Summarize each girl's sales by location and use the Report Filter to change the calculations to include any subset of products.

2. The `Station.xlsx` file contains data for each family including the family size (large or small), income (high or low), and whether the family bought a station wagon. Use this file to perform the following exercises:

   a. Does it appear that family size or income is a more important determinant of station wagon purchases?

   b. Compute the percentage of station wagon purchasers that are high or low income.

c. Compute the fraction of station wagon purchasers that come from each of the following four categories: High Income Large Family, High Income Small Family, Low Income Large Family, and Low Income Small Family.

3. The `cranberrydata.xlsx` file contains data for each quarter in the years 2006–2011 detailing the pounds of cranberries sold by a small grocery store. You also see the store's price and the price charged by the major competitor. Use this file to perform the following exercises:

a. Ignoring price, create a chart that displays the seasonality of cranberry sales.

b. Ignoring price, create a chart that shows whether there is an upward trend in sales.

c. Determine average sales per quarter, breaking it down based on whether your price was higher or lower than the competitor's price.

4. The `tapedata.xlsx` file contains data for weeks during 2009–2011 for the unit sales of 3M tape, price charged, whether an ad campaign was run that week (1 = ad campaign), and whether the product was displayed on the end of the aisle (1 = end cap). Use this file to perform the following exercises:

a. Does there appear to be an upward trend in sales?

b. Analyze the nature of the monthly seasonality of tape sales.

c. Does an ad campaign appear to increase sales?

d. Does placing the tape in an end-cap display appear to increase sales?

5. The files `EAST.xlsx` and `WEST.xlsx` contain information on product sales (products A–H) that you sell in January, February, and March. You want to use a PivotTable to summarize this sales data. The Field List discussed in this chapter does not enable you to create PivotTables on data from multiple ranges. If you hold down the ALT key and let go and hold down the D key and let go of the D key and hold down the P key, you can see the Classic PivotTable Wizard that enables you to select multiple ranges of data to key a PivotTable. Let Excel create a single page field for you and create a PivotTable to summarize total sales in the East and West during each month. Use the Filters so that the PivotTable shows only January and March sales of products A, C, and E.

2

Using Excel Charts to Summarize Marketing Data

An important component of using analytics in business is a push towards "visualization." Marketing analysts often have to sift through mounds of data to draw important conclusions. Many times these conclusions are best represented in a chart or graph. As Confucius said, "a picture is worth a thousand words." This chapter focuses on developing Excel charting skills to enhance your ability to effectively summarize and present marketing data. This chapter covers the following skills:

- Using a combination chart and a secondary axis
- Adding a product picture to your column graphs
- Adding labels and data tables to your graphs
- Using the Table feature to ensure your graphs automatically update when new data is added
- Using PivotCharts to summarize a marketing survey
- Making chart labels dynamic
- Using Sparklines to summarize sales at different stores
- Using Custom Icon Sets to summarize trends in sales force performance
- Using a check box to control the data series that show in a graph
- Using the Table feature and GETPIVOTDATA function to automate creation of end-of-month sales reports

Combination Charts

Companies often graph actual monthly sales and targeted monthly sales. If the marketing analyst plots both these series with straight lines it is difficult to differentiate between actual and target sales. For this reason analysts often summarize actual sales versus targeted sales via a combination chart in which the two series are displayed using different formats (such as a line and column graph.) This section explains how to create a similar combination chart.

All work for this chapter is located in the file Chapter2charts.xlsx. In the worksheet Combinations you see actual and target sales for the months January through July. To begin charting each month's actual and target sales, select the range F5:H12 and choose a line chart from the Insert tab. This yields a chart with both actual and target sales displayed as lines. This is the second chart shown in Figure 2-1; however, it is difficult to see the difference between the two lines here. You can avoid this by changing the format of one of the lines to a column graph. To do so, perform the following steps:

1. Select the Target sales series line in the line graph by moving the cursor to any point in this series.

2. Then right-click, and choose Change Series Chart Type...

3. Select the first Column option and you obtain the first chart shown in Figure 2-1.

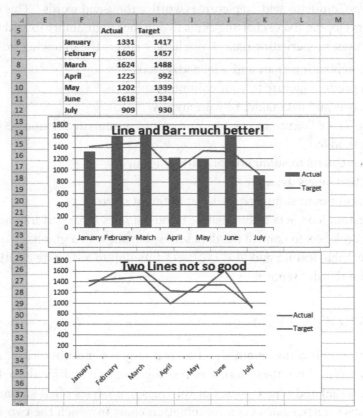

Figure 2-1: Combination chart

With the first chart, it is now easy to distinguish between the Actual and Target sales for each month. A chart like this with multiple types of graphs is called a *combination chart*.

You'll likely come across a situation in which you want to graph two series, but two series differ greatly in magnitude, so using the same vertical axis for each series results in one series being barely visible. In this case you need to include a secondary axis for one of the series. When you choose a secondary axis for a series Excel tries to scale the values of the axis to be consistent with the data values for that series. To illustrate the creation of a secondary axis, use the data in the `Secondary Axis` worksheet. This worksheet gives you monthly revenue and units sold for a company that sells expensive diamonds.

Because diamonds are expensive, naturally the monthly revenue is much larger than the units sold. This makes it difficult to see both revenue and units sold with only a single vertical axis. You can use a secondary axis here to more clearly summarize the monthly units sold and revenue earned. To do so, perform the following steps:

1. In the `Secondary Axis` worksheet select D7:F16, click the Insert tab, click the Line menu in the Charts section, and select the first Line chart option. You obtain the chart shown in Figure 2-2.

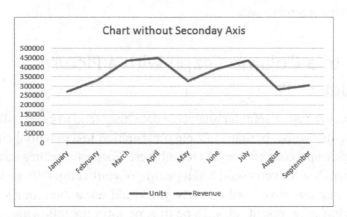

Figure 2-2: Line graph shows need for Secondary Axis

2. You cannot see the units' data though, because it is so small relative to the revenue. To remedy this problem, select the Revenue series line in the graph and right-click.

3. Choose Format Data Series, and select Secondary Axis.

4. Then select any point in the Revenue series, right-click, and change the chart type for the Revenue series to a column graph.

The resulting chart is shown in Figure 2-3, and you can now easily see how closely units and revenue move together. This occurs because Revenue=Average price*units sold, and if the average price during each month is constant, the revenue and units sold series will move in tandem. Your chart indeed indicates that average price is consistent for the charted data.

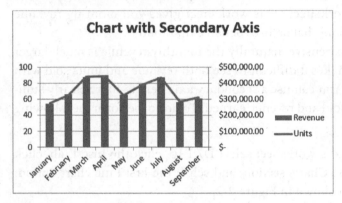

Figure 2-3: Chart with a secondary axis

Adding Bling to a Column Graph with a Picture of Your Product

While column graphs are quite useful for analyzing data, they tend to grow dull day after day. Every once in a while, perhaps in a big presentation to a potential client, you might want to spice up a column graph here and there. For instance, in a column graph of your company's sales you could add a picture of your company's product to represent sales. Therefore if you sell Ferraris, you could use a .bmp image of a Ferrari in place of a bar to represent sales. To do this, perform the following steps:

1. Create a Column graph using the data in the `Picture` worksheet. This data shows monthly sales of cars at an L.A. Ferrari dealer.

2. After creating a Column graph, right-click on any column and choose Format Data Series... followed by Fill.

3. Click Picture or texture fill, as shown in Figure 2-4.

4. Next click File below the Insert from query and choose the `Ferrari`
`.bmp` file (available for download from the companion site).

5. Choose Stack and Scale with **200** units per picture. This ensures each car represents sales of 200 cars.

The resulting chart is shown in Figure 2-5, as well as in the `Picture` worksheet.

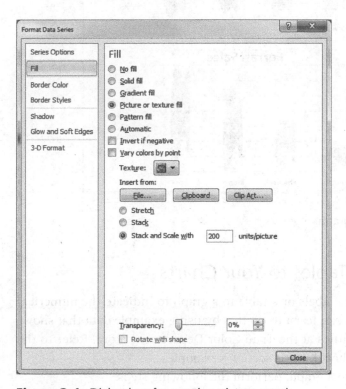

Figure 2-4: Dialog box for creating picture graph

NOTE   If you choose Stretch in the Fill tab of the Format Data Series dialog, you can ensure that Excel represents each month's sales by a single car whose size is proportional to that month's sales.

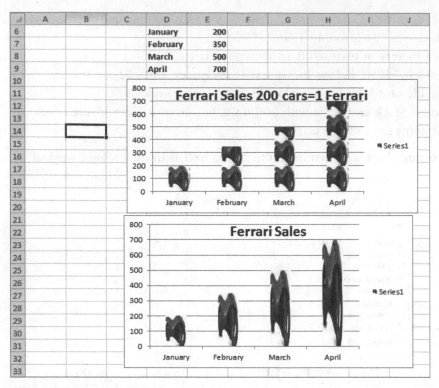

Figure 2-5: Ferrari picture graph

Adding Labels or Tables to Your Charts

Often you want to add data labels or a table to a graph to indicate the numerical values being graphed. You can learn to do this by using example data that shows monthly sales of product lines at the True Color Department Store. Refer to the Labels and Tables worksheet for this section's examples.

To begin adding labels to a graph, perform the following steps:

1. Select the data range C5:D9 and choose the first Column chart option (Clustered Column) from the Charts section of the Insert tab.

2. Now click on any column in the graph and choose Layout from the Chart Tools section of the ribbon.

3. Choose the Data Labels option from the Layout section of Chart Tools and select More Data Label Options... Fill in the dialog boxes as shown in Figure 2-6.

4. Include the Value and Category Name in the label, and put them on a different line.

The resulting graph with data labels is shown in Figure 2-7.

Figure 2-6: Dialog Box for creating chart with data labels

You can also add a Data Table to a column graph. To do so, again select any of the columns within the graph and perform the following steps:

1. From the Chart Tools tab, select Layout.

2. Choose Data Table.

3. Choose the Show Data Table option to create the table shown in the second chart in Figure 2-7.

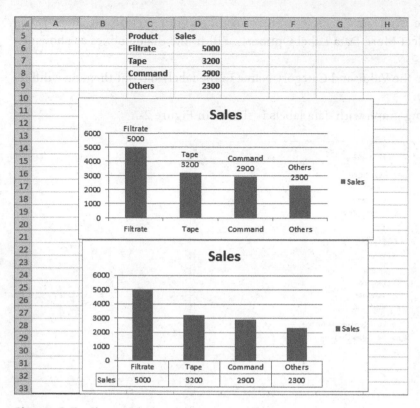

Figure 2-7: Chart with data labels or data tables

Using a PivotChart to Summarize Market Research Surveys

To determine a new product's viability, market researchers often ask potential customers questions about a new product. PivotTables (discussed in Chapter 1, "Slicing and Dicing Marketing Data with PivotTables") are typically used to summarize this type of data. A PivotChart is a chart based on the contents of a PivotTable. As you will see, a PivotChart can be a highly effective tool to summarize any data gathered from this type of market research. The Survey PivotChart worksheet in the Chapter2chart.xlsx file uses a PivotChart to summarize a market research survey based on the data from the Survey Data worksheet (see Figure 2-8). The example data shows the answer to seven questions about a product (such as Likely to Buy) that was recorded on a 1–5 scale, with a higher score indicating a more favorable view of the product.

	I	J	K
5	Response	Question	
6	5	Likely To Buy	
7	3	Easy to cook	
8	3	Attractive packaging	
9	2	Too expensive	
10	5	Easy to cook	
11	1	Easy to cook	
12	3	Too expensive	
13	1	Likely To Buy	
14	2	Likely To Buy	
15	3	Better tasting	
16	2	Too expensive	
17	5	Too expensive	
18	3	Nutritious meal	
19	2	Recommend to friend	
20	2	Nutritious meal	
21	4	Likely To Buy	
22	2	Likely To Buy	
23	5	Attractive packaging	
24	4	Likely To Buy	
25	2	Likely To Buy	
26	5	Easy to cook	
27	5	Attractive packaging	
28	3	Too expensive	
29	4	Recommend to friend	
30	4	Likely To Buy	

Figure 2-8: Data for PivotChart example

To summarize this data, you can perform the following steps:

1. Select the data from the Survey Data worksheet and from the Tables section of the Insert tab choose PivotTable ➢ PivotTable and click OK.
2. Next drag the Question field heading to the Row Labels zone and the Response field heading to the Column Labels and Values zones.
3. Assume you want to chart the fraction of 1, 2, 3, 4, and 5 responses for each question. Therefore, use Value Field Settings to change the Summarize Values By tab field to Count and change the Show Values As tab field to % of Row Total. You then obtain the PivotTable shown first in Figure 2-9.
4. You can now create a Pivot Chart from this table. Select PivotChart from the Options tab and choose the first Column chart option. This process yields the PivotChart shown second in Figure 2-9.
5. This chart is a bit cluttered however, so click the drop-down arrow by the Question button, and choose to display only responses to Likely to Buy and Recommend to a Friend. The resulting uncluttered chart is shown in Figure 2-10.

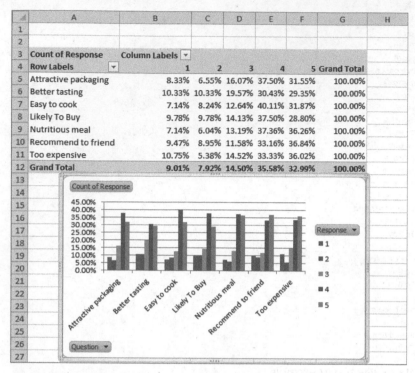

Figure 2-9: PivotTable and cluttered PivotChart

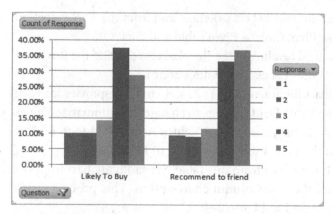

Figure 2-10: Uncluttered PivotChart

You can see that for both questions more than 60 percent of the potential customers gave the new product a 4 or 5, which is quite encouraging.

Ensuring Charts Update Automatically When New Data is Added

Most marketing analysts download sales data at the end of each month and individually update a slew of graphs that include the new data. If you have Excel 2007 or later, an easy way to do this is to use the TABLE feature to cause graphs to automatically update to include new data. To illustrate the idea, consider the Housing starts worksheet, which contains U.S. monthly housing starts (in 000s) for the time period January 2000 through May 2011. From the Insert tab, you can create the X-Y scatter chart, as shown in Figure 2-11. Just click anywhere in the data and then choose the first scatter plot option.

Figure 2-11: Housing chart through May 2011

If you add new data in columns D and E as it currently stands, the chart does not automatically incorporate the new data. To ensure that new data is automatically charted, you can instead make your data a TABLE before you create the chart. To do this, simply select the data (including headers) and press Ctrl+T. You can try this for yourself in the New Data worksheet by following these steps:

1. Select the data (D2:E141) and press Ctrl+T to make it a table.
2. Insert a scatter chart.
3. Add two new data points for June 2011 and July 2011 in Row 142 and Row 143.
4. The chart (as shown in Figure 2-12) automatically updates to include the new data. The difference between the two charts is apparent because June and July 2011 housing starts are much larger than April and May 2011 housing

starts. Imagine the time-savings if you have 15 or 20 charts keying off this data series!

Figure 2-12: Housing chart through July 2011

You can use the Ctrl+T trick for PivotTables too. If you use data to create a PivotTable, you should make the data a TABLE before creating the PivotTable. This ensures that when you right-click and select Refresh (to update a PivotTable) the PivotTable automatically incorporates the new data.

Making Chart Labels Dynamic

Data in your charts comes from data in your spreadsheet. Therefore changes to your spreadsheet will often alter your chart. If you do not set up the chart labels to also change, your chart will certainly confuse the user. This section shows how to make chart labels dynamically update to reflect changes in the chart.

Suppose you have been asked to project sales of a new product. If sales in a year are at least 2,000 units, the company will break even. There are two inputs in the Dynamic Labels worksheet: Year 1 sales (in cell D2) and annual growth in sales (in cell D3). The break-even target is given in cell D1. Use the Excel Create from Selection feature to name the data in D1:D3 with the names in the cell range C1:C3. To accomplish this, perform the following steps:

1. Select the cell range D1:D3.
2. Under the Formulas tab in the Defined Names section, select Create from Selection.

3. Choose the Left Column. Now, for example, when you use the name Year1sales in a formula, Excel knows you are referring to D2.

NOTE A important reason for using range names is the fact that you can use the F3 key to Paste Range Names in formulas. This can save you a lot of time moving back and forth in your spreadsheet. For example, if your data is in Column A and you have named it you can use the F3 key to quickly and easily paste the data into a formula that is far away from Column A (for example, Column HZ.)

You can continue by graphing the annual sales that are based on initial sales and annual sales growth. As these assumptions change, the graph title and vertical axis legend need to reflect those changes. To accomplish this goal proceed as follows:

4. Enter the Year 1 sales in cell F5 with the formula =Year1sales. Copy the formula =F5*(1+anngrowth) from F6 to F7:F15 to generate sales in Years 2–11.
5. You want to find the year in which you break even, so copy the formula =IF(F5>=target,"yes","no") from G5 to G6:G15 to determine if you have broken even during the current year. For example, you can see that during Years 5–11 you broke even.

The key to creating dynamic labels that depend on your assumed initial sales and annual sales growth is to base your chart title and series legend key off formulas that update as your spreadsheet changes.

Now you need to determine the first year in which you broke even. This requires the use of the Excel MATCH function. The MATCH function has the following syntax: MATCH(lookup_value,lookup_range,0). The lookup_range must be a row or column, and the MATCH function will return the position of the first occurrence of the lookup_value in the lookup_range. If the lookup_value does not occur in the lookup_range, the MATCH function returns an #N/A error. The last argument of 0 is necessary for the MATCH function to work properly.

In cell E19 the formula =MATCH("yes",G5:G15,0) returns the first year (in this case 5) in which you meet the breakeven target. In cell D22 several Excel functions are used to create the text string that will be the dynamic chart title. The formula entered in cell D22 is as follows:

```
=IFERROR("We will break even in year "&TEXT(E19,"0"),"Never break
even")
```

The functions used in this formula include the following:

- IFERROR evaluates the formula before the comma. If the formula does not evaluate to an error, IFERROR returns the formula's result. If the formula evaluates to an error, IFERROR returns what comes after the comma.
- The & or concatenate sign combines what is before the & sign with what comes after the & sign.
- The TEXT function converts the contents of a cell to text in the desired format. The two most commonly used formats are "0", which that indicates an integer format, and "0.0%", which indicates a percentage format.

If the MATCH formula in cell E19 does not return an error, the formula in cell D22 returns the text string We Will Break Even in Year followed by the first year you break even. If you never make it to break even, the formula returns the phrase Never Break Even. This is exactly the chart title you need.

You also need to create a title for the sales data that includes the annual sales growth rate. The series title is created in cell D23 with the following formula:

```
="Sales (growth rate="&TEXT(anngrowth,"0.0")&")".
```

NOTE Note that the growth rate has been changed to a single decimal.

Now you are ready to create the chart with dynamic labels. To do so, perform the following steps:

1. Select the source data (cell range E4:F15 in the Dynamic Labels worksheet) from the chart.
2. Navigate to the Insert tab and choose an X-Y Scatter Chart (the second option).
3. Go to the Layout section of the Chart Tools Group and select Chart Title and Centered Overlay Chart.
4. Place the cursor in the formula bar and type an equal sign (=), point to the chart title in D22, and press Enter. You now have a dynamic chart title that depends on your sales assumptions.
5. To create the series title, right-click any plotted data point, and choose Select Data.
6. Click Edit and choose Series name.

7. Type an equals sign, point to the title in D23, and press Enter. You now have a dynamic series label. Figure 2-13 shows the resulting chart.

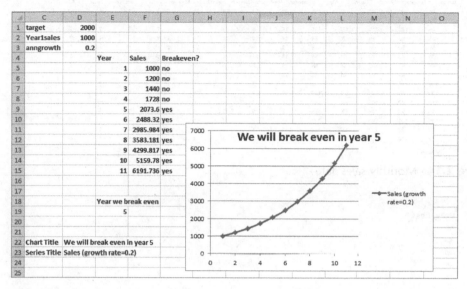

Figure 2-13: Chart with dynamic labels

Summarizing Monthly Sales-Force Rankings

If you manage a sales force, you need to determine if a salesperson's performance is improving or declining. Creating customized icon sets provides an easy way to track a salesperson's performance over time.

The data in the Sales Tracker worksheet list sales of salespeople during each month (see Figure 2-14). You can track each month with icons (up arrow, down arrow, or flat arrow) to determine whether a salesperson's ranking has improved, worsened, or stayed the same. You could use Excel's Conditional Formatting icon sets (see Chapter 24 of Winston's *Data Analysis and Business Modeling with Excel 2010* for a description of the Conditional Formatting icon sets), but then you would need to insert a set of icons separately for each column. A more efficient (although not as pretty) way to create icons is to use Wingdings 3 font and choose an "h" for an up arrow, an "i" for a down arrow, and a "g" for a flat arrow (see Figure 2-15).

	D	E	F	G	H	I	J	K	L	M	N	O	P	Q	R
1	p	h	up												
2	q	i	down												
3	u	g	flat												
4							rank	rank	rank	rank	rank	trend	trend	trend	trend
5		January	February	March	April	May	January	February	March	April	May	Feb	March	April	May
6	Lebron	85	66	81	61	56	10	14	13	15	15	↓	↑	↓	→
7	Wade	82	63	74	78	75	12	15	15	12	14	↓	→	↑	↓
8	Dirk	45	100	115	127	150	15	4	3	2	1	↑	↑	↑	↑
9	Manning	75	88	89	76	83	13	10	11	13	12	↑	↓	↓	↑
10	Brady	96	90	98	76	93	9	9	9	13	10	→	→	↓	↑
11	Halliday	75	73	79	91	95	13	13	14	10	9	→	↓	↑	↑
12	Britney	98	91	109	99	84	8	8	4	8	11	→	↑	↓	↓
13	Lindsay	83	84	97	81	98	11	12	10	11	8	↓	↑	↓	↑
14	Paris	106	98	84	93	82	5	5	12	9	13	→	↓	↑	↓
15	JLO	104	88	109	101	115	6	10	4	6	3	↓	↑	↓	↑
16	Emma	115	94	105	101	107	3	7	6	6	6	↓	↑	→	→
17	Melo	118	98	128	126	108	2	5	1	3	4	↓	↑	↓	↓
18	KD	100	114	104	116	131	7	2	7	5	2	↑	↓	↑	↑
19	Vick	112	122	102	124	107	4	1	8	4	6	↑	↓	↑	↓
20	Rodgers	127	114	116	139	108	1	2	2	1	4	↓	→	↑	↓
21															

Figure 2-14: Monthly sales data

J	K	L
Letter	Wingdings 3	
a	⇨	
b	⇦	
c	⇨	
d	⇦	
e	⇨	
f	←	
g	→	
h	↑	
i	↓	
j	↖	
k	↗	
l	↙	
m	↘	
n	↔	
o	↕	
p	▲	
q	▼	
r	△	
s	▽	
t	◄	
u	►	
v	◁	
w	▷	
x	◣	
y	◢	
z	◥	

Figure 2-15: Icon sets created with Wingdings 3 font

To begin creating up, down, or flat arrows that reflect monthly changes in each salesperson's performance, perform the following steps:

1. Create each salesperson's rank during each month by copying the formula =RANK(E6,E$6:E$20,0) from J6 to J6:N20.

The last argument of 0 in the RANK function indicates that the largest number in E6:E20 will receive a rank of 1, the second largest number a rank of 2, and so on. If the last argument of the RANK function is 1, the smallest number receives a RANK of 1.

2. Next create the h, i, and g that correspond to the arrows by copying the formula =IF(K6<J6,"h",IF(K6>J6,"i","g")) from O6 to O6:R20.

3. Finally change the font in O6:R20 to Wingdings3.

You can now follow the progress of each salesperson (relative to her peers). For example, you can now see that Dirk Nowitzki improved his ranking each month.

Using Check Boxes to Control Data in a Chart

Often the marketing analyst wants to plot many series (such as sales of each product) in a single chart. This can result in a highly cluttered chart. Often it is convenient to use *check boxes* to control the series that are charted. The Checkboxes worksheet illustrates this idea. The data here shows weekly sales of chocolates, DVDs, magazines, soda, and hot dogs at the Quickie Mart convenience store. You can easily summarize this data in a single chart with five lines, as shown in Figure 2-16

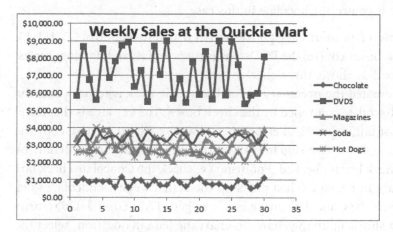

Figure 2-16: Sales at Quickie Mart

Now this chart is a good start, however, you might notice that the presence of five series appears cluttered, and therefore you would probably be better off if you did not show the sales of every product. Check boxes make it easy to control which series show up in a chart. To create a check box, perform the following steps:

1. Ensure you see the Developer tab on the ribbon. If you do not see the Developer tab in Excel 2010 or 2013, select File ➤ Options, and from Customize Ribbon select the Developer tab.

2. To place a check box in a worksheet, select the Developer tab and chose Insert.

3. From the Form Controls (Not ActiveX) select the check box that is third from the left in the top row.

4. After releasing the left mouse in the worksheet, you see a drawing tool. Hold down the left mouse to size the check box. If you want to resize the check box again later, simply hold down the control key and click the check box. A check box simply puts a TRUE or FALSE in a cell of your choosing. It serves as a Toggle switch that can be used to turn Excel features (such as a Function argument or Conditional Formatting) on or off.

5. Next, select the cell controlled by the check box by moving the cursor to the check box until you see the Pointer (a hand with a pointing finger).

6. Right-click, select the Format Control dialog box, and select cell F3 (by pointing) as the cell link. Click OK.

7. Now when this check box is selected, F3 shows TRUE, and when the check box is not selected, cell F3 shows FALSE. Label this check box with the name of the series it controls, Chocolate in this case.

In a similar fashion four more check boxes were created that control G3, H3, I3, and J3. These check boxes control the DVDs, magazines, sodas, and hot dogs series, respectively. Figure 2-17 shows these check boxes.

After you have created the necessary check boxes, the trick is to not chart the original data but chart data controlled by the check boxes. The key idea is that Excel will ignore a cell containing an #N/A error when charting. To get started, copy the formula = IF(F$3,F6,NA()) from O6 to O6:S35 to ensure that a series will only be charted when its check box is checked. For instance, check the Chocolate check box and a TRUE appears in F3, so O6 just picks up the actual week 1 chocolate sales in F6. If you uncheck the Chocolate check box, you get a FALSE in F3, O6 returns #N/A, and nothing shows up in the chart. To chart the data in question, select the modified data in the range O5:S35 and choose from the Insert tab the second X Y Scatter option. If you check only the Chocolate and Magazines check boxes, you can obtain the chart shown in Figure 2-18, which shows only sales of Chocolate and Magazines.

	B	C	D	E	F	G	H	I	J
1									
2									
3					TRUE	FALSE	TRUE	FALSE	FALSE
4					Original Data				
5				Week	Chocolate	DVDS	Magazine:	Soda	Hot Dogs
6				1	$857.00	$5,820.00	$3,374.00	$3,036.00	$2,564.00
7				2	$1,050.00	$8,656.00	$3,821.00	$3,589.00	$2,615.00
8	☑ Chocolate			3	$863.00	$6,749.00	$2,857.00	$3,279.00	$2,512.00
9				4	$933.00	$5,580.00	$3,284.00	$3,981.00	$2,705.00
10				5	$905.00	$8,534.00	$3,923.00	$3,411.00	$2,386.00
11	☐ DVDS			6	$901.00	$6,837.00	$3,837.00	$3,484.00	$2,977.00
12				7	$597.00	$7,794.00	$2,713.00	$3,498.00	$2,946.00
13				8	$1,185.00	$8,708.00	$3,375.00	$3,169.00	$2,729.00
14				9	$565.00	$8,892.00	$3,674.00	$3,660.00	$2,977.00
15				10	$964.00	$6,338.00	$2,640.00	$3,797.00	$2,322.00
16	☑ Magazines			11	$982.00	$7,258.00	$2,926.00	$3,201.00	$2,939.00
17				12	$658.00	$5,468.00	$2,360.00	$3,738.00	$2,648.00
18				13	$961.00	$8,690.00	$3,466.00	$3,374.00	$2,619.00
19	☐ Soda			14	$691.00	$7,054.00	$2,888.00	$3,371.00	$2,449.00
20				15	$695.00	$8,988.00	$2,433.00	$3,211.00	$2,589.00
21				16	$1,065.00	$5,658.00	$2,085.00	$3,622.00	$2,919.00
22				17	$851.00	$6,781.00	$3,392.00	$3,812.00	$2,533.00
23	☐ Hot dogs			18	$636.00	$5,423.00	$3,714.00	$3,458.00	$2,590.00
24				19	$989.00	$7,763.00	$2,534.00	$3,101.00	$2,596.00

Figure 2-17: Check boxes for controlling which products show in chart

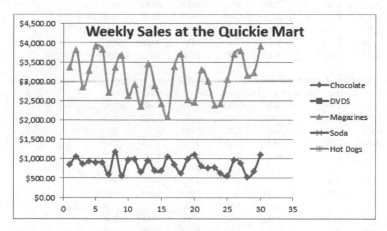

Figure 2-18: Charting only selected data

Using Sparklines to Summarize Multiple Data Series

Suppose you are charting daily sales of French Fries at each of the over 12,000 US McDonald's. Showing the sales for each restaurant in a single chart would result in a useless, cluttered graph. But think of the possibilities if you could summarize daily sales for each restaurant in a single cell! Fortunately, Excel 2010 and later enables you to create *sparklines*. A sparkline is a graph that summarizes a row or column of data in a single cell. This section shows you how to use Excel 2010 to easily create sparklines.

The Sparklines worksheet contains data that can be used to illustrate the concept of Sparklines. The data gives the number of engagement rings sold each day of the week in each city for a national jewelry store chain (see Figure 2-19).

	C	D	E	F	G	H	I	J	K
1									
2		Different scale for each sparkline							
3		Monday	Tuesday	Wednesday	Thursday	Friday	Saturday	Sunday	
4	Chicago	2520	3680	3852	3816	4800	5668	3600	
5	New York	6804	9630	8262	7290	10044	11700	9630	
6	Los Angeles	6489	8640	8910	8181	11340	12753	8550	
7	San Francisco	2184	3000	2673	2646	3528	4134	2970	
8	Dallas	3325	4650	4050	4050	6540	6630	5200	
9	Houston	4494	6120	5724	5778	6840	8580	5700	
10	Atlanta	3052	4240	3384	3924	4512	4680	4400	
11	Seattle	1890	3300	2700	2619	3960	3939	3030	
12	Miami	1316	1820	1800	1728	2328	2678	2120	
13	Boston	3948	6180	5562	5670	7056	7488	5940	
14	Nashville	1498	2020	1818	1962	2352	2600	1880	
15									
16		Same Scale for each sparkline							
17		Monday	Tuesday	Wednesday	Thursday	Friday	Saturday	Sunday	
18	Chicago	2520	3680	3852	3816	4800	5668	3600	
19	New York	6804	9630	8262	7290	10044	11700	9630	
20	Los Angeles	6489	8640	8910	8181	11340	12753	8550	
21	San Francisco	2184	3000	2673	2646	3528	4134	2970	
22	Dallas	3325	4650	4050	4050	6540	6630	5200	
23	Houston	4494	6120	5724	5778	6840	8580	5700	
24	Atlanta	3052	4240	3384	3924	4512	4680	4400	
25	Seattle	1890	3300	2700	2619	3960	3939	3030	
26	Miami	1316	1820	1800	1728	2328	2678	2120	
27	Boston	3948	6180	5562	5670	7056	7488	5940	
28	Nashville	1498	2020	1818	1962	2352	2600	1880	

Figure 2-19: Sparklines Example

You can summarize the daily sales by graphing the daily counts for each city in a single cell. To do so, perform the following steps:

1. First, select where you want your Sparklines to go (the Sparklines worksheet uses K4:K14: you can use L4:L14) and then from the Insert tab, select Line from the Sparklines section.

2. Fill in the dialog box shown in Figure 2-20 with the data range on which the Sparklines are based (D4:J14).

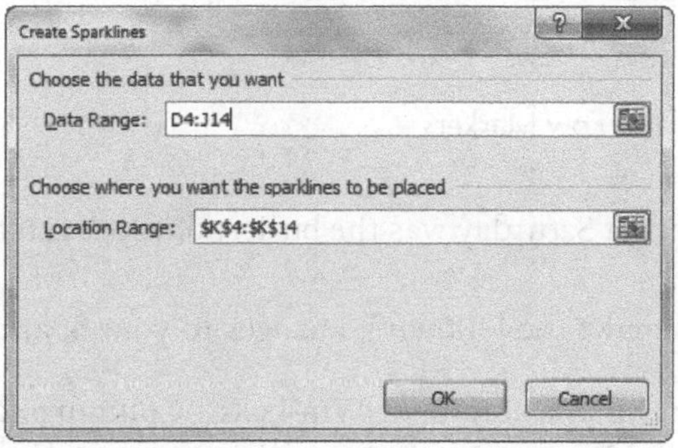

Figure 2-20: Sparkline dialog box

You now see a line graph (refer to Figure 2-19) that summarizes the daily sales in each city. The Sparklines make it clear that Saturday is the busiest day of the week.

If you click in any cell containing a Sparkline, the Sparkline Tools Design tab appears. Here, after selecting the Design tab, you can make many changes to your Sparklines. For example, Figure 2-21 shows selections for the high and low points to be marked and Figure 2-22 shows the Sparklines resulting from these selections.

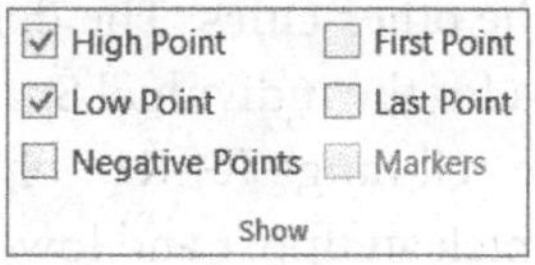

Figure 2-21: Selecting High and Low Point Markers

	N	O	P	Q	R	S	T	U	V
1									
2		Different scale for each sparkline							
3		Monday	Tuesday	Wednesd	Thursday	Friday	Saturday	Sunday	
4	Chicago	2520	3680	3852	3816	4800	5668	3600	
5	New York	6804	9630	8262	7290	10044	11700	9630	
6	Los Angel	6489	8640	8910	8181	11340	12753	8550	
7	San Franci	2184	3000	2673	2646	3528	4134	2970	
8	Dallas	3325	4650	4050	4050	6540	6630	5200	
9	Houston	4494	6120	5724	5778	6840	8580	5700	
10	Atlanta	3052	4240	3384	3924	4512	4680	4400	
11	Seattle	1890	3300	2700	2619	3960	3939	3030	
12	Miami	1316	1820	1800	1728	2328	2678	2120	
13	Boston	3948	6180	5562	5670	7056	7488	5940	
14	Nashville	1498	2020	1818	1962	2352	2600	1880	

Figure 2-22: Sparklines with High and Low Markers

These Sparklines make it clear that Saturday was the busiest day for each branch and Monday was the slowest day.

The Design tab enables you to make the following changes to your Sparklines:

- Alter the type of Sparkline (Line, Column, or Win-Loss). Column and Win-Loss Sparklines are discussed later in the chapter.
- Use the Edit Data choice to change the data used to create the Sparkline. You can also change the default setting so that hidden data is included in your Sparkline.
- Select any combination of the high point, low point, negative points, first point, or last point to be marked.
- Change the style or color associated with the Sparklines and markers.
- Use the Axis menu to change the way the axes are set for each Sparkline. For example, you may make the x-axis or y-axis scale the same for each Sparkline. This is the scaling used in the cell range K18:K28. Note this choice shows that Nashville, for example, sells fewer rings than the other cities. The default is for the scale for each axis to be based on the data for the individual Sparkline. This is the scaling used in the Sparklines in the cell range K4:K14 of Figure 2-22. The Custom Value choice enables you to pick an upper and lower limit for each axis.
- When data points occur at irregularly spaced dates, you can select Data Axis Type from the Axis menu so that the graphed points are separated by an amount of space proportional to the differences in dates.

NOTE   By clicking any of the Sparklines, you could change them to Column Sparklines simply by selecting Column from the Sparklines Design tab.

Excel also can create Win-Loss Sparklines. A Win-Loss Sparkline treats any positive number as an *up block* and any negative number as a *down block*. Any 0s are graphed as a gap. A Win-Loss Sparkline provides a perfect way to summarize performance against sales targets. In the range D32:J42 you can see a list of the daily targets for each city. By copying the formula = IF(D18>D32−1−1) from D45 to D45:J55, you can create a 1 when a target is met and *a* −1 when a target is not met. To create the Win-Loss Sparklines, select the range where the Sparklines should be placed (cell range K45:K55) and from the Insert menu, select Win-Loss Sparklines. Then choose the data range D45:J55. Figure 2-23 shows your Win-Loss Sparklines.

	C	D	E	F	G	H	I	J	K
30		Target							
31		Monday	Tuesday	Wednesday	Thursday	Friday	Saturday	Sunday	
32	Chicago	3193	3592	3592	3991	3991	5188	3991	
33	New York	7241	8146	8146	9051	9051	11767	9051	
34	Los Angeles	7413	8340	8340	9266	9266	12046	9266	
35	San Francisco	2415	2717	2717	3019	3019	3925	3019	
36	Dallas	3937	4429	4429	4921	4921	6397	4921	
37	Houston	4941	5559	5559	6177	6177	8030	6177	
38	Atlanta	3222	3625	3625	4027	4027	5236	4027	
39	Seattle	2450	2756	2756	3063	3063	3981	3063	
40	Miami	1576	1773	1773	1970	1970	2561	1970	
41	Boston	4782	5380	5380	5978	5978	7771	5978	
42	Nashville	1615	1817	1817	2019	2019	2624	2019	
43		Monday	Tuesday	Wednesday	Thursday	Friday	Saturday	Sunday	
44		Met Goal?							
45	Chicago	-1	1	1	-1	1	1	-1	
46	New York	-1	1	1	-1	1	-1	1	
47	Los Angeles	-1	1	1	-1	1	1	-1	
48	San Francisco	-1	1	-1	-1	1	1	-1	
49	Dallas	-1	1	-1	-1	1	1	1	
50	Houston	-1	1	1	-1	1	1	-1	
51	Atlanta	-1	1	-1	-1	1	-1	1	
52	Seattle	-1	1	-1	-1	1	-1	-1	
53	Miami	-1	1	1	-1	1	1	1	
54	Boston	-1	1	1	-1	1	-1	-1	
55	Nashville	-1	1	1	-1	1	-1	-1	

Figure 2-23: Win-Loss Sparklines

NOTE   If you want your Sparklines to automatically update to include new data, you should make the data a table.

Using GETPIVOTDATA to Create the End-of-Week Sales Report

Many marketing analysts download weekly sales data and want to summarize it in charts that update as you download the new data. The Excel Table feature and GETPIVOTDATA function can greatly ease this process. To illustrate this process, download the source data in columns D through G in the End of Month dashboard worksheet. Each row (see Figure 2-24) gives the week of sales, the sales category, the store in which sales were made, and the revenue generated. The goal is to create a line graph to summarize sales of selected product categories (for each store) that automatically update when new data is downloaded. The approach is as follows:

	D	E	F	G
4	WEEK	Catego	Store	Revenue
5	3	Abrasives	Lowe's	2043
6	12	Safety	Menards	2343
7	3	Tape	Home Depo	1414
8	12	Command	Target	1820
9	9	Tape	Home Depo	943
10	7	Tape	Target	1219
11	7	Command	Menards	1156
12	11	Abrasives	Lowe's	2127
13	12	Safety	Menards	1315
14	3	Tape	Target	1580
15	10	Abrasives	Home Depo	1598
16	4	Command	Lowe's	1000
17	7	Tape	Menards	1087
18	7	Abrasives	Menards	1728
19	1	Abrasives	Target	1911
20	7	Abrasives	Menards	1563
21	2	Tape	Target	2482
22	7	Safety	Lowe's	1534
23	12	Safety	Menards	1471
24	2	Abrasives	Lowe's	990
25	11	Tape	Lowe's	1580
26	1	Safety	Target	2389

Figure 2-24: Weekly sales data

1. Make the source data a table; in this example you can do so by selecting Table from the Insert tab after selecting the range D4:G243.
2. Create a PivotTable based on the source data by dragging Week to the Row Labels zone, Store and Category to the Column Labels zone, and Revenue to the Values zone. This PivotTable summarizes weekly sales in each store for each product category. Figure 2-25 shows a portion of this PivotTable.

	J	K	L	M	N	O	P	Q	R	S	T	U
11	Column Labels											
12	Lowe's				Lowe's Total	Menards				Menards Total	Home Depot	
13	Abrasives	Safety	Tape	Command		Abrasives	Safety	Tape	Command		Abrasives	Safety
14			1065		1247	2312	3772	526	3466		7764	3272	1984
15	2349	4510			6859	6220	3296	2159		11675	1921	2167
16	2797	1233	2046	6335	12411	3472		959	2369	6800		3352
17	1501	3822	1180	1000	7503	6018	2212			8230		
18	1940		833	2945	5718	708		501	597	1806	1758	3755
19			1918	6494	8412	4145	6205	4653		15003		2253
20	3049	3228			6277	3291	2303	6472	1156	13222	3580	4218
21	4208	2890	1873		8971	910		1494	3776	6180	2445	5496
22			2052	2825	4877	6265		1888		8153		
23	6117		1875		7992			2138		2138	4807	2325
24	2127	1971	4461	2394	10953	3596	1169			4765		810
25		1542	4786	850	7178	1124	7565	7264	2491	18384	2471	
26				1196	1196				3400	3400		
27	1455				1455							
28	25543	20261	21024	25286	92114	39521	23276	30994	13729	107520	20254	26360

Figure 2-25: PivotTable for Weekly sales report

3. Create a drop-down box in cell AG8 from which a store can be selected. To accomplish this, navigate to the Data tab and select Data Validation from the Data Tools group.

4. Choose Settings and fill in the Data Validation dialog box, as shown in Figure 2-26. This ensures that when the cursor is placed in cell AG8 you can see a drop-down box that lists the store names (pulled from cell range F5:F8)

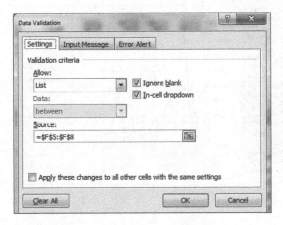

Figure 2-26: Creating Data Validation drop-down box

5. Enter week numbers in the range AG11:AG24 and product categories in AG10:AK10. Then use the GETPIVOTDATA function to pull the needed data from the PivotTable. Before entering the key formula, simply click anywhere in the PivotTable to get a GETPIVOTDATA function. Then copy that function and

paste it in the following formula to modify the arguments for Week, Category, and Store, as shown here. Enter this important formula in cell AH11:

```
=IF(AH$9=FALSE,NA(),IFERROR(GETPIVOTDATA("Revenue",$I$11,"WEEK"
,$AG11,"Category",AH$10,"Store",$AG$8)," ")).
```

6. Copy this formula to the range AH11:AK24. This formula uses GETPIVOTDATA to pull revenue for the store listed in AG8 and the category listed in row 10 if row 9 has a TRUE. The use of IFERROR ensures a blank is entered if the category were not sold in the selected store during the given week.

7. Make the source data for the chart, AG10:AK24, a table, so new data is automatically included in the graph. The Table feature can also ensure that when you enter a new week the GETPIVOTDATA formulas automatically copy down and pull needed information from the updated PivotTable.

8. Use check boxes to control the appearance of TRUE and FALSE in AH9:AK9. After making the range AG10:AK24 a table, the chart is simply an X-Y scatter graph with source data AG10:AK24. Figure 2-27 shows the result.

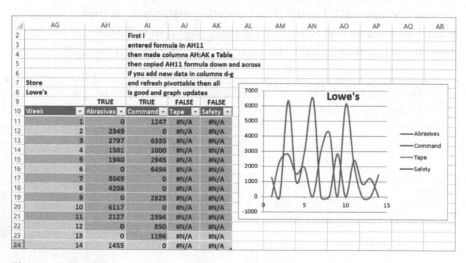

Figure 2-27: Sales summary report

9. Now add new data for Week 15 and refresh the PivotTable. If you add Week 15 in cell AG25, the graph automatically updates. Because you made the source data for the chart a table, when you press Enter Excel "knows" you want the formulas copied down.

Summary

In this chapter you learned the following:

- Right-clicking a series in a chart enables you to change the series' chart type and create a Combination chart.
- Right-clicking a chart series and choosing Format Data Series enables you to create a secondary axis for a chart.
- Right-clicking a chart series in a Column graph and selecting Fill followed by Picture or Texture Fill enables you to replace a bland column with a picture from a file or Clip Art.
- On Chart Tools from the Layout tab, you can easily insert Data Labels and a Data Table in the chart.
- If you make the source data for a chart a table (from the Insert tab choose Table) before creating a chart, the chart automatically updates to include new data.
- PivotCharts are a great way to summarize a lengthy market research survey. Filtering on the questions enables you customize the results shown in your chart.
- If you base your chart title and series labels on cell formulas, they dynamically update as you change the inputs or assumptions in your spreadsheet.
- Clever use of IF formulas and the Wingdings 3 font can enable you to create a visually appealing summary of trends over time in sales data.
- Use check boxes to control the series that appear in a chart.
- Combining the Table feature, PivotTables, GETPIVOTDATA, check boxes, and Data Validation drop-down boxes makes it easy to create charts with customized views that automatically update to include new data.

Exercises

Exercises 1–6 use data in the file Chapter2exercisesdata.xlsx.

1. The Weather worksheet includes monthly average temperature and rainfall in Bloomington, Indiana. Create a combination chart involving a column and line graph with a secondary axis to chart the temperature and rainfall data.
2. The Weather worksheet includes monthly average temperature and rainfall in Bloomington, Indiana. Create a combination chart involving a column and area graph with a secondary axis to chart the temperature and rainfall data.

3. The `Pictures and Labels` worksheet includes monthly tomato sales on Farmer Smith's farm. Summarize this data with pictures of tomatoes, data labels, and a data table.

4. The `Survey` worksheet contains results evaluating a training seminar for salespeople. Use a PivotChart to summarize the evaluation data.

5. The data in the `checkboxes` worksheet contains monthly sales during 2010 and 2011. Use check boxes to set up a chart in which the user can choose which series are charted.

6. The `Income` worksheet contains annual data on median income in each state for the years 1984–2010. Use Sparklines to summarize this data.

7. Jack Welch's GE performance evaluation system requires management to classify the top 20 percent of all workers, middle 70 percent of all workers, and bottom 10 percent of all workers. Use Icon sets to classify the salespeople in the `Sales Tracker` worksheet of file `Chapter2data.xlsx` according to the 20-70-10 rule.

NOTE You need the `PERCENTILE` function. For example, the function `PERCENTILE(A1:A50,.9)` would return the 90th percentile of the data in the cell range A1:A50.

Exercises 8 and 9 deal with the data in the file `LaPetitbakery.xlsx` that was discussed in Chapter 1.

8. Use the Excel Table feature to set up a chart of daily cake sales that updates automatically when new data is included.

9. Set up a chart that can be customized to show total monthly sales for any subset of La Petit Bakery's products. Of course, you want the chart to update automatically when new data appears in the worksheet.

10. The marketing product life cycle postulates that sales of a new product will increase for a while and then decrease. Specify the following five inputs:

   - Year 1 sales
   - Years of growth
   - Years of decline
   - Average annual growth rate during growth period
   - Average annual decline during decline period

Set up a Data Validation drop-down box that allows years of growth and decline to vary between 3 and 10. Then determine sales during Years 1–20. Suppose 10,000 units need to be sold in a year to break even. Chart your annual sales, and set up a dynamic chart title that shows the year (if any) in which you break even. Your series label should include the values of the five input parameters.

3

Using Excel Functions to Summarize Marketing Data

In Chapter 1, "Slicing and Dicing Marketing Data with PivotTables," and Chapter 2, "Using Excel Charts to Summarize Marketing Data," you learned how to summarize marketing data with PivotTables and charts. Excel also has a rich library of powerful functions that you can use to summarize marketing data. In this chapter you will learn how these Excel functions enable marketers to gain insights for their data that can aid them to make informed and better marketing decisions.

This chapter covers the following:

- Using the Excel Table feature to create dynamic histograms that summarize marketing data and update automatically as new data is added.
- Using Excel statistical functions such as AVERAGE, STDEV, RANK, PERCENTILE, and PERCENTRANK to summarize marketing data.
- Using the powerful "counting and summing functions" (COUNTIF, COUNTIFS, SUMIF, SUMIFS, AVERAGEIF, and AVERAGEIFS) to summarize marketing data.
- Writing array formulas to perform complicated statistical calculations on any subset of your data.

Summarizing Data with a Histogram

A *histogram* is a commonly used tool to summarize data. A histogram essentially tells you how many data points fall in various ranges of values. Several Excel functions, including *array functions* such as the TRANSPOSE and the FREQUENCY function, can be used to create a histogram that automatically updates when new data is entered into the spreadsheet.

When using an array function, you need to observe the following rules:

1. Select the range of cells that will be populated by the array function. Often an array function populates more than one cell, so this is important.
2. Type in the function just like an ordinary formula.
3. To complete the entry of the formula, do not just press Enter; instead press Control+Shift+Enter. This is called *array entering* a formula.

Because the FREQUENCY function is a rather difficult array function, let's begin with a discussion of a simpler array function, the TRANSPOSE function.

Using the TRANSPOSE Function

The TRANSPOSE function is a great place to start when illustrating the use of array functions. To begin, take a look at the Histogram worksheet in the Chapter3bakery. xlsx file. In Figure 3-1, cells N27:Q27 list some of my best students. This list would be easier to digest though if the names were listed in a column. To do this, copy N27:Q27 and move the cursor to R28, then right-click and select Paste Special... Select the Transpose checkbox to paste the names in a column.

	N	O	P	Q	R	S
27	Scarlett	Lindsay	Britney	Paris	PASTE SPECIAL	TRANSPOSE FUNCTION
28					Scarlett	Scarlett
29					Lindsay	Lindsay
30					Britney	Britney
31					Paris	Paris

Figure 3-1: Use of the Transpose function

Unfortunately, if you change the source data (for example, Scarlett to Blake) the transposed data in column R does not reflect the change. If you want the transposed data to reflect changes in the source data, you need to use the TRANSPOSE function. To do so perform the following steps:

1. Select S28:S31.
2. Enter in cell S28 the formula =TRANSPOSE(N27:Q27) and press Control+Shift+Enter. You will know an array formula has been entered when you see a { in the Formula bar.
3. Change Scarlett in N27 to Blake, and you can see that Scarlett changes to Blake in S28 but not in R28.

Using the FREQUENCY Function

The FREQUENCY function can be used to count how many values in a data set fit into various ranges. For example, given a list of heights of NBA basketball players the FREQUENCY function could be used to determine how many players are at least 7' tall, how many players are between 6' 10" and 7' tall, and so on. The syntax of the FREQUENCY function is FREQUENCY(array,bin range). In this section you will utilize the FREQUENCY function to create a histogram that charts the number of days in which cake sales fall into different numerical ranges. Moreover, your chart will automatically update to include new data.

On the Histogram worksheet you are given daily sales of cakes at La Petit Bakery. You can summarize this data with a histogram. The completed histogram is provided for you in the worksheet, but if you want to follow along with the steps simply copy the data in D7:E1102 to the same cell range in a blank worksheet. Begin by dividing a range of data into 5–15 equal size ranges (called a *bin range*) to key a histogram. To do so, perform the following steps:

1. Select your data (the range D7:E1102) and make this range a table by selecting Insert ➤ Table. If a cell range is already a table then under Insert the table option will be grayed out.

2. In cell E5, point to all the data and compute the minimum daily cake sales with the formula =MIN(Table1[Cakes]).

3. Similarly, determine the maximum daily cake sales in E6. The range of daily cake sales is between 32 and 165. Select your bin ranges to be <= 30, 31–50, 51–70, …, 151–170…, > 170 cakes.

4. List the boundaries for these bin ranges in the cell range I9:I17. Figure 3-2 shows this process in action.

You can now use the FREQUENCY function to count the number of days in which cake sales fall in each bin range. The syntax of the FREQUENCY function is FREQUENCY(array,bin range). When an array is entered, this formula can count how many values in the array range fall into the bins defined by the bin range. In this example the function will count the number of days in which cake sales fall in each bin range. This is exemplified in Figure 3-2. To begin using the FREQUENCY function, perform the following steps:

1. Select the range J9:J17 in the Histogram worksheet and type the formula =FREQUENCY(E8:E1102,I9:I17).

2. Array enter this formula by pressing Control+Shift+Enter. This formula computes how many numbers in the table are ≤30, between 31 and 50,..., between 151 and 170, and more than 170.

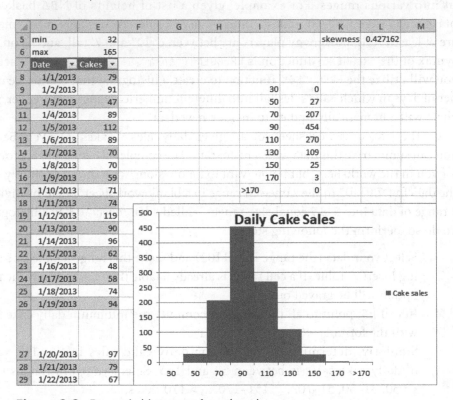

	D	E	F	G	H	I	J	K	L	M
5	min	32						skewness	0.427162	
6	max	165								
7	Date	Cakes								
8	1/1/2013	79								
9	1/2/2013	91				30	0			
10	1/3/2013	47				50	27			
11	1/4/2013	89				70	207			
12	1/5/2013	112				90	454			
13	1/6/2013	89				110	270			
14	1/7/2013	70				130	109			
15	1/8/2013	70				150	25			
16	1/9/2013	59				170	3			
17	1/10/2013	71				>170	0			
18	1/11/2013	74								
19	1/12/2013	119								
20	1/13/2013	90								
21	1/14/2013	96								
22	1/15/2013	62								
23	1/16/2013	48								
24	1/17/2013	58								
25	1/18/2013	74								
26	1/19/2013	94								
27	1/20/2013	97								
28	1/21/2013	79								
29	1/22/2013	67								

Figure 3-2: Dynamic histogram for cake sales

For example, you can find that there were three days in which between 151 and 170 cakes were sold. The counts update automatically if new days of sales are added.

3. Select the range I9:J17, and from the Insert tab, select the first Column Graph option.

4. Right-click any column, select Format Data Series..., and change Gap Width to 0. This enables you to obtain the histogram, as shown in Figure 3-2.

5. If you enter more data in Column E (say 10 numbers >170) you can see that the histogram automatically updates to include the new data. This would not have happened if you had failed to make the data a Table.

Skewness and Histogram Shapes

There are a variety of histograms that are seen when examining marketing data, but the three most commonly seen histogram shapes are listed here (see Figure 3-3 and file Skewexamples.xlsx):

- *Symmetric histogram:* A histogram is symmetric and looks approximately the same to the left of the peak and the right of the peak. In Figure 3-3 the IQ scores yield an asymmetric histogram.
- *Positively skewed:* (skewed right) A histogram is positively skewed (or skewed right) if it has a single peak and the values of the data set extend much further to the right of the peak than to the left of the peak. In Figure 3-3 the histogram of family income is positively skewed.
- *Negatively skewed:* (skewed left) A histogram is negatively skewed if it has a single peak and the values of the data set extend much further to the left of the peak than to the right of the peak. In Figure 3-3, the histogram of Days from Conception to Birth is negatively skewed.

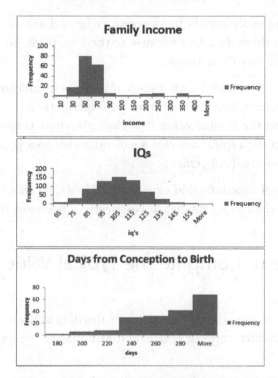

Figure 3-3: Symmetric, positively skewed, and negatively skewed histograms

The Excel SKEW function provides a measure of the skewness of a data set. A skewness value > +1 indicates mostly positive skewness, < −1 mostly negative skewness, and a skewness value between −1 and +1 indicates a mostly symmetric histogram. This function can be used to obtain a quick characterization of whether a histogram is symmetric, positively skewed, or negatively skewed. To see this function in action, enter the formula =SKEW(Table1[Cakes]) into cell L5 in the Histogram worksheet to yield a skewness of .43, implying that cake cells follow a symmetric distribution. Because you made the source data an Excel table, the skewness calculation in L5 would automatically update if new data is added.

In the next section you will see that the degree of skewness (or lack thereof) in a data set enables the marketing analyst to determine how to best describe the typical value in a data set.

Using Statistical Functions to Summarize Marketing Data

In her daily work the marketing analyst will often encounter large datasets. It is often difficult to make sense of these data sets because of their vastness, so it is helpful to summarize the data on two dimensions:

- **A typical value of the data:** For example, what single number best summarizes the typical amount a customer spends on a trip to the supermarket.
- **Spread or variation about the typical value:** For example, there is usually much more spread about the typical amount spent on a visit to a grocery superstore than a visit to a small convenience store.

Excel contains many statistical functions that can summarize a data set's typical value and the spread of the data about its mean. This section discusses these statistical functions in detail.

Using Excel Functions to Compute the Typical Value for a Data Set

The file Chapter3bakery.xlsx contains the La Petit Bakery sales data that was discussed in Chapter 1. For each product, suppose you want to summarize the typical number of that product sold in a day. Three measures are often used to summarize the *typical value* for a data set.

- The mean, or *average*, is simply the sum of the numbers in the data set divided by the number of values in the dataset. The average is computed with the Excel AVERAGE function. For example, the average of the numbers 1, 3, and 5 is $\frac{1+3+5}{3}$ = 3. You can often use $\bar{x}$ to denote the mean or average of a data set.
- The *median* is approximately the 50th percentile of the data set. Roughly one-half the data is below the median and one-half the data is above the median. More precisely, suppose there are n values that when ordered from smallest to largest are $x_1, x_2, \ldots, x_n$. If n is odd the median is $x_{.5(n+1)}$, and if n is even, the median is $(x_{.5n} + x_{.5n+1})/2$. For example, for the data set 1, 3, 5, the median is 3, and for the data set 1, 2, 3, 4 the median is 2.5. The MEDIAN function can be used to compute the median for a data set.
- The *mode* of a data set is simply the most frequently occurring value in the data set. If no value appears more than once, the data set has no mode. The MODE function can be used to compute the mode of a data set. A data set can have more than one mode. If you have Excel 2010 or later, then the array function MODE.mult (see *Excel 2010 Data Analysis and Business Modeling* by Wayne Winston [Microsoft Press, 2011]) can be used to compute all modes. For example, the data set 1, 3, and 5 has no mode, whereas the data set 1, 2, 2, 3 has a mode of 2.

The Descriptive stats worksheet uses Excel functions to compute three measures of typical value for daily sales of cakes, pies, cookies, smoothies, and coffee. Complete the following steps and see Figure 3-4 for details.

1. To compute the average for daily cake sales in cell H5, enter the formula =AVERAGE(H12:H1106).
2. To compute the median for daily cake sales in cell H6, enter the formula =MEDIAN(H12:H1106).
3. To, compute the mode of daily cake sales in cell H7, enter the formula =MODE(H12:H1106).
4. Copy these formulas to the range I5:L7 to compute these measures for La Petit Bakery's other products.

You find, for example, that on average 86.28 cakes were sold each day, around one-half the time fewer than 85 cakes were sold, and the most frequently occurring number of cakes sold in a day is 90.

	G	H	I	J	K	L	M
1	5th largest cake day	148					
2	3rd smallest cake day	38					
3	rank of 136 cakes	0.979					
4							
5	mean	86.28037	53.54795	540.4511	218.4666667	391.6265	
6	median	85	52	533	206	388	
7	mode	90	46	397	166	375	
8	standard deviation	20.27667	13.37189	132.3544	74.35093017	102.9305	
9	95th percentile	122	77.2	764.8	352.2	568.4	
10	Skewness	0.427162	0.474088	0.440287	0.785999912	0.360745	
11	Date	Cakes	Pies	Cookies	Smoothies	Coffee	promotion
12	1/1/2013	79	46	518	60	233	none
13	1/2/2013	91	50	539	161	427	none
14	1/3/2013	47	60	222	166	347	none
15	1/4/2013	89	64	734	153	358	none
16	1/5/2013	112	73	764	240	392	none
17	1/6/2013	89	57	922	259	510	none
18	1/7/2013	70	50	476	120	334	none
19	1/8/2013	70	48	496	222	316	none
20	1/9/2013	59	37	587	181	156	none
21	1/10/2013	71	36	488	178	298	none
22	1/11/2013	74	50	645	100	490	none
23	1/12/2013	119	71	438	162	416	none
24	1/13/2013	90	51	568	137	434	none
25	1/14/2013	96	48	585	194	573	promotion

Figure 3-4: Descriptive statistics

Which Measure of Typical Value Is Best?

Although there is no single best answer to this question, there are a few rules of thumb that are summarized here. The mode might be relevant if a hat store wanted to maximize sales and was going to stock only one size of hats. In most cases, however, the analyst who wants to summarize a data set by a single number must choose either the mean or the median. In the presence of substantial positive or negative skewness, extreme values tend to distort the mean, and the median is a better choice as a summary of a typical data value. In other situations using the median throws out important information, so the mean should be used to summarize a data set. To summarize:

■ If a skew statistic is greater than 1 or less than −1, substantial skewness exists and you should use median as a measure of typical value.

■ If skew statistic is between −1 and 1, use mean as a measure of typical value.

For the cake example, data skewness is between −1 and 1, so you would use the mean of 86.28 cakes as a summary value for daily cake sales.

For an example of how skewness can distort the mean, consider the starting salaries of North Carolina students who graduated in 1984. Geography majors had by far the highest average starting salary. At virtually every other school, business majors had the highest average starting salary. You may guess that Michael Jordan was a UNC geography major, and his multimillion dollar salary greatly distorted the average salary for geography majors. The median salary at UNC in 1984 was, as expected, highest for business majors.

Using the VAR and STDEV Functions to Summarize Variation

Knowledge of the typical value characterizing a data set is not enough to completely describe a data set. For example, suppose every week Customer 1 spends $40 on groceries and during a week Customer 2 is equally likely to spend $10, $20, $30, or $100 on groceries. Each customer spends an average of $40 per week on groceries but we are much less certain about the amount of money Customer 2 will spend on groceries during a week. For this reason, the description of a data set is not complete unless you can measure the spread of a data set about its mean. This section discusses how the variance and standard deviation can be used to measure the spread of a data set about its mean.

Given a data set $x_1, x_2, \ldots, x_n$ the *sample variance* (s^2) of a data set is approximately the average squared deviation of the mean and may be computed with the formula $s^2 = \frac{1}{n-1}\sum_{i=1}^{i=n}(x_i - \bar{x})^2$. Here $\bar{x}$ is the average of the data values. For example, for the data set 1, 3, 5 the average is 3, so the sample variance is as follows:

$$\frac{1}{2}\{(1-3)^2 + (3-3)^2 + (5-3)^2\} = 4$$

Note that if all data points are identical, then the sample variance is 0. You should square deviations from the mean to ensure that positive and negative deviations from the mean will not cancel each other out.

Because variance is not in the same units as dollars, the analyst will usually take the square root of the sample variance to obtain the *sample standard deviation*(s). Because the data set 1, 3, and 5, has a sample variance of 4, s=2.

The Excel VAR function computes sample variance, and the Excel STDEV function computes sample standard deviation. As shown in Figure 3-4 (see Descriptive stats worksheet), copying the formula =STDEV(H12:H1106) from H8 to K8:L8 computes the standard deviation of each product's daily sales. For example, the standard deviation of daily cake sales was 20.28 cakes.

The Rule of Thumb for Summarizing Data Sets

If a data set does not exhibit substantial skewness, then the statisticians' interesting and important rule of thumb lets you easily characterize a data set. This rule states the following:

- Approximately 68 percent of all data points are within 1 sample standard deviation of the mean.
- Approximately 95 percent of all data points are within 2 standard deviations (2s) of the mean.
- Approximately 99.7 percent of the data points are within 3 standard deviations of the mean.

Any data point that is more than two sample standard deviations (2s) from the mean is unusual and is called an *outlier*. Later in the chapter (see the "Verifying the Rule of Thumb" section) you can find that for daily cake sales, the rule of thumb implies that 95 percent of all daily cake sales should be between 45.3 and 126.83. Thus cake sales less than 45 or greater than 127 would be an outlier. You can also find that 95.62 percent of all daily cake sales are within 2s of the mean. This is in close agreement with the rule of thumb.

The Percentile.exc and Percentrank.exc Functions

A common reorder policy in a supply chain is to produce enough to have a low percent chance, say, a 5 percent, of running out of a product. For cakes, this would imply that you should produce x cakes, where there is a 5 percent chance demand for cakes that exceed x or a 95 percent chance demand for cakes that is less than or equal to x. The value x is defined to be the 95th percentile of cake demand. The Excel 2010 and later function PERCENTILE.EXC(range, k) (here k is between 0 and 1) returns the 100*kth percentile for data in a range. In earlier versions of Excel, you should use the PERCENTILE function. By copying the formula =PERCENTILE. EXC(H12:H1106,0.95) from H9 to I9:L9 of the Descriptive stats worksheet you can obtain the 95th percentile of daily sales for each product. For example, there is a 5 percent chance that more than 122 cakes will be sold in a day.

Sometimes you want to know how unusual an observation is. For example, on December 27, 2015, 136 cakes were sold. This is more than two standard deviations above average daily cake sales, so this is an outlier or unusual observation. The PERCENTRANK.EXC function in Excel 2010 or later (or PERCENTRANK in earlier versions of Excel) gives the ranking of an observation relative to all values in a data set. The syntax of `PERCENTRANK.EXC` is `PERCENTRANK(range, x,[significance])`. This returns the percentile rank (as a decimal) of *x* in the given range. Significance is an optional argument that gives the number of decimal points returned by the function. Entering in cell H3 the formula `=PERCENTRANK.EXC(H12:H1106,H1102)`, you find that you sold more than 136 cakes on only 2.1 percent of all days.

The LARGE and SMALL Functions

Often you want to find, say, the fifth largest or third smallest value in an array. The function `LARGE(range,k)` returns the *k*th largest number in a range, whereas the function `SMALL(range,k)` returns the *k*th smallest number in a range. As shown in Figure 3-4, entering in cell H1 the formula `=LARGE(H12:H1106,5)` tells you the fifth largest daily sales of cakes was 148. Similarly, entering in cell H2 the formula `=SMALL(H12:H1106,3)` tells you the third smallest daily demand for cakes was 38.

These same powerful statistical functions can be used by marketing managers to gain important insights such as who are the 5 percent most profitable customers, who are the three most costly customers, or even what percentage of customers are unprofitable.

Using the COUNTIF and SUMIF Functions

In addition to mathematical functions such as `SUM` and `AVERAGE`, the `COUNTIF` and `SUMIF` functions might be (or should be!) two of the most used functions by marketing analysts. These functions provide powerful tools that enable the analyst to select a subset of data in a spreadsheet and perform a calculation (`count`, `sum`, or `average`) on any column in the spreadsheet. The wide variety of computations performed in this section should convince the marketer that these functions are a necessary part of your toolkit.

The first few examples involve the `COUNTIF` and `SUMIF` functions. The `COUNTIF` function has the syntax `COUNTIF(range, criteria)`. Then the `COUNTIF` function counts how many cells in the range meet the criteria. The `SUMIF` function has the syntax `SUMIF (range, criteria, and sum_range)`. Then the `SUMIF` function adds up the entries in the sumrange column for every row in which the cell in the range column meets the desired criteria.

The following sections provide some examples of these functions in action. The examples deal with the La Petit Bakery data, and the work is in the `Sumif Countif` worksheet. The work is also shown in Figure 3-5. The Create From Selection feature (discussed in Chapter 2) is used in the examples to name columns F through O with their row 10 headings.

	F	G	H	I	J	K	L	M	N	O	P	Q	R
1													
2			Outside										
3	MEAN-2SIGMA	45.72702047	13										
4	MEAN+2SIGMA	126.8337101	35										
5	TOTAL	1095											
6	WITHIN 2 SIGMA	1047											
7	FRACTION	95.62%											
8													
9													
10	weekday	Date	Cakes	Pies	Cookies	Smoothies	Coffee	promotion	month	Namemonth			
11	2	1/1/2013	79	46	518	60	233	none	1	January			
12	3	1/2/2013	91	50	539	161	427	none	1	January			
13	4	1/3/2013	47	60	222	166	347	none	1	January		How many promotions?	
14	5	1/4/2013	89	64	734	153	358	none	1	January		Promotion	110
15	6	1/5/2013	112	73	764	240	392	none	1	January		None	985
16	7	1/6/2013	89	57	922	259	510	none	1	January			
17	1	1/7/2013	70	50	476	120	334	none	1	January		Days sold>=122 cakes	56

Figure 3-5: Illustrating the Rule of Thumb

Counting the Number of Promotions

The Excel COUNTIF function can be used to count the number of rows in a range of cells that meet a single criterion. For example, you can compute the number of days on which La Petit Bakery had a promotion and did not have a promotion by using the COUNTIF function. Simply copy the formula =COUNTIF(promotion,Q14) from R14 to R15. You will see that there were 110 days with a promotion and 985 without a promotion. Note that Q14 as a criterion ensures that you only count days on which there was a promotion and Q15 as a criterion ensures that you only count days on which there was no promotion.

Verifying the Rule of Thumb

In the "Rule of Thumb" section of this chapter you learned that the rule of thumb tells you that for approximately 95 percent of all days, cake sales should be within 2s of the mean. You can use the COUNTIF function to check if this is the case. In cell G3 you can compute for daily cake sales the Average −2s with the formula AVERAGE(Cakes)−2*STDEV(Cakes). In G4 you can compute the Average +2s with the formula AVERAGE(Cakes)+2*STDEV(Cakes).

You can also find the number of days (13) on which cakes were more than 2s below the mean. To do so, enter in cell H3 the formula COUNTIF(Cakes,"<"&G3). The & (or concatenate) sign combines with the less than sign (in quotes because < is text) to ensure you only count entries in the Cakes column that are more than 2s (s = sample standard deviation) below the mean.

In cell H4 the formula COUNTIF(Cakes,">"&G4) computes the number of days (35) on which cake sales were more than 2s above the mean. Any data point that differs from the dataset's mean by more than 2s is called an outlier. Chapters 10 and 11 will make extensive use of the concept of an outlier.

The COUNT function can be used to count the number of numeric entries in a range while the COUNTA function can be used to count the number of non-blanks in a range. Also the COUNTBLANK function counts the number of blank cells in a range. For example, the function =COUNT(Cakes) in cell G5 counts how many numbers appear in the Cake column (1095). The COUNTA function counts the number of nonblank (text or numbers) cells in a range, and the COUNTBLANK function counts the number of blanks in a range. In G6 compute (with formula =G5−H3−H4) the number of cells (1047) within 2s of the mean. In G7 you find that 95.62 percent of the days had cake cells within 2s of the mean. This is in close agreement with the rule of thumb.

Computing Average Daily Cake Sales

You can also use SUMIF and COUNTIF functions to calculate the average sales of cakes for each day of the week. To do so, perform the following steps:

1. Copy the formula =SUMIF(daywk,Q20,Cakes) from S20 to S21:S26 to compute the total cake sales for each day of the week.
2. Copy the formula =COUNTIF(daywk,Q20) from R20 to R21:R:26 to compute for each day of the week the number of times the day of the week occurs in your data set.
3. Finally, in Column T, divide the SUMIF result for each day by the COUNTIF result, and this gives the average cake sales for each day of the week.

To rank the average cake sales for each day of the week, copy the formula =RANK(T20,$T$20:$T$26,0) from U20 to U21:U26. The formula in U20 ranks the Monday average sales among all days of the week. Dollar signing the range T20:T26 ensures that when you copy the formula in U21, each day's average sales is ranked against all 7 days of the week. If you had not dollar signed the range T20:T26, then in U21 the range would have changed to T21:T27, which would be incorrect because this range excludes Monday's average sales. The last argument of 0 ensures that the day of the week with the largest sales is given a rank of 1. If you use a last argument of 1, then sales are ranked on a basis that makes the smallest number have a rank of 1, which is not appropriate in this situation. Note that Saturday is the best day for sales and Wednesday was the worst day for sales.

In an identical manner, as shown in Figure 3-6 you can compute the average daily sales of smoothies during each month of the year in the cell range Q28:U40. The results show that the summer months (June–August) are the best for smoothie sales.

	Q	R	S	T	U
18	Cakes				
19	Total Sales by day of week	How many days	Total Sales	Average Daily sales	Rank
20	Monday	156	12259	78.58333	4
21	Tuesday	157	12079	76.93631	6
22	Wednesday	157	11986	76.34395	7
23	Thursday	157	12148	77.3758	5
24	Friday	156	14770	94.67949	3
25	Saturday	156	16181	103.7244	1
26	Sunday	156	15054	96.5	2
27	Smoothies				
28	Total sales by month of year	How many days	Total Sales	Average Daily Sales	Rank
29	January	93	15955	171.5591	12
30	February	84	14692	174.9048	10
31	March	93	16930	182.043	8
32	April	90	19016	211.2889	7
33	May	93	22434	241.2258	4
34	June	90	24971	277.4556	3
35	July	93	26654	286.6022	2
36	August	93	26724	287.3548	1
37	September	90	19737	219.3	5
38	October	93	19813	213.043	6
39	November	90	15463	171.8111	11
40	December	93	16832	180.9892	9

Figure 3-6: Daily summary of cake sales

In the next section you will learn how the AVERAGEIF function makes these calculations a bit simpler.

Using the COUNTIFS, SUMIFS, AVERAGEIF, and AVERAGEIFS Functions

COUNTIF and SUMIF functions are great, but they are limited to calculations based on a single criteria. The next few examples involve the use of four Excel functions that were first introduced in Excel 2007: COUNTIFS, SUMIFS, AVERAGEIF, and AVERAGEIFS (see the New 2007 Functions worksheet). These functions enable you to do calculations involving multiple (up to 127!) criteria. A brief description of the syntax of these functions follows:

■ The syntax of COUNTIFS is COUNTIFS(range1,criteria1, range2,critieria2, .. range_n, criteria_n). COUNTIFS counts the number of rows in which the *range1* entry meets *criteria1*, the *range2* entry meets *criteria2*, and ... the *range_n* entry meets *criteria_n*.

- The syntax of SUMIFS is SUMIFS(sum_range, range1, criteria1, range2, criteria2, ...,range_n,criteria_n). SUMIFS sums up every entry in the sum_range for which *criteria1* (based on *range1*), *criteria2* (based on *range2*), ... *criteria_n* (based on *range_n*) are all met.

- The AVERAGEIF function has the syntax AVERAGEIF(range, criteria, average_range). AVERAGEIF averages the range of cells in the average range for which the entry in the range column meets the criteria.

- The syntax of AVERAGEIFS is AVERAGEIFS(average_range, criteria_range1, criteria_range2, ..., criteria_range_n). AVERAGEIFS averages every entry in the average range for which *criteria1* (based on *range1*), *criteria2* (based on *range2*), ... *criteria_n* (based on *range_n*) are all met.

Now you can use these powerful functions to perform many important computations. The following examples are shown in the New 2007 Functions worksheet. The work is shown in Figure 3-7.

	Q	R	S	T	U	V
1	Promotions on each day of week			Average Cookies Sales by day of week		
2	COUNTIFS	How Many		AVERAGEIF	Mean sales	
3	Monday	23		Monday	482.0962	
4	Tuesday	14		Tuesday	480.6242	
5	Wednesday	17		Wednesday	486.8662	
6	Thursday	13		Thursday	488.6752	
7	Friday	13		Friday	597.3397	
8	Saturday	14		Saturday	654.7179	
9	Sunday	16		Sunday	593.8974	
10						
11	Total Sales					
12	SUMIFS					
13		Cakes	Pies	Cookies	Smoothie	Coffee
14	January	7726	4803	48070	15955	37039
15	February	7089	4507	44886	14692	33514
16	March	7848	4999	50764	16930	36317
17	April	7601	4647	46740	19016	34550
18	May	8360	4846	49865	22434	34396
19	June	7760	4948	47298	24971	34938
20	July	8085	4881	50228	26654	37015
21	August	7898	5130	50674	26724	37784
22	September	7842	4712	49605	19737	34081
23	October	8041	5117	51527	19813	36518
24	November	8045	4955	51617	15463	35713
25	December	8182	5090	50520	16832	36966

Figure 3-7: Monthly sales summary

Calculating the Number of Promotions on Each Day of the Week

In R3 the formula COUNTIFS(daywk,O3,promotion,"promotion") counts the number of promotions (23) on Monday. Copying this formula to R4:R9 calculates the number of promotions on each day of the week.

Calculating the Average Cookie Sales on Each Day of the Week

The formula in U3 =AVERAGEIF(daywk,T3,Cookies) averages the number of cookie sales on Monday. Copying this formula to the range U4:U9 calculates average cookie sales for all other days of the week.

Computing Monthly Sales for each Product

The formula =SUMIFS(INDIRECT(R$13),Namemonth,$Q14) in cell R14 computes total cake sales in January (7726).

1. Place the INDIRECT function before the reference to R13 to enable Excel to recognize the word "Cakes" as a range name.
2. Copy this formula to the range R14:V25. This calculates the total sales for each product during each month.

> **NOTE**   Note the INDIRECT function makes it easy to copy formulas involving range names. If you do not use the INDIRECT function then Excel will not recognize text in a cell such as R13 as a range name.

Computing Average Daily Sales by Month for Each Product

The formula =AVERAGEIFS(INDIRECT(R$28),Namemonth,$Q29) in cell R29 computes average cake sales in January. Copying this formula to the range R29:V40 calculates average sales during each month for each product. Figure 3-8 shows this example.

Summarizing Data with Subtotals

The final method to summarize market data discussed in this chapter is with *subtotals*. The subtotals feature yields a great looking summary of data. Unfortunately, if new data is added, subtotals are difficult to update. Suppose you want to get a breakdown for each day of the week and for each product showing how sales differ on days with and without promotions (see the Subtotals Bakery worksheet). Before computing subtotals you need to sort your data in the order in which you want your subtotals to be computed. In the subtotals you want to see the day of the week, and then "promotion" or "not promotion." Therefore, begin by sorting the data in this order. The dialog box to create this sort is shown in Figure 3-9.

	Q	R	S	T	U	V
27	Average Sales					
28	AVERAGEIFS	Cakes	Pies	Cookies	Smoothie	Coffee
29	January	83.0752688	51.64516	516.8817204	171.5591	398.2688
30	February	84.3928571	53.65476	534.3571429	174.9048	398.9762
31	March	84.3870968	53.75269	545.8494624	182.043	390.5054
32	April	84.4555556	51.63333	519.3333333	211.2889	383.8889
33	May	89.8924731	52.10753	536.1827957	241.2258	369.8495
34	June	86.2222222	54.97778	525.5333333	277.4556	388.2
35	July	86.9354839	52.48387	540.0860215	286.6022	398.0108
36	August	84.9247312	55.16129	544.8817204	287.3548	406.2796
37	September	87.1333333	52.35556	551.1666667	219.3	378.6778
38	October	86.4623656	55.02151	554.0537634	213.043	392.6667
39	November	89.3888889	55.05556	573.5222222	171.8111	396.8111
40	December	87.9784946	54.73118	543.2258065	180.9892	397.4839

Figure 3-8: Using AVERAGEIFS to summarize monthly sales

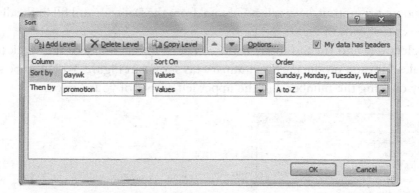

Figure 3-9: Sorting in preparation for subtotals

After performing the sort you see all the Sundays with no promotion, followed by the Sundays with a promotion, then the Mondays with no promotion days, and so on. Perform the following steps to continue:

1. Place your cursor anywhere in the data and select Subtotal from the Data tab on the ribbon.
2. Compute Subtotals for each product for each day of the week by filling in the Subtotals dialog box, as shown in Figure 3-10.

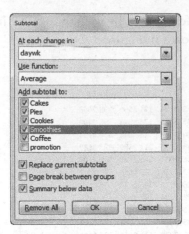

Figure 3-10: Subtotals settings for daily summary

3. Next you "nest" these subtotals with totals each day of the week for no promotion and promotion days. To compute the nested subtotals giving the breakdown of average product sales for each day of the week on promotion and no promotion days, select Subtotal from the Data tab and fill in the dialog box, as shown in Figure 3-11.

4. Select OK and the Subtotals feature creates for each day of the week total sales for each product. This summary (as shown in Figure 3-12) can be seen by clicking the number 2 in the upper left corner of your screen.

Figure 3-11: Final subtotals dialog box

By unchecking Replace Current Subtotals, you ensure that the subtotals on Promotions will build on and not replace the daily calculations. By clicking the 3 in the upper-left corner of the screen, you can find the final breakdown (see Figure

3-13) of average sales on no promotion versus promotion sales for each day of the week. It is comforting to note that for each product and day of week combination, average sales are higher with the promotion than without.

	D	E	F	G	H	I	J	K	L	M
9										
10		daywk	weekday	Date	Cakes	Pies	Cookies	Smoothies	Coffee	promotion
169		Sunday Average			96.5	59.46795	593.8974	240.2820513	434.5128	
328		Monday Average			78.58333	48.19231	482.0962	195.3653846	353.7564	
488		Tuesday Average			76.93631	46.76433	480.6242	198.5732484	348.3631	
648		Wednesday Average			76.34395	47.75159	486.8662	198.2101911	347.5287	
808		Thursday Average			77.3758	48.10828	488.6752	197.1719745	362.9427	
967		Friday Average			94.67949	59.6859	597.3397	235.0064103	427.0321	
1126		Saturday Average			103.7244	64.98077	654.7179	265.0512821	467.9936	
1127		Grand Average			86.28037	53.54795	540.4511	218.4666667	391.6265	

Figure 3-12: Daily subtotals summary

	D	E	F	G	H	I	J	K	L	M	N
9											
10		daywk	weekday	Date	Cakes	Pies	Cookies	Smoothies	Coffee	promotion	
151					95.37857	58.67857	584.7571	236.0428571	428.4786	none Average	
168					106.3125	66.375	673.875	277.375	487.3125	promotion Average	
169		Sunday Average			96.5	59.46795	593.8974	240.2820513	434.5128		
303					76.04511	47.30827	469.015	194.4135338	342.6241	none Average	
327					93.26087	53.30435	337.7391	200.8695652	418.1304	promotion Average	
328		Monday Average			78.58333	48.19231	482.0962	195.3653846	353.7564		
472					76.13986	46.33566	469.9441	194.8391608	346.014	none Average	
487					85.07143	51.14286	589.7143	236.7142857	372.3571	promotion Average	
488		Tuesday Average			76.93631	46.76433	480.6242	198.5732484	348.3631		
629					75.02143	47.06429	476.9786	195.75	343.2643	none Average	
647					87.23529	53.41176	568.2941	218.4705882	382.6471	promotion Average	
648		Wednesday Average			76.34395	47.75159	486.8662	198.2101911	347.5287		
793					76.56944	47.34722	478.25	194.1597222	360.9722	none Average	
807					86.30769	56.53846	604.1538	230.5384615	384.7692	promotion Average	
808		Thursday Average			77.3758	48.10828	488.6752	197.1719745	362.9427		
952					93.96503	59.07692	589.8392	227.2377622	421.8112	none Average	
966					102.5385	66.38462	679.8462	320.4615385	484.4615	promotion Average	
967		Friday Average			94.67949	59.6859	597.3397	235.0064103	427.0321		
1110					102.1479	63.78169	650.7183	258.028169	459.5775	none Average	
1125					119.7143	77.14286	695.2857	336.2857143	553.3571	promotion Average	
1126		Saturday Average			103.7244	64.98077	654.7179	265.0512821	467.9936		
1127		Grand Average			86.28037	53.54795	540.4511	218.4666667	391.6265		

Figure 3-13: Final subtotals summary

USING EXCEL OUTLINES WITH THE SUBTOTALS FEATURE

Whenever you use the Subtotals feature you will see numbers (in this case 1,2, 3, and 4) in the upper left hand corner of your spreadsheet. This is an example of an Excel outline. The higher the number in the outline, the less aggregated is the data. Thus selecting 4 gives the original data (with subtotals below the relevant data), selecting 3 gives a sales breakdown by day of week and promotion and lack thereof, selecting 2 gives a sales breakdown by day of the week, and selecting 1 gives an overall breakdown of average sales by product. If your cursor is within the original data you can click the Remove All button in the dialog box to remove all subtotals.

Using Array Formulas to Summarize *ESPN The Magazine* Subscriber Demographics

The six wonderful functions previously discussed are great ways to calculate conditional counts, sums, and averages. Sometimes, however, you might want to compute a conditional median, standard deviation, percentile, or some other statistical function. Writing your own array formulas you can easily create your own version of a MEDIANIF, STDEVIF, or other conditional statistical functions.

NOTE The rules for array formulas discussed in "Summarizing Data with a Histogram" also apply to array formulas that you might write.

To illustrate the idea, look at the Chapter 1 data on ESPN subscribers located in the Slicing with arrays worksheet (see also Figure 3-14).

▲	A	B	C	D	E	F	G	H	I	J	K
1											
2											
3											
4											
5											
6											
7											
8	Age	Gender	Income	Location							
9	72	m	72	rural		77	Median income subscibers >= 50				
10	29	m	68	suburban		80	Median incomesubscribers <50				
11	33	m	57	suburban		27.36277	Standard deviation income rural subscribers				
12	25	m	62	suburban							
13	38	m	164	urban							
14	33	m	44	urban							
15	18	f	62	rural							
16	17	m	68	urban							
17	32	f	53	urban							
18	24	f	92	urban							
19	26	f	54	suburban							
20	40	m	88	urban							
21	26	f	46	rural							
22	21	m	83	suburban							
23	29	m	144	rural							
24	51	f	30	suburban							

Figure 3-14: Using arrays to compute conditional medians and standard deviations

Suppose you have been asked to determine the median income for subscribers over 50. To accomplish this goal, perform the following steps:

1. Array enter in cell F9 the formula =MEDIAN(IF(Age>=50,Income,"")). This formula loops through the Income column and creates an array as follows: whenever the Age column contains a number greater than or equal to 50, the array returns the income value; otherwise the array returns a blank. Now the MEDIAN function is simply being applied to the rows corresponding to subscribers who are at least 50 years old. The median income for subscribers who are at least 50 is $77,000. Note that since your array formula populates a single cell you do not need to select a range containing more than one cell before typing in the formula.

2. In a similar fashion, array enter in cell F10 the formula =MEDIAN(IF(Age<50,Income,"")) to compute the median salary ($80,000) for subscribers who are under 50 years old.

3. Finally, in cell F11, array enter the formula =STDEV(IF(Location="rural", Income,"")) to compute (27.36) the standard deviation of the Income for Rural subscribers. This formula produces an array that contains only the Income values for rural subscribers and takes the standard deviation of the values in the new array.

Summary

In this chapter you learned the following:

- Using the FREQUENCY array function and the TABLE feature, you can create a histogram that summarizes data and automatically updates to include new data.

- The median (computed with the MEDIAN function) is used to summarize a typical value for a highly skewed data set. Otherwise, the mean (computed with the AVERAGE function) is used to summarize a typical value from a data set.

- To measure a data set's spread about the mean, you can use either variance (computed with the Excel VAR function) or standard deviation (computed with the Excel STDEV function). Standard deviation is the usual measure because it is in the same units as the data.

- For data sets that do not exhibit significant skewness, approximately 95 percent of your data is within two standard deviations of the mean.
- The PERCENTILE.EXC function returns a given percentile for a data set.
- The PERCENTRANK.EXC function returns the percentile rank for a given value in a data set.
- The LARGE and SMALL functions enable you to compute either the kth largest or kth smallest value in a data set.
- The COUNTIF and COUNTIFS functions enable you to count how many rows in a range meet a single or multiple criteria.
- The SUMIF and SUMIFS enable you to sum a set of rows in a range that meets a single or multiple criteria.
- The AVERAGEIF and AVERAGEIFS functions enable you to average a set of rows in a range that meets a single or multiple criteria.
- The SUBTOTALS feature enables you to create an attractive summary of data that closely resembles a PivotTable. Data must be sorted before you invoke the SUBTOTALS feature.
- Using array functions you can create formulas that mimic a STDEVIF, MEDIANIF, or PERCENTILEIF function.

Exercises

1. Exercises 1-6 use the data in the Descriptive stats worksheet of the Chapter3bakery.xlsx workbook. Create a dynamically updating histogram for daily cookie sales.
2. Are daily cookie sales symmetric or skewed?
3. Fill in the blank: By the rule of thumb you would expect on 95 percent of all days daily smoothie demand will be between ___ and ___.
4. Determine the fraction of days for which smoothie demand is an outlier.
5. Fill in the blank: There is a 10 percent chance daily demand for smoothies will exceed ____.
6. Fill in the blank: There is a____ chance that at least 600 cookies will be sold in a day.
7. Exercises 7 and 8 use the data in the Data worksheet of the ESPN.xlsx workbook. Find the average age of all ESPN subscribers who make at least $100,000 a year.
8. For each location and age group (under 25, 25–39, 40–54, 55, and over) determine the fraction of ESPN subscribers for each location that are in each age group.

9. Exercises 9-12 use the data in the `Descriptive stats` worksheet of the `Chapter3bakery.xlsx` workbook. Determine the percentage of La Petit Bakery cookie sales for each day of the week and month combination. For example, your final result should tell you the fraction of cookie sales that occur on a Monday in January, and so on.

10. Determine the average profit earned for each day of the week and month combination. Assume the profit earned by La Petit Bakery on each product is as follows:

   - Cakes: $2
   - Cookie: $0.50
   - Pie: $1.50
   - Smoothie: $1.00
   - Coffee: $0.80

11. Find the median cake sales on days in which at least 500 cookies were sold.

12. Fill in the blank: On days in which at least 500 cookies are sold there is a 5 percent chance at least _____ cookies are sold.

13. In the years 1980–2012 median U.S. family income (after inflation) has dropped but mean family income has sharply increased. Can you explain this seeming anomaly?

14. Compute and interpret the skewness for the three data sets in the file `Skewexamples.xlsx`.

II Pricing

Chapter 4: Estimating Demand Curves and Using
Solver to Optimize Price

Chapter 5: Price Bundling

Chapter 6: Nonlinear Pricing

Chapter 7: Price Skimming and Sales

Chapter 8: Revenue Management

4

Estimating Demand Curves and Using Solver to Optimize Price

Understanding how pricing impacts revenues and profitability is one of the most important issues faced by managers. To do so, managers need to understand how consumers' willingness to purchase changes at different price levels and how these changes impact profitability. (That is, managers need to understand the demand curve.) To do so effectively, this chapter covers the following topics:

- Using the Excel Trend Curve and Goal Seek to obtain back-of-the-envelope estimation of a demand curve.
- Using the Excel Solver to determine the profit maximizing price.
- Examining the effect of product tie-ins on the optimal product price.
- Using the SolverTable add-in to quickly price thousands of products!

Estimating Linear and Power Demand Curves

In this section you learn how to fit the two most frequently used demand curves (linear and power) to a particular marketing situation. These estimations are used to determine a profit-maximizing price, and to do so you need to know two things:

- The variable cost to produce each unit of the product. (Call this UC.)
- The product's demand curve. Simply put, a demand curve tells you the number of units of your product a customer will demand at each price. In short, if you charge a price of p per unit, the demand curve gives you a number $D(p)$, which equals the number of units of your product that will be demanded at price p. Of course, a firm's demand curve is constantly changing and often depends on factors beyond the firm's control (such as the state of the economy and a competitor's price). Part III, "Forecasting," addresses these factors.

When you know UC and the demand curve, the profit corresponding to a price of p is simply $(p - UC) * D(p)$. After you have an equation for $D(p)$, which gives the quantity of the product demanded for each price, you can use the Microsoft Office Excel Solver feature to find the profit-maximizing price.

Price Elasticity

Given a demand curve, the *price elasticity* for demand is the percentage of decrease in demand resulting from a 1 percent increase in price. When elasticity is larger than 1, demand is price elastic. When demand is price elastic, a price cut will increase revenue. When elasticity is less than 1, demand is price inelastic. When demand is price inelastic, a price cut will decrease revenue. Studies by economists have obtained the following estimates of elasticity:

- **Salt:** 0.1 (very inelastic)
- **Coffee:** 0.25 (inelastic)
- **Legal fees:** 0.4 (inelastic)
- **TV sets:** 1.2 (slightly elastic)
- **Restaurant meals:** 2.3 (elastic)
- **Foreign travel:** 4.0 (very elastic)

A 1 percent decrease in the cost of foreign travel, for example, can result in a 4 percent increase in demand for foreign travel. Managers need to understand the price elasticity at each price point to make optimal pricing decisions. In the next section you will use price elasticity to estimate a product's demand curve.

Forms of Demand Curves

There are multiple forms of demand curves that you can use to analyze marketing data. Using q to represent the quantity demanded of a product, the two most commonly used forms for estimating demand curves are as follows:

- **Linear demand curve:** In this case, demand follows a straight line relationship of the form $q = a - bp$. Here q = quantity demanded and p = unit price. For example, $q = 10 - p$ is a linear demand curve. (Here a and b can be determined by using a method described in the "Estimating a Linear Demand Curve" section of this chapter.) When the demand curve is linear, the elasticity is changing.
- **Power demand curve:** In this situation, the demand curve is described by a power curve of the form $q = ap^b$, $a>0$, $b<0$. Again, a and b can be determined by the method described later in the chapter. The equation $q = 100p^{-2}$ is an example of a power demand curve. If demand follows a power curve, for any price, the elasticity equals $-b$. See Exercise 11 for an explanation of this

important property of the power demand curve. Thus, for the demand curve $q = 100p^{-2}$ the price elasticity of demand always equals 2.

Estimating a Linear Demand Curve

Suppose that a product's demand curve follows a linear demand curve. Given the current price and demand for a product and the product's price elasticity of demand, determining the product's demand curve is a simple matter. The following example illustrates how to fit a linear demand curve.

Suppose a product is currently selling for $100 and demand equals 500 units. The product's price elasticity for demand is 2. Assuming the demand curve is linear, you can determine the equation of the demand curve. The solution is in the Linearfit .xls file, which is shown in Figure 4-1.

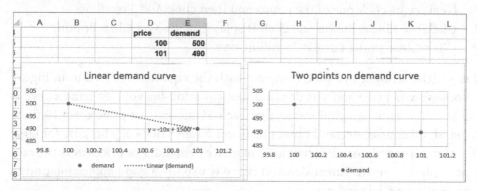

Figure 4-1: Fitting linear demand curve

Given two points, you know that there is a unique straight line that passes through those two points. You actually know two points on your demand curve. One point is p=100 and q=500. Because elasticity of demand equals 2, a 1 percent increase in price results in a 2 percent decrease in demand. Thus, if p=101 (a 1 percent increase), demand drops by 2 percent of 500 (10 units) to 490. Thus p=101 and q=490 is a second point on the demand curve. You can now use the Excel Trendline to find the straight line that passes through the points (100,500) and (101,490).

Begin by entering these points in the worksheet in the cell range D5:E6 (refer to Figure 4-1). Then select the range D4:E6, and on the Ribbon, in the Charts group choose Scatter ➤ Scatter with Only Markers.

1. Begin by entering the points in the Linearfit.xls worksheet in the cell range D5:E6 (refer to Figure 4-1).
2. Select the range D4:E6.

3. Go to the Insert tab and in the Charts group choose Scatter ➤ Scatter with Only Markers. You should now see that the graph has a positive slope. This would imply that higher prices lead to higher demand, which cannot be correct. The problem is that with only two data points, Excel assumes that the data points you want to graph are in separate columns, not separate rows.

4. To ensure Excel understands that the individual points are in separate rows, click inside the graph.

5. On the Ribbon click the Design tab in the Chart Tools section.

6. Click Switch Row/Column in the Data section of the Design tab.

NOTE   Note that by clicking the Select Data button, you can change the source data that generates your chart.

7. Next, right-click one of the points and then click Add Trendline.

8. Click the Linear button and click Display Equation on Chart option.

9. Click Close in the Format Trendline box.

You see the straight line plot, complete with the equation referred to in Figure 4-1. Because x is price and y is demand, the equation for your demand curve is $q = 1500 - 10p$. This equation means that each \$1 increase in price costs 10 units of demand. Of course, demand cannot be linear for all values of p because for large values of p, a linear demand curve yields negative demand. For prices near the current price, however, the linear demand curve is usually a good approximation to the product's true demand curve.

Estimating a Power Demand Curve

Recall that for a linear demand curve the price elasticity is different for each price point. If the marketing analyst believes that elasticity remains relatively constant as price changes, then she can use a power demand curve (which has constant price elasticity) to model demand for a product.

Again assume that a product is currently selling for \$100 and demand equals 500 units. Assume also that the product's price elasticity for demand is known to equal 2. (In Chapters 31 and 32 you will learn some more advanced methods to estimate price elasticity). You can fit a power demand curve to this information by performing the following steps in the Powerfit.xls file, as shown in Figure 4-2.

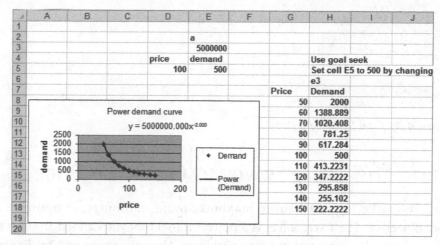

	A	B	C	D	E	F	G	H	I	J
1										
2					a					
3					5000000					
4				price	demand			Use goal seek		
5				100	500			Set cell E5 to 500 by changing		
6								e3		
7							Price	Demand		
8							50	2000		
9							60	1388.889		
10							70	1020.408		
11							80	781.25		
12							90	617.284		
13							100	500		
14							110	413.2231		
15							120	347.2222		
16							130	295.858		
17							140	255.102		
18							150	222.2222		
19										
20										

Figure 4-2: Fitting Power Demand Curve

1. After naming cell E3 as *a*, enter a trial value for *a*.

2. In cell D5, enter the current price of $100. Because elasticity of demand equals 2, you know that the demand curve has the form $q=ap^{-2}$ where *a* is unknown.

3. In cell E5, enter a formula that computes the demand when the unit price equals $100. The demand is linked to your choice of the value of *a* in cell E3 with the formula `a*D5^-2`.

4. Now use the `Global Seek` command to determine the value of *a*. This formula makes the demand for price $100 equal to 500 units. Goal Seek enables you to find a value of a cell in a spreadsheet (called the By Changing Cell) that makes a formula (called the Set Cell) hit a wanted Value. In the example you want to change cell E3 so that the formula in cell E5 equals 500. Set cell E5 to the value of 500 by changing cell E3.

5. To invoke Goal Seek, switch to the Data tab and select What-If analysis from the Data Tools Group, then choose Goal Seek from the drop down arrow. Fill the dialog box as shown in Figure 4-3. With these settings, Excel changes the changing cell (E3) until the value of the set cell (E5) matches your desired value of 500.

A value for a = 5 million yields a demand of 500 at a price of $100. Thus, the demand curve (refer to Figure 4-2) is given by $q = 5,000,000p^{-2}$. For any price, the price elasticity of demand on this demand curve equals 2.

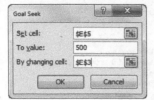

Figure 4-3: Goal Seek dialog box

Using the Excel Solver to Optimize Price

Often in marketing you want to maximize profit, minimize, or optimize some other objective. The *Excel Solver* is a powerful tool that you can use to solve many marketing (and other!) optimization problems. The Solver is an add-in. To activate the Solver proceed as follows:

For Excel 2010 or Excel 2013:

1. Select File and then Options.
2. Select Add-Ins, click Go, check the Solver add-in, and select OK.
3. Now click the Data tab and you should see the Solver add-in on the right side of the Ribbon.

For Excel 2007:

1. Click the Office Button (the oval in the left side of the ribbon) and choose Excel Options.
2. Selecting Add-Ins, click Go, check the Solver add-in, and select OK.
3. Now click the Data tab and you should see the Solver add-in on the right side of the Ribbon.

In this chapter the examples work with the Excel 2010 Solver, which is more powerful than the Solver included with previous versions of Excel. If you select Solver from the Data tab, the Solver window appears, as shown in Figure 4-4.

To define a Solver model, you must specify in the Solver dialog box the following three parts of the model:

- **Set Objective or Target Cell:** The objective cell contains the goal you want to maximize (like profit) or minimize (production cost).

■ **Changing Variable Cells:** These cells are the cells that you can change or adjust to optimize the target cell. In this chapter the changing cells will be each product's price.

■ **Constraints:** These are restrictions on the changing cells. For example, you might want to constrain the price for each of your products to be within 10 percent of the competitor's price.

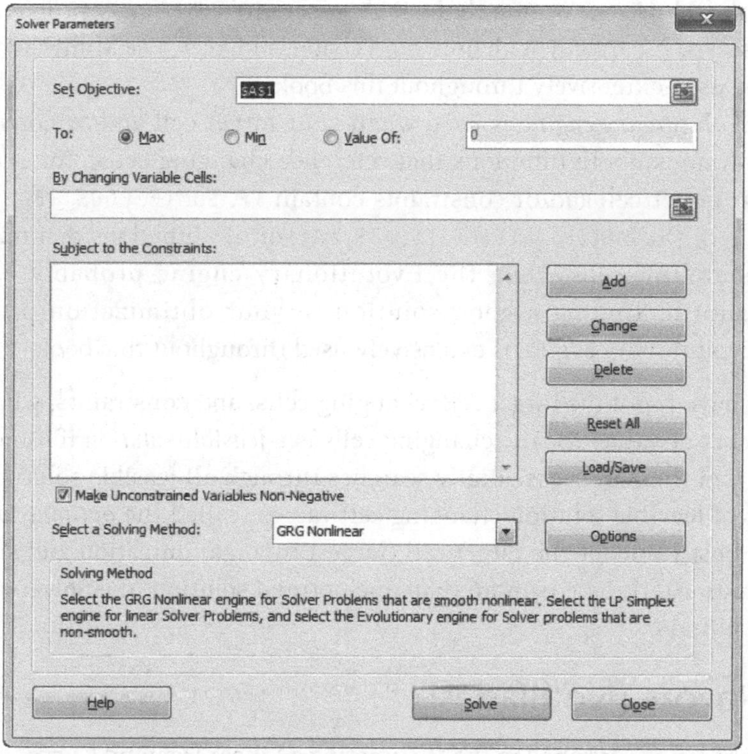

Figure 4-4: Solver window

The Excel Solver has been greatly revamped and improved in Excel 2010. The primary change is the presence of the Select a Solving Method drop-down list. From this list you must select the appropriate solution engine for your optimization problem. You can choose from the following options:

■ The *Simplex LP engine* is used to solve linear optimization problems. A linear optimization problem is one in which the target cell and constraints are all created by adding together terms of the form *(changing cell)***(constant)*. Most marketing models are not linear. An exception is the classic advertising media selection model discussed in Chapter 35, "Media Selection Models."

- The *GRG Nonlinear engine* is used to solve optimization problems in which the target cell and/or some of the constraints are not linear and are computed by using typical mathematical operations such as multiplying or dividing changing cells, raising changing cells to a power, using exponential or trig functions involving changing cells, and so on. The GRG engine includes a powerful Multistart option that enables users to solve many problems that were solved incorrectly with previous versions of Excel. The Multistart option will be used extensively throughout this book.

- The *Evolutionary engine* is used when your target cell and/or constraints contain nonsmooth functions that reference changing cells. For example, if your target cell and/or constraints contain IF, SUMIF, COUNTIF, SUMIFS, COUNTIFS, AVERAGEIF, AVERAGEIFS, ABS, MAX, or MIN functions that reference the changing cells, then the Evolutionary engine probably has the best shot at finding a good solution to your optimization problem. The Evolutionary engine is extensively used throughout this book.

After you have input the target cell, changing cells, and constraints, what does Solver do? A set of values for the changing cells is a *feasible solution* if it meets all constraints, and the Solver essentially searches through all feasible solutions and finds the set of feasible solution changing cell values (called the *optimal solution*) that has the best value for the target cell (largest in a maximization and smallest in a minimization). If there is more than one optimal solution, the Solver stops at the first one it finds.

Pricing Razors (No Blades!)

Using the techniques described in the "Estimating a Linear Demand Curve" section, it's easy to determine a demand curve for the product that's originally purchased. You can then use the Microsoft Office Excel Solver to determine the original product price that maximizes the sum of the profit earned from razors. Then you can show how the fact that purchasers of razors also buy blades reduces the profit maximizing price for razors.

Suppose that you currently charge $5.00 for a razor and you sell 6 million razors. Assume that the variable cost to produce a razor is $2.00. Finally, suppose that the price elasticity of demand for razors is 2, and the demand curve is linear. What price should you charge for razors?

You can determine a demand curve (assuming a linear demand curve), as shown in Figure 4-5. (You can find this data and the chart on the no blades worksheet in the file razorsandblades.xls.) Two points on the demand curve are price = $5.00, demand = 6 million razors and price = $5.05 (an increase of 1 percent), demand = 5.88 million (2 percent less than 6 million).

1. Begin by drawing a chart and inserting a linear trend line, as shown in the section "Estimating a Linear Demand Curve." You'll find the demand curve equation is $y = 18 - 2.4x$. Because x equals price and y equals demand, you can write the demand curve for razors as follows:

$$\text{Demand (in millions)} = 18 - 2.4(\text{price})$$

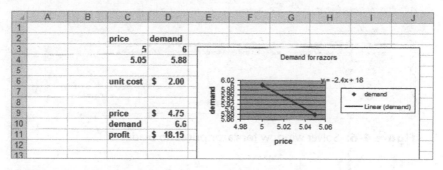

Figure 4-5: Optimizing razor price: no blades

2. Associate the names in cell C6 and the range C9:C11 with cells D6 and D9:D11.

3. Next, enter a trial price in D9 to determine demand for that price in cell D10 with the formula =18-2.4*price.

4. Determine in cell D11 the profit for razors by using the formula =demand*(price-unit_cost).

5. You can now use Solver to determine the profit-maximizing price. The Solver Parameters dialog box is shown in Figure 4-6. Choose to maximize the profit cell (cell D11) by changing the price (cell D9).

6. The model is not linear because the target cell multiplies together two quantities—*demand* and (*price–cost*)—each depending on the changing cell. Therefore choose the GRG Nonlinear option. Solver finds that by charging $4.75 for a razor, you can maximize the profit. (The maximum profit is $18.15 million.)

Figure 4-6: Solver window for razor price: no blades

Incorporating Complementary Products

Certain consumer product purchases frequently result in the purchase of related products, or *complementary products*. Table 4-1 provides some examples:

Table 4-1: Examples of Complementary Product

Original Purchase	Tie-in Complementary Product
Men's suit	Tie or shirt
Inkjet printer	Printer cartridge
Xbox console	Video game
Cell phone	Case

If the profit from complementary products is included in the target cell, the profit maximizing price for the original product will decrease. Suppose that the average purchaser of a razor buys 50 blades and you earn $0.15 of profit per blade purchased. You can use the Excel Solver to determine how this changes the price you should charge for a razor. Assume that the price of a blade is fixed. (In Exercise 3 at the end of the chapter, the blade price changes.) The analysis is in the `blades` worksheet of the `razorsandblades.xls` file, as shown in Figure 4-7.

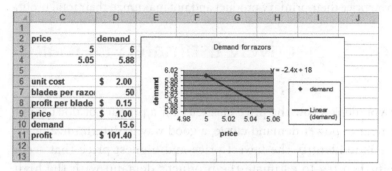

Figure 4-7: Optimizing razor price: blade profit included

To maximize profit perform the following steps:

1. Use the Create from Selection command in the Defined Names group on the Formulas tab to associate the names in cells C6:C11 with cells D6:D11. (For example, cell D10 is named Demand.)

NOTE   Recall that cell D10 of the `no blades` worksheet is also named Demand. When you use the range name Demand in a formula Excel simply refers to the cell named Demand in the current worksheet. In other words, when you use the range name Demand in the `blades` worksheet, Excel refers to cell D10 of that worksheet, and not to cell D10 in the `no blades` worksheet.

2. In cells D7 and D8, enter the relevant information about blades.
3. In D9, enter a trial price for razors, and in D10, compute the demand with the formula `18-2.4*price`.
4. Next, in cell D11, compute the total profit from razors and blades with the following formula:

    `demand*(price-unit_cost)+demand*blades_per_razor*profit_per_blade`

    Here the `demand*blades_per_razor*profit_per_blade` is the profit from blades.

5. The Solver setup is exactly as shown earlier in Figure 4-6: Change the price to maximize the profit. Of course, now the profit formula includes the profit earned from blades.

Profit is maximized by charging only $1.00 (half the variable cost!) for a razor. This price results from making so much money from the blades. You are much better off ensuring that many people have razors even though you lose $1.00 on each razor sold. Many companies do not understand the importance of the profit from tie-in products. This leads them to overprice their primary product and not maximize their total profit.

Pricing Using Subjectively Estimated Demand Curves

In situations when you don't know the price elasticity for a product or don't think you can rely on a linear or power demand curve, a good way to determine a product's demand curve is to identify the lowest price and highest price that seem reasonable. You can then try to estimate the product's demand with the high price, the low price, and a price midway between the high and low prices. This approach is based on a discussion in the book *Power Pricing*, by Robert Dolan. Given these three points on the product's demand curve, you can use the Microsoft Office Excel Trendline feature to fit a quadratic demand curve with the following equation:

$$(1)\ \text{Demand} = a(\text{price})^2 + b(\text{price}) + c$$

Fitting a quadratic demand curve in this manner enables the slope of the demand curve to either become steeper or flatter, which is much more realistic than the linear demand curve that requires the slope to remain constant.

For any three specified points on the demand curve, values of a, b, and c exist that makes Equation 1 *exactly* fit the three specified points. Because Equation 1 fits three points on the demand curve, it seems reasonable to believe that the equation can give an accurate representation of demand for other prices. You can then use Equation 1 and Solver to maximize profit, which is given by the formula (price- unit cost)*demand. The following example shows how this process works.

Suppose that a drugstore pays $0.90 for each unit of ChapStick it orders. The store is considering charging from $1.50 through $2.50 for a unit of ChapStick. It thinks that at a price of $1.50, it can sell 60 units per week. (See the ChapStickprice.xls file.) At a price of $2.00, it thinks it can sell 51 units per week and at a price of $2.50, 20 units per week. To determine what price the store should charge for ChapStick, perform the following steps.

1. Begin by entering the three points with which to chart your demand curve in the cell range E3:F6.
2. Select E3:F6, click the Scatter option on the Charts group on the Ribbon, and then select the first option for a Scatter chart.

3. Right-click a data point and select Add Trendline.

4. In the Format Trendline dialog box, choose Polynomial, and select 2 in the Order box to obtain a quadratic curve of the form of Equation 1. Then select the option Display Equation on Chart. Figure 4-8 shows the required Trend Curve Settings. The chart containing the demand curve is shown in Figure 4-9.

    The estimated demand curve Equation 2 is as follows:

    $$(2)\ \text{Demand} = -44 * \text{Price}^2 + 136 * \text{Price} - 45$$

5. Next, insert a trial price in cell I2. Compute the product demand by using Equation 2 in cell I3 with the formula =-44*price^2+136*price-45. (Cell I2 is named Price.)

Figure 4-8: Pricing with a quadratic demand curve

6. Compute the weekly profit from ChapStick sales in cell I4 with the formula =demand*(price-unit_cost). (Cell E2 is named Unit_Cost and cell I3 is named Demand.)

7. Use Solver to determine the price that maximizes profit. The Solver Parameters dialog box is shown in Figure 4-10. The price is constrained to be from the lowest through the highest specified prices ($1.50 through $2.50). If you allow Solver to consider prices outside this range, the quadratic demand curve

might slope upward, which implies that a higher price would result in larger demand. This result is unreasonable, which is why you constrain the price.

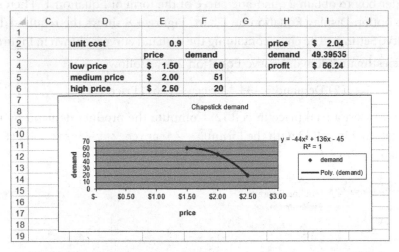

Figure 4-9: ChapStick demand curve

Figure 4-10: Solver window for quadratic demand curve example

You find that the drugstore should charge $2.04 for a ChapStick unit. This yields sales of 49.4 units per week and a weekly profit of $56.24.

NOTE   The approach to pricing outlined in this section requires no knowledge of the concept of price elasticity. Inherently, the Solver considers the elasticity for each price when it determines the profit-maximizing price.

NOTE   For the quadratic demand model to be useful, the minimum and maximum prices must be consistent with consumer preferences. A knowledgeable sales force should be able to come up with realistic minimum and maximum prices.

Using SolverTable to Price Multiple Products

The approach developed to price a product in the preceding section can be extended to enable a company to easily price hundreds or thousands of products. The only information required for each product is the unit cost, estimated demand for lowest possible price, estimated demand for an intermediate price, and estimated demand. Using the SolverTable add-in written by Chris Albright (available for download at www.kelley.iu.edu/albright/Free_downloads.htm) you can easily fit the quadratic demand curve to each product. SolverTable is an Excel add-in that enables you to easily vary the inputs to a Solver model and track a wanted set of outputs.

After fitting the demand curves, you can use Solver to set a price for each product to maximize the total product generated from all products by completing the following steps (the Data worksheet in the Fittingmultipledemandcurves.xls file shows the estimated demand for three products at a low ($1.10), medium ($1.30), and high ($1.50) price):

1. Use an HLOOKUP function that keys off the entry in cell A11 to place the demands for each product in E14:E16. The Solver model chooses constant a, a coefficient b for price, and a coefficient c for price^2 that exactly passes through the demand points for each product.
2. Use SolverTable to loop through each product by changing the value in cell A11 in the range 1, 2, …, where n = number of products.
3. Name the range F6:H10 Lookup.
4. Copy the formula =HLOOKUP($A$11,Lookup,C14) from E14 to E15:E16 to pull the demand for each product corresponding to the product index in A11.
5. Copy the formula =E$3+$E$4*D14+$E$5*(D14^2) from F14 to F15:F16 to compute the forecasted demand based on the quadratic demand curve based on the values in E3:E5.

6. Copy the formula =(E14-F14)^2 from G14 to G15:G16 to compute the squared error in the demand forecast for each price. For each price the estimation error is simply actual demand minus demand estimated from quadratic demand curve.

7. In cell G12 use the formula =SUM(G14:G16) to compute the sum of the squared estimation errors.

8. If you minimize G12 by changing E3:E5, Solver finds the values of *a*, *b*, and *c* that make the sum of squared errors equal to 0. You minimize the sum of squared errors instead of minimizing the sum of errors because if you do not square errors, then the sum of positive and sum of negative errors cancels each other out. Minimizing the sum of squared errors mimics the action of the Trend Curve Polynomial option described in the preceding section. The appropriate Solver Window is shown in Figure 4-11.

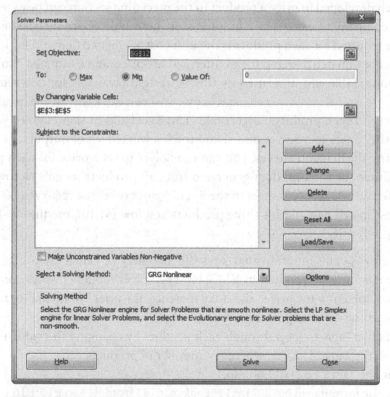

Figure 4-11: Solver window for SolverTable example

9. Choose the GRG Nonlinear option because the target cell is not constructed by adding up terms of the form (changing cell)*constant.

10. For Solver to obtain a correct solution to this problem, go to Options and check Use Automatic Scaling; then go to the GRG tab and select Central Derivatives.

11. Select Solve and you find the answer (see Figure 4-12). The Sum of Squared errors is 0 to 26 decimal places and the quadratic demand curve is $-73.625+195 \text{price}+87.5 \text{price}^2$. Because a, b, and c can be negative, do not check the Make Unconstrained Variables Non-Negative box.

⬚	A	B	C	D	E	F	G	H
1								
2								
3				a	-73.625			
4				b	195			
5				c	-87.5			
6						1	2	3
7					Price	Product 1 demand	Product 2 demand	Product 3 demand
8				Low	1.1	35	32	24
9				Medium	1.3	32	27	17
10	Data set			High	1.5	22	16	9
11		1					SSE	
12							1.00974E-27	
13				Price	Demand	Forecast	Squared Error	
14			3	1.1	35	35	2.01948E-28	
15			4	1.3	32	32	8.07794E-28	
16			5	1.5	22	22	0	

Figure 4-12: Use of SolverTable for price optimization

Using SolverTable to Find the Demand Curve for All Products

After you have a Solver model in a worksheet, you can use SolverTable to "loop through" the values of one (in a One-way SolverTable) or two (in a Two-way SolverTable) inputs and track any wanted outputs. To get started, assuming you have installed SolverTable, select SolverTable from the Ribbon, choose a One-way Table, and fill in the SolverTable dialog box, as shown in Figure 4-13.

To begin Solver place a 1 in the input cell (A11) and run the Solver to track the output cells (a, b, and c and Sum of Squared Errors [SSE]). Then Solver places a 2 in A11 and finally a 3 in A11. The results are placed in a new worksheet (STS_1), as shown in Figure 4-14.

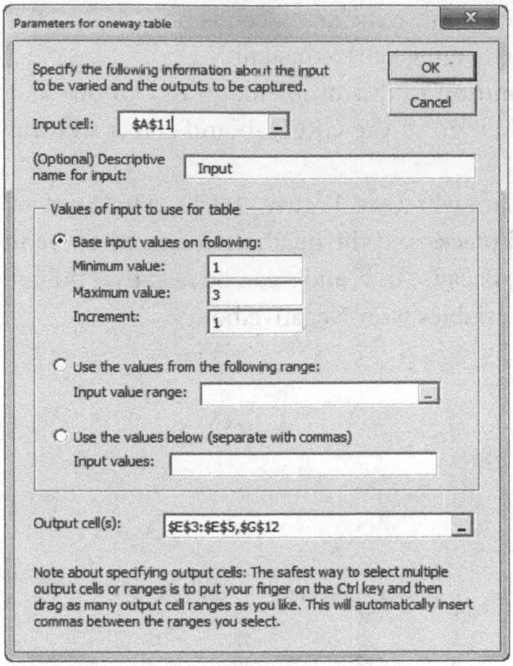

Figure 4-13: SolverTable settings

	A	B	C	D	E	F	G	H	I
1	Oneway analysis for Solver model in data worksheet								
2									33.23375
3	Input (cell $A$11) values along side, output cell(s) along top								
4		a	b	c	$G$12	Price	demand	unit cost	Profit
5	1	-73.625	195	-87.5	1.04441E-22	1.389493	28.3907	0.8	16.73611
6	2	-47.75	155	-75	6.31897E-25	1.370568	23.80379	0.9	11.2013
7	3	44.625	-5	-12.5	7.98128E-21	1.367619	14.40715	1	5.296336

Figure 4-14: SolverTable results

You can now set up a Solver model that determines the profit maximizing price for each product. Proceed as follows:

1. Enter trial prices for each product in the range F5:F7.

2. Based on the prices in F5:F7, compute the demand for each product by copying the formula =B5+C5*F5+F5^2*D5 from G5 to G6:G7.

3. Enter the unit cost for each product in H5:H7, and compute the profit for each product as *(price-unit cost)*demand* by copying the formula =(F5-H5)*G5 from I5 to I6:I7.

4. Compute the total profit for all products in cell I2 with the formula =SUM(I5:I7).

5. Now use Solver (see Figure 4-15) to choose the prices in F5:F7 to maximize total profit (I2). This, of course, chooses the profit maximizing price for each product.

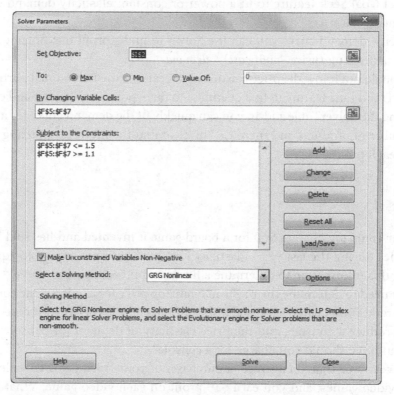

Figure 4-15: Finding profit maximizing price for each product

You find that you should charge $1.39 for Product 1 and $1.37 for Products 2 and 3. The SolverTable provides a powerful tool that can enable the marketing analyst to quickly estimate a demand curve for several products and determine a profit maximizing price for each product.

Summary

In this chapter you learned the following:

- Price elasticity of demand is the percentage decrease in demand for a 1 percent increase in price.
- Given the current price and demand and price elasticity, you can use the Excel Trend Line feature to fit a linear demand curve (*Demand = a -b*price*).

For a linear demand curve price, elasticity is different at every point on the demand curve.

- Given the current price and demand and price elasticity, you can use the Excel Goal Seek feature to fit a power or constant elasticity demand curve (*Demand =a(price)*$^{-b}$)
- Given a demand curve you can use Solver to find a profit maximizing price by maximizing *(price – unit cost) * demand.*
- If you do not know the price elasticity, you can use the Polynomial portion of the Trend Line feature to fit a quadratic to three points on the demand curve.
- Using the SolverTable add-in you can quickly fit the demand curve for a huge number of products and then use Solver to find the profit maximizing price for each product.

Exercises

1. Your company charges $60 for a board game it invented and has sold 3,000 copies during the last year. Elasticity for board games is known to equal 3. Use this information to determine a linear and power demand curve.

2. You need to determine the profit-maximizing price for a video game console. Currently you charge $180 and sell 2 million consoles per year. It costs $150 to produce a console, and the price elasticity of demand for consoles is 3. What price should you charge for a console?

3. Now assume that, on average, a purchaser of your video game console buys 10 video games, and you earn $10 profit on each video game. What is the correct price for consoles?

4. In the razorsandblades.xls file example, suppose the cost to produce a blade is $0.20. If you charge $0.35 for a blade, a customer buys an average of 50 blades from you. Assume the price elasticity of demand for blades is 3. What price should you charge for a razor and for a blade?

5. You manage a movie theater that can handle up to 8,000 patrons per week. The current demand, price, and elasticity for ticket sales, popcorn, soda, and candy are given in Figure 4-16. The theater keeps 45 percent of ticket revenues. Unit cost per ticket, popcorn sales, candy sales, and soda sales are also given. Assuming linear demand curves, how can the theater maximize profits? Demand for foods is the fraction of patrons who purchase the given food.

	B	C	D	E	F	G	H	I
2								
3			elasticity	current price	demand	cost	ticket percentage	
4	keep 45%	ticket	3	8	3000	0	0.45	
5		popcorn	1.3	3.5	0.5	0.4		
6		soda	1.5	3	0.6	0.6		
7		candy	2.5	2.5	0.2	1		

Figure 4-16: Data for Exercise 5

6. A prescription drug is produced in the United States and sold internationally. Each unit of the drug costs $60 to produce. In the German market, you sell the drug for 150 euros per unit. The current exchange rate is 0.667 U.S. dollars per euro. Current demand for the drug is 100 units, and the estimated elasticity is 2.5. Assuming a linear demand curve, determine the appropriate sales price (in euros) for the drug.

7. Suppose it costs $250 to produce a video game console. A price between $200 and $400 is under consideration. Estimated demand for the game console is shown in the following table. What price should you charge for game console?

Price	Demand
$200	50,000
$300	25,000
$400	12,000

8. Use the demand information given in Exercise 7 for this exercise. Each game owner buys an average of 10 video games. You earn $10 profit per video game. What price should you charge for the game console?

9. You want to determine the correct price for a new weekly magazine. The variable cost of printing and distributing a copy of the magazine is $0.50. You are thinking of charging from $0.50 through $1.30 per copy. The estimated weekly sales of the magazine are shown in the following table. What price should you charge for the magazine?

Price	Demand (in Millions)
$0.50	2
$0.90	1.2
$1.30	.3

10. Given the following information in the table for four products, find the profit-maximizing price for each product.

Product	Lowest Price	Medium Price	High Price	Low Price Demand	Medium Price Demand	High Price Demand	Unit cost
Product 1	$1.40	$2.20	$3.00	100	40	5	$1.10
Product 2	$2.20	$3.00	$4.00	200	130	25	$1.50
Product 3	$45	$75	$95	400	300	130	$40
Product 4	$200	$250	$300	600	300	50	$120

11. (Requires calculus) Show that if the demand for a product is given by the power curve $q = ap^{-b}$, then for any price a, a 1 percent increase in price will decrease demand by 1 percent.

12. For the demand curve $q = 100p^{-2}$ show that for $p = 1, 2, 4, 8$, and 16 that a 1 percent increase in price will result in approximately a 2 percent decrease in demand.

5

Price Bundling

hapter 4, "Estimating Demand Curves and Using Solver to Optimize Price," discussed situations in which a customer pays the same price for each unit she purchases of a product. When a customer pays the same price for each unit the seller is using *linear pricing*. This chapter and Chapter 6, "Nonlinear Pricing," describe some *nonlinear pricing* models in which the total amount a customer pays for a set of products is not equal to the sum of the individual product prices. One of the most common instances of nonlinear pricing is price bundling. This chapter shows that analytic models can help companies use bundling to maximize their profits.

Why Bundle?

Companies often bundle products in an attempt to get customers to purchase more products than they would have without bundling. A few examples of bundling include the following:

- Cable companies bundle landlines, cell phone service, TV service, and Internet service.
- Automobile companies often bundle popular options such as navigation, satellite radio, and keyless entry.
- Computer mail order companies often bundle computers with printers, scanners, and monitors.
- Microsoft Office has been a highly successful bundling of software products such as Excel, Word, Access and Outlook.

In this chapter you will make the assumption that customers make decisions based on the concept of *consumer surplus*. The consumer surplus of a product is simply the value a consumer attaches to an available product minus the actual cost of the product.

> **NOTE**   In Chapters 16, "Conjoint Analysis" and 18, "Discrete Choice Analysis," you learn how to determine the value a consumer attaches to a particular product or combination of products.

The consumer's goal is to make a choice that maximizes her consumer surplus. Therefore, if each product combination has a negative surplus, no product combination is purchased; however, as long as at least one option has a non-negative consumer surplus, the consumer will choose the option with the largest consumer surplus. The possibility of ties can be ignored. This section examines three examples that portray how bundling can increase profits.

Bundling Products to Extract Consumer Surplus

Suppose you own Disney World and each customer values the five rides in the park as follows:

- Space Mountain: $10
- Matterhorn: $8
- Tower of Terror: $6
- Small World: $4
- Mr. Toad: $2

How can Disney World maximize revenue from these rides? First assume a single price is charged for each ride. If Disney World charges $10 a ride, each customer would go on only Space Mountain and you make $10 per customer. If Disney World charges $8 per ride, each customer would go on two rides, and you make $16. If you charge $6 per ride, then each customer goes on three rides and you make $18. If you charge $4 per ride, then each customer goes on four rides and you make $16. Finally, charging $2 per ride, you make $10 in revenue. Therefore with a single price for each ride, revenue is maximized at $18 per customer.

Now suppose Disney World does not offer per ride tickets but simply offers a five-ride ticket for $30. Because the consumer values all five rides at $30 (the sum of the ride values) he will pay $30 for park admission. This is a 67 percent increase in revenue. Of course, single park admission is the strategy Disney World has adapted. Single park admission has other benefits such as reducing lines, but this simple example shows that product bundling can help companies "extract" consumer surplus from customers. Later in the chapter you see that the assumption that all customers are identical is not important to your analysis.

Pure Bundling

Now consider another example. Suppose you sell two products and have two potential customers that value each product, as shown in Table 5-1:

Table 5-1: Pure Bundling Works Well with Negatively Correlated Valuations

Product	Customer 1	Customer 2
Computer	$1,000	$500
Monitor	$500	$1,000

For simplicity, assume the cost of producing each product is negligible and can be assumed to equal $0. Therefore revenue and profit are identical. In this example customer valuations are negatively correlated; Customer 1 values the computer more than Customer 2 but values the monitor less. If you price each product separately, you would charge $1,000 for each product and make $2,000 revenue; however, if you charge $1,500 for a bundle of both products, you make $3,000. Thus, when customer valuations for products are negatively correlated, bundling can result in a significant increase in profit.

The reason bundling works in this case is that bundling enables the seller to entirely extract the value the consumers attach to the products. If the seller only offers the customer a choice between purchasing all products or nothing, the situation is called *pure bundling*. Movie rental companies usually give theatres a choice between renting an assortment of some blockbuster movies and some not-so-popular movies, or renting no movies at all. In this case if the theatre owner wants the blockbuster movies she has to also rent the less-popular movies.

If customer valuations are positively correlated then bundling usually offers no benefit, because bundling does not allow the seller to extract more surplus than separate prices. For example, in Table 5-2 valuations are positively correlated because Customer 2 is willing to pay more for each product than Customer 1. In this case, if the seller offers only separate prices she would charge $1,000 for the computer and $500 for the monitor. Then each customer buys both products and total revenue is $3,000. If the seller offers a pure bundle she should charge $1,500 for the bundle. Then both customers purchase the bundle for $1,500 yielding a total revenue of $3,000. In this this case pure bundling and separate prices yield identical profits.

Table 5-2: Pure Bundling Works Poorly with Positively Correlated Valuations

Product	Customer 1	Customer 2
Computer	$1,000	$1,250
Monitor	$500	$750

Mixed Bundling

Mixed bundling means the seller offers a different price for each available combination of products. For the data in Table 5-3 mixed bundling is optimal.

Table 5-3: Mixed Bundling is Optimal

Customer	Computer	Monitor
1	$900	$800
2	$1,100	$600
3	$1,300	$400
4	$1,500	$200
Unit Cost	$1,000	$300

To maximize profits, the seller can do the following (see also Exercise 7):

- To maximize profit from separate prices the seller charges $600 for the monitor and $1,300 for the computer. In this scenario Customers 3 and 4 buy the computer and Customers 1 and 2 buy the monitor yielding a profit of $1,200.
- To maximize profit with mixed bundling the seller can charge $799 for the monitor, $1,499 for the computer, and $1,700 for the bundle. Then Customer 1 buys just a monitor, Customer 4 buys just a computer, and Customers 2 and 3 buy the product bundle. The seller earns a profit of $1,798.
- If only the monitor and computer pure bundle is offered, the seller should sell the pure bundle for $1,700. Then each customer will purchase the pure bundle and the seller earns a profit of $1,600.

Using Evolutionary Solver to Find Optimal Bundle Prices

When you combine the consumer surplus decision-making assumptions explained in the previous section with the power of the Evolutionary Solver Engine of Excel 2010 or later, you can easily solve complex bundling problems.

For this section's example, suppose Verizon sells cell phone service, Internet access, and FIOS TV service to customers. Customers can buy any combination of these three products (or not buy any). The seven available product combinations include the following:

- Internet (Combination 1)
- TV (Combination 2)
- Cell phone (Combination 3)
- Internet and TV (Combination 4)
- Internet and cell phone (Combination 5)
- TV and cell phone (Combination 6)
- All three products (Combination 7)

The file phone.xls gives the amount 77 representative customers are willing to pay per month for each service. Use the model in the initial solver worksheet to follow along with the example (also shown in Figure 5-1). In row 6 you see that the first customer is willing to pay up to $3.50 per month for Internet, $7 per month for TV service, and $3.50 per month for cell phone service. (It's hard to make money off this customer!) You can use the Evolutionary Solver Engine and the willingness to pay data to determine a price for each product combination that maximizes revenue.

	A	B	C	D	E	F	G	H	I	J	K	L	M	N	O	P
3			Product	1	2	3	4	5	6	7		total	3413.696			
4			Price	74.35303	35	82.16	69.9942	69.99101	69.991	89.945						
5	Internet	TV	Cell Phon	Internet	TV	Cell	Internet +TV	Internet +Cell	TV+Cell I	All 3	max surp	bought?	revenue			
6	$3.50	$7.00	$3.50	-70.853	-28	-78.7	-59.494	-62.991	-59.491	-75.945	-27.9987	0	0			
7	$17.50	$35.00	$3.50	-56.853	0	-78.7	-17.494	-48.991	-31.491	-33.945	0.0013	2	34.9987			
8	$28.00	$28.00	$49.00	-46.353	-7	-33.2	-13.994	7.008987	7.0087	15.055	15.05482	7	89.94518		Product	Frequenc
9	$70.00	$70.00	$0.00	-4.35303	35	-82.2	70.0058	0.008987	0.0087	50.055	70.00576	4	69.99424		0	25
10	$0.00	$7.00	$14.00	-74.353	-28	-68.2	-62.994	-55.991	-48.991	-68.945	-27.9987	0	0		1	0
11	$0.00	$70.00	$0.00	-74.353	35	-82.2	0.00576	-69.991	0.0087	-19.945	35.0013	2	34.9987		2	19
12	$21.00	$35.00	$10.50	-53.353	0	-71.7	-13.994	-38.491	-24.491	-23.445	0.0013	2	34.9987		3	0
13	$7.00	$21.00	$0.00	-67.353	-14	-82.2	-41.994	-62.991	-48.991	-61.945	-13.9987	0	0		4	8
14	$5.25	$7.00	$2.10	-69.103	-28	-80.1	-57.744	-62.641	-60.891	-75.595	-27.9987	0	0		5	2
15	$21.00	$28.00	$28.00	-53.353	-7	-54.2	-20.994	-20.991	-13.991	-12.945	-6.9987	0	0		6	1
16	$35.00	$49.00	$21.00	-39.353	14	-61.2	14.0058	-13.991	0.0087	15.055	15.05482	7	89.94518		7	22
17	$21.00	$21.00	$21.00	-53.353	-14	-61.2	-27.994	-27.991	-27.991	-26.945	-13.9987	0	0			
18	$14.00	$35.00	$21.00	-60.353	0	-61.2	-20.994	-34.991	-13.991	-19.945	0.0013	2	34.9987			
19	$35.00	$35.00	$14.00	-60.353	0	-68.2	-20.994	-41.991	-20.991	-26.945	0.0013	2	34.9987			
20	$70.00	$0.00	$49.00	-4.35303	-35	-33.2	0.00576	49.00899	-20.991	29.055	49.00899	5	69.99101			
21	$7.00	$35.00	$14.00	-67.353	0	-68.2	-27.994	-48.991	-20.991	-33.945	0.0013	2	34.9987			
22	$21.00	$35.00	$42.00	-53.353	0	-40.2	-13.994	-6.99101	7.0087	8.0548	8.054824	7	89.94518			

Figure 5-1: Verizon Internet example

The key to your model is to set up a spreadsheet that tells you, for any set of prices for each possible product combination, how much revenue you can obtain from your sample of customers. Then you can use the Evolutionary Solver to find the set of prices for the product combinations that maximize your revenue. To find how much revenue you can generate for any set of product combination prices, proceed as follows:

1. In D4:J4 enter trial prices for each of the possible seven product combinations.
2. In Row 6, determine the first's customer's consumer surplus by computing her value for the products in a combination and subtracting the cost of the product combination. For example, the first customer's consumer surplus for the Internet +TV product combination is computed in cell G6 with the formula =A6+B6-G$4. Copy the formulas in row 6 to the cell range D7:J82 to compute each customer's consumer surplus for each product combination.
3. Determine for the set of prices in row 4 which product combination, if any, is purchased. Copy the formula =MAX(D6:J6) from K6 to K7:K82 to find each consumer's surplus.
4. Now here's the key to your spreadsheet. In Column L you use the MATCH function (introduced in Chapter 2, "Using Excel Charts to Summarize Marketing Data") combined with an IF statement to determine which product combination each customer purchases. Use product combination 0 to denote no purchase, whereas the actual product combinations are indicated by the integers 1–7. Copy the formula =IF(K6<0,0,MATCH(K6,D6:J6,0)) from L6 to L7:L82 yields the product combination (if any) bought by each customer.
5. Copy the formula =IF(L6=0,0,HLOOKUP(L6,$D$3:$J$4,2)) from M6 to M7:M82 to compute for each person the revenue generated.
6. In cell M4, compute your total revenue with the formula =SUM(M6:M82).

To find the product combination prices that maximize revenue you need to use the Evolutionary Solver, so some discussion of the Evolutionary Solver is in order.

Introduction to the Evolutionary Solver

As explained in Chapter 4, "Estimating Demand Curves and Using Solver to Optimize Price," the Evolutionary Engine is used when your target cell and constraints contain nonsmooth functions that reference changing cells. For example, if your target cell and constraints contain IF, SUMIF, COUNTIF, SUMIFS, COUNTIFS, AVERAGEIF, AVERAGEIFS, ABS, MAX, or MIN functions that reference the changing cells, then the Evolutionary engine probably has the best chance to find a good solution to your optimization problem. The model makes extensive use of IF statements, so it is a good choice to use the Evolutionary Solver. The target cell is to maximize revenue (cell M3) by changing the product prices (cell range D4:J4).

When using the Evolutionary Solver, you should follow these rules:

- Place upper and lower bounds on each of your changing cells. This makes the Solver's search for an optimal solution much easier. In the Verizon bundling model use a lower bound of 0 for each price and an upper bound of 100.

NOTE   If, when running Evolutionary Solver, a changing cell hits an upper or lower bound, you should relax that bound because Solver was trying to push the changing cell outside the range you specified.

- Use no constraints other than the bounds on the changing cells. You will soon see how to use penalties in the target cell to enforce constraints.
- In the Options tab increase Max Time to 3600 seconds. This causes Solver to run for 60 minutes, even if you leave the room. This should be plenty of time for Solver to find a good solution. Also add a few 000s to Max Subproblems and Max Feasible Solutions. This ensures that Solver does not stop when you leave the room. Figure 5-2 summarizes these settings.
- In the Options tab select the Evolutionary Solver tab and change Mutation Rate to 0.5 and Maximum Time Without Improvement to 300 seconds. (Mutation rate is explained soon.) Setting a Maximum Time Without Improvement to 5 minutes ensures that if Solver fails in 5 minutes to improve the current solution, the Solver stops. Hitting the Escape key at any time stops the Solver.

Evolutionary algorithms (often called *genetic algorithms*) were discovered by John Holland, a Michigan computer science processor. Evolutionary Solver begins with between 50 and 200 "solutions," which are randomly chosen values of the changing cells that lie between the lower and upper bounds for each changing cell. The exact number of solutions used is specified in the Population Size field in Figure 5-3. The default value is 100, which is fine. Then the target cell value is computed for each solution. By a process of "reproduction" explained in David Goldberg's textbook *Genetic Algorithms* (Addison-Wesley, 1989), a new set of 100 solutions is obtained. Previous solutions that have "good" values (large in a Max problem and small in a Min problem) have a better chance of surviving to the next generation of solutions. This is the mathematical implementation of Darwin's survival of the fittest principle.

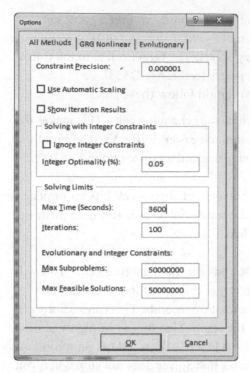

Figure 5-2: Evolutionary Solver settings

The Excel Solver also enables solutions to improve via Mutation. To understand how Mutation works you need to know that Excel codes each value of a changing cell in binary notation. For example, the number 9 is coded as 1001 ($1 * 2^3 + 0 * 2^2 + 0 * 2^1 + 1$).

A Mutation in the Evolutionary Solver changes a 0 to a 1 or a 1 to a 0. A higher value for the Mutation rate moves you around more in the feasible region but exposes you to a larger probability of being led on a wild goose chase after moving to a part of the feasible region with poor changing cell values. A Mutation rate of .5 usually yields the best results. Figure 5-3 shows the Mutation rate changed to .5. The amazingly simple Evolutionary Solver search procedure based on survival of the fittest can solve extraordinarily complex problems! When solving a problem the Evolutionary Solver must make many random choices. This means that if two different people run the same model, then after 5 minutes or so they may see different optimal solutions. Eventually they should see target cell values that are virtually identical.

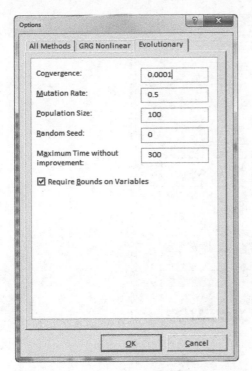

Figure 5-3: Changing the Mutation rate

Finding the Optimal Bundle Prices

The Solver window shown in Figure 5-4 enables you to find revenue maximizing the set of prices for each product combination. A maximum profit of $3,413.70 (see worksheet `initial solver`) is found with the product combination prices, as shown in Figure 5-5.

> **NOTE**   Unlike the GRG or Simplex Solver engine, the Evolutionary Solver engine is only guaranteed to find a near optimal solution (as opposed to an optimal solution). Therefore, when you run the Evolutionary Solver on the book's examples, do not be surprised if your optimal target cell value differs slightly from the target cell value shown in the book.

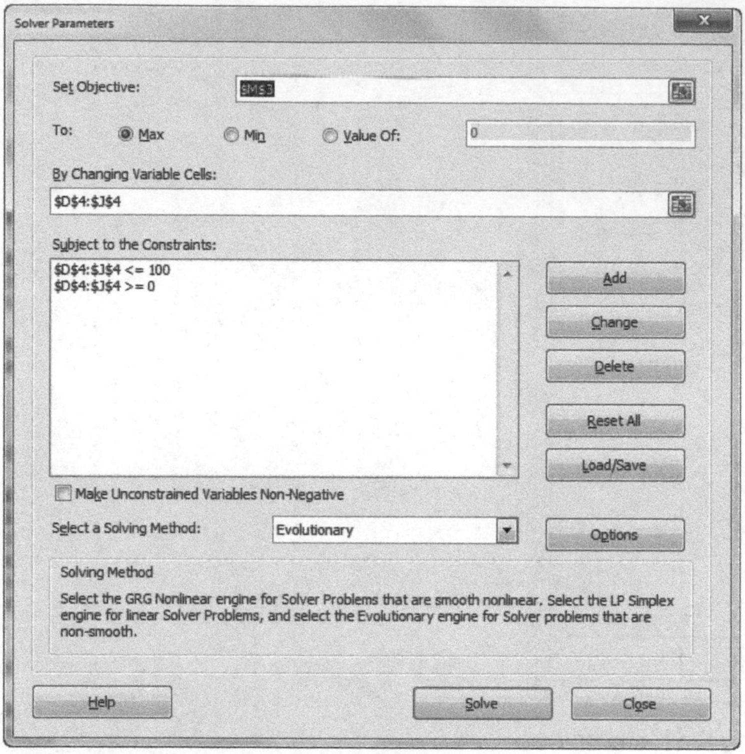

Figure 5-4: Initial bundling Solver model

	C	D	E	F	G	H	I	J
3	Product	1	2	3	4	5	6	7
4	Price	74.35303	35	82.16	69.9942	69.99101	69.991267	89.945
5	Cell Phone	Internet	TV	Cell	Internet +TV	Internet +Cell	TV+Cell	All 3

Figure 5-5: Solution to initial bundling model

Unfortunately, you could not go to market charging $74.35 for Internet service and $69.99 for Internet + TV service because it is unreasonable to provide two services for a lower price than a single service. This situation is called a *price reversal*. As you soon see, the reason Solver charged a higher price for Internet service than for Internet and TV service is because the revenue maximizing prices involve nobody just buying Internet service, so a high price helps ensure that nobody buys just Internet service.

Take a look at the final solver worksheet, and you see it contains the same prices found in the initial solver worksheet. The cell range P70:Q81 in the final `solver` worksheet (as shown in Figure 5-6) computes the price reversals for each possible combination of a product with a larger combination of products. In column P, the price of the smaller product combination is subtracted from the price of the larger product combination. For example, in P71 the formula =D4-G4 computes the Internet Price – (Internet + TV Price). The difference of $4.36 indicates that the Internet + TV price is $4.36 lower than the Internet price. To ensure that no price reversals occur, the target cell is penalized $500 for each dollar of price reversal. Then, survival of the fittest should ensure that no price reversals survive. The choice of penalty amount is an art, not a science. Too large a penalty (such as $1 million) seems to work poorly, and too small a penalty does not "kill off" the things you want to avoid.

	O	P	Q
68			
69	Penalty	dev	penalty
70	TV-(I+TV)	-34.9955	0
71	I-(I+TV)	4.358796	4.358796
72	Cell-(I+Cell)	12.16776	12.16776
73	I-(I+C)	4.36202	4.36202
74	TV-(TV+Cell)	-34.9926	0
75	Cell-(TV+Cell)	12.1675	12.1675
76	(I+TV)-All	-19.9509	0
77	(I+C)-All	-19.9542	0
78	(TV+Cell)-All	-19.9539	0
79	TV-All	-54.9465	0
80	Cell-All	-7.7864	0
81	I-All	-15.5921	0
82	Total		33.05608

Figure 5-6: Price reversals for initial Solver solution

You can copy the formula =IF(P70>0,P70,0) from Q70 to Q71:Q82, to track the price reversal because it yields a value of 0 if the product comparison does not have a price reversal. With the formula =SUM(M6:M82)-500*Q82 you can incorporate your penalty in the target cell. The Solver window is the same (refer to Figure 5-4). After running the Solver you can find the optimal solution, as shown in Figure 5-7.

Therefore, after completing all the calculations, a maximum profit of $3,413.90 is obtained by charging the following:

- $47.41 for Internet service
- $35 for TV service
- $67.87 for cell phone service
- $70 for any two product combination
- $89.95 for all three products

									total	3413.9
	1	**2**	**3**	**4**	**5**	**6**	**7**			
Price	47.41	35	67.87	70	70	70	89.95			
Cell Phone	Internet	TV	Cell	Internet +TV	Internet +Cell	TV+Cell	All 3	max surp	bought?	revenue
$3.50	-43.91	-28	-64.4	-59.5	-63	-59.5	-75.95	-28	0	0
$3.50	-29.91	0	-64.4	-17.5	-49	-31.5	-33.95	1.39E-09	2	35
$49.00	-19.41	-7	-18.9	-14	7.000001	7	15.05	15.05	7	89.95
$0.00	22.59	35	-67.9	70	6.01E-07	5E-08	50.05	70	4	70
$14.00	-47.41	-28	-53.9	-63	-56	-49	-68.95	-28	0	0
$0.00	-47.41	35	-67.9	1.9E-08	-70	5E-08	-19.95	35	2	35
$10.50	-26.41	0	-57.4	-14	-38.5	-24.5	-23.45	1.39E-09	2	35
$0.00	-40.41	-14	-67.9	-42	-63	-49	-61.95	-14	0	0
$2.10	-42.16	-28	-65.8	-57.75	-62.65	-60.9	-75.6	-28	0	0
$28.00	-26.41	-7	-39.9	-21	-21	-14	-12.95	-7	0	0
$21.00	-12.41	14	-46.9	14	-14	5E-08	15.05	15.05	7	89.95
$21.00	-26.41	-14	-46.9	-28	-28	-28	-26.95	-14	0	0

Figure 5-7: Final bundling solution

The consumer is given a substantial discount if she buys two or more products. You can copy the formula =COUNTIF($L$6:$L$82,N9) from O9 to O10:O16 to find the number of people purchasing each product combination. As shown in Figure 5-8, 25 people buy nothing; nobody buys just the Internet; 19 buy just TV; nobody buys just the cell phone; 8 buy the Internet + TV; 2 buy Internet + cell phone; 1 buys TV + cell phone; and 22 people buy the bundle! Your pricing helped extract the high value people place on the Internet and cell phone service by incentivizing these people to buy more than one service. Note the high prices for the Internet and cell phone are designed to give customers an incentive to purchase more products.

Product	Frequency
0	25
1	0
2	19
3	0
4	8
5	2
6	1
7	22

Figure 5-8: Number of purchases of each product combination

This method will automatically determine whether separate prices, mixed bundling, or pure bundling is optimal.

Summary

In this chapter you learned the following:

- Bundling products often allows companies to extract more consumer surplus from customers by incentivizing the customers to purchase more products.
- If you assume that each customer will purchase the product with the largest (non-negative) surplus, then you can set up a spreadsheet that tells you the revenue obtained from your customers for any set of prices.
- You can use Evolutionary Solver to maximize Revenue (or Profit) obtained from customers.
- When using Evolutionary Solver you need to implement bounds on changing cells, use a Mutation rate of 0.5, and handle other constraints by incorporating penalties in the target cell.

Exercises

1. A German machine company sells industrial machinery and maintenance policies for the machine. There are four market segments. Figure 5-9 shows the size of each market segment and the amount each segment will pay for the machine separately, maintenance separately, or the bundle of machinery + maintenance. The variable cost is $550 per machine and $470 per maintenance agreement. What set of prices maximize profits?

	B	C	D	E
1	**fixed**	Machine	Maintenance	Bundle
2	Costs	550	470	1020
3	Size	Machine Use Max	Maintenance Max	Bundle Max
4	12	1250	1500	2600
5	23	1450	540	1750
6	22	1080	1200	2090
7	43	1390	1100	2350

Figure 5-9 Data for Exercise 1

2. The file songdata.xlsx gives the values several hundred people place on 15 downloadable songs. A subset of the data is shown in Figure 5-10.

> **a.** If you charge a single price for all songs, how can you maximize revenue?
>
> **b.** If you can charge two different prices for songs, how can you maximize revenue?

	C	D	E	F	G	H	I	J
10	Person	Song 1	Song 2	Song 3	Song 4	Song 5	Song 6	Song 7
11	1	$0.76	$0.68	$1.61	$1.82	$0.26	$0.66	$1.51
12	2	$0.74	$0.89	$1.78	$1.87	$0.49	$0.68	$1.42
13	3	$0.36	$0.49	$1.40	$1.42	-$0.02	$0.33	$1.14
14	4	$0.34	$0.45	$1.42	$1.50	$0.07	$0.34	$1.14
15	5	$1.27	$1.31	$2.14	$2.38	$1.02	$1.19	$2.05
16	6	$1.46	$1.55	$2.53	$2.52	$1.15	$1.38	$2.18
17	7	$0.57	$0.70	$1.51	$1.48	$0.11	$0.46	$1.23
18	8	$0.62	$0.74	$1.48	$1.71	$0.31	$0.47	$1.29
19	9	$1.37	$1.50	$2.31	$2.57	$1.09	$1.31	$2.14
20	10	$0.47	$0.38	$1.39	$1.51	$0.10	$0.31	$1.11
21	11	$1.50	$1.61	$2.42	$2.56	$1.13	$1.43	$2.10
22	12	$0.57	$0.73	$1.53	$1.65	$0.37	$0.62	$1.36
23	13	$0.92	$0.87	$1.76	$1.82	$0.51	$0.82	$1.63
24	14	$1.02	$1.13	$2.07	$2.22	$0.65	$1.11	$1.91
25	15	$1.27	$1.32	$2.10	$2.28	$0.77	$1.23	$1.94

Figure 5-10 Data for Exercise 2

3. Kroger is trying to determine which types of Vanilla Wafer cookies to stock. The wholesale cost Kroger is charged for a box of each type of cookie is shown in the following table:

National 1	National 2	Generic	Copycat
$1.5	$2.00	$0.90	$1.25

The wholesale price of a box of cookies is assumed equal to the product's quality. Each customer assigns a different value to quality, as shown in file Wafersdata.xlsx and Figure 5-11. For example, Customer 7 would value National 1 at 1.02 * (1.5), and so on. Your task is to determine how to price each type of cookie and then to recommend which brands Kroger should stock to maximize profit from cookies.

⊿	E	F	G
7	Customer	Quality value	
8	1	1	
9	2	1.003333	
10	3	1.006667	
11	4	1.01	
12	5	1.013333	
13	6	1.016667	
14	7	1.02	
15	8	1.023333	
16	9	1.026667	
17	10	1.03	
18	11	1.033333	
19	12	1.036667	
20	13	1.04	
21	14	1.043333	
22	15	1.046667	
23	16	1.05	

Figure 5-11 Valuations for Exercise 3

4. Microsoft is going to sell a Student version of Office (excluding Access and Outlook) and a full version of Office. Assume there are three market segments whose size and valuations for each version of Office are given in the following table. What price for each version of Office can maximize Microsoft's revenue?

Segment	Student Version	Full Version	Size
Students	110	160	20%
Individuals (nonstudent)	170	300	40%
Businesses	240	500	40%

5. *The New York Times* wants to price home subscriptions and web access. Of course, people can buy both home subscriptions and web access. Assume there are three market segments whose size and valuations (per month) for each product combination are given here. The cost to provide a home subscription is $15 and the variable cost to provide web access is $1.

Segment	Home Subscription	Web Access	Home +Web	Size
1	$30	$35	$50	25%
2	$35	$15	$40	40%
3	$20	$20	$25	35%

What prices maximize monthly profits?

6. Before publishing a hardcover book, a publisher wants to determine the proper price to charge for the hardcover and paperback versions. The file paperback .xlsx contains the valuations of 50 representative potential purchasers of the book. Suppose the unit cost of the hardcover book is $4 and the unit cost of the paperback is $2. If the bookstore charges double what it pays the publisher, what price should the publisher charge the bookstore for each version of the book?

7. For the data in Table 5-3 verify that the given mixed bundling strategy maximizes the seller's profit.

8. Describe a situation in which a bank can benefit from a bundling strategy.

9. Suppose your company sells four products and during a year a customer will buy each product at most once. Your company would like to give an end-of-year rebate of 10 percent off to customers who purchase at least $1,000 of products. How can the methods of this chapter be used to maximize your company's profits?

6

Nonlinear Pricing

onlinear pricing is used in a situation in which the cost of purchasing q units is not equal to the unit cost c per unit times q. Bundling (discussed in Chapter 5, "Price Bundling") is a special type of nonlinear pricing because the price of three items is not equal to the sum of the individual prices.

Other common examples of nonlinear pricing strategies include:

■ **Quantity discounts:** If customers buy ≤*CUT* units, they pay high price (*HP*) per unit, and if they buy >*CUT* units, they pay low price (*LP*) per unit. *CUT* is simply the "cutoff point at which the charged price changes." For example, if customers buy ≤*1000* units, you charge $10 a unit, but if they buy more than 1000 units, you charge $8 per unit for all units bought. This form of nonlinear pricing is called the *nonstandard quantity discount*. Another type of quantity discount strategy is as follows: Charge *HP* for the first *CUT* units bought, and charge *LP* for remaining units bought. For example, you charge $10 per unit for first 1000 units and $8 per unit for remaining units bought. This form of nonlinear pricing is called the *standard quantity discount*. In both examples the value of *CUT* = *1000*.

■ **Two-part tariff:** The cost of buying q units is a fixed charge K plus c per unit purchased. For example, it may cost $500 to join a golf club and $30 per round of golf.

Many companies use quantity discounts and two-part tariffs. Microsoft does not charge twice as much for 200 units, for example, as for 100 units. Supermarkets charge less per ounce for a 2-pound jar of peanut butter as for a 1-pound jar of peanut butter. Golf courses often use a two-part tariff by charging an annual membership fee and a charge for each round of golf.

Just as in Chapter 5 you used the Evolutionary Solver to find optimal price bundling strategies, you can use the Evolutionary Solver to find the profit maximizing parameters of a nonlinear pricing strategy. As in Chapter 5, you can assume the consumer will choose an option giving her the maximum (non-negative) consumer surplus. You can see that nonlinear pricing can often significantly increase your profits, seemingly creating profits out of nothing at all.

In this chapter you will first learn how a consumer's demand curve yields the consumer's willingness to pay for each unit of a product. Using this information you will learn how to use the Evolutionary Solver to determine profit or revenue maximizing nonlinear pricing strategies.

Demand Curves and Willingness to Pay

A demand curve tells you for each possible price how many units a customer is willing to buy. A consumer's willingness to pay curve is defined as the maximum amount a customer is willing to pay for each unit of the product. In this section you will learn how to extract the willingness to pay curve from a demand curve.

Suppose you want to sell a software program to a Fortune 500 company. Let q equal the number of copies of the program the company demands, and let p equal the price charged for the software. Suppose you estimated that the demand curve for software is given by $q = 400 - p$. Clearly, your customer is willing to pay less for each additional unit of your software program. Locked inside this demand curve is information about how much the company is willing to pay for each unit of your program. This information is crucial to maximize profitability of sales.

Now rewrite your demand curve as $p = 400 - q$. Thus, when $q = 1$, $p = \$399$, and so on. Now try to figure out the value your customer attaches to each of the first two units of your program. Assuming that the customer is rational, the customer will buy a unit if and only if the value of the unit exceeds your price. At a price of \$400, demand equals 0, so the first unit cannot be worth \$400. At a price of \$399, however, demand equals 1 unit. Therefore, the first unit must be worth somewhere between \$399 and \$400. Similarly, at a price of \$399, the customer does not purchase the second unit. At a price of \$398, however, the customer is purchasing two units, so the customer does purchase the second unit. Therefore, the customer values the second unit somewhere between \$399 and \$398. The customer's willingness to pay for a unit of a product is often referred to as the unit's *reservation price*.

It can be shown that a good approximation to the value of the ith unit purchased by the customer is the price that makes demand equal to $i - 0.5$. For example, by setting q equal to 0.5, you can find that the value of the first unit is 400 − 0.5 = \$399.50. Similarly, by setting $q = 1.5$, you can find that the value of the second unit is 400 − 1.5 = \$398.50.

Suppose the demand curve can be written as $p = D(q)$. In your example this looks like $D(q) = 400 - q$. The reader who knows integral calculus can exactly determine the value a consumer places on the first n items by computing $\int_0^n D(q)dq$. In your example you would find the value of the first two units to be the following:

$$\int_0^2 (400-q)dq = [400q - .5q^2]_0^2 = 800 - 2 = 798$$

This agrees with your approximate method that yields a value of 399.5 + 398.5 = 798 for the first two units.

Profit Maximizing with Nonlinear Pricing Strategies

Throughout this chapter assume a power company (Atlantis Power and Light, APL for short) wants to determine how to maximize the profit earned from a customer whose demand in kilowatt hours (kwh) for power is given by $q = 20 - 2p$. It costs $2 to produce a unit of power. Your analysis begins by assuming APL will use linear pricing; that is, charging the same price for each unit sold. You will find that with linear pricing the maximum profit that can be obtained is $32. Then you will find the surprising result that proper use of quantity discounts or a two-part tariff doubles APL's profit! The work for this chapter is in the file `Powerblockprice.xls`. To determine the profit maximizing linear pricing rule, you simply want to maximize $(20 - 2p) \times (p - 2)$. In the `oneprice` worksheet from the `Powerblockprice.xls` file, a price of $6 yields a maximum profit of $32 (see Figure 6-1). The Solver model simply chooses a non-negative price (changing the cell that maximizes profit [Cell D12]). Charging $6 per kwh yields a maximum profit of $32.00.

	C	D	E
8	price	$6.00	
9	demand	8	
10	unit cost	$2.00	
11			
12	profit	$32.00	
13			

Figure 6-1: Finding the profit maximizing single price strategy

Optimizing the Standard Quantity Discount

To determine a profit maximizing pricing strategy that uses the standard quantity discount, assume the quantity discount pricing policy is defined as follows: All units up to a value *CUT* are sold at a high price (*HP*). Recall that *CUT* is simply the cutoff point at which the per unit price is lowered. All other units sell at a lower price (*LP*). Assuming the customer chooses the number of kwh with the highest non-negative surplus, you can use the Evolutionary Solver to determine profit maximizing values of *CUT*, *HP*, and *LP*. The work for this task is shown in sheet qd of file Powerblockprice.xls. Also, Figure 6-2 shows that the demand curve may be written as $p = 10 - (q/2)$, so the first unit is valued at $10 - (.5/2) = \$9.75$, the second unit is valued at $10 - (1.5/2) = \$9.25$, and so on.

	C	D	E	F	G	H	I	J
1			cutoff	5		Units bought	16	
2	cost		HP	14.30422		Revenue	$ 96.00	
3	2		LP	2.2253		Prod Cost	$ 32.00	
4					Max surplus	0.000611745		
5	Midpoint	Unit	Value	Cum Valu	Price paid	Surplus		Profit
6	0.5	1	9.75	9.75	14.30421665	-4.554216652		$ 64.00
7	1.5	2	9.25	19	28.6084333	-9.608433303		
8	2.5	3	8.75	27.75	42.91264995	-15.16264995		
9	3.5	4	8.25	36	57.21686661	-21.21686661		
10	4.5	5	7.75	43.75	71.52108326	-27.77108326		
11	5.5	6	7.25	51	73.74638371	-22.74638371		
12	6.5	7	6.75	57.75	75.97168417	-18.22168417		
13	7.5	8	6.25	64	78.19698462	-14.19698462		
14	8.5	9	5.75	69.75	80.42228508	-10.67228508		
15	9.5	10	5.25	75	82.64758553	-7.647585529		
16	10.5	11	4.75	79.75	84.87288598	-5.122885984		
17	11.5	12	4.25	84	87.09818644	-3.098186438		
18	12.5	13	3.75	87.75	89.32348689	-1.573486892		
19	13.5	14	3.25	91	91.54878735	-0.548787347		
20	14.5	15	2.75	93.75	93.7740878	-0.024087801		
21	15.5	16	2.25	96	95.99938826	0.000611745		
22	16.5	17	1.75	97.75	98.22468871	-0.47468871		
23	17.5	18	1.25	99	100.4499892	-1.449989164		
24	18.5	19	0.75	99.75	102.6752896	-2.925289618		
25	19.5	20	0.25	100	104.9005901	-4.900590073		

Figure 6-2: Finding the profit maximizing standard quantity discount strategy

To complete the determination of the profit maximizing standard quantity discount strategy, complete the following steps:

1. Copy the formula =10-0.5*C6 from E6 to E7:E25 to determine the value of each unit.

2. In column F compute the cumulative value associated with buying 1, 2,…19 units. In F6 compute the value of the first unit with formula =E6. Copy the formula =F6+E7 from F7 to F8:F25 to compute the cumulative value of buying 2, 3,…20 units.

3. Copy the formula =IF(D6<=cutoff,HP*D6,HP*cutoff+LP*(D6-cutoff)) from G6 to G7:G25 to compute the total cost the consumer pays for purchasing each number of units. If you want to analyze different nonlinear pricing strategies, just change this column to a formula that computes the price the customer is charged for each number of units purchased.

4. Copy the formula =F6-G6 from H6 to H7:H25 to compute the consumer surplus associated with each purchase quantity. In cell H4 compute the maximum surplus with the formula =IF(MAX(H6:H25)>= 0,MAX(H6:H25),0); if it is negative no units will be bought, and in this case you enter a surplus of 0.

5. In cell I1 use the match function to compute the number of units bought with the function =IF(H4>0,MATCH(H4,H6:H25,0),0).

6. In cell I2 compute the sales revenue with the formula =IF(I1=0,0,VLOOKUP (I1,lookup,4)). The range D5:G25 is named Lookup.

7. In cell I3 compute production cost with the formula =I1*C3.

8. In cell J6 compute profit with the formula =I2-I3.

9. Use Solver to find the values of *CUT*, *HP*, and *LP* that maximize profit. The Solver window is shown in Figure 6-3.

You can constrain the value of *CUT* and each price to be at most $20. To do so, charge $14.30 per unit for the first 5 units and $2.22 for remaining units. A total profit of $64 is earned. The quantity discount pricing structure here is an incentive for the customer to purchase 16 units, whereas linear pricing results in the customer purchasing only 6 units. After all, how can the customer stop at 6 units when later units are so inexpensive?

Optimizing the Nonstandard Quantity Discounts

Now assume that your quantity discount strategy is to charge a high price (*HP*) if at most *CUT* units are purchased, and if more than *CUT* units are purchased, all units are sold at a low price (LP). The only change needed to solve for the profit maximizing strategy of this form (see sheet qd2) is to copy the formula =IF(D6<=cutoff,HP*D6,LP*D6) from G6 to G7:G25. Then just rerun the Solver window, as shown in Figure 6-3. This pricing strategy, shown in Figure 6-4, maximizes the profit: If the customer buys up to 15 units, he pays $16.79, and if he buys at least 16 units, he pays $6 per unit. Then the customer buys 16 units, and you make $64 in profit.

Figure 6-3: Determining the profit maximizing standard quantity discount

	C	D	E	F	G	H	I	J
1			cutoff	15		Units bought		16	
2	cost		HP	16.79609		Revenue	$ 96.00	
3	2		LP	5.999873		Prod Cost	$ 32.00	
4					Max surplus	0.002031561		
5	Midpoint	Unit	Value	Cum Valu	Price paid	Surplus		Profit
6	0.5	1	9.75	9.75	16.79608788	-7.046087876		$ 64.00
7	1.5	2	9.25	19	33.59217575	-14.59217575		
8	2.5	3	8.75	27.75	50.38826363	-22.63826363		
9	3.5	4	8.25	36	67.1843515	-31.1843515		
10	4.5	5	7.75	43.75	83.98043938	-40.23043938		
11	5.5	6	7.25	51	100.7765273	-49.77652726		
12	6.5	7	6.75	57.75	117.5726151	-59.82261513		
13	7.5	8	6.25	64	134.368703	-70.36870301		
14	8.5	9	5.75	69.75	151.1647909	-81.41479088		
15	9.5	10	5.25	75	167.9608788	-92.96087876		
16	10.5	11	4.75	79.75	184.7569666	-105.0069666		
17	11.5	12	4.25	84	201.5530545	-117.5530545		
18	12.5	13	3.75	87.75	218.3491424	-130.5991424		
19	13.5	14	3.25	91	235.1452303	-144.1452303		
20	14.5	15	2.75	93.75	251.9413181	-158.1913181		
21	15.5	16	2.25	96	95.99796844	0.002031561		
22	16.5	17	1.75	97.75	101.9978415	-4.247841466		
23	17.5	18	1.25	99	107.9977145	-8.997714493		
24	18.5	19	0.75	99.75	113.9975875	-14.24758752		
25	19.5	20	0.25	100	119.9974605	-19.99746055		

Figure 6-4: Profit maximizing nonstandard quantity discount

Optimizing a Two-Part Tariff

Organizations such as a golf country club or Sam's Club find it convenient to give the consumer an incentive to purchase many units of a product by charging a fixed fee to purchase any number of units combined with a low constant per unit cost. This method of nonlinear pricing is called a *two-part tariff*. To justify paying the fixed fee the customer needs to buy many units. Of course, the customer will not buy any units whose unit cost exceeds the consumer's reservation price, so the organization must be careful to not charge a unit price that is too high.

For example, when you join a country club, you often pay a fixed fee for joining and then a constant fee per round of golf. You might pay a $500 per year fixed fee to be a club member and also pay $30 per round of golf. Therefore one round of golf would cost $530 and two rounds of golf would cost $560. If a two-part tariff were linear then for any number of purchased units, the cost per unit would be the same, but because one round cost $530 per round and two rounds costs $530/2 = $265, the two-part tariff is not consistent with linear pricing.

To dig a little deeper into the concept of a two-part tariff, look at the worksheet tpt. You will see how a power company can optimize a two-part tariff by performing the following steps:

1. To begin, make a copy of your QD or QD2 worksheet.
2. In F2 enter a trial value for the fixed fee, and in F3 enter a trial value for the price per unit. Name cell F2 Fixed and cell F3 var. The only formulas that you need to change are the formulas in the Price Paid formula in Column G (see Figure 6-5).
3. Copy the formula =Fixed+D6*Var from G6 to G7:G25, to compute the cost of buying each number of units.
4. Adjust the Solver window, as shown in Figure 6-6.

You need to constrain the fixed and variable costs between $0 and $100. The profit is maximized by charging a fixed fee of $60.27 and a cost of $2.21 per unit. Again a maximum profit of $64 is made, and the customer purchases 16 units.

	C	D	E	F	G	H	I	J
1				0		Units bought	16	
2	cost		Fixed	60.57433887		Revenue	$ 96.00	
3	2		var	2.214067061		Prod Cost	$ 32.00	
4					Max surplus	0.000588158		
5	Midpoint	Unit	Value	Cum Value	Price paid	Surplus		Profit
6	0.5	1	9.75	9.75	62.78840593	-53.03840593		$ 64.00
7	1.5	2	9.25	19	65.00247299	-46.00247299		
8	2.5	3	8.75	27.75	67.21654005	-39.46654005		
9	3.5	4	8.25	36	69.43060711	-33.43060711		
10	4.5	5	7.75	43.75	71.64467417	-27.89467417		
11	5.5	6	7.25	51	73.85874123	-22.85874123		
12	6.5	7	6.75	57.75	76.07280829	-18.32280829		
13	7.5	8	6.25	64	78.28687535	-14.28687535		
14	8.5	9	5.75	69.75	80.50094241	-10.75094241		
15	9.5	10	5.25	75	82.71500948	-7.715009476		
16	10.5	11	4.75	79.75	84.92907654	-5.179076537		
17	11.5	12	4.25	84	87.1431436	-3.143143598		
18	12.5	13	3.75	87.75	89.35721066	-1.607210659		
19	13.5	14	3.25	91	91.57127772	-0.57127772		
20	14.5	15	2.75	93.75	93.78534478	-0.035344781		
21	15.5	16	2.25	96	95.99941184	0.000588158		
22	16.5	17	1.75	97.75	98.2134789	-0.463478903		
23	17.5	18	1.25	99	100.427546	-1.427545964		
24	18.5	19	0.75	99.75	102.641613	-2.891613025		
25	19.5	20	0.25	100	104.8556801	-4.855680086		

Figure 6-5: Optimizing a two-part tariff

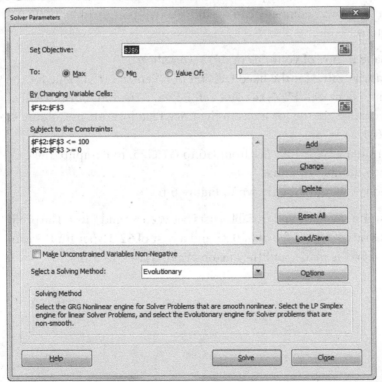

Figure 6-6: Solver window for two-part tariff

All three of the fairly simple nonlinear pricing strategies result in doubling the linear price profit to $64. There is no nonlinear pricing plan that can make more than $64 off the customer. You can easily show the exact value of the sixteenth unit is $2.25, and the exact value of the seventeenth unit is $1.75, which is less than the unit cost of $2.00. Because the customer values unit 16 more than the cost, you should be able to get her to buy 16 units. Because the area under the demand curve (see Exercise 5) from 0 to 16 is 96, the most you can make the consumer pay for 16 units is $96. Therefore your maximum profit is $96 − ($2)(16) = $64, which is just what you obtained using all three nonlinear pricing strategies. The problem with the linear pricing strategy is that it does not extract the surplus value in excess of the $2 cost that the customer places on earlier units. The nonlinear pricing strategies manage to extract all available consumer surpluses.

For a monopolist (like a power company) it may be realistic to assume that an organization can extract all consumer surplus. In the presence of competition, it may be unrealistic to assume that an organization can extract all consumer surplus. To illustrate how the models of this chapter can be modified in the presence of competition, suppose you are planning to enter a business where there is already a single company selling a product. Assume that this company is currently extracting 80 percent of the consumer surplus and leaving 20 percent of the consumer surplus with the consumer. By adding a constraint to your models that leaves, say 25 percent of the consumer surplus in the hands of the customer, you can derive a reasonable nonlinear pricing strategy that undercuts the competition. For an illustration of this idea see Exercise 8.

Summary

In this chapter you learned the following:

- Nonlinear pricing strategies involve not charging the same price for each unit sold.
- If you assume customers purchase the available option with the largest (if non-negative) surplus, then you can use the Evolutionary Solver to find profit maximizing nonlinear pricing strategies such as quantity discounts and two-part tariffs.
- For a linear demand curve, nonlinear pricing earns twice as much profit as linear pricing.

Exercises

1. You own a small country club. You have three types of customers who value each round of golf they play during a month as shown in the following table:

Round	Segment 1	Segment 2	Segment 3
1	$60	$60	$40
2	$50	$45	$30
3	$40	$30	$20
4	$30	$15	$10
5	$20	$0	$0
6	$10	$0	$0

It costs you $5 in variable costs to provide a customer with a round of golf. Find a profit maximizing a two-part tariff. Each market segment is of equal size.

2. The demand curve for a product is $q = 4000 - 40p$. It costs $5 to produce each unit.

   a. If you charge a single price for each unit, how can you maximize profit?
   b. If you use a two-part tariff, how can you maximize the profit?

3. Using the data in Exercise 1, determine the profit maximizing the quantity discount scheme in which all units up to a point sell for a high price, and all remaining units sell for a low price.

4. The file Finalmusicdata.xls (available on the companion website) contains data showing the most 1,000 people were willing to pay for 10 songs. For example, as shown in Figure 6-7, Person 1 is willing to pay up to 38 cents for Song 1.

	C	D	E	F	G	H	I	J	K	L	M
3		Song 1	Song 2	Song 3	Song 4	Song 5	Song 6	Song 7	Song 8	Song 9	Song 10
4	1	$0.38	$0.94	$1.32	$1.85	$0.57	$1.16	$1.39	$2.23	$1.95	$1.88
5	2	$1.02	$1.83	$2.23	$0.56	$0.30	$2.12	$2.09	$1.63	$1.65	$1.50
6	3	$0.60	$1.44	$1.91	$1.67	$0.82	$2.41	$0.64	$1.00	$1.80	$1.46
7	4	$0.31	$2.10	$1.12	$0.84	$1.30	$0.61	$0.84	$1.95	$0.88	$0.51
8	5	$1.71	$1.22	$1.76	$2.35	$0.99	$1.96	$2.04	$0.65	$2.33	$1.56
9	6	$1.44	$2.35	$2.27	$0.94	$1.20	$0.43	$0.51	$1.97	$1.85	$1.51
10	7	$0.22	$1.04	$1.77	$1.51	$0.91	$2.11	$1.33	$2.10	$2.14	$0.61
11	8	$1.27	$0.93	$2.40	$1.57	$1.91	$0.35	$1.14	$1.24	$1.70	$0.63
12	9	$1.85	$0.36	$0.28	$0.61	$1.75	$1.59	$1.55	$1.00	$0.43	$1.37
13	10	$0.85	$2.12	$1.29	$2.41	$1.02	$0.42	$1.18	$2.32	$1.27	$0.58
14	11	$2.07	$2.24	$1.26	$1.49	$0.25	$0.42	$0.75	$2.09	$1.65	$1.14

Figure 6-7: Data for Problem 4

a. If you charge a single price for each song, what price can maximize your revenue?

b. If you use a two-part tariff pricing scheme (for example $3 to download any songs + 40 cents per song), how can you maximize revenue?

c. How much more money do you make with the two-part tariff?

NOTE   For the second part, you must realize that a person will buy either nothing, their top-valued song, their top 2 songs, their top 3 songs,…their top 9 songs or top 10 songs.

5. Show that for the demand curve $q = 40 - 2p$ the consumer places a value of exactly $256 on the first 16 units.

6. (Requires calculus) Suppose the demand for a computer by a leading corporate client (for $p \geq 100$) is given by $200000 / p^2$. Assume the cost of producing a computer is $100.

a. If the same price is charged for each computer, what price maximizes profit?

b. If you charge HP for the first CUT computers and LP for remaining computers purchased, how can you maximize profit?

7. Suppose Verizon has only three cell phone customers. The demand curve for each customer's monthly demand (in hours) is shown here:

Customer	Demand curve
1	$Q = 60 - 20p$
2	$Q = 70 - 30p$
3	$Q = 50 - 8p$

Here p = price in dollars charged for each hour of cell phone usage. It costs Verizon 25 cents to provide each hour of cell phone usage.

   a. If Verizon charges the same price for each hour of cell phone usage, what price should they charge?

   b. Find the profit maximizing a two-part tariff for Verizon. How much does the best two-part tariff increase the profit over the profit maximizing the single price?

8. For the power company example construct a standard quantity discount pricing strategy that leaves the customer with 25 percent of the consumer surplus.

7

Price Skimming and Sales

To solve many interesting pricing problems, you can use the assumption that consumers choose the option that gives them the maximum consumer surplus (if it is non-negative) as discussed in Chapter 5, "Price Bundling," and Chapter 6, "Nonlinear Pricing." This chapter uses this assumption and the Evolutionary Solver to explain two pricing strategies that are observed often:

- Why do prices of high tech products usually drop over time?
- Why do many stores have sales or price promotions?

Dropping Prices Over Time

The prices of most high-tech products as well as other products such as new fashion styles tend to drop over time. You might be too young to remember that when VCRs were first introduced, they sold for more than $1,000. Then the price of VCRs quickly dropped. There are a few reasons for this behavior in prices, and this section examines three of them.

Learning Curve

The most common reason that prices of products—high-tech items in particular—drop over time is due to a learning or experience curve. As first observed by T.P. Wright in 1936 during his study of the costs of producing airplanes, it is often the case that the unit cost to produce a product follows a *learning curve*. Suppose y = unit cost to produce the xth unit of a product. In many situations $y = ax^{-b}$ where $a > 0$ and $b > 0$. If the unit cost of a product follows this equation, the unit cost of production follows a learning curve. If it can easily be shown (see Exercise 3) that if a product's cost follows a learning curve, then whenever cumulative product doubles, unit cost drops by the same percentage $(1 - 2^{-b}$, see Exercise 1). In most observed cases, costs drop between 10 percent and 30 percent when cumulative production doubles.

If unit costs follow a learning curve, costs drop as more units are sold. Passing this drop in costs on to the consumer results in prices dropping over time. The learning curve also gives an incentive to drop prices and increase capacity so your company sells more, increases your cost advantage over competitors, and perhaps puts them out of business. This strategy was popularized in the 1970s by Bruce Henderson of the Boston Consulting Group. Texas Instruments followed this strategy with pocket calculators during the 1980s.

Competition

Aside from a learning curve causing these types of reductions, prices also drop over time as competitors enter the market; this increases supply that puts a downward pressure on prices.

Price Skimming

A third reason why prices of products drop over time is *price skimming*. When a new product comes out, everyone in the market places a different value on the product. If a company starts with a low price, it foregoes the opportunity to have the high-valuation customers pay their perceived product value. As time passes, the high-valuation customers leave the market, and the company must lower the price to sell to the remaining lower valuation customers.

The following example shows how price skimming works. Suppose there are 100 people who might be interested in buying a product. One person values the product at $1; one person values the product at $2; one person values the product at $100. At the beginning of each of the next 10 years, you set a price for the product. Anyone who values the product at an amount at least what you charge buys the product. The work in the Skim.xls file shows the pricing strategy that maximizes your total revenue over the next 10 years. The following steps walk you through the maximization.

1. Enter trial prices for each year in C5:C14.
2. Copy the formula =C5-1 from D5 to D6:D14 to keep track of the highest price valuation person that is left after a given year. For example, after Year 1 people valuing the product at $91 or less are left.
3. Copy the formula =D4-D5 from E5 to E6:E14 to track the unit sale for each year. For example, in Year 1 all people valuing the product at $92 or more (9 people) buy the product.
4. Copy the formula =E5*C5 from F5 to F6:F14 to compute each year's revenue.
5. In cell F15 compute the total revenue with the formula =SUM(F5:F14).

6. Use the Solver to find revenue-maximizing prices. The Solver window is shown in Figure 7-1. Choose each year's price to be an integer between $1 and $100 with a goal to maximize revenue. Figure 7-2 shows the sequence of prices shown in C5:C14.

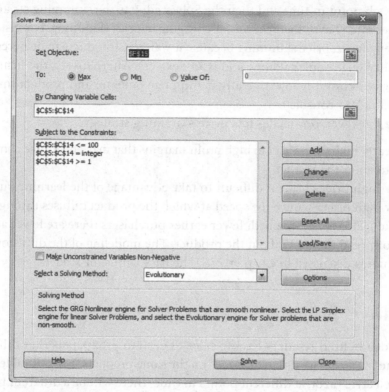

Figure 7-1 Solver window for price skimming model

	A	B	C	D	E	F
1		Skimming				
2						
3		Year	Price	Left<=	Unit sales	Revenue
4		0		100		
5		1	$ 92.00	91	9	828
6		2	$ 83.00	82	9	747
7		3	$ 74.00	73	9	666
8		4	$ 65.00	64	9	585
9		5	$ 56.00	55	9	504
10		6	$ 46.00	45	10	460
11		7	$ 37.00	36	9	333
12		8	$ 27.00	26	10	270
13		9	$ 18.00	17	9	162
14		10	$ 9.00	8	9	81
15					Total	4636

Figure 7-2: Price skimming model

You should discover that prices decline as you "skim" the high-valuation customers out of the market early. You could model prior purchasers coming into market after, say, three years, if the product wears out. You just need to track the status of the market (that is, how many people with each valuation are currently in the market) at each point in time and then the Solver adjusts the skimming strategy.

Companies often have other reasons for engaging in price skimming. For instance, a firm may engage in price skimming because it wants its products to be perceived as high quality (e.g. Apple's iPhone and iPad devices). Alternatively, the firm may engage in price skimming to artificially manipulate demand and product interest (e.g. Nintendo's Wii console.)

There are, however, downsides to a price skimming strategy:

- The early high prices lead to high profit margins that may encourage competitors to enter the market.
- Early high prices make it difficult to take advantage of the learning curve.
- Early high prices reduce the speed at which the product diffuses through the market. This is because with fewer earlier purchasers there are fewer adopters to spread the word about the product. The modeling of the diffusion of a product is discussed in Chapter 27, "The Bass Diffusion Model."

Why Have Sales?

The main idea behind retailers having sales of certain products is that different people in the market place different values on the same products. For a durable good such as an electric razor, at different points in time, there will be a different mix of people wanting to buy. When people with low product valuations predominate in the market, you should charge a low price. When people with high product valuations predominate in the market, you should charge a higher price. The following example develops a simple spreadsheet model which illustrates this idea.

Assume that all customers value an electric razor at $30, $40, or $50. Currently, there are 210 customers in the market, and an equal number value the razor at $30, $40, or $50. Each year 20 new customers with each valuation enter the market. A razor is equally likely to last for one or two years. The work in the sales worksheet of the Sales.xls workbook (see Figure 7-3) determines a pricing policy that maximizes your profit over the next 20 years. These steps are outlined in the following list:

1. Enter a code and the valuation associated with each code in D4:E6. The code for each year is the changing cell and determines the price charged that year. For instance, a code of 2 for one year means a price of $40 will be charged.

2. Enter a trial set of codes in B8:B27.

	A	B	C	D	E	F	G	H	I	J	K	L	M
1				New	20								
2		Why Have Sales?					Buyerst+1=Nonbuyerst+(buyerst-salest)+.5*salest+.5new						
3				Code	Price		Nonbuyerst+1=.5New+.5Salest						totalrevenue
4				1	30								401662.964
5				2	40								
6				3	100						100	40	30
7	Period	Code	Price	High buyers	High nonbuyers	Medium buyers	Medium nonbuyers	Low buyers	Low nonbuyers	High sales	Medium sales	Low sales	Revenue
8	1	3	100	45	45	45	45	45	45	45	0	0	4500
9	2	1	30	77.5	32.5	100	10	100	10	77.5	100	100	8325
10	3	3	100	81.25	48.75	70	60	70	60	81.3	0	0	8125
11	4	1	30	99.375	50.625	140	10	140	10	99.4	140	140	11381.25
12	5	3	100	110.313	59.6875	90	80	90	80	110	0	0	11031.25
13	6	1	30	124.844	65.15625	180	10	180	10	125	180	180	14545.3125
14	7	3	100	137.578	72.42188	110	100	110	100	138	0	0	13757.8125
15	8	1	30	151.211	78.78906	220	10	220	10	151	220	220	17736.3281
16	9	3	100	164.395	85.60547	130	120	130	120	164	0	0	16439.4531
17	10	1	30	177.803	92.19727	260	10	260	10	178	260	260	20934.082
18	11	3	100	191.099	98.90137	150	140	150	140	191	0	0	19109.8633
19	12	1	30	204.451	105.5493	300	10	300	10	204	300	300	24133.5205
20	13	3	100	217.775	112.2253	170	160	170	160	218	0	0	21777.4658
21	14	1	30	231.113	118.8873	340	10	340	10	231	340	340	27333.3801
22	15	3	100	244.444	125.5563	190	180	190	180	244	0	0	24444.3665
23	16	1	30	257.778	132.2218	380	10	380	10	258	380	380	30533.345
24	17	3	100	271.111	138.8891	210	200	210	200	271	0	0	27111.0916
25	18	1	30	284.445	145.5555	420	10	420	10	284	420	420	33733.3363
26	19	3	100	297.778	152.2223	230	220	230	220	298	0	0	29777.7729
27	20	1	30	311.111	158.8889	460	10	460	10	311	460	460	36933.3341

Figure 7-3 Why Have Sales? model

3. Compute the price charged each year in the cell range C8:C27. The Year 1 price is computed in C8 with the formula =VLOOKUP(B8,lookup2).

4. Copy this formula to the cell range C8:C27 to compute the price charged each year.

5. Enter the number of people valuing a razor at $30, $40, and $50 (classified as buyers and nonbuyers) in Year 1 in D8:I8. Half of all new people are classified as buyers and half as nonbuyers. Also 50 percent of holdovers are buyers and 50 percent are nonbuyers.

6. The key to the model is to accurately track each period for the number of buyers and nonbuyers of each valuation. The key relationships include the following two equations:

(1) Buyers(t+1) = Non buyers(t) + (buyers(t) – Sales(t))
       + .5 * Sales(t) + .5 * New
(2) Nonbuyers(t + 1) = .5 * New + .5 * Sales(t)

7. Copy the formula =E8+(D8-J8)+0.5*J8+0.5*New from D9 to D10:D28 to use Equation 1 to compute the number of high-valuation buyers in periods 2–20.

8. Copy the formula 0.5*New+0.5*J8 from E9 to E10:E28 to use Equation 2 to compute the number of high-valuation nonbuyers in periods 2–20.

9. In J8:L8 determine the number of people of each type (High, Medium, and Low valuation) who purchase during Year 1. Essentially, all members of High, Medium, or Low in the market purchase if the price does not exceed their valuation. Thus in K8 the formula =IF(C8<=$E$5,F8,0) determines the number of Medium valuation people purchasing during Year 1. The Solver window for the sales example is shown in Figure 7-4.

Figure 7-4 Solver window for Why Have Sales?

In the Solver model the target cell is meant to maximize the total profit (cell M4). The changing cells are the codes (B8:B27). Constrain the codes to be integers between 1 and 3. You use codes as changing cells rather than prices because prices need to be constrained as integers between 30 and 50. This would cause the Solver to consider silly options such as charging $38. During most years a price of $30 is optimal, but during some years a price of $40 is optimal. The price of $40 is optimal only during years in which the number of $40 customers in the market exceeds the number of $30 customers in the market. The $50 people get off easy! They never pay what the product is worth. Basically, the razors are on sale 50 percent of the time. (Ten of the 20 years' price is $30!)

It is interesting to see how changing the parameters of this example can change the optimal pricing policy. Suppose the high-valuation customers value the product at $100. Then the Solver finds the optimal solution, as shown in Figure 7-5 (see the `high price` worksheet in the `Sales.xls` file). You cycle between an expensive price and a fire sale!

Of course stores have sales for other reasons as well:

■ Drugstores and supermarkets often put soda on sale as a loss leader to draw people into the store in the hope that the customer will buy other products on their current trip to the store or return to the store in the future.

■ Stores often have sales to clear out excess inventory to make room for products that have better sales potential. This is particularly true when a new version of a product comes out (like a new PC or phone.)

	A	B	C	D	E	F	G	H	I	J	K	L	M
1				New	20								
2		Why Have Sales?					Buyerst+1=Nonbuyerst+(buyerst-salest)+.5*salest+.5new						
3			Code	Price			Nonbuyerst+1=.5New+.5Salest						totalrevenue
4			1	30									401662.964
5			2	40									
6			3	100						100	40	30	
7	Period	Code	Price	High buyers	High nonbuyers	Medium buyers	Medium nonbuyers	Low buyers	Low nonbuyers	High sales	Medium sales	Low sales	Revenue
8	1	3	100	45	45	45	45	45	45	45	0	0	4500
9	2	1	30	77.5	32.5	100	10	100	10	77.5	100	100	8325
10	3	3	100	81.25	48.75	70	60	70	60	81.3	0	0	8125
11	4	1	30	99.375	50.625	140	10	140	10	99.4	140	140	11381.25
12	5	3	100	110.313	59.6875	90	80	90	80	110	0	0	11031.25
13	6	1	30	124.844	65.15625	180	10	180	10	125	180	180	14545.3125
14	7	3	100	137.578	72.42188	110	100	110	100	138	0	0	13757.8125
15	8	1	30	151.211	78.70906	220	10	220	10	151	220	220	17736.3281
16	9	3	100	164.395	85.60547	130	120	130	120	164	0	0	16439.4531
17	10	1	30	177.803	92.19727	260	10	260	10	178	260	260	20934.082
18	11	3	100	191.099	98.90137	150	140	150	140	191	0	0	19109.8633
19	12	1	30	204.451	105.5493	300	10	300	10	204	300	300	24133.5205
20	13	3	100	217.775	112.2253	170	160	170	160	218	0	0	21777.4658
21	14	1	30	231.113	118.8873	340	10	340	10	231	340	340	27333.3801
22	15	3	100	244.444	125.5563	190	180	190	180	244	0	0	24444.3665
23	16	1	30	257.778	132.2218	380	10	380	10	258	380	380	30533.345
24	17	3	100	271.111	138.8891	210	200	210	200	271	0	0	27111.0916
25	18	1	30	284.445	145.5555	420	10	420	10	284	420	420	33733.3363
26	19	3	100	297.778	152.2223	230	220	230	220	298	0	0	29777.7729
27	20	1	30	311.111	158.8889	460	10	460	10	311	460	460	36933.3341

Figure 7-5 Sales solution when high valuation = $100

■ Stores often have a sale on a new product to get customers to sample the product in the hopes of maximizing long-term profits from sales on the product. The importance of long-term profits in marketing analytics will be discussed in Chapters 19-22, which cover the concept of lifetime customer value.

Summary

In this chapter you learned the following:

- Prices of high-tech products often drop over time because when the product first comes out, companies want to charge a high price to customers who value the product highly. After these customers buy the product, the price must be lowered to appeal to customers who have not yet purchased the product.
- Because customers have heterogeneous valuations for a product, if you do not have sales, you never can sell your product to customers with low valuations for the product.

Exercises

1. Joseph A. Bank often has a deal in which men can buy one suit and get two free. The file Banks.xlsx contains the valuations of 50 representative customers for one, two, or three suits. Suppose it costs Joseph A. Banks $150 to ready a suit for sale. What strategy maximizes Joseph A. Banks profit: charging a single price for each suit, charging a single price for two suits, or charging a single price for three suits?

2. The file Coupons.xlsx gives the value that a set of customers associates with a Lean Cuisine entree. The file also gives the "cost" each person associates with clipping and redeeming a coupon. Assume it costs Lean Cuisine $1.50 to produce a dinner and 10 cents to redeem a coupon. Also the supermarket sells the entrée for twice the price it pays for the entrée. Without coupons what price should Lean Cuisine charge the store? How can Lean Cuisine use coupons to increase its profit?

3. Show that if the unit cost to produce the xth unit of a product is given by ax^{-b}, then doubling the cumulative cost to produce a unit always drops by the same fraction.

4. If unit cost drops by 20 percent, when cumulative production doubles, then costs follow an 80 percent learning curve. What value of b corresponds to an 80 percent learning curve?

5. (Requires calculus). Suppose the first computer of a new model produced by Lenovo costs $800 to produce. Suppose previous models follow an 85 percent learning curve and it has produced 4,000 computers. Estimate the cost of producing the next 1,000 computers.

8 Revenue Management

Often you purchase an item that seems identical and the price changes. Here are some examples:

- When I fly from Indianapolis to Los Angeles to visit my daughter, the price I have paid for a roundtrip ticket has varied between $200 and $900.
- When I stay in LA at the downtown Marriott, I usually pay $300 per night for a weekday and under $200 a night for a weekend.
- When I rent a car from Avis on a weekend I pay much less than the weekday rate.
- The day after Easter I can buy Easter candy much cheaper than the day before!
- My local steakhouse offers a second entrée for half price on Monday–Wednesday.
- It is much cheaper to rent a house in Key West, Florida in the summer than during the winter.
- The Indiana Pacers charge much more for a ticket when they play the Heat.
- Movies at my local theater cost $5 before 7 p.m. and $10 after 7 p.m.

All these examples illustrate the use of *revenue management*. Revenue management (often referred to as *yield management*) is used to describe pricing policies used by organizations that sell goods whose value is time-sensitive and usually perishable. For example, after a plane takes off, a seat on the plane has no value. After Easter, Easter candy has reduced value. On April 2, an April 1 motel room has no value.

Revenue management has increased the bottom line for many companies. For example:

- American Airlines credits revenue management with an annual revenue increase of $500 million.
- In 2003, Marriott reported revenue management increased profit by $6.7 million.
- Revenue management is credited with saving National Rental Car from bankruptcy.

This chapter explains the basic ideas behind revenue management. The reader who wants to become an expert in revenue management should read Kalyan Talluri and Garrett Ryzin's treatise (*The Theory and Practice of Revenue Management* (Springer-Verlag, 2004).

The main revenue management concepts discussed in this chapter are the following:

- **Making people pay an amount close to their actual valuation for a product.** For example, business travelers are usually willing to pay more for a plane ticket, so revenue management should somehow charge most business travelers a higher price than leisure travelers for a plane ticket.

- **Understanding how to manage the uncertainty about usage of the perishable good.** For example, given that some passengers do not show up for a flight, an airline needs to sell more tickets than seats on the plane, or else the plane leaves with some empty seats.

- **Matching a variable demand to a fixed supply.** For example, power companies will often charge more for power during a hot summer day in an attempt to shift some of the high power demand during the afternoon to the cooler evening or morning hours.

Estimating Demand for the Bates Motel and Segmenting Customers

In many industries customers can be segmented based on their differing willingness to pay for a product. For example, business travelers (who do not stay in their destination on Saturday nights) are usually willing to pay more for a plane ticket than non-business travelers (who usually stay in their destination on Saturday.) Similarly business travelers (who often reserve a room near the reservation date) often are willing to pay more for a hotel room than a non-business traveler (who usually reserves the room further in advance.) This section uses an example from the hotel industry to show how a business can increase revenue and profit by utilizing the differing valuations of different market segments.

Estimating the Demand Curve

Suppose the 300-room Bates Motel wants to maximize its revenue for June 15, 2016. They asked 2 percent (10 people) of the potential market (business has dropped at the Bates Motel since an incident in 1960) their valuation for a stay at the Motel on

June 15, 2016, and found the results shown in Figure 8-1. This work is in the demand curve worksheet of the file Batesmotel.xlsx.

	D	E	F	G
3			2% of market	
4	Customer	Value		
5	1	323		
6	2	151		
7	3	534		
8	4	378		
9	5	358		
10	6	284		
11	7	50		
12	8	113		
13	9	225		
14	10	456		
15				
16				
17		Price	Demand	Price
18		323	5	323
19		151	8	151
20		534	1	534
21		378	3	378
22		358	4	358
23		284	6	284
24		50	10	50
25		113	9	113
26		225	7	225
27		456	2	456

Figure 8-1: Estimating Bates Motel demand curve

You can estimate a demand curve for June 15, 2016, after you have 10 points on the demand curve. For example, 5 of the 10 people have valuations of at least $323, so if you charge $323 for a room, 2 percent of your demand equals 5. To compute 10 points on the demand curve, simply list the 10 given valuations in E18:E27. Then copy the formula =COUNTIF($E$5:$E$14,">="&E18) from F18 to F19:F27. In cell F18, for example, this formula counts how many people have valuations at least as large as $323.

You can now use the Excel Trend Curve to find the straight-line demand curve that best fits the data. To do so, follow these steps:

1. Enter the prices again in the cell range G18:G27 so that you can fit a demand curve with quantity on the x-axis and price on the y-axis.

2. Select the range F18:G27 and then on the ribbon navigate to Insert ➤ Charts ➤ Scatter. Choose the first option (just dots) to obtain a plot of demand against price.

3. Right-click the series; select Add Trendline... and choose the Linear option. Then check Display Equation on chart. This yields the chart shown in Figure 8-2, which shows the best-fitting linear demand curve $p = 564.87-50.49 * q$.

4. Round this off to simplify calculations; you can assume the demand curve is $p = 565 - 50q$.

5. Solve for q in terms of p; you find: $q = \dfrac{565 - p}{50}$.

6. Because this is 2 percent of your demand, multiply the previous demand estimate by 50. This cancels out the 50 in the denominator and you find your entire demand is given by $q = 565 - p$.

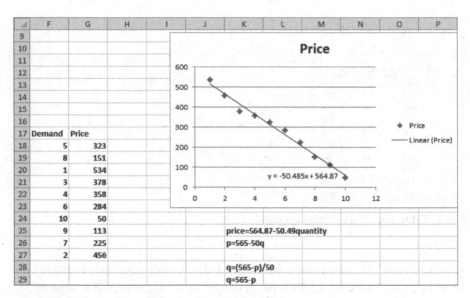

Figure 8-2: Chart of Bates Motel demand curve

Optimal Single Price

To show how revenue management increases profits, you need to determine profits when revenue management is not applied; that is, when each customer is charged the same price.

To simplify your approach, temporarily ignore the 300-room capacity limitation. Under this assumption, if the Bates Motel wants to maximize profit, it should simply choose a price to maximize: profit = price * (565-price). The approach described in Chapter 4, "Estimating Demand Curves and Using Solver to Optimize Price" is now used to determine a single profit maximizing price. The work is in the single price worksheet of the Batesmotel.xslx file as shown in Figures 8-3 and the Solver window in Figure 8-4. Maximum revenue of $79,806.25 is obtained by charging a price of $282.50.

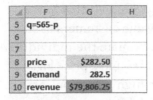

	F	G	H
5	q=565-p		
6			
7			
8	price	$282.50	
9	demand	282.5	
10	revenue	$79,806.25	

Figure 8-3: Computing the best single price

Figure 8-4: Solver window to find best single price

Using Two Prices to Segment Customers

To maximize revenue the Bates Motel would love to charge each customer an individual valuation. However, this is illegal; each customer must be charged the same price. Yield management, however, provides a legal way to price discriminate and increase profits.

If there is a variable highly correlated with a customer's willingness to pay, then Bates can approximate the individual pricing strategy. Suppose that low-valuation customers are willing to purchase early, and high-value customers usually purchase near the date of the reservation. Bates can approximate the individual pricing strategy by charging a price *low* for advance purchases and a price *high* for last minute purchases. Assuming that all customers with high valuations arrive at the last minute this would result in a demand 565 – *high* for last-minute sales and a demand (565 – *low*) – (565 – *high*) for advance sales. The Solver model to determine the revenue maximizing high and low prices is in the Segmentation worksheet (see Figure 8-5.) You proceed as follows:

	E	F	G	H	I	J	K
1							
2							
3							
4							
5							
6	q=565-p			For			
7				all customers >=high charge high			
8				rest charge low			
9							
10	high	$376.67					
11	low	$188.33					
12	highdemand	188.33366					
13	lowdemand	188.333449					
14	highrevenue	$70,938.95					
15	Lowrevenue	$35,469.38					
16	Totalrevenue	$106,408.33					

Figure 8-5: Model for computing prices with segmentation

1. In cell F12 compute the demand for last-minute reservations with the formula =565-high.
2. In cell F13 compute the advance demand with the formula =(565-low)-(565-high).
3. In cell F14 compute the revenue from last-minute reservations with the formula =high*highdemand.
4. In cell F15 compute the revenue from advance reservations with the formula =lowdemand*low.
5. In cell F16 compute the total revenue with the formula =SUM(F14:F15).
6. As shown in the Solver window (refer to Figure 8-6), you choose non-negative high and low prices to maximize total revenue.

Figure 8-6: Solver window with segmentation

You'll find that a high price of $376.67 should be charged for last-minute reservations and a low price of $188.33 for advance reservations. Bates' revenue has now increased by 33 percent to $106,408.33. Of course, this revenue increase would be realized only if there were a perfect correlation between willingness to pay and a customer wanting to buy in advance at the last minute. If this correlation existed, it provides a legal way for Bates to charge higher prices to high-valuation customers. In this situation, Bates can add a qualifying restriction (say, reserve rooms at least 2 weeks in advance) or a *fence,* that separates high-valuation and low-valuation customers. Airlines often use similar tactics by using the qualifying restriction of "staying over a Saturday night" as an imperfect fence to separate leisure and business travelers.

This solution, however, resulted in more people showing up than the hotel has rooms. You can resolve this issue by adding constraints on received reservations.

Segmentation with Capacity Constraints

In Figure 8-7, you can see how to ensure that the number of rooms reserved will not exceed capacity. After all you don't want Norman to stay in his mother's room. To avoid this problem, copy the Segmentation worksheet to a new worksheet named Segmentation with capacity. Then compute total rooms reserved in cell H16 and add a constraint that H16<=J16. As shown in Figure 8-7, $415 should be charged for last-minute reservations and $265 for advance reservations. One hundred and fifty reservations of each type will be purchased and the revenue drops by approximately 4 percent to $102,000. Note that the new prices result in the number of reservations equaling capacity.

	E	F	G	H	I	J	K
6	q=565-p						
7				All customers >=high charge high			
8				rest charge low			
9							
10	high	$415.00					
11	low	$265.00					
12	advancedemand	150.00					
13	lastmindemand	150.00					
14	advancerevenue	$62,250.00					
15	lastminrevenue	$39,750.00		Usage		Capacity	
16	Totalrevenue	$102,000.00		300.00 <=		300	

Figure 8-7: Optimal prices with capacity restriction

Handling Uncertainty

The analysis of the Bates Motel in the previous section implicitly assumed that when prices were set Bates knew *exactly* how many people would reserve in advance and at the last minute. Of course, this is not the case. In this section you learn how Bates should deal with this uncertainty. When developing revenue management systems, airlines also deal with uncertainty, such as the number of people that will fail to show up for a flight.

Determining a Booking Limit

To illustrate the role of uncertainty in revenue management, assume all advance reservations arrive before all last-minute reservations. Bates charges $105 for an advance reservation and $159 for a last-minute reservation. Also assume that sufficient customers want to reserve in advance to fill all the rooms. Because Bates does not know how many last-minute reservations will occur, it "protects" a certain number of rooms for last-minute reservations. A *protection limit* is the number of rooms *not* sold to advance reservations because late arrivals are willing to pay more for a room. Alternatively, a *booking limit* is the maximum number of rooms reserved for advance purchases. For example, a booking limit of 200 means Bates will allow at most 200 rooms to be reserved at the $105 price. Of course a booking limit of 200 rooms is equivalent to a protection limit of 300 − 200 = 100 rooms.

Assume the number of last-minute reservations that Bates receives is unknown and follows a normal random variable with a mean of 100 and a standard deviation of 20. This implies there is a 68 percent chance that between 80 and 120 last-minute reservations will be received, and a 95 percent chance that between 60 and 140 last-minute reservations will be received.

Now you can determine the protection level Q that maximizes Bates' expected profit using the powerful concept of *marginal analysis*. In marginal analysis you try and determine an optimal value of a decision variable by comparing the benefits of a unit change in the variable to the cost incurred from a unit change in a variable. To apply marginal analysis to the determination of the optimal protection level you check if for a given value of Q, Bates can benefit by reducing the protection level from $Q + 1$ to Q. To do so perform these steps:

1. Define `F(Q)` the probability number of last-minute reservations as less than or equal to Q, or `F(Q)=`*n*`(last minute reservations)≥Q`.

2. Because you assumed all rooms could be filled at the discounted price, reducing the protection level by 1 would surely gain Bates $105.

3. With probability $1 − F(Q)$ Bates would sell the $Q +1$ protected room at a $159 price, so on average Bates would lose `(1-F(Q))*159+F(`*Q*`)*0` `−(1 F(Q))*159` if it reduces the protection level by 1. Therefore Bates should reduce the protection level from $Q+1$ to Q if and only if `105>=(1-F(Q))*159` or `F(Q)>=54/159=.339`.

4. You can find the 33.9 percentile of last-minute reservations using the Excel `NORMINV` function. `NORMINV(probability, mean, standard_dev)` gives the value Q for a normal random variable with a given mean and standard deviation such that `F(Q)=p`. Enter `=NORMINV(0.339,100,20)` into Excel. This yields 91.70. Therefore F(91)<.339 and F(92)>.339, so Bates Motel should protect 92 rooms.

Overbooking Models

Airlines usually have several fare classes, so they must determine more than one booking limit. As the time of the flight approaches, airlines update the booking limits based on the number of reservations received. This updating requires lots of past data on similar flights. In most cases, revenue management requires a large investment in information technology and data analysis, so the decision to institute a revenue management program should not be taken lightly.

Airlines always deal with the fact that passengers who have a ticket may not show up. If airlines do not "overbook" the flight by selling more tickets than seats, most flights leave with empty seats that could have been filled. Of course, if they sell too many tickets, they must give "bumped" passengers compensation, so airlines must trade off the risk of empty seats against the risk of overbooking. Marginal analysis can also be used to analyze this trade-off problem.

To illustrate the idea, suppose the price for a New York to Indianapolis flight on Fly by Night (FBN) airlines is $200. The plane seats 100 people. To protect against no-shows, FBN tries to sell more than 100 tickets. Federal Law requires that any ticketed customer who cannot board the plane is entitled to $100 compensation. Past data indicates the number of no-shows for this flight follows a normal random variable with mean 20 and standard deviation 5. To maximize expected revenue less compensation costs for the flight, how many tickets should FBN try to sell for each flight? Assuming that unused tickets are refundable, follow these steps:

1. Let Q equal number of tickets FBN will try to sell and NS equal number of no shows. You can model NS as a continuous random variable, so NS can assume a fractional value. Therefore assume, for example, that if $Q - NS$ is between 99.5 and 100.5, then 100 passengers will show up.

2. For a given value of Q, consider whether you should reduce Q from $Q + 1$ to Q. If $Q - NS >= 99.5$, then you save $100 by reducing ticket limit from $Q + 1$ to Q. This is because one less person will be overbooked. On the other hand, if $Q - NS < 99.5$, then reducing the ticket limit from $Q + 1$ to Q results in one less ticket sale, which reduces revenue by $200. If $F(x)$ = Probability number of no-shows is less than or equal to x, then

   ■ With Probability $F(Q - 99.5)$ reducing the ticket limit from $Q + 1$ to Q saves $100.
   ■ With probability $1 - F(Q - .99.5)$ reducing the ticket limit from $Q + 1$ to Q costs $200.

Therefore reducing the ticket limit from $Q + 1$ to Q benefits you if:

$$100F(Q - 99.5) - 200(1 - F(Q - 99.5)) >= 0$$

or

$$F(Q - 99.5) >= \frac{200}{200+100} = .667$$

3. Now `NORMINV(0.667,20,5)=22.15`. This implied that if and only if $Q - 99.5 >= 22.15$ or $Q >= 121.65$ you should reduce Q from $Q + 1$ to Q. Therefore you should reduce tickets sold from 123 to 122 and stop there. In short, to maximize expected revenue less compensation costs, FBN should cut ticket sales off at 122 tickets.

The problem faced by the airlines is much more complicated than this simple overbooking model. At every instant the airline must update their view of how many tickets will be sold for the flight and use this information to determine optimal decisions on variables such as booking limits.

Markdown Pricing

Many retailers practice revenue management by reducing a product's price based on season or timing. For example, bathing suits are discounted at the end of the summer. Also Easter candy and Christmas cards are discounted after the holiday. The now defunct Filene's Basement of Boston for years used the following markdown policy:

- Twelve days after putting an item on sale, the price was reduced by 25%.
- Six selling days later, the price is cut by 50%.
- After an additional 6 selling days, the items were offered at 75% off the original price.
- After 6 more selling days, the item was given to charity.

The idea behind markdown pricing is that as time goes on, the value of an item to customers often falls. This logic especially applies to seasonal and perishable goods. For example, a bathing suit purchased in April in Indiana has much more value than a bathing suit purchased in September because you can wear the April-purchased suit for many more upcoming summer days. Likewise, to keep perishable items from going bad before they are sold supermarkets markdown prices when a perishable item gets near its expiration date. Because customers only buy products if perceived value exceeds cost, a reduction in perceived value necessitates a reduction in price if you still want to maintain a reasonable sales level. The following example further illustrates mark-down pricing.

Consider a store that sells a product (such as swimsuits) over a three-month period. The product is in demand most when it first hits the stores. In the workbook `Markdownpricing.xlsx` you will determine how pricing strategy maximizes profit. Figure 8-8 shows the markdown pricing spreadsheet model.

Suppose you have 400 swimsuits to sell and the methods of Chapter 4 have been used to estimate the following demand curves:

- Month 1 Demand = 300 − *price*
- Month 2 Demand = 300 − 1.3*price*
- Month 3 Demand = 300 − 1.8*price*

	C	D	E	F	G	H	I	J	K
1									
2	Markdown Pricing								
3	Sell our 400 swimsuits								
4									
5		Month	1	2	3				
6		intercept	300	300	300				
7		slope	-1	-1.3	-1.8		total sold		available
8		price	$162.20	$127.58	$95.53		400	<=	400
9		demand	137.80488	134.1463408	128.0487804				
10		revenue	$22,351.28	$17,114.35	$12,232.30				
11									
12			total revenue						
13			$51,697.94						

Figure 8-8: Markdown pricing model

To determine the sequence of prices that maximizes your revenue, proceed as follows (see the order 400 worksheet):

1. Solver requires you to start with numbers in the changing cells, so in E8:G8 enter trial values for each week's price.
2. Copy the formula =E6+E7*E8 from E9 to E9:G9 to generate the actual demand each month.
3. Copy the formula =E8*E9 from E10 to F10:G10 to compute each month's revenue.
4. The total revenue is computed in cell E13 with the formula =SUM(E10:G10).

You can maximize revenue (E13) by changing prices (E8:G8) and constrain units sold (I8) to equal 400. The Solver window is shown in Figure 8-9.

A maximum revenue of $51,697.94 is obtained by charging $162.20 during Month 1, $127.58 during Month 2, and $95.53 during Month 3. Of course, the prices are set to ensure that all 400 swimsuits are sold.

Your model would be more realistic if the store realizes that it should also try to optimize the number of swimsuits it buys at the beginning of the season. Assume the store must pay $100 per purchased swimsuit. In the how many worksheet (see Figure 8-10) you can use Solver to determine prices that maximize profit.

In E10:G10 you can revise the profit formulas to include the purchase cost by copying the formula =(E8 -cost)*E9 from E10 to F10:G10. After deleting the constraint I8 = 400, the Solver window is identical to Figure 8-9. Profit is maximized at a value of $17,557.69 by buying 245 swimsuits and charging $200 in Month 1, $165.38 in Month 2, and $133.33 in Month 3.

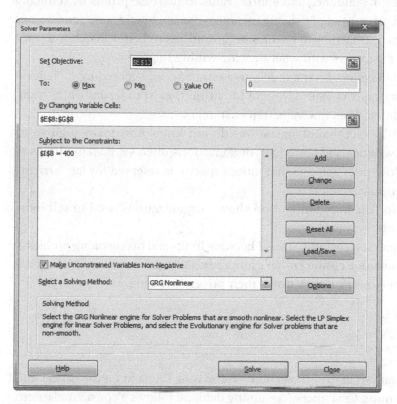

Figure 8-9: Solver window for markdown pricing

	C	D	E	F	G	H	I
1	Maximize Profit						
2	Dynamic Pricing						
3		cost	$100.00				
4							
5		Month	1	2	3		
6		intercept	300	300	300		
7		slope	-1	-1.3	-1.8		total
8		price	$200.00	$165.38	$133.33		245
9		demand	100	85.00000009	60		
10		profit	$10,000.00	$5,557.69	$2,000.00		
11							
12			total profit				
13			$17,557.69				

Figure 8-10: Markdown pricing and purchase decision

Summary

In this chapter you learned the following:

- Revenue management enables organizations including airlines, hotels, rental car agencies, restaurants, and sports teams to increase profits by reducing the unused amount of perishable inventory (seats, hotel rooms, and so on) Revenue management also enables organizations to better match the price charged to customers with what they are willing to pay.

- Revenue management has a much greater chance of succeeding if "fences" (such as staying over Saturday night for airlines) exist to separate high-valuation customers from low-valuation customers.

- To handle the fact that organizations do not know how many high-value customers will demand a product, organizations often set booking limits to constrain low-price sales so that more capacity is reserved for late arriving high-valuation customers.

- To adjust for the possibility of no shows, organizations need to sell more capacity than is available.

- Marginal analysis is helpful to solve booking limits and overbooking problems.

- Often the valuation customers have for products drops over time. This requires that retailers lower or mark down their prices over time.

Exercises

1. Redo the analysis in the first section, "Estimating Demand for the Bates Motel and Segmenting Customers," assuming demand follows a constant elasticity demand curve. Use the Power Curve option on the Excel Trendline to fit the demand curve.

2. How can TV networks use revenue management?

3. How can Broadway plays use revenue management?

4. A flight from New York to Atlanta has 146 seats. Advance tickets purchased cost $74. Last-minute tickets cost $114. Demand for full-fare tickets is normally distributed with a mean of 92 and standard deviation of 30. What booking limit maximizes expected revenues? Assume there are no no-shows and always enough advanced purchasers to fill the flight.

5. Suppose a Marriot offers a $159 discount rate for a midweek stay. Its regular rate is $225. The hotel has 118 rooms. Suppose it is April 1 and the Marriott wants to maximize profit from May 29 bookings. The Marriott knows it can

fill all rooms at the discounted price, but to maximize profit it must reserve or protect some rooms at the high price. Because business travelers book late, the hotel decides to protect or reserve rooms for late-booking business customers. The question is how many rooms to protect. The number of business travelers who will reserve a room is unknown, and you can assume it is normal with the mean = 27.3 and a standard deviation of 6. Determine the Protection Limit that maximizes the expected profit. Again assume that there are always enough leisure travelers to pay the discount rate for the unsold rooms.

6. The Atlanta to Dallas FBN flight has 210 seats and the fare is $105. Any overbooked passenger costs $300. The number of no-shows is normal with a mean of 20 and standard deviation of 5. All tickets are nonrefundable. How many reservations should FBN accept on this flight?

7. The pre-Christmas demand for Christmas cards at a local Hallmark stores is given by $q = 2000 - 300p$. The demand for Christmas cards after Christmas is given by $q = 1000 - 400p$. If the store pays $1 per card, how can they maximize profits from Christmas cards? Assume they want all inventory sold.

III Forecasting

Chapter 9: Simple Linear Regression and Correlation

Chapter 10: Using Multiple Regression to Forecast Sales

Chapter 11: Forecasting in the Presence of Special Events

Chapter 12: Modeling Trend and Seasonality

Chapter 13: Ratio to Moving Average Forecast Method

Chapter 14: Winter's Method

Chapter 15: Using Neural Networks to Forecast Sales

9

Simple Linear Regression and Correlation

Often the marketing analyst needs to determine how variables are related, and much of the rest of this book is devoted to determining the nature of relationships between variables of interest. Some commonly important marketing questions that require analyzing the relationships between two variables of interest include:

- How does price affect demand?
- How does advertising affect sales?
- How does shelf space devoted to a product affect product sales?

This chapter introduces the simplest tools you can use to model relationships between variables. It first covers finding the line that best fits the hypothesized causal relationship between two variables. You then learn to use correlations to analyze the nature of non-causal relationships between two or more variables.

Simple Linear Regression

Every business analyst should have the ability to estimate the relationship between important business variables. In Microsoft Office Excel, the Trendline feature can help you determine the relationship between two variables. The variable you want to predict is the *dependent variable*. The variable used for prediction is the *independent variable*. Table 9-1 shows some examples of business relationships you might want to estimate.

Table 9-1: Examples of Relationships

Independent Variable	Dependent Variable
Units produced by a plant in 1 month	Monthly cost of operating a plant
Dollars spent on advertising in 1 month	Monthly sales
Number of employees	Annual travel expenses
Daily sales of cereal	Daily sales of bananas
Shelf space devoted to chocolate	Sales of chocolate
Price of bananas sold	Pounds of bananas sold

The first step to determine how two variables are related is to graph the data points so that the independent variable is on the x-axis and the dependent variable is on the y-axis. You can do this by using the Scatter Chart option in Microsoft Excel and performing the following steps:

1. With the Scatter Chart option selected, click a data point (displayed in blue) and click Trendline in the Analysis group on the Chart Tools Layout tab.

2. Next click More Trendline Options…, or right-click and select Add Trendline… You'll see the Format Trendline dialog box, which is shown in Figure 9-1.

3. If your graph indicates that a straight line can be drawn that provides a reasonable fit (a reasonable fit will be discussed in the "Defining R^2" section of this chapter) to the points, choose the Linear option. Nonlinear relationships are discussed in the "Modeling Nonlinearities and Interactions" section of Chapter 10, "Using Multiple Regression to Forecast Sales."

Analyzing Sales at Mao's Palace Restaurant

To illustrate how to model a linear relationship between two variables, take a look at the daily sales of products at Mao's Palace, a local Chinese restaurant (see Figure 9-2). Mao's main product is bowls filled with rice, vegetables, and meat made to the customer's order. The file Maospalace.xlsx gives daily unit sales of bowl price, bowls, soda, and beer.

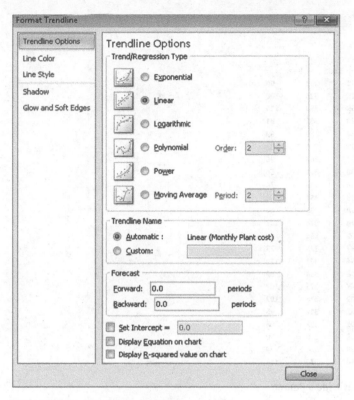

Figure 9-1: Trendline dialog box

Now suppose you want to determine how the price of the bowls affects daily sales. To do this you create an XY chart (or a scatter plot) that displays the independent variable (price) on the x-axis and the dependent variable (bowl sales) on the y-axis. The column of data that you want to display on the x-axis must be located to the left of the column of data you want to display on the y-axis. To create the graph, you perform two steps:

1. Select the data in the range E4:F190 (including the labels in cells E4 and F4).
2. Click Scatter in the Charts group on the Insert tab of the Ribbon, and select the first option (Scatter with only Markers) as the chart type. Figure 9-3 shows the graph.

◢	E	F	G	H
1				
2				
3				
4	Bowl Price	Bowls	Soda	Beer
5	$9.30	391	313	90
6	$9.10	418	326	100
7	$8.50	459	358	115
8	$9.50	424	331	81
9	$8.70	447	380	89
10	$9.70	383	291	92
11	$9.80	399	307	96
12	$8.80	440	361	66
13	$8.60	436	344	74
14	$9.60	413	351	62
15	$8.20	428	338	64
16	$8.00	479	374	101
17	$8.10	462	388	69
18	$9.80	387	325	77
19	$8.90	454	341	114
20	$9.40	418	314	88
21	$8.30	447	375	107
22	$9.60	442	376	102
23	$9.90	381	312	95
24	$9.30	401	301	68
25	$8.10	468	370	70
26	$8.70	428	321	64
27	$8.10	480	374	115

Figure 9-2: Sales at Mao's Palace

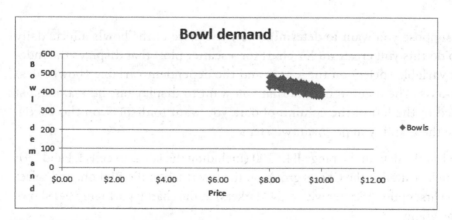

Figure 9-3: Scatterplot of Bowl demand versus Price

If you want to modify this chart, you can click anywhere inside the chart to display the Chart Tools contextual tab. Using the commands on the Chart Tools Design tab, you can do the following:

- Change the chart type.
- Change the source data.
- Change the style of the chart.
- Move the chart.

Using the commands on the Chart Tools Layout tab, you can do the following:

- Add a chart title.
- Add axis labels.
- Add labels to each point that gives the x and y coordinate of each point.
- Add gridlines to the chart.

Looking at the scatter plot, it seems reasonable that there is a straight line (or linear relationship) between the price and bowl sales. You can see the straight line that "best fits" the points by adding a trend line to the chart. To do so, perform the following steps:

1. Click within the chart to select it, and then click a data point. All the data points display in blue with an X covering each point.
2. Right-click and then click Add Trendline...
3. In the Format Trendline dialog box, select the Linear option, and then check the Display Equation on chart and the Display R-squared value on chart boxes, as shown in Figure 9-4. The R-Squared Value on the chart is defined in the "Defining R^2" section of this chapter.
4. Click Close to see the results shown in Figure 9-5. To add a title to the chart and labels for the x-and y-axes, select Chart Tools, click Chart Title, and then click Axis Titles in the Labels group on the Layout tab.
5. To add more decimal points to the equation, select the trend-line equation; after selecting Layout from Chart Tools, choose Format Selection.
6. Select Number and choose the number of decimal places to display.

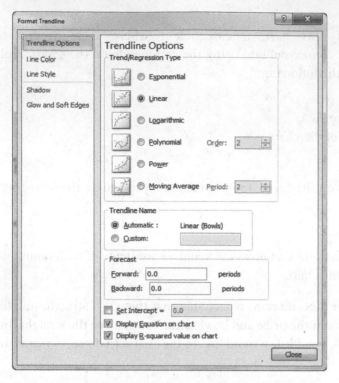

Figure 9-4: Trendline settings for Bowl demand

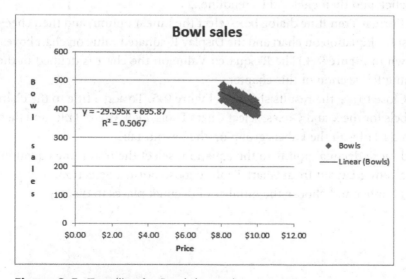

Figure 9-5: Trendline for Bowl demand

How Excel Determines the Best-Fitting Line

When you create a scatter chart and plot a trend line using the Trendline feature, it chooses the line that minimizes (over all lines that could be drawn) the sum of the squared vertical distance from each point to the line. The vertical distance from each point to the line is an *error*, or *residual*. The line created by Excel is called the *least-squares line*. You minimize the sum of squared errors rather than the sum of the errors because in simply summing the errors, positive and negative errors can cancel each other out. For example, a point 100 units above the line and a point 100 units below the line cancel each other if you add errors. If you square errors, however, the fact that your predictions for each point are wrong will be used by Excel to find the best-fitting line. Another way to see that minimizing the sum of squared errors is reasonable is to look at a situation in which all points lie on one line. Then minimizing the least squares line would yield this line and a sum of squared errors equal to 0.

   Thus, Excel calculates that the best-fitting straight line for predicting daily bowl sales from the price by using the equation `Daily Bowl Sales=-29.595*Price + 695.87`. The -29.595 slope of this line indicates that the best guess is that a $1 increase in the price of a bowl reduces demand by 29.595 bowls.

> **WARNING**   You should not use a least-squares line to predict values of an independent variable that lies outside the range for which you have data. Your line should be used only to predict daily bowl sales for days in which the bowl price is between $8 and $10.

Computing Errors or Residuals

Referring back to the Mao's Palace example, you can compute predicted bowl sales for each day by copying the formula `=-29.595*E5+695.87` from C5 to C6:C190. Then copy the formula `=F5-C5` from D5 to D6:D190. This computes the errors (or residuals). These errors are shown in Figure 9-6. For each data point, you can define the error by the amount by which the point varies from the least-squares line. For each day, the error equals the observed demand minus the predicted demand. A positive error indicates a point is above the least-squares line, and a negative error indicates that the point is below the least-squares line. In cell D2, the sum of the errors is computed, which obtained 1.54. In reality, for any least-squares line, the sum of the errors should equal 0. 1.54 is obtained because the equation is rounded to three decimal points.) The fact that errors sum to 0 implies that the least-squares line has the intuitively satisfying property of splitting the points in half.

B	C	D	E	F	G	H
		sum errors				
		1.537				
	Predicted					
	Bowl Sales	Error	Bowl Price	Bowls	Soda	Beer
	420.6365	-29.6365	$9.30	391	313	90
	426.5555	-8.5555	$9.10	418	326	100
	444.3125	14.6875	$8.50	459	358	115
	414.7175	9.2825	$9.50	424	331	81
	438.3935	8.6065	$8.70	447	380	89
	408.7985	-25.7985	$9.70	383	291	92
	405.839	-6.839	$9.80	399	307	96
	435.434	4.566	$8.80	440	361	66
	441.353	-5.353	$8.60	436	344	74
	411.758	1.242	$9.60	413	351	62
	453.191	-25.191	$8.20	428	338	64
	459.11	19.89	$8.00	479	374	101

Figure 9-6: Errors in predicting Bowl demand

Defining R^2

As you can see in the Mao's Palace example, each day both the bowl price and bowl sales vary. Therefore it is reasonable to ask what percentage of the monthly variation in sales is explained by the daily variation in price. In general the percentage of the variation in the dependent variable explained by the least squares line is known as R^2. For this regression the R^2 value is 0.51, which is shown in Figure 9-5. You can state that the linear relationship explains 51 percent of the variation in monthly operating costs.

Once you determine the R^2 value, your next question might be what causes the other 49 percent of the variation in daily bowl sales costs. This value is explained by various other factors. For example, the day of the week and month of the year might affect bowl sales. Chapter 10, "Using Multiple Regression to Forecast Sales" explains how to use *multiple regression* to determine other factors that influence operating costs. In most cases, finding factors that increase R^2 increases prediction accuracy. If a factor only results in a slight increase in R^2, however, using that factor to predict the dependent variable can actually decrease forecast accuracy. (See Chapter 10 for further discussion of this idea.)

Another question that comes up a lot in reference to R^2 values is what is a good R^2 value? There is no definitive answer to this question. As shown in Exercise 5 toward the end of the chapter, a high R^2 can occur even when a trend line is not a good predictor of *y*. With one independent variable, of course, a larger R^2 value indicates a better fit of the data than a smaller R^2 value. A better measure of the accuracy of your predictions is the *standard error of the regression*, described in the next section.

Accuracy of Predictions from a Trend Line

When you fit a line to points, you obtain a standard error of the regression that measures the *spread* of the points around the least-squares line. You can compute the standard error associated with a least-squares line with the STEYX function. The syntax of this function is STEYX(known_y's, known_x's), where *yrange* contains the values of the dependent variable, and *xrange* contains the values of the independent variable. To use this function, select the range E4:F190 and use FORMULAS CREATE FROM SELECTION to name your price data Bowl_Price and your sales data Bowls. Then in cell K1, compute the standard error of your cost estimate line with the formula =STEYX(Bowls,Bowl_Price). Figure 9-7 shows the result.

	J	K	L
1			
2	STD ERROR	17.41867	
3	SLOPE	-29.5945	
4	INTERCEPT	695.8741	
5	RSQ	0.506748	

Figure 9-7: Computing standard error of the regression

Approximately 68 percent of your points should be within one standard error of regression (SER) of the least-squares line, and approximately 95 percent of your points should be within two SER of the least-squares line. These measures are reminiscent of the descriptive statistics rule of thumb described in Chapter 2, "Using Excel Charts to Summarize Marketing Data." In your example, the absolute value of approximately 68 percent of the errors should be 17.42 or smaller, and the absolute value of approximately 95 percent of the errors should be 34.84, or 2 * 17.42, or smaller. You can find that 57 percent of your points are within one SER of the least-squares line, and all (100 percent) of the points are within two standard SER of the least-squares line. Any point that is more than two SER from the least-squares line is called an *outlier*.

Looking for causes of outliers can often help you to improve the operation of your business. For example, a day in which actual demand was 34.84 higher than anticipated would be a demand outlier on the high side. If you ascertain the cause of this high sales outlier and make it recur, you would clearly improve profitability.

Similarly, consider a month in which actual sales are over 34.84 less than expected. If you can ascertain the cause of this low demand outlier and ensure it occurred less often, you would improve profitability. Chapters 10 and 11 explain how to use outliers to improve forecasting.

The Excel Slope, Intercept, and RSQ Functions

You have learned how to use the Trendline feature to find the line that best fits a linear relationship and to compute the associated R^2 value. Sometimes it is more convenient to use Excel functions to compute these quantities. In this section, you learn how to use the Excel SLOPE and INTERCEPT functions to find the line that best fits a set of data. You also see how to use the RSQ function to determine the associated R^2 value.

The Excel SLOPE(*known_y's, known_x's*) and INTERCEPT(*known_y's, known_x's*) functions return the slope and intercept, respectively, of the least-squares line. Thus, if you enter the formula SLOPE(Bowls, Bowl_Price) in cell K3 (see Figure 9-7) it returns the slope (–29.59) of the least-squares line. Entering the formula INTERCEPT(Bowls, Bowl_Price) in cell K4 returns the intercept (695.87) of the least-squares line. By the way, the RSQ(*known_y's, known_x's*) function returns the R^2 value associated with a least-squares line. So, entering the formula RSQ(Bowls, Bowl_Price) in cell K5 returns the R^2 value of 0.507 for your least-squares line. Of course this R^2 value is identical to the RSQ value obtained from the Trendline.

Using Correlations to Summarize Linear Relationships

Trendlines are a great way to understand how two variables are related. Often, however, you need to understand how more than two variables are related. Looking at the correlation between any pair of variables can provide insights into how multiple variables move up and down in value together. Correlation measures linear association, not causation.

The correlation (usually denoted by r) between two variables (call them x and y) is a unit-free measure of the strength of the linear relationship between x and y. The correlation between any two variables is always between –1 and +1. Although the exact formula used to compute the correlation between two variables isn't very important, interpreting the correlation between the variables is.

A correlation near +1 means that x and y have a strong positive linear relationship. That is, when x is larger than average, y is almost always larger than average, and when

x is smaller than average, y is almost always smaller than average. For example, for the data shown in Figure 9-8, (x = units produced and y = monthly production cost), x and y have a correlation of +0.95. You can see that in Figure 9-8 the least squares line fits the points very well and has a positive slope which is consistent with large values of x usually occurring with large values of y.

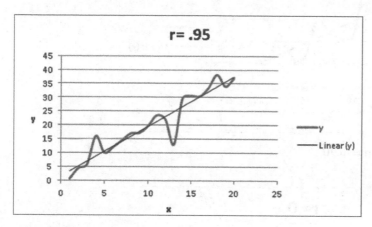

Figure 9-8: Correlation = +0.95

If x and y have a correlation near –1, this means that there is a strong negative linear association between x and y. That is, when x is larger than average, y is usually be smaller than average, and when x is smaller than average, y is usually larger than average. For example, for the data shown in Figure 9-9, x and y have a correlation of –0.90. You can see that in Figure 9-9 the least squares line fits the points very well and has a negative slope which is consistent with large values of x usually occurring with small values of y.

A correlation near 0 means that x and y have a weak linear association. That is, knowing whether x is larger or smaller than its mean tells you little about whether y will be larger or smaller than its mean. Figure 9-10 shows a graph of the dependence of unit sales (y) on years of sales experience (x). Years of experience and unit sales have a correlation of 0.003. In the data set, the average experience is 10 years. You can see that when a person has more than 10 years of sales experience, sales can be either low or high. You also see that when a person has fewer than 10 years of sales experience, sales can be low or high. Although experience and sales have little or no linear relationship, there is a strong nonlinear relationship (see the fitted curve in Figure 9-10) between years of experience and sales. Correlation does not measure the strength of nonlinear associations.

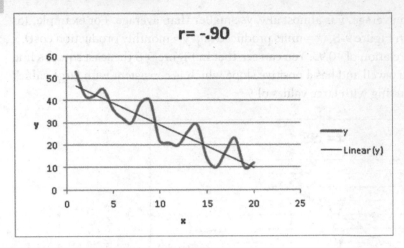

Figure 9-9: Correlation = -0.90

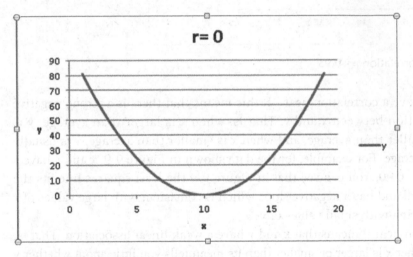

Figure 9-10: Correlation near 0

Finding a Correlation with the Data Analysis Add-In

You will now learn how Excel's Data Analysis Add-in and the Excel Correlation function can be used to compute correlations. The Data Analysis Add-In makes it easy to find correlations between many variables. To install the Data Analysis Add-in, perform the following steps:

1. Click the File tab and select Options.
2. In the Manage box click Excel Add-Ins, and choose Go.
3. In the Add-Ins dialog box, select Analysis ToolPak and then click OK.

Now you can access the Analysis ToolPak functions by clicking Data Analysis in the Analysis group on the Data tab.

You can use this functionality to find the correlations between each pair of variables in the Mao's Palace data set. To begin select the Data Analysis Add-In, and choose Correlation. Then fill in the dialog box, as shown in Figure 9-11.

Figure 9-11: Correlation dialog box

To compute correlations with the Data Analysis Add-in proceed as follows:

1. Select the range which contains the relevant data and data labels. The easiest way to accomplish this is to select the upper-left cell of the data range (E5) and then press Ctrl+Shift+Right Arrow, followed by Ctrl+Shift+Down Arrow.
2. Check the Labels In First Row option because the first row of the input range contains labels. Enter cell M9 as the upper-left cell of the output range.
3. After clicking OK, you see the results, as shown in Figure 9-12.

	M	N	O	P	Q
3					
4					
5		Price Bowl Correlation			
6		-0.71186			
7					
8					
9		Bowl Price	Bowls	Soda	Beer
10	Bowl Price	1			
11	Bowls	-0.71186	1		
12	Soda	-0.58095	0.831008	1	
13	Beer	-0.19367	0.338691	0.246803	1

Figure 9-12: Correlation matrix

From Figure 9-12, you find there is a –0.71 correlation between Bowl Price and Bowl Sales, indicating a strong negative linear association The .0.83 correlation between Soda Sales and Bowl Sales indicates a strong positive linear association. The +0.25 correlation between beer and soda sales indicates a slight positive linear association between beer and soda sales.

Using the CORREL Function

As an alternative to using the Correlation option of the Analysis Toolpak, you can use the CORREL function. For example, enter the formula =CORREL(Bowl_Price,F5:F190) in cell N6 and you can confirm that the correlation between price and bowl sales is -0.71.

Relationship Between Correlation and R^2

The correlation between two sets of data is simply $-\sqrt{R^2}$ for the trend line, where you choose the sign for the square root to be the same as the sign of the slope of the trend line. Thus the correlation between bowl price and bowl sales is $-\sqrt{.507} = -0.711$.

Correlation and Regression Toward the Mean

You have probably heard the phrase "regression toward the mean." Essentially, this means that the predicted value of a dependent variable will be in some sense closer to its average value than the independent variable. More precisely, suppose you try to predict a dependent variable y from an independent variable x. If x is k standard deviations above average, then your prediction for y will be $r \times k$ standard deviations above average. (Here, r = correlation between x and y.) Because r is between -1 and $+1$, this means that y is fewer standard deviations away from the mean than x. This is the real definition of "regression toward the mean." See Exercise 9 for an interesting application of the concept of regression toward the mean.

Summary

Here is a summary of what you have learned in this chapter:

- The Excel Trendline can be used to find the line that best fits data.
- The R^2 value is the fraction of variation in the dependent variable explained by variation in the independent variable.
- Approximately 95 percent of the forecasts from a least-squares line are accurate within two standard errors of the regression.
- Given two variables x and y, the correlation r (always between -1 and $+1$) between x and y is a measure of the strength of the linear association between x and y.

- Correlation may be computed with the Analysis ToolPak or the CORREL function.
- If x is k standard deviations above the mean, you can predict y to be rk standard deviations above the mean.

Exercises

1. The file `Delldata.xlsx` (available on the companion website) contains monthly returns for the Standard & Poor's stock index and for Dell stock. The *beta* of a stock is defined as the slope of the least-squares line used to predict the monthly return for a stock from the monthly return for the market. Use this file to perform the following exercises:

    a. Estimate the beta of Dell.

    b. Interpret the meaning of Dell's beta.

    c. If you believe a recession is coming, would you rather invest in a high-beta or low-beta stock?

    d. During a month in which the market goes up 5 percent, you are 95 percent sure that Dell's stock price will increase between which range of values?

2. The file `Housedata.xlsx` (available on the companion website) gives the square footage and sales prices for several houses in Bellevue, Washington. Use this file to answer the following questions:

    a. You plan to build a 500-square-foot addition to your house. How much do you think your home value will increase as a result?

    b. What percentage of the variation in home value is explained by the variation in the house size?

    c. A 3,000-square-foot house is listed for $500,000. Is this price out of line with typical real estate values in Bellevue? What might cause this discrepancy?

3. You know that 32 degrees Fahrenheit is equivalent to 0 degrees Celsius, and that 212 degrees Fahrenheit is equivalent to 100 degrees Celsius. Use the trend curve to determine the relationship between Fahrenheit and Celsius temperatures. When you create your initial chart, before clicking Finish, you must indicate (using Switch Rows and Columns from the Design Tab on Chart Tools) that data is in columns and not rows because with only two data points, Excel assumes different variables are in different rows.

4. The file Electiondata.xlsx (available on the companion website) contains, for several elections, the percentage of votes Republicans gained from voting machines (counted on election day) and the percentage Republicans gained from absentee ballots (counted after election day). Suppose that during an election, Republicans obtained 49 percent of the votes on election day and 62 percent of the absentee ballot votes. The Democratic candidate cried "Fraud." What do you think?

5. The file GNP.xls (available on the companion website) contains quarterly GNP data for the United States in the years 1970–2012. Try to predict next quarter's GNP from last quarter's GNP. What is the R^2? Does this mean you are good at predicting next quarter's GNP?

6. Find the trend line to predict soda sales from daily bowl sales.

7. The file Parking.xlsx contains the number of cars parked each day both in the outdoor lot and in the parking garage near the Indiana University Kelley School of Business. Find and interpret the correlation between the number of cars parked in the outdoor lot and in the parking garage.

8. The file Printers.xlsx contains daily sales volume (in dollars) of laser printers, printer cartridges, and school supplies. Find and interpret the correlations between these quantities.

9. NFL teams play 16 games during the regular season. Suppose the standard deviation of the number of games won by all teams is 2, and the correlation between the number of games a team wins in two consecutive seasons is 0.5. If a team goes 12 and 4 during a season, what is your best prediction for how many games they will win next season?

10

Using Multiple Regression to Forecast Sales

A common need in marketing analytics is forecasting the sales of a product. This chapter continues the discussion of *causal forecasting* as it pertains to this need. In causal forecasting, you try and predict a dependent variable (usually called Y) from one or more independent variables (usually referred to as X_1, X_2, …, X_n). In this chapter the dependent variable Y usually equals the sales of a product during a given time period.

Due to its simplicity, univariate regression (as discussed in Chapter 9, "Simple Linear Regression and Correlation") may not explain all or even most of the variance in Y. Therefore, to gain better and more accurate insights about the often complex relationships between a variable of interest and its predictors, as well as to better forecast, one needs to move towards multiple regression in which more than one independent variable is used to forecast Y. Utilizing multiple regression may lead to improved forecasting accuracy along with a better understanding of the variables that actually cause Y.

For example, a multiple regression model can tell you how a price cut increases sales or how a reduction in advertising decreases sales. This chapter uses multiple regression in the following situations:

- Setting sales quotas for computer sales in Europe
- Predicting quarterly U.S. auto sales
- Understanding how predicting sales from price and advertising requires knowledge of nonlinearities and interaction
- Understanding how to test whether the assumptions needed for multiple regression are satisfied
- How multicollinearity and/or autocorrelation can disturb a regression model

Introducing Multiple Linear Regression

In a multiple linear regression model, you can try to predict a dependent variable Y from independent variables $X_1, X_2, \ldots X_n$. The assumed model is as follows:

$$(1) \; Y = B_0 + B_1X_1 + B_2X_2 + \ldots B_nX_n + \text{error term}$$

In Equation 1:

- B_0 is called the *intercept* or *constant term*.
- B_i is called the *regression coefficient* for the independent variable X_i.

The *error term* is a random variable that captures the fact that regression models typically do not fit the data perfectly; rather they approximate the relationships in the data. A positive value of the error term occurs if the actual value of the dependent variable exceeds your predicted value $(B_0 + B_1X_1 + B_2X_2 + \ldots B_nX_n)$. A negative value of the error term occurs when the actual value of the dependent variable is less than the predicted value.

The error term is required to satisfy the following assumptions:

- The error term is normally distributed.
- The variability or spread of the error term is assumed not to depend on the value of the dependent variable.
- For time series data successive values of the error term must be independent. This means, for example, that if for one observation the error term is a large positive number, then this tells you nothing about the value of successive error terms.

In the "Testing Validity of Multiple Regression Assumptions," section of this chapter you will learn how to determine if the assumptions of regression analysis are satisfied, and what to do if the assumptions are not satisfied.

To best illustrate how to use multiple regression, the remainder of the chapter presents examples of its use based on a fictional computer sales company, HAL Computer. HAL sets sales quotas for all salespeople based on their territory. To set fair quotas, HAL needs a way to accurately forecast computer sales in each person's territory. From the 2011 *Pocket World in Figures* by *The Economist*, you can obtain the following data from 2007 (as shown in Figure 10-1 and file `Europe.xlsx`) for European countries:

- Population (in millions)
- Computer sales (in millions of U.S. dollars)

■ Sales per capita (in U.S. dollars)
■ GNP per head
■ Average Unemployment Rate 2002–2007
■ Percentage of GNP spent on education

	F	G	H	I	J	K	L
3				Source Economist Pocket World in Figures 2011			
4	Country	Pop (millions)	Computer Sales	Sales/Capita	GNP per head	Unemployment rate	%age spend on education
5	Austria	8.4	941.2	$112.05	$49,600	4.2	5.8
6	Belgium	10.5	1681.9	$160.18	$47,090	8.1	5.9
7	Bulgaria	7.6	154	$20.26	$6,550	13.5	3.5
8	Czech Rep.	10.2	1028.7	$100.85	$20,670	6.6	4.4
9	Denmark	5.5	935.4	$170.07	$62,120	5.2	8.4
10	Finland	5.3	1971	$371.89	$51,320	9.9	6.3
11	France	61.9	5928.9	$95.78	$44,510	10	5.7
12	Germany	82.5	6824.3	$82.72	$44,450	9.1	4.6
13	Greece	11.2	813	$72.59	$31,670	9.9	3.9
14	Hungary	10	449	$44.90	$15,410	7.3	5.1
15	Ireland	4.4	576.9	$131.11	$60,460	6.3	4.3
16	Italy	58.9	3858.2	$65.50	$38,490	9.3	5
17	Netherlands	16.5	2168.5	$131.42	$52,960	4.4	5
18	Poland	38	2847	$74.92	$13,850	14.4	5.6
19	Portugal	10.7	728.6	$68.09	$22,920	6.3	5.9
20	Romania	21.3	687.2	$32.26	$9,300	7	3.3
21	Spain	44.8	4745.8	$105.93	$35,220	14.2	4.4
22	Switzerland	7.5	1130.4	$150.72	$64,430	3.6	5.6
23	Sweden	9.2	2113.4	$229.72	$51,950	6.3	7.6
24	Turkey	75.8	2879	$37.98	$9,940	8.6	3.7

Figure 10-1: HAL computer data

This data is *cross-sectional data* because the same dependent variable is measured in different locations at the same point in time. In *time series data*, the same dependent variable is measured at different times.

In order to apply the multiple linear regression model to the example, Y = Per Capital Computer spending, $n = 3$, X_1 = Per Capita GNP, X_2 = Unemployment Rate, and X_3 = Percentage of GNP spent on education.

Running a Regression with the Data Analysis Add-In

You can use the Excel Data Analysis Add-In to determine the best-fitting multiple linear regression equation to a given set of data. See Chapter 9 for a refresher on installation instructions for the Data Analysis Add-In.

To run a regression, select Data Analysis in the Analysis Group on the Data tab, and then select Regression. When the Regression dialog box appears, fill it in, as shown in Figure 10-2.

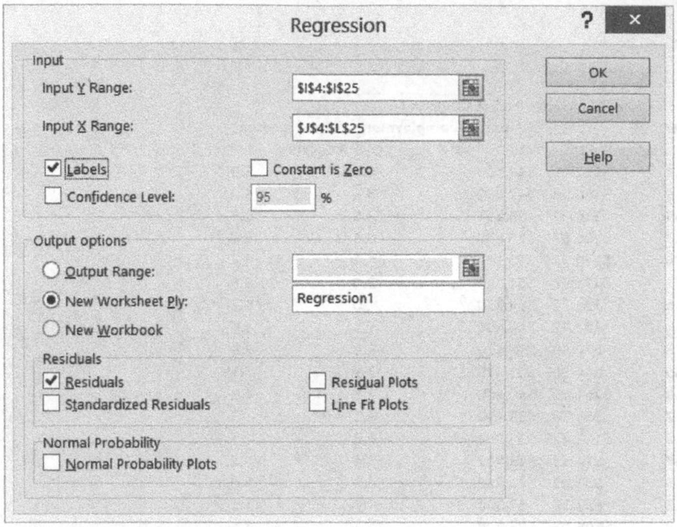

Figure 10-2: Regression dialog box

- The Y Range (I4:I25) includes the data you want to predict (computer per capita sales), including the column label.
- The X Range (J4:L25) includes those values of the independent variables for each country, including the column label.
- Check the Labels box because your X range and Y range include labels. If you do not include labels in the X and Y range, then Excel will use generic labels like Y, X_1, X_2,...,X_n which are hard to interpret.
- The worksheet name Regression1 is the location where the output is placed.
- By checking the Residuals box, you can ensure Excel will generate the error (for each observation error = actual value of Y – predicted value for Y).

After selecting OK, Excel generates the output shown in Figures 10-3 and 10-4. For Figure 10-4, the highlighted text indicates data that is thrown out later in the chapter.

	A	B	C	D	E	F	G	H	I
1	SUMMARY OUTPUT								
2									
3	*Regression Statistics*								
4	Multiple R	0.731106465							
5	R Square	0.534516664							
6	Adjusted R Square	0.452372545							
7	Standard Error	58.42625704							
8	Observations	21							
9									
10	ANOVA								
11		*df*	*SS*	*MS*	*F*	*Significance F*			
12	Regression	3	66638.03186	22212.68	6.507059	0.003940222			
13	Residual	17	58031.66769	3413.628					
14	Total	20	124669.6996						
15									
16		*Coefficients*	*Standard Error*	*t Stat*	*P-value*	*Lower 95%*	*Upper 95%*	*Lower 95.0%*	*Upper 95.0%*
17	Intercept	-114.8351503	78.28996449	-1.46679	0.160688	-280.012537	50.34224	-280.0125369	50.3422364
18	GNP per head	0.002297712	0.00095193	2.413741	0.027355	0.000289316	0.004306	0.000289316	0.004306108
19	Unemployment rate	4.219524573	4.840005896	0.871802	0.395463	-5.99199526	14.43104	-5.991995264	14.43104441
20	%age spend on education	21.4226983	12.73611957	1.682043	0.110837	-5.44816518	48.29356	-5.448165177	48.29356178

Figure 10-3: First multiple regression output

	A	B	C	D
24	RESIDUAL OUTPUT			
25				
26	*Observation*	*Predicted Sales/Capita*	*Residuals*	
27	1	141.105011	-29.0574	
28	2	153.9361699	6.244782	
29	3	32.15788817	-11.8947	
30	4	54.76728846	46.08565	
31	5	229.7909036	-59.7182	
32	6	179.8197146	192.0671	Finland
33	7	151.7406304	-55.9587	
34	8	124.2402274	-41.5214	
35	9	83.25520078	-10.6659	
36	10	60.63088012	-15.7309	
37	11	142.7851159	-11.6715	
38	12	119.958849	-54.4546	
39	13	132.5310691	-1.10683	
40	14	97.71642325	-22.7954	
41	15	90.80533021	-22.7119	
42	16	6.765146383	25.49776	
43	17	120.2673827	-14.3343	
44	18	168.3638234	-17.6438	
45	19	193.9264924	35.7909	
46	20	23.55600061	14.42553	
47	21	112.9313707	49.15388	

Figure 10-4: Residuals from first regression

Interpreting the Regression Output

After you run a regression, you next must interpret the output. To do this you must analyze a variety of elements listed in the output. Each element of the output affects the output in a unique manner. The following sections explain how to interpret the important elements of the regression output.

Coefficients

The Coefficients column of the output (cells B17:B20) gives the best fitting estimate of the multiple regression equation. Excel returns the following equation:

(2) Predicted Computer Sales / Capita = –114.84 + .002298 * (Per Capita GNP) + 4.22 * (Unemployment Rate) + 21.42(Percentage Spent on Education)

Excel found this equation by considering all values of B_0, B_1, B_2, and B_3 and choosing the values that minimize the sum over all observations of (Actual Dependent Variable – Predicted Value)^2. The coefficients are called the *least squares estimates* of B_0, B_1,...,B_n. You square the errors so positive and negative values do not cancel. Note that if the equation perfectly fits each observation, then the sum of squared errors is equal to 0.

F Test for Hypothesis of No Linear Regression

Just because you throw an independent variable into a regression does not mean it is a helpful predictor. If you used the number of games each country's national soccer team won during 2007 as an independent variable, it would probably be irrelevant and have no effect on computer sales. The ANOVA section of the regression output (shown in Figure 10-3) in cells A10:F14 enables you to test the following hypotheses:

- **Null Hypothesis:** The *Hypothesis of No Linear Regression*: Together all the independent variables are not useful (or significant) in predicting Y.
- **Alternative Hypothesis:** Together all the independent variables are useful (or significant).

To decide between these hypotheses, you must examine the *Significance F Value* in cell F12. The Significance F value of .004 tells you that the data indicates that there are only 4 chances in 1000 that your independent variables are not useful in predicting Y, so you would reject the null hypothesis. Most statisticians agree that a Significance F (often called *p-value*) of .05 or less should cause rejection of the Null Hypothesis.

Accuracy and Goodness of Fit of Regression Forecasts

After you conclude that the independent variables together are significant, a natural question is, how well does your regression equation fit the data? The R^2 value in B5 and *Standard Error* in B7 (see Figure 10-3) answer this question.

- The R^2 value of .53 indicates that 53 percent of the variation in Y is explained by Equation 1. Therefore, 47 percent of the variation in Y is unexplained by the multiple linear regression model.
- The Standard Error of 58.43 indicates that approximately 68 percent of the predictions for Y made from Equation 2 are accurate within one standard error ($58.43) and 95 percent of your predictions for Y made from Equation 2 are accurate within two standard errors ($116.86.)

Determining the Significant Independent Variables

Because you concluded that together your independent variables are useful in predicting Y, you now must determine which independent variables are useful. To do this look at the *p-values* in E17:E20. A p-value of .05 or less for an independent variable indicates that the independent variable is (after including the effects of all other independent variables in the equation) a significant predictor for Y. It appears that only GNP per head (p-value .027) is a significant predictor. At this point you want to see if there are any *outliers* or unusual data points. Outliers in regression are data points where the absolute value of the error (actual value of y – predicted value of y) exceeds two standard errors. Outliers can have a drastic effect on regression coefficients, and the analyst must decide whether to rerun the regression without the outliers.

The Residual Output and Outliers

For each data point or observation, the Residual portion of the regression output, as shown in Figure 10-4, gives you two pieces of information.

- The Predicted Value of Y from Equation 2. For example, Austria predicted per capita expenditures are given by the following:

$$(\$116.86) + (0.00229) * (49,600) + (4.22) * (4.2) + 21.52 (5.8)$$
$$= \$141.10$$

- The Residuals section of the output gives for each observation the error = Actual value of Y – Predicted Value of Y. For Austria you find the residual is $112.05 – $141.10 = $–29.05. The regression equation found by least squares has the intuitively pleasing property that the sum of the residuals equals 0. This implies that overestimates and underestimates of Y cancel each other out.

Dealing with Insignificant Independent Variables

In the last section you learned that GNP per head was the only significant independent variable and the other two independent variables were insignificant. When an independent variable is insignificant (has a p-value greater than .05) you can usually drop it and run the regression again. Before doing this though, you must decide what to do with your outlier(s). Because the standard error or the regression is 58.4, any error exceeding 116.8 in absolute value is an outlier. Refer to Figure 10-4 and you can see that Finland (which is highlighted) is a huge outlier. Finland's spending on computers is more than three standard errors greater than expected. When you delete Finland as an outlier, and then rerun the analysis, the result is in the worksheet Regression2 of file Europe.xlsx, as shown in Figure 10-5.

Checking the residuals you find that Switzerland is an outlier. (You under predict expenditures by slightly more than two standard errors.) Because Switzerland is not an outrageous outlier, you can choose to leave it in the data set in this instance. Unemployment Rate is insignificant (p-value of .84 > .05) so you can delete it from the model and run the regression again. The resulting regression is in worksheet Regression 3, of file Europe.xlsx as shown in Figure 10-6.

◢	A	B	C	D	E	F	G
1	SUMMARY OUTPUT						
2							
3	*Regression Statistics*						
4	Multiple R	0.860805637					
5	R Square	0.740986344					
6	Adjusted R Square	0.692421283					
7	Standard Error	29.9835813					
8	Observations	20					
9							
10	ANOVA						
11		*df*	*SS*	*MS*	*F*	*Significance F*	
12	Regression	3	41150.44477	13716.81	15.2576	5.93265E-05	
13	Residual	16	14384.24236	899.0151			
14	Total	19	55534.68713				
15							
16		*Coefficients*	*Standard Error*	*t Stat*	*P-value*	*Lower 95%*	*Upper 95%*
17	Intercept	-32.20876114	41.89082135	-0.76887	0.453169	-121.0133353	56.595813
18	GNP per head	0.001678416	0.000496537	3.380244	0.003816	0.000625805	0.002731
19	Unemployment rate	-0.527867146	2.575579641	-0.20495	0.840195	-5.987852075	4.9321178
20	%age spend on education	15.22764461	6.596202921	2.308547	0.034658	1.244319079	29.21097

Figure 10-5: Regression results: Finland outlier removed

	A	B	C	D	E	F	G
1	SUMMARY OUTPUT						
2							
3	*Regression Statistics*						
4	Multiple R	0.860410573					
5	R Square	0.740306355					
6	Adjusted R Square	0.709754161					
7	Standard Error	29.12650434					
8	Observations	20					
9							
10	ANOVA						
11		*df*	*SS*	*MS*	*F*	*Significance F*	
12	Regression	2	41112.68179	20556.34	24.23087	1.0542E-05	
13	Residual	17	14422.00534	848.3533			
14	Total	19	55534.68713				
15							
16		*Coefficients*	*Standard Error*	*t Stat*	*P-value*	*Lower 95%*	*Upper 95%*
17	Intercept	-38.48026121	27.79129164	-1.38462	0.184076	-97.1147612	20.154239
18	GNP per head	0.001723168	0.000433202	3.977751	0.000973	0.000809193	0.0026371
19	%age spend on education	15.30973984	6.395825812	2.393708	0.028487	1.815726905	28.803753

Figure 10-6: Regression output: unemployment rate removed

Both independent variables are significant, so use the following equation to predict Per Capita Computer Spending:

(3) -38.48 + 0.001723 * (GNP Per Capita) + 15.30974 * (Percentage GNP Spent on Education)

Because $R^2 = 0.74$, the equation explains 74 percent of the variation in Computer Spending. Because the Standard error is 29.13, you can expect 95 percent of your forecasts to be accurate within $58.26. From the Residuals portion of the output, you can see that Switzerland (error of $62.32) is the only outlier.

Interpreting Regression Coefficients

The regression coefficient of a variable estimates the effect (after adjusting for all other independent variables used to estimate the regression equation) of a unit increase in the independent variable. Therefore Equation 3 may be interpreted as follows:

- After adjusting for a fraction of GNP spent on education, a $1,000 increase in Per Capita GNP yields a $1.72 increase in Per Capital Computer spending.
- After adjusting for Per Capita GNP, a 1 percent increase in the fraction of GNP spent on education yields a $15.31 increase in Per Capita Computer spending.

Setting Sales Quotas

Often part of a salesperson's compensation is a commission based on whether a salesperson's sales quota is met. For commission payments to be fair, the company needs to ensure that a salesperson with a "good" territory has a higher quota than a salesperson with a "bad" territory. You'll now see how to use the multiple regression model to set fair sales quotas. Using the multiple regression, a reasonable annual sales quota for a territory equals the population * company market share * regression prediction for per capita spending.

Assume that a province in France has a per capita GNP of $50,000 and spends 10 percent of its GNP on education. If your company has a 30 percent market share, then a reasonable per capita annual quota for your sales force would be the following:

$$0.30(-38.48 + 0.001723 * (50,000) + 15.30974 * (10)) = \$60.23$$

Therefore, a reasonable sales quota would be $60.23 per capita.

Beware of Blind Extrapolation

While you can use regressions to portray a lot of valuable information, you must be wary of using them to predict values of the independent variables that differ greatly from the values of the independent variables that fit the regression equation. For example, the Ivory Coast has a Per Capita GNP of $1,140, which is far less than any country in your European data set, so you could not expect Equation 3 to give a reasonable prediction for Per Capita Computer spending in the Ivory Coast.

Using Qualitative Independent Variables in Regression

In the previous example of multiple regression, you forecasted Per Capita Computer sales using Per Capita GNP and Fraction of GNP spent on education. Independent variables can also be quantified with an exact numerical value and are referred to as *quantitative independent variables*. In many situations, however, independent variables can't be easily quantified. This section looks at ways to incorporate a qualitative factor, such as seasonality, into a multiple regression analysis.

Suppose you want to predict quarterly U.S. auto sales to determine whether the quarter of the year impacts auto sales. Use the data in the file Autos.xlsx, as shown in Figure 10-7. Sales are listed in thousands of cars, and GNP is in billions of dollars.

You might be tempted to define an independent variable that equals 1 during the first quarter, 2 during the second quarter, and so on. Unfortunately, this approach would force the fourth quarter to have four times the effect of the first quarter, which might not be true. The quarter of the year is a qualitative independent variable. To model a qualitative independent variable, create an independent variable (called a *dummy variable*) for all but one of the qualitative variable's possible values. (It is arbitrary which value you leave out. This example omits Quarter 4.) The dummy variables tell you which value of the qualitative variable occurs. Thus, you have a dummy variable for Quarter 1, Quarter 2, and Quarter 3 with the following properties:

- Quarter 1 dummy variable equals 1 if the quarter is Quarter 1 and 0 if otherwise.
- Quarter 2 dummy variable equals 1 if the quarter is Quarter 2 and 0 if otherwise.
- Quarter 3 dummy variable equals 1 if the quarter is Quarter 3 and 0 if otherwise.

	A	B	C	D	E	F
9	Historical data					
10	Year	Quarter	Sales	GNP	Unemp	Int
11	79	1	Sales	2541	5.9	9.4
12	79	2	2910	2640	5.7	9.4
13	79	3	2562	2595	5.9	9.7
14	79	4	2385	2701	6	12
15	80	1	2520	2785	6.2	13
16	80	2	2142	2509	7.3	9.6
17	80	3	2130	2570	7.7	9.2
18	80	4	2190	2667	7.4	14
19	81	1	2370	2878	7.4	14
20	81	2	2208	2835	7.4	15
21	81	3	2196	2897	7.4	15
22	81	4	1758	2744	8.3	12
23	82	1	1944	2582	8.8	13
24	82	2	2094	2613	9.4	12
25	82	3	1911	2529	10	9.3
26	82	4	2031	2544	10.7	7.9
27	83	1	2046	2633	10.4	7.8
28	83	2	2502	2878	10.1	8.4
29	83	3	2238	3051	9.4	9.1
30	83	4	2394	3274	8.5	8.8
31	84	1	2586	3594	7.9	9.2
32	84	2	2898	3774	7.5	9.8
33	84	3	2448	3861	7.5	10
34	84	4	2460	3919	7.2	8.8
35	85	1	2646	4040	7.4	8.2
36	85	2	2988	4133	7.3	7.5
37	85	3	2967	4303	7.1	7.1
38	85	4	2439	4393	7	7.2
39	86	1	2598	4560	7.1	8.9
40	86	2	3045	4587	7.1	7.7
41	86	3	3213	4716	6.9	7.4
42	86	4	2685	4796	6.8	7.4

Figure 10-7: Auto sales data

A Quarter 4 observation can be identified because the dummy variables for Quarter 1 through Quarter 3 equal 0. It turns out you don't need a dummy variable for Quarter 4. In fact, if you include a dummy variable for Quarter 4 as an independent variable in your regression, Microsoft Office Excel returns an error message. The reason you get an error is because if an exact linear relationship exists between any set of independent variables, Excel must perform the mathematical equivalent of dividing by 0 (an impossibility) when running a multiple regression. In this situation, if you include a Quarter 4 dummy variable, every data point satisfies the following exact linear relationship:

```
(Quarter 1 Dummy)+(Quarter 2 Dummy)+(Quarter 3 Dummy)
+(Quarter 4 Dummy)=1
```

NOTE   An exact linear relationship occurs if there exists constants $c_0, c_1, \ldots c_N$, such that for each data point $c_0 + c_1 x_1 + c_2 x_2 + \ldots c_N x_N = 0$. Here $x_1, \ldots x_N$ are the values of the independent variables.

You can interpret the "omitted" dummy variable as a "baseline" scenario; this is reflected in the "regular" intercept. Therefore, you can think of dummies as changes in the intercept.

To create your dummy variable for Quarter 1, copy the formula IF(B12=1,1,0) from G12 to G13:G42. This formula places a 1 in column G whenever a quarter is the first quarter, and places a 0 in column G whenever the quarter is not the first quarter. In a similar fashion, you can create dummy variables for Quarter 2 (in H12:H42) and Quarter 3 (in I12:I42). Figure 10-8 shows the results of the formulas.

In addition to seasonality, you'd like to use macroeconomic variables such as gross national product (GNP, in billions of 1986 dollars), interest rates, and unemployment rates to predict car sales. Suppose, for example, that you want to estimate sales for the second quarter of 1979. Because values for GNP, interest rate, and unemployment rate aren't known at the beginning of the second quarter 1979, you can't use the second quarter 1979 GNP, interest rate, and unemployment rate to predict Quarter 2 1979 auto sales. Instead, you use the values for the GNP, interest rate, and unemployment rate lagged one quarter to forecast auto sales. By copying the formula =D11 from J12 to J12:L42, you can create the lagged value for GNP, the first of your macroeconomic-independent variables. For example, the range J12:L12 contains GNP, unemployment rate, and interest rate for the first quarter of 1979.

You can now run your multiple regression by clicking Data Analysis on the Data tab and then selecting Regression in the Data Analysis dialog box. Use C11:C42 as the Input Y Range and G11:L42 as the Input X Range; check the Labels box (row 11 contains labels), and also check the Residuals box. After clicking OK, you can obtain the output, which you can see in the Regression worksheet of the file Autos. xlsx and in Figure 10-9.

	G	H	I	J	K	L
9						
10	Q1	Q2	Q3	LagGNP	LagUnemp	LagInt
11	Q1	Q2	Q3	LagGNP	LagUnemp	LagInt
12	0	1	0	2541	5.9	9.4
13	0	0	1	2640	5.7	9.4
14	0	0	0	2595	5.9	9.7
15	1	0	0	2701	6	11.9
16	0	1	0	2785	6.2	13.4
17	0	0	1	2509	7.3	9.6
18	0	0	0	2570	7.7	9.2
19	1	0	0	2667	7.4	13.6
20	0	1	0	2878	7.4	14.4
21	0	0	1	2835	7.4	15.3
22	0	0	0	2897	7.4	15.1
23	1	0	0	2744	8.3	11.8
24	0	1	0	2582	8.8	12.8
25	0	0	1	2613	9.4	12.4
26	0	0	0	2529	10	9.3
27	1	0	0	2544	10.7	7.9
28	0	1	0	2633	10.4	7.8
29	0	0	1	2878	10.1	8.4
30	0	0	0	3051	9.4	9.1
31	1	0	0	3274	8.5	8.8
32	0	1	0	3594	7.9	9.2
33	0	0	1	3774	7.5	9.0
34	0	0	0	3861	7.5	10.3
35	1	0	0	3919	7.2	8.8
36	0	1	0	4040	7.4	8.2
37	0	0	1	4133	7.3	7.5
38	0	0	0	4303	7.1	7.1
39	1	0	0	4393	7	7.2
40	0	1	0	4560	7.1	8.9
41	0	0	1	4587	7.1	7.7
42	0	0	0	4716	6.9	7.4

Figure 10-8: Dummy and lagged variables

	A	B	C	D	E	F	G
1	SUMMARY OUTPUT						
2							
3	Regression Statistics						
4	Multiple R	0.884139126					
5	R Square	0.781701994					
6	Adjusted R Square	0.727127492					
7	Standard Error	190.5240756					
8	Observations	31					
9							
10	ANOVA						
11		df	SS	MS	F	Significance F	
12	Regression	6	3119625.193	519937.5322	14.32357552	6.79746E-07	
13	Residual	24	871186.1616	36299.4234			
14	Total	30	3990811.355				
15							
16		Coefficients	Standard Error	t Stat	P-value	Lower 95%	Upper 95%
17	Intercept	3154.700285	462.6530922	6.818716525	4.7214E-07	2199.83143	4109.56914
18	Q1	156.833091	98.87110703	1.586237838	0.125774521	-47.22680256	360.8929846
19	Q2	379.7835116	96.08921514	3.95240518	0.000594196	181.4651595	578.1018637
20	Q3	203.035501	95.40891864	2.128055783	0.043800625	6.12121161	399.9497905
21	LagGNP	0.174156906	0.05842	2.981117865	0.006490201	0.053583977	0.294729835
22	LagUnemp	-93.83233214	28.32328716	-3.312904029	0.002918487	-152.2887117	-35.37595254
23	LagInt	-73.9167147	17.78851573	-4.155305358	0.000355622	-110.6303992	-37.20303822

Figure 10-9: Summary regression output for auto example

In Figure 10-9, you can see that Equation 1 is used to predict quarterly auto sales as follows:

```
Predicted quarterly sales=3154.7+156.833Q1+379.784Q2+203.03
6Q3+.174(LAGGNP in billions)-93.83(LAGUNEMP)-73.91(LAGINT)
```

Also in Figure 10-9, you see that each independent variable except Q1 has a p-value less than or equal to 0.05. The previous discussion would indicate that you should drop the Q1 variable and rerun the regression. Because Q2 and Q3 are significant, you know there is significant seasonality, so leave Q1 as an independent variable because this treats the seasonality indicator variables as a "package deal." You can therefore conclude that all independent variables have a significant effect on quarterly auto sales. You interpret all coefficients in your regression equation *ceteris paribus* (which means that each coefficient gives the effect of the independent variable after adjusting for the effects of all other variables in the regression).

Each regression coefficient is interpreted as follows:

- A $1 billion increase in last quarter's GNP increases quarterly car sales by 174.
- An increase of 1 percent in last quarter's unemployment rate decreases quarterly car sales by 93,832.
- An increase of 1 percent in last quarter's interest rate decreases quarterly car sales by 73,917.

To interpret the coefficients of the dummy variables, you must realize that they tell you the effect of seasonality relative to the value left out of the qualitative variables. Therefore

- In Quarter 1, car sales exceed Quarter 4 car sales by 156,833.
- In Quarter 2, car sales exceed Quarter 4 car sales by 379,784.
- In Quarter 3, car sales exceed Quarter 4 car sales by 203,036.

Car sales are highest during the second quarter (April through June; tax refunds and summer are coming) and lowest during the third quarter. (October through December; why buy a new car when winter salting will ruin it?)

You should note that each regression coefficient is computed after adjusting for all other independent variables in the equation (this is often referred to as ceteris paribus, or all other things held equal).

From the Summary output shown in Figure 10-9, you can learn the following:

- The variation in your independent variables (macroeconomic factors and seasonality) explains 78 percent of the variation in your dependent variable (quarterly car sales).

■ The standard error of your regression is 190,524 cars. You can expect approximately 68 percent of your forecasts to be accurate within 190,524 cars and about 95 percent of your forecasts to be accurate within 381,048 cars (2 * 190,524).

■ There are 31 observations used to fit the regression.

The only quantity of interest in the ANOVA portion of Figure 10-9 is the significance (0.00000068). This measure implies that there are only 6.8 chances in 10,000,000, that when taken together, all your independent variables are useless in forecasting car sales. Thus, you can be quite sure that your independent variables are useful in predicting quarterly auto sales.

Figure 10-10 shows for each observation the predicted sales and residual. For example, for the second quarter of 1979 (observation 1), predicted sales from Equation 1 are 2728.6 thousand, and your residual is 181,400 cars (2910 – 2728.6). Note that no residual exceeds 381,000 in absolute value, so you have no outliers.

	A	B	C
27	RESIDUAL OUTPUT		
28			
29	Observation	Predicted Sales	Residuals
30	1	2728.588616	181.4113836
31	2	2587.848606	-25.84860587
32	3	2336.034563	48.96543676
33	4	2339.328281	180.6717193
34	5	2447.266343	-305.2663429
35	6	2400.118977	-270.1189769
36	7	2199.7408	-9.740800106
37	8	2076.383266	293.6167341
38	9	2276.947422	-68.94742189
39	10	2026.185621	169.8143789
40	11	1848.731191	-90.73119119
41	12	2138.394335	-194.3943352
42	13	2212.298456	-118.2984563
43	14	2014.216596	-103.2165964
44	15	1969.394332	61.60566841
45	16	2160.040544	-120.6405443
46	17	2440.632301	61.3676994
47	18	2290.352403	-52.35240272
48	19	2131.386979	262.6130214
49	20	2433.681173	152.3188271
50	21	2739.094517	158.9054833
51	22	2586.877653	-138.8776532
52	23	2362.035446	97.96455439
53	24	2667.994409	-21.99440885
54	25	2937.601377	50.39862257
55	26	2838.174893	128.8251074
56	27	2713.079218	-274.0792178
57	28	2887.577992	-289.5779921
58	29	3004.570968	40.42903226
59	30	2921.225251	291.7747488
60	31	2781.597472	-96.59747188

Figure 10-10: Residual output for Auto example

Modeling Interactions and Nonlinearities

Equation 1 assumes that each independent variable affects Y in a linear fashion. This means, for example, that a unit increase in X^1 will increase Y by B_1 for any values of $X_1, X_2, ..., X_n$. In many marketing situations this assumption of linearity is unrealistic. In this section, you learn how to model situations in which an independent variable can interact with or influence Y in a nonlinear fashion.

Nonlinear Relationship

An independent variable can often influence a dependent variable through a nonlinear relationship. For example, if you try to predict product sales using an equation such as the following, price influences sales linearly.

$$Sales = 500 - 10 * Price$$

This equation indicates that a unit increase in price can (at any price level) reduce sales by 10 units. If the relationship between sales and price were governed by an equation such as the following, price and sales would be related nonlinearly.

$$Sales = 500 + 4 * Price - .40 * Price^2$$

As shown in Figure 10-11, larger increases in price result in larger decreases in demand. In short, if the change in the dependent variable caused by a unit change in the independent variable is not constant, there is a nonlinear relationship between the independent and dependent variables.

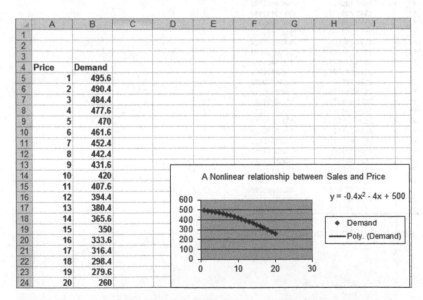

Figure 10-11: Nonlinear relationship between Sales and Price

Interaction

If the effect of one independent variable on a dependent variable depends on the value of another independent variable, you can say that the two independent variables exhibit *interaction*. For example, suppose you try to predict sales using the price and the amount spent on advertising. If the effect to change the level of advertising dollars is large when the price is low and small when the price is high, price and advertising exhibit interaction. If the effect to change the level of advertising dollars is the same for any price level, sales and price do not exhibit any interaction. You will encounter interactions again in Chapter 41, "Analysis of Variance: Two-way ANOVA."

Testing for Nonlinearities and Interactions

To see whether an independent variable has a nonlinear effect on a dependent variable, simply add an independent variable to the regression that equals the square of the independent variable. If the squared term has a low p-value (less than 0.05), you have evidence of a nonlinear relationship.

To check whether two independent variables exhibit interaction, simply add a term to the regression that equals the product of the independent variables. If the term has a low p-value (less than 0.05), you have evidence of interaction. The file `Priceandads.xlsx` illustrates this procedure. In worksheet `data` from this file (see Figure 10-12), you have the weekly unit sales of a product, weekly price, and weekly ad expenditures (in thousands of dollars).

With this example, you'll want to predict weekly sales from the price and advertising. To determine whether the relationship is nonlinear or exhibits any interactions, perform the following steps:

1. Add in Column H *Advertising*Price*, in Column I *Price²*, and in Column J *Ad²*.
2. Next, run a regression with *Y* Range E4:E169 and *X* Range F4:J169. You can obtain the regression output, as shown in the worksheet `nonlinear` and Figure 10-13.
3. All independent variables except for *Price²* have significant p-values (less than .05). Therefore, drop *Price²* as an independent variable and rerun the regression. The result is in Figure 10-14 and the worksheet `final`.

⊿	E	F	G	H	I	J
1						
2						
3						
4	Sales	Price	Ad	A*P	Price^2	Ad^2
5	22845	8	1	8	64	1
6	20417	9	8	72	81	64
7	23761	5	3	15	25	9
8	22674	4	12	48	16	144
9	22782	7	5	35	49	25
10	23807	5	3	15	25	9
11	18924	10	9	90	100	81
12	21855	9	5	45	81	25
13	21749	10	4	40	100	16
14	22683	4	12	48	16	144
15	20968	6	11	66	36	121
16	22202	10	2	20	100	4
17	23241	6	5	30	36	25
18	19004	10	9	90	100	81
19	23978	4	1	4	16	1
20	20497	8	9	72	64	81
21	22322	9	3	27	81	9
22	22628	8	4	32	64	16
23	21051	10	6	60	100	36
24	24515	3	3	9	9	9
25	22126	10	2	20	100	4
26	22141	5	11	55	25	121
27	21151	9	7	63	81	49
28	22558	5	10	50	25	100

Figure 10-12: Nonlinearity and interaction data

⊿	A	B	C	D	E	F	G	H	I
1	SUMMARY OUTPUT								
2									
3	*Regression Statistics*								
4	Multiple R	0.996924531							
5	R Square	0.99385852							
6	Adjusted R Square	0.993665392			Price^2 has high p value so delete it and rerun analysis				
7	Standard Error	135.2764087							
8	Observations	165							
9									
10	ANOVA								
11		*df*	*SS*	*MS*	*F*	*Significance F*			
12	Regression	5	470861057.7	94172212	5146.105	7.9582E-174			
13	Residual	159	2909653.375	18299.71					
14	Total	164	473770711.1						
15									
16		*Coefficients*	*Standard Error*	*t Stat*	*P-value*	*Lower 95%*	Upper 95%	ower 95.0%	pper 95.0%
17	Intercept	24005.74767	111.4951345	215.3076	5.5E-198	23785.54521	24225.95	23785.55	24225.95
18	Price	-135.6678621	32.18950019	-4.21466	4.18E-05	-199.242002	-72.0937	-199.242	-72.0937
19	Ad	660.0035108	16.15110952	40.86428	3.07E-86	628.1051313	691.9019	628.1051	691.9019
20	A*P	-74.12725368	1.425595543	-51.9974	1E-101	-76.94279942	-71.3117	-76.9428	-71.3117
21	Price^2	-0.178202781	2.349205511	-0.07586	0.939629	-4.817874684	4.461469	-4.81787	4.461469
22	Ad^2	-37.37381917	1.019418942	-36.6619	1.84E-79	-39.38716769	-35.3605	-39.3872	-35.3605

Figure 10-13: First regression output for Nonlinearity and Interaction example

	A	B	C	D	E	F	G	H	I
1	SUMMARY OUTPUT								
2									
3	*Regression Statistics*								
4	Multiple R	0.996924419							
5	R Square	0.993858298		All ind variables have low p value so use this equation to predict sales					
6	Adjusted R Squ:	0.993704755		Ads have nonlinear effect and Price and ads interact.					
7	Standard Error	134.8554475		At higher price ads have less effect on sales					
8	Observations	165							
9									
10	ANOVA								
11		*df*	*SS*	*MS*	*F*	*Significance F*			
12	Regression	4	470860952.4	117715238.1	6472.852287	9.3099E-176			
13	Residual	160	2909758.675	18185.99172					
14	Total	164	473770711.1						
15									
16		*Coefficients*	*Standard Error*	*t Stat*	*P-value*	*Lower 95%*	*Upper 95%*	*Lower 95.0%*	*Upper 95.0%*
17	Intercept	24012.24758	71.11479957	337.6547179	3.3475E-230	23871.80286	24152.69231	23871.80286	24152.69231
18	Price	-137.997013	9.633696108	-14.32441001	1.78044E-30	-157.0226141	-118.9714118	-157.0226141	-118.9714118
19	Ad	660.0418883	16.09294845	41.01435424	8.35145E-87	628.2598999	691.8238767	628.2598999	691.8238767
20	A*P	-74.12897476	1.420979292	-52.16752641	2.3559F-102	-76.93526893	71.32268059	-76.93526893	-71.32268059
21	Ad^2	-37.37288222	1.016172056	-36.77810466	5.94521E-80	-39.37972197	-35.36604248	-39.37972197	-35.36604248

Figure 10-14: Final regression output for Nonlinearity and Interaction example

The Significance F Value is small, so the regression model has significant predictive values. All independent variables have extremely small p-values, so you can predict the weekly unit sales with the equation

$$\text{Predicted Unit Sales} = 24{,}012 - 138 * \text{Price} + 660.04 * \text{Ad} - 74.13 * \text{Ad} * \text{P} - 37.33 \text{AD}^2$$

The $-37.33\ Ad^2$ term implies that each additional \$1,000 in advertising can generate fewer sales (diminishing returns). The $-74.13*Ad*P$ term implies that at higher prices additional advertising has a smaller effect on sales.

The R^2 value of 99.4 percent implies your model explains 99.4 percent of the variation in weekly sales. The Standard Error of 134.86 implies that roughly 95 percent of your forecasts should be accurate within 269.71. Interactions and nonlinear effects are likely to cause multicollinearity, which is covered in the section "Multicollinearity" later in this chapter.

Testing Validity of Regression Assumptions

Recall earlier in the chapter you learned the regression assumptions that should be satisfied by the error term in a multiple linear regression. For ease of presentation, these assumptions are repeated here:

- The error term is normally distributed.
- The variability or spread of the error term is assumed not to depend on the value of the dependent variable.

■ For time series data, successive values of the error term must be independent. This means, for example, that if for one observation the error term is a large positive number, then this tells you nothing about the value of successive error terms.

This section further discusses how to determine if these assumptions are satisfied, the consequences of violating the assumptions, and how to resolve violation of these assumptions.

Normally Distributed Error Term

You can infer the nature of an unknown error term through examination of the residuals. If the residuals come from a normal random variable, the normal random variable should have a symmetric density. Then the skewness (as measured by Excel SKEW function described in Chapter 2) should be near 0.

Kurtosis, which may sound like a disease but isn't, can also help you identify if the residuals are likely to have come from a normal random variable. Kurtosis near 0 means a data set exhibits "peakedness" close to the normal. Positive kurtosis means that a data set is more peaked than a normal random variable, whereas negative kurtosis means that data is less peaked than a normal random variable. The kurtosis of a data set may be computed with the Excel KURT function.

For different size data sets, Figure 10-15 gives 95 percent confidence intervals for the skewness and kurtosis of data drawn from a normal random variable.

Sample Size	Kurtosis 2.5	Kurtosis 97.5	Skewness 2.5	Skewness 97.5
10	-1.74	3.41	-1.37	1.36
20	-1.27	2.46	-1.02	1.03
30	-1.09	2.06	-0.86	0.85
40	-0.99	1.77	-0.73	0.75
50	-0.91	1.62	-0.66	0.67
60	-0.85	1.49	-0.61	0.62
70	-0.80	1.36	-0.57	0.57
80	-0.77	1.27	-0.53	0.54
90	-0.73	1.20	-0.51	0.51
100	-0.71	1.13	-0.48	0.48

Figure 10-15: 95 percent confidence interval for skewness and kurtosis for sample from a normal distribution

For example, it is 95 percent certain that in a sample of size 50 from a normal random variable, kurtosis is between −0.91 and 1.62. It is also 95 percent certain that in a sample of size 50 from a normal random variable, skewness is between −0.66 and 0.67. If your residuals yield a skewness or kurtosis outside the range shown in Figure 10-15, then you have reason to doubt the normality assumption.

In the computer spending example for European countries, you obtained a skewness of 0.83 and a kurtosis of 0.18. Both these numbers are inside the ranges specified in Figure 10-15, so you have no reason to doubt the normality of the residuals.

Non-normality of the residuals invalidates the p-values that you used to determine significance of independent variables or the entire regression. The most common solution to the problem of non-normal random variables is to transform the dependent variable. Often replacing y by Ln y, $\sqrt{y}$, or $\frac{1}{y}$ can resolve the non-normality of the errors.

Heteroscedasticity: A Nonconstant Variance Error Term

If larger values of an independent variable lead to a larger variance in the errors, you have violated the constant variance of the error term assumption, and *heteroscedasticity* is present. Heteroscedasticity, like non-normal residuals, invalidates the p-values used earlier in the chapter to test for significance. In most cases you can identify heteroscedasticity by graphing the predicted value on the x-axis and the absolute value of the residual on the y-axis. To see an illustration of this, look at the file Heteroscedasticity.xlsx. A sample of the data is shown in Figure 10-16.

In this file, you are using the data in Heteroscedasticity.xlsx and trying to predict the amount a family spends annually on food from their annual income. After running a regression, you can graph the absolute value of the residuals against predicted food spending. Figure 10-17 shows the resulting graph.

The upward slope of the line that best fits the graph indicates that your forecast accuracy decreases for families with more income, and heteroscedasticity is clearly present. Usually heteroscedasticity is resolved by replacing the dependent variable Y by Ln Y or $\sqrt{Y}$. The reason why these transformations often resolve heteroscedasticity is that these transformations reduce the spread in the dependent variable. For example, if three data points have $Y = 1$, $Y = 10,000$ and $Y = 1,000,000$ then after using the $\sqrt{Y}$ transformation the three points now have a dependent variable with values 1, 100, and 1000 respectively.

	I	J
4	Income	Food spending
5	$74,201.00	$9,646.13
6	$41,659.00	$8,331.80
7	$44,085.00	$9,698.70
8	$63,529.00	$10,799.93
9	$48,436.00	$9,202.84
10	$82,481.00	$13,196.96
11	$35,243.00	$4,934.02
12	$57,563.00	$9,210.08
13	$39,589.00	$5,938.35
14	$53,826.00	$10,226.94
15	$78,861.00	$14,194.98
16	$87,406.00	$11,362.78
17	$74,020.00	$15,544.20
18	$82,290.00	$9,874.80
19	$38,921.00	$4,670.52
20	$80,960.00	$17,001.60
21	$37,107.00	$8,163.54
22	$80,531.00	$14,495.58
23	$79,760.00	$13,559.20
24	$57,427.00	$12,633.94
25	$67,657.00	$9,471.98
26	$75,449.00	$14,335.31
27	$71,390.00	$10,708.50

Figure 10-16: Heteroscedasticity data

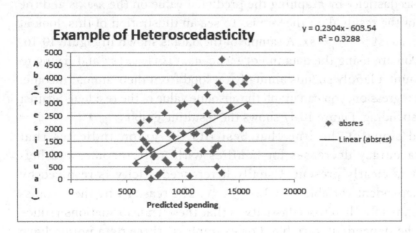

Figure 10-17: Example of Heteroscedasticity

Autocorrelation: The Nonindependence of Errors

Suppose your data is times series data. This implies the data is listed in chronological order. The auto data is a good example. The p-values used to test the hypothesis of no linear regression and the significance of an independent variable are not valid if your error terms appear to be dependent (nonindependent). Also, if your error terms are nonindependent, you can say that *autocorrelation* is present. If autocorrelation is present, you can no longer be sure that 95 percent of your forecasts will be accurate within two standard errors. Probably fewer than 95 percent of your forecasts will be accurate within two standard errors. This means that in the presence of autocorrelation, your forecasts can give a false sense of security. Because the residuals mirror the theoretical value of the error terms in Equation 1, the easiest way to see if autocorrelation is present is to look at a plot of residuals in chronological order. Recall the residuals sum to 0, so approximately half are positive and half are negative. If your residuals are independent, you would expect sequences of the form ++, + −, − +, and − − to be equally likely. Here + is a positive residual and − is a negative residual.

Graphical Interpretation of Autocorrelation

You can use a simple time series plot of residuals to determine if the error terms exhibit autocorrelation, and if so, the type of autocorrelation that is present.

Figure 10-18 shows an illustration of independent residuals exhibiting no autocorrelation.

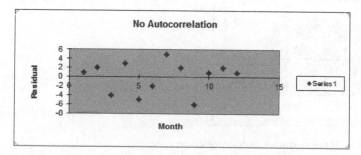

Figure 10-18: Residuals indicate no autocorrelation

Here you can see 6 changes in sign out of 11 possible changes.

Figure 10-19, however, is indicative of *positive autocorrelation*. Figure 10-19 shows only one sign change out of 11 possible changes. Positive residuals are followed by positive residuals, and negative residuals are followed by negative residuals. Thus, successive residuals are positively correlated. When residuals exhibit few sign changes (relative to half the possible number of sign changes), positive autocorrelation is suspected. Unfortunately, positive autocorrelation is common in business and economic data.

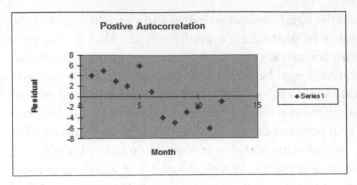

Figure 10-19: Residuals indicate positive autocorrelation

Figure 10-20 is indicative of *negative autocorrelation*. Figure 10-20 shows 11 sign changes out of a possible 11. This indicates that a small residual tends to be followed by a large residual, and a large residual tends to be followed a small residual. Thus, successive residuals are negatively correlated. This shows that many sign changes (relative to half the number of possible sign changes) are indicative of negative autocorrelation.

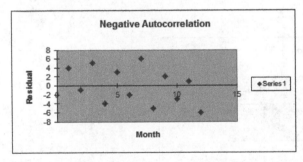

Figure 10-20: Residuals indicate negative autocorrelation

To help clarify these three different types of graphical interpretation, suppose you have n observations. If your residuals exhibit no correlation, then the chance of seeing either less than $\frac{n-1}{2} - \sqrt{n-1}$ or more than $\frac{n-1}{2} + \sqrt{n-1}$ sign changes is approximately 5 percent. Thus you can conclude the following:

- If you observe less than or equal to $\frac{n-1}{2} - \sqrt{n-1}$ sign changes, conclude that positive autocorrelation is present.
- If you observe at least $\frac{n-1}{2} + \sqrt{n-1}$ sign changes, conclude that negative autocorrelation is present.
- Otherwise you can conclude that no autocorrelation is present.

Detecting and Correcting for Autocorrelation

The simplest method to correct for autocorrelation is presented in the following steps. To simplify the presentation, assume there is only one independent variable (Call it X):

1. Determine the correlation between the following two time series: your residuals and your residuals lagged one period. Call this correlation p.
2. Run a regression with the dependent variable for time t being $Y_t - pY_{t-1}$ and independent variable $X_t - pX_{t-1}$.
3. Check the number of sign changes in the new regression's residuals. Usually, autocorrelation is no longer a problem, and you can rearrange your equation to predict Y_t from Y_{t-1}, X_t, and X_{t-1}.

To illustrate this procedure, you can try and predict consumer spending (in billions of $) during a year as a function of the money supply (in billions of $). Twenty years of data are given in Figure 10-21 and are available for download from the file autocorr.xls.

Now complete the following steps:

1. Run a regression with X Range B1:B21 and Y Range A1:A21, and check the Labels and Residuals box. Figure 10-22 shows the residuals.
2. Observe that a sign change in the residuals occurs if, and only if, the product of two successive residuals is <0. Therefore, copying the formula =IF(I27*I26<0,1,0) from J27 to J28:J45 counts the number of sign changes. Compute the total number of sign changes (4) in cell J24 with the formula =SUM(J27:J45).

	A	B
1	Exp	Money stock
2	214.6	159.3
3	217.7	161.2
4	219.6	162.8
5	227.2	164.6
6	230.9	165.9
7	233.3	167.9
8	234.1	168.3
9	232.3	169.7
10	233.7	170.5
11	236.5	171.6
12	238.7	173.9
13	243.2	176.1
14	249.4	178
15	254.3	179.1
16	260.9	180.2
17	263.3	181.2
18	265.6	181.6
19	268.2	182.5
20	270.4	183.3
21	275.6	184.3

Figure 10-21: Data for Autocorrelation example

	E	F	G	H	I	J	K
23			RESIDUAL OUTPUT			sign changes	
24						4	
25			Observation	Predicted Exp	Residuals		Residual(t-1)
26	correlation		1	211.7298848	2.87012	Sign change	
27	Residual(t)		2	216.1005891	1.59941	0	2.87012
28	and Residual(t-1)		3	219.7811822	-0.18118	1	1.59941
29	0.8227		4	223.9218494	3.27815	1	-0.18118
30			5	226.9123312	3.98767	0	3.27815
31			6	231.5130725	1.78693	0	3.98767
32			7	232.4332208	1.66678	0	1.78693
33			8	235.6537397	-3.35374	1	1.66678
34			9	237.4940363	-3.79404	0	-3.35374
35			10	240.024444	-3.52444	0	-3.79404
36			11	245.3152965	-6.6153	0	-3.52444
37			12	250.376112	-7.17611	0	-6.6153
38			13	254.7468163	-5.34682	0	-7.17611
39			14	257.277224	-2.97722	0	-5.34682
40			15	259.8076317	1.09237	1	-2.97722
41			16	262.1080024	1.192	0	1.09237
42			17	263.0281506	2.57185	0	1.192
43			18	265.0984842	3.10152	0	2.57185
44			19	266.9387808	3.46122	0	3.10152
45			20	269.2391514	6.36085	0	3.46122

Figure 10-22: Residuals for Autocorrelation example

3. In cell J22 compute the "cutoff" for the number of sign changes that indicates the presence of positive autocorrelation. If the number of sign changes is <5.41, then you can suspect the positive autocorrelation is present: =9.5-SQRT(19).

4. Because you have only four sign changes, you can conclude that positive autocorrelation is present.

5. To correct for autocorrelation, find the correlation between the residuals and lagged residuals. Create the lagged residuals in K27:K45 by copying the formula =I26 from K27 to K28:K45.

6. Find the correlation between the residuals and lagged residuals (0.82) in cell L26 using the formula =CORREL(I27:I45, K27:K45).

7. To correct for autocorrelation run a regression with dependent variable $Expenditures_t - .82\ Expenditures_{t-1}$ and independent variable $Money\ Supply_t - .82\ Money\ Supply_{t-1}$. See Figure 10-23.

	A	B	C	D
1	Exp	Money stock	Exp(t)-.82Exp(t-	MS(t)-.82(MS(t-1)
2	214.6	159.3		
3	217.7	161.2	41.728	30.574
4	219.6	162.8	41.086	30.616
5	227.2	164.6	47.128	31.104
6	230.9	165.9	44.596	30.928
7	233.3	167.9	43.962	31.862
8	234.1	168.3	42.794	30.622
9	232.3	169.7	40.338	31.694
10	233.7	170.5	43.214	31.346
11	236.5	171.6	44.866	31.79
12	238.7	173.9	44.77	33.188
13	243.2	176.1	47.466	33.502
14	249.4	178	49.976	33.598
15	254.3	179.1	49.792	33.14
16	260.9	180.2	52.374	33.338
17	263.3	181.2	49.362	33.436
18	265.6	181.6	49.694	33.016
19	268.2	182.5	50.408	33.588
20	270.4	183.3	50.476	33.65
21	275.6	184.3	53.872	33.994

Figure 10-23: Transformed data to correct for autocorrelation

8. In Column C create your transformed dependent variable by copying the formula =A3-0.82*A2 from C3 to C4:C21.

9. Copy this same formula from D3 to D4:D21 to create the transformed independent variable $Money\ Supply_t - .82Money\ Supply_{t-1}$.

10. Now run a regression with the Y Range as C3:C21 and X Range as D3:D21. Figure 10-24 shows the results.

Because the p-value for your independent variable is less than .15, you can conclude that your transformed independent variable is useful for predicting your transformed independent variable. You can find the residuals from your new regression change sign seven times. This exceeds the positive autocorrelation cutoff of 4.37 sign changes. Therefore you can conclude that you have successfully removed the positive autocorrelation. You can predict period t expenditures with the following equation:

$$Period\ t\ expenditures - 0.82Period(t-1)\ Expenditures = -41.97 + 2.74(Period(t)\ Money\ Supply - .82Period(t-1)\ Money\ Supply)$$

H	I	J	K	L	M	N
1						
2 SUMMARY OUTPUT						
3		Exp(t)-.82Exp(t-1)=-41.98+2.74*(MS(t)-.82MS(t-1))				
4 *Regression Statistics*		or				
5 Multiple R	0.82491	Exp(t)=.82Exp(t-1)-41.98+2.74*(MS(t)-.82MS(t-1))				
6 R Square	0.68048					
7 Adjusted R Square	0.66051					
8 Standard Error	2.30236					
9 Observations	18					
10						
11 ANOVA						
12	*df*	*SS*	*MS*	*F*	*Significance F*	
13 Regression	1	180.6254254	180.625	34.0748	2.5233E-05	
14 Residual	16	84.81364059	5.30085			
15 Total	17	265.439066				
16						
17	*Coefficient*	*Standard Error*	*t Stat*	*P-value*	*Lower 95%*	*Upper 95%*
18 Intercept	-41.9766	15.25392438	-2.75186	0.01418	-74.313504	-9.6397687
19 Var 1	2.74079	0.469526345	5.83736	2.5E-05	1.74544379	3.7361461

Figure 10-24: Regression output for transformed data

You can rewrite this equation as the following:

Period t expenditures = .82Period($t − 1$) Expenditures − 41.97 + 2.74(Period(t) Money Supply − .82Period($t − 1$) Money Supply)

Because everything on the right hand side of the last equation is known at Period t, you can use this equation to predict Period t expenditures.

Multicollinearity

If two or more independent variables in a regression analysis are highly correlated, a regression analysis may yield strange results. Whenever two or more independent variables are highly correlated and the regression coefficients do not make sense, you can say that *multicollinearity* exists.

Figure 10-25 (see file housing.xls) gives the following data for the years 1963–1985: the number of housing starts (in thousands), U.S. population (in millions), and mortgage rate. You can use this data to develop an equation that can forecast housing starts by performing the following steps:

1. It seems logical that housing starts should increase over time, so include the year as an independent variable to account for an upward trend. The more people in the United States, the more housing starts you would expect, so include Housing Starts as an independent variable. Clearly, an increase in mortgage rates decreases housing starts, so include the mortgage rate as an independent variable.

	A	B	C	D
1	Housing data			
2	thousand	millions		
3	Starts	Pop	Mort Rate	Year
4	1635	189	5.89	1963
5	1561	192	5.82	1964
6	1510	194	5.81	1965
7	1196	197	6.25	1966
8	1322	199	6.46	1967
9	1545	201	6.97	1968
10	1600	203	7.8	1969
11	1434	205	8.45	1970
12	2085	208	7.74	1971
13	2379	210	7.6	1972
14	2057	212	7.96	1973
15	1353	214	8.92	1974
16	1171	216	9	1975
17	1548	218	9	1976
18	2002	220	9.02	1977
19	2036	223	9.56	1978
20	1760	225	10.78	1979
21	1312	228	12.66	1980
22	1100	230	14.7	1981
23	1072	232	15.14	1982
24	1712	234	12.57	1983
25	1756	236	12.38	1984
26	1745	238	11.55	1985

Figure 10-25: Multicollinearity data

2. Now run a multiple regression with the Y range being A3:A26 and the X Range being B3:D26 to obtain the results shown in Figure 10-26.

3. Observe that neither POP nor YEAR is significant. (They have p-values of .59 and .74, respectively.) Also, the negative coefficient of YEAR indicates that there is a downward trend in housing starts. This doesn't make sense though. The problem is that POP and YEAR are highly correlated. To see this, use the DATA ANALYSIS TOOLS CORRELATION command to find the correlations between the independent variables.

	A	B	C	D	E	F	G
1	SUMMARY OUTPUT						
2							
3	*Regression Statistics*						
4	Multiple R	0.660983152					
5	R Square	0.436898728					
6	Adjusted R Squ	0.347988001					
7	Standard Error	279.5855911					
8	Observations	23					
9							
10	ANOVA						
11		*df*	*SS*	*MS*	*F*	*Significance F*	
12	Regression	3	1152331.526	384110.5087	4.913903437	0.010796446	
13	Residual	19	1485193.952	78168.10274			
14	Total	22	2637525.478				
15							
16		*Coefficients*	*Standard Error*	*t Stat*	*P-value*	*Lower 95%*	*Upper 95%*
17	Intercept	221794.5255	661959.9507	0.335057318	0.741252754	-1163704.005	1607293.056
18	Pop	90.39255757	162.9146358	0.554846145	0.585473195	-250.5917998	431.376915
19	Mort Rate	-206.8964396	55.49611616	-3.728124668	0.00142535	-323.0511818	-90.74169748
20	Year	-120.3847361	352.8922741	-0.341137352	0.736743719	-858.9969839	618.2275117

Figure 10-26: First regression output: Multicoillinearity example

4. Select Input Range B3:D26.
5. Check the labels box.
6. Put the output on the new sheet Correlation.

You should obtain the output in Figure 10-27.

	A	B	C	D
1		Pop	Mort Rate	Year
2	Pop	1		
3	Mort Rate	0.913679	1	
4	Year	0.999655	0.90995	1

Figure 10-27: Correlation matrix for Multicollinearity example

The .999 correlation between POP and YEAR occurs because both POP and YEAR increase linearly over time. Also note that the correlation between Mort Rate and the other two independent variables exceeds .9. Due to this, *multicollinearity* exists. What has happened is that the high correlation between the independent variables has confused the computer about which independent variables are important. The solution to this problem is to drop one or more of the highly correlated independent variables and hope that the independent variables remaining in the regression will be significant. If you decide to drop YEAR, change your X Range to B3:C26 to obtain the output shown in Figure 10-28. If you have access to a statistical package, such as SAS or SPSS, you can identify the presence of multicollinearity by looking at the Variance Inflation Factor (VIF) of each independent variable. A general rule of thumb is that any independent variable with a variance inflation factor exceeding 5 is evidence of multicollinearity.

	A	B	C	D	E	F	G
1	SUMMARY OUTPUT						
2							
3	Regression Statistics						
4	Multiple R	0.658369001					
5	R Square	0.433449742					
6	Adjusted R Squa	0.376794716					
7	Standard Error	273.3396002					
8	Observations	23					
9							
10	ANOVA						
11		df	SS	MS	F	Significance F	
12	Regression	2	1143234.737	571617.3685	7.650684739	0.003407096	
13	Residual	20	1494290.741	74714.53706			
14	Total	22	2637525.478				
15							
16		Coefficients	Standard Error	t Stat	P-value	Lower 95%	Upper 95%
17	Intercept	-4024.025797	1627.113433	-2.473107108	0.022486161	-7418.123366	-629.9282276
18	Pop	34.91659242	9.564839902	3.650515092	0.001590215	14.96469527	54.86848956
19	Mort Rate	-200.8475581	51.41238103	-3.906599034	0.000875172	-308.0918558	-93.60326032

Figure 10-28: Final regression output for Multicollinearity example

POP is now highly significant (p-value = .001). Also, by dropping YEAR you actually decreased s_e from 280 to 273. This decrease is because dropping YEAR reduced the confusion the computer had due to the strong correlation between POP and YEAR. The final predictive equation is as follows:

$$\text{Housing Starts} = -4024.03 + 34.92\text{POP} - 200.85\text{MORT RAT}$$

The interpretation of this equation is that after adjusting for interest rates, an increase in U.S. population of one million people results in $34,920 in housing starts. After adjusting for Population, an increase in interest rates of 1 percent can reduce housing starts by $200,850. This is valuable information that could be used to forecast the future cash flows of construction-related industries.

NOTE   After correcting for multicollinearity, the independent variables now have signs that agree with common sense. This is a common by-product of correcting for multicollinearity.

Validation of a Regression

The ultimate goal of regression analysis is for the estimated models to be used for accurate forecasting. When using a regression equation to make forecasts for the future, you must avoid over fitting a set of data. For example, if you had seven data points and only one independent variable, you could obtain an $R^2 = 1$ by fitting a sixth degree polynomial to the data. Unfortunately, such an equation would probably work poorly in fitting future data. Whenever you have a reasonable amount of data, you should hold back approximately 20 percent of your data (called the *Validation Set*) to validate your forecasts. To do this, simply fit regression to 80 percent of your data (called the *Test Set*). Compute the standard deviation of the errors for this data. Now use the equation generated from the Test Set to compute forecasts and the standard deviation of the errors for the Validation Set. Hopefully, the standard deviation for the Validation Set will be fairly close to the standard deviation for the Test Set. If this is the case, you can use the regression equation for future forecasts and be fairly confident that the accuracy of future forecasts will be approximated by the s_e for the Test Set. You can illustrate the important idea of validation with the data from your housing example.

Using the years 1963–1980 as your Test Set and the years 1981–1985 as the Validation Set, you can determine the suitability of the regression with independent variables *POP* and *MORT RAT* for future forecasting using the powerful TREND function. The syntax of the TREND function is TREND(known_y's,[known_x's],[new_x's] ,[const]). This function fits a multiple regression using the known *y*'s and known *x*'s and then uses this regression to make forecasts for the dependent variable using the new *x*'s data. [Constant] is an optional argument. Setting [Constant]=False causes Excel to fit the regression with the constant term set equal to 0. Setting [Constant]=True or omitting [Constant] causes Excel to fit a regression in the normal fashion.

The TREND function is an array function (see Chapter 2) so you need to select the cell range populated by the TREND function and finally press Ctrl+Shift+Enter to enable TREND to calculate the desired results. As shown in Figure 10-29 and worksheet Data, you will now use the TREND function to compare the accuracy of regression predictions for the 1981-1985 validation period to the accuracy of regression predictions for the fitted data using the following steps.

	A	B	C	D	E	F	G	H
1	Housing data						Std Dev	
2	thousand millions						1963-1980	285.701
3	Starts	Pop	Mort Rate	Year	Predictions	Error	1981-1985	255.886
4	1635	189	5.89	1963	1329.1723	305.828		
5	1561	192	5.82	1964	1490.6514	70.3486		
6	1510	194	5.81	1965	1587.9926	-77.9926		
7	1196	197	6.25	1966	1606.047	-410.047		
8	1322	199	6.46	1967	1641.5187	-319.519		
9	1545	201	6.97	1968	1592.6229	-47.6229		
10	1500	203	7.8	1969	1453.7352	46.2648		
11	1434	205	8.45	1970	1365.468	68.532		
12	2085	208	7.74	1971	1706.931	378.069		
13	2379	210	7.6	1972	1840.8314	538.169		
14	2057	212	7.96	1973	1834.1193	222.881		
15	1353	214	8.92	1974	1658.6724	-305.672		
16	1171	216	9	1975	1730.7033	-559.703		
17	1548	218	9	1976	1825.2322	-277.232		
18	2002	220	9.02	1977	1914.1366	87.8634		
19	2036	223	9.56	1978	1904.0686	131.931		
20	1760	225	10.78	1979	1655.5031	104.497		
21	1312	228	12.66	1980	1268.5938	43.4062		
22	1100	230	14.7	1981	789.42395	310.576		
23	1072	232	15.14	1982	760.21392	311.786		
24	1712	234	12.57	1983	1577.4907	134.509		
25	1756	236	12.38	1984	1725.4524	30.5476		
26	1745	238	11.55	1985	2053.3979	-308.398		

Figure 10-29: Use of Trend function to validate regression

1. To generate forecasts for the years 1963–1985 using the 1963–1980 data, simply select the range E4:E26 and enter in E4 the array formula =TREND(A4:A21, B4:C21,B4:C26) (refer to Figure 10-29). Rows 4-21 contain the data for the years 1963-1980 and Rows 4-26 contain the data for the years 1963-1985.

2. Compute the error for each year's forecast in Column F. The error for 1963 is computed in F4 with the formula =A4-F4.

3. Copy this formula down to row 26 to compute the errors for the years 1964–1985.

4. In cell H2 compute the standard deviation (285.70) of the errors for the years 1963–1980 with the formula =STDEV(F4:F21).

5. In cell H3 compute the standard deviation (255.89) of the forecast errors for the years 1981–1985 with the formula =AVERAGE(F22:F26).

The forecasts are actually more accurate for the Validation Set! This is unusual, but it gives you confidence that 95 percent of all future forecasts should be accurate within $2s_e$ = 546,700 housing starts.

Summary

In this chapter you learned the following:

- The multiple linear regression model models a dependent variable Y as $B_0 + B_1X_1 + B_2X_2 + ...B_nX_n$ + *error term*.
- The error term is required to satisfy the following assumptions:
    - The error term is normally distributed.
    - The variability or spread of the error term is assumed not to depend on the value of the dependent variable.
    - For time series data, successive values of the error term must be independent. This means, for example, that if for one observation the error term is a large positive number, then this tells you nothing about the value of successive error terms.
- Violation of these assumptions can invalidate the p-values in the Excel output.
- You can run a regression analysis using the Data Analysis Tool.
- The Coefficients portion of the output gives the least squares estimates of $B_0, B_1, ..., B_n$.
- A Significance F in the ANOVA section of the output less than .05 causes you to reject the hypothesis of no linear regression and conclude that your independent variables have significant predictive value.
- Independent variables with p-value greater than .05 should be deleted, and the regression should be rerun until all independent variables have p-values of .05 or less.
- Approximately 68 percent of predictions from a regression should be accurate within one standard error and approximately 95 percent of predictions from a regression should be accurate within two standard errors.
- Qualitative independent variables are modeled using indicator variables.
- By adding the square of an independent variable as a new independent variable, you can test whether the independent variable has a nonlinear effect on Y.

- By adding the product of two independent variables (say X_1 and X_2) as a new independent variable, you can test whether X_1 and X_2 interact in their effect on Y.
- You can check for the presence of autocorrelation in a regression based on time series data by examining the number of sign changes in the residuals; too few sign changes indicate positive autocorrelation and too many sign changes indicate negative autocorrelation.
- If independent variables are highly correlated, then their coefficients in a regression may be misleading. This is known as multicollinearity.

Exercises

1. Fizzy Drugs wants to optimize the yield from an important chemical process. The company thinks that the number of pounds produced each time the process runs depends on the size of the container used, the pressure, and the temperature. The scientists involved believe the effect to change one variable might depend on the values of other variables. The size of the process container must be between 1.3 and 1.5 cubic meters; pressure must be between 4 and 4.5 mm; and temperature must be between 22 and 30 degrees Celsius. The scientists patiently set up experiments at the lower and upper levels of the three control variables and obtain the data shown in the file Fizzy.xlsx.

   a. Determine the relationship between yield, size, temperature, and pressure.
   b. Discuss the interactions between pressure, size, and temperature.
   c. What settings for temperature, size, and pressure would you recommend?

2. For 12 straight weeks, you have observed the sales (in number of cases) of canned tomatoes at Mr. D's Supermarket. (See the file Grocery.xlsx.) Each week, you keep track of the following:

   a. Was a promotional notice for canned tomatoes placed in all shopping carts?
   b. Was a coupon for canned tomatoes given to each customer?
   c. Was a price reduction (none, 1, or 2 cents off) given?

Use this data to determine how the preceding factors influence sales. Predict sales of canned tomatoes during a week in which you use a shopping cart notice, a coupon, and reduce price by 1 cent.

3. The file `Countryregion.xlsx` contains the following data for several under-developed countries:

   ■ Infant mortality rate
   ■ Adult literacy rate
   ■ Percentage of students finishing primary school
   ■ Per capita GNP

   Use this data to develop an equation that can be used to predict infant mortality. Are there any outliers in this set of data? Interpret the coefficients in your equation. Within what value should 95 percent of your predictions for infant mortality be accurate?

4. The file `Baseball96.xlsx` gives runs scored, singles, doubles, triples, home runs, and bases stolen for each major league baseball team during the 1996 season. Use this data to determine the effects of singles, doubles, and other activities on run production.

5. The file `Cardata.xlsx` provides the following information for 392 different car models:

   ■ Cylinders
   ■ Displacement
   ■ Horsepower
   ■ Weight
   ■ Acceleration
   ■ Miles per gallon (MPG)

   Determine an equation that can predict MPG. Why do you think all the independent variables are not significant?

6. Determine for your regression predicting computer sales whether the residuals exhibit non-normality or heteroscedasticity.

7. The file `Oreos.xlsx` gives daily sales of Oreos at a supermarket and whether Oreos were placed 7" from the floor, 6" from the floor, or 5" from the floor. How does shelf position influence Oreo sales?

8. The file `USmacrodata.xlsx` contains U.S. quarterly GNP, Inflation rates, and Unemployment rates. Use this file to perform the following exercises:

    a. Develop a regression to predict quarterly GNP growth from the last four quarters of growth. Check for non-normality of residuals, heteroscedasticity, autocorrelation, and multicollinearity.

    b. Develop a regression to predict quarterly inflation rate from the last four quarters of inflation. Check for non-normality of residuals, heteroscedasticity, autocorrelation, and multicollinearity.

    c. Develop a regression to predict quarterly unemployment rate from the unemployment rates of the last four quarters. Check for non-normality of residuals, heteroscedasticity, autocorrelation, and multicollinearity.

9. Does our regression model for predicting auto sales exhibit autocorrelation, non-normality of errors, or heteroscedasticity?

11

Forecasting in the Presence of Special Events

Often special factors such as seasonality and promotions affect demand for a product. The Excel Regression tool can handle 15 independent variables, but many times that isn't enough. This chapter shows how to use the Excel Solver to build forecasting models involving up to 200 changing cells. The discussion is based on a student project (admittedly from the 1990s) that attempted to forecast the number of customers visiting the Eastland Plaza Branch of the Indiana University (IU) Credit Union each day. You'll use this project to learn how to forecast in the face of special factors.

Building the Basic Model

In this section you will learn how to build a model to forecast daily customer count at the Indiana University Credit Union. The development of the model should convince you that careful examination of outliers can result in more accurate forecasting.

The data collected for this example is contained in the `original` worksheet in the `Creditunion.xlsx` file and is shown in Figure 11-1. It is important to note that this data is before direct deposit became a common method to deposit paychecks. For each day of the year the following information is available:

■ Month of the year
■ Day of the week
■ Whether the day was a faculty or staff payday
■ Whether the day before or the day after was a holiday

If you try to run a regression on this data by using dummy variables (as described in Chapter 10, "Using Multiple Regression to Forecast Sales,") the dependent variable would be the number of customers arriving each day (the data in column E). Nineteen independent variables are needed:

■ 11 to account for the month (12 months minus 1)
■ 4 to account for the day of the week (5 business days minus 1)

- 2 to account for the types of paydays that occur each month
- 2 to account for whether a particular day follows or precedes a holiday

	B	C	D	E	F	G	H	I	J
1								RSQ	0.771
2									
3	MONTH	DAYMON	DAYWEEK	CUST	SPECIAL	SP	FAC	BH	AH
4	1	2	2	1825	SP,FAC,AF	1	1	0	1
5	1	3	3	1257	0	0	0	0	0
6	1	4	4	969	0	0	0	0	0
7	1	5	5	1672	SP	1	0	0	0
8	1	8	1	1098	0	0	0	0	0
9	1	9	2	691	0	0	0	0	0
10	1	10	3	672	0	0	0	0	0
11	1	11	4	754	0	0	0	0	0
12	1	12	5	972	0	0	0	0	0
13	1	15	1	816	0	0	0	0	0
14	1	16	2	717	0	0	0	0	0
15	1	17	3	728	0	0	0	0	0
16	1	18	4	711	0	0	0	0	0
17	1	19	5	1545	SP	1	0	0	0
18	1	22	1	873	0	0	0	0	0
19	1	23	2	713	0	0	0	0	0
20	1	24	3	626	0	0	0	0	0
21	1	25	4	653	0	0	0	0	0
22	1	26	5	1080	0	0	0	0	0
23	1	29	1	650	0	0	0	0	0
24	1	30	2	644	0	0	0	0	0
25	1	31	3	803	0	0	0	0	0

Figure 11-1: Data for Credit Union example

Microsoft Office Excel enables only 15 independent variables, so when a regression forecasting model requires more you can use the Excel Solver feature to estimate the coefficients of the independent variables. As you learned earlier, Excel's Solver can be used to optimize functions. The trick here is to apply Solver to minimize the sum of squared errors, which is the equivalent to running a regression. Because the Excel Solver allows up to 200 changing cells, you can use Solver in situations where the Excel Regression tool would be inadequate. You can also use Excel to compute the R-squared values between forecasts and actual customer traffic as well as the standard deviation for the forecast errors. To analyze this data, you create a forecasting equation by using a lookup table to "look up" the day of the week, the month, and other factors. Then you use Solver to choose the coefficients for each level of each factor that yields the minimum sum of squared errors. (Each day's error equals actual customers minus forecasted customers.) The following steps walk you through this process:

1. First, create indicator variables (in columns G through J) for whether the day is a staff payday (SP), faculty payday (FAC), before a holiday (BH), or after a holiday (AH). (Refer to Figure 11-1). For example, cells G4, H4, and J4 use 1 to indicate that January 2 was a staff payday, faculty payday, and after a holiday. Cell I4 contains 0 to indicate that January 2 was not before a holiday.

2. The forecast is defined by a constant (which helps to center the forecasts so that they will be more accurate), and effects for each day of the week, each month, a staff payday, a faculty payday, a day occurring before a holiday, and a day occurring after a holiday. Insert Trial values for all these parameters (the Solver changing cells) in the cell range O4:O26, as shown in Figure 11-2. Solver can then choose values that make the model best fit the data. For each day, the forecast of customer count will be generated by the following equation:

```
Predicted customer count=Constant+(Month effect)+(Day of
week effect)+(Staff payday effect, if any)+(Faculty payday
effect, if any)+(Before holiday effect, if any)+(After
holiday effect, if any)
```

	I	J	K	L	M	N	O	P	Q	R
1	RSQ	0.771		stdeverr	163.1772					
2			SSE	6736582						
3	BH	AH	Forecast	Sq Err	Error	Day of Week			average	
4	0	1	1766.78	3389.56	58.21993	1	103.357		dayweek	0
5	0	0	709.603	299643	547.3965	2	-139.19		month	-4E-09
6	0	0	745.698	49863.78	223.302	3	-150.34			
7	0	0	1557.22	13174.18	114.7788	4	-114.25			
8	0	0	963.303	18143.29	134.697	5	300.424			
9	0	0	720.753	885.2568	-29.7533	SP	396.851			
10	0	0	709.603	1414.02	-37.6035	FAC	394.894			
11	0	0	745.698	68.92317	8.301998	BH	205.293			
12	0	0	1160.37	35483.19	-188.37	AH	254.281			
13	0	0	963.303	21698.16	-147.303	Month				
14	0	0	720.753	14.08701	-3.75327	1	-110.69			
15	0	0	709.603	338.4326	18.39654	2	-75.715			
16	0	0	745.698	1203.951	-34.698	3	-40.341			
17	0	0	1557.22	149.3565	-12.2212	4	0.02839			
18	0	0	963.303	8154.623	-90.303	5	87.8157			
19	0	0	720.753	60.11313	-7.75327	6	133.341			
20	0	0	709.603	6989.539	-83.6035	7	115.803			
21	0	0	745.698	8592.92	-92.698	8	28.7743			
22	0	0	1160.37	6459.308	-80.3698	9	-87.563			
23	0	0	963.303	98158.74	-313.303	10	-53.002			
24	0	0	720.753	5891.064	-76.7533	11	-42.761			
25	0	0	709.603	8722.913	93.39654	12	44.3091			
26	0	0	1175.57	11328.02	106.4332	constant	970.635			
27	0	0	1592.2	203224.6	450.8044					

Figure 11-2: Changing cells for Credit Union example

3. Using this model, compute a forecast for each day's customer count by copying the following formula from K4 to K5:K257:

```
$O$26+VLOOKUP(B4,$N$14:$O$25,2)+VLOOKUP(D4,$N$4:$O$8,2) +G4*$O$
9+H4*$O$10+I4*$O$11+J4*$O$12.
```

Cell O26 picks up the constant term. VLOOKUP(B4,$N$14:$O$25,2) picks up the month coefficient for the current month, and VLOOKUP(D4,$N$4:$O$8,2) picks up the day of the week coefficient for the current week. =G4*$O$9+H4*$O$10+I4*$O$11+J4*$O$12 picks up the effects (if any) when the current day is SP, FAC, BH, or AH.

4. Copy the formula =(E4-K4)^2, from L4 to L5:L257 to compute the squared error for each day. Then, in cell L2, compute the sum of squared errors with the formula =SUM(L4:L257).

5. In cell R4, average the day of the week changing cells with the formula =AVERAGE(O4:O8), and in cell R5, average the month changing cells with the formula =AVERAGE(O14:O25). Later in this section you will add constraints to your Solver model which constrain the average month and day of the week effects to equal 0. These constraints ensure that a month or day of the week with a positive effect has a higher than average customer count, and a month or day of the week with a negative effect has a lower than average customer count.

6. Use the Solver settings shown in Figure 11-3 to choose the forecast parameters to minimize the sum of squared errors.

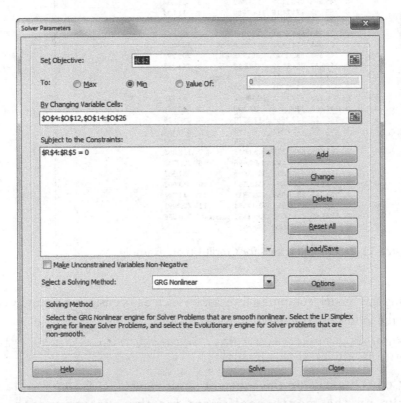

Figure 11-3: Solver settings for Credit Union example

The Solver model changes the coefficients for the month, day of the week, BH, AH, SP, FAC, and the constant to minimize the sum of square errors. It also constrains the average day of the week and month effect to equal 0. The Solver enables you to obtain the results shown in Figure 11-2. These show that Friday is the busiest day of the week and June is the busiest month. A staff payday raises the forecast (all else being equal—in the Latin, *ceteris paribus*) by 397 customers.

Evaluating Forecast Accuracy

To evaluate the accuracy of the forecast, you compute the R^2 value between the forecasts and the actual customer count in cell J1. You use the formula =RSQ(E4:E257,K4:K257) to do this. This formula computes the percentage of the actual variation in customer count that is explained by the forecasting model. The independent variables explain 77 percent of the daily variation in customer count.

You can compute the error for each day in column M by copying the formula =E4-K4 from M4 to M5:M257. A close approximation to the standard error of the forecast is given by the standard deviation of the errors. This value is computed in cell M1 by using the formula =STDEV(M4:M257). Thus, approximately 68 percent of the forecasts should be accurate within 163 customers, 95 percent accurate within 326 customers, and so on.

After you evaluate the accuracy of your forecasts and compute the error, you will want to try and spot any outliers. Recall that an observation is an outlier if the absolute value of the forecast error exceeds two times the standard error of the regression. To locate the outliers, perform the following steps:

1. Select the range M4:M257, and then click Conditional Formatting on the Home tab.
2. Select New Rule and in the New Formatting Rule dialog box, choose Use a Formula to Determine Which Cells to Format.
3. Fill in the rule description in the dialog box, as shown in Figure 11-4.

This procedure essentially copies the formula from M4 to M5:M257 and formats the cell in red if the formula is true. This ensures that all outliers are highlighted in red.

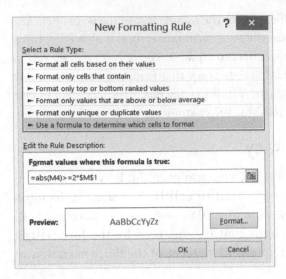

Figure 11-4: Highlighting outliers

After choosing a format with a red font, the conditional formatting settings display in red any error whose absolute value exceeds 2 * (standard deviation of errors). Looking at the outliers, you see that the customer count for the first three days of the month is often under forecast. Also, during the second week in March (spring break), the data is over forecast, and the day before spring break, it is greatly under forecast.

Refining the Base Model

To remedy this problem, the 1st three days worksheet from the Creditunion.xlsx file shows additional changing cells for each of the first three days of the month and for spring break and the day before spring break. There are also additional trial values for these new effects in cells O26:O30. By copying the following formula from K4 to K5:K257 you can include the effects of the first three days of the month:

```
=$O$25+VLOOKUP(B4,$N$13:$O$24,2)+VLOOKUP(D4,$N$4:$O$8,2)+G4*$O$
9+H4* $O$10+I4*$O$11+J4*$O$12+IF(C4=1,$O$26,IF(C4=2,$O$27,IF(C4=3
,$O$28,0)))
```

NOTE The term =IF(C4=1,$O$26,IF(C4=2,$O$27,IF(C4=3,$O$28,0))) picks up the effect of the first three days of the month. For example, if Column C indicates that the day is the first day of the month, the First Day of the Month effect from O26 is added to the forecast.

You can now manually enter the spring break coefficients in cells K52:K57. For this example, you add +029 to the formula in cell K52 and +030 in cells K52:K57.

After including the new changing cells in the Solver dialog box, you can find the results shown in Figure 11-5. Notice that the first three days of the month greatly increase customer count (possibly because of government support and Social Security checks) and that spring break reduces customer count. Figure 11-5 also shows the improvement in forecasting accuracy. The R^2 value is improved to 87 percent and the standard error is reduced to 122 customers.

	H	I	J	K	L	M	N	O	P	Q	R	S
1		RSQ	0.871		stdeverr	122.285						
2				SSE	3783269							
3	FAC	BH	AH	Forecast	Sq Err	Error	Day of Week			average		
4	1	0	1	1879.63	2984.54	-54.631		1 107.706		dayweek	0	
5	0	0	0	995.4	68434.5	261.6		2 -138.93		month	2.5E-14	
6	0	0	0	722.934	60548.4	246.066		3 -153.32				
7	0	0	0	1554.45	13818.2	117.551		4 -115.08				
8	0	0	0	945.724	23188.1	152.276		5 299.624				
9	0	0	0	699.086	65.3826	-8.08595	SP	416.808				
10	0	0	0	684.701	161.326	-12.7014	FAC	96.6442				
11	0	0	0	722.934	965.091	31.0659	BH	196.457				
12	0	0	0	1137.64	27436.9	-165.641	AH	299.116				
13	0	0	0	945.724	16828.2	-129.724		1 -105.51				
14	0	0	0	699.086	320.913	17.9141		2 -81.763				
15	0	0	0	684.701	1874.77	43.2986		3 -27.856				
16	0	0	0	722.934	142.422	-11.9341		4 -7.2892				
17	0	0	0	1554.45	89.2902	-9.44935		5 83.8453				
18	0	0	0	945.724	5288.71	-72.7235		6 130.672				
19	0	0	0	699.086	193.601	13.9141		7 106.616				
20	0	0	0	684.701	3445.86	-58.7014		8 13.2601				
21	0	0	0	722.934	4890.78	-69.9341		9 -64.687				
22	0	0	0	1137.64	3322.49	-57.641		10 -68.305				
23	0	0	0	945.724	87452.4	-295.724		11 -33.753				
24	0	0	0	699.086	3034.46	-55.0859		12 54.7719				
25	0	0	0	684.701	13994.6	118.299	constant	943.528				
26	1	0	0	1396.77	13173.2	-114.775	d1	553.449				
27	0	0	0	1946.17	9375.37	96.8265	d2	367.977				
28	0	0	0	969.471	31162.5	176.529	d3	310.699				
29	0	0	0	722.834	294.688	17.1665	day before sp break	223.704				
30	0	0	0	708.449	109.181	-10.449	sp break	-57.035				

Figure 11-5: Credit Union model including Spring Break and First Three Days of Month factors

By looking at the forecast errors for the week 12/24 through 12/31 (see Figure 11-6), you see that you've greatly over forecasted the customer counts for the days in this week. You've also under forecasted customer counts for the week before Christmas. Further examination of the forecast errors (often called residuals) also shows the following:

- Thanksgiving is different than a normal holiday in that the credit union is far less busy than expected the day after Thanksgiving.
- The day before Good Friday is busy because people leave town for Easter.

■ Tax day (April 16) is also busier than expected.

■ The week before Indiana University starts fall classes (last week in August) is not busy, possibly because many staff and faculty take a "summer fling vacation" before the hectic onrush of the fall semester.

A	B	C	D	E	F	G	H	I	J	K	L	M
								RSQ	0.871		stdeverr	122.285
										SSE	3783269	
	MONTH	DAYMON	DAYWEE	CUST	SPECIAL	SP	FAC	BH	AH	Forecast	Sq Err	Error
	12	18	2	1058		0	0	0	0	859.369	39454.4	198.631
	12	19	3	1104		0	0	0	0	844.984	67089.1	259.016
	12	20	4	1018		0	0	0	0	883.217	18166.5	134.783
	12	21	5	1955	SP	1	0	0	0	1714.73	57728.6	240.268
	12	24	1	941	BH	0	0	1	0	1302.46	130656	-361.463
	12	26	3	999	AH	0	0	0	1	1144.1	21054.1	-145.1
	12	27	4	619		0	0	0	0	883.217	69810.6	-264.217
	12	28	5	937		0	0	0	0	1297.92	130266	-360.924
	12	31	1	1146	BH		0	0	1	1302.46	24480.7	-156.463

Figure 11-6: Pre- and post-Christmas forecasts are way off!

In the `Christmas week` worksheet, these additional factors are included as changing cells in the forecast models. After adding the new parameters as changing cells, run Solver again. The results are shown in Figure 11-7. The R^2 is up to 92 percent and the standard error is down to 98.61 customers! Note that the post-Christmas week reduced the daily customer count by 359; the day before Thanksgiving added 607 customers; the day after Thanksgiving reduced customer count by 161, and so on.

Notice that you improve the forecasting model by using outliers. If your outliers have something in common (such as being the first three days of the month), include the common factor as an independent variable and your forecasting error drops.

The forecasting model can provide useful insights in a variety of situations. For instance, a similar analysis was performed to predict daily customer count for dinner at a major restaurant chain. The special factors corresponded to holidays. Super Bowl Sunday was the least busy day and Valentine's Day and Mother's Day were the busiest. Also, Saturday was the busiest day of the week for dinner, and Friday was the busiest day of the week for lunch. Using the model described in this section, after adjusting for all other factors the restaurant chain found the following:

■ On Saturdays 192 more people than average ate dinner and on Mondays 112 fewer people than average ate dinner.

■ On Super Bowl Sunday 212 fewer people than average ate dinner and on Mother's Day and Valentine's Day 350 more people ate dinner. Since an average of 401 people ate dinner daily, the model shows that business almost doubles on Mother's Day and Valentine's Day, and business is cut in half on Super Bowl Sunday.

In contrast, for pizza delivery companies such as Domino's, Super Bowl Sunday is the busiest day of the year. Given daily counts of delivered pizzas, it would be easy to come up with an accurate estimate of the effect of Super Bowl Sunday on pizza deliveries.

F	SP	FAC	BH	AH	Forec	Sq Err	Error	Day of Week	O	sign change	average	R
			RSQ	0.916		stdeverr	98.61		cutoff	110.56262		
					SSE	2460390			aotual	125		
SPECIAL												
SP,FAC.	1	1	0	1	1981	24363.99	-156	1	108		dayweek	-0
0	0	0	0	0	976	78914.97	280.9	2	-155	1	month	0
0	0	0	0	0	718	63163.6	251.3	3	-165	0		
SP	1	0	0	0	1539	17577.99	132.6	4	-121	0		
0	0	0	0	0	947	22839.22	151.1	5	332	0		
0	0	0	0	0	684	46.55953	6.823	SP	368	0		
0	0	0	0	0	674	3.925658	-1.98	FAC	97.1	1		
0	0	0	0	0	718	1319.41	36.32	BH	273	1		
0	0	0	0	0	1171	39631.63	-199	AH	478	1		
0	0	0	0	0	947	17127.87	-131	1	-111	0		
0	0	0	0	0	684	1077.379	32.82	2	-82.1	1		
0	0	0	0	0	674	2918.017	54.02	3	-26.4	0		
0	0	0	0	0	718	44.57311	-6.68	4	-34.8	1		
SP	1	0	0	0	1539	31.15878	5.582	5	71	1		
0	0	0	0	0	947	5457.293	-73.9	6	127	1		
0	0	0	0	0	684	830.7915	28.82	7	94	1		
0	0	0	0	0	674	2302.208	-48	8	60.9	1		
0	0	0	0	0	718	4183.025	-64.7	9	-75.3	0		
0	0	0	0	0	1171	8295.008	-91.1	10	-67.9	0		
0	0	0	0	0	947	88133.87	-297	11	-35.9	0		
0	0	0	0	0	684	1614.155	-40.2	12	80.3	0		
0	0	0	0	0	674	16645.82	129	constant	950	1		
FAC	0	1	0	0	1388	11207.14	-106	d1	544	1		
SP	1	0	0	0	1922	14631.65	121	d2	354	1		
0	0	0	0	0	976	28935.87	170.1	d3	302	0		
0	0	0	0	0	713	718.3699	26.8	day before sp br	183	0		
0	0	0	0	0	703	25.02358	-5	sp break	-55.2	1		
0	0	0	0	0	747	2672.615	-51.7	christmas week	-359	0		
0	0	0	0	0	1200	1689.043	-41.1	before xmas we	183	0		
0	0	0	0	0	976	9004.971	-94.9	before thanks	607	0		
0	0	0	0	0	713	3003.306	54.8	after thanks	-161	1		
0	0	0	0	0	703	2401.231	-49	good thurday	320	1		
0	0	0	0	0	747	12388.28	111.3	summerfling	-165	1		
SP	1	0	0	0	1568	6171.827	78.56	tax day	244	0		

Figure 11-7: Final forecast model

Checking the Randomness of Forecast Errors

A good forecasting method should create forecast errors or residuals that are random. Random errors mean that the errors exhibit no discernible pattern. If forecast errors are random, the sign of your errors should change (from plus to minus or minus to plus) approximately half the time. Therefore, a commonly used test to evaluate the randomness of forecast errors is to look at the number of sign changes in the errors. If you have n observations, nonrandomness of the errors is indicated if you find either fewer than $\frac{n-1}{2} - \sqrt{n}$ or more than $\frac{n-1}{2} + \sqrt{n}$ n changes in sign. The Christmas week worksheet, as shown in Figure 11-7, determines the number of sign changes in the residuals by copying the formula =IF(M5*M4<0,1,0) from cell P5 to P6:P257. A sign change in the residuals occurs if, and only if, the product of two consecutive residuals is negative. Therefore, the formula yields 1 whenever a change in the sign of the residuals occurs. In this worksheet example, there were 125 changes in sign. Cell P1 computes $\frac{254-1}{2} - \sqrt{254} = 110.6$ changes in sign as the cutoff for nonrandom residuals. Therefore there are random residuals here.

Summary

In this chapter you learned the following:

- The Excel Solver can be used to mimic regression analysis and work around the 15 independent variable limitations of Excel's Regression tool.
- Using the Excel Solver you can often forecast daily demand with the model *Base Level + Day of Week Effect + Month Effect + Effect of Special Factors*.
- You can use outliers to spot omitted special factors.
- If the signs of residuals change much less than half the time, then forecast errors are not random.

Exercises

1. How can you use the techniques outlined in this chapter to predict the daily sales of pens at Staples?
2. If you had several years of data, how would you incorporate a trend in the analysis?
3. The file `Dinner.xls` contains a model to predict daily dinner sales at a well-known chain restaurant. Column Q of the worksheet `outliers removed` contains the final forecast equation.

   a. Explain in words the equation used to forecast daily dinner sales.
   b. Explain how the day of the week affects dinner sales.
   c. Explain how the time of year affects dinner sales.
   d. Explain the special factors that affect dinner sales.
   e. What other data might you want to collect to improve forecast accuracy?

4. The file `Promotiondata.xlsx` contains monthly sales (in pounds) of ice cream at a Kroger's supermarket for three years. The file also tells you when promotions occurred. Promotions are known to increase sales during the month of the promotion but decrease sales during the month after the promotion. Develop a model that can be used to predict monthly ice cream sales. Hint:

Add a term to your model involving the month number; the coefficient of this term will model the trend in ice cream sales.

a. What percentage of variation in ice cream sales is explained by your model?

b. Fill in the blank: 95 percent of forecasts for monthly sales will be accurate within _____.

c. What month appears to be the best for ice cream sales?

d. Describe the trend of ice cream sales.

e. Describe the effect of a promotion on ice cream sales.

12

Modeling Trend and Seasonality

Whether the marketing analyst works for a car manufacturer, airline, or consumer packaged goods company, she often must forecast sales of her company's product. Whatever the product, it is important to understand the trends (either upward or downward) and seasonal aspects of the product's sales. This chapter discusses how to determine the trends and seasonality of product sales. Using monthly data on U.S. air passenger miles (2003–2012) you will learn how to do the following:

- Use moving averages to eliminate seasonality to easily see trends in sales.
- Use the Solver to develop an additive or multiplicative model to estimate trends and seasonality.

Using Moving Averages to Smooth Data and Eliminate Seasonality

Moving averages smooth out noise in the data. For instance, suppose you work for Amazon.com and you are wondering whether sales are trending upward. For each January sales are less than the previous month (December sales are always high because of Christmas), so the unsuspecting marketing analyst might think there is a downward trend in sales during January because sales have dropped. This conclusion is incorrect, though, because it ignores the fact that seasonal influences tend to drop January sales below December sales. You can use moving averages to smooth out seasonal data and better understand the trend and seasonality characteristics of your data.

NOTE All work in this chapter uses the file `airlinemiles.xlsx`, which contains monthly airlines miles (in thousands) traveled in the United States during the period from January 2003 through April 2012. A sample of this data is shown in Figure 12-1.

	D	E	F
8	MonthNumber	Month	AirlineMiles (000'S)
9	1	Jan2003	32,854,790.00
10	2	Feb2003	30,814,269.00
11	3	Mar2003	37,586,654.00
12	4	Apr2003	35,226,398.00
13	5	May2003	36,569,670.00
14	6	Jun2003	39,750,216.00
15	7	Jul2003	43,367,508.00
16	8	Aug2003	42,092,669.00
17	9	Sep2003	32,549,732.00
18	10	Oct2003	36,442,428.00
19	11	Nov2003	34,350,366.00
20	12	Dec2003	37,389,382.00
21	13	Jan2004	33,537,392.00
22	14	Feb2004	33,909,139.00
23	15	Mar2004	40,805,211.00
24	16	Apr2004	40,172,829.00
25	17	May2004	39,671,007.00
26	18	Jun2004	43,652,277.00
27	19	Jul2004	46,262,249.00
28	20	Aug2004	44,701,691.00
29	21	Sep2004	35,470,844.00
30	22	Oct2004	39,627,851.00
31	23	Nov2004	37,567,116.00
32	24	Dec2004	39,117,678.00

Figure 12-1: US airline miles

To further illustrate the concept of moving averages, take a look at the graph of United States airline miles shown in Figure 12-2. To obtain this graph select the data from the `Moving average` worksheet of the `airlinemiles.xlsx` file in the range E8:F120 and select Insert ➢ Charts ➢ Scatter and choose the second option (Scatter with Smooth Lines and Markers). You obtain the graph shown in Figure 12-2.

Due to seasonality (primarily because people travel more in the summer), miles traveled usually increase during the summer and then decrease during the winter. This makes it difficult to ascertain the trend in airline travel. Graphing the *moving average* of airline miles can help to better understand the trend in this data. A 12-month moving average, for example, graphs the average of the current month's miles and the last 11 months. Because moving averages smooth out noise in the data, you can use a 12-month moving average to eliminate the influence of seasonality. This is because a 12-month moving average includes one data point for each month. When analyzing a trend in quarterly data, you should plot a four-quarter moving average.

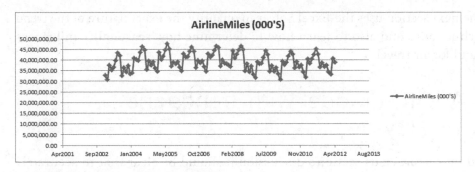

Figure 12-2: Graph of US airline miles

To overlay a 12-month moving average on the scatterplot, you return to an old friend, the Excel Trendline. Right-click the data series and select Add Trendline... Choose Moving Average and select 12 periods. Then you can obtain the trendline, as shown in Figure 12-3.

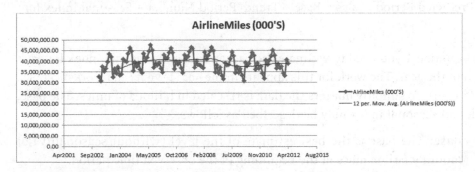

Figure 12-3: Moving average trendline

The moving average trendline makes it easy to see how airline travel trended between 2003 and 2012. You can now see the following:

- In 2003 and 2004 there was a sharp upward trend in airline travel (perhaps a rebound from 9/11).
- In 2005–2008 airline travel appeared to stagnate.
- In late 2008 there was a sharp drop in airline travel, likely due to the financial crisis.
- In 2010 a slight upward trend in air travel occurred.

The next section uses the Excel Solver to quantify the exact nature of the trend in airline miles and also to learn how to determine how seasonality influences demand for air travel.

An Additive Model with Trends and Seasonality

Based on the previous section's discussion it should be clear that to accurately forecast sales when the data has seasonality and trends, you need to identify and separate these from the data series. In this section you learn how this process can be modeled using Excel's Solver. These analyses enable you to identify and separate between the baseline, seasonality, and trend components of a data series.

When predicting product sales, the following additive model is often used to estimate the trend and seasonal influence of sales:

(1) Predicted Period t Sales = Base + Trend*Period Number + Seasonal Index for Month t

In Equation 1 you need to estimate the base, trend, and seasonal index for each month of the year. The work for this appears in the `Additive trend` worksheet (see Figure 12-4). To simplify matters the data is rescaled in billions of miles. The base, trend, and seasonal index may be described as follows:

- **Base:** The base is the best estimate of the level (without seasonality) of monthly airline miles at the beginning of the observed time period.
- **Trend:** The trend is the best estimate of the monthly rate of increase in airline miles traveled. A trend of 5, for example, would mean that the level of airline travel is increasing at a rate of 5 billion miles per month.
- **Seasonal Index:** Each month of the year has a seasonal index to reflect if travel during the month tends to be higher or lower than average. A seasonal index of +5 for June would mean, for example, that June airline travel tends to be 5 billion miles higher than an average month.

NOTE The seasonal indices must average to 0.

	A	B	C	D	E	F	G	H	I	J	K
1											
2	baseadd	37.37856									
3	trendadd	0.059026									
4										stddeverr	0.386323
5	1	-4.45733								RSQ	0.988934
6	2	-6.62334								SSE	4.9251
7	3	1.601041									
8	4	-0.319		MonthNumber	Month		Month	Airline Miles (billion	Forecast	Error	Sq Error
9	5	1.274636		1	7/1/2009	7		44.22	43.7288	0.49	0.236896
10	6	3.795057		2	8/1/2009	8		42.40	41.95583	0.44	0.194662
11	7	6.291206		3	9/1/2009	9		34.68	35.12698	-0.45	0.203932
12	8	4.459215		4	10/1/2009	10		37.32	37.69339	-0.38	0.140881
13	9	-2.42866		5	11/1/2009	11		34.58	35.31697	-0.74	0.54817
14	10	0.078726		6	12/1/2009	12		36.46	36.41789	0.04	0.001696
15	11	-2.35673		7	1/1/2010	1		33.49	33.33441	0.15	0.023327
16	12	-1.31482		8	2/1/2010	2		30.72	31.22743	-0.51	0.259421
17				9	3/1/2010	3		39.37	39.51084	-0.14	0.019948
18	mean	0		10	4/1/2010	4		37.76	37.64982	0.11	0.012653
19				11	5/1/2010	5		38.88	39.30248	-0.42	0.175395
20				12	6/1/2010	6		41.90	41.88193	0.02	0.000401
21				13	7/1/2010	7		44.02	44.43711	-0.42	0.172428
22				14	8/1/2010	8		42.81	42.66414	0.15	0.02222
23				15	9/1/2010	9		36.13	35.8353	0.30	0.087799
24				16	10/1/2010	10		39.18	38.4017	0.78	0.611145
25				17	11/1/2010	11		36.67	36.02528	0.65	0.41766

Figure 12-4: Additive trend model

To estimate base, trend, and seasonal indices, you need to create formulas based on trial values of the parameters in Column H. Then in Column I, you will determine the error for each month's forecast, and in Column J, you compute the squared error for each forecast. Finally, you use the Solver to determine the parameter values that minimize squared errors. To execute this estimation process, perform the following steps:

1. Enter trial values of the base and trend in cells B2 and B3. Name cell B2 baseadd and cell B3 trend.

2. Enter trial seasonal indices in the range B5:B16.

3. In cell B18, average the seasonal indices with the formula =AVERAGE(B5:B16). The Solver model can set this average to 0 to ensure the seasonal indices average to 0.

4. Copy the formula =baseadd+trend*D9+VLOOKUP(F9,$A$5:$B$16,2) from H9 to H10:H42 to compute the forecast for each month.

5. Copy the formula =G9-H9 from I9 to I10:I42 to compute each month's forecast error.

6. Copy the formula =(I9^2) from J9 to J10:J42 to compute each month's squared error.

7. In cell K6, compute the Sum of Squared Errors (SSE) using the formula =SUM(J9:J42).

8. Now set up the Solver model, as shown in Figure 12-5. Change the parameters to minimize SSE and constrain the average of the seasonal indices to 0. Do not check the non-negative box because some seasonal indices must be negative. The forecasting model of Equation 1 is a *linear forecasting model* because each unknown parameter is multiplied by a constant. When the forecasts are created by adding together terms that multiply changing cells by constants, the GRG Solver Engine always finds a unique solution to the least square minimizing parameter estimates for a forecasting model.

Figure 12-5: Additive trend Solver model

Refer to the data shown in Figure 12-4 and you can make the following estimates:

- At the beginning of July 2009, the base level of airline miles is 37.38 billion.
- An upward trend in airline miles is 59 billion miles per month.
- The busiest month is July (6.29 billion miles above average) and the slowest month is February with 6.62 billion miles below average.

Cell K5 uses the formula =RSQ(G9:G42,H9:H42) to show that the model explains 98.9 percent of the variation in miles traveled. Cell K4 also computes the standard deviation of the errors (989 billion) with the formula =STDEV(I9:I42). You should expect 95 percent of the predictions to be accurate within 2 * 0.386 = 0.772 billion miles. Looking at Column I, no outliers are found.

A Multiplicative Model with Trend and Seasonality

When predicting product sales, the following multiplicative model is often used to estimate the trend and seasonal influence of sales:

(2) Predicted Period t Sales = Base * (Trend^t) * (Seasonal Index for Month t)

As in the additive model, you need to estimate the base, trend, and seasonal indices. In Equation 2 the trend and seasonal index have different meanings than in the additive model.

- **Trend:** The trend now represents the percentage monthly increase in the level of airline miles. For example, a trend value of 1.03 means monthly air travel is increasing 3 percent per month, and a trend value of .95 means monthly air travel is decreasing at a rate of 5 percent per month. If per period growth is independent of the current sales value, the additive trend model will probably outperform the multiplicative trend model. On the other hand, if per period growth is an increasing function of current sales, the multiplicative trend model will probably outperform the additive trend model.
- **Seasonal Index:** The seasonal index for a month now represents the percentage by which airline travel for the month is above or below an average month. For example, a seasonal index for July of 1.16 means July has 16 percent more air travel than an average month, whereas a seasonal index for February of .83 means February has 17 percent less air travel than an average month. Of course, multiplicative seasonal indices must average to 1. This is because months with above average sales are indicated by a seasonal index exceeding 1, while months with below average sales are indicated by a seasonal index less than 1.

The work for this equation appears in the Multiplicative trend worksheet. All the formulas are the same as the additive model with the exception of the monthly forecasts in Column H. You can implement Equation 2 by copying the formula =base*(trend^D9)*VLOOKUP(F9,$A$5:$B$16,2)from H9 to H10:H42.

The forecasting model in Equation 2 is a nonlinear forecasting model because you can raise the trend to a power and multiply, rather than add terms involving the seasonal indices. For nonlinear forecasting models, the GRG Solver Engine often fails to find an optimal solution unless the starting values for the changing cells are close to the optimal solution. The remedy to this issue is as follows:

1. In Solver select Options, and from the GRG tab, select Multistart. This ensures the Solver will try many (between 50 and 200) starting solutions and find the optimal solution from each starting solution. Then the Solver reports the "best of the best" solutions.

2. To use the Multistart option, input lower and upper bounds on the changing cells. To speed up solutions, these bounds should approximate sensible values for the estimated parameters. For example, a seasonal index will probably be between 0 and 3, so an upper bound of 100 would be unreasonable. As shown in Figure 12-6, you can choose an upper bound of 3 for each seasonal index and an upper bound of 2 for the trend. For this example, choose an upper bound of 100 for the base.

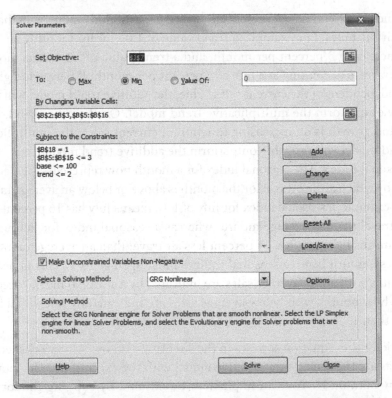

Figure 12-6: Solver window for multiplicative trend model

3. Cell B18 averages the seasonal indices, so in the Solver window add the constraint $B$18 =1 to ensure that the seasonal indices average to 1.

4. Select Solve, and the Solver will then find the optimal solution (refer to Figure 12-7).

	A	B		D	E		G	H	I	J	K
1											
2	base	3.74E+01									
3	trend	1.001493569					1.00E+06				
4										stddeverrors	0.411756002
5	1	0.884049011								RSQ	0.987429707
6	2	0.82837254								SSE	
7	3	1.041400111									5.59
8	4	0.991684904		MonthNumber	Month	Month	AirlineMiles (b	Forecast	Error	Sq Error	
9	5	1.03315296		1	7/1/2009	7	44.22	43.63945105	0.58	0.33	
10	6	1.098599337		2	8/1/2009	8	42.40	41.89570886	0.50	0.25	
11	7	1.164327734		3	9/1/2009	9	34.68	35.19980697	-0.52	0.28	
12	8	1.116136195		4	10/1/2009	10	37.32	37.71609694	-0.40	0.16	
13	9	0.936353544		5	11/1/2009	11	34.58	35.38768125	-0.81	0.66	
14	10	1.00179316		6	12/1/2009	12	36.46	36.46161088	0.00	0.00	
15	11	0.938545346		7	1/1/2010	1	33.49	33.43255124	0.05	0.00	
16	12	0.965585734		8	2/1/2010	2	30.72	31.37379361	-0.66	0.43	
17				9	3/1/2010	3	39.37	39.50091231	-0.13	0.02	
18	mean	0.999999998		10	4/1/2010	4	37.76	37.67136647	0.09	0.01	
19				11	5/1/2010	5	38.88	39.30524076	-0.42	0.18	
20				12	6/1/2010	6	41.90	41.85750467	0.04	0.00	
21				13	7/1/2010	7	44.02	44.4280508	-0.41	0.16	
22				14	8/1/2010	8	42.81	42.65279779	0.16	0.03	
23				15	9/1/2010	9	36.13	35.8358956	0.30	0.09	
24				16	10/1/2010	10	39.18	38.39765695	0.79	0.62	
25				17	11/1/2010	11	36.67	36.03716402	0.64	0.42	

Figure 12-7: Multiplicative trend model

NOTE If the Solver assigns a changing cell, a value near its lower or upper bound should be relaxed. For example, if you set the upper bound for the base to 30, the Solver will find a value near 30, thereby indicating the bound should be relaxed.

From the optimal Solver solution you find the following:

- The estimated base level of airline miles is 37.4 billion.
- You can estimate airline miles increase at a rate of 0.15 percent per month or $1.00149^{12} - 1 = 1.8$ percent per year.
- The busiest month for the airlines is July, when miles traveled are 16 percent above average, and the least busy month is February, during which miles traveled are 17 percent below average.

A natural question is whether the additive or multiplicative model should be used to predict airline miles for future months. Because the additive model has a lower standard deviation of residuals, you should use the additive model to forecast future airline miles traveled.

Summary

In this chapter you learned the following:

- Using a 12-month or 4-quarter moving average chart enables you to easily see the trend in a product's sales.
- You can often use seasonality and trend to predict sales by using the following equation:

$$\text{Predicted Period } t \text{ Sales} = \text{Base} + \text{Trend} * \text{Period Number} + \text{Seasonal Index for Month } t$$

- You can often use the following equation to predict sales of a product:

$$\text{Predicted period } t \text{ Sales} = \text{Base} * (\text{Trend}^t) * (\text{Seasonal Index for Month } t)$$

Exercises

The following exercises use the file `airlinedata.xlsx`, which contains monthly U.S. domestic air miles traveled during the years 1970–2004.

1. Determine the trend and seasonality for the years 1970–1980.
2. Determine the trend and seasonality for the years 1981–1990.
3. Determine the trend and seasonality for the years 1995–2004.

13

Ratio to Moving Average Forecasting Method

In Chapter 12, "Modeling Trend and Seasonality," you learned how to estimate trend and seasonal indices. Naturally you would like to use your knowledge of trend and seasonality to make accurate forecasts of future sales. The *Ratio to Moving Average Method* provides an accurate, easy-to-use forecasting method for future monthly or quarterly sales. This chapter shows how to use this method to easily estimate seasonal indices and forecast future sales.

Using the Ratio to Moving Average Method

The simple Ratio to Moving Average Forecasting Method is described in this section via examples using data from the `Ratioma.xlsx` file, which includes sales of a product during 20 quarters (as shown in Figure 13-1 in rows 5 through 24). This technique enables you to perform two tasks:

- Easily estimate a time series' trend and seasonal indices.
- Generate forecasts of future values of the time series.

Using the first 20 quarters for the data exemplified in this chapter, you will be able to forecast sales for the following four quarters (Quarters 21 through 24). Similar to the one in Chapter 12, this time series data has both trend and seasonality.

The Ratio to Moving Average Method has four main steps:

- Estimate the deseasonalized level of the series during each period (using centered moving averages).
- Fit a trend line to your deseasonalized estimates (in Column G).
- Determine the seasonal index for each quarter and estimate the future level of the series by extrapolating the trend line.
- Predict future sales by reseasonalizing the trend line estimate.

	B	C	D	E	F	G	H	I	J	K	L
1				slope	6.9387868						
2				intercept	30.166176				quarter	seasonal index	normalized
3									1	0.818547	0.81373678
4	Quarter#	Year	Quarter	Sales	4 period MA	Centered MA	Actual/CMA	Forecast	2	0.93934	0.9338196
5	1	1	1	24					3	1.067364	1.06109143
6	2	1	2	44	52				4	1.198394	1.19135219
7	3	1	3	61	58	55.00	1.11				
8	4	1	4	79	63.5	60.75	1.30				
9	5	2	1	48	71	67.25	0.71				
10	6	2	2	66	77.5	74.25	0.89				
11	7	2	3	91	82.5	80.00	1.14				
12	8	2	4	105	87.25	84.88	1.24				
13	9	3	1	68	89.5	88.38	0.77				
14	10	3	2	85	94.5	92.00	0.92				
15	11	3	3	100	104.25	99.38	1.01				
16	12	3	4	125	114.25	109.25	1.14				
17	13	4	1	107	123.75	119.00	0.90				
18	14	4	2	125	132.25	128.00	0.98				
19	15	4	3	138	139.25	135.75	1.02				
20	16	4	4	159	146.75	143.00	1.11				
21	17	5	1	135	156	151.38	0.89				
22	18	5	2	155	164.25	160.13	0.97				
23	19	5	3	175							
24	20	5	4	192							
25	21	6	1			175.880699		143.121			
26	22	6	2			182.819485		170.72			
27	23	6	3			189.758272		201.351			
28	24	6	4			196.697059		234.335			

Figure 13-1: Example of Ratio to Moving Average Method

The following sections walk you through each main part of this process.

Calculating Moving Averages and Centered Moving Averages

To begin, you compute a four-quarter (four quarters eliminates seasonality) moving average for each quarter by averaging the prior quarter, current quarter, and next two quarters. To do this you copy the formula =AVERAGE(E5:E8) down from cell F6 to F7:F22. For example, for Quarter 2, the moving average is $(24 + 44 + 61 + 79) / 4 = 52$.

Because the moving average for Quarter 2 averages Quarters 1 through 4 and the numbers 1–4 average to 2.5, the moving average for Quarter 2 is centered at Quarter 2.5. Similarly, the moving average for Quarter 3 is centered at Quarter 3.5. Therefore, averaging these two moving averages gives a centered moving average that estimates the level of the process at the end of Quarter 3. To estimate the level of the series during each series (without seasonality), copy the formula =AVERAGE(F6:F7) down from cell G7.

Fitting a Trend Line to the Centered Moving Averages

You can use the centered moving averages to fit a trend line that can be used to estimate the future level of the series. To do so, follow these steps:

1. In cell F1 use the formula =SLOPE(G7:G22,B7:B22) to find the slope of the trend line.
2. In cell F2 use the formula =INTERCEPT(G7:G22,B7:B22) to find the intercept of the trend line.
3. Estimate the level of the series during Quarter t to be $6.94t \, c + 30.17$.
4. Copy the formula =intercept + slope*B25 down from cell G25 to G26:G28 to compute the estimated level (excluding seasonality) of the series from Quarter 21 onward.

Compute the Seasonal Indexes

Recall that a seasonal index of 2 for a quarter means sales in that quarter are twice the sales during an average quarter, whereas a seasonal index of .5 for a quarter would mean that sales during that quarter were one-half of an average quarter. Therefore, to determine the seasonal indices, begin by determining for each quarter for which you have sales *(Actual Sales) / Centered Moving Average*. To do this, copy the formula =E7/G7 down from cell H7 to H8:H22. You find, for example, that during Quarter 1 sales were 77 percent, 71 percent, 90 percent and 89 percent of average, so you could estimate the seasonal index for Quarter 1 as the average of these four numbers (82 percent). To calculate the initial seasonal index estimates, you can copy the formula =AVERAGEIF($D$7:$D$22,J3,$H$7:$H$22) from cell K3 to K4:K6. This formula averages the four estimates you have for Q1 seasonality.

Unfortunately, the seasonal indices do not average exactly to 1. To ensure that your final seasonal indices average to 1, copy the formula =K3/AVERAGE($K$3:$K$6) from cell L3 to L4:L6.

Forecasting Sales during Quarters 21–24

To create your sales forecast for each future quarter, simply multiply the trend line estimate for the quarter's level (from Column G) by the appropriate seasonal index. Copy the formula =VLOOKUP(D25,season,3)*G25 from cell G25 to G26:G28 to compute the final forecast for Quarters 21–24. This forecast includes estimates of trend and seasonality.

If you think the trend of the series has changed recently, you can estimate the series' trend based on more recent data. For example, you could use the centered moving averages for Quarters 13–18 to get a more recent trend estimate by using the formula =SLOPE(G17:G22,B17:B22). This yields an estimated trend of 8.09 units per quarter. If you want to forecast Quarter 22 sales, for example, you take the last centered moving average you have (from Quarter 18) of 160.13 and add 4 (8.09) to estimate the level of the series in Quarter 22. Then multiply the estimate of the Quarter 22 level by the Quarter 2 seasonal index of .933 to yield a final forecast for Quarter 22 sales of (160.13 + 4(8.09)) * (.933) = 179.6 units.

Applying the Ratio to Moving Average Method to Monthly Data

Often the Ratio to Moving Average Method is used to forecast monthly sales as well as quarterly sales. To illustrate the application of this method to monthly data, let's look at U.S. housing starts.

The Housingstarts.xlsx file gives monthly U.S. housing starts (in thousands) for the period January 2000 through May 2011. Based on the data through November 2010, you can apply the Ratio to Moving Average Method to forecast monthly U.S. housing starts for the period December 2010 through May 2011. You can forecast a total of 3.5 million housing starts, and in reality there were 3.374 million housing starts. The key difference between applying the method to monthly and quarterly data is that for monthly data you need to use 12-month moving averages to eliminate seasonality.

Summary

In this chapter you learned the following:

- Applying the Ratio to Moving Average Method involves the following tasks:
  - Compute four-quarter moving averages and then determine the centered moving averages.
  - Fit a trend line to the centered moving averages.
  - Compute seasonal indices.
  - Compute forecasts for future periods.

- You can apply the Ratio to Moving Average Method to monthly data as well by following the same process but use 12-month moving averages to eliminate seasonality.

Exercises

1. The file `Walmartdata.xls` contains quarterly revenues of Wal-Mart during the years 1994–2009. Use the Ratio to Moving Average Method to forecast revenues for Quarters 3 and 4 in 2009 and Quarters 1 and 2 in 2010. Use Quarters 53–60 to create a trend estimate that you use in your forecasts.

2. Based on the data in the file `airlinemiles.xlsx` from Chapter 12, use the Ratio to Moving Average Method to forecast airline miles for the remaining months in 2012.

14

Winter's Method

Predicting future values of a time series is usually difficult because the characteristics of any time series are constantly changing. For instance, as you saw in Chapter 12, "Modeling Trend and Seasonality," the trend in U.S. airline passenger miles changed several times during the 2000–2012 period. *Smoothing* or *adaptive* methods are usually best suited for forecasting future values of a time series. Essentially, smoothing methods create forecasts by combining information from a current observation with your prior view of a parameter, such as trend or a seasonal index. Unlike many other smoothing methods, Winter's Method incorporates both trend and seasonal factors. This makes it useful in situations where trend and seasonality are important. Because in an actual situation (think U.S. monthly housing starts) trend and seasonality are constantly changing, a method such as Winter's Method that changes trend and seasonal index estimates during each period has a better chance of keeping up with changes than methods like the trend and seasonality approaches based on curve fitting discussed in Chapter 12, which use constant estimates of trend and seasonal indices.

To help you understand how Winter's Method works, this chapter uses it to forecast airline passenger miles for April through December 2012 based on the data studied in Chapter 12. This chapter describes the three key characteristics of a time series (level, trend, and seasonality) and explains the initialization process, notation, and key formulas needed to implement Winter's Method. Finally, you explore forecasting with Winter's Method and the concept of Mean Absolute Percentage Error (MAPE).

Parameter Definitions for Winter's Method

In this chapter you will develop Winter's exponential smoothing method using the three time series characteristics, level (also called base), trend, and seasonal index, discussed in Chapter 12 in the "Multiplicative Model with Trend and Seasonality" section. After observing data through the end of month t you can estimate the following quantities of interest:

- L_t = Level of series
- T_t = Trend of series
- S_t = Seasonal index for current month

The key to Winter's Method is the use of the following three equations, which are used to update L_t, T_t, and S_t. In the following equations, *alp*, *bet*, and *gam* are called *smoothing parameters*. The values of these parameters will be chosen to optimize your forecasts. In the following equations, c equals the number of periods in a seasonal cycle ($c = 12$ months for example) and x_t equals the observed value of the time series at time t.

(1) $L_t = alp(x_t) / (s_{t-c}) + (1 - alp)(L_{t-1} * T_{t-1})$

(2) $T_t = bet(L_t / L_{t-1}) + (1 - bet) T_{t-1}$

(3) $S_t = gam(x_t / L_t) + (1 - gam)s_{(t-c)}$

Equation 1 indicates that the new base estimate is a weighted average of the current observation (deseasonalized) and last period's base is updated by the last trend estimate. Equation 2 indicates that the new trend estimate is a weighted average of the ratio of the current base to last period's base (this is a current estimate of trend) and last period's trend. Equation 3 indicates that you update the seasonal index estimate as a weighted average of the estimate of the seasonal index based on the current period and the previous estimate. In equations 1–3 the first term uses an estimate of the desired quantity based on the current observation and the second term uses a past estimate of the desired quantity.

NOTE Note that larger values of the smoothing parameters correspond to putting more weight on the current observation.

You can define $F_{t,k}$ as your forecast (F) after period t for the period $t + k$. This results in the following equation:

(4) $F_{t,k} = L_t*(T_t)^k s_{t+k-c}$

Equation 4 first uses the current trend estimate to update the base k periods forward. Then the resulting base estimate for period $t + k$ is adjusted by the appropriate seasonal index.

Initializing Winter's Method

To start Winter's Method, you must have initial estimates for the series base, trend, and seasonal indices. You can use the data from the `airlinewinters.xls` file, which contains monthly U.S. airline passenger miles for the years 2003 and 2004 to obtain initial estimates of level, trend, and seasonality. See Figure 14-1.

	A	B	C	D	E	F	G	H	I
1									
2	base	3.51E+01						SSE	
3	trend	1.006491							5.63
4			MonthNu	Month	Month	AirlineMiles (billions)	Forecast	Error	Sq Error
5	1	0.90305	1	Jan2003	1	32.85	31.87289	0.98	0.96
6	2	0.875947	2	Feb2003	2	30.81	31.11699	-0.30	0.09
7	3	1.053815	3	Mar2003	3	37.59	37.6785	-0.09	0.01
8	4	1.008006	4	Apr2003	4	35.23	36.27456	-1.05	1.10
9	5	1.011706	5	May2003	5	36.57	36.644	-0.07	0.01
10	6	1.099865	6	Jun2003	6	39.75	40.09572	-0.35	0.12
11	7	1.173706	7	Jul2003	7	43.37	43.06529	0.30	0.09
12	8	1.129149	8	Aug2003	8	42.09	41.69932	0.39	0.15
13	9	0.879644	9	Sep2003	9	32.55	32.696	-0.15	0.02
14	10	0.977359	10	Oct2003	10	36.44	36.5638	-0.12	0.01
15	11	0.918146	11	Nov2003	11	34.35	34.57155	-0.22	0.05
16	12	0.969609	12	Dec2003	12	37.39	36.74627	0.64	0.41
17			13	Jan2004	1	33.54	34.44595	-0.91	0.83
18	mean	1	14	Feb2004	2	33.91	33.62903	0.28	0.08
19			15	Mar2004	3	40.81	40.72023	0.08	0.01
20			16	Apr2004	4	40.17	39.20296	0.97	0.94
21			17	May2004	5	39.67	39.60222	0.07	0.00
22			18	Jun2004	6	43.65	43.33259	0.32	0.10
23			19	Jul2004	7	46.26	46.54189	-0.28	0.08
24			20	Aug2004	8	44.70	45.06565	-0.36	0.13
25			21	Sep2004	9	35.47	35.3355	0.14	0.02
26			22	Oct2004	10	39.63	39.51555	0.11	0.01
27			23	Nov2004	11	37.57	37.36247	0.20	0.04
28			24	Dec2004	12	39.12	39.71275	-0.60	0.35

Figure 14-1: Data for Winter's Method

In the `Initial` worksheet you can fit the Multiplicative Trend Model from Chapter 12 to the 2003–2004 data. As shown in Figure 14-2, you use the trend and seasonal index from this fit as the original seasonal index and the December 2004 trend. Cell C25 determines an estimate of the base for December 2004 by deseasonalizing the observed December 2004 miles. This is accomplished with the formula `=(B25/H25)`.

	A	B	C	D	E	F	G	H	I	J	K
1	DATE	Airline Miles(billions)									
2	Jan2003	32.85									
3	Feb2003	30.81									
4	Mar2003	37.59									
5	Apr2003	35.23									
6	May2003	36.57									
7	Jun2003	39.75									
8	Jul2003	43.37									
9	Aug2003	42.09									
10	Sep2003	32.55						alp	bet	gam	
11	Oct2003	36.44						0.548512014	0.049142	0.58877279	
12	Nov2003	34.35									
13	Dec2003	37.39									
14	Jan2004	33.54						0.903049602			
15	Feb2004	33.91						0.875947455			
16	Mar2004	40.81						1.053814727			
17	Apr2004	40.17						1.00800602			
18	May2004	39.67						1.011705575			
19	Jun2004	43.65						1.099865309			
20	Jul2004	46.26						1.173705527			
21	Aug2004	44.70				SSE	77.8196	1.129148564			
22	Sep2004	35.47				stdeverro	0.9369659	0.879643964		34 sign changes of 87	
23	Oct2004	39.63						0.977358616		MAPE	
24	Nov2004	37.57	Base	Trend	Forecast	Error	Sq Eerror	0.918146041	34	0.02062096	
25	Dec2004	39.12	40.34378	1.006491				0.969608616	Sign char	APE	
26	Jan2005	36.12	40.27083	1.006083	36.6689	-0.55	0.3038	0.899411078		0.01526167	
27	Feb2005	34.56	39.93414	1.005373	35.4897	-0.93	0.8628	0.869764432	0	0.02687615	
28	Mar2005	43.64	40.8425	1.006227	42.3093	1.33	1.7767	1.062490091	1	0.03054212	
29	Apr2005	40.24	40.45404	1.005453	41.42583	-1.18	1.3953	1.000244124	1	0.02935135	
30	May2005	41.80	41.02748	1.005882	41.15077	0.65	0.4235	1.015922148	1	0.01556855	
31	Jun2005	44.68	40.91303	1.005456	45.39013	-0.71	0.5089	1.095230183	1	0.0159679	
32	Jul2005	47.56	40.80036	1.005052	48.28184	-0.72	0.5166	1.169022868	0	0.01511097	

Figure 14-2: Initialization of Winter's Method

The next part of Winter's Method includes choosing the smoothing parameters to optimize the one-month-ahead forecasts for the years 2005 through 2012.

Estimating the Smoothing Constants

After observing each month's airline miles (in billions), you are now ready to update the smoothing constants. In Column C, you will update the series base; in Column D, the series trend; and in Column H, the seasonal indices. In Column E, you compute the forecast for next month, and in Column G, you compute the squared error for each month. Finally, you'll use Solver to choose smoothing constant values that minimize the sum of the squared errors. To enact this process, perform the following steps:

1. In H11:J11, enter trial values (between 0 and 1) for the smoothing constants.
2. In C26:C113, compute the updated series level with Equation 1 by copying the formula =alp*(B26/H14)+(1-alp)*(C25*D25) from cell C26 to C27:C113.
3. In D26:D113, use Equation 2 to update the series trend. Copy the formula =bet*(C26/C25)+(1-bet)*D25 cell from D26 to D27:D113.

4. In H26:H113, use Equation 3 to update the seasonal indices. Copy the formula `=gam*(B26/C26)+(1-gam)*H14` from cell H26 to H27:H113.

5. In E26:E113, use Equation 4 to compute the forecast for the current month by copying the formula `=(C25*D25)*H14` from cell E26 to E27:E113.

6. In F26:F113 compute each month's error by copying the formula `=(B26-E26)` from cell E26 to E27:E113.

7. In G26:G113, compute the squared error for each month by copying the formula `=F26^2` from cell F26 to F27:F113. In cell G21 compute the Sum of Squared Errors (SSE) using the formula `=SUM(G26:G113)`.

8. Now use the Solver to determine smoothing parameter values that minimize SSE. The Solver Parameters dialog box is shown in Figure 14-3.

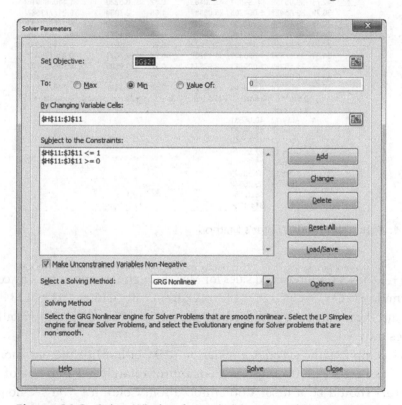

Figure 14-3: Solver Window for optimizing smoothing constants

9. Choose the smoothing parameters (H11:J11) to minimize SSE (cell G21). The Excel Solver ensures you can find the best combination of smoothing constants. Smoothing constants must be α. The Solver finds that alp = 0.55, bet = 0.05, and gamma = 0.59.

Forecasting Future Months

Now that you have estimated the Winter's Method smoothing constants (α, β, γ, etc.), you are ready to use these estimates to forecast future airline miles. This can be accomplished using the formula in cell D116. Copying this formula down to cells D117:D123 enables you to forecast sales for the months of May through December of 2012. Figure 14-4 offers a visual summary of the forecasted sales.

	A	B	C	D	E	F	G	H
101	Apr2011		38.51	38.09331	0.999196	38.63321	-0.13	0.0162	1.011448481
102	May2011		40.43	38.7357	1.000064	39.16698	1.26	1.5942	1.03767775
103	Jun2011		42.57	38.84163	1.000195	42.36397	0.21	0.0425	1.095009094
104	Jul2011		45.07	39.00168	1.000388	44.75388	0.32	0.1025	1.154171797
105	Aug2011		42.78	38.66139	0.99994	43.50483	-0.72	0.5220	1.110060016
106	Sep2011		36.70	39.65425	1.001205	35.05387	1.65	2.7064	0.917771587
107	Oct2011		38.70	39.72586	1.001235	38.66143	0.04	0.0018	0.974072493
108	Nov2011		36.83	40.16433	1.001716	36.182	0.65	0.4171	0.913943328
109	Dec2011		37.49	39.82658	1.001219	38.1972	-0.70	0.4955	0.944695094
110	Jan2012		34.31	39.32558	1.000541	35.19792	-0.88	0.7821	0.876725748
111	Feb2012		33.26	39.53299	1.000773	32.97971	0.28	0.0809	0.840092107
112	Mar2012		40.78	38.94334	1.000002	41.9811	-1.20	1.4396	1.05291499
113	Apr2012		38.81	38.6274	0.999604	39.38927	-0.58	0.3396	1.00743814
114				Base	Trend	Forecast	Error	Sq Eerror	Seasonal Indices
115				forecasts					
116			1	May-12	40.06691				
117			2	Jun-12	42.26383				
118			3	Jul-12	44.52966				
119			4	Aug-12	42.81079				
120			5	Sep-12	35.38093				
121			6	Oct-12	37.53649				
122			7	Nov-12	35.20542				
123			8	Dec-12	36.37556				
124				total	314.1696				

Figure 14-4: Forecasting with Winter's Method

Figure 14-4 shows the forecasted sales for May through December 2012 by copying the formula =($C$113*$D$113^B116)*H102 from cell D116 to D117:D123. Cell D124 adds up these forecasts and predicts the rest of 2012 to see 314.17 billion airline miles traveled.

Cell G22 computes the standard deviation (0.94 billion) of the one-month-ahead forecast errors. This implies that approximately 95 percent of the forecast errors should be at most 1.88 billion. From Column F you see none of the one-month-ahead forecasts are outliers.

Mean Absolute Percentage Error (MAPE)

Statisticians like to estimate parameters for a forecast model by minimizing squared errors. In reality, however, most people are more interested in measuring forecast accuracy by looking at the Mean of Absolute Percentage Error (MAPE). This is probably because MAPE, unlike SSE, is measured in the same units as the data. Figure 14-5 shows that the one-month-ahead forecasts are off by an average of 2.1 percent. To compute the Absolute Percentage Error (APE) for each month, copy the formula =ABS(B26-E26)/B26 from cell G26 to J26:J113. In cell J24 the formula =AVERAGE(J26:J113) computes the MAPE.

	C	D	E	F	G	H	I	J	K	L
22				stdeverrors	0.9369659	0.879643964		34 sign changes of 87		
23						0.977358616		MAPE		
24	Base	Trend	Forecast	Error	Sq Eerror	0.918146041	34	0.0206		
25	40.34378	1.006491				0.969608616	Sign change	APE		
26	40.27083	1.006083	36.6689	-0.55	0.3038	0.899411078		0.0153		
27	39.93414	1.005373	35.4897	-0.93	0.8628	0.869764432	0	0.0269		
28	40.8425	1.006227	42.3093	1.33	1.7767	1.062490091	1	0.0305		
29	40.45404	1.005453	41.42583	-1.10	1.3953	1.000244124	1	0.0294		
30	41.02748	1.005882	41.15077	0.65	0.4235	1.015922148	1	0.0156		
31	40.91303	1.005456	45.39013	-0.71	0.5089	1.095230183	1	0.016		
32	40.80036	1.005052	48.28184	-0.72	0.5166	1.169022868	0	0.0151		
33	40.43957	1.00437	46.30243	-1.17	1.3621	1.121476998	0	0.0259		
34	41.43753	1.005368	35.72786	1.32	1.7346	0.888092908	1	0.0356		
35	40.61218	1.004125	40.71671	-1.87	3.4855	0.965138667	1	0.0481		
36	41.20776	1.004643	37.44173	0.72	0.5134	0.922768159	1	0.0188		
37	40.85333	1.003992	40.14091	-0.96	0.9307	0.963331236	1	0.0246		
38	40.88625	1.003835	36.89062	-0.21	0.0456	0.898023391	0	0.0058		
39	40.44253	1.003114	35.6978	-0.95	0.9068	0.863505332	0	0.0274		
40	40.45961	1.002981	43.10358	-0.21	0.0445	1.061104844	0	0.0049		

Figure 14-5: Computation of MAPE

Winter's Method is an attractive forecasting method for several reasons:

- Given past data, the method can easily be programmed to provide quick forecasts for thousands of products.
- Winter's Method catches changes in trend or seasonality.
- Smoothing methods "adapt" to the data. That is, if you underforecast you raise parameter estimates and if you overforecast you lower parameter estimates.

Summary

In this chapter you learned the following:

- Exponential smoothing methods update time series parameters by computing a weighted average of the estimate of the parameter from the current observation with the prior estimate of the parameter.
- Winter's Method is an exponential smoothing method that updates the base, trend, and seasonal indices after each equation:

  (1) $L_t = alp(x_t) / (s_{t-c}) + (1-alp)(L_{t-1} * T_{t-1})$

  (2) $T_t = bet(L_t / L_{t-1}) + (1-bet)T_{t-1}$

  (3) $S_t = gam(x_t / L_t) + (1-gam)s_{(t-c)}$

- Forecasts for k periods ahead at the end of period t are made with Winter's Method using Equation 4:

$$(4)\ F_{t,k} = L_t * (T_t)^k s_{t+k-c}$$

Exercises

All the data for the following exercises can be found in the file `Quarterly.xlsx`.

1. Use Winter's Method to forecast one-quarter-ahead revenues for Wal-Mart.
2. Use Winter's Method to forecast one-quarter-ahead revenues for Coca-Cola.
3. Use Winter's Method to forecast one-quarter-ahead revenues for Home Depot.
4. Use Winter's Method to forecast one-quarter-ahead revenues for Apple.
5. Use Winter's Method to forecast one-quarter-ahead revenues for Amazon.com.
6. Suppose at the end of 2007 you were predicting housing starts in Los Angeles for the years 2008 and 2009. Why do you think Winter's Method would provide better forecasts than multiple regression?

15

Using Neural Networks to Forecast Sales

Recall from Chapter 10 "Using Multiple Regression to Predict Sales," that to use multiple regression you had to posit the form of the relationship between the dependent and independent variables. Usually you assumed that the independent variables influenced the dependent variable via a linear relationship. However, if the relationship between the independent variables and the dependent variable is highly complex, there is little chance that multiple regression can find the relationship. Neural nets are an amazing form of artificial intelligence that can capture these complex relationships. Essentially a neural network is a "black box" that searches many models (including nonlinear models involving interactions) to find a relationship involving the independent variables that best predict the dependent variable. In a neural network the independent variables are called *input cells* and the dependent variable is called an *output cell* (more than one output is OK).

This chapter shows how to use Palisade Corporation's great Excel add-in, NeuralTools, to easily fit a neural network to data. You can download a 15-day trial version of NeuralTools at Palisade.com.

Regression and Neural Nets

As in regression, neural nets have a certain number of observations (say, *N*). Each observation contains a value for each independent variable and dependent variable. Also similar to regression, the goal of the neural network is to make accurate predictions for the output cell or dependent variable. As you will see, the usage of neural networks is increasing rapidly because neural networks are great at finding patterns. In regression you only find a pattern if you know what to look for. For example, if $y = Ln\ x$ and you simply use x as an independent variable, you cannot predict y very well. A neural network does not need to be "told" the nature of the relationship between the independent variables and the dependent variable. If a relationship or pattern exists and you provide the neural network enough data, it can find the pattern on its own by "learning" it from the data. A major advantage of neural networks over regression is that this method requires no statistical assumptions about your data. For example, unlike regression you do not assume that your errors are independent and normally distributed.

Using Neural Networks

Neural networks have been successfully applied in many situations. This section briefly describes some actual applications of neural networks.

Predicting the Stock Market

The efficient market hypothesis of financial markets states that the "past history" of a stock's returns yields no information about the future return of the stock. The late Halbert White, formerly an economics professor at UC San Diego, examines returns on IBM to see if the market is efficient in his 1988 white paper "Economic Prediction Using Neural Networks: The Case of IBM Daily Stock Returns" (see http://goo.gl/8vG9W). He begins by estimating a multiple regression where the dependent variable is the next day's return on IBM stock and the five independent variables are the return on IBM during each of the last five days. This regression yielded $R^2 = .0079$, which is consistent with the efficient market hypothesis. White then estimated a neural network (containing one hidden layer) with the output cell corresponding to the next day's return on IBM and five input cells corresponding to the last five days' return on IBM. This neural network yielded $R^2 = .179$. This implies that the past five days of IBM returns do contain information that can be used to make predictions about tomorrow's return on IBM. This lends support to those investors who believe that *momentum* or trends in recent returns can be used to improve predictions of future market changes.

Fidelity, a financial services corporation specializing in investment banking, also uses neural networks for predicting trends in the stock market. According to the October 9, 1993 *Economist*, Fidelity managed $2.6 billion in assets using neural networks.

For another example of an investment firm that uses neural networks to guide their investing strategy, see the following Ward Systems Group, Inc. article "Interviews with Real Traders" describing a hedge fund that had success using neural networks: http://www.neuroshell.com/traders .asp?task=interviews&id=15.

Driving Your Car

In 1995, researchers at Carnegie-Mellon University developed ALVINN (short for Automated Land Vehicle in a Neural Network, a neural network that can drive a car! ALVINN can tell if a car is nearby and then slow down the car based on information received via video cameras installed in the car. Using improved versions of ALVINN, in 10 years a neural network may be driving your car! Exercise 1 at the end of this chapter prompts you to look deeper into this scenario. The following article from *Discover* magazine discusses the future of computer driven cars: `http://discovermagazine.com/2011 /apr/10-future-tech-finally-ready-self-driving-cars`.

Direct Market Targeting

Although most of us would not guess it based on the number of pieces of direct/junk mail delivered to our mailboxes, marketers often put a lot of effort into determining who receives direct mail offers. Direct mail campaigns target people who are most likely to respond to the mailing. An article from SSRN found at `http://papers .ssrn.com/sol3/papers.cfm?abstract_id=370877` shows how neural networks were used to determine who a Dutch charity should target to maximize the response rate. The following independent variables were chosen to reflect the RFM method:

- **Recency:** Time since last donation
- **Frequency:** How many donations were made in the last five years
- **Monetary Value:** How much money has been donated in the last five years

The neural network outperformed all other methods used to identify the members of the mailing list who received a donor request. When mailing to 10 percent of the mailing list as chosen by the neural network, a 70 percent response rate was achieved, compared to a 30 percent overall response rate.

Bankruptcy Prediction

In finance and accounting it is helpful and important to accurately predict whether a company will go bankrupt during the next year. Edward Altman, an NYU finance professor, developed a method called Altman's Z-statistic in 1968 to predict whether a firm will go bankrupt during the next year based on the firm's financial ratios. This method uses a version of regression called *discriminant analysis* that Chapter 39, "Classification Algorithms: Naive Bayes Classifier and Discriminant Analysis," discusses in greater detail. As discussed by Rick Wilson and Ramesh Sharda ("Bankruptcy Prediction Using Neural Networks," *Decision Support Systems Journal*, 1994, pages 545–57), neural networks that use financial ratios as input cells have been more accurate than Altman's Z in their determination of whether a firm will go bankrupt during the next year.

Analyzing Scanner Data

Ann Furr Peterson and Thomas Grucca of the University of Iowa and Bruce Klemz of the University of Nebraska used neural networks to predict catsup market share based on price, which products were on display, and recent market share in 1999. The neural network outperformed (had a higher R^2 and a lower MAPE) other statistical techniques. You can read more about the study here: http://dl.acm.org/citation.cfm?id=846174.

Neural Networks and Elevators

On September 22, 1993, the *New York Times* reported that Otis Elevator used neural networks to direct elevators. For example, if elevator 1 is on floor 10 and going up, elevator 2 is on floor 6 and going down, and elevator 3 is on floor 2 and going up, the neural network will recommend which elevator should answer a call to go down from floor 8. This system is used, for example, in the Marriott Hotel in Times Square.

Credit Cards and Loans

Many banks (Mellon and Chase are two examples) and credit card companies use neural networks to predict (on the basis of past usage patterns) whether a credit card transaction should be disallowed. If you have ever had a stop put on your credit card when you visit another city, there is a neural network to blame. Essentially the neural network attempts to spot patterns that indicate a credit card has been stolen before the theft is reported. This often happens to the author when he visits his daughter in Los Angeles and takes her shopping at the 3rd Street Promenade Mall in Santa Monica.

AVCO Financial also uses a neural net to determine whether to lend people money. The inputs to the neural network include information used to create credit scores (such as time at same address, annual income, number of times mortgage or credit card payments are late, etc.) By utilizing the neural network to determine if a person is a good or bad risk and giving loans only to people who are predicted to be good risks, AVCO increased its loan volume by 25 percent and decreased its default rate by 20 percent!

Using NeuralTools to Predict Sales

To demonstrate how neural networks can find patterns in data, you can use the data in the Data worksheet of the Neuralpriceads.xlsx file. A subset of this data is shown in Figure 15-1. You are given weekly sales of a product, the price, and advertising amount (in hundreds of dollars). You can construct sales under the assumption that when the price is high, advertising has no effect. More specifically, you can create weekly sales with the following rules:

- If Price is less than or equal to $8, then Sales = 500 − 15 * Price + 0.1 * Advertising.
- If Price is greater than $8, then Sales = 500 − 15 * Price. In this case advertising has no effect on sales.

	C	D	E
3	Sales	Price	Advertisin
4	400.3	7	53
5	365	9	68
6	387.6	8	76
7	432	5	70
8	401.4	7	64
9	387.8	8	78
10	431	5	60
11	400.1	7	51
12	404.7	7	97
13	388.8	8	88
14	388.9	8	89
15	415.2	6	52
16	416.5	6	65
17	365	9	51

Figure 15-1: Price and advertising neural networks example

To get started, perform the following steps:

1. Run a multiple linear regression to predict Sales from Price and Advertising. The result is in the regression worksheet, as shown in Figure 15-2. The regression has a high R^2 and a standard error of 2.03 units. You soon see that a neural network can find much better forecasts with a standard deviation of forecast errors under .03!

2. From the Start Menu select Programs and then choose Palisade Decision Tools. Click NeuralTools; you'll see the toolbar, as shown in Figure 15-3.

	A	B	C	D	E	F	G
1	SUMMARY OUTPUT						
2							
3	*Regression Statistics*						
4	Multiple R	0.997413					
5	R Square	0.994833					
6	Adjusted R Square	0.994802					
7	Standard Error	2.034422					
8	Observations	332					
9							
10	ANOVA						
11		df	SS	MS	F	gnificance F	
12	Regression	2	262191.2	131095.6	31674.24	0	
13	Residual	329	1361.689	4.138871			
14	Total	331	263552.9				
15							
16		Coefficient	andard Err	t Stat	P-value	Lower 95%	Upper 95%
17	Intercept	513.1581	0.812466	631.6054	0	511.5598	514.7564
18	Price	-16.7327	0.067173	-249.099	0	-16.8648	-16.6005
19	Advertising	0.064978	0.007716	8.421615	1.16E-15	0.0498	0.080156

Figure 15-2: Regression model to predict sales

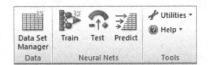

Figure 15-3: Neural Nets toolbar

3. Select the data that will be analyzed. In this case select the data in the range C3:E335, and NeuralTools can automatically recognize the data. Columns of data may be classified as Independent or Dependent Variables and as Categorical (such as subscriber or nonsubscriber) or Numeric.

4. After selecting the data click on the NeuralTools tab on the Ribbon. Then select the Data Set Manager. The Data Set Manager enables you to specify the nature of the input variables and dependent variable (categorical or numeric.) All the variables are numeric, so fill in the Data Set Manager dialog box, as shown in Figure 15-4.

5. Select NeuralTools again from the Ribbon, then select Train and fill in the dialog box as shown in Figure 15-5 and click Next.

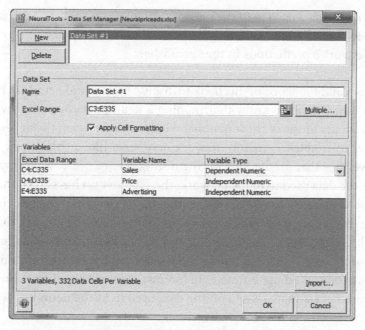

Figure 15-4: NeuralTools Data Set Manager dialog box

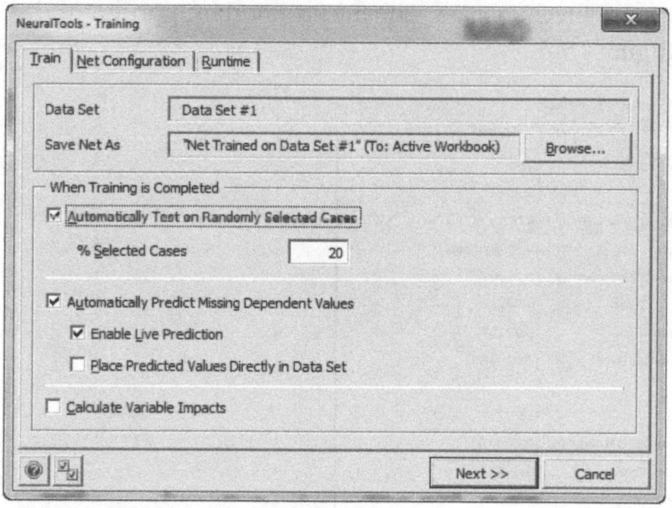

Figure 15-5: Training dialog box

6. As also shown in Figure 15-5, check Automatically Test on Randomly Selected Cases to have NeuralTools "hold out" a randomly chosen 20 percent of the data for testing the network. This helps avoid a network

that overfits the data used to fit the network and performs poorly on data that has not been seen by the network. Check Enable Live Prediction to place the Neural Network's predictions in the spreadsheet.

NOTE   It is beyond the scope of this book to discuss how neural networks create predictions. It is sufficient to know that training a neural network is equivalent to trying many, many forms of the functional relationship between the dependent and independent variables. A neural network may seem like a "black box," but if the analyst verifies that predictions for the testing set are nearly as accurate as predictions for the data used to fit the network, then the analyst has shown that the neural network works almost as well on data that has not yet been seen as on data used for fitting the neural network. This gives the analyst some confidence that the neural network is not simply overfitting data and will be useful for making predictions using unseen data. When estimating the accuracy of a forecast from a neural network, the analyst should use estimates of forecast accuracy based on the testing set, rather than error estimates based on the data used to fit the neural network.

7. Select Next and NeuralTools will fit a neural network to your data. At this point Train NeuralTools uses 80 percent of the data set to train the network. A summary report sheet appears. The most important portion of this report is shown in Figure 15-6.

	B	C
15	*Training*	
16	Number of Cases	266
17	Training Time	0:00:00
18	Number of Trials	67
19	Reason Stopped	Auto-Stopped
20	% Bad Predictions (30% Tolerance)	0.0000%
21	Root Mean Square Error	0.03238
22	Mean Absolute Error	0.02137
23	Std. Deviation of Abs. Error	0.02432
24	*Testing*	
25	Number of Cases	66
26	% Bad Predictions (30% Tolerance)	0.0000%
27	Root Mean Square Error	0.05476
28	Mean Absolute Error	0.03369
29	Std. Deviation of Abs. Error	0.04317

Figure 15-6: NeuralTools report

You can find that 266 data points were used to train the network, and 67 data points were used to test the network. The observations used for the testing and training sets are randomly chosen. That is, each observation has an 80 chance of being in the training set and a 20 percent chance of being in the testing set. In the training set the mean of the absolute errors is 0.02, and in the testing set the mean absolute error is worse (0.03) but still impressive. Also note that the Root Mean Square error (which approximates the Standard Error of the Regression) for the training set is 0.03 and for the testing set is 0.05. Recall that for the multiple regression the standard error was 2.03, far inferior to the neural net.

If you now select Predict from the Neural Net toolbar and fill in the dialog box, as shown in Figure 15-7, NeuralTools places predictions in the spreadsheet, as shown in Figure 15-8. You can see Columns C and H are nearly identical, indicating that the neural net figured out the pattern in the data.

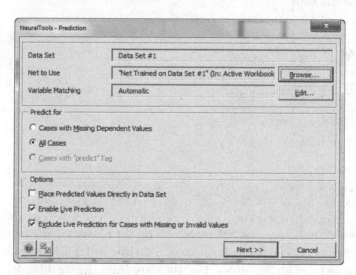

Figure 15-7: Prediction dialog box

To create forecasts for new data, you simply enter the values of Price and Advertising below the original data and copy down the formula in Column H. Figure 15-9 shows the forecasts for two new data points. Note that the forecasts are extremely accurate.

	C	D	E	F	G	H
1						
2					Prediction Report: "Ne	
3	Sales	Price	Advertising		Tag Used	Prediction
4	400.3	7	53		predict	400.29
5	365	9	68		predict	365.00
6	387.6	8	76		predict	387.57
7	432	5	70		predict	431.94
8	401.4	7	64		predict	401.39
9	387.8	8	78		predict	387.84
10	431	5	60		predict	430.99
11	400.1	7	51		predict	400.08
12	404.7	7	97		predict	404.67
13	388.8	8	88		predict	388.83
14	388.9	8	89		predict	388.86
15	415.2	6	52		predict	415.23
16	416.5	6	65		predict	416.54

Figure 15-8: NeuralTools predictions

	C	D	E	F	G	H
3	Sales	Price	Advertising		Tag Used	Prediction
334	432.7	5	77		predict	432.66
335	385.1	8	51		predict	385.10
336	350	10	49			350.00
337	400.4	7	54			400.37

Figure 15-9: New forecasts of sales

Using NeuralTools to Forecast Airline Miles

In Chapter 14, "Winter's Method," you used Winter's Method to forecast airline miles. You can also use neural networks to forecast U.S airline miles (in thousands) from the last 12 months of airline miles. Use the data from the workbook neuralnetsairlinemiles.xlsx to make this prediction. A subset of the data is shown in Figure 15-10.

	B	C	D	E	F	G	H	I	J	K	L	M	N	O
7	Month	Miles	Miles-1	Miles-2	Miles-3	Miles-4	Miles-5	Miles-6	Miles-7	Miles-8	Miles-9	Miles-10	Miles-11	Miles-12
8	Jan1971	7.97E+06	7.99E+06	6.66E+06	8.02E+06	7.37E+06	7.73E+06	9.18E+06	9.57E+06	1.03E+07	7.75E+06	7.44E+06	7.03E+06	8.47E+06
9	Feb1971	6.78E+06	6.66E+06	8.02E+06	7.37E+06	7.73E+06	9.18E+06	9.57E+06	1.03E+07	7.75E+06	7.44E+06	7.03E+06	8.47E+06	7.97E+06
10	Mar1971	7.71E+06	8.02E+06	7.37E+06	7.73E+06	9.18E+06	9.57E+06	1.03E+07	7.75E+06	7.44E+06	7.03E+06	8.47E+06	7.97E+06	6.78E+06
11	Apr1971	8.48E+06	7.37E+06	7.73E+06	9.18E+06	9.57E+06	1.03E+07	7.75E+06	7.44E+06	7.03E+06	8.47E+06	7.97E+06	6.78E+06	7.71E+06
12	May1971	7.89E+06	7.73E+06	9.18E+06	9.57E+06	1.03E+07	7.75E+06	7.44E+06	7.03E+06	8.47E+06	7.97E+06	6.78E+06	7.71E+06	8.48E+06
13	Jun1971	8.91E+06	9.18E+06	9.57E+06	1.03E+07	7.75E+06	7.44E+06	7.03E+06	8.47E+06	7.97E+06	6.78E+06	7.71E+06	8.48E+06	7.89E+06
14	Jul1971	9.71E+06	9.57E+06	1.03E+07	7.75E+06	7.44E+06	7.03E+06	8.47E+06	7.97E+06	6.78E+06	7.71E+06	8.48E+06	7.89E+06	8.91E+06
15	Aug1971	1.01E+07	1.03E+07	7.75E+06	7.44E+06	7.03E+06	8.47E+06	7.97E+06	6.78E+06	7.71E+06	8.48E+06	7.89E+06	8.91E+06	9.71E+06
16	Sep1971	7.85E+06	7.75E+06	7.44E+06	7.03E+06	8.47E+06	7.97E+06	6.78E+06	7.71E+06	8.48E+06	7.89E+06	8.91E+06	9.71E+06	1.01E+07
17	Oct1971	8.10E+06	7.44E+06	7.03E+06	8.47E+06	7.97E+06	6.78E+06	7.71E+06	8.48E+06	7.89E+06	8.91E+06	9.71E+06	1.01E+07	7.85E+06
18	Nov1971	7.52E+06	7.03E+06	8.47E+06	7.97E+06	6.78E+06	7.71E+06	8.48E+06	7.89E+06	8.91E+06	9.71E+06	1.01E+07	7.85E+06	8.10E+06
19	Dec1971	9.07E+06	8.47E+06	7.97E+06	6.78E+06	7.71E+06	8.48E+06	7.89E+06	8.91E+06	9.71E+06	1.01E+07	7.85E+06	8.10E+06	7.52E+06

Figure 15-10: Airline miles data

You first run a multiple linear regression to predict Column C from Columns D through O. You can see that in Column D of the `regression` worksheet this returns a MAD (Mean Absolute Deviation, which is the average of the absolute forecast errors) of 961,855. After running NeuralTools you find that the neural net yields a MAD of 497,000. To compute the MAD you simply average over all observations the absolute value of (Actual miles − Neural Network prediction). Note that the neural net has one-half the average error of the multiple regression and yields more accurate forecasts.

Whenever you are using a neural net and you find that it yields forecasts that are not much better than a multiple regression, this tells you that the multiple linear regression is just about as good as any other functional relationship, and you are justified in modeling the relationship between the dependent and independent variables as a linear relationship.

Summary

In this chapter you learned the following:

- You can use neural networks to search for a nonlinear relationship that best explains the relationship between a dependent variable and a set of independent variables.
- Neural nets have been used to forecast stock prices, sales of consumer packaged goods, and even to drive a car!
- The Palisades add-in, NeuralTools, makes it easy to fit a neural set to data.
- If the MAD for the testing set is far larger than the MAD for the training set, then the neural net is overfitting the data and should not be used for forecasting.
- If the MAD for a neural net is not much better than the MAD for a multiple linear regression, then you can be confident that the relationship between the dependent and independent variables can be accurately modeled as a linear relationship.

Exercises

1. What independent variables and dependent variables would be used to train a neural network that can drive a car? Hint: Assume the car has video cameras that can see in front of, in back of, and to the side of the car.

2. The file `windchill.xlsx` gives the wind chill index (a measure of the danger from wind and temperature) for a variety of winds and temperatures. Use a neural network to predict the wind chill index based on temperature and wind speed. How much better is the neural network at predicting wind chill than a multiple linear regression?

3. The file `movierevenue.xls` gives revenue for several movies during weeks 1 and 2 of release as well as their total revenue. Use a neural network to predict total revenue from week 1 and week 2 revenues.

4. For the neural network you found in Problem 3, predict total revenue for the following two movies:
   a. **Movie 1**: Week 1 revenue $50 million; Week 2 revenue $50 million
   b. **Movie 2**: Week 1 revenue: $80 million; Week 2 revenue $20 million

   Note that both movies made a total of $100 million during their first two weeks of release. Why is your prediction for total revenue from Movie 2 higher than your predicted revenue for Movie 1?

5. The file `Quarterly.xlsx` discussed in Chapter 14 gives quarterly revenues and quarterly profits for several U.S. companies. Use a neural network to predict next quarter's revenues based on the last eight quarters.

IV What do Customers Want?

Chapter 16: Conjoint Analysis
Chapter 17: Logistic Regression
Chapter 18: Discrete Choice Analysis

16 Conjoint Analysis

Often the marketing analyst is asked to determine the attributes of a product that are most (and least) important in driving a consumer's product choice. For example, when a soda drinker chooses between Coke and Pepsi, what is the relevant importance of the following:

- Price
- Brand (Coke or Pepsi)
- Type of soda (diet or regular)

After showing a consumer several products (called *product profiles*) and asking the consumer to rank these product profiles, the analyst can use *full profile conjoint analysis* to determine the relative importance of various attributes. This chapter shows how the basic ideas behind conjoint analysis are simply an application of multiple regression as explained in Chapter 10, "Using Multiple Regression to Forecast Sales."

After understanding how to estimate a conjoint model, you will learn to use conjoint analysis to develop a market simulator, which can determine how a product's market share can change if the product's attributes are changed or if a new product is introduced into the market.

The chapter closes with a brief discussion of two other forms of conjoint analysis: *adaptive/hybrid conjoint* and *choice-based conjoint*.

Products, Attributes, and Levels

Essentially, conjoint analysis enables the marketing analyst to determine the product characteristics that drive a consumer's preference for products. For example, in purchasing a new car what matters most: brand, price, fuel efficiency, styling, or engine power? Conjoint analysis analyzes the consumer decision process by identifying the number of product choices available; listing the main characteristics used by consumers when choosing among products; and ranking each attribute offered in each product. After learning a few definitions, you will work through a detailed illustration of conjoint analysis.

The *product set* is a set of objects from which the consumer must make a choice (choosing no product is often an option). For example, a product set might be luxury sedans, laptop computers, shampoos, sodas, and so on. Conjoint analysis is also used in fields such as human resources, so product sets don't necessarily have to be consumer goods. For example, the HR analyst might want to determine what type of compensation mix (salary, bonus, stock options, vacation days, and telecommuting) is most attractive to prospective hires.

Each product is defined by the *level* of several *product attributes*. Attributes are the variables that describe the product. The levels for each attribute are the possible values of the attributes. Table 16-1 shows four examples of levels and attributes.

Table 16-1: Examples of Product Attributes and Levels

Product	Attribute 1	Attribute 2	Attribute 3
Blood Pressure Drug	Price: Low, Medium, High	Efficacy: Reduces Systolic 5, 10, or 15 points	Side Effects: Percentage with serious side effects: 5%, 8%, and 11%
Plane Flight	Airline: USAir, Delta, United	Price: $200, $300, $400	Number of Stops: 0, 1, or 2
Compensation for Microsoft Programmer	Starting Salary: 100K, 130K, 160K	Days of Vacation: 10, 20, 30	6-Month Sabbatical after 5 Years: Yes or No
Soda	Brand: Coke or Pepsi	Calories: 0 or 150	Price: High, Medium, or Low

The purpose of conjoint analysis is to help the marketing analyst understand the relative importance of the attributes and within each attribute the ranking of the levels. For example, a customer might rank the attributes in order of importance for price, brand, and food service. The customer might rank the brands in the order of Marriott, Hilton, and Holiday Inn. The best-known application of conjoint analysis is its use to design the Courtyard Marriott Hotel chain. This study is described in Wind, Green, Shifflet, and Scarborough's journal article, "Courtyard by Marriott: Designing a Hotel Facility with Consumer-Based Marketing Models" (*Interfaces*, 1989, pp. 25–47). This study used the following product attributes:

■ External décor
■ Room décor

- Food service
- Lounge facilities
- General services
- Leisure facilities
- Security features

Other industries in which conjoint analysis has been used to ascertain how consumers value various product attributes include comparisons of the following:

- Credit card offers
- Health insurance plans
- Automobiles
- Overnight mail services (UPS versus FedEx)
- Cable TV offerings
- Gasoline (Shell versus Texaco)
- Ulcer drugs
- Blood pressure drugs
- E-ZPass automated toll paying versus toll booths

The best way to learn how to use conjoint analysis is to see it in action. The following section works through a complete example that shows how conjoint analysis can give you knowledge of customer preferences.

Full Profile Conjoint Analysis

To illustrate the use of full profile conjoint analysis, this section uses a classic example that is described in Paul Green and Yorman Wind's article "New Way to Measure Consumers' Judgments" (*Harvard Business Review*, August 1975, pp. 107–17, http:// hbr.org/1975/07/new-way-to-measure-consumers-judgments/ar/1). The goal of this conjoint study was to determine the role that five attributes play in influencing a consumer's preference for carpet cleaner. The five attributes (and their levels) deemed relevant to the consumer preference are as follows:

- Package design (either A, B, or C)
- Brand (1, 2, or 3)
- Price (either $1.19, $1.39, or $1.59)
- Did *Good Housekeeping* magazine approve product?
- Is product guaranteed?

These attributes were chosen not just because they are measurable, but because the researchers believed these attributes were likely to drive consumer product choices.

Determining the Product Profiles

In full profile conjoint analysis, the consumer is shown a set of products (called *product profiles*) and asked to rank them in order from best (#1) to worst. In the carpet cleaning situation there are a total of $3 \times 3 \times 3 \times 2 \times 2 = 108$ possible product profiles. It seems unlikely that any consumer could rank the order of 108 product combinations; therefore, the marketing analyst must show the consumer a much smaller number of combinations. Green and Wind chose to show the consumer the 18 possible combinations shown in Figure 16-1. After being shown these combinations, the consumer ranked the product profiles (refer to Figure 16-1). Here a rank of 1 indicates the most preferred product profile and a rank of 18 the least preferred product profile. For example, the consumer felt the most preferred product was Package C, Brand 3, $1.19 price, with a guarantee and Good Housekeeping Seal. This data is available in the Data worksheet of the conjoint.xls file that is available for download from the companion website.

The 18 product profiles cannot be randomly chosen. For example, if every profile with a guarantee also had *Good Housekeeping* approval, then the analyst could not determine whether the consumer preferred a profile due to a guarantee or a *Good Housekeeping* approval. Essentially, you want the attributes to be uncorrelated, so with few product profiles, a multiple regression will be less likely to be "confused" by the correlation between attributes. Such a combination of product profiles is called an *orthogonal design*. Figure 16-2 shows that the product profiles from Figure 16-1 yield an orthogonal design.

	A	B	C	D	E	F
1	Design	Brand	Price	Approved	Guarantee?	Rank
2	A	1	1.19	No	No	13
3	A	2	1.39	No	Yes	11
4	A	3	1.59	Yes	No	17
5	B	1	1.39	Yes	Yes	2
6	B	2	1.59	No	No	14
7	B	3	1.19	No	No	3
8	C	1	1.59	No	Yes	12
9	C	2	1.19	Yes	No	7
10	C	3	1.39	No	No	9
11	A	1	1.59	Yes	No	18
12	A	2	1.19	No	Yes	8
13	A	3	1.39	No	No	15
14	B	1	1.19	No	No	4
15	B	2	1.39	Yes	No	6
16	B	3	1.59	No	Yes	5
17	C	1	1.39	No	No	10
18	C	2	1.59	No	No	16
19	C	3	1.19	Yes	Yes	1

Figure 16-1: Data for conjoint example

	H	I	J	K	L	M	N	O	P	Q	R
1											
2											
3	Design	Brand	Price	Approval	Guarantee						
4	1	1	1	0	0						
5	1	2	2	1	1						
6	1	3	3	0	0						
7	2	1	2	1	1						
8	2	2	3	0	0						
9	2	3	1	0	0						
10	3	1	3	1	1						
11	3	2	1	0	0						
12	3	3	2	0	0		Design	Brand	Price	Approval	Guarantee
13	1	1	3	0	0	Design	1				
14	1	2	1	1	1	Brand	0	1			
15	1	3	2	0	0	Price	0	0	1		
16	2	1	1	0	0	Approval	0	0	0	1	
17	2	2	2	0	0	Guarantee	0	0	0	1	1
18	2	3	3	1	1						
19	3	1	2	0	0						
20	3	2	3	0	0						
21	3	3	1	1	1						

Figure 16-2: Proof design is orthogonal.

Sidney Adelman's article "Orthogonal Main-Effect Plans for Asymmetrical Factorial Experiments" (*Technometric*, 1962, Vol. 4 No. 1, pp. 36–39) is an excellent source on orthogonal designs. Table 16-2 illustrates an orthogonal design with nine product profiles and four attributes, each having three levels. For example, the first product profile sets each attribute to level 1.

Table 16-2: Example of an Orthogonal Design

Product Profile	Attribute 1	Attribute 2	Attribute 3	Attribute 4
1	1	1	1	1
2	1	2	2	3
3	1	3	3	1
4	2	1	2	2
5	2	2	3	1
6	2	3	1	3
7	3	1	3	3
8	3	2	1	2
9	3	3	2	1

Running the Regression

You can determine the relative importance of product attributes by using regression with dummy variables. You begin by rescaling the consumer's rankings so that the highest ranked product combination receives a score of 18 and the lowest ranked product combination receives a score of 1. This ensures that the larger regression coefficients for product attributes correspond to more preferred attributes. Without the rescaling, the larger regression coefficients would correspond to less preferred attributes. The analysis applies the following steps to the information in the Data worksheet:

1. Rescale the product profile rankings by subtracting 19 from the product combination's actual ranking. This yields the rescaled rankings called the *inverse rankings*.
2. Run a multiple linear regression using dummy variables to determine the effect of each product attribute on the inverse rankings.
3. This requires leaving out an arbitrarily chosen level of each attribute; for this example you can leave out Design C, Brand 3, a $1.59 price, no Good Housekeeping Seal, and no guarantee.

After rescaling the rankings a positive coefficient for a dummy variable indicates that the given level of the attribute makes the product more preferred than the omitted level of the attribute, and a negative coefficient for a dummy variable indicates that the given level of the attribute makes the product less preferred than the omitted level of the attribute. Figure 16-3 displays the coding of the data.

	A?	B?	Brand 1?	Brand 2?	1.19?	1.39?	Approved	Guarantee	Rank(1=Best)	Rank(1=worst)	Forecast
20	A?	B?	Brand 1?	Brand 2?	1.19?	1.39?	Approved	Guarantee	Rank(1=Best)	Rank(1=worst)	Forecast
21	1	0	1	0	1	0	0	0	13	6	6.5
22	1	0	0	1	0	1	0	1	11	8	7.666667
23	1	0	0	0	0	0	1	0	17	2	1.833333
24	0	1	1	0	0	1	1	1	2	17	17.66667
25	0	1	0	1	0	0	0	0	14	5	6.333333
26	0	1	0	0	1	0	0	0	3	16	16
27	0	0	1	0	0	0	0	1	12	7	7.833333
28	0	0	0	1	1	0	1	0	7	12	12
29	0	0	0	0	0	1	0	0	9	10	9.666667
30	1	0	1	0	0	0	1	0	18	1	0.333333
31	1	0	0	1	1	0	0	1	8	11	10.5
32	1	0	0	0	0	1	0	0	15	4	5.166667
33	0	1	1	0	1	0	0	0	4	15	14.5
34	0	1	0	1	0	1	1	0	6	13	12.66667
35	0	1	0	0	0	0	0	1	5	14	12.83333
36	0	0	1	0	0	1	0	0	10	9	8.166667
37	0	0	0	1	0	0	0	0	16	3	2.833333
38	0	0	0	0	1	0	1	1	1	18	18.5

Figure 16-3: Coding of conjoint data

Notice how Row 21 indicates that if you charge $1.19 for Brand 1 and Package design A with no guarantee or *Good Housekeeping* approval, the combination is rated 6th from worst (or 13th overall). If you run a regression with Y-range J21:J38 and X-range A21:H38, you can obtain the equation shown in Figure 16-4 (see the Regression worksheet).

	A	B	C	D	E	F	G
1	SUMMARY OUTPUT						
2							
3	*Regression Statistics*						
4	Multiple R	0.99153625					
5	R Square	0.983144135					
6	Adjusted R Square	0.968161144					
7	Standard Error	0.952579344					
8	Observations	18					
9							
10	ANOVA						
11		*df*	*SS*	*MS*	*F*	gnificance F	
12	Regression	8	476.3333333	59.54167	65.61735	4.49E-07	
13	Residual	9	8.166666667	0.907407			
14	Total	17	484.5				
15							
16		*Coefficients*	*Standard Error*	*t Stat*	*P-value*	Lower 95%	Upper 95%
17	Intercept	4.833333333	0.635052896	7.610915	3.29E-05	3.396743	6.269924
18	A?	-4.5	0.549971941	-8.18224	1.85E-05	-5.74412	-3.25588
19	B?	3.5	0.549971941	6.363961	0.000131	2.255876	4.744124
20	Brand 1?	-1.5	0.549971941	-2.72741	0.023323	-2.74412	-0.25588
21	Brand 2?	-2	0.549971941	-3.63655	0.00543	-3.24412	-0.75588
22	1.19?	7.666666667	0.549971941	13.94011	2.13E-07	6.422543	8.910791
23	1.39?	4.833333333	0.549971941	8.788327	1.04E-05	3.589209	6.077457
24	Approved?	1.5	0.476289672	3.149344	0.01175	0.422557	2.577443
25	Guarantee?	4.5	0.476289672	9.448032	5.73E-06	3.422557	5.577443

Figure 16-4: Conjoint regression data

All independent variables are significant at the .05 level. (All p-values are smaller than .05.) The R^2 value of 0.98 indicates that the attributes explain 98 percent of the variation in this consumer's ranking. As discussed in Chapter 10, "Using Multiple Regression to Forecast Sales," the standard error of 0.95 indicates that 95 percent of the predicted ranks would be accurate within 1.9. Thus it appears that the multiple linear regression model adequately captures how this consumer processes a product and creates a product ranking.

If the multiple linear regression model for a conjoint analysis does not produce a high R^2 and a low standard error, it is likely that one of the following must have occurred:

- You omitted some attributes that the consumer feels are important.
- The consumer's preferences are related to the current set of attributes via an interaction and nonlinear relationship. You can test for interactions or nonlinear relationships using the techniques described in Chapter 10.

The best prediction for the rescaled rank of a product is as follows:

(1) Predicted Rescaled Rank = $4.833 - 4.5A + 3.5B - 1.5(Brand\ 1) - 2(Brand\ 2) + 7.667(\$1.19\ Price) + 4.83(\$1.39\ Price) + 1.5(Approved?) + 4.5(Guarantee)$

To interpret this equation, recall from the discussion of dummy variables in Chapter 11 that all coefficients are interpreted relative to the level of the attribute that was coded with all 0s. This observation implies the following:

- Design C leads to a rank 4.5 higher than Design A and 3.5 lower than Design B.
- Brand 3 leads to a rank 1.5 higher than Brand 1 and 2 higher than Brand 2.
- A $1.19 price leads to a rank 7.67 higher than $1.59 and 2.83 higher than $1.39.
- A *Good Housekeeping* approval yields a rank 1.5 better than no approval.
- A guarantee yields a rank 4.5 higher than no guarantee.

By array entering the formula =TREND(J21:J38,A21:H38,A21:H38) in the range K21:K38, you create the predicted inverse rank for each product profile. The close agreement between Columns J and K shows how well a simple multiple linear regression explains this consumer's product profile rankings.

Ranking the Attributes and Levels

Which attributes have the most influence on the customer's likelihood to purchase the product? To rank the importance of the attributes, order the attributes based on the attributes' spread from the best level of the attribute to the worst level of the attribute. Table 16-3 displays this ranking.

Table 16-3: Product Attribute Rankings

Attribute	Spread	Ranking
Design	4.5 – (-3.5) = 8	1st
Brand	0 – (-2) = 2	4th
Price	7.67 – 0 = 7.67	2nd
Approval	1.5 – 0 = 1.5	5th
Guarantee	4.5 – 0 = 4.5	3rd

For example, you can see the package design is the most important attribute and the *Good Housekeeping* approval is the least important attribute. You can also rank the levels within each attribute. This customer ranks levels as follows:

- Design: B, C, A
- Price: $1.19, $1.39, $1.59

- Brand: Brand 3, Brand 1, Brand 2
- Guarantee: Guarantee, No Guarantee
- Approval: Approval, No Approval

Within each attribute, you can rank the levels from most preferred to least preferred. In this customer's example, Brand 3 is most preferred, Brand 1 is second most preferred, and Brand 2 is least preferred.

Using Conjoint Analysis to Segment the Market

You can also use conjoint analysis to segment the market. To do so, simply determine the regression equation described previously for 100 representative customers. Let each row of your spreadsheet be the weights each customer gives to each attribute in the regression. Thus for the customer analyzed in the preceding section, his row would be (–4.5, 3.5, -1.5, –2, 7.67, 4.83, 1.5, 4.5). Then perform a *cluster analysis* (see Chapter 23, "Cluster Analysis") to segment customers. This customer, for example, would be representative of a brand-insensitive, price-elastic decision maker who thought package design was critical.

Value-Based Pricing with Conjoint Analysis

Many companies price their products using *cost plus pricing*. For example, a cereal manufacturer may mark up the cost of producing a box of cereal by 20 percent when selling to the retailer. Cost plus pricing is prevalent for several reasons:

- It is simple to implement, even if your company sells many different products.
- Product margins are maintained at past levels, thereby reducing shareholder criticism that "margins are eroding."
- Price increases can be justified if costs increase.

Unfortunately, cost plus pricing ignores the voice of the customer. Conjoint analysis, on the other hand, can be used to determine the price that can be charged for a product feature based on the value consumers attach to that feature. For example, how much is a Pentium 4 worth versus a Pentium 2? How much can a hotel charge for high-speed wireless Internet access? The key idea is that Equation 1 enables you to impute a monetary value for each level of a product attribute. To illustrate how conjoint analysis can aid in value-based pricing, assume the preferences of all customers in the carpet cleaning example are captured by Equation 1. Suppose the carpet cleaning fluid without guarantee currently sells for $1.39. What can you charge if you add a guarantee? You can implement value-based pricing by keeping the product with a guarantee at the same value as a product without a guarantee at the current price of $1.39.

The regression implies the following:

- $1.19 has a score of 7.67.
- $1.39 has a score of 4.83.
- $1.59 has a score of 0.

Thus, increasing the product price (in the range $1.39 to $1.59) by 1 cent costs you 4.83/20 = 0.24 points.

Because a guarantee increases ranking by 4.5 points, value-based pricing says that with a guarantee you should increase price by x cents where $0.24x = 4.5$ or $x = 4.5/0.24 = 19$ cents.

You should check that if the product price is increased by 19 cents (to $1.58) and the product is guaranteed, the customer will be as happy as she was before. This shows that you have priced the guarantee according to the customer's imputed value. Although this approach to value-based pricing is widely used, it does not ensure profit maximization. When you study discrete choice in Chapter 18, "Discrete Choice Analysis," you will see how choice-based conjoint analysis can be used to incorporate consumer preferences into profit maximization. Of course, this analysis assumes that for a price between $1.39 and $1.59 the effect of price on product ranking is a linear function of price. If this is not the case then $Price^2$ should have been added to the regression as an independent variable. This would allow the regression to capture the nonlinear effect of price on the consumer's product rankings.

Using Evolutionary Solver to Generate Product Profiles

The leading statistical packages (SAS and SPSS) enable a user to input a desired number of product profiles, the number of attributes, and the number of levels, and output (if one exists) an orthogonal design. In many situations the user must exclude product profiles that are unreasonable. For example, in analyzing an automobile it is unreasonable to set the car's size to a Mini Cooper and assume the car can carry six passengers. This section shows how to use the Excel 2010 or 2013 Evolutionary Solver to easily design something that is close to being orthogonal but that excludes unreasonable product profiles. The work here is based on Steckel, DeSarbo, and Mahajan's study "On the Creation of Acceptable Conjoint Analysis Experimental Designs" (*Decision Sciences*, 1991, pp. 436–42, `http://goo.gl/2P00J`) and can be found in the `evconjoint.xlsx` file. If desired, the reader may omit this advanced section without loss of continuity.

Assume that you want to use a conjoint analysis to evaluate how consumers value the following attributes for a new car:

- Miles per gallon (MPG): 20 or 40
- Maximum speed in miles per hour (MPH): 100 or 150
- Length: 12 feet or 14 feet
- Price: $25,000 or $40,000
- Passenger capacity: 4, 5, or 6

Now suppose the analyst wants to create 12 product profiles and exclude the following types of product profiles as infeasible:

- 40 MPG, 6 passengers, 14-foot car
- 14-foot car, 150 MPH, and $20,000 price
- 40 MPG and 150 MPH

You can now see how to design 12 product profiles that include each level of an attribute an equal number of times, which are close to orthogonal and exclude infeasible product profiles.

1. To begin, list in B3:G28 each attribute and level the number of times you want the combination to occur in the profiles. For example, Figure 16-5 lists 20 MPG six times and four passengers four times.

2. Give a range name to each listing of attribute values. For the example file the range D16:E28 is named `lookpassengers`.

3. The key to the model is to determine in cells K5:O16 how to "scramble" (as shown in Figure 16-6) for each attribute the integers 1 through 12 to select for each product profile the level for each attribute.

   For example, the 7 in K5 in `evconjoint.xlsx` (to be selected by Solver) means "look up the attribute level for MPG in the 7th row of B4:C15." This yields 40 MPG in Q5. The formulas in Q5:U16 use a little known Excel function: the `INDIRECT` function. With this function a cell reference in an Excel formula after the word `INDIRECT` tells Excel to replace the cell reference with the contents of the cell. (If the contents of the cell are a range name, Excel knows to use the named range in the formula.) Therefore, copying the formula =VLOOKUP(K5,INDIRECT(Q$2),2, FALSE) from Q5:U16 translates the values 1–12 in K5:O16 into actual values of the attributes.

	B	C	D	E	F	G
3		MPG		MPH		Length
4	1	20	1	100	1	12
5	2	20	2	100	2	12
6	3	20	3	100	3	12
7	4	20	4	100	4	12
8	5	20	5	100	5	12
9	6	20	6	100	6	12
10	7	40	7	150	7	14
11	8	40	8	150	8	14
12	9	40	9	150	9	14
13	10	40	10	150	10	14
14	11	40	11	150	11	14
15	12	40	12	150	12	14
16		Price		Passengers		
17	1	25	1	4		
18	2	25	2	4		
19	3	25	3	4		
20	4	25	4	4		
21	5	25	5	5		
22	6	25	6	5		
23	7	30	7	5		
24	8	30	8	5		
25	9	30	9	6		
26	10	30	10	6		
27	11	30	11	6		
28	12	30	12	6		

Figure 16-5: Listing attribute-level combinations

	K	L	M	N	O	P	Q	R	S	T	U
3	Coded						Actual				
4	MPG	MPH	Length	Price	Passengers		MPG	MPH	Length	Price	Passenger
5	7	1	8	4	6		40	100	14	25	5
6	2	10	9	12	9		20	150	14	30	6
7	1	12	2	10	7		20	150	12	30	5
8	3	7	4	5	2		20	150	12	25	4
9	9	3	11	1	1		40	100	14	25	4
10	5	11	10	2	11		20	150	14	25	6
11	6	9	7	7	3		20	150	14	30	4
12	10	5	6	11	4		40	100	12	30	4
13	4	8	3	6	5		20	150	12	25	5
14	12	6	12	8	8		40	100	14	30	5
15	8	2	1	3	12		40	100	12	25	6
16	11	4	5	9	10		40	100	12	30	6

Figure 16-6: Selecting attribute levels

4. Next, in the cell range V5:W16 (see Figure 16-7), you can determine if a product profile represents an infeasible combination. Copy the formula =COUNTIFS(Q5,40,U5,6,S5,14) from V5 to V6:V16. This determines if the product profile is infeasible due to getting 40 MPG in a six-passenger 14-foot car. In a similar fashion Columns W and X yield a 1 if a product profile is infeasible for being either 14-foot, 150 MPH, and $20,000 price or 40 MPG with 150 MPH.

	Q	R	S	T	U	V	W	X
3	Actual					Excluded	Excluded	Excluded
						40 MPG 6	14 ft 150	40 MPG
4	MPG	MPH	Length	Price	Passenger	PASS 14 FT	MPH $20	150 MPH
5	40	100	14	25	5	0	0	0
6	20	150	14	30	6	0	0	0
7	20	150	12	30	5	0	0	0
8	20	150	12	25	4	0	0	0
9	40	100	14	25	4	0	0	0
10	20	150	14	25	6	0	0	0
11	20	150	14	30	4	0	0	0
12	40	100	12	30	4	0	0	0
13	20	150	12	25	5	0	0	0
14	40	100	14	30	5	0	0	0
15	40	100	12	25	6	0	0	0
16	40	100	12	30	6	0	0	0

Figure 16-7: Excluding infeasible product profiles

5. Determine the correlations between each pair of attributes. A slick use of the INDIRECT function makes this easy: apply Create from Selection to the range Q4:U16 names Q5:Q16 MPG, R5:R16 MPH, and so on. Then, as shown in Figure 16-8, compute the absolute value of the correlation between each pair of attributes by copying the formula =ABS(CORREL(INDIRECT(O$19),INDIRECT($N20))) from O20 to O20:S24.

	L	M	N	O	P	Q	R	S	T
19				MPG	MPH	Length	Price	Passengers	
20			MPG	1	1	0	0	0	
21			MPH	1	1	0	0	0	
22			Length	0	0	1	0	0	
23			Price	0	0	0	1	0	
24			Passengers	0	0	0	0	1	
25									
26		avgcorr	penalties	target					
27		0.1	0	0.1					

Figure 16-8: Correlations and target cell

6. Now set up a target cell for Solver to minimize the sum of the average of the nondiagonal correlations (all diagonal correlations are 1) added to the number of infeasible product profiles. In cell M27 the formula =(SUM(O20:S24)-5)/20 calculates the average absolute value of the nondiagonal correlations. The target cell tries to minimize this average. This minimization moves you closer to an orthogonal design. Then determine the number of infeasible product profiles used in cell N27 with the formula =SUM(V5:X16). The final target cell is computed in cell O27 with the formula =N27+M27.

7. Finally, you are ready to invoke Solver! Figure 16-9 shows the Solver window. Simply change K5:O16 and invoke the AllDifferent option for each column. This ensures that columns K through O will contain the integers 1–12 once. In general, if you constrain a range of *n* cells to be AllDifferent, Excel ensures that these cells always assume the integer values 1, 2, ..., *n* and each value will be used once. From the way you set up the formulas in Columns Q through U, this ensures that each level of all attributes appear the wanted number of times. After going to Evolutionary Solver options and resetting the Mutation rate to .5, you obtain the solution shown in Figures 16-7 and 16-8. Note that no infeasible product profiles occur, and all correlations except for MPH and MPG are 0. MPH and MPG have a correlation of –1 because the infeasible profiles force a low MPG to be associated with a large MPH, and vice versa.

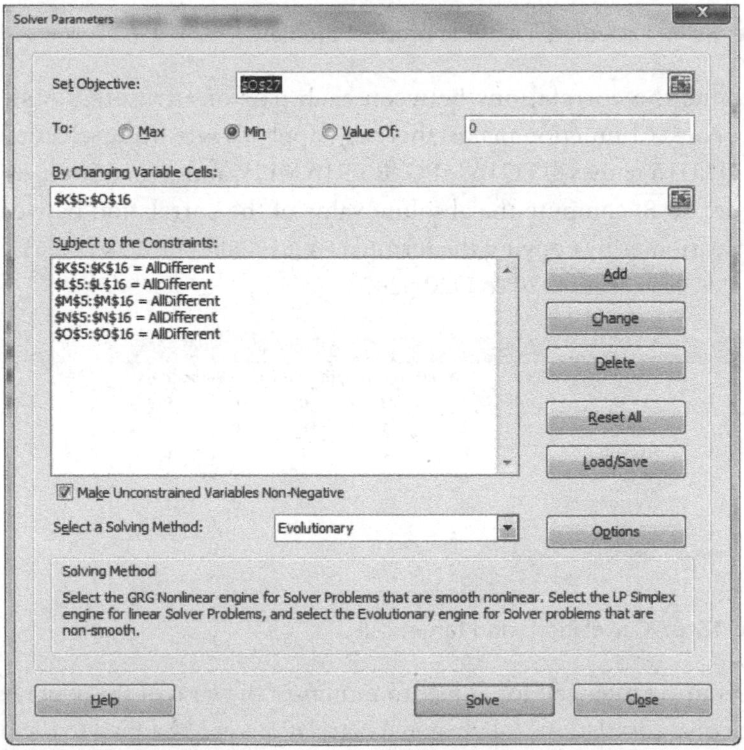

Figure 16-9: Solver window for selecting product profiles

Developing a Conjoint Simulator

Conjoint analysis is often used to predict how the introduction of a new product (or changes in existing products) result in changes in product market share. These insights require the marketing analyst to develop a *conjoint simulator* that predicts how changes in product attributes change market share. This section illustrates how to calibrate a conjoint simulator to current share data and how to make predictions about how changes in products or the introduction of a new product can change market share. The work for this section is in the Segments worksheet of the conjoint.xls file and is shown in Figure 16-10.

	A	B	C	D	E	F	G	H	I	J	K	L	M	N	O	P	Q	R
1	Current share			A	B	Brand	Brand?	1.19?	1.39?	Approved?	Guarantee	Alpha	2.07561					SSE
2		0.3 Our brand		1	0	1	0	1	0	0	0			Squared Error	0.00193	0.00035	0.00063	0.00291
3		0.5 Comp 1		0	1	0	1	0	1	1	0			Actual Share	0.3	0.5	0.2	
4		0.2 Comp 2		0	0	0	0	0	0	0	1			Predicted Share	0.3439	0.48124	0.17486	

	Segment	Size(000)	Intercept	A	B	Brand	Brand?	1.19?	1.39?	Approved?	Guarantee	Our Brand Score	Comp 1 score	Comp 2 Score	Our share	Comp 1 share	Comp 2 Share
6	1	10	4.83	-4.5	3.5	-1.5	-2	7.7	4.83	1.5	4.5	6.5	12.66	9.33	0.14071	0.56136	0.29793
7	2	15	2	-6	5	1	2	9	6	2	3	6	17	5	0.09643	0.83753	0.06605
8	3	20	5	-2	2	-4	-6	8	5	3	6	7	9	10	0.20914	0.35236	0.43849
9	4	12	2	4	1	4	2	7	4	1	4	17	10	6	0.69082	0.22964	0.07954
10	5	22	4.7	1	4	3	2	6	4	2	2	14.7	16.7	6.7	0.40018	0.52148	0.07834
11	6	14	9	-6	-4	2	1	5	3	2	3	10	11	12	0.27183	0.3313	0.39687
12	7	10	8	1	3	0	-2	4	3	1	2	13	13	10	0.38758	0.38758	0.22483
13	8	15	2	4	-3	5	-3	9	7	2	1	20	5	3	0.92956	0.05232	0.01812
14	9	8	2	-2	4	2	6	7	4	3	4	9	18	6	0.17711	0.74655	0.07634
15	10	12	7	-4	-2	1	3	6	4	2	2	10	14	9	0.26219	0.52713	0.21069
16	11	9	2	1	2	2	4	8	5	4	3	13	17	5	0.34689	0.60537	0.04774
17	12	11	4.4	-6	5	-4	-2	6	4	5	2	0.4	16.4	6.4	0.00039	0.87544	0.12416
18	13	8	7	-4	3	-1	3	4	3	2	3	6	18	10	0.07317	0.71557	0.21126
19	14	14	2	2	2	2	-1	8	5	3	4	14	11	6	0.56228	0.34085	0.09687

Figure 16-10: Conjoint simulator

Suppose you're using cluster analysis (as shown in Chapter 23) and through a conjoint analysis the analyst has identified 14 market segments for a carpet cleaner. The regression equation for a typical member of each segment is given in the cell range D6:K19 and the size of each segment (in thousands) is the cell range B6:B19. For example, Segment 1 consists of 10,000 people and has Equation 1 as representative of consumer preferences for Segment 1. The range D2:K4 describes the product profile associated with the three products currently in the market. The brand currently has a 30 percent market share, Comp 1 has a 50 percent market share, and Comp 2 has a 20 percent market share.

To create a market simulator, you need to take the score that each segment associates with each product and translate these scores for each segment to a market share for each product. You can then calibrate this rule, so each product gets the observed market share. Finally, you can change attributes of the current products or introduce new products and "simulate" the new market shares for each product.

Consider Segment 1. Given that there are *n* products, you can assume the fraction of people in Segment 1 that will purchase Product *i* is given by the following:

$$\frac{(Product\ i\ Score\ for\ Segment\ 1)^{\alpha}}{\sum_{K=n}^{K=n}(Product\ \kappa\ Score\ for\ Segment\ 1)^{\alpha}}$$

When you choose the value of α, ensure that the predicted market share over all segments for each product matches as closely as possible the observed market share. To complete this process proceed as follows:

1. Copy the formula =SUMPRODUCT($D$2:$K$2,D6:K6)+C6 from L6 to L7:L19 to compute each segment's score for the product. Similar formulas in Columns M and N compute each segment's score for Comp 1 and Comp 2.
2. Copy the formula =L6^Alpha/($L6^Alpha+$M6^Alpha+$N6^Alpha) from O6 to the range O6:Q19 to compute for each segment the predicted market share for each product.
3. Copy the formula =SUMPRODUCT(O6:O19,$B$6:$B$19)/SUM($B$6:$B$19) from O4 to P4:Q4 to compute the predicted market share for each product by accounting for the size of each segment.
4. Copy the formula =(O4-O3)^2 from O2 to P2:Q2 to compute (based on the trial value of α) the squared error in trying to match the actual market share for each product.
5. Use the Solver window, as shown in Figure 16-11, to yield the value of α (2.08) that "calibrates" the simulator to actual market share data.

Suppose you consider adding (with no price increase) a guarantee and believe you can obtain *Good Housekeeping* approval. In the worksheet GuaranteeApp you can change J2 and K2 to 1, and see that the conjoint simulator predicts that the market share will increase from 34 percent to 52 percent.

As an illustration of the use of a conjoint simulator, consider the problem of estimating the fraction of motorists who would use E-ZPass (an electronic method to collect tolls). Before New York and New Jersey implemented E-ZPass a conjoint simulator was used to choose the levels of the following attributes:

- Lanes available
- Method used to acquire E-ZPass
- Toll prices
- Other uses of E-ZPass

The conjoint simulator predicted that 49 percent of motorists would use E-ZPass. In reality, after seven years 44 percent of all motorists used E-ZPass.

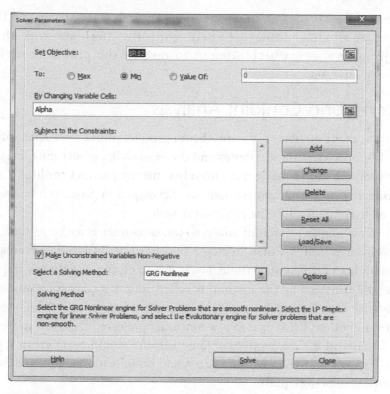

Figure 16-11: Solver window to calibrate conjoint simulator

Examining Other Forms of Conjoint Analysis

The approach to conjoint analysis thus far in this chapter involves using a set of a few (in the chapter example, five) product attributes to generate product profiles (in the chapter example, 18) which are ranked by a group of customers. Then multiple regression is used to rank the importance of the product attributes and rank the levels of each attribute. This approach to conjoint analysis is called *full profile conjoint*. The two shortcomings of full profile conjoint are as follows:

- Full profile conjoint has difficulty dealing with many attributes because the number of profiles that must be ranked grows rapidly with the number of attributes.
- Consumers have difficulty ranking product profiles. Rather than having a consumer rank product profiles, it is much easier for a consumer to choose the best available option.

This section provides a brief description of two alternate forms of conjoint analysis: adaptive/hybrid conjoint analysis and choice-based conjoint analysis, which attempt to resolve the problems with full profile conjoint analysis.

Adaptive/Hybrid Conjoint Analysis

If a product has many attributes, the number of product profiles needed to analyze the relative importance of the attributes and the desirability of attribute levels may be so large that consumers cannot accurately rank the product profiles. In such situations *adaptive* or *hybrid conjoint analysis* (developed by Sawtooth Software in 1985) may be used to simplify the consumer's task.

In step 1 of an adaptive conjoint analysis, the consumer is asked to rank order attribute levels from best to worst. In step 2 the consumer is asked to evaluate the relative desirability of different attribute levels. Based on the consumer's responses in steps 1 and 2 (this is why the method is called adaptive conjoint analysis), the consumer is asked to rate on a 1–9 scale the strength of his preference for one product profile over another. If, for example, a consumer preferred Design A to Design B and Brand 1 to Brand 2, the adaptive conjoint software would never create a paired comparison between a product with Design A and Brand 1 to Design B and Brand 2 (all other attributes being equal).

Choice-Based Conjoint Analysis

In *choice-based conjoint analysis*, the consumer is shown several product profiles and is not asked to rank them but simply to state which profile (or none of the available choices) she would choose. This makes the consumer's task easier, but an understanding of choice-based conjoint analysis requires much more mathematical sophistication then ordinary conjoint analysis. Also, choice-based conjoint analysis cannot handle situations in which attributes such as price or miles per gallon for a car are allowed to assume a range of values. In Chapter 18 you will learn about the theory of *discrete choice*, which is mathematically more difficult than multiple linear regression. Discrete choice generalizes choice-based conjoint analysis by allowing product attributes to assume a range of values.

Summary

In this chapter you learned the following:

- Conjoint analysis is used to determine the importance of various product attributes and which levels of the attributes are preferred by the customer.
- In full profile conjoint analysis, the consumer is asked to rank a variety of product profiles.
- To make the estimates of each attribute's importance and level preferences more accurate, it is usually preferable to make the correlation between any pair of attributes in the product profiles close to 0.
- Multiple linear regression (often using dummy variables) can easily be used to rank the importance of attributes and the ranking of levels within each attribute.
- A conjoint simulator can predict how changes in existing products (or introduction of new products) will change product market shares.
- Adaptive/hybrid conjoint analysis is often used when there are many product attributes. After having the consumer answer questions involving ranking attributes and levels, the software adapts to the consumer's preferences before asking the consumer to make paired comparisons between product profiles.
- Choice-based conjoint analysis ascertains the importance of attributes and the ranking of levels within each attribute by asking the consumer to simply choose the best of several product profiles choices (usually including an option to choose none of the available product profiles.) The extension of choice-based conjoint analysis to a situation where an attribute such as price is continuous is known as discrete choice and will be covered in Chapter 18.

Exercises

1. Determine how various attributes impact the purchase of a car. There are four attributes, each with three levels:

- Brand: Ford = 0, Chrysler = 1, GM = 2
- MPG: 15 MPG = 0, 20 MPG = 1, 25 MPG = 2
- Horsepower (HP): 100 HP = 0, 150 HP = 1, 200 HP = 2
- Price: $18,000 = 0, $21,000 = 1, $24,000 = 2

The nine product profiles ranked in Figure 16-12 were evaluated by a consumer.

	A	B	C	D	E	F
1		(F,C,GM)	(15,20,25)	(100,150,200)	(18000,21000,24000)	
2	Trial	Brand	MPG	Power	Price	Rank
3	1	0	0	0	0	4
4	2	0	1	1	2	7
5	3	0	2	2	1	3
6	4	1	0	1	1	6
7	5	1	1	2	0	2
8	6	1	2	0	2	9
9	7	2	0	2	2	8
10	8	2	1	0	1	5
11	9	2	2	1	0	1

Figure 16-12: Auto data for Exercise 1

a. For this market segment, rank the product attributes from most important to least important.

b. Consider a car currently getting 20 MPG selling for $21,000. If you could increase MPG by 1 mile, how much could you increase the price of the car and keep the car just as attractive to this market segment?

c. Is this design orthogonal?

NOTE When you run the regression in Excel, you can obtain a #NUM error for the p-values. You still may use the Coefficients Column to answer the exercise.

2. The soda.xlsx file (see Figure 16-13) gives a consumer's ranking on an orthogonal design with 12 product profiles involving a comparison of Coke and Pepsi. The attributes and levels are as follows:

- Brand: Coke or Pepsi
- Packaging: 12 oz. can or 16 oz. bottle
- Price per ounce: 8 cents, 10 cents, 12 cents
- Calories per ounce: 0 or 15

Determine the ranking of the attributes' importance and the ranking of all attribute levels.

Profile	Brand	Packaging	per oz Calories	per oz Price	Rank
1	coke	can	0	8	4
2	coke	bottle	0	8	2
3	pepsi	can	15	8	6
4	pepsi	bottle	15	8	5
5	coke	can	15	10	11
6	coke	bottle	15	10	9
7	pepsi	can	0	10	3
8	pepsi	bottle	0	10	1
9	coke	can	15	12	12
10	coke	bottle	0	12	8
11	pepsi	can	0	12	7
12	pepsi	bottle	15	12	10

Figure 16-13: Soda data for Exercise 2

3. Show that the list of product profiles in the following table yields an orthogonal design.

Product Profile	Attribute 1	Attribute 2	Attribute 3	Attribute 4
1	1	1	1	1
2	1	2	2	3
3	1	3	3	2
4	2	1	2	2
5	2	2	3	1
6	2	3	1	3
7	3	1	3	3
8	3	2	1	2
9	3	3	2	1

17

Logistic Regression

Many marketing problems and decisions deal with understanding or estimating the probability associated with certain events or behaviors, and frequently these events or behaviors tend to be dichotomous—that is, of one type or of another type. When this is the case, the marketing analyst must predict a binary dependent variable (one that assumes the value 0 or 1, representing the inherent dichotomy) from a set of independent variables. Some examples follow:

- Predicting from demographic behavior whether a person will (dependent variable = 1) or will not (dependent variable = 0) subscribe to a magazine or use a product.

- Predicting whether a person will (dependent variable = 1) or will not (dependent variable = 0) respond to a direct mail campaign. Often the independent variables used are recency (time since last purchase), frequency (how many orders placed in last year), and monetary value (total amount purchased in last year.

- Predicting whether a cell phone customer will "churn" (dependent variable = 1) by end of year and switch to another carrier. The dependent variable = 0 if you retain the customer. You will see in Chapters 19, "Calculating Lifetime Customer Value," and 20, "Using Customer Value to Value a Business," that a reduction in churn can greatly increase the value of a customer to the company.

In this chapter you learn how to use the widely used tool of *logistic regression* to predict a binary dependent variable. You learn the following:

- Why multiple linear regression is not equal to the task of predicting a binary dependent variable
- How the Excel Solver may be used to implement the technique of maximum likelihood to estimate a logistic regression model

- How to interpret the coefficients in a logistic regression model
- How Palisade's StatTools program can easily be used to estimate a logistic regression model and test hypotheses about the individual coefficients

Why Logistic Regression Is Necessary

To explain why you need logistic regression, suppose you want to predict the chance (based on the person's age) that a person will subscribe to a magazine. The linear regression worksheet in the subscribers.xlsx file provides the age and subscription status (1 = subscriber, 0 = nonsubscriber) for 41 people. Figure 17-1 displays a subset of this data.

	D	E
6	Age	Subscribe
7	20	0
8	23	0
9	24	0
10	25	0
11	25	1
12	26	0
13	26	0
14	28	0
15	28	0
16	29	0
17	30	0
18	30	0
19	30	0
20	30	0
21	30	0
22	30	1
23	32	0
24	32	0
25	33	0
26	33	0
27	34	0
28	34	0
29	34	1
30	34	0
31	34	0

Figure 17-1: Age and subscriber status

Using this data, you can run a linear regression to predict a subscriber's status from the subscriber's age. The Y-range is E6:E47 and the X-range is E6:E47. Check the residual box because you will soon see that the residuals indicate two of the key assumptions (from Chapter 10, "Using Multiple Regression to Forecast Sales") of regression are violated. Figure 17-2 and Figure 17-3 show the results of running this regression.

	H	I	J	K	L	M	N
6							
7							
8							
9	SUMMARY OUTPUT						
10							
11	*Regression Statistics*						
12	Multiple R	0.413481783					
13	R Square	0.170967185					
14	Adjusted R Square	0.149709934					
15	Standard Error	0.400905926					
16	Observations	41					
17							
18	ANOVA						
19		*df*	*SS*	*MS*	*F*	*gnificance F*	
20	Regression	1	1.292678718	1.292678718	8.04277	0.007207	
21	Residual	39	6.268296892	0.160725561			
22	Total	40	7.56097561				
23							
24		*Coefficients*	*Standard Error*	*t Stat*	*P-value*	*Lower 95%*	*Upper 95%*
25	Intercept	-0.543019266	0.284454263	-1.908986215	0.063642	-1.11838	0.032344
26	Age	0.023194673	0.008178722	2.83597778	0.007207	0.006652	0.039738

Figure 17-2: Flawed linear regression

	H	I	J	K
32	*Observation*	*Predicted Subscribe?*	*Residuals*	*abs(Residuals)*
33	1	-0.07912581	0.07912581	0.07912581
34	2	-0.009541791	0.009541791	0.009541791
35	3	0.013652882	-0.013652882	0.013652882
36	4	0.036847555	-0.036847555	0.036847555
37	5	0.036847555	0.963152445	0.963152445
38	6	0.060042228	-0.060042228	0.060042228
39	7	0.060042228	-0.060042228	0.060042228
40	8	0.106431573	-0.106431573	0.106431573
41	9	0.106431573	-0.106431573	0.106431573
42	10	0.129626246	-0.129626246	0.129626246
43	11	0.152820919	-0.152820919	0.152820919
44	12	0.152820919	-0.152820919	0.152820919
45	13	0.152820919	-0.152820919	0.152820919
46	14	0.152820919	-0.152820919	0.152820919
47	15	0.152820919	-0.152820919	0.152820919
48	16	0.152820919	0.847179081	0.847179081
49	17	0.199210265	-0.199210265	0.199210265
50	18	0.199210265	-0.199210265	0.199210265
51	19	0.222404937	-0.222404937	0.222404937
52	20	0.222404937	-0.222404937	0.222404937
53	21	0.24559961	-0.24559961	0.24559961

Figure 17-3: Residuals for flawed regression

From Figure 17-2 you can find the following equation:

(Predicted subscriber status) = -0.543 + .0231 * Age

Using the Residuals column shown in Figure 17-3, you can see three problems with this equation.

■ Some observations predicted a negative subscriber status. Because the subscriber status must be 0 or 1, this is worrisome. Particularly, if you want to predict the probability that a person is a subscriber, a negative probability does not make sense.

■ Recall from Chapter 10 that the residuals should indicate that the error term in a regression should be normally distributed. Figure 17-4, however, shows a histogram of the residuals in which this is not the case.

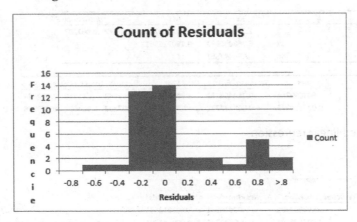

Figure 17-4: Histogram of residuals

■ Figure 17-5 gives the standard deviation of the residuals as a function of the predicted value of the subscriber variable. The spread of the residuals is not independent of the predicted value of the dependent variable. This implies that the assumption of homoscedasticity is violated. It can be shown that the variance of the error term in predicting a binary dependent variable is largest when the probability of the dependent variable being 1 (or 0) is near .5 and decreases as this probability moves away from .5.

	P	Q	R
41	Prediction	Sigma Residuals	
42	<.13	0.32544	
43	.13-.25	0.325747	
44	.26-.31	0.419726	
45	.31-.74	0.507828	

Figure 17-5: Residual spread as function of predicted dependent variable

The Logistic Regression Model, described in the following section, resolves these three problems.

Logistic Regression Model

Let p = probability and a binary dependent variable = 1. In virtually all situations it appears that the relationship between p and the independent variable(s) is nonlinear. Analysts have often found that the relationship in Equation 1 does a good job of explaining the dependence of a binary-dependent variable on an independent variable.

$$(1)\ Ln\ \frac{p}{1-p} = \beta_0 + \beta_1 x_1 + \beta_2 x_2 + \ldots \beta_n x_n$$

The transformation of the dependent variable described by Equation 1 is often called the *logit transformation*.

In this magazine example, Equation 1 takes on the following form:

$$(2)\ Ln\ \frac{p}{1-p} = Intercept + Slope * Age$$

In Equation 2, $Ln\ \frac{p}{1-p}$ is referred to as the *log odds ratio*, because $\frac{p}{1-p}$ (the *odds ratio*) is the ratio of the probability of success (dependent variable = 1) to the probability of failure (dependent variable = 0.)

If you take e to both sides of Equation 2 and use the fact that $e^{Ln\ x} = x$, you can rewrite Equation 2 as one of the following:

$$(3)\ p = \frac{1}{1 + e^{-\ (Intercept + Slope * Age)}}$$

or

$$(4)\ p = \frac{e^{(Intercept + Slope * Age)}}{1 + e^{-\ (Intercept + Slope * Age)}}$$

Equation 3 is often referred to as the *logistic regression model* (or sometimes the *logit regression model*) because the function $y = \frac{1}{1 + e^{-x}}$ is known as the logistic function. Note that $0 < p < 1$. Because p is a probability, this is desirable. In the next section you find the best estimate of slope and intercept to be slope = 0.1281 and intercept = 5.662. Substituting these values into Equation 3 shows that as a function of age, a person's chance of being a subscriber varies according to the S-curve, as shown in Figure 17-6. Note that this relationship is highly nonlinear.

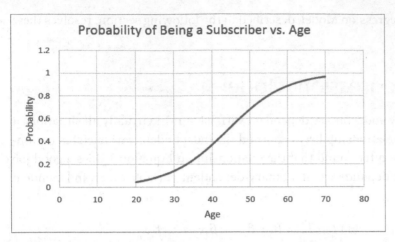

Figure 17-6: S-curve for Being a Subscriber versus Age relationship

Maximum Likelihood Estimate of Logistic Regression Model

This section demonstrates how to use the maximum likelihood method to estimate the coefficients in a logistic regression model. Essentially, in the magazine example, the maximum likelihood estimation chooses the slope and intercept to maximize, given the age of each person, the probability or likelihood of the observed pattern of subscribers and nonsubscribers. For each observation in which the person was a subscriber, the probability that the person was a subscriber is given by Equation 4, and for each observation in which the person is not a subscriber, the probability that the person is not a subscriber is given by 1 – (right side of Equation 4). If you choose slope and intercept to maximize the product of these probabilities, then you are "maximizing the likelihood" of what you have observed. Unfortunately, the product of these probabilities proves to be a small number, so it is convenient to maximize the natural logarithm of this product. The following equation makes it easy to maximize the log likelihood.

$$(5)\ Ln\ (p_1 {}^* p_2 {}^* \dots p_n) = Ln\ p_1 + Ln\ p_2 + \dots Ln\ p_n$$

The work for this equation is shown in Figure 17-7 and is located in the `data` worksheet.

	C	D	E	F	G	H	I	J
1	intercept	-5.661581					product	
2	slope	0.128134					3.85064E-09	-19.3750
3	Person#	Age	Subscribe?	Score	Prob	1-Prob	Likelihood	Ln Likelihood
4	1	20	0	-3.0989	0.043	0.95685	0.9568	-0.0441
5	2	23	0	-2.7145	0.062	0.93788	0.9379	-0.0641
6	3	24	0	-2.58637	0.07	0.92998	0.9300	-0.0726
7	4	25	0	-2.45824	0.079	0.92116	0.9212	-0.0821
8	5	25	1	-2.45824	0.079	0.92116	0.0788	-2.5404
9	6	26	0	-2.3301	0.089	0.91134	0.9113	-0.0928
10	7	26	0	-2.3301	0.089	0.91134	0.9113	-0.0928
11	8	28	0	-2.07383	0.112	0.88833	0.8883	-0.1184
12	9	28	0	-2.07383	0.112	0.88833	0.8883	-0.1184
13	10	29	0	-1.9457	0.125	0.87498	0.8750	-0.1336
14	11	30	0	-1.81757	0.14	0.86027	0.8603	-0.1505
15	12	30	0	-1.81757	0.14	0.86027	0.8603	-0.1505
16	13	30	0	-1.81757	0.14	0.86027	0.8603	-0.1505
17	14	30	0	-1.81757	0.14	0.86027	0.8603	-0.1505
18	15	30	0	-1.81757	0.14	0.86027	0.8603	-0.1505
19	16	30	1	-1.81757	0.14	0.86027	0.1397	-1.9681
20	17	32	0	-1.5613	0.173	0.82654	0.8265	-0.1905

Figure 17-7: Maximum likelihood estimation

To perform the maximum likelihood estimation of the slope and intercept for the subscriber example, proceed as follows:

1. Enter trial values of the intercept and slope in D1:D2, and name D1:D2 using Create from Selection.

2. Copy the formula =intercept+slope*D4 from F4 to F5:F44, to create a "score" for each observation.

3. Copy the formula =EXP(F4)/(1+EXP(F4)) from G4 to G5:G44 to use Equation 4 to compute for each observation the estimated probability that the person is a subscriber.

4. Copy the formula =1-G4 from H4 to H5:H44 to compute the probability of the person not being a subscriber.

5. Copy the formula =IF(E4=1,G4,1-G4) from I4 to I5:I44 to compute the likelihood of each observation.

6. In I2 the formula =PRODUCT(I5:I44) computes the likelihood of the observed subscriber and nonsubscriber data. Note that this likelihood is a small number.

7. Copy the formula =LN(I4) from J4 to J5:J44, to compute the logarithm of each observation's probability.

8. Use Equation 5 in cell J2 to compute the Log Likelihood with the formula =SUM(J4:J44).

9. Use the Solver window (in Figure 17-8), to determine the slope and intercept that maximize the Log Likelihood.

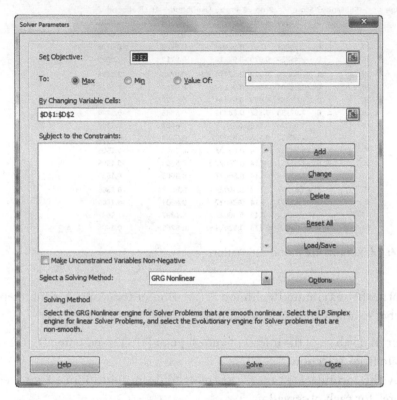

Figure 17-8: Maximum Likelihood Solver window

10. Press Solve and you find the maximum likelihood estimates of slope = -5.661 and Intercept = 0.1281.

Using a Logistic Regression to Estimate Probabilities

You can use logistic regression with Equation 4 to predict the chance that a person will be a subscriber based on her age. For example, you can predict the chance that a 44-year-old is a subscriber with the following equation:

$$\frac{e(-5.661 + 44 * 1281)}{1 + e^{-((-5.6661 + 44 * .1281))}} = .494$$

Since e raised to any power is a positive number, you can see that unlike ordinary least squares regression, logistic regression can never give a negative number for a probability. In Exercise 7 you will show that logistic regression also resolves the problems of heteroscedasticity and non-normal residuals.

Interpreting Logistic Regression Coefficients

In a multiple linear regression, you know how to interpret the coefficient of an independent variable: If βi is the coefficient of an independent variable x_i, then a unit increase in the independent variable can increase the dependent variable by βi. In a logistic regression, the interpretation of the coefficient of an independent variable is much more complex: Suppose in a logistic regression βi is the coefficient of an independent variable x_i. It can be shown (see Exercise 6) that a unit increase in x_i increases the odds ratio $(\frac{Probability\ Y=1}{Probability\ Y=0})$ by $e^{\beta i}$ percent. In the magazine example, this means that for any age a one-year increase in age increases the odds ratio by $e^{.1281} = 13.7$ percent.

Using StatTools to Estimate and Test Logistic Regression Hypotheses

Chapter 10 explains how easy it is to use the Excel Analysis ToolPak to estimate a multiple linear regression and test relevant statistical hypotheses. The last section showed that it is relatively easy to use the Excel Solver to estimate the coefficients of a logistic regression model. Unfortunately, it is difficult to use "garden variety" Excel to test logistic regression statistical hypotheses. This section shows how to use Palisade's add-in StatTools (a 15-day trial version is downloadable from Palisade .com) to estimate a logistic regression model and test hypotheses of interest. You can also use full-blown statistical packages such as SAS or SPSS to test logistic regression statistical hypotheses. The work for this section is in the data worksheet of the subscribers.xlsx workbook.

Running the Logistic Regression with StatTools

To start StatTools simply click it on the desktop or start it from the All Programs menu. After bringing up StatTools, proceed as follows:

1. Choose Data Set Manager from the StatTools Toolbar, and select the data range (D3:E44), as shown in Figure 17-9.
2. From the Regression and Classification menu, select Logistic Regression..., and fill in the dialog box, as shown in Figure 17-10.

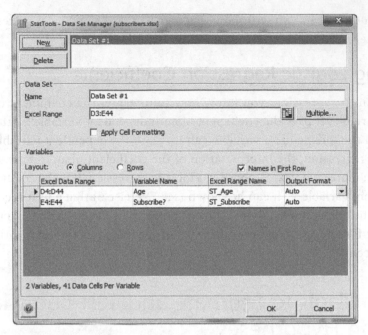

Figure 17-9: Selecting data for the subscriber example

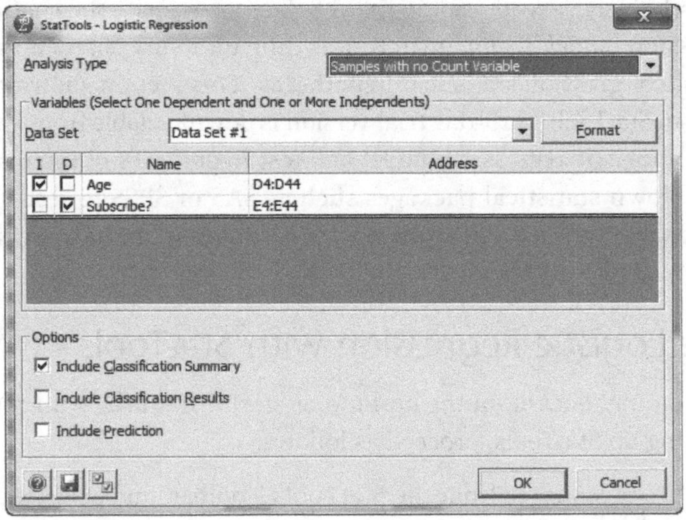

Figure 17-10: Dialog box for Logistic Regression

This dialog box tells StatTools to use Logistic Regression to predict Subscribe from Age. After selecting OK you can obtain the StatTools printout, as shown in Figure 17-11.

	M	N	O	P	Q	R	S	T
16	*Summary Measures*							
17	Null Deviance	45.554						
18	lo	38.75005						
19	Improvement	6.803948						
20	p-Value	0.0091						
21								
22		Coefficient	Standard	Wald	p-Value	Lower	Upper	Exp(Coef)
23	*Regression Coefficients*		Error	Value		Limit	Limit	
24	Constant	-5.66156	2.017251	-2.80657	0.0050	-9.61537	-1.70775	0.003477
25	Age	0.128133	0.054733	2.34107	0.0192	0.020857	0.235409	1.136704

Figure 17-11: StatTools logistic regression output

Interpreting the StatTools Logistic Regression Output

It is not necessary for the marketing analyst to understand all numbers in the StatTools output, but the key parts of the output are explained here:

- The maximum likelihood estimates of the intercept (-5.661 in cell N24) and slope (0.1281 in cell N25) agree with the maximum likelihood estimates you obtained with the Excel Solver.
- The p-value in cell N20 is used to test the null hypothesis: Adding the age variable improves the prediction of the subscriber over predicting the subscriber with just an intercept. The p-value of 0.009 indicates (via a Likelihood Ratio Chi Squared test) there are only 9 chances in 1,000 that age does not help predict whether a person is a subscriber.
- The p-value in Q25 (0.0192) uses a different test (based on Wald's Statistic) to test whether the age coefficient is significantly different from 0. This test indicates there is a 1.9 percent chance that the age coefficient is significantly different from 0.
- T24:T25 exponentiates each coefficient. This data is useful for using Equation 4 to predict the probability that a dependent variable equals 1.

If you are interested in a more complete discussion of hypothesis testing in logistic regression, check out Chapter 14 of *Introduction to Linear Regression Analysis* (Montgomery, Peck, and Vining, 2006).

A Logistic Regression with More Than One Independent Variable

The subscribers2.xlsx workbook shows how to use StatTools to run a logistic regression with more than one independent variable. As shown in Figure 17-12, you can try to predict the likelihood that people will subscribe to a magazine (indicated by a 1 in the Subscribe column) based on their age and annual income (in thousands of dollars). To do so, perform the following steps:

	D	E	F	G	H
1					
2	constant	age	income		
3	-3.231111	0.023059	0.015936		
4	Subscribe	Age	Income	Score	Prob
5	0	25	132	-0.55103	0.365624
6	0	64	84	-0.41668	0.39731
7	0	31	100	-0.92265	0.284419
8	0	66	72	-0.5618	0.36313
9	0	39	78	-1.08878	0.251849
10	1	53	54	-1.14842	0.240777
11	1	49	102	-0.47571	0.383265
12	1	63	145	0.532377	0.630037
13	0	66	130	0.362508	0.589647
14	0	72	87	-0.1844	0.454029
15	0	35	89	-1.00571	0.26782
16	0	42	97	-0.71681	0.328096
17	1	65	90	-0.29801	0.426045
18	1	48	90	-0.69001	0.334031
19	0	28	67	-1.51772	0.179797
20	0	46	98	-0.60864	0.352371
21	0	31	55	-1.63978	0.162495
22	0	41	103	-0.64425	0.344287
23	0	57	128	0.123105	0.530737
24	0	70	72	-0.46957	0.384719
25	0	53	81	-0.71814	0.327802
26	0	49	134	0.034252	0.508562
27	1	51	142	0.207861	0.551779

Figure 17-12: Logistic data with two independent variables

1. In StatTools use the Data Set Manager to select the range D4:F411.
2. From Regression and Classification select Logistic Regression....
3. Fill in the dialog box, as shown in Figure 17-13.

You should obtain the output shown in Figure 17-14.

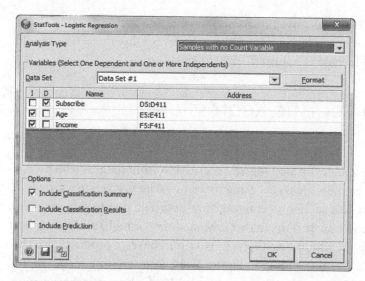

Figure 17-13: Variable selection for a Two Variable Logistic Model

	J	K	L	M	N	O	P	Q
10	*Summary Measures*							
11	Null Deviance	553.7964						
12	Model Deviance	514.5033						
13	Improvement	39.29306						
14	p-Value	< 0.0001						
15								
16		Coefficient	Standard Error	Wald Value	p-Value	Lower Limit	Upper Limit	Exp(Coef)
17	*Regression Coefficients*							
18	Constant	-3.23111	0.534179	-6.04874	< 0.0001	-4.2781	-2.18412	0.039514
19	Age	0.023059	0.007163	3.219241	0.0013	0.00902	0.037098	1.023327
20	Income	0.015936	0.002993	5.324267	< 0.0001	0.01007	0.021803	1.016064

Figure 17-14: Output for Two Variable Logistic Regression

The p-value in K14 (< 0.0001) indicates that age and income together have less than 1 chance in 1,000 of not being helpful to predict whether a person is a subscriber. The small p-values in N19 and N20 indicate that each individual independent variable has a significant impact on predicting whether a person is a subscriber. Your estimate of the chance that a person is a subscriber is given by the following equation:

$$(5) \text{ Probability person is a subscriber} = \frac{e^{-3.23 + .023 * Age + .016 * Income}}{1 + e^{-3.23 + .023 * Age + .016 * Income}}$$

In the cell range H5:H411, you use Equation 5 to compute the probability that a person is a subscriber. For example, from H6 you see the probability that a 64-year-old with an $84,000 annual income is a subscriber is 39.7 percent.

Performing a Logistic Regression with Count Data

In the previous section you performed logistic regression from data in which each data point was listed in an individual row. Sometimes raw data is given in a grouped, or *count format*. In count data each row represents multiple data points. For example, suppose you want to know how income (either low, medium, or high) and age (either young or old) influence the likelihood that a person purchases a product. Use the data from `countdata2.xlsx`, also shown in Figure 17-15. You can find, for example, that the data includes 500 young, low-income people, 35 of whom purchased your product.

	A	B	C	D	E	F	G	H	I	J	K
1						0.8625	1.48651	1.00484			
2	Joint category	Age	Income	Number	Purchasers	Young	LowInc	MidInc	Score	Predicted Prob	Actual Prob
3	1	Young	Low	500	35	1	1	0	-2.54	0.0731	0.07
4	2	Young	Middle	300	15	1	0	1	-3.022	0.0465	0.05
5	3	Young	High	200	4	1	0	0	-4.026	0.0175	0.02
6	4	Old	Low	200	8	0	1	0	-3.402	0.0322	0.04
7	5	Old	Middle	400	7	0	0	1	-3.884	0.0202	0.0175
8	6	Old	High	200	1	0	0	0	-4.889	0.0075	0.005
9											
10	*Summary Measures*										
11	Null Deviance	29.58									
12	Model Deviance	0.92									
13	Improvement	28.66									
14	p-Value	#####									
15											
16		Coefficien	Standard Error	Wald Value	p-Value	Lower Limit	Upper Limit	Exp(Coef)			
17	*Regression Coefficients*										
18	Constant	-4.889	0.496323	-9.85023	< 0.0001	-5.8617	-3.9161	0.00753			
19	Young	0.863	0.298032	2.89411	0.0038	0.2784	1.446679	2.36916			
20	LowInc	1.487	0.479329	3.101233	0.0019	0.547	2.425994	4.42164			
21	MidInc	1.005	0.500595	2.007282	0.0447	0.0237	1.986002	2.73146			

Figure 17-15: Count data for logistic regression

In F3:H8 IF statements are used to code age and income as dummy variables. The data omits old in the age variable and high in the income variable. For example, the range F8:H8 tells StatTools that row 8 represents old, high-income people.

To run a logistic regression with this count data, perform the following steps:

1. Use the Data Set Manager to select the range D2:H8.
2. Select Logistic Regression... from Regression and Classification, and fill in the dialog box, as shown in Figure 17-16. Note now the upper-left corner of the dialog box indicates that you told StatTools that count data was used.

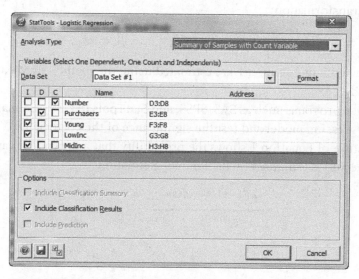

Figure 17-16: Variable selection with count data

3. Select Number as the raw Count column and tell StatTools to predict purchasers using the *Young*, *LowInc*, and *MidInc* variables.
4. The p-values in E19:E21 indicate that each independent variable is a significant predictor of purchasing behavior. If you generalize Equation 4 you can predict in Column J the probability that a person would subscribe with the formula. Use the following equation to do so:

$$\text{Probability of subscribing} = \frac{e^{-4.89 + .8663 * Young + 1.487 * LowInc * 1.005 * MidINC}}{1 + e^{-4.89 + .8663 * Young + 1.487 * LowInc * 1.005 * MidINC}}$$

Refer to Figure 17-15 to see that the actual and predicted probabilities for each grouping are close.

Summary

In this chapter you learned the following:

- When the dependent variable is binary, the assumptions of multiple linear regression are violated.
- To predict the probability p that a binary-dependent variable equals 1, use the logit transformation:

$$(1)\ Ln\ \frac{p}{1-p} = \beta_0 + \beta_1 x_1 + \beta_2 x_2 + \cdots \beta_n x_n$$

- The coefficients in Equation 1 are estimated using the method of Maximum Likelihood.
- You can use programs such as SAS, SPSS, and StatTools to easily estimate the logistic regression model and test the significance of the coefficients.
- Manipulation of Equation 1 shows the probability that a dependent variable equals one and is estimated by the following equation:

$$\frac{e^{\beta_0 + \beta_1 x_1 + \cdots \beta_n x_n}}{1 + e^{\beta_0 + \beta_1 x_1 + \cdots \beta_n x_n}}$$

Exercises

1. For 1,022 NFL field goal attempts the file FGdata.xlsx contains the distance of the field goal and whether the field goal was good. How does the length of the field goal attempt affect the chance to make the field goal? Estimate the chance of making a 30, 40, or 50 yard field goal.

2. The file Logitsubscribedata.xls gives the number of people in each age group who subscribe and do not subscribe to a magazine. How does age influence the chance of subscribing to the magazine?

3. The file Healthcaredata.xlsx gives the age, party affiliation, and income of 300 people. You are also told whether they favor Obamacare. Develop a model to predict the chance that a person favors Obamacare. For each person generate a prediction of whether the person favors Obamacare. Interpret the coefficients of the independent variables in your logistic regression.

4. How would you incorporate nonlinearities and/or interactions in a logistic regression model?

5. The file `RFMdata.xlsx` contains the following data:

- Whether a person responded (dependent variable = 1) or did not respond (dependent variable = 0) to the most recent direct mail campaign.
- R: recency (time since last purchase) measured on a 1–5 scale; 5 indicates a recent purchase.
- F: frequency (how many orders placed in the last year) measured on a 1–5 scale with a 5 indicating many recent purchases.
- M: monetary value (total amount purchased in last year) measured on a 1–5 scale with a 5 indicating the person spent a lot of money in the last year on purchases.

Use this data to build a model to predict based on R, F, and M whether a person will respond to a mailing. What percentage of people responded to the most recent mailing? If you mailed to the top 10 percent (according to the logistic regression model) what response would be obtained?

6. Show that in a logistic regression model if an independent variable x_i is increased by 1, then the odds ratio will increase by a factor of e^{β_i}.

7. Using the data in the `data` worksheet of the file `subscribers.xlsx`, show that for the magazine example logistic regression resolves the problems of non-normal residuals and heteroscedasticity.

8. The file `shuttledata.xlsx` contains the following data for several launches of the space shuttle:

- Temperature (degrees Fahrenheit)
- Number of O-rings on the shuttle and the number of O-rings that failed during the mission

Use logistic regression to determine how temperature affects the chance of an O-ring failure. The *Challenger* disaster was attributed to O-ring failure. The temperature at launch was 36 degrees. Does your analysis partially explain the *Challenger* disaster?

9. In 2012 the Obama campaign made extensive use of logistic regression. If you had been working for the Obama campaign how would you have used logistic regression to aid his re-election campaign?

18

Discrete Choice Analysis

In Chapter 16, "Conjoint Analysis," you learned how the marketing analyst could use a customer's ranking of product profiles to determine the relative importance the customer attaches to product attributes and how a customer ranks the level of each product attribute. In this chapter you will learn how to use *discrete choice analysis* to determine the relative importance the customer attaches to product attributes and how a customer ranks the level of each product attribute. To utilize discrete choice analysis, customers are asked to make a choice among a set of alternatives (often including none of the given alternatives). The customer need not rank the product attributes. Using maximum likelihood estimation and an extension of the logit model described in Chapter 17, "Logistic Regression," the marketing analyst can estimate the ranking of product attributes for the population represented by the sampled customers and the ranking of the level of each product attribute.

In this chapter you learn how discrete choice can be used to perform the following:

- Estimate consumer preferences for different types of chocolate.
- Estimate price sensitivity and brand equity for different video games, and determine the profit maximizing price of a video game.
- Model how companies should dynamically change prices over time.
- Estimate price elasticity.
- Determine the price premium a national brand product can command over a generic product.

Random Utility Theory

The concept of *random utility theory* provides the theoretical basis for discrete choice analysis. Suppose a decision maker must choose among *n* alternatives. You can observe certain attributes and levels for each alternative.

The decision maker associates a utility U_j with the jth alternative. Although the decision maker knows these utilities, the marketing analyst does not. The random utility model assumes the following:

$$U_j = V_j + \varepsilon_j$$

Here V_j is a deterministic "score" based on the levels of the attributes that define the alternative, and the ε_j's are random unobservable error terms. The decision maker is assumed to choose the alternative j ($j = 1, 2, ..., n$) having the largest value of U_j. Daniel McFadden showed (see "Conditional Logit Analysis of Qualitative Choice Behavior" in *Frontiers of Econometric Behavior*, Academic Press, 1974) that if the ε_j's are independent *Gumbel* (also known as *extreme value*) random variables, each having the following distribution function: `F(x)=Probability` ε_j `<= x)=` $e^{-e^{-x}}$, then the probability that the decision maker chooses alternative j (that is, $U_j = max_{k=1,2,...,n} U_k$) is given by the following:

$$(1) \quad \frac{e^{V_j}}{\sum_{i=n}^{i=n} e^{V_i}}$$

Of course, Equation 1 is analogous to the logit model of Chapter 17 and is often called the *multinomial logit model*. Equation 1 is of crucial importance because it provides a reasonable method for transforming a customer's score for each product into a reasonable estimate of the probability that the person will choose each product. In the rest of this chapter you will be given the alternative chosen by each individual in a set of decision makers. Then you use Equation 1 and the method of maximum likelihood (introduced in Chapter 17) to estimate the importance of each attribute and the ranking of the levels within each attribute.

> **NOTE** If this discussion of random utility theory seems too technical, do not worry; to follow the rest of the chapter all you really need to know is that Equation 1 can be used to predict the probability that a decision maker chooses a given alternative.

> **NOTE** Another commonly used assumption is that the errors in Equation 1 are not independent and have marginal distributions that are normal. This assumption can be analyzed via *probit regression*, which is beyond the scope of this book. In his book *Discrete Choice Methods with Simulation*, 2nd ed. (Cambridge University Press, 2009), Kenneth Train determined how changes in

the price of different energy sources (gas, electric, and so on) affect the fraction of homes choosing different sources of energy. You can refer to his book for an extensive discussion of probit regression.

Discrete Choice Analysis of Chocolate Preferences

Suppose that eight alternative types of chocolate might be described by the levels of the following attributes:

- Dark or milk
- Soft or chewy
- Nuts or no nuts

The eight resulting types of chocolate are listed here:

- Milk, chewy, no nuts
- Milk, chewy, nuts
- Milk, soft, no nuts
- Milk, soft, nuts
- Dark, chewy, no nuts
- Dark, chewy, nuts
- Dark, soft, no nuts
- Dark, soft, nuts

Ten people were asked which type of chocolate they preferred. (People were not allowed to choose none of the above.) The following results were obtained:

- Two people chose milk, chewy, nuts.
- Two people chose dark, chewy, no nuts.
- Five people chose dark, chewy, nuts.
- One person chose dark, soft, nuts.

You can use discrete choice analysis to determine the relative importance of the attributes and, within each attribute, rank the levels of the attributes. The work for this process is shown in Figure 18-1 and is in the chocolate.xls file.

	A	B	C	D	E	F	G	H
2								
3			Dark	Milk	Soft	Chewy	Nuts	No Nuts
4		weights	0	-1.38629458	2.401382	4.598606	5.923627529	5.07633
5		number choosing						
6				exp(score)				
7	Score	milk chewy no nuts	8.288641	3978.42311		we set dark weight =0		
8	Score	milk chewy nuts	9.135939	9282.98697				
9	Score	milk soft nonuts	6.091417	442.047234				
10	Score	milk soft nuts	6.938715	1031.44351				
11	Score	dark chewy no nuts	9.674935	15913.6959				
12	Score	dark chewy nuts	10.52223	37131.9559			sum	
13	Score	dark soft nonuts	7.477711	1768.18932			-14.36349699	
14	Score	dark soft nuts	8.325009	4125.77494	Number choosing			
15	Prob	milk chewy no nuts	0.054		0			
16	Prob	milk chewy nuts	0.126		2			
17	Prob	milk soft nonuts	0.006		0			
18	Prob	milk soft nuts	0.014		0			
19	Prob	dark chewy no nuts	0.216		2			
20	Prob	dark chewy nuts	0.504		5			
21	Prob	dark soft nonuts	0.024		1			
22	Prob	dark soft nuts	0.056		0			
23		milk chewy no nuts						

Figure 18-1: Chocolate discrete choice example

Assume the score for each of the eight types of chocolate will be determined based on six unknown numbers which represent the "value" of various chocolate characteristics.

- Value for dark
- Value for milk
- Value for soft
- Value for chewy
- Value for nuts
- Value for no nuts

The score, for example of milk, chewy, no nuts chocolate, is simply determined by the following equation:

(2) (Value of Milk) + (Value of Chewy) + (Value of No Nuts)

To estimate the six unknowns proceed as follows:

1. In cells C4:H4 enter trial values for these six unknowns.
2. In cells C7:C14 compute the score for each type of chocolate. For example, in C7 Equation 2 is used to compute the score of milk, chewy, no nuts with the formula =D4+F4+H4.
3. Use Equation 1 to compute the probability that a person will choose each of the eight types of chocolate. To do so copy the formula =EXP(C7) from D7 to D8:D14 to compute the numerator of Equation 1 for each type of chocolate.

Then copy the formula =D7/SUM($D$7:$D$14) from C15 to C16:C22 to implement Equation 1 to compute the probability that a person will choose each type of chocolate.

4. Use the technique of maximum likelihood (actually maximizing the logarithm of maximum likelihood) to determine the six values that maximize the likelihood of the observed choices. Note that Equation 2 implies that if you add the same constant to the score of each alternative, then for each alternative the probabilities implied by Equation 2 remain unchanged. Therefore when you maximize the likelihood of the observed choices, there is no unique solution k. Therefore you may arbitrarily set any of the changing cells to 0. For this example suppose the value of dark = 0.

The likelihood of what you have observed is given by the following equation:

$$(3)\ (P\ of\ M,C,N)^2(P\ of\ D,C,NN)^2(P\ of\ D,C,N)^5(P\ of\ D,S,N)^1$$

Essentially you find the likelihood of what has been observed by taking the probability of each selected alternative and raising it to a power that equals the number of times the selected alternative is observed. For example, in the term $(P\ of\ D,C,N)^5$, (P of D,C,N) is raised to the fifth power because five people preferred dark and chewy with nuts.

Equation 3 uses the following abbreviations:

- ■ *P* = Probability
- ■ *M* = Milk
- ■ *D* = Dark
- ■ *N* = Nuts
- ■ *NN* = No Nuts
- ■ *C* = Chewy
- ■ *S* = Soft

Recall the following two basic laws of logarithms:

$$(4)\ Ln\ (x * y) = Ln\ x + Ln\ y$$
$$(5)\ Ln\ p^n = nLn\ p$$

You can apply Equations 4 and 5 to Equation 3 to show that the natural logarithm of the likelihood of the observed choices is given by the following equation:

$$(6)\ 2*Ln(P\ of\ M,C,N) + 2*(P\ of\ D,\ C,\ NN) + 5*P(D,\ C,\ N) + P(D,\ S,\ N)$$

Cell G13 computes the Log Likelihood with the formula =E16*LN(C16)+E19*LN(C19)+E20*LN(C20)+E21*LN(C21).

You can use the Solver window in Figure 18-2 to determine the maximum likelihood estimates of the values for each level of each attribute. The values enable you to determine the importance of each attribute and the rankings within each attribute of the attribute levels.

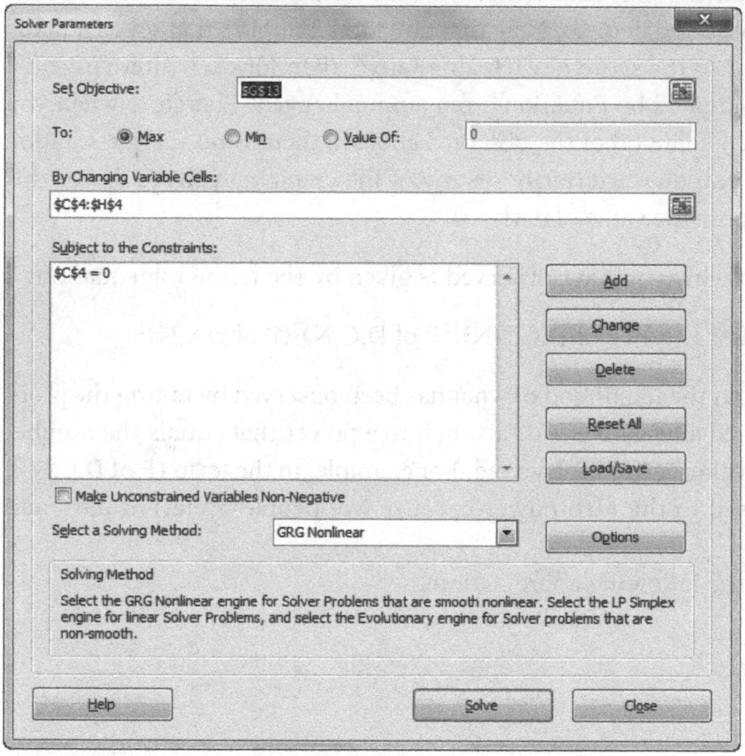

Figure 18-2: Solver window for chocolate example

Refer to Figure 18-1 and you can find the following maximum likelihood estimates:

- Dark = 0, Milk = −1.38, so Dark is preferred to Milk overall and the difference between the Dark and Milk values is 1.38.
- Chewy = 4.59 and Soft = 2.40, so Chewy is preferred to Soft overall and the difference between the Chewy and Soft scores is 2.19.
- Nuts = 5.93 and No Nuts = 5.08, so Nuts is preferred to No Nuts and the difference between the Nuts and No Nuts scores is 0.85.

You can rank the importance of the attributes based on the difference in scores within the levels of the attribute. This tells you that the attributes in order of importance are Chewy versus Soft, Dark versus Milk, and Nuts versus No Nuts. This is consistent with the fact that nine people prefer Chewy, eight prefer Dark, and seven prefer Nuts.

Incorporating Price and Brand Equity into Discrete Choice Analysis

In this section you learn how to incorporate price and brand equity into a discrete choice analysis. The first model is in the file Xbox1.xls and the data is shown in Figure 18-3.

⬜	A	B		C	D	E	F	G	H	I	J
1		cost		$180	$160	$155					
2											
3							Nothing				
4		Brand		1.879	4.967	0.489	0				
5		price		-0.012	-0.024	-0.01					
6		Choice#		Xbox	PS	Wii		Pick Xbox	Pick PS	Pick Wii	Pick nothing
7			1	$221	$267	$275		28	11	14	47
8			2	$193	$295	$275		38	1	14	47
9			3	$278	$294	$176		10	2	43	45
10			4	$288	$191	$250		2	44	10	44
11			5	$162	$224	$221		30	16	17	37
12			6	$172	$249	$157		23	15	24	38
13			7	$167	$251	$169		24	12	25	39
14			8	$213	$255	$158		21	25	9	45

Figure 18-3: Video game data

The data indicates that 100 people were shown eight price scenarios for Xbox, PlayStation (PS), and Wii. Each person was asked which product they would buy (or none) for the given prices. For example, if Xbox sold for $221, PS for $267, and Wii for $275, 28 people chose Xbox, 11 chose PS, 14 chose Wii, and 47 chose to buy no video game console. You are also given the cost to produce each console.

You will now learn how to apply discrete choice analysis to estimate price sensitivity and product brand equity in the video game console market. For each possible product choice, assume the value may be computed as follows:

- Value Xbox = Xbox brand weight + (Xbox price) * (Xbox price sensitivity)
- Value PS = PS brand weight + (PS price) * (PS price sensitivity)
- Value Wii = Wii brand weight + (Wii price) * (Wii price sensitivity)
- Assume Weight for Nothing = 0, so Value Nothing = 0

Now you can use maximum likelihood estimation to estimate the brand weight for each product and the price sensitivity for each product. The strategy is to find the Log Likelihood of the data for each set of prices, and then, because of Equation 4, add the Log Likelihoods. By maximizing the Log Likelihood you can obtain the set of weights that maximize the chance to observe the actual observed choice data. The work is shown in Figure 18-4. Proceed as follows:

	G	H	I	J	K	L	M	N	O	P	Q	R	S
4													sum
5													-984.7550485
6	Pick Xbox	Pick PS	Pick Wii	Pick nothing	XBox score	PS Score	Wii Score	Nothing Score	XBox prob	PS prob	Wii Prob	Nothing Prob	Ln(Likelihood)
7	28	11	14	47	-0.882	-1.5539	-1.218	0	0.2155	0.11004	0.154	0.52045	-124.1354628
8	38	1	14	47	-0.532	-2.2376	-1.218	0	0.2952	0.053621	0.1487	0.5025	-108.3181076
9	10	2	43	45	-1.594	-2.2132	-0.603	0	0.1092	0.058804	0.2942	0.53777	-108.3357813
10	2	44	10	44	-1.719	0.30214	-1.062	0	0.0623	0.470087	0.1201	0.3475	-106.4650498
11	30	16	17	37	-0.145	-0.5038	-0.882	0	0.3001	0.209578	0.1435	0.34683	-133.2964867
12	23	15	24	38	-0.27	-1.1143	-0.485	0	0.2821	0.121213	0.2274	0.36938	-134.1584807
13	24	12	25	39	-0.207	-1.1631	-0.56	0	0.3014	0.115888	0.2119	0.37083	-132.1271517
14	21	25	9	45	-0.782	-1.2608	-0.492	0	0.1945	0.120471	0.26	0.42505	-137.918528

Figure 18-4: Maximum likelihood estimation for video console example

1. In C4:E5 enter trial values for brand coefficients and price sensitivities for each product. In F4 set the Nothing "brand" coefficient equal to 0.

2. Copy the formula =C$4+C$5*C7 from K7 to K7:M14 to generate scores for each product for each scenario.

3. Copy the formula =$F$4 from N7 to N7:N14 to generate for each scenario the score for no purchase.

4. Copy the formula =EXP(K7)/(EXP($K7)+EXP($L7)+EXP($M7)+EXP($N7)) from O7 to O7:R14 to utilize Equation 1 to compute for each price scenario the probability that each product (or no purchase) is chosen.

5. To see how to compute the likelihood of the observed results for each scenario, note that in the first scenario the likelihood is as follows:

(Prob. Xbox chosen) [28] (Prob. PS chosen) [11] (Prob. GC chosen) [14] (Prob. nothing chosen) [47]

The goal is to maximize the sum of the logarithms of the likelihoods for each scenario. For the first scenario the logarithm of the likelihood is as follows:

28 * Ln(Prob. Xbox chosen) + 11 * Ln(Prob. PS chosen) + 14 * Ln(Prob. GC chosen) + 47 * Ln(Prob. nothing chosen)

This follows from Equations 4 and 5. Therefore copy the formula G7*LN (O7)+H7*LN(P7)+I7*LN(Q7)+J7*LN(R7) from S7 to S7:S14 to compute the logarithm of the likelihood for each scenario.

5. In cell S5 you can create the target cell needed to compute maximum likelihood estimates for the changing cells (the range C4:E5 and F4). The target cell is computed as the sum of the Log Likelihoods with the formula =SUM(S7:S14).

6. Use the Solver window shown in Figure 18-5 to determine the brand weights and price sensitivities that maximize the sum of the Log Likelihoods. This is equivalent, of course, to maximizing the likelihood of the observed choices given by Equation 3. Note that you constrained the score for the Nothing choice to equal 0 with the constraint $F$4 = 0.

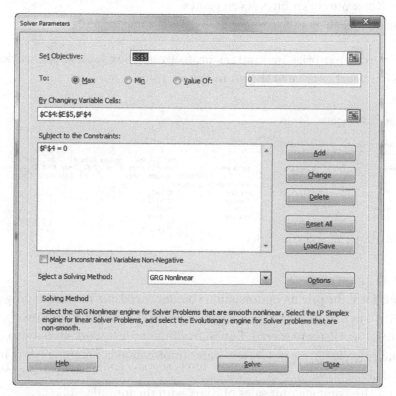

Figure 18-5: Solver window for maximum likelihood estimation

The weights and price sensitivities are shown in the cell range C4:E5 of Figure 18-3. At first glance it appears that PS has the highest brand equity, but because PS also has the most negative price sensitivity, you are not sure. In the "Evaluating Brand Equity" section you constrain each product's price weight to be identical so that you can obtain a fair comparison of brand equity for each product.

Pricing Optimization

After you have estimated the brand weights and price sensitivities, you can create a market simulator (similar to the conjoint simulator of Chapter 16) to help a company price to maximize profits. Suppose you work for Xbox and want to determine a profit maximizing price. Without loss of generality, assume the market consists of 100 customers. Then your goal is to price Xbox to maximize profit earned per 100 customers in the market. Make the following assumptions:

- Xbox price is $180.
- PS price is $215 and Wii price is $190.
- Each Xbox purchaser buys seven games.
- Xbox sells each game for $40 and buys each game for $30.

To determine what price maximizes profit from Xbox look at the worksheet pricing in file Xbox1.xls (also shown in Figure 18-6).

	A	B	C	D	E	F	G	H	I	J	K	L	M	N
1		cost	$180.00	$160.00	$155.00									
2														
3						Nothing								
4		Brand	1.87892	4.9665	0.488912494	0								
5		price	-0.0125	-0.0244	-0.00620515									
6		Price	X BOX	PS 2	Game Cube		XBOX score	PS Score	Wii Score	Nothing Score	XBox Prob	PS Prob	Wii Prob	Nothing Prob
7			1	$207.46	$215.00		$190.00	-0.712715307	-0.28396	-0.69	0	0.179	0.274	0.183	0.36435
8							XBOX Profit Computation							
9							unit sales	17.86425						
10	Games sold	7					Revenues	$8,708.12						
11	Game price	$40.00					Costs	$6,967.06						
12	Game cost	$30.00					Total Profit	$1,741.07						

Figure 18-6: Determining Xbox price

Proceed as follows:

1. To perform the pricing optimization you only need one row containing probability calculations from the model worksheet. Therefore in Row 7 of the pricing worksheet recreate Row 7 from the model worksheet. Also insert a trial price for Xbox in C7, and enter information concerning Xbox in B10 and B11.

2. In cell H9, compute unit sales of Xbox with the formula =100*K7.

3. In cell H10, compute Xbox revenue from consoles and games with the formula =C7*H9+H9*B10*B11.

4. In cell H11, enter the cost of Xbox consoles and games with the formula =H9*C1+B10*H9*B12.

5. In cell H12, compute the profit with the formula =H10-H11.

6. Use the Solver window in Figure 18-7 to yield a profit-maximizing price of $207.47 for Xbox.

Figure 18-7: Solver window for Xbox price

Evaluating Brand Equity

Based on the pricing analyses performed in the previous section, you can also estimate the value of each brand, or brand equity, by forcing the price weight to be identical across all competitors. For instance, you might say PS has the largest brand equity because its brand coefficient is the largest. As previously pointed out, however, PS has the most negative price weight, so it is not clear that PS has the largest brand equity. For example, if PS had the largest brand equity then you would think that the scores and choice mechanism would indicate that the market would prefer a PS over an Xbox or Wii at a $200 price. Due to the large negative price coefficient for PS, it is unclear whether PS would be preferred if all products sold for the same price. To correctly determine brand equity, you must rerun the Solver model assuming that the price weight is the same for each product. Setting the price weights equal for all products ensures that if all products sell for the same price the market would prefer the product with the largest brand weight. The results are in the worksheet Brand equity and price of workbook Xbox2.xls, and the changes from the previous model are shown in Figure 18-8.

Set D5 and E5 equal to C5, and delete D5 and E5 as changing cells. After running Solver, you find that PS has the largest brand equity, followed by Xbox and Wii.

	A	B	C	D	E	F
1		Cost	$180.00	$160.00	$155.00	
2						
3						pick nothing
4		Brand	1.904231	2.10939	1.74652854	0
5		Price	-0.01254	-0.01254	-0.01253911	
6		Price#	X Box	PS 2	Wii	
7		1	$221.00	$267.00	$275.00	
8		2	$193.00	$295.00	$275.00	
9		3	$278.00	$294.00	$176.00	
10		4	$288.00	$191.00	$250.00	
11		5	$162.00	$224.00	$221.00	
12		6	$172.00	$249.00	$157.00	
13		7	$167.00	$251.00	$169.00	
14		8	$213.00	$255.00	$158.00	

Figure 18-8: PS has the largest brand equity

Testing for Significance in Discrete Choice Analysis

Once you have estimated the brand values and price weights, you can plug the product prices into Equation 2 and forecast market shares. You might wonder whether including a factor such as price in market share forecasts improves the quality of the forecasts. To determine whether or not adding a factor such as price to a discrete choice analysis significantly improves the model's predictions for product market shares, proceed as follows:

1. Let $LL(Full)$ = Log Likelihood when all changing cells are included.
2. Let $LL(Full - q)$ = Log Likelihood when changing cell q is omitted from the model.
3. Let $DELTA(q) = 2 * (LL(FULL) - LL(FULL - q))$. Then $DELTA(q)$ follows a Chi-Square random variable with 1 degree of freedom, and a p-value for the significance of q may be computed with the Excel formula `=CHIDIST(DELTA(q),1)`.
4. If this formula yields a p-value less than .05, you may conclude that the changing cell q is of significant use (after adjusting for other changing cells in the model) in predicting choice.

You can use this technique to test if incorporating price in your choice model is a significant improvement over just using the brand weights. In the Brand Equity and Price worksheet of workbook Xbox2.xls, you can find $LL(Full\ Model) = -996.85$. In worksheet Brand equity and price the model is run with the price weight set to 0, which obtains $LL(Model(no\ price)) = -1045.03$. Then $Delta(q) = 96.37$ and

CHIDIST(96.37,1) = 10^{-22}. It is therefore virtually certain that price is a significant factor in the choice of a video game console.

Dynamic Discrete Choice

Although the previous sections and analyses offer important insights regarding the drivers of consumer choice, as well as pricing and brand equity implications, they do not represent the "real world" in the sense that the previous analyses do not address competitive dynamics. In the real world, if one firm changes its price, it should expect competitors to react. This section addresses competitive dynamics in discrete choice analysis.

If Xbox sets a price of $207 as recommended previously, then PS and Wii would probably react by changing their prices. In this section you will learn how to follow through the dynamics of this price competition. Usually one of two situations occurs:

- A price war in which competitors continually undercut each other
- A *Nash equilibrium* in which no competitor has an incentive to change its price. Nash equilibrium implies a stable set of prices because nobody has an incentive to change their price.

The file Xbox3.xls contains the analysis. The model of competitive dynamics is shown in Figure 18-9.

	B	C	D	E	F	G	H	I	J	K	L	M	N
1	Cost	$180.00	$160.00	$155.00									
2													
3					Nothing								
4	Brand	1.87892	4.966548	0.48891	0								
5	Price#	-0.01249	-0.024421	-0.0062									
6	Price	Xbox	PS	Wii		Xbox score	PS Score	Wii Score	Nothing Score	XBox Prob	PS Prob	Wii Prob	Nothing Prob
7		1	$207.46	$215.00	$190.00		-0.712715	-0.284	-0.6900664	0	0.17864	0.274	0.183	0.364345
8							Xbox	PS	Wii				
9						unit sales	17.86	27.43	18.27				
10						revenue	3706.13	5896.97	3471.96				
11						cost	3215.56	4388.44	2832.39				
12						profit	1741.07	3428.47	1918.71				
13													
14													
15	Xbox	$207.46	$215.00	$190.00									
16	PS	$207.46	$173.55	$190.00									
17	Wii	$207.46	$173.55	$260.74									
18	Xbox	$202.38	$173.55	$260.74									
19	PS	$202.38	$175.16	$260.74									
20	Wii	$202.38	$175.16	$260.92									
21	Xbox	$202.64	$175.16	$260.92									
22	PS	$202.64	$175.18	$260.92									
23	Wii	$202.64	$175.18	$260.94									

Figure 18-9: Dynamic pricing of Video game consoles

1. To begin, copy the formulas in H9:H12 to I9:J12. This computes profit for PS and Wii, respectively.
2. Change Solver to maximize I12 by changing D7. The resulting Solver solution shows that PS should now charge $173.55.
3. Next, change the target cell to maximize J12 by changing E7. The resulting Solver solution shows that given current prices of other products, Wii should charge $260.74.
4. Now it is Xbox's turn to change the Xbox price: maximize H12 by changing C7. Xbox now sells for $202.38. Repeating the process, you find that prices appear to stabilize at the following levels:

   ■ Xbox: $202.64
   ■ PS: $175.18
   ■ Wii: $260.94

With this set of prices, no company has an incentive to change its price. If it changes its price, its profit will drop. Thus you have found a stable Nash equilibrium.

Independence of Irrelevant Alternatives (IIA) Assumption

Discrete choice analysis implies that the ratio of the probability of choosing alternative j to the chance of choosing alternative i is independent of the other available choices. This property of discrete choice modeling is called the *Independence of Irrelevant Alternatives (IIA)* assumption. Unfortunately, in many situations you will learn that IIA is unreasonable.

From Equation 2 you can show (see Exercise 6) that for any two alternatives i and j, Equation 7 holds.

$$(7) \quad \frac{Prob\ Choose\ i}{Prob\ Choose\ j} = \frac{e^{Score_i}}{e^{Score_j}}$$

Equation 7 tells you that the ratio of the probability of choosing alternative i to the probability of choosing alternative j is independent of the other available choices. This property of discrete choice modeling is called the *Independence of Irrelevant Alternatives (IIA)* assumption. The following paradox (called the Red Bus/Blue Bus Problem) shows that IIA can sometimes result in unrealistic choice probabilities.

Suppose people have two ways to get to work: a Blue Bus or a Car. Suppose people equally like buses and cars so the following is true:

Probability of Choosing Blue Bus = Probability of Choosing Car = 0.5

Now add a third alternative: a Red Bus. Clearly the Red and Blue Buses should divide the 50-percent market share for buses and the new probabilities should be:

- Probability Car = 0.5
- Probability Blue Bus = 0.25
- Probability Red Bus = 0.25

The IIA assumption implies that the current ratio of Probability Blue Bus/ Probability Car will remain unchanged. Because Probability Red Bus = Probability Blue Bus, you know that discrete choice will produce the following unrealistic result:

- Probability Car = 1/3
- Probability Blue Bus = 1/3
- Probability Red Bus = 1/3

The IIA problem may be resolved by using more advanced techniques including mixed logit, nested logit, and probit. See Train (2009) for details.

Discrete Choice and Price Elasticity

In Chapter 4, "Estimating Demand Curves and Using Solver to Optimize Price," you learned that a product's price elasticity is the percentage change in the demand for a product resulting from a 1 percent increase in the product's price. In this section you will learn how discrete choice analysis can be used to estimate price elasticity. Define the following quantities as indicated:

- $Prob(j)$ = Probability product j is chosen.
- $Price(j)$ = Price of product j.
- $\beta(j)$ = Price coefficient in score equation.

From Equation 2 it can be shown that:

(8) Price Elasticity for Product j = $(1 - Prob(j)) * Price(j) * \beta(j)$

The cross elasticity (call it $E(k,j)$) of product k with respect to product j is the percentage change in demand for product k resulting from a 1 percent increase in the price of product j. From Equation 2 it can be shown that:

(9) $E(k,j) = - Prob(j) * Price(j) * \beta(j)$

> **NOTE** All products other than product *j* have the same cross elasticity. This is known as the *property of uniform cross elasticity.*

The file Xbox4.xls illustrates the use of Equations 8 and 9. Return to the video game example and assume that the current prices are Xbox = $200, PS = $210, and Wii = $220, as shown in Figure 18-10.

	A	B	C	D	E	F	G	H	I	J	K	L	M
1	Cost	$180.00	$160.00	$155.00									
2													
3						Pick Nothing							
4	Brand	1.9042314	2.1093899	1.74653	0								
5	Price	-0.0125391	-0.012539	-0.0125									
6		Xbox	PS	Wii		XBox score	PS Score	Wii Score	Nothing Score	XBox Prob	PS Prob	Wii Prob	Nothing Prob
7	Price	$200.00	$210.00	$220.00		-0.60359	-0.524	-1.012	0	0.219	0.24	0.145	0.39959
8													
9													
10		Xbox elasticity	-1.96										
11		PS Cross elasticity with Xbox	0.55										
12		Wii Cross elasticity with Xbox	0.55										

Figure 18-10: Elasticities for Xbox example

The price elasticity for Xbox is -1.96 (a 1 percent increase in Xbox price reduces Xbox sales by 1.96 percent) and the cross elasticities for Xbox price are .55. (A 1 percent increase in Xbox price increases demand for other products by 0.55 percent)

Summary

In this chapter you learned the following:

- A discrete choice analysis helps the marketing analyst determine what attributes matter most to decision makers and how levels of each attribute are ranked by decision makers.
- To begin a discrete choice analysis, decision makers are shown a set of alternatives and asked to choose their most preferred alternative.

- The analyst must determine a model that is used to "score" each alternative based on the level of its attributes.
- The fraction of decision makers that choose alternative j is assumed to follow the multinomial logit model:

(1) $\quad \dfrac{e^{V_j}}{\sum_{i=n}^{i=n} e^{V_i}}$, where V_j = score for alternative j

- Maximum Likelihood is used to estimate the parameters (such as brand equity and price sensitivity) in the scoring equation.
- In a discrete analysis, a Chi Square Test based on the change in the Log Likelihood Ratio can be used to assess the significance of a changing cell.
- The Independence of Irrelevant Alternatives (IIA) that follows from Equation 2 implies that the ratio of the probability to choose alternative i to the probability to choose alternative j is independent of the other available choices. In situations like the Red Bus/Blue Bus example, discrete choice analysis may lead to unrealistic results.
- The multinomial logit version of discrete choice enables you to easily compute price elasticities using the following equations:

(8) *Price Elasticity for Product j = (1 − Prob(j)) * Price(j) * β(j)*
(9) E(k,j) = − Prob(j) * Price(j) * β(j)

Exercises

1. In her book *Discrete Choice Modeling and Air Travel Demand* (Ashgate Publishing, 2010), Per Laurie Garrow details how airlines have predicted how changes in flight prices will affect their market share. Use this example to perform some similar analysis. Delta Airlines wants to determine the profit maximizing price to charge for a 9 a.m. New York to Chicago flight. A focus group has been shown 16 different flights and asked if it would choose a flight if the flight were available. The results of the survey are in file Airlinedata .xlsx, and a sample is shown in Figure 18-11. For example, when shown a Delta 8 a.m., four-hour flight with no music (audio), video, or meals, priced at $300, 78 people chose that flight over choosing not to take a flight at all (Delta = 0, United = 1).

	F	G	H	I	J	K	M	N	O	P	Q	R
13	Price	Leave 8	Leave 9	Leave Noon	Leave other time	Length of flight	Audio	Video	Meals	Airline	Like flight?	Not?
14	300	1	0	0	0	4	0	0	0	0	78	22
15	300	0	1	0	0	5	0	1	1	0	60	40
16	300	0	0	1	0	6	1	0	1	1	50	50
17	300	0	0	0	1	7	1	1	0	1	28	72
18	400	1	0	0	0	5	1	0	1	1	60	40
19	400	0	1	0	0	4	1	1	0	1	50	50
20	400	0	0	1	0	7	0	0	0	0	20	80
21	400	0	0	0	1	6	0	1	1	0	33	67
22	500	1	0	0	0	6	0	1	0	1	10	90
23	500	0	1	0	0	7	0	0	1	1	13	87
24	500	0	0	1	0	4	1	1	1	0	38	60
25	500	0	0	0	1	5	1	0	0	0	22	78
26	600	1	0	0	0	7	1	1	1	0	30	70
27	600	0	1	0	0	6	1	0	0	0	7	93
28	600	0	0	1	0	5	0	1	0	1	12	88
29	600	0	0	0	1	4	0	0	1	1	15	85

Figure 18-11: Data for Exercise 1

a. Which airline (Delta or United) has more brand equity on this route?

b. Delta wants to optimally design a 9 a.m. flight. The flight will have audio and take six hours. There are 500 potential flyers on this route each day. The plane can seat at most 300 people. Determine the profit maximizing price, and whether Delta should offer a movie and/or meals on the flight. The only other flight that day is a $350 United 8 a.m., five-hour flight with audio, movies, and no meals. Delta's cost per person on the flight breaks down as follows:

Item	Cost Per Person
Fuel	$60
Food	$40
Movie	$15

Help Delta maximize its profit on this flight.

2. P&G is doing a discrete choice analysis to determine what price to charge for a box of Tide. It collected the data shown in Figure 18-12. For example, when people were asked which they prefer: Generic for $5, Tide for $8, or None, 35 people said generic, 22 picked Tide, and 43 chose None.

	F	G	H	I	J
5	Generic	P and G	Generic	P and G	None
6	$ 5.00	$ 8.00	35	22	43
7	$ 5.50	$ 7.00	29	29	42
8	$ 7.00	$ 9.00	24	18	59
9	$ 7.50	$ 8.00	17	28	33
10	$ 0.85	$ 10.00	56	4	28
11	$ 4.00	$ 7.00	37	26	28
12	$ 3.50	$ 6.50	38	28	27

Figure 18-12: Data for Exercise 2

Using a discrete choice model with the same price weight for each product, answer the following questions:

a. Using the value-based approach to pricing outlined in Chapter 16, "Conjoint Analysis," what price premium can Tide command over the generic product?

b. If the generic product sold for $5, what price would you recommend for Tide?

3. P&G wants to determine if it should introduce a new, cheaper version of Head and Shoulders shampoo. It asked a focus group which of three products it would prefer at different prices (see Figure 18-13). For example, if all three products cost $3.60, 70 people prefer Head and Shoulders, 13 prefer Head and Shoulders Lite, 4 prefer CVS, and 13 would buy no dandruff shampoo.

a. Use this data to calibrate a discrete choice model. Use the same price weight for each product.

b. Suppose the CVS shampoo sells for $3.00. If the unit cost to produce Head and Shoulders is $2.20 and the unit cost to produce Head and Shoulders Lite is $1.40, what pricing maximizes P&G's profit?

c. By what percentage does the introduction of Head and Shoulders Lite increase P&G's profit?

Scanario	HS	HSLite	CVS	HS Share	HS lite share	CVS share	None share
1	3.6	3.6	3.6	70	13	4	13
2	3.8	2.8	2.6	59	22	7	13
3	4	3	2.7	58	21	7	14
4	4.2	3	2.7	54	23	8	15
5	4.4	3.1	2.6	51	23	9	17
6	4.6	2.9	2.5	46	27	10	17
7	4.8	3	2.8	44	28	9	19
8	5	3	2.9	41	30	9	20
9	5.2	3	2.6	37	31	11	21
10	5.4	3.1	3	35	32	9	23
11	5.6	3.3	2.8	33	30	12	25
12	5.8	3.5	3.1	32	29	11	28
13	6	3.7	3.2	31	28	11	31
14	6.2	4	3.2	29	25	12	34
15	6.4	4.5	3.4	29	20	12	39
16	6.6	4.7	3.6	28	19	11	42

Figure 18-13: Data for Exercise 3

4. CVS wants to determine how to price Listerine with whitener (LW), Listerine (LIST), and CVS mouthwash. One hundred people were shown the following price scenarios, and their choices are listed in Figure 18-14. For example, with LW at $6.60, LIST at $5, and CVS at $3.25, 37 picked no mouthwash, 18 chose LISTW, 20 preferred LIST, and 25 chose CVS.

	E	F	G	H	I	J	K
18	LISTW	LIST	CVS	Pick Nothing	Pick LISTW	Pick LIST	Pick CVS
19	$6.60	$5.00	$3.25	37	18	20	25
20	$7.00	$5.80	$3.50	40	17	17	25
21	$6.90	$6.00	$3.75	41	18	17	24
22	$6.80	$5.90	$3.10	38	18	16	27
23	$8.40	$6.75	$4.25	46	14	16	24

Figure 18-14: Data for Exercise 4

a. Fit a discrete choice model to this data. Use only a single price variable.
b. Using Value-Based Pricing, estimate the value customers place on the whitening feature.
c. Using Value-Based Pricing, estimate the brand equity of P&G.

NOTE LIST and CVS have the same features; the only difference is the name on the bottle.

d. Suppose the price of CVS mouthwash must be $6. Also assume CVS pays $4 for a bottle of LISTW, $3 for a bottle of LIST, and $2.50 for a bottle of CVS. What price for LISTW and LIST maximizes profits for CVS?

5. Armed Forces recruiting has asked for your help to allocate recruiting bonuses among the Air Force, Navy, and Army. During the next year, 1,000,000 people are expected to show interest in enlisting. The United States needs 100,000 enlistees in the Air Force and Navy and 250,000 enlistees in the Army. Recruiting bonuses of up to $30,000 are allowed. A discrete choice study has been undertaken to determine the minimum cost recruiting budget that will obtain the correct number of enlistees. The information shown in Figure 18-15 is available:

	C	D	E	F	L	M	N	O
7		Thousands of $s						
8								
9		Bonus	Bonus	Bonus				
10	Set	AF	NAVY	ARMY	No Enlist	AF	NAVY	ARMY
11	1	$10.00	$10.00	$10.00	59	25	10	6
12	2	$10.00	$20.00	$20.00	52	11	27	10
13	3	$10.00	$30.00	$30.00	3	3	47	14
14	4	$20.00	$10.00	$20.00	49	43	1	7
15	5	$20.00	$20.00	$30.00	42	28	12	18
16	6	$20.00	$30.00	$10.00	37	20	37	6
17	7	$30.00	$10.00	$30.00	31	60	0	9
18	8	$30.00	$20.00	$10.00	33	59	2	6
19	9	$30.00	$30.00	$20.00	29	44	21	6

Figure 18-15: Data for Exercise 5

For example, 100 potential recruits were offered $10,000 to enlist in each service. Fifty-nine chose not to enlist, 25 chose the Air Force, 10 chose the Navy, and 6 chose the Army.

a. Develop a discrete choice model that can determine how the size of the bonuses influences the number of recruits each service obtains. Assume the following:

Score for Not Enlisting = Weight for Not Enlisting
Score for Each Service = Weight for Each Service + (Bonus Weight) * (Size of Bonus)

Use the same bonus weight for each service.

b. Assuming the bonus for each service can be at most $30,000, determine the minimum cost bonus plan that will fill the U.S. recruiting quotas.

6. Verify Equation 7.

V Customer Value

Chapter 19: Calculating Lifetime Customer Value

Chapter 20: Using Customer Value to Value a Business

Chapter 21: Customer Value, Monte Carlo Simulation, and Marketing Decision Making

Chapter 22: Allocating Marketing Resources between Customer Acquisition and Retention

19

Calculating Lifetime Customer Value

I f a company continually spends more money to acquire customers than a customer generates, the company often goes out of business. Therefore, it is important to calculate a *customer's lifetime value* and use these calculations to increase the company's profitability.

For instance, in October 2009, Groupon offered its first deal. For $13 (one half the normal price of $26) a customer could purchase two pizzas from the Chicago Motel Bar pub. Groupon took one half of the $13 and gave Motel Bar one half of the $13. On average the variable cost of a pizza is approximately 35 percent of the pizza's retail price. Motel Bar received $6.50 for pizza that had a variable cost of $9.10. At first glance it seems that Motel Bar would lose $2.60 for each customer who took the Groupon deal; however, Motel Bar understood that the Groupon deal might bring in new customers who would earn Motel Bar a significant future profit that would more than make up for the $2.60 on the customer's first pizza purchase. If the merchants using Groupon did not understand the importance of the long-term value generated by a customer, then Groupon would have never existed.

In this chapter you learn how to easily estimate a customer's lifetime value and use estimates of lifetime value to justify important business decisions. You will see how the concept of customer value could have been used to economically justify DIRECTV's decision to save the author's favorite TV show, *Friday Night Lights*. Finally, you see how to estimate (based on the customer's past purchase history) the probability that a customer is still active.

Basic Customer Value Template

You can use a Customer Value template to easily estimate the value of a customer. To do so, first assume that each year a customer generates a $1 profit margin. Keep in mind the two following parameters:

- **Per period discount rate (typically 10 percent to 16 percent per year):** An annual discount rate of 10 percent means, for example, that $1 received a year from now is equivalent to 1/1.10 dollars received today. Most analysts use *i* to denote the per period discount rate.

NOTE The discount rate and retention rate must refer to the same length of time. For example, if an annual retention rate is used, then an annual discount rate must be used.

- **Per period retention rate:** A retention rate of 60 percent per year means that during any year you lose 40 percent of the customers and you retain 60 percent of your customers. The quantity 1– retention rate is known as the *churn rate*. Most analysts let *r* = retention rate.

Following the work of Gupta and Lehmann in *Managing Customers as Investments* (2005, Pearson Prentice-Hall), you will learn how to use the discount and retention rates to calculate the *customer value multiplier*. A multiplier of 4 means, for example, that a customer's long-term value is four times the profit she generates during the first period. To determine a customer value multiplier, you can begin (see worksheet `basic model` of workbook `customervalue.xls`) in first period with an arbitrary number of customers. (Choose 100 for convenience.) Assume the following:

- A fraction (1– retention rate) of the customers is lost each period. The fraction of customers lost each period is known as the churn rate.
- The customer generates the same profit margin each year.
- The number of periods considered is limited to 360. Even if a period is a month, this covers 30 years. As churn and discount rate effects are compounded, the per period value of an initial customer becomes small after this number of periods, so you can neglect it.

If you move the cursor to cell E1 (refer to Figure 19-1) you see a Data Validation drop-down box, which enables the user to determine if you assume profits are generated at the end, beginning, or middle of a period. If the time period is a month or shorter, then selecting the end, beginning, or middle of the period is of little importance. The drop-down box shows up whenever you click in cell E1. To create this drop-down box, perform the following steps:

	A	B	C	D	E	F	G	H	I	J
1	discount rate		0.1		time frame	beginning				
2	retention rate		0.8		assume constant margins					
3								end		0
4	Period		Customer	df		multiplier		beginning		1
5		1	100	1		3.66666667		middle		0.5
6		2	80	0.909091						
7		3	64	0.826446						
8		4	51.2	0.751315						
9		5	40.96	0.683013						
10		6	32.768	0.620921						
11		7	26.2144	0.564474				df		
12		8	20.97152	0.513158		3.666667		0.1	0.12	0.14	0.16
13		9	16.77722	0.466507		0.6		2.2	2.153846	2.111111	2.071429
14		10	13.42177	0.424098		retention	0.7	2.75	2.666667	2.590909	2.521739
15		11	10.73742	0.385543			0.8	3.666667	3.5	3.352941	3.222222
16		12	8.589935	0.350494			0.9	5.5	5.090909	4.75	4.461538
17		13	6.871948	0.318631	1834.14						
18		14	5.497558	0.289664				Managing Customers as Investments			
19		15	4.398047	0.263331				Gupta and Lehmann			

Figure 19-1 Customer Value template with constant margins

1. Place the cursor in cell E1, and from the Data tab, select Data Validation.
2. From the Settings tab, select the List option; then select the cell range H3:H5 as the source.
3. In cell B5 determine the number of customers generating profits during the first period:

   - 100 for beginning of year
   - 100*(1– retention rate) for end of year)
   - .5*100*(1+ retention rate) for middle of year)

4. Copy the formula B5*retention_rate from B6 to B7:B360 to generate the number of customers for periods 2–360. For example, if you assume beginning-of-year profits, then in period 2 you can retain 80 percent of the customers and have 80 customers left; in period 3 you can retain 80 percent of the 64 customers and have 51.2 customers left.
5. Copy the formula =(1/(1+discount_rate)^A5)*(1+discount_rate)^(VLOOKUP($E$1,lookdis,2,FALSE))from C5 to C6:C364 to generate the discount factor for each year. For example, during year 1 if the annual discount rate is 10 percent then the following are true:

   - End-of-year discount factor for year 1 is 1/1.10.
   - Beginning-of-year discount factor for year 1 is 1.
   - Middle-of-year discount factor for year 1 is $\dfrac{1}{1.10^5}$.

6. In cell E5 use the formula =SUMPRODUCT(C5:C364,B5:B364)/100 to compute the multiplier by summing up for each period (# of customers left)*(discount factor) and dividing by beginning number of customers.

Measuring Sensitivity Analysis with Two-way Tables

Every model has inputs (In the current model the discount rate and retention rate are the inputs.) and output(s). (In the current model the output is the multiplier.) *Sensitivity analysis* of a model involves determining how "sensitive" model outputs are to changes in model inputs. Sensitivity analysis is important because estimates of the model inputs may be wrong, so you need to have an idea how errors in your input estimates will affect the model's outputs. This can be accomplished by using Excel's best sensitivity tool, the *Data Table*. In particular, a two-way Data Table enables you to determine how any formula (in this case the multiplier) varies as two inputs (retention n rate and discount rate) are changed. To create the two-way data table, perform the following steps:

1. Begin by listing values of the retention rate (0.6–0.9) in the range F13:F16, and list values of the other input (discount rate) in the range G12:J12.
2. Place in the upper-left corner (cell F12) the *output formula*. The output formula is simply the multiplier (=E5).
3. Select the table range as F12:J16. Then from the Data tab, choose What-If Analysis and select Data Table....
4. Select the column input cell as B2 and row input cell as B1. Press OK.

Excel places each retention rate in B2 and each discount rate in B1. For each combination of retention rate and discount rate, Excel computes the output cell (the multiplier.) For example, a 10 percent discount rate and 60 percent retention rate yields a multiplier of 2.2, but a 10 percent discount rate and 90 percent discount factor yields a multiplier of 5.5. This shows the importance of increasing the retention rate!

NOTE The concept of customer value took off after Frederic Reichfeld pointed out that for a credit card company, an increase in an annual retention rate from 80 percent to 90 percent could double the multiplier (see *Loyalty Effect*, Reichfeld and Teal, 2001).

An Explicit Formula for the Multiplier

If you assume the per-period profit generated by a customer does not depend on how long he has been a customer, you simply compute the value of the customer as:

(Profit per Period) * (Multiplier)

Therefore, suppose the annual retention rate for cable TV subscribers is 80 percent and the annual discount rate is 10 percent. Assuming end-of-year cash flows, the multiplier is 3.666667. Assuming an annual profit margin of $300, a customer's value would equal ($300)*(3.666667) = $1,100.

Now take a closer look at the multiplier. Let i = per period discount rate and r = per period retention rate. If you assume that for an infinite number of periods each customer generates $1 of profit at the beginning of each period, then you can derive an explicit formula for the multiplier. If you begin period 1 with a single customer, then at the beginning of period 1, you receive $1 from one customer; at the beginning of period 2, you receive $1 from r customers; at the beginning of period 3, you receive $1 from r^2 customers, and so on. Discounting these profits by $1 / (1 + i)$ during period 2, $1 / (1 + i)^2$ during period 3, and so on results in the total profit generated by your initial customer, which may be written as Equation 1:

$$(1)\ \text{Multiplier} = 1 + r / (1 + i) + r^2 / (1 + i)^2 + r^3 / (1 + i)^3 + \ldots$$

Multiplying Equation 1 by $r / (1 + i)$ yields Equation 2:

$$(2)\ r * \text{Multiplier} / (1 + i) = r / (1 + i) + r^2 / ((1 + i)^2 + r^3 / (1 + i)^3 + \ldots$$

Subtracting Equation 2 from Equation 1 yields $(1 + i - r) / (1 + i) * \text{Multiplier} = 1$ or Equation 3:

$$(3)\ \text{Multiplier} = (1 + i) / (1 + i - r).$$

Varying Margins

Lehmann and Gupta make a persuasive case that if the retention rate varies with the length of tenure, using an overall average retention rate is sufficient to accurately estimate customer value. For example, if for newer customers the initial retention rate is 70 percent, and in later years retention rate trends to 90 percent, an average retention rate (See Exercise 5 for an example of how to compute a retention rate.) of approximately 80 percent can be used to accurately estimate the multiplier.

In many cases, however, customer margins tend to increase with the length of a customer's tenure. You can see this occur in the `growing margins` worksheet (also see Figure 19-2). To handle growing customer margins, values are needed for the following three parameters.

- **Year 1 margin per customer:** This is the margin at the beginning of year 1, say, $1 in this case.
- **Steady state margin per customer:** This is the per period profit margin for a customer who is with the company for a long period of time. Assume the steady state margin increases from $1 to $1.50.
- **Periods** until margin per customer is halfway to the steady state margin ($1.25). Call this T^*. Now assume that $T^* = 3$ periods.

	A	B	C	D	E	F	G	H	I	J	K	L
1	discount rate	0.1				time frame	middle					
2												
3						year 1 margin	1					
4						steady state margin	1.5 k		0.231			
5	retention rate	0.6				improve half way(years needed)	3					
6										end	0	
7	Year		Customer	df	begin margin	end marg	margin	multiplier			beginning	1
8		1	0.8	0.953463	1	1.10313	1.0515651	1.913928			middle	0.5
9		2	0.48	0.866784	1.103130267	1.184989	1.1440595					
10		3	0.288	0.787986	1.18498883	1.249963	1.217476					
11		4	0.1728	0.716351	1.249963202	1.301536	1.2757496					
12		5	0.10368	0.651228	1.301535926	1.342471	1.3220036					
13		6	0.062208	0.592025	1.342471232	1.374963	1.3587172					
14		7	0.037325	0.538205	1.374963199	1.400753	1.3878583				years	
15		8	0.022395	0.489277	1.400753357	1.421224	1.4109887	1.913928		2	4	7	10
16		9	0.013437	0.444797	1.421224022	1.437472	1.4293482		0.6	1.987181	1.868623	1.798879	1.766493
17		10	0.008062	0.404361	1.437472398	1.450369	1.4439209	retention	0.7	2.714178	2.540711	2.431588	2.378985
18		11	0.004837	0.367601	1.450369374	1.460606	1.4554878		0.8	3.965608	3.702864	3.52168	3.429446
19		12	0.002902	0.334183	1.460606214	1.468732	1.4646689		0.9	6.555422	6.136496	5.806145	5.62265

Figure 19-2 Customer Value template with increasing margins

Using these parameters, you can compute year n margin as follows:

Year n margin = Year 1 margin + (Steady state margin – Year 1 margin) * $(1 - e^{-kn})$

Here $k = -\text{Ln}(0.5) / T^* = -.69 / T^*$. Thus for $T^* = 3$, $k = 0.231$.

Now assume you measure the number of customers and margins mid-year. Copy the formula `=year_1_margin+(steady_state_margin-year_1_margin)*(1-EXP(-k*(A8-1)))` from D8 to D9:D367 to compute the beginning of period margin. Then copy the formula

`=year_1_margin+(steady_state_margin-year_1_margin)*(1-EXP(-k*(A8)))` from E8 to E9:E367 to compute the end-of-period margin. Column F averages these two numbers to obtain a mid-period margin.

As with the constant margins example, it is very important to verify how robust the multiplier is to varying inputs. In the varying margins example, one of the most relevant issues is to estimate how customer value changes if the firm keeps the customer over different lengths of time. Figure 19-2 displays a two-way data table that shows how varying the retention rate and speed of margin change (measured by T^*) influences the Customer Value multiplier. As T^* increases margins increase more slowly, and the customer value multiplier decreases (but not by a large amount).

DIRECTV, Customer Value, and *Friday Night Lights (FNL)*

As previously mentioned, the author's favorite TV show was *Friday Night Lights* (*FNL*). Although ostensibly a sports show, *FNL* did a terrific job of showing how everyday people struggle with everyday problems and overcome these problems that are often not of their own making. During the 2006–2007 and 2007–2008 TV seasons, *FNL* struggled with low ratings on NBC and was about to be canceled when DIRECTV stepped in and saved the show. This enabled *FNL* to run for three more seasons, which were capped by Kyle Chandler's (Coach Taylor) Emmy® for Best Actor and an Emmy for Best Episode (the show's final episode "Always"). DIRECTV agreed to split production costs with NBC, and DIRECTV obtained the rights to run the show in the fall before NBC ran it during the following spring. In explaining DIRECTV's move, Executive Vice President Eric Shanks spoke about their acquisition:

> We have exclusive content around sports with the NFL, college basketball and NASCAR. Why can't that same model work with entertainment? Why can't we go out and get exclusive entertainment properties and use that as a differentiator as well? If fans are passionate enough to ditch cable and come to DIRECTV, we can help keep shows alive.

It costs $2 million to produce an episode of *FNL*. DIRECTV split the cost with NBC; saving FNL costs DIRECTV $13 million per year. Using your knowledge you can estimate the value of a new subscriber and reverse engineer the number of new subscribers needed to cover the $13 million cost to DIRECTV. The work for this exercise is in the file DirecTV.xls.

> **NOTE** According to an article on *FNL* and DIRECTV (http://fueled.com /blog/the-end-of-friday-night-lights-and-how-directv-saved-it/), DIRECTV hoped that showing *FNL* would generate tens of thousands of new subscribers.

The following information is from DIRECTV's 2008 annual report:

- Monthly churn rate .0151 implies that the chance of retaining a customer for a year is $(1 - .0151)^{12} = .8331$.
- Operating profit = $2.4 billion
- Subscribers 16.8 million
- Acquisition Costs $1.9 billion

Now assume (conservatively) that all other DIRECTV costs are variable costs. Then conservatively, a new subscriber would generate (after acquisition costs) at least 4.3 billion/16.8 million = $255 per year in profits. If you assume an annual discount rate of 10 percent mid-year profits and the annual retention rate of .8331, you find a multiplier of 3.60 and can estimate a customer lifetime value of 3.6($255) = $920. Therefore, to recoup the annual production costs of $13 million, *FNL* would need to create 13,000,000/920 = 14,100 new subscribers. Because *FNL* averages approximately 6 million viewers per week on NBC, you can see why DIRECTV thought saving the show was a worthwhile investment. Of course, there were other benefits such as a perception that DIRECTV supports "quality TV." Your analysis assumes that new customers generated by *FNL* would generate the same profit as current customers. DIRECTV may have actually thought *FNL* would generate more affluent customers who spend more on sports packages and movies than the typical subscriber.

Estimating the Chance a Customer Is Still Active

A marketing analyst is often given a list of customers and their past purchase history. If you want to predict the company's future profits, you need to predict which customers are still active. In their article, "Counting Your Customers: Who Are They and What Will They Do Next?" (*Management Science*, p.33 [1987], pp. 1-24),

Schmittlein, Morrison, and Colombo provide a simple method to estimate the probability that a customer is still active. The following data is needed:

- N = Number of purchases
- t = Time of last purchase
- T = Time elapsed between acquisition of customer and present time

After defining $T^* = t / T$, the authors show that $(T^*)^n$ estimates the probability that the customer is still active. For example, suppose that $T = 10$ and a customer has made a purchase at times 1, 5, 6, and 9. You can estimate the probability that a customer is still active to equal $.9^4 = 0.6561$. Section 5.4 of Blattberg, Kim, and Neslin's book *Database Marketing* (Springer, 2008) contains a more advanced discussion of recent work on determining the probability a customer is still active.

Going Beyond the Basic Customer Lifetime Value Model

Many valuable insights can be gleaned from Gupta and Lehmann's basic customer value model. Following are some ideas that can make the basic customer value concept even more useful to a 21st-century corporation.

- Not all customers generate the same customer value. Several of the author's former students have used multiple regression (see Chapter 10, "Using Multiple Regression to Forecast Sales") to predict from information such as demographic variables the value generated by a potential customer. This enables companies to focus attention on trying to attract more profitable customers. Banks in particular can profit from this type of analysis. See `http://bankblog.optirate.com /bank-and-credit-union-business-strategy-and-customer- life-time-value/#axzz266PyVmgT` for more details of how banks can use the concept of customer value to increase profits.
- In addition to trying to estimate the probability that a customer is still active, the corporation wants to predict the value generated in the future by each customer. In his book *Customer Lifetime Value: Foundations and Trends in Marketing* (Now Publishing, 2008), V. Kumar discusses how a software manufacturer accurately predicted the future value of customers and used this information to allocate marketing resources between customers to maximize future profits.

■ The sensitivity analysis of the basic customer value model showed that increasing the retention rate (or equivalently reducing churn) is a key to increasing lifetime customer value. Logistic regression (see Chapter 17, "Logistic Regression") is a very useful tool to predict who will churn (see `http://analyticstoday.wordpress.com/2010/03/24/churn-analytics-in-the-telecom-industry/`.) Independent variables such as education level, location (rural, urban, or suburban), and customer satisfaction have been found as significant predictors of whether a customer will churn. In an interesting study (before the era of cell phone dominance), Ameritech found that the best predictor of a customer dropping their landline service was that the customer had a repair service call that did not fix the problem. Using the customer lifetime value model, Ameritech could quantify the benefits derived from improved repair service. Once you have identified customers who are likely to churn, preemptive measures (giving coupons, free gifts, etc.) can be used to prevent profitable customers from churning.

Summary

In this chapter you learned the following:

■ Given the retention rate, discount rate, and profit per period generated by a customer, the `customervalue.xls` workbook can be used to easily compute the value of a customer.

■ Given N = Number of purchases, t = Time of last purchase, T = Time elapsed between acquisition of customer and present time, and $T^* = t / T$, $(T^*)^n$ estimates the probability a customer is still active at time T.

Exercises

1. AOL bought customers from CD Now for $60 per customer. CD Now's annual retention rate was 60 percent, and customers generated $15 of profit per year. Assuming an annual discount rate of 12 percent, evaluate AOL's purchase of CD Now customers.

2. It costs Ameritrade $203 to acquire a customer. Ameritrade earned $200 per year from a customer and had an annual retention rate of 95 percent. Assuming cash flows are discounted at 12 percent, estimate the value of a customer and the net of acquisition costs.

3. Assume the annual retention rate for a cell phone subscriber is 70 percent and the customer generates $300 per year in profit. Assuming an annual discount rate of 8 percent, compute the value of a customer.

4. Each year Capital Two retains 75 percent of its customers, and the annual discount rate is 5 percent. What annual retention rate doubles the value of a customer?

5. The file `retentiondata.xlsx` gives retention data on a sample of magazine subscribers. Some of this data is shown in Figure 19-3. For example, the first person was a subscriber for 7 years and is no longer a subscriber, while the 13th person has been a subscriber for one year and is still a subscriber. Use this data to estimate the magazine's annual retention rate for a customer.

Person	Years	Still
1	7	no
2	6	no
3	4	no
4	1	no
5	7	no
6	8	no
7	3	no
8	7	no
9	8	no
10	1	no
11	7	no
12	1	no
13	1	yes
14	1	no
15	6	no
16	1	no
17	3	no
18	6	no

Figure 19-3 Retention data for Problem 5

6. Assume a customer has been with a company for 10 years and has made purchases at times .2, 1.2, .8, and 3. Estimate the probability the customer is still active.

7. Customers 1 and 2 have been with a company for 12 months. Customer 1 has made four purchases and Customer 2 has made two purchases. Each customer's last purchase was at the end of month 8. Which customer is most likely to still be active? Can you explain this result?

8. Modify Equation 3 if $1 of profit is generated at the end, not the beginning of each period.

20 Using Customer Value to Value a Business

Today many companies raise money via venture capital. To raise money, you need to present a business plan that shows how your idea will generate an acceptable level of cash flow. Because a company's customers generate cash flow, a model of how a company's number of customers evolves, coupled with estimates of per customer profitability and acquisition costs, can help generate reasonable predictions for future cash flows. This chapter illustrates the customer-centric approach to valuation, often called the *eyeball approach* (see Exercise 4), combining it with a customer-centric model that values cash flows generated by a new health club.

A Primer on Valuation

You can model the profitability of a business as the discounted value of the cash flows generated by the business. During years in which the business receives revenue, computing cash flows requires use of the following accounting relationships:

(1) Before-Tax Profits = Revenues – (Variable and Nondepreciated Costs) – Depreciation

(2) After-Tax Profits = (1 – Tax Rate) * Before-Tax Profits

(3) Working Capital = Current Assets – Current Liabilities will be modeled as a fixed percentage of revenue

(4) Cash Flow = After-Tax Profits + Depreciation – Change in Working Capital

You can compute the Net Present Value (NPV) of cash flows using the XNPV function. The syntax XNPV(annual discount rate, cash flows, dates of cash flows) computes the NPV of a sequence of irregularly spaced cash flows as of the first listed date. Some investors are interested in the *IRR (Internal Rate of Return)* on an investment. The IRR of a sequence of cash flows is the discount rate that makes the NPV of a sequence of cash flows equal to 0. Technical problems can arise if a sequence of cash flows has no IRR or more than one IRR.

If a sequence of cash flows begins with a negative cash flow followed by a sequence of all non-negative cash flows, the sequence of cash flows will have a unique IRR. This condition is satisfied by most new businesses, which begin with a large up-front capital investment. The syntax XIRR(values, dates, [guess]) computes the IRR of a sequence of irregularly spaced cash flows.

NOTE Guess is an optional argument (usually in the range -50 percent to 50 percent) that gives Excel a starting point, which is used to start the search for the IRR.

The valuation model in this chapter is based on estimating the size of a firm's customer base during each period. Equation 5 is the key to modeling the size of a firm's future customer base.

(5) End Period $t + 1$ customers = Beginning Period $t + 1$ Customers + New Period $t + 1$ customers − (1 − Retention rate) * (Beginning Period t customers)

The next section provides a detailed numerical example that estimates the value of a company by combining the customer value concepts of Chapter 19, "Calculating Lifetime Customer Value" with accounting valuation concepts.

Using Customer Value to Value a Business

If you want to raise money to start a new business, you must present a business plan that makes a convincing case that your investors will recoup their investment. Suppose you want to start a new health club called The Iron Pit Health Club in the idyllic "small town" of Bloomington, Indiana. You have asked noted Bloomington resident John Cougar Mellencamp to invest in the project. To convince John that the health club is an attractive investment, you are going to project 10 years of cash flows. The retention rate of your members will be a crucial input into your model because if 90 percent of your members quit each year, it is unlikely that the health club will be profitable. The assumptions underlying this valuation analysis are summarized in the following list, also shown in Figure 20-1:

- It will cost $900,000 in capital expense (incurred on 1/1/2014) to build the health club and buy equipment. This capital expense will be depreciated on a straight-line basis for 10 years: 2014–2023. For simplicity you assume the $90,000 (.1 * $900,000) annual depreciation is taken mid-year on July 1.
- Variable costs of $100 per year are associated with each member.
- The annual membership fee is $400.
- Annual fixed costs of $350,000 are incurred by Iron Pit.

- 1,000 new members will join each year.
- Iron Pit has an 80 percent annual retention rate.
- Working capital is 10 percent of annual revenues.
- Profits are taxed at 40 percent.

	A	B	C	D	E
1					
2					
3			**buildcost**	**$900,000.00**	
4			**anncostpermember**	**$100.00**	
5			**annfee**	**$400.00**	
6			**annfixedcost**	**$350,000.00**	
7			**newmembersperyear**	**1000**	
8			**retentionrate**	**0.8**	
9			**discountrate**	**0.1**	
10			**workingcappercentage**	**0.1**	
11			**taxrate**	**0.4**	

Figure 20-1: Assumptions for Iron Pit cash flow analysis

As shown in Figure 20-2, the file `Ironpit.xlsx` contains the calculations of 10 years of cash flows.

O13   *fx* 7/1/2023

	D	E	F	G	H	I	J	K	L	M	N	O
13		1/1/2014	7/1/2014	7/1/2015	7/1/2016	7/1/2017	7/1/2018	7/1/2019	7/1/2020	7/1/2021	7/1/2022	7/1/2023
14	fixedcost	$900,000.00										
15	beginning customers		0	1000	1800	2440	2952	3361.6	3689.28	3951.424	4161.1392	4328.91136
16	new customers		1000	1000	1000	1000	1000	1000	1000	1000	1000	1000
17	quits		0	200	360	488	590.4	672.32	737.856	790.2848	832.22784	865.782272
18	end customers		1000	1800	2440	2952	3361.6	3689.28	3951.424	4161.1392	4328.91136	4463.129088
19	revenue		$200,000.00	$560,000.00	$848,000.00	$1,078,400.00	$1,262,720.00	$1,410,176.00	$1,528,140.80	$1,622,512.64	$1,698,010.11	$1,758,408.09
20	Annual fixed cost		$350,000.00	$350,000.00	$350,000.00	$350,000.00	$350,000.00	$350,000.00	$350,000.00	$350,000.00	$350,000.00	$350,000.00
21	variable cost		$50,000.00	$140,000.00	$212,000.00	$269,600.00	$315,680.00	$352,544.00	$382,035.20	$405,628.16	$424,502.53	$439,602.02
22	depreciation		$90,000.00	$90,000.00	$90,000.00	$90,000.00	$90,000.00	$90,000.00	$90,000.00	$90,000.00	$90,000.00	$90,000.00
23	before tax profits		-$290,000.00	-$20,000.00	$196,000.00	$368,800.00	$507,040.00	$617,632.00	$706,105.60	$776,884.48	$833,507.58	$878,806.07
24	after tax profits		-$174,000.00	-$12,000.00	$117,600.00	$221,280.00	$304,224.00	$370,579.20	$423,663.36	$466,130.69	$500,104.55	$527,283.64
25	working capital	$0.00	$20,000.00	$56,000.00	$84,800.00	$107,840.00	$126,272.00	$141,017.60	$152,814.08	$162,251.26	$169,801.01	$175,840.81
26	change in working capital		$20,000.00	$36,000.00	$28,800.00	$23,040.00	$18,432.00	$14,745.60	$11,796.48	$9,437.18	$7,549.75	$6,039.80
27	cash flow	-$900,000.00	-$104,000.00	$42,000.00	$178,800.00	$288,240.00	$375,792.00	$445,833.60	$501,866.88	$546,693.50	$582,554.80	$611,243.84
28												
29		NPV	$937,113.25									
30		IRR	23.14%									

Figure 20-2: Iron Pit cash flow analysis

To create this spreadsheet, perform the following steps:

1. In cell E14 enter the fixed cost of $900,000.
2. In cell F15 enter a 0 indicating you have 0 initial customers.
3. Copy the formula `=newmembersperyear` from F16 to G16:O16 to enter each year's number of new customers.
4. Copy the formula `=(1-retentionrate)*F15` from F17 to G17:O17 to compute the number of customers churning each year.
5. Copy the formula `=F18` from G15 to H15:O15 to enter each year's beginning number of customers.

6. Copy the formula =0.5*annfee*(F15+F18) from F19 to G19:O19 to compute Iron Pit's annual revenue based on averaging each year's beginning and ending customers.

7. Copy the formula =0.5*annfixedcost from F20 to G20:O20 to enter each year's annual fixed cost.

8. Copy the formula =0.5*(F15+F18)*anncostpermember from F21 to G21:O21 to compute each year's variable cost.

9. Copy the formula =buildcost/10 from F22 to G22:O22 to compute each year's depreciation.

10. Copy the formula =F19-F20-F21-F22 from F23 to G23:O23, and use equation (1) to compute each year's before tax profits.

11. Copy the formula =(1-taxrate)*F23 from F24 to G24:O24 and use Equation 2 to compute each year's after-tax profits. Assume Iron Pit is part of a profitable corporation, so even though the 2014 before-tax profit is negative, Iron Pit's loss can contribute a tax shield to the rest of the company.

12. In cell E25 enter an initial working capital level of 0. Copy the formula =workingcappercentage*F19 from F25 to G25:O25 to compute each year's working capital.

13. Copy the formula =F25-E25 from F26 to G26:O26 to compute each year's change in working capital.

14. In cell E28 compute the cash flow due to the initial capital costs with the formula =-E14.

15. Copy the formula =F24-F26+F22 from F27 to G27:O27-and use Equation 4 to compute each year's cash flow.

16. In cell F29 compute the NPV of all cash flows (as of 1/1/2014) with the formula =XNPV(discountrate,E27:O27,E13:O13). Given your assumptions, your health club will generate a cash flow of $4,924,240.41.

17. In cell F30 compute the IRR of the health club's cash flows with the formula =XIRR(E27:O27,E13:O13). Your assumptions yield an IRR of 61.6 percent. This means that the current assumptions imply that John's investment would earn a 61.6 percent annual return.

This analysis shows that for the given assumptions, the health club will yield a great rate of return on investment within a relatively short 10 year period. Of course, the assumptions may be wrong, so you will next examine how large an error in your assumptions will compromise the attractiveness of the health club investment.

Measuring Sensitivity Analysis with a One-way Table

Recall from Chapter 19 that the sensitivity analysis of a model involves determining how "sensitive" model outputs are to changes in model inputs. Of course, John Cougar Mellencamp realizes that the assumptions may not actually pan out. Anticipating John's objection, you can use a one-way Data Table (see Figure 20-3) to determine the sensitivity of Iron Pit's NPV and IRR to the annual retention rate. In Chapter 19 you used a two-way table to measure sensitivity analysis, but you only need a one-way table here because you are varying a single parameter. To create the one-way Data Table, proceed as follows:

1. In the cell range J3:J9 enter reasonable values for the health club's retention rate. (You can choose 70 percent–95 percent.) These values might be derived from the annual retention rates experienced by other health clubs.
2. A one-way Data Table can have more than one output cell. The output cells for a one-way Data Table are listed beginning one row above the first input value and one column to the right of the input values. Your two output cells will be the health club's NPV (enter in cell K2 with the formula =F29) and the health club's IRR (enter in cell L2 with the formula =F30).
3. Select the table range (J2:L10), which includes the input values, output cell formulas, and the range where the Data Table places its calculations.
4. From the Data tab on the ribbon, select What If Analysis from the Data Tools group and then select Data Table.... In a one-way table there is no row input cell because no input values exist in the first row of the table. Because the values in the first column of the table range are retention rates, choose D8 as the column input cell.
5. Click OK and you see the one-way Data Table shown in Figure 20-3.

You find, for example, that increasing the annual retention rate from 70 percent to 90 percent doubles the NPV of Iron Pit and increases the IRR from 17 percent to 33 percent. This Data Table shows that even if the retention rate were a relatively low 70 percent, the investment would still be a good one. This sensitivity analysis should make John feel much better about investing in Iron Pit.

	J	K	L
1		NPV	IRR
2		$937,113.25	23.14%
3	0.7	$423,919.73	17%
4	0.75	$660,397.29	20%
5	0.8	$937,113.25	23%
6	0.85	$1,262,399.22	26%
7	0.9	$1,646,340.76	30%
8	0.95	$2,101,112.89	33%
9			

Figure 20-3: Iron Pit sensitivity analysis

Using Customer Value to Estimate a Firm's Market Value

Gupta and Zeithaml (*Marketing Science*, 2006, pp. 718–739) used a customer-centric approach similar to the Iron Pit analysis to value the future cash flows generated by Amazon.com, TD Ameritrade, Capital One, eBay, and E*TRADE. Their method parallels the Iron Pit analysis (see Exercise 3 for an example). Their method closely approximated the actual market values of E*TRADE, Ameritrade, and Capital One. Rust, Lemon and Zeithaml (*Journal of Marketing*, 2004, pp. 109–126) used a customer value approach to estimate the value of American Airlines and found their value came close to American Airlines' actual market value.

The key to both these papers was the method used to model the evolution of each company's number of customers. The authors used S curves (see Chapter 26, "Using S Curves to Forecast Sales of a New Product") to model the evolution of each firm's customers.

Summary

In this chapter you learned the following:

- A firm's customers drive the firm's revenues and profits. Therefore, if you can build a model that accurately generates a firm's number of customers, you can model the firm's future cash flows and estimate the firm's value. Key relationships used in this type of model include the following equations:

(1) Before-Tax Profits = Revenues – (Variable and Nondepreciated Costs) – Depreciation

(2) After-Tax Profits = (1 – Tax Rate) * Before-Tax Profits

(3) Working Capital = Current Assets – Current Liabilities will be modeled as a fixed percentage of revenue.

(4) Cash Flow = After-Tax Profits + Depreciation – Change in Working Capital

(5) End Period t + 1 Customers = Beginning Period t + 1 Customers + New Period t + 1 Customers – (1– Retention rate) * (Beginning Period t Customers)

■ The Excel XNPV and XIRR functions can determine the NPV or IRR of a stream of irregularly spaced cash flows.

Exercises

1. Assume that for N years the number of new customers will grow at G percent per year, and thereafter the number of new customers will drop by D percent per year. Modify the Ironpit.xlsx file to incorporate this customer dynamic.

2. Modify the Ironpit.xlsx analysis to incorporate an annual growth rate in membership fees, annual fixed cost, and annual costs per customer.

3. A nice way to value new companies is to say Company Value = NPV of customer value from all current and future customers. Gupta and Lehmann (2006) used this approach to value Amazon.com as of March 2002. Using a method (S curves) (to be discussed in Chapter 26, "Using S Curves to Forecast Sales of a New Product"), they projected the total number of customers N(t) to have tried Amazon.com by the end of month t to be as given in file newamazondata.xls. In this file t = 1 is March 1997 and so on. For example, through the end of March 1997, 1.39 million people had tried Amazon.com; through April 1997, 1.81 million people had tried Amazon.com and so on.

You are given the following information (as of March 1997):

■ Cost of acquiring customer: $7.70
■ Monthly profit margin from customer: $1.29

■ Tax rate: 38 percent
■ Annual retention rate: 70 percent
■ Costs and revenues grow at 2.5 percent annually.
■ Discount profits at 10 percent per year

    a. Assume the profit during the month is based on the ending number of customers. Use this information to get a value of Amazon.com as of March 2002. Market value at the beginning of March 2002 was $5.4 billion. For each month you might have the following columns:

      ■ $N(t)$ = Total number of customers who have tried Amazon.com by end of month t
      ■ Quits = Number of customers leaving Amazon.com during each month
      ■ New customers
      ■ Ending customers
      ■ Acquisition costs
      ■ Profit margin
      ■ After-tax profits

    b. Run 420 total months (35 years) and determine whether you believe that at the beginning of March 2002 Amazon.com was fairly valued.

4. Why do you think that our customer-centric approach to valuation is often called the eyeball approach?

5. For the Iron Pit example, suppose that during year 1 Iron Pit would gain 2,000 new customers, but each year the number of new customers dropped 10 percent. Would this increase or decrease the attractiveness of the investment?

6. In your analysis of Iron Pit, you assumed the annual fee was $400. How would you determine whether the assumed $400 annual fee was appropriate?

7. Use a one-way Data Table to analyze how sensitive the attractiveness of the investment is to a change in the assumption that working capital = 10 percent of annual revenue.

21

Customer Value, Monte Carlo Simulation, and Marketing Decision Making

I n many situations the results of a marketing decision are highly uncertain. For example, when Land's End mails a catalog, it does not know how many dollars of profit will be generated by the catalog. The profit generated on a mailing often depends on the customer's past response to catalog mailings. Likewise, consider a merchant who is considering using a Groupon offer. The amount of profit or loss obtained is uncertain because it depends on the number of people taking the offer who become loyal customers as well as the long-term value generated by the customers. *Monte Carlo simulation* is a method for determining the range of outcomes that can occur in a situation. Using Monte Carlo simulation you may find that a Groupon offer has a 90 percent chance of earning a profit.

In this chapter you learn how combining Monte Carlo simulation and the concept of long-term customer value can improve a company's decision making by allowing the marketer to estimate the range of outcomes that can result from a marketing decision.

A Markov Chain Model of Customer Value

Often a customer passes through various stages of a *customer life cycle*. For example, a Progressive car insurance policy holder may start as a teenager who has several accidents and turn into a 30-year-old who never has another accident. A Land's End catalog customer may begin as someone who bought a sweater last month and turn into someone who has not made another purchase in the last two years.

The value of a customer therefore depends on where the customer is currently in this life cycle. Calculating customer value based on this cycle can be achieved using Monte Carlo simulation. Monte Carlo simulation is a method to model uncertainty and estimate a range of outcomes under uncertainty by replaying a situation out many times (even millions of times). Monte Carlo simulation began during World

War II when scientists tested to see if the random neutron diffusion in the nuclear fission involved in the atomic bomb would actually result in a bomb that worked. Mathematicians James von Neumann and Stanislaw Ulam the simulation procedure named Monte Carlo after the gambling casinos in Monaco. As you will learn, Monte Carlo simulation bears a resemblance to repeatedly tossing "electronic dice" or repeatedly spinning an "electronic roulette wheel."

The following example shows how you can use Monte Carlo simulation to model customer value in situations in which customers pass through stages.

Imagine that a small mail-order firm mails out catalogs every three months (at a cost of $1). Based on analyses performed on historical purchase data (probably using PivotTables!), the marketing analyst found that each time a customer places an order, the profit earned (exclusive of mailing cost) follows a normal random variable with mean $60 and standard deviation $10. The probability that a customer orders from a catalog depends on recency (number of catalogs since last order) and frequency (total number of orders placed), as shown in Figure 21-1.

	C	D	E	F	G	H
1		Frequency				
2						
3	Recency	1	2	3	4	>=5
4	1	0.103	0.121	0.143	0.151	0.163
5	2	0.076	0.09	0.106	0.112	0.121
6	3	0.059	0.069	0.081	0.086	0.093
7	4	0.045	0.053	0.062	0.066	0.071
8	5	0.038	0.045	0.053	0.056	0.061
9	6	0.035	0.041	0.049	0.051	0.056
10	7	0.03	0.035	0.041	0.043	0.047
11	8	0.027	0.032	0.038	0.04	0.043
12	9	0.025	0.029	0.035	0.037	0.04
13	10	0.021	0.025	0.03	0.031	0.034
14	11	0.021	0.024	0.028	0.03	0.033
15	12	0.02	0.024	0.028	0.03	0.032
16	13	0.017	0.02	0.024	0.025	0.027
17	14	0.017	0.02	0.024	0.025	0.027
18	15	0.016	0.019	0.022	0.024	0.026
19	16	0.015	0.018	0.021	0.022	0.024
20	17	0.014	0.017	0.02	0.021	0.022
21	18	0.013	0.016	0.018	0.019	0.021
22	19	0.013	0.015	0.018	0.019	0.02
23	20	0.012	0.014	0.017	0.018	0.019
24	21	0.012	0.014	0.016	0.017	0.018
25	22	0.011	0.013	0.015	0.016	0.017
26	23	0.011	0.012	0.015	0.015	0.017
27	24	0.01	0.012	0.014	0.015	0.016

Figure 21-1: Chance of purchasing from Land's End catalog

For example, based on the preceding analysis, a customer (call her Miley) who has ordered twice and whose last order was three catalogs ago has a 6.9 percent chance of ordering. This assumes that a customer's future evolution depends only on her present state. For example, in analyzing Miley's future purchases you need only know she has ordered twice and her last order was three catalogs ago. You do not need to know, for example, the timing of other orders that were placed before the last order. This model is an example of a *Markov Chain*. In a Markov Chain a process evolves from one state to another state, with the probability of going to the next state depending only on the current state. In this example the customer's current state is the number of periods in the past when last order occurred and the number of previous orders. Given this information you can determine how the value of a customer who has ordered once depends on recency.

Assume you stop mailing to a customer after she fails to order 24 consecutive times. Also assume the annual discount rate (often called the weighted average cost of capital [WACC]) is 3 percent per period (or 1.03^4) per year. The following steps describe how to determine the customer value for a customer who has bought one time (frequency = 1) and bought from the last received catalog (recency = 1). The work for this example is in the `Markov.xls` file (see Figure 21-2).

1. In cell C30 enter the recency level (in this case 1) with the formula `=Initial_recency`.
2. In cell D30 enter the initial frequency with the formula `=Original_Frequency`.
3. In cell E30 determine the probability that the customer orders in with the formula `=IF(B30="no",0,INDEX(probs,C30,D30))`. If you have ended the relationship with the customer, the order probability is 0.

The key to performing a Monte Carlo simulation is the `RAND()` function. When you enter the `RAND()` function in a cell, Excel enters a number that is equally likely to assume any value greater than 0 and less than 1. For example, there is a 10 percent chance that a number less than or equal to 0.10 appears in a cell; a 30 percent chance that a number greater than or equal to 0.4 and less than or equal to 0.7 appears in the cell; and so on. Values in different cells containing a `RAND()` function are independent; that is, the value of a `RAND()` in one cell does not have influence on the value of a `RAND()` in any other cell. In a Monte Carlo simulation, you use `RAND()` functions to model sources of uncertainty. Then you recalculate the spreadsheet many times (say 10,000) to determine the range of outcomes that can occur. The `RAND()` function plays the role of "electronic dice."

	C	D	E	F	G	H	I	K	L
17	14	0.017	0.02	0.024	0.025	0.027		Original Frequency	1
18	15	0.016	0.019	0.022	0.024	0.026		Initial recency	1
19	16	0.015	0.018	0.021	0.022	0.024		wacc	0.03
20	17	0.014	0.017	0.02	0.021	0.022		cost	1
21	18	0.013	0.016	0.018	0.019	0.021		salesprofit	60
22	19	0.013	0.015	0.018	0.019	0.02		meanprofit	60
23	20	0.012	0.014	0.017	0.018	0.019		stddevprofit	10
24	21	0.012	0.014	0.016	0.017	0.018			
25	22	0.011	0.013	0.015	0.016	0.017			
26	23	0.011	0.012	0.015	0.015	0.017			1
27	24	0.01	0.012	0.014	0.015	0.016	value		
28							$129.34		

	A Period	B still goin	C Recency	D Frequency	E Prob buy	F Buy?	G Cost	H Net contribution from sale	I total profit	J Random number for Ordering	K Random Number for Order Profit
30	1	yes	1	1	0.103	0	1	$ -	$ (1.00)	0.619823407	0.508273348
31	2	yes	2	1	0.076	0	1	$ -	$ (1.00)	0.352922719	0.751903009
32	3	yes	3	1	0.059	0	1	$ -	$ (1.00)	0.784000303	0.302748458
33	4	yes	4	1	0.045	0	1	$ -	$ (1.00)	0.779155415	0.292283242
34	5	yes	5	1	0.038	0	1	$ -	$ (1.00)	0.564459144	0.405582301
35	6	yes	6	1	0.035	1	1	$ 41.65	$ 40.65	0.033278537	0.487694534
36	7	yes	1	2	0.121	0	1	$ -	$ (1.00)	0.520523773	0.876439516
37	8	yes	2	2	0.09	0	1	$ -	$ (1.00)	0.801084665	0.531285222
38	9	yes	3	2	0.069	0	1	$ -	$ (1.00)	0.125746486	0.721864745
39	10	yes	4	2	0.053	0	1	$ -	$ (1.00)	0.405850062	0.30842148
40	11	yes	5	2	0.045	1	1	$ 31.33	$ 30.33	0.002071541	0.988193167
41	12	yes	1	3	0.143	0	1	$ -	$ (1.00)	0.638149249	0.599977121
42	13	yes	2	3	0.106	1	1	$ 42.60	$ 41.60	0.040954151	0.846907576
43	14	yes	1	4	0.151	0	1	$ -	$ (1.00)	0.680405052	0.02076187
44	15	yes	2	4	0.112	0	1	$ -	$ (1.00)	0.480151067	0.000581978
45	16	yes	3	4	0.086	0	1	$ -	$ (1.00)	0.742269962	0.850630577
46	17	yes	4	4	0.066	0	1	$ -	$ (1.00)	0.184001115	0.86990783
47	18	yes	5	4	0.056	0	1	$ -	$ (1.00)	0.203105044	0.635954588
48	19	yes	6	4	0.051	0	1	$ -	$ (1.00)	0.242354818	0.047300115
49	20	yes	7	4	0.043	1	1	$ 36.36	$ 35.36	0.009030817	0.209660576
50	21	yes	1	5	0.163	0	1	$ -	$ (1.00)	0.987141979	0.179800981
51	22	yes	2	5	0.121	1	1	$ 43.12	$ 42.12	0.045725851	0.873710957
52	23	yes	1	5	0.163	1	1	$ 49.74	$ 48.74	0.152474115	0.355900659
53	24	yes	1	5	0.163	0	1	$ -	$ (1.00)	0.991131139	0.307565164
54	25	yes	2	5	0.121	0	1	$ -	$ (1.00)	0.375441459	0.201176465
55	26	yes	3	5	0.093	0	1	$ -	$ (1.00)	0.633093379	0.835821261

Figure 21-2: Land's End Customer Value model

During each three-month period, the Monte Carlo simulation uses two RAND() functions. One RAND() determines if the customer places an order. If the customer orders, the second RAND() function determines the profit (excluding mailing cost) generated by the order. The following steps continue the Markov .xls example, now walking you through using the RAND() function to perform the Monte Carlo simulation:

1. In cell F30 you can determine if the customer orders during period 1 by using the formula =IF(B30="no",0,IF(J30<E30,1,0)). If you mailed a catalog and the random number in Column J is less than or equal to the chance of the customer placing an order, then an order is placed. Because the RAND() value is equally likely to be any number between 0 and 1, this gives a probability of E30 that an order is placed.

2. Book the cost of mailing the catalog (if the customer is still with you) by using the formula =IF(B30="yes",$L$20,0) in cell G30.

3. Book the profit from an order by using the formula `=IF(AND(B30="yes",` `F30=1),NORMINV(J30,meanprofit,stddevprofit),0)` in cell H30. If an order is received, then the profit of the order is generated with the `NORMINV(J30,meanprofit,stddevprofit,0)` portion of the formula. If the random number in Column J equals x, then this formula returns the xth percentile of a normal random variable with the given mean and standard deviation. For example, if J30 contains a 0.5, you generate a profit equal to the mean, and if J30 contains a 0.841, you generate a profit equal to one standard deviation above the mean.

4. Calculate the total profit for the period in cell I30 with the formula `=H30-G30`.

5. In cells C31 and D31 update recency and frequency based on what happened with the last catalog mailing. *This is the key step in your model because it determines how the customer's state changes.* In C31 the formula `=IF(F30=1,1,C30+1)` increases recency by 1 if a customer did not buy last period. Otherwise, recency returns to 1. In cell D31 the formula `=IF(D30=5,5,D30+F30)` increases frequency by 1 if and only if the customer placed an order last period. If the customer has ordered five times frequency remains at $> = 5$.

6. In cell B31 end the relationship with the customer if she has not ordered for 24 months with the formula `=IF(C30>=24,"no","yes")`. When there is a "No" in Column B, all future cash flows are 0.

7. Copy the formulas from E30:K30 to E31:K109 and copy the formulas from B31:D31 to B32:D109 to arbitrarily cut off profits after 80 quarters (20 years).

8. In cell I28 compute the present value of all profits (assuming end-of-period profits) with the formula `=NPV(wacc,I30:I109)`.

You can now use a two-way data table to "trick" Excel into running your spreadsheet 10,000 times and tabulating the results for all possible recency values (1–24). This is the step where you "perform" the Monte Carlo simulation. To do so complete the following steps:

NOTE Because a data table takes a while to recalculate, go to the Formulas tab, and from Calculation Options select Automatic Except for Data Tables. After you choose this option, data tables recalculate only when you select the F9 key. This option enables you to modify the spreadsheet without waiting for data tables to recalculate.

1. Enter the possible recency values (1–24) in the range Q5:AN5.
2. Enter the integers 1 through 10,000 (corresponding to the 10,000 "iterations" of recalculating the spreadsheet) in the range P6:P10005. To accomplish this enter a 1 in P6, and from the Home tab, select Fill and then Series. Then complete the dialog box, as shown in Figure 21-3.

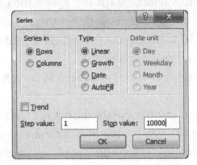

Figure 21-3: Filling in iteration numbers 1–10,000

3. Enter the output formula =I28 in the upper-left corner (cell P5) of the table range.
4. From the Data tab select What-If Analysis and then choose Data Table...
5. Fill in the Row input cell as L18 (Initial Recency Level).
6. For the Column input cell choose any blank cell (such as AD2). In each column Excel sequentially places 1, 2, …10,000 in the blank cell and recalculates the RAND() values for the column's recency level. After a few minutes you have "played out" 10,000 customers for each recency level. (Recall you have fixed Frequency = 1.)
7. Copy the formula =AVERAGE(Q6:Q10005) from Q4 to R4:AN4 to compute an estimate of the average profit for each recency level. The results are shown in Figure 21-4.

You can now estimate that a customer who purchased from the last received catalog is worth $14.48; a customer who last purchased two catalogs ago is worth $8.76; and so on. Customers who last ordered seven or more catalogs ago have negative value, so you should stop mailing to these customers.

	P	Q	R	S	T	U	V	W	X	Y	Z	AA
1												
2	frequency =1											
3												
4	mean profit	$14.48	$8.76	$4.57	$2.42	$0.79	$0.21	-$0.29	-$0.85	-$1.79	-$2.80	-$2.44
5	($16.94)	1	2	3	4	5	6	7	8	9	10	11
6	1	$99.31	$4.64	$20.04	-$15.42	-$14.88	-$14.32	-$13.75	-$13.17	-$12.56	-$11.94	-$11.30
7	2	$94.40	-$16.44	$23.48	-$15.42	$1.25	-$14.32	-$13.75	$100.87	-$12.56	-$11.94	-$11.30
8	3	-$16.94	$44.92	-$15.94	-$15.42	$186.04	$21.98	-$13.75	-$13.17	-$12.56	-$11.94	-$11.30
9	4	$7.93	-$16.44	-$15.94	-$15.42	$17.19	-$14.32	$18.94	-$13.17	-$12.56	-$11.94	-$11.30
10	5	-$16.94	-$16.44	-$15.94	-$15.42	-$14.88	$20.43	-$13.75	-$13.17	$79.70	-$11.94	-$11.30
11	6	$18.90	-$16.44	$29.76	$6.27	-$14.88	-$14.32	$36.04	-$13.17	-$12.56	-$11.94	$10.66
12	7	$1.29	-$16.44	-$15.94	-$15.42	-$14.88	$18.18	$4.27	-$13.17	-$12.56	$6.38	-$11.30
13	8	-$16.94	-$16.44	-$15.94	-$15.42	-$14.88	-$14.32	-$13.75	-$13.17	-$12.56	-$11.94	$96.57
14	9	$122.50	-$16.44	-$15.94	-$0.83	-$14.88	-$14.32	-$13.75	-$13.17	$17.88	-$11.94	$24.29
15	10	$125.81	-$16.44	-$15.94	-$15.42	-$14.88	-$14.32	-$13.75	$52.19	-$12.56	-$11.94	-$11.30
16	11	$117.76	$52.02	-$15.94	$46.97	-$14.88	-$14.32	-$13.75	-$13.17	-$12.56	-$11.94	-$11.30
17	12	$54.03	$8.29	-$15.94	-$15.42	$66.78	$7.03	$33.38	-$13.17	-$12.56	$75.49	-$11.30
18	13	$68.79	-$16.44	-$15.94	$12.29	-$14.88	-$14.32	-$13.75	-$13.17	-$12.56	$16.28	-$11.30
19	14	$9.72	-$16.44	-$15.94	-$15.42	$2.91	$10.70	-$13.75	-$1.52	-$12.56	-$11.94	-$11.30
20	15	$40.58	$30.75	-$15.94	$115.56	-$14.88	$9.68	-$13.75	-$13.17	-$12.56	-$11.94	-$11.30
21	16	$51.17	-$16.44	-$15.94	-$15.42	-$14.88	$123.73	-$13.75	-$13.17	-$12.56	-$11.94	-$11.30
22	17	$4.02	$19.84	$51.08	$36.85	-$14.88	-$14.32	-$13.75	-$13.17	$17.88	-$11.94	-$11.30
23	18	-$16.94	$43.52	$44.90	-$15.42	-$14.88	-$14.32	-$13.75	$21.54	$8.26	-$11.94	-$11.30
24	19	-$16.94	-$16.44	-$15.94	-$15.42	-$14.88	-$14.32	-$13.75	-$13.17	-$12.56	-$11.94	-$11.30
25	20	$18.15	-$16.44	$52.36	-$15.42	-$14.88	-$14.32	-$13.75	-$13.17	-$12.56	-$11.94	$29.71
26	21	-$16.94	-$3.41	$76.47	-$15.42	$28.66	-$14.32	-$13.75	-$13.17	-$12.56	-$11.94	-$0.64
27	22	-$16.94	-$16.44	-$15.94	-$15.42	$80.05	-$14.32	-$13.75	-$0.01	-$12.56	-$11.94	-$11.30
28	23	-$16.94	-$16.44	$25.66	$34.71	-$14.88	-$14.32	-$13.75	$14.06	-$12.56	-$11.94	-$11.30

Figure 21-4: Land's End data table

Using Monte Carlo Simulation to Predict Success of a Marketing Initiative

When a company is considering a marketing decision, they never know with 100 percent certainty that their decision will make the company better off. If a company repeatedly chooses marketing decisions that have much more than a 50 percent probability of making the company better off, then in the long run the company will succeed as result of marketing decisions. You can use Monte Carlo simulation to evaluate the probability that a marketing decision will improve a company's bottom line. In this section you will learn how to do this by analyzing whether a pizza parlor will benefit from a Groupon offer.

Carrie has just been fired from the CIA and has purchased a suburban Virginia pizza parlor. She is trying to determine whether she should offer the local residents a Groupon offer. As discussed in Chapter 19, "Calculating Lifetime Customer Value," Groupon offers customers pizza for less than cost. The restaurant hopes to recoup the loss on the pizzas sold with a Groupon offer via the customer value of new customers who become return customers. To be specific, the terms of the Groupon offer follow:

- Customers are offered two pizzas (usually sold for $26) for $10.
- Carrie keeps half of the revenue ($5).
- Carrie's profit margin is 50 percent.

In deciding whether to use Groupon, Carrie faces many sources of uncertainty:

- Fraction of customers who take the offer who are new customers
- Fraction of people who spend more than the deal size ($26)
- For customers who spend more than $26, the amount spent in excess of $26
- Fraction of new customers who return
- Annual profit generated by new customers who return
- Retention rate for new customers

To help Carrie determine the range of outcomes that will result from the Groupon offer, you can use the Monte Carlo simulation to model these sources of uncertainty and in doing so, estimate the chances that the Groupon offer will increase profitability. The key to the analysis is using the customer value concepts of Chapter 19 and the Monte Carlo simulation to estimate the probability that the benefit the pizza parlor gains from new customers will outweigh the lost profit on pizzas sold to customers who redeem the Groupon offer.

To simplify modeling, assume each of the six uncertain quantities is equally likely to assume any value between a low value and a high value. The low and high values for these quantities are shown in Figure 21-5.

When trying to determine these values, the marketing analyst can use historical information to establish upper and lower bounds. In his 2011 paper "What Makes Groupon Promotions Profitable for Businesses?", Utpal Dhoakia surveyed 324 businesses that used Groupon and obtained estimates for some of the previously listed quantities:

- 75 percent of people taking the deal are new customers.
- 36 percent of all deal takers spent more than the deal size.
- 20 percent of new customers returned later.

	B	C	D	E	F	G
1		Groupon				
2						
3		margin	0.5			
4		2pizzas	$26.00			
5		weget	$5.00			
6		cost	$13.00	Low	High	
7		probnewcustomer	0.76	0.65	0.85	
8		newspendmorethandeal	0.4	0.3	0.42	
9		newpeoplewhoreturn	0.17	0.1	0.3	
10						
11		Look at 100 people who take deal				
12	new	76				
13	returnees	24				
14	howmanyspendmore	40	Low	High		
15	howmuchmore	$7.00	$3.00	$17.00		
16	valuenewcustomer	$59.07	Low	High		
17	anncustomerprofit	$21.00	$20.00	$40.00		
18	retentionrate	0.77	0.55	0.85		
19	newcomeback	12.92				
20						
21						
22						
23						
24	Loss					
25	fromnew	$608.00				
26	fromreturning	$504.00	assume they would have come anyway			
27	total loss	$1,112.00				
28	Benefits					
29	extraprofittoday	$140.00				
30	valuenewcustomers	$763.15				
31	total	$903.15				
32						
33	Net Gain	-$208.85				

Figure 21-5: Analysis of Groupon for Carrie's Pizza

Based on this information and on past Groupon offers, Carrie believes the following:

- Between 65 percent and 85 percent of customers taking the deal will be new customers.
- Between 30 percent and 42 percent of customers will spend an amount in excess of $26.
- Those who spend in excess of $26 will spend on average between $3 and $17 beyond $26.

- Between 10 percent and 30 percent of new customers will return.
- Average annual profit generated by a new customer is between $20 and $40.
- Average annual retention rate for new customers generated by Groupon is between 55 percent and 85 percent.

You can use the Excel RANDBETWEEN function to ensure that an uncertain quantity (often called a *random variable*) is equally likely to lie between a lower limit L and an upper limit U. For integers, entering the formula RANDBETWEEN(L,U) in a cell makes it equally likely that any integer between L and U inclusive will be entered in the cell. For example, entering the formula =RANDBETWEEN(65,85) in a cell ensures that it is equally likely that any of 65, 66, …, 84, or 85 is entered in the cell.

Complete the following steps (see the file Groupon.xlsx) to model the range of outcomes that will ensue if Carrie introduces a Groupon offer:

1. In D3:D5 enter Carrie's profit margin, the price of two pizzas without Groupon, and what Carrie receives from Groupon for two pizzas.

2. In D6 compute the cost of producing two pizzas with the formula =(1-margin)*_2pizzas.

3. In cell D7 enter the fraction of Groupon offer takers who are new customers with the formula =RANDBETWEEN(100*E7,100*F7)/100. This is equally likely to enter a .65, .66, …, .84, .85 in cell D7.

4. In cell D8 generate the fraction of new customers who spend more than $26 with the formula =RANDBETWEEN(100*E8,100*F8)/100.

5. Copy this formula from cell D8 to D9 to generate the fraction of new Groupon customers who return.

6. Assume without loss of generality that 100 customers take the Groupon offer and you generate the random net gain (or loss) in profit from these 100 offer takers. Include gains or losses today and gains from added new customers.

7. In cell C12 compute the number of your 100 offer takers who will be new customers with the formula =100*probnewcustomer.

8. In cell C13 compute the number of offer takers who are returnees with the formula =100*(1-probnewcustomer).

9. In cell C14 compute the number of offer takers who spend more than the deal with the formula =100*newspendmorethandeal.

10. In cell C15 determine the average amount spent in excess of $26 by those spending more than $26 with the formula =RANDBETWEEN(D15,E15). Copy this formula to C17 to determine the average level of annual customer profit for new customers created by the Groupon offer.

11. In the worksheet `basic model`, attach your Customer Value template, as discussed in Chapter 19. Then in C16 use the formula `='basic model'!E5*C17` to compute the lifetime value of a customer based on mid-year cash flows.

12. In cell C18 compute the average retention rate for new customers with the formula `=RANDBETWEEN(100*D18,100*E18)/100`.

13. In cell C19 compute the number of the 100 offer takers who are returning new customers with the formula `=C12*newpeoplewhoreturn`.

In the range C25:C33 you can compute your gain or loss from the 100 offer takers:

1. To begin in cell C25, use the formula `=(cost-weget)*C12` to compute your loss today from the new customers among the offer takers as $8 * *number of new customers*.

2. To simplify your work assume all offer takers who were previous customers would have shown up anyway. Because each of these returning customers would have paid $26, you lose $26 – $5 = $21 on each of these customers.

3. Then in cell C26 use the formula `=C13*(_2pizzas-weget)` to compute your loss on these customers.

4. In cell C27 the formula `=SUM(C25:C26)` computes your total loss today on the 100 people who took the Groupon offer.

5. In C29 with the formula `=margin*C15*C14`, compute the extra profit earned today by multiplying your 50 percent profit margin by the amount in excess of $26 spent today by offer takers.

6. In C30 use the formula `=C19*C16` to compute the value of the new customers by multiplying the number of returning new customers times the average value for each new customer.

7. In cell C31 use the formula `=C29+C30` to compute the total benefits created by the Groupon offer.

8. In cell C33 use the formula `=C31-C27` to compute the total benefits less today's losses.

Using a One-Way Data Table to Simulate the Groupon Deal

You can now use Monte Carlo simulation (via a one-way data table) to "play out" the spreadsheet 10,000 times. Then tabulate your average gain per offer taker and the probability that the Groupon offer will increase Carrie's long-term bottom line.

1. Use FILL SERIES (from the Home tab) to enter the iteration numbers (1, 2, ..., 10,000) in the range I9:I10008.

2. Use a one-way data table to "trick" Excel into replaying your spreadsheet 10,000 times. Recalculate your total gain on the 100 offer takers, so enter the total gain in cell J8 with the formula =C33.

3. Select the data table range (I8:J10008), and from the Data tab, choose What-If Analysis and select Data Table... In a one-way data table, there is no row input cell, so all you need to do is choose any blank cell (such as N7) as the column input cell. Then Excel places 1, 2, ..., 10,000 in N7 and each time recalculates Carrie's net gain. During each recalculation each RANDBETWEEN function recalculates, so you play out the modeled uncertainty 10,000 times. The resulting simulated profits are shown in the range J9:J10008 of Figure 21-6.

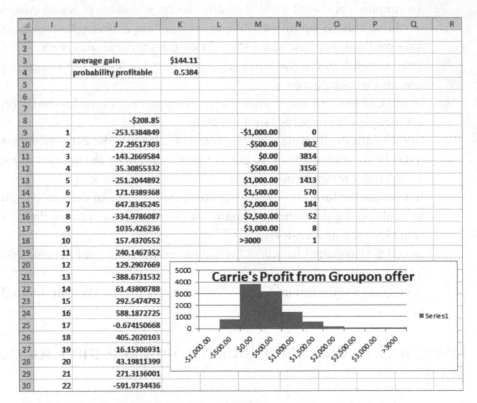

Figure 21-6: Simulation results for Carrie's Pizza

4. In cell K3 compute the average profit over your 10,000 iterations earned from the 100 deal takers with the formula =AVERAGE(J9:J10008). You find

an average gain of $144.11, which indicates that on average the Groupon deal can improve Carrie's bottom line.

5. In cell K4 compute the probability that the deal increases profits with the formula =COUNTIF(J9:J10008,">0")/10000. There is a 53.8 percent chance the deal yields a favorable result.

This finding indicates that the deal is of marginal value to the pizza parlor. From cell K3, you find that the average profit per customer equals $144.11. This again indicates that on average, the Groupon deal does just a little better than breaking even.

Using a Histogram to Summarize the Simulation Results

As the Chinese say, "A picture is worth a thousand words." With this in mind use a bar graph or histogram to summarize your simulation results. To create a bar graph of your simulation results, proceed as follows:

1. Enter the boundaries of bin ranges (−$1000, −$500, …, $3000) in M9:M17. Append a label >3000 for all iterations in which profit is more than $3000.

2. Select the range N9:N18 and array enter by selecting Ctrl+Shift+Enter (see Chapter 2, "Using Excel Charts to Summarize Marketing Data") the formula =FREQUENCY(J9:J10008,M9:M17). In N9 this computes the number of iterations in which profit is <=$1000; in N10 this array formula computes the number of iterations in which profit is >−$1000 and <=−$500 (802); in N18 this array formula computes the number of iterations (1) in which profit is >$3000.

A column graph summarizing these results is shown in Figure 21-6.

Summary

You can use the Excel data table feature combined with Excel's RAND() and RANDBETWEEN functions to simulate uncertainty in situations in which customer value involves uncertain quantities (random variables).

- If an uncertain event has a probability x of occurring, then the event occurs if a value of RAND() is less than or equal to x.
- If an uncertain quantity (such as annual retention rate) is normally distributed with a given mean and sigma, then the function =NORMINV(RAND(),mean,standard dev) generates a normal random variable with the given mean and sigma.

■ If an uncertain quantity (such as annual profit generated by a customer) is equally likely to be between two integers L and U, then it can be modeled with the function RANDBETWEEN(L,U).

Exercises

1. Suppose each customer purchase of a product generates $10 in profit. Each month a customer either buys 0 or 1 unit of the product. If a customer bought last month, there is a 0.5 chance she will buy next month. If she last bought two months ago, there is a 0.2 chance she will buy next month. If she last bought three months ago, there is a 0.1 chance that she will buy next month. If a customer has not bought for four months, there is no chance she will ever buy in the future. Determine the value of a customer who last purchased the product last month, two months ago or three months ago. Assume profits are discounted at 1 percent per month.

2. You own a business magazine CY. At the beginning of year 1, you have 300,000 subscribers and 700,000 nonsubscribers who are considered possible subscribers in the future. Determine whether it is a good idea to give prospective subscribers their first year subscription for free. The file Customerdata.xlsx gives for a random sample of subscribers the number of years they subscribed. A sample of the data is shown in Figure 21-7. For example, Person 2 subscribed for six years before canceling, and Person 13 has subscribed for one year and is still a subscriber. To begin, use this data to estimate the annual retention rate, assuming that retention rate does not depend on how long a person has subscribed.

   a. Currently the annual subscription fee is $55 and you make $50 annual profit per subscriber (based on beginning of year subscribers.) You discount cash flows at 10 percent per year. At present 5 percent of the nonsubscribers at the beginning of a year become subscribers at the beginning of the next year. At the beginning of each year, 20,000 new nonsubscribers enter the market. After a person stops being a subscriber, assume he will never subscribe again. Determine the value of the status quo. Use 20 years and assume at the beginning of year 21 each current subscriber is credited with a salvage value based on the Customer Value template.

Person	Years	Still here?
1	7	no
2	6	no
3	4	no
4	1	no
5	7	no
6	8	no
7	3	no
8	7	no
9	8	no
10	1	no
11	7	no
12	1	no
13	1	yes

Figure 21-7: Retention data for CY magazine

b. CY is considering giving new subscribers their first year for free. You are not sure how this will increase the fraction of nonsubscribers you get each year above the current level of 5 percent, but you estimate the new recruitment percentage will be normally distributed with a mean of 6 percent and a standard deviation of 1 percent. Assume that the recruitment rate of new subscribers will be the same each year. Also assume that all cash flows occur at the beginning of a year and there is no customer acquisition cost. Use the output from 10,000 iterations of a Monte Carlo simulation to determine whether you should give the new subscribers the first year for free.

3. You work for OJ's Orange Juice. Currently there are 10 million customers, and each week a customer buys 1 gallon of orange juice from OJ or a competitor. The current profit margin is $2 per gallon. Last week six million customers bought from you, and four million bought from the competition.

The file OJdata.xlsx gives the purchase history for a year for several customers. For example, in week three, Person 5 did not buy from you (0 = bought from competition, 1 = bought from you). The data is scrambled so you need to manipulate it. From this data you should figure out the chance customers will buy from you next week if they bought from you last week and the chance customers will buy from you next week if they bought from a competitor last week. Solve the following situations:

a. Evaluate the profitability of the status quo (for 52 weeks including the current week). No need for discounting!

b. OJ Orange Juice is considering a quality improvement. This improvement will reduce per-gallon profitability by 30 cents. This will increase customer loyalty, but you are not sure by how much. Assume it is equally likely that the customer retention rate will increase by between 0 percent and 10 percent. Use 10,000 iterations of a Monte Carlo simulation to determine whether OJ should make the quality improvement. Use a single RANDBETWEEN random variable to model the average improvement in customer loyalty created by the quality improvement.

4. GM wants to determine whether to give a $1,000 incentive this year to buyers of Chevy Malibus. Here is relevant information for the base case:

   - Year 1 price: $20,000
   - Year 1 cost: $16,000
   - Each year 30 percent of the market buys a Malibu or a car from the competition.
   - Seventy percent of people who last bought a Malibu will make their next purchase a Malibu.
   - Twenty-five percent of people who last bought a car from the competitor will make their next purchase a Malibu.
   - Inflation is 5 percent per year (on costs and price).
   - Currently 50 percent of the market is loyal to Malibu, and 50 percent is loyal to the competition.
   - Profits are accrued at the beginning of the year and are discounted at 10 percent per year.

   GM is considering giving a $1,000 incentive to any year 1 purchaser. The only change in the base numbers are as follows:

   - The percentage of the market buying a Malibu or a car from the competition in year 1 will increase by between 2 percent and 10 percent.
   - The fraction of loyal people who will make their next purchase in year 1 a Malibu will increase by between 5 percent and 15 percent.
   - The fraction of non-loyal people who will make their next purchase in year 1 a Malibu will increase by between 6 percent and 13 percent.

   Answer the following questions:

   a. Assuming end of year cash flows and a 30-year planning horizon, should Chevy give the $1,000 incentive? To answer this question, use the output from 10,000 iterations of a Monte Carlo simulation.
   b. Suppose the discount rate decreased to 7 percent. Would your decision change? Explain your answer without any calculations.

c. Suppose the year 1 price increased to $22,000. Would your decision change? Explain your answer without any calculations.

5. The local Ford dealer wants to determine whether to give all purchasers of new cars free oil changes. The Forddata.xlsx contains information on loyalty of car purchasers. A sample of this data is shown in Figure 21-8. For example, the data in row 7 indicates that customer number 113 bought a non-Ford on 8/15/1990.

	D	E	F
6	Date bought	Customer	Bought
7	8/15/1990	113	other
8	8/16/1990	64	other
9	8/18/1990	49	ford
10	8/18/1990	54	ford
11	8/18/1990	83	other
12	8/20/1990	42	other
13	8/20/1990	79	other
14	8/21/1990	51	other
15	8/23/1990	4	ford
16	8/23/1990	116	other
17	8/25/1990	25	other
18	8/26/1990	31	other
19	8/26/1990	33	other
20	8/27/1990	72	ford
21	8/28/1990	7	other
22	8/28/1990	60	other
23	8/28/1990	89	ford
24	8/28/1990	105	ford

Figure 21-8: Purchase data for Ford dealer

Use this data to determine the current chance that a Ford purchaser will next buy a Ford and the current chance a purchaser of another type of car will next buy a Ford. You have the following information:

- The length of time a person keeps a new car is equally likely to be between 700 and 2,000 days.
- Ford makes $2,000 on the purchase of a new car.
- Without free oil changes Ford earns $350 profit per year from servicing a car.
- Currently customers pay $100 per year for oil changes, which cost Ford $60 to perform. Assume all Ford purchasers always have their oil changed at the dealer.
- All purchase and service profits are booked at the time the car is purchased, and profits are discounted at 10 percent per year.

■ If you give free oil changes, loyalty percentages and switch percentages will improve by an unknown amount, equally likely to be between 2 percent and 15 percent.

Suppose a customer has bought a car from a competitor today. Determine the 20-year value of this customer to Ford without the free oil changes. What is the chance that the free oil changes increase the value of this customer?

22

Allocating Marketing Resources between Customer Acquisition and Retention

In the discussion of customer value so far, the retention rate has been assumed as a given. In reality, a firm can increase its retention rate by spending more money on customer retention. For example, Verizon could put more customer service representatives in stores to provide customers with better technical support and reduce store waiting times. This would cost Verizon money, but would likely increase its customer retention rate. Verizon could also increase the number of new customers by spending more money on customer acquisition. Robert Blattberg and John Deighton (*Manage Marketing by the Customer Equity Test*, Harvard Business Review, 1996, Vol. 74, No. 4, pp. 136–144) were the first to realize that companies could optimize profits by adjusting expenditures on retention and acquisition. This chapter explains and extends their model to show how companies can determine if they are spending too much (or too little) on customer retention and customer acquisition.

Modeling the Relationship between Spending and Customer Acquisition and Retention

Companies need to determine how much money to spend acquiring new customers and how much money to spend retaining current customers. The first step in optimizing spending is to develop a functional relationship that explains how increased spending leads to more customer retention or acquisition. Following Blattberg and Deighton (1996), assume the following equations are true:

(1) Fraction of potential customers retained in year =
$$ceilingRet * (1 - e^{-KRet * spentpercustomer})$$

(2) Fraction of potential prospects acquired in year =
$$ceilingAcq * (1 - e^{-KAcq * spentperprospect})$$

The *ceilingRet* is the fraction of current customers you would retain during a year if you spent a saturation level of money on retention. Note that as *spentpercustomer* grows large, the fraction of potential customers retained in a year approaches *ceilingRet*. Given an estimate of *ceilingRet* and current *retentionrate* (based on current spending) you can use Equation 1 to solve for *kRet* (see Exercise 3.) You can find that the following is true:

$$(3) \quad kREt = -LN(1 - (currentretentionrate/ceilingret)) / currentspendpercustomer$$

Given the *currentretentionrate*, *ceilingRet*, and *currentspendpercustomer*, you can use the file `Retentiontemplate.xlsx` (see Figure 22-1) to calculate *kRet*. For example, if you are given that current spending of $40 per customer yields a retention rate of 60 percent and a saturation level of spending yields an 80 percent retention rate, then *kRet* = 0.034657. Figure 22-1 shows how additional spending on retention yields diminishing returns in improving the retention rate. In essence the value of *kRet* governs the speed at which the retention rate approaches its ceiling. The larger the value of *kRet*, the faster the retention rate approaches its ceiling value.

The *ceilingAcq* is a fraction of the potential prospects you would attract in a year if you spent a saturation level of money on customer acquisition. Note that as *spendperprospect* grows large, the annual fraction of prospects acquired in a year approaches the ceiling. Given an estimate for the ceiling and current acquisition rate (based on current spending) you can use Equation 2 to solve for the value of *k* in Equation 4, as shown in the `acquisition` worksheet of the `Retentiontemplate.xlsx` file:

$$(4) \quad KAcq = -LN(1 - (currentacquisitionrate/ceiling)) / currentspendperprospect$$

For example, suppose that spending $40 a year per prospective customer yielded an annual acquisition rate of 5 percent of potential customers (shown in Figure 22-2). Also suppose that spending a saturation level of money on acquisition raises the acquisition rate to 10 percent. Then *k* = 0.01732868.

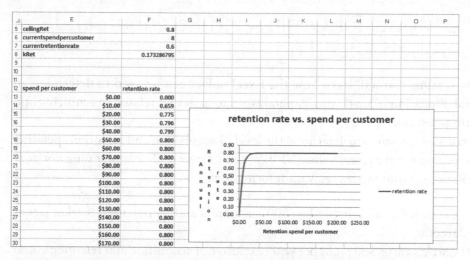

Figure 22-1: Retention rate as a function of retention spend per customer

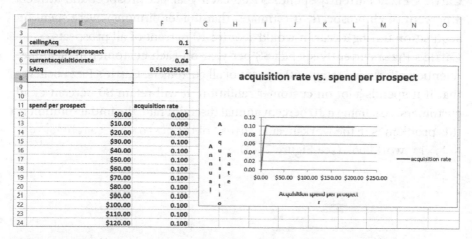

Figure 22-2: Acquisition rate as a function of acquisition spend per prospect

After you have fit Equations 1 and 2, you can use Solver to optimize acquisition and retention spending over a time horizon of arbitrary length.

Basic Model for Optimizing Retention and Acquisition Spending

In this section you will learn how the Excel Solver can be used to determine an optimal allocation of marketing expenditures to activities related to acquiring and retaining customers.

Carrie's Pizza wants to determine the level of acquisition and retention spending that maximizes net present value (NPV) of profits over a 20-year planning horizon. The following summarizes relevant information:

- Carrie's Pizza currently has 500 customers and its potential market size is 10,000.
- Carrie's earns $50 profit per year (exclusive of acquisition and retention costs) per customer.
- Carrie's Pizza currently spends $1.00 each year per prospect and attracts 4 percent of all prospects. It estimates that if a lot of money were spent on acquisition during a year, it would acquire 10 percent of all prospects.
- Carrie's Pizza currently spends $8 per year on each customer in customer retention efforts and retains 60 percent of all customers. Carrie's Pizza believes that if it spends a lot on customer retention, it will retain 80 percent of all customers. Assuming a 10 percent annual discount rate, the initial solution to this problem is in the worksheet `original` of the `customerretentionorigi-nal.xls` workbook (see Figure 22-3).

	C	D	E	F	G	H	I	J	K	L	M
2	getting new			retention							
3	ceilingAcq	0.1		ceilingRet	0.8						
4	cost	$	1.00	cost1	$	8.00					
5											
6	kAcq	0.510825624		kRet	0.1732868						
7	market size	1.00E+04									
8	profitpercustomer	$	50.00							npv	
9	discountrate	0.1								$375,752.22	
10	Year	beginning customers	$s per prospect	$s per customer	start potential customers	prospect %age	retention percentage	end actual customers	end potential customers	profit	marketing cost
11	1	5.00E+02	3.257969	14.5628945	9500	0.08106585	0.735860894	1138.05599	8861.94401	2720.138806	38231.20095
12	2	1138.05599	3.188619	14.69526897	8861.94401	0.08038407	0.737315409	1551.465339	8448.534661	22256.63356	44981.39968
13	3	1551.465339	3.119916	14.69932235	8448.53466	0.07968343	0.737359423	1817.195775	8182.804225	35052.31777	49164.21008
14	4	1817.195775	3.085715	14.69810923	8182.80423	0.07932536	0.737346253	1999.006402	8010.993590	43195.90818	51959.14623
15	5	1999.006402	3.06725	14.65850679	8010.9936	0.07912943	0.736914808	2099.633604	7900.366396	48488.41441	53727.58573
16	6	2099.633604	3.057163	14.6214633	7900.3664	0.07902761	0.736508553	2170.697795	7829.302205	51905.8579	54852.42708
17	7	2170.697795	3.047899	14.6171275	7829.3022	0.0789221	0.736468831	2216.538848	7783.461152	54088.62693	55592.28915
18	8	2216.538848	3.042911	14.64248461	7783.46115	0.07886833	0.736739413	2246.88008	7753.11992	55445.45441	56140.01879
19	9	2246.88008	3.031937	14.67257236	7753.11992	0.07874953	0.737068383	2266.650806	7733.341194	56363.99054	56474.48161
20	10	2266.650806	3.046761	14.6790809	7733.34119	0.07890994	0.73713932	2281.080054	7718.919946	56859.3604	56834.1111
21	11	2281.080054	3.023653	14.64522076	7718.91995	0.07865941	0.7367694	2287.795688	7712.204312	57475.63771	56746.25583
22	12	2287.795688	3.008787	14.57069847	7712.20431	0.07849674	0.735947562	2289.080561	7710.919439	57882.74253	56539.1637
23	13	2289.080561	2.961589	14.46712715	7710.91944	0.07797199	0.7347876	2283.223773	7716.776227	58354.61508	55952.99326
24	14	2283.223773	2.986126	14.34782810	7716.77623	0.07710627	0.733425437	2269.586259	7730.413741	58789.35702	55030.09377
25	15	2269.586259	2.818825	14.21428834	7730.41374	0.07630552	0.731866892	2250.908259	7749.091741	58961.12735	54051.23559
26	16	2250.908259	2.754887	14.0395924	7749.09174	0.07551885	0.729772796	2227.854086	7772.145914	59019.35579	52949.70283
27	17	2227.854086	2.62831	13.74655626	7772.14591	0.07380363	0.726114614	2191.911794	7808.088216	59441.21936	51952.3284
28	18	2191.911794	2.388012	13.1600752	7808.00822	0.07047279	0.71821886	2124.51259	7875.48741	60419.07441	47491.53456
29	19	2124.51259	1.922096	11.01966626	7875.48741	0.06253849	0.696825715	1972.936058	8027.063942	62187.74108	40248.47514
30	20	1972.936058	0.528272	6.537706523	8027.06394	0.02365097	0.542321295	1259.813079	8740.186921	63679.77832	17138.95012

Figure 22-3: Basic model for optimizing retention and acquisition spending

From cell F7 of the worksheet `acquisition` (see Figure 22-2) in the workbook `Retentiontemplate.xlsx` you find that $kAcq = 0.510825824$, and from cell F8 of the worksheet `retention` (see Figure 22-1) in the workbook `Retentiontemplate.xlsx` you find that $kRet = 0.173287$. Once you find this, you can enter trial values for years 1–20 of acquisition per prospect and retention spending per customer in E11:F30. This will track Carrie's Pizza's number of customers each year and the associated profits and costs.

Begin with any trial values for annual expenditures on acquisition and retention spending entered in the range E11:F30. You can then use Solver to determine the annual spending that maximizes Carrie's Pizza's 20-year NPV. No matter what the starting point, the Solver will find the values of annual spending on acquisition and retention that maximize Carrie's 20-year NPV. Proceed as follows:

1. Enter the beginning customers in D11, enter trial acquisition spending per prospect in E11:E30, and enter trial retention spending per customer in F11:F30.

2. Compute the beginning potential customers in G11 with formula `=market_size-D11`.

3. Copy the formula `=ceiling*(1-EXP(-kAcq*E11))` from H11 to H12:H30 to compute the percentage of prospects acquired during each year.

4. Copy the formula `=ceilingRet*(1-EXP(-Ret_*F11))` from I11 to I12:I30 to compute the fraction of all customers retained during each year.

5. Copy the formula `=I11*D11+H11*G11` from J11 to J12:J30 to add together new and retained customers to compute the number of customers at the end of each year.

6. Copy the formula `=market_size-J11` from K11 to K12:K30 to compute the number of prospects at the end of each year.

7. Copy the formula `=0.5*profitpercustomer*(D11+J11)-E11*G11-F11*D11` from L11 to L12:L30 to compute the profit for each year. Note that you average beginning and ending customers to get a more accurate estimate of the average number of customers present during the period.

8. Copy the formula `=E11*G11-F11*D11` from M11 to M12:M30 to compute the total marketing cost during each year.

9. Copy the formula `=J11` from D12 to D13:D30 to ensure that each month's beginning customers equal the previous month's ending customers.

10. Assuming end-of-year cash flows, compute total NPV of profits in cell L9 with the formula `=NPV(D9,L11:L30)`.

11. Use the Solver settings shown in Figure 22-4 to choose the annual levels of retention and acquisition spending that maximize the 20-year NPV end-of-year profits.

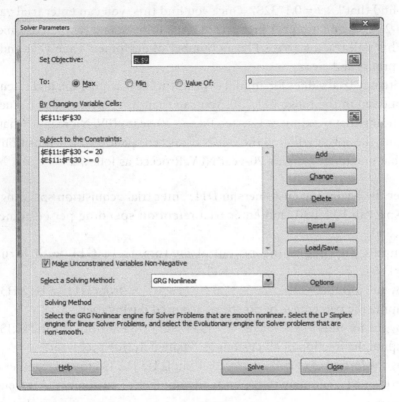

Figure 22-4: Solver settings for basic model

You bounded spending on acquisition and retention per person during each year by $20. (This bound was unnecessary, however, because the optimization did not recommend spending that much money). Note that if during any month the per capita expenditure recommended by Solver were $20, you would have increased the upper bound.

Solver found a maximum NPV of approximately $376,000. During most years you spend approximately $3 per prospect on acquisition and $14 per customer on retention. Given the cost structure you try during most years, you retain 73 percent of the customers and acquire 8 percent of the prospects.

An Improvement in the Basic Model

The basic model discussed in the last section has a small flaw: in the last few years the spending drops. This is because a customer acquired in, say, year 19, generates only one year of profit in the model. Because a customer acquired in year 19 yields little profit, you do not spend much to get her. If the model is valid, the spending on acquisition or retention should not sharply decrease near the end of the planning horizon. To remedy this problem you need to give an *ending credit* or *salvage value* for a customer left at the end of the planning horizon. To accurately determine the value of a customer, follow these steps using the `customerretentionsalvage.xls` workbook shown in Figure 22-5.

1. To begin, copy the formulas from the `original` worksheet down to row C34 (see Figure 22-5) and add in cell I8 as a trial value for the value of a single customer who has just been acquired.

2. Using a Solver constraint, force the customer value for the second set of formulas (listed in cell I40) to equal I8.

3. Add one more initial customer to cell D41 and start with 501 customers.

4. In both parts of the spreadsheet, assign each ending customer a salvage value by adding the term J63*I40 to cell L63 and adding the term J31*I8 to cell L31.

5. In cell L2 compute the difference between the two situations with the formula =L42-L10 (see Figure 22-6). Also constrain the spending levels in rows 44–63 to equal the spending levels in rows 12–31. The Solver window is shown in Figure 22-7.

	C	D	E	F	G	H	I	J	K	L	M
1										DIFF	
2	getting new			retention						$67.51	
3	ceilingAcq	0.1		ceilingRet	0.8						
4	cost	$ 1.00		cost1	$ 8.00						
5	result	0.04		result1	0.6					L8 chANGES	
6	kAcq	0.510825432		kRet	0.17328679					L8=12	
7	fitted result	0.039999988		fitted result1	0.6		CUST VALUE				
8	market size	10000					67.5092066				
9	profitpercustomer	$ 50.00								npv	
10	discountrate	0.1								$395,848.01	
11	Year	beginning customers	$s per prospect	$s per customer	start potential customers	prospect %age	retention percentage	end actual customers	end potential customers	profit	marketing cost
12	1	500	3.04018	14.7233096	9500	0.07783883	0.737619258	1117.77951	8882.22149	4201.07898	36243.3839
13	2	1117.778514	3.04017	14.7233218	8882.22149	0.07883067	0.73761939	1524.75764	8475.24236	22602.55203	43460.8518
14	3	1524.75764	3.04015	14.7233339	8475.24236	0.07883851	0.73761952	1792.86644	8207.13356	34725.06119	48215.5408
15	4	1792.866441	3.04018	14.7233239	8207.13356	0.07883882	0.737619412	1969.49384	8030.50616	42710.87916	51348.1279
16	5	1969.493842	3.04018	14.7233273	8030.50616	0.07883854	0.73761945	2085.85032	7914.14968	47972.11882	53411.4853
17	6	2085.850321	3.04018	14.7233111	7914.14968	0.07883884	0.737619274	2162.50576	7837.49424	51437.81782	54771.0842
18	7	2162.505761	3.04017	14.7233312	7837.49424	0.07883868	0.737619492	2213.00412	7786.99588	53721.15641	55666.5906
19	8	2213.004119	3.04017	14.7233512	7786.99588	0.07893068	0.737619707	2246.27193	7753.72807	55225.20769	56256.6135
20	9	2246.271926	3.04017	14.7233331	7753.72807	0.07883866	0.737619512	2268.18756	7731.81244	56216.25191	56645.2353
21	10	2268.187564	3.04018	14.7232931	7731.81244	0.07883882	0.737619079	2282.62541	7717.37459	56869.02221	56901.3023
22	11	2282.625414	3.04017	14.7232822	7717.37459	0.07883074	0.737618962	2292.13586	7707.86414	57299.13595	57069.896
23	12	2292.135862	3.04017	14.7232843	7707.86414	0.07883874	0.737618984	2298.40119	7701.59881	57582.41603	57181.0102
24	13	2298.401186	3.04017	14.7233235	7701.59881	0.07883875	0.737619408	2302.52972	7697.47028	57768.9655	57254.3072
25	14	2302.529722	3.04016	14.7233046	7697.47028	0.07883056	0.737619203	2305.24763	7694.75237	57892.06748	57302.3663
26	15	2305.247628	3.04018	14.723236	7694.75237	0.07883882	0.737618463	2307.03842	7692.96158	57973.00457	57334.1466
27	16	2307.03842	3.04017	14.7232575	7692.96158	0.07883871	0.737618694	2308.21782	7691.78218	58026.36866	57355.0374
28	17	2308.217021	3.04016	14.7233736	7691.78218	0.07883058	0.737619949	2308.99666	7691.00334	58061.37218	57368.9898
29	18	2308.996661	3.04016	14.72325	7691.00334	0.07883863	0.737618614	2309.50708	7690.49292	58084.75112	57377.8423
30	19	2309.507077	3.04022	14.7234814	7690.49292	0.0788392	0.737621115	2309.8535	7690.1465	58099.26818	57384.7462
31	20	2309.853497	3.04016	14.7234483	7690.1465	0.07883063	0.737620758	2310.07649	7689.92351	214061.3704	57388.31

Figure 22-5: Model with customer salvage value

⬚	K	L
1		DIFF
2		$67.51
3		
4		
5		L8 chANGES
6		L8=I2
7		
8		
9		npv
10		$395,848.01

Figure 22-6: Customer value for salvage value model

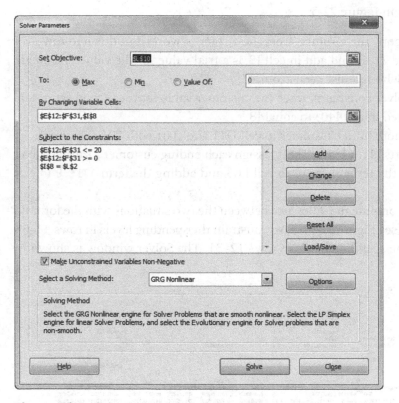

Figure 22-7: Solver settings for salvage value model

The Solver window changes in two ways:

- The value of an individual customer (I8) is added as a changing cell.
- A constraint that L2=I8 is added. This constraint ensures that the customer value in cell I8 indeed equals the amount you gain by adding one more customer. This consistency constraint ensures that Solver will make the value in cell I8 equal the true value of a customer. Because you are now properly accounting for the ending value of a customer, the model now ensures you do not reduce spending near the end of the planning horizon.

Running Solver yields the spending levels shown in Figure 22-5 and the individual customer value shown in Figure 22-6. The optimal spending for the acquisition is approximately $3.04 per customer every year, and approximately $14.71 per customer is spent each year on retention. The value of a customer is $67.51.

Summary

In this chapter you have learned the following:

- To determine the profit maximizing expenditures on customer acquisition and retention, assume the following equations are true:

  (1) Fraction of potential customers retained in year =
  $ceilingRet * (1 - e^{-KRet\ *\ spentpercustomer})$

  (2) Fraction of potential prospects acquired in year =
  $ceilingAcq * (1 - e^{-KAcq\ *\ spentperprospect})$

- Given assumptions on the maximum attainable retention (*ceilingRet*) and acquisition (*ceilingAcq*) rates and the current spending on retention and acquisition, you can use Equations 3 and 4 or the workbook Retentiontemplate .xlsx to solve for *kRet* and *kAcq*.
- The Solver can determine the annual levels of per capita retention and acquisition spending that maximizes the NPV of profits.
- If desired you may account for the salvage value of a customer to ensure that spending levels remain unchanged throughout the planning horizon.

Exercises

1. Verizon is trying to determine the value of a cell phone subscriber in Bloomington, Indiana, and the optimal levels of acquisition and retention spending. Currently Verizon has 20,000 customers and 30,000 potential customers. You are given the following information:

   - Profits are discounted at 10 percent per year.
   - Annual profit per customer is $400.
   - Currently Verizon is spending $12 per prospect on acquisition and capturing 4 percent annually of prospective customers.
   - Currently Verizon is spending $30 per customer on customer retention and has a retention rate of 75 percent.
   - Verizon believes that with a saturation level of spending, the annual acquisition rate would increase to 10 percent and the annual retention rate would increase to 85 percent.

   a. Determine the value of a customer and the profit maximizing annual level of acquisition and retention spending.

   b. Use SolverTable to determine how the optimal level of retention and acquisition spending in Exercise 1 varies with an increase in annual profit.

2. Verify Equation 3.

VI Market Segmentation

Chapter 23: Cluster Analysis

Chapter 24: Collaborative Filtering

Chapter 25: Using Classification Trees for Segmentation

23 Cluster Analysis

Often the marketer needs to categorize objects into groups (or *clusters*) so that the objects in each group are similar, and the objects in each group are substantially different from the objects in the other groups. Here are some examples:

■ When Procter & Gamble test markets a new cosmetic, it may want to group U.S. cities into groups that are similar on demographic attributes such as percentage of Asians, percentage of Blacks, percentage of Hispanics, median age, unemployment rate, and median income level.

■ An MBA chairperson naturally wants to know the segment of the MBA market in which her program belongs. Therefore, she might want to cluster MBA programs based on program size, percentage of international students, GMAT scores, and post-graduation salaries.

■ A marketing analyst at Coca-Cola wants to segment the soft drink market based on consumer preferences for price sensitivity, preference of diet versus regular soda, and preference of Coke versus Pepsi.

■ Microsoft might cluster its corporate customers based on the price a given customer is willing to pay for a product. For example, there might be a cluster of construction companies that are willing to pay a lot for Microsoft Project but not so much for Power Point.

■ Eli Lilly might cluster doctors based on the number of prescriptions for each Lilly drug they write annually. Then the sales force could be organized around these clusters of physicians: a GP cluster, a mental health cluster, and so on.

This chapter uses the first and third examples to learn how the Evolutionary version of the Excel Solver makes it easy to perform a cluster analysis. For example, in the U.S. city illustration, you can find that every U.S. city is similar to Memphis, Omaha, Los Angeles, or San Francisco. You can also find, for example, that the cities in the Memphis cluster are dissimilar to the cities in the other clusters.

Clustering U.S. Cities

To illustrate the mechanics of cluster analysis, suppose you want to "cluster" 49 of America's largest cities (see the `cluster.xls` file for the data and analysis, as well as Figure 23-1). For each city you have the following demographic data that will be used as the basis of your cluster analysis:

- Percentage Black
- Percentage Hispanic
- Percentage Asian
- Median age
- Unemployment rate
- Per capita income

	A	B	C	D	E	F	G	H
9	City #	City	%age Black	%age Hispanic	%age Asian	Median Age	Unemployment rate	Per capita income(000's)
10	1	Albuquerque	3	35	2	32	5	18
11	2	Atlanta	67	2	1	31	5	22
12	3	Austin	12	23	3	29	3	19
13	4	Baltimore	59	1	1	33	11	22
14	5	Boston	26	11	5	30	5	24
15	6	Charlotte	32	1	2	32	3	20
16	7	Chicago	39	20	4	31	9	24
17	8	Cincinnati	38	1	1	31	8	21
18	9	Cleveland	47	5	1	32	13	22
19	10	Columbus	23	1	2	29	3	13
20	11	Dallas	30	21	2	30	9	22
21	12	Denver	13	23	2	34	7	23
22	13	Detroit	76	3	1	31	9	21
23	14	El Paso	3	69	1	29	11	13
24	15	Fort Worth	22	20	2	30	9	20
25	16	Fresno	9	30	13	28	13	16
26	17	Honolulu	1	5	71	37	5	24
27	18	Houston	28	28	4	30	7	22
28	19	Indianapolis	22	1	1	32	5	21
29	20	Jacksonville	25	3	2	32	7	19
30	21	Kansas City	30	4	1	33	6	21
31	22	Las Vegas	11	13	4	33	5	20
32	23	Long Beach	14	24	14	30	8	21
33	24	Los Angeles	14	40	10	31	11	21

Figure 23-1: Data for clustering U.S. cities

For example, Atlanta's demographic information is as follows: Atlanta is 67 percent Black, 2 percent Hispanic, 1 percent Asian, has a median age of 31, a 5 percent unemployment rate, and a per capita income of $22,000.

For now assume your goal is to group the cities into four clusters that are demographically similar. Later you can address the issue of why you used four clusters. The basic idea used to identify the clusters is to choose a city to "anchor," or "center," each cluster. You assign each city to the "nearest" cluster center. Your target cell is then to minimize the sum of the squared distances from each city to the closest cluster anchor.

Standardizing the Attributes

In the example, if you cluster using the attribute levels referred to in Figure 23-1, the percentage of Blacks and Hispanics in each city will drive the clusters because these values are more spread out than the other demographic attributes. To remedy this problem you can *standardize* each demographic attribute by subtracting off the attribute's mean and dividing by the attribute's standard deviation. For example, the average city has 24.34 percent Blacks with a standard deviation of 18.11 percent. This implies that after standardizing the percentage of Blacks, Atlanta has 2.35 standard deviations more Blacks (on a percentage basis) than a typical city. Working with standardized values for each attribute ensures that your analysis is unit-free and each attribute has the same effect on your cluster selection. Of course you may give a larger weight to any attribute.

Choosing Your Clusters

You can use the Solver to identify a given number of clusters. The key in doing so is to ensure that the cities in each cluster are demographically similar and cities in different clusters are demographically different. Using few clusters enables the marketing analyst to reduce the 49 U.S. cities into a few (in your case four) easily interpreted market segments. To determine the four clusters, as shown in Figure 23-2, begin by computing the mean and standard deviation for Black percentage in C1:G2.

1. Compute the Black mean percentage in C1 with the formula =AVERAGE(C10:C58).

2. In C2 compute the standard deviation of the Black percentages with the formula =STDEV(C10:C58).

3. Copy these formulas to D1:G2 to compute the mean and standard deviation for each attribute.

4. In cell I10 (see Figure 23-3) compute the standardized percentage of Blacks in Albuquerque (often called a z-score) with the formula =STANDARDIZE(C10,C$1,C$2). This formula is equivalent, of course, to $\frac{C10-C\$1}{C\$2}$. The reader can verify (see Exercise 6) that for each demographic attribute the z-scores have a mean of 0 and a standard deviation of 1.

	A	B	C	D	E	F	G	H
1		Mean	24.3469	14.5918	6.04082	31.8776	7.020408163	20.9184
2		Std dev	18.1103	16.4721	11.1448	1.99617	2.688631901	3.3344
3								Column
4							City	Cluster
5							Los Angeles	24
6							Omaha	34
7							Memphis	25
8							San Francisco	43
9	City #	City	%age Black	%age Hispanic	%age Asian	Median Age	Unemployment rate	Per capita income(000's)

Figure 23-2: Means and standard deviations for U.S. cities

	A	B	C	D	E	F	G	H	I
9	City #	City	%age Black	%age Hispanic	%age Asian	Median Age	Unemployment rate	Per capita income(000's)	z Black
10	1	Albuquerque	3	35	2	32	5	18	-1.17872
11	2	Atlanta	67	2	1	31	5	22	2.35519
12	3	Austin	12	23	3	29	3	19	-0.68177
13	4	Baltimore	59	1	1	33	11	22	1.91345
14	5	Boston	26	11	5	30	5	24	0.09128
15	6	Charlotte	32	1	2	32	3	20	0.42258
16	7	Chicago	39	20	4	31	9	24	0.8091
17	8	Cincinnati	38	1	1	31	8	21	0.75389
18	9	Cleveland	47	5	1	32	13	22	1.25084
19	10	Columbus	23	1	2	29	3	13	-0.07437
20	11	Dallas	30	21	2	30	9	22	0.31215
21	12	Denver	13	23	2	34	7	23	-0.62655
22	13	Detroit	76	3	1	31	9	21	2.85214
23	14	El Paso	3	69	1	29	11	13	-1.17872
24	15	Fort Worth	22	20	2	30	9	20	-0.12959
25	16	Fresno	9	30	13	28	13	16	-0.84742
26	17	Honolulu	1	5	71	37	5	24	-1.28916

Figure 23-3: Standardized demographic attributes

5. Copy this formula from I10 to N58 to compute z-scores for all cities and attributes.

How Solver Finds the Optimal Clusters

To determine n clusters (in this case $n = 4$) you define a changing cell for each cluster to be a city that "anchors" the cluster. For example, if Memphis is a cluster anchor, each city in the Memphis cluster should be similar to Memphis demographically, and all cities not in the Memphis cluster should be different demographically from Memphis. You can arbitrarily pick four cluster anchors, and for each city in the data set, you can determine the squared distance (using z-scores) of each city from each of the four cluster anchors. Then you assign each city the squared distance to the closest anchor and have your Solver target cell equal the sum of these squared distances.

To illustrate how this approach can find optimal clusters, suppose you ask a set of moviegoers who have seen both *Fight Club* and *Sea Biscuit* to rate these movies on a 0–5 scale. The ratings of 40 people for these movies are shown in Figure 23-4 (see file `Clustermotivation.xlsx`).

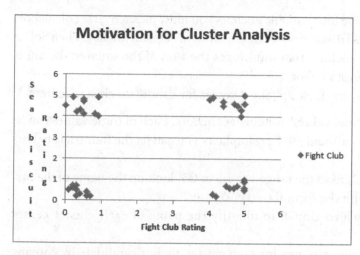

Figure 23-4: Movie ratings

Looking at the chart it is clear that the preference of each moviegoer falls into one of four categories:

- **Group 1:** People who dislike *Fight Club* and *Sea Biscuit* (lower-left corner)
- **Group 2:** People who like both movies (upper-right corner)
- **Group 3:** People who like *Fight Club* and dislike *Sea Biscuit* (aka people with no taste in the lower-right corner)
- **Group 4:** People who like *Sea Biscuit* and hate *Fight Club* (aka smart people in the upper-left corner)

Suppose you take this data and set up four changing cells, with each changing cell or anchor allowed to represent the ratings of any person (refer to Figure 23-4). Let each point's contribution to the target cell be the squared distance to the closest anchor. Then choose one anchor from each group to minimize the target cell. This ensures each point is "close" to an anchor. If, for example, Solver considers two anchors from Group 1, one from Group 3, and one from Group 4, this cannot be optimal because swapping out one Group 1 anchor for a Group 2 anchor would lessen the target cell contribution from the 10 Group 2 points, while hardly changing the target cell contribution from the Group 1 points. Therefore you must only have one anchor for each group. You can now implement this approach for the Cities example.

Setting Up the Solver Model for Cluster Analysis

For the Solver to determine four suitable anchors you must pick a trial set of anchors and figure out the squared distance of each city from the closest anchor. Then Solver can pick the set of four anchors that minimizes the sum of the squared distances of each city from its closest anchor.

To begin, set up a way to "look up" the z-scores for candidate cluster centers:

1. In H5:H8 enter "trial values" for cluster anchors. Each of these values can be any integer between 1 and 49. For simplicity you can let the four trial anchors be cities 1–4.

2. After naming A9:N58 as the range lookup in G5, look up the name of the first cluster anchor with the formula =VLOOKUP(H5,Lookup,2).

3. Copy this formula to G6:G8 to identify the name of each cluster center candidate.

4. In I5:N8 identify the z-scores for each cluster anchor candidate by copying from I5 to I5:N8 the formula =VLOOKUP($H5,Lookup,I$3).

	G	H	I	J	K	L	M	N
3		Column	9	10	11	12	13	14
4	City	Cluster	z *Black*	z *Hispanic*	z *Asian*	z *Age*	z *Unemp*	z *income*
5	Los Angeles	24	-0.57133	1.542497	0.355249	-0.43962	1.480155	0.024482
6	Omaha	34	-0.62655	-0.70373	-0.4523	0.061342	-0.75146	-0.27542
7	Memphis	25	1.69258	-0.82514	-0.4523	0.061342	0.736282	-0.27542
8	San Francisco	43	-0.73698	-0.03593	2.06008	2.06518	-0.37953	3.023526

Figure 23-5: Look up z-scores for cluster anchors

You can now compute the squared distance from each city to each cluster candidate (see Figure 23-6.)

1. To compute the distance from city 1 (Albuquerque) to cluster candidate anchor 1, enter in O10 the formula =SUMXMY2($I$5:$N$5,$I10:$N10). This cool Excel function computes the following:

$$(I5-I10)^2+(J5-J10)^2+(K5-K10)^2+(L5-L10)^2+(M5-M10)^2+(N5-N10)^2$$

2. To compute the squared distance of Albuquerque from the second cluster anchor, change each 5 in O10 to a 6. Similarly, in Q10 change each 5 to a 7. Finally, in R10 we change each 5 to an 8.

3. Copy from O10:R10 to O11:R58 to compute the squared distance of each city from each cluster anchor.

	A	B	O	P	Q	R	S	T	U
7									
8						Sum Dis^2	165.3482		
9	City #	City	Distance ^2 to 1	Distance ^2 to 2	Distance ^2 to 3	Distance^2 to 4	Min Distance	Assigned to	City
10	1	Albuquerque	7.016897	4.44672	15.08608	27.04371987	4.44672	2	Albuquerqu
11	2	Atlanta	19.60865	9.505167	3.266853	30.10200048	3.266853	3	Atlanta
12	3	Austin	11.68898	4.411405	14.78223	32.237947	4.411405	2	Austin
13	4	Baltimore	13.52578	12.05718	1.212861	26.96212426	1.212861	3	Baltimore
14	5	Boston	9.780438	3.32289	7.717853	18.93671521	3.32289	2	Boston
15	6	Charlotte	16.3033	1.676812	6.601068	23.98015278	1.676812	2	Charlotte
16	7	Chicago	5.032486	7.102106	3.873518	19.4812244	3.873518	3	Chicago
17	8	Cincinnati	9.259088	3.506272	1.360387	24.97922616	1.360387	3	Cincinnati
18	9	Cleveland	9.381499	12.75265	2.827259	28.64125199	2.827259	3	Cleveland
19	10	Columbus	21.98167	7.546867	14.77613	49.61465911	7.546867	2	Columbus
20	11	Dallas	3.520536	5.660316	4.751479	24.71547105	3.520536	1	Dallas
21	12	Denver	6.415243	3.848943	9.536884	13.07848391	3.848943	2	Denver
22	13	Detroit	17.97118	14.65559	1.700234	36.15314763	1.700234	3	Detroit
23	14	El Paso	10.88078	28.0051	32.50553	62.55287039	10.88078	1	El Paso
24	15	Fort Worth	3.078873	4.537368	5.662687	27.53351539	3.078873	1	Fort Worth
25	16	Fresno	5.577794	18.2029	18.37833	46.09382815	5.577794	1	Fresno
26	17	Honolulu	49.81239	47.61727	58.32659	19.60205136	19.60205	4	Honolulu
27	18	Houston	3.972443	4.978902	6.898872	23.09371445	3.972443	1	Houston

Figure 23-6: Computing squared distances from cluster anchors

4. In S10:S58 compute the distance from each city to the "closest" cluster anchor by entering the formula =MIN(O10:R10) in cell S10 and copying it to the cell range S10:S59.

5. In S8 compute the sum of squared distances of all cities from their cluster anchor with the formula =SUM(S10:S58).

6. In T10:T58 compute the cluster to which each city is assigned by entering in T10 the formula =MATCH(S10,O10:R10,0) and copying this formula to T11:T58. This formula identifies which element in columns O:R gives the smallest squared distance to the city.

7. Use the Solver window, as shown in Figure 23-7, to find the optimal cluster anchors for the four clusters.

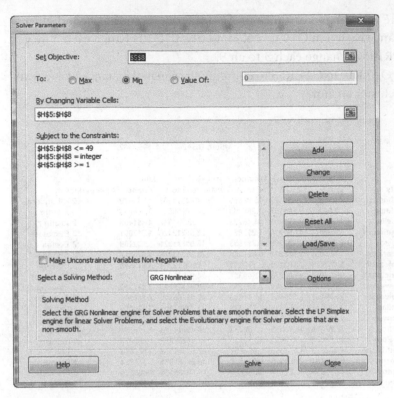

Figure 23-7: Solver window for cluster anchors

> **NOTE** Cell S8 (sum of squared distances) is minimized in the example. The cluster anchors (H5:H8) are the changing cells. They must be integers between 1 and 49.

8. Choose the Evolutionary Solver. Select Options from the Solver window, navigate to the Evolutionary tab, and increase the Mutation rate to 0.5. This setting of the Mutation rate usually improves the performance of the Evolutionary Solver.

The Evolutionary Solver finds that the cluster anchors are Los Angeles, Omaha, Memphis, and San Francisco. Figure 23-8 shows the members of each cluster.

Interpretation of Clusters

The z-scores of the anchors represent a typical member of a cluster. Therefore, examining the z-scores for each anchor enables you to easily interpret your clusters.

	W	X	Y
9	Assigned	City	Anchor
10	1	Dallas	LA
11	1	El Paso	LA
12	1	Fort Worth	LA
13	1	Fresno	LA
14	1	Houston	LA
15	1	Long Beach	LA
16	1	Los Angeles	LA
17	1	Miami	LA
18	1	NY	LA
19	1	San Antonio	LA
20	1	San Diego	LA
21	1	San Jose	LA
22	2	Albuquerque	Omaha
23	2	Austin	Omaha
24	2	Boston	Omaha
25	2	Charlotte	Omaha
26	2	Columbus	Omaha
27	2	Denver	Omaha
28	2	Indianapolis	Omaha
29	2	Jacksonville	Omaha
30	2	Kansas City	Omaha
31	2	Las Vegas	Omaha
32	2	Milwaukee	Omaha
33	2	Minneapolis	Omaha
34	2	Nashville	Omaha
35	2	Oklahoma City	Omaha
36	2	Omaha	Omaha
37	2	Phoenix	Omaha
38	2	Pittsburgh	Omaha
39	2	Portland	Omaha
40	2	Sacramento	Omaha
41	2	Toledo	Omaha
42	2	Tucson	Omaha
43	2	Tulsa	Omaha
44	2	Virginia Beach	Omaha
45	3	Atlanta	Memphis
46	3	Baltimore	Memphis
47	3	Chicago	Memphis
48	3	Cincinnati	Memphis
49	3	Cleveland	Memphis
50	3	Detroit	Memphis
51	3	Memphis	Memphis
52	3	New Orleans	Memphis
53	3	Oakland	Memphis
54	3	Philadelphia	Memphis
55	3	St. Louis	Memphis
56	4	Honolulu	SF
57	4	San Francisco	SF
58	4	Seattle	SF

Figure 23-8: Assignment of cities to clusters

You can find that the San Francisco cluster consists of rich, older, and highly Asian cities. The Memphis cluster consists of highly Black cities with high unemployment rates. The Omaha cluster consists of average income cities with few minorities. The Los Angeles cluster consists of highly Hispanic cities with high unemployment rates.

From your clustering of U.S. cities a company like Procter & Gamble that often engages in test marketing of a new product could now predict with confidence that if a new product were successfully marketed in the San Francisco, Memphis, Los Angeles, and Omaha areas, the product would succeed in all 49 cities. This is because the demographics of each city in the data set are fairly similar to the demographics of one of these four cities.

Determining the Correct Number of Clusters

After a while, adding clusters often yields a diminishing improvement in the target cell. To determine the "correct" number of clusters, you can add one cluster at a time and see if the additional complexity of adding a cluster yields improved insights into the demographic structure of U.S. cities. You can usually start by running three clusters (see Exercise 1) and in this case you can find a Sum of Distances Squared of 212.5 with anchors of Philadelphia (corresponding to the Memphis cluster), Omaha, and San Diego (corresponding to the Los Angeles cluster). When you use four clusters, the San Francisco cluster is added, thereby reducing the Sum of Distances Squared to 165.35. This large improvement justifies the use of four clusters. If you increase to five clusters (see Exercise 2) all that happens is that Honolulu receives its own cluster and the Sum of Distances Squared decreases to 145.47. With deference to Honolulu, this doesn't justify an extra cluster, so you can stop at four clusters.

The problem of determining the correct number of clusters involves trading off parsimony against specificity. After all, you could simply choose each city as a cluster. In this case you have high specificity but no parsimony. The importance of cluster analysis is that the clusters often yield a parsimonious representation of large data sets that leads to an understanding of market segments. In your study of principal components in Chapter 37, "Principal Components Analysis (PCA)," you will again encounter the parsimony vs. specificity tradeoff.

Using Conjoint Analysis to Segment a Market

As explained in Chapter 16, "Conjoint Analysis," you can use conjoint analysis to segment the customers in a given market. Recall from Chapter 16 that for each customer you run a regression to predict the customer's ranking of a product from the levels of each product attribute. In this section you learn how the coefficients of these regressions can be used to identify market segments.

To illustrate how cluster analysis can be used to segment the market, suppose you are a market analyst for Coca-Cola and you ask 132 soda drinkers (see the worksheet

Conjoint Data in the `CokePepsi.xlsx` file) to rank the 20 product profiles (shown in Figure 23-9) describing a six-pack of soda.

	D	E	F	G
1				
2				
3				
4				
5	Choice	Price	Coke or Pepsi	Diet or Regular
6	1	$3.50	C	D
7	2	$3.75	C	D
8	3	$4.00	C	D
9	4	$4.25	C	D
10	5	$4.50	C	D
11	6	$3.50	C	R
12	7	$3.75	C	R
13	8	$4.00	C	R
14	9	$4.25	C	R
15	10	$4.50	C	R
16	11	$3.50	P	D
17	12	$3.75	P	D
18	13	$4.00	P	D
19	14	$4.25	P	D
20	15	$4.50	P	D
21	16	$3.50	P	R
22	17	$3.75	P	R
23	18	$4.00	P	R
24	19	$4.25	P	R
25	20	$4.50	P	R

Figure 23-9: Product profiles for Coke and Pepsi

Each customer's ranking (with rank of 20 indicating the highest rated product and a rank of 1 the lowest rated product) of the 20 product profiles are in the range AC29:AW160. For example, customer 1 ranked profile 6 ($3.50 Regular Coke) highest and profile 15 ($4.50 Diet Pepsi) lowest. You can use this data and cluster analysis to segment the market.

1. Determine the regression equation for each customer. Let each row of your spreadsheet be the regression coefficients the customer gives to each attribute in the regression. Then do a cluster analysis on these regression coefficients.

2. Next, determine the regression coefficients for each customer where the dependent variable is the customer's rank and the independent variables describe the product profile. Figure 23-10 shows the data needed to run the regression for customer 1. Coke = 1 indicates a product profile was Coca-Cola

(so Coke = 0 indicates Pepsi) and Diet = 1 to indicate that a product profile was diet (so Diet = 0 indicates the product profile was regular soda).

	J	K	L	M	R	S	T	U
1								
2	Customer							
3	1							
4								
5	Rank	Price	Coke	Diet				
6	18	$3.50	0	1				
7	16	$3.75	1	1				
8	13	$4.00	1	1				
9	10	$4.25	1	1				
10	7	$4.50	1	1				
11	20	$3.50	1	0	Diet	Coke	Price	Const
12	19	$3.75	1	0	-3.8	6.6	-9.6	47.5
13	17	$4.00	1	0	1.344433	1.344433	1.901315	7.693869
14	15	$4.25	1	0	0.782556	3.006244	#N/A	#N/A
15	12	$4.50	1	0	19.1941	16	#N/A	#N/A
16	9	$3.50	1	1	520.4	144.6	#N/A	#N/A
17	6	$3.75	0	1				
18	4	$4.00	0	1				
19	2	$4.25	0	1				
20	1	$4.50	0	1				
21	14	$3.50	0	0				
22	11	$3.75	0	0				
23	8	$4.00	0	0				
24	5	$4.25	0	0				
25	3	$4.50	0	0				

Figure 23-10: Setting up regression for Coke-Pepsi cluster analysis

3. Enter the customer number in cell J3. Then copy the formula =INDEX(ranks,$J$3,D6) from cell J6 to J7:J25 to pick off the customer's ranking of the product profiles. (The range ranks refers to the range AD29:AW160.)

To get the regression coefficients, you need to run a regression based on each customer's rankings. Therefore you need to run 132 regressions. Combining Excel's array LINEST function with the Data Table feature makes this easy. In Chapter 10, "Using Multiple Regression to Forecast Sales," you learned how to run a regression with the Data Analysis tool. Unfortunately, if the underlying data changes, this method does not update the regression results. If you run a regression with LINEST, the regression coefficients update if you change the underlying data.

1. To run a regression with LINEST when there are *m* independent variables, select a blank range with five rows and *m* + 1 columns. The syntax of LINEST is LINEST(knowny's,knownx's,const,stats).

2. To make any array function work you must use the Control+Shift+Enter key sequence. After selecting the cell range R12:U16 with the cursor in R12, enter

=LINEST(J6:J25,K6:M25,TRUE,TRUE) and the array enters the formula with the Control+Shift+Enter key sequence.

3. Now in R12:U12 you can find the least-squares regression equation; with the coefficients read right to left, starting with the Intercept. For example, for customer 1 the best fit to her rankings is 47.5 − 3.8 Diet + 6.6 Coke − 9.6 Price. This indicates that customer 1 prefers Regular to Diet and Coke to Pepsi. You do not need to be concerned with the remainder of the LINEST output.

You can now use a one-way data table to loop LINEST through each customer and track each customer's regression equation. You can do so by completing the following steps. The results are shown in Figure 23-11.

	AY	AZ	BA	BB
8				
9		Diet	Coke	Price
10		-3.8	6.6	-9.6
11	1	-3.8	6.6	-9.6
12	2	1	-1.6	-16
13	3	4.6	-6	-11.2
14	4	5.8	6	-10
15	5	4.6	-6	-11.2
16	6	-5.8	5.8	-8.8
17	7	4.4	-4.8	-12.8
18	8	-8.4	-2.8	-9.6
19	9	6.8	-5.2	-10
20	10	3.97E-16	1.6	-16
21	11	-6.8	-3.4	-11.2
22	12	7.6	-5.2	-8.8
23	13	-1	1.6	-16
24	14	4.4	4.8	-12.8
25	15	8.4	3.4	-9.6
26	16	5.8	6.2	-9.4
27	17	4.6	6	-11.2
28	18	3.8	-6.6	-10.8
29	19	1	-1.6	-16
30	20	-4.4	-5.2	-11.6
31	21	-2.5	-1.1	-15.8
32	22	6.8	-4.2	-11.2
33	23	-2	-2E-16	-16
34	24	4.6	6	-11.2
35	25	-7.2	-4.4	-9.4
36	26	-7.6	-4.4	-8.8

Figure 23-11: Regression coefficients for Coke-Pepsi cluster analysis

1. Enter the customer numbers in AY11:AY130. The customer numbers are the input into a one-way data table (so called because the table has only one input cell: customer number.) As you vary the customer number, the one-way data table uses the LINEST function to compute the coefficients of each customer's regression equation.

2. Copy the formula =R12 from AZ10 to BA10:BB10 to create output cells, which pick up each regression coefficient.
3. Select the Table range AY10:BB130, and select What-If Analysis from the Data Tools Group on the Data tab.
4. Next select Data Table... and as shown in Figure 23-12, choose J3 as the column input cell. This causes Excel to loop through each customer and use LINEST to run a regression based on each customer's rank.

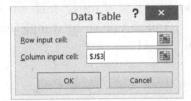

Figure 23-12: $J$3 is the column input cell for a one-way data table.

5. Copy the regression results from your data table to the worksheet cluster, and run a cluster analysis with five clusters on the regression coefficients. Use customers 1–5 as the initial set of anchors. The results are shown in Figure 23-13.

	J	K	L	M	N	O
1		5	6	7		
2	Anchor	z Diet	z Coke	z Price		
3	27	1.092289	1.287635545	0.633988	Diet Coke	
4	117	1.273207	-1.091955351	0.402277	Diet Pepsi	
5	72	-0.21032	-0.328690346	-1.68313	Just Price	
6	40	-1.09681	-1.159302263	0.633988	Regular Pepsi	
7	98	-1.00635	1.10804378	0.633988	Regular Coke	

Figure 23-13: Cluster results for Coke-Pepsi cluster analysis

You can find the following clusters:

- The first cluster represents people with a strong preference for Diet Coke.
- The second cluster represents people with a strong preference for Diet Pepsi.
- The third cluster represents people who make their soda choice based primarily on price.
- The fourth cluster represents people who prefer Regular Pepsi.
- The fifth cluster represents people who prefer Regular Coke.

NOTE The final target cell value for the cluster analysis was 37.92. When you run an Evolutionary Solver model multiple times, the Solver may find a slightly different target cell value. Thus in the current situation Solver might find a target cell value of, say, 38. The changing cells might also be different, but the interpretation of the cluster anchors would surely remain the same.

Summary

To construct a cluster analysis with n clusters, do the following:

- Choose n trial anchors.
- For each data point standardize each attribute.
- Find the squared distance from each anchor to each data point.
- Assign each data point the squared distance to the closest anchor.
- Increase the Mutation rate to 0.5 and use the Evolutionary Solver to minimize the Sum of the Squared Distances.
- Interpret each cluster based on the attribute z-scores for the cluster anchor.

Exercises

1. Run a three-cluster analysis on your U.S. City data.
2. Run a five-cluster analysis on your U.S City data.
3. When you ran your four-cluster U.S. City analysis, you did not put in a constraint to ensure that Solver would not pick the same city twice. Why was it not necessary to include such a constraint?
4. The file `cereal.xls` contains calories, protein, fat, sugar, sodium, fiber, carbs, sugar, and potassium content per ounce for 43 breakfast cereals. Use this data to perform a cluster analysis with five anchors.
5. The file `NewMBAdata.xlsx` contains average undergrad GPA, average GMAT score, percentage acceptance rate, average starting salary, and out of state tuition and fees for 54 top MBA programs. Use this data to perform a cluster analysis with five anchors.
6. Verify that the z-scores for each attribute in the file `cluster.xlsx` have a mean of 0 and a standard deviation of 1.
7. Do an Internet search for Claritas. How are Claritas's services based on cluster analysis?

24 Collaborative Filtering

In today's world you have so many choices. What book should you read next? What movie should you rent? What hot, new song should you download to your iPod or iPhone? *Collaborative filtering* is the buzzword for methods used to "filter" choices using the collective intelligence of other people's product choices. The web has made it easy to store the purchasing history and preferences of thousands, and in some cases, millions of consumers. The question is how to use this data to recommend products to you that you will like but didn't know you wanted. If you ever rented a movie from a Netflix recommendation, bought a book from an Amazon.com recommendation, or downloaded an iTunes song from a Genius recommendation, you have used a result generated by a collaborative filtering algorithm.

In this chapter you'll see simple examples to illustrate the key concepts used in two types of collaborative filtering: *user-based* and *item-based collaborative filtering algorithms*.

User-Based Collaborative Filtering

Suppose you have not seen the movie *Lincoln* and you want to know if you would like it. In user-based collaborative filtering, you look for moviegoers whose rating of movies you have seen is most similar to yours. After giving a heavier weighting to the most similar moviegoers, you can use their ratings to generate an estimate of how well you would like *Lincoln*.

NOTE Despite the title, Badrul Sarwar et al.'s article "Item-Based Collaborative Filtering Recommendation Algorithms" (*Transactions of the Hong Kong ACM*, 2001, pp. 1-11) contains a detailed discussion of user-based collaborative filtering.

You can use the following simple example to further illustrate how user-based collaborative filtering works. Suppose seven people (Lana, George, Manuel, Charles,

Noel, James, and Theresa) have each rated on a 1–5 scale a subset of six movies (*Sixth Sense*, *Flight*, *Amour*, *Superman*, *Dodge Ball*, and *The Others*). Figure 24-1 (see file `finaluserbased.xlsx`) shows the ratings.

	C	Sixth Sense	Flight	Amour	Superman	Dodge Ball	The Others	Mean	K	L	M
8	Lana	2.5	3.5	3	3.5	2.5		3			
9	George	3	3.5	1.5	5	3.5	3	3.25			
10	Manuel	2.5	3		3.5		4	3.25			
11	Charles		3.5	3	4	2.5	4.5	3.5			
12	Noel	3	4	2	3	2	3	2.833			
13	James	3	4		5	3.5	3	3.7			
14	Theresa		4.5		4	1		3.167			
15		1	2	3	4	5	6				
16	Lana	2.5	3.5	3	3.5	2.5	0				
17	Theresa	0	4.5	0	4	1	0				
18	Lana		3.5		3.5	2.5		3.5	3.5		2.5 Correlation
19	Theresa		4.5		4	1		4.5	4		1 0.991241

Figure 24-1: Movie ratings

Now suppose you want to predict Theresa's rating for the tearjerker *Amour*, which she has not seen. To generate a reasonable member-based forecast for Theresa's rating for *Amour*, proceed as follows:

1. Begin with Theresa's average rating of all movies she has seen.
2. Identify the people whose ratings on movies seen by Theresa are most similar to Theresa's ratings.
3. Use the ratings of each person who has seen *Amour* to adjust Theresa's average rating. The more similar the person's other ratings are to Theresa's, the more weight you give their ratings.

Evaluating User Similarity

There are many measures used to evaluate the similarity of user ratings. You can define the similarity between two users to equal the correlation between their ratings on all movies seen by both people. Recall that if two people's ratings have a correlation near +1, then if one person rates a movie higher than average, it is more likely that the other person will rate the movie higher than average, and if one person rates a movie lower than average, then it is more likely that the other person rates the movie lower than average.

NOTE See pp. 356–58 of Blattberg's *Database Marketing*, Springer, 2008 for an excellent discussion of similarity measures.

On the other hand, if two people's ratings have a correlation near −1, then if one person rates a movie higher than average, it is more likely that the other person will rate the movie lower than average, and if one person rates a movie lower than average, then it is more likely that the other person rates the movie higher than average. The Excel `CORREL` function can determine the correlation between two data sets. To find the correlation between each pair of moviegoers, proceed as follows:

1. In cells C16 and C17, type in the cells the names of any two moviegoers. (The worksheet `Correlation sim` uses Lana and Theresa.)

2. Copy the formula =INDEX($D$8:$I$14,MATCH($C16,$C$8:$C$14,0),D$15) from D16 to D16:I17 to place Lana's and Theresa's ratings in rows 16 and 17.

3. You cannot use the `CORREL` function on the data in rows 16 and 17 because Excel will use the 0s (corresponding to unseen movies) in its calculations. Therefore, copy the formula =IF(COUNTIF(D$16:D$17,">0") = 2,D16,"_") from D18 to D18:I19 to replace all 0s in rows 16 and 17 with a _. This ensures that when you measure similarity between two people's movie ratings via correlation you use only movies that were rated by both people.

4. Enter the formula =CORREL(D18:I18,D19:I19) in cell M19 to compute the correlation, or similarity between Lana's and Theresa's ratings. The correlation of 0.991241 indicates that Lana and Theresa have similar tastes in movies.

5. Now use a two-way data table to compute for each pair of people the correlations between their movie ratings. List all people's names in the ranges H24:H30 and I23:O23.

6. In H23 reenter the correlation formula =CORREL(D18:I18,D19:I19).

7. Select the table range of H23:O30, select Data Table... from the What-If portion of the Data Tools Group on the Data tab, and select C16 as the row input cell and C17 as the column input cell. This enables Excel to loop through all pairs of movie viewers and yields the correlations shown in Figure 24-2.

	H	I	J	K	L	M	N	O
21								
22	Correlations							
23	0.991240707	Lana	George	Manuel	Charles	Noel	James	Theresa
24	Lana	1	0.398	0.866025	0.94388	0.597614	0.845154255	0.991241
25	George	0.398409536	1	0.204598	0.31497	0.411765	0.963795682	0.381246
26	Manuel	0.866025404	0.205	1	1	-0.2582	0.134839972	-1
27	Charles	0.943879807	0.315	1	1	0.566947	0.028571429	0.893405
28	Noel	0.597614305	0.412	-0.2582	0.566947	1	0.211288564	0.924473
29	James	0.845154255	0.964	0.13484	0.028571	0.211289	1	0.662849
30	Theresa	0.991240707	0.381	-1	0.893405	0.924473	0.66284898	1

Figure 24-2: User similarities

Estimating Theresa's Rating for *Amour*

You can use the following formula to estimate Theresa's rating for *Amour*. All summations are for moviegoers who have seen *Amour*.

(1) Estimate of Theresa's Rating for *Amour* = (Theresa's Mean Rating) +

$$\frac{\sum_{Other\ moviegoers}(Similarity\ of\ moviegoer\ to\ Theresa) * (Moviegoer's\ rating\ for\ Amour\ -\ Moviegoer's\ average\ rating)}{\sum_{All\ moviegoers}|Moviegoer's\ similarity\ to\ Theresa|}$$

To generate your estimate of Theresa's rating for *Amour*, start with Theresa's average rating of all movies and use the following types of moviegoers to increase your estimate of Theresa's rating for *Amour*:

- People who have a positive similarity to Theresa and like *Amour* more than their average movie.
- People who have a negative similarity to Theresa and like *Amour* less than their average movie.

Use the following types of moviegoers to decrease your estimate of Theresa's rating for *Amour*:

- People who have a positive similarity to Theresa and like *Amour* less than their average movie.
- People who have a negative similarity to Theresa and like *Amour* more than their average movie.

The denominator of Equation 1 ensures that the sum of the absolute value of the weights given to each moviegoer adds up to 1. The calculations used to determine your estimate of Theresa's rating for *Amour* are as follows:

1. Copy the formula =AVERAGE(D8:I8) from J8 to J9:J14 to compute the average rating for each person. For example (refer to Figure 24-1), Theresa's average movie rating is 3.167.
2. The remaining calculations are shown in Figure 24-3. In H34 and I34 choose (via drop-down boxes) the movie-person combination for which you want to estimate a rating.
3. Copy the formula =VLOOKUP(N34,$C$8:$J$14,8,FALSE) from O34 to O35:O40 to copy each person's average rating. For example, in cell O34 your formulas extract Lana's average rating (3).
4. Copy the formula =INDEX(correlations,MATCH($I$34,$H$24:$H$30,0),MATCH(N34,$I$23:$O$23,0)) from P34 to P35:P40 to pull the similarity of each person to the selected person. The first MATCH function ensures you pull the

correlations for Theresa, whereas the second MATCH function ensures that you pull the similarity of Theresa to each other person. For example, the formula in cell P35 extracts the 0.38 correlation between George and Theresa.

	H	I	J	N	O	P	Q	R	S
33	Predict rating for	Person	Mean		Mean	Similarity	Movie Rating	Adjustment	Abs. Correlation
34	Amour	Theresa	3.167	Lana	3	0.991241	3	0	0.991240707
35				George	3.25	0.381246	1.5	-1.75	0.381246426
36				Manuel	3.25	-1	0	0	0
37				Charles	3.5	0.893405	3	-0.5	0.893405147
38				Noel	2.833333	0.924473	2	-0.833333333	0.924473452
39				James	3.7	0.662849	0	0	0
40				Theresa	3.166667	1	0	0	0
41									
42				Total Adjustment	-0.59062				
43				Final Rating	2.576052				

Figure 24-3: Estimating Theresa's rating for *Amour*

5. The anchoring of H34 in the second MATCH function ensures that copying the formula =INDEX(ratings,MATCH(N34,$N$34:$N$40,0),MATCH($H$34,$D$7 :$I$7,0))from Q34 to Q35:Q40 pulls each person's rating for *Amour*. If the person has not seen *Amour*, enter a value of 0. For example, the formula in Q35 extracts George's 1.5 rating for *Amour*.

6. Copy the formula =IF(AND(N34<>$I$34,Q34>0),(Q34-O34),0) from R34 to R35:R40 to compute for each person who has seen *Amour* an adjustment equal to the amount by which the person's rating for *Amour* exceeds their average movie rating. For example, George gave movies an average rating of 3.25 and rated *Amour* only a 1.5, so George's adjustment factor is 1.5 – 3.25 = –1.75. Anyone who has not seen *Amour* has an adjustment factor of 0.

7. Copy the formula =IF(AND(N34<>$I$34,Q34>0),ABS(P34),0) from S35:S40 to enter the absolute value of the correlation between Theresa and each person who has seen *Amour*.

8. In O42 the formula =SUMPRODUCT(R34:R40,P34:P40)/SUM(S34:S40) computes (–0.591) the second term in Equation 1, which is used to compute the total amount by which you can adjust Theresa's average rating to obtain an estimate of Theresa's rating for *Amour*.

9. Finally, enter the formula =J34+O42 in cell Q43 to compute your estimate (2.58) for Theresa's rating.

NOTE You adjusted Theresa's average rating downward because George's, Charles's, and Noel's tastes were similar to Theresa's tastes, and all of them rated *Amour* below their average movie rating.

Item-Based Filtering

An alternative method to user-based collaborative filtering is *item-based collaborative filtering*. Think back to the *Lincoln* movie example. In item-based collaborative filtering (first used by Amazon.com) you first determine how similar all the movies you have seen are to *Lincoln*. Then you can create an estimated rating for *Lincoln* by giving more weight to your ratings for the movies most similar to *Lincoln*.

Now return to the *Amour* example, and again assume that you want to estimate Theresa's rating for *Amour*. To apply item-based filtering in this situation, look at each movie Theresa has seen and proceed as follows:

1. For each movie that Theresa has seen, use the correlation of the user ratings to determine the similarity of these movies to the unseen movie (*Amour*).

2. Use the following Equation 2 to estimate Theresa's rating for *Amour*.

$$\text{(2) Theresa's Estimated Rating for } Amour$$
$$= \text{(Theresa's Average Rating)}$$
$$+$$
$$\frac{\sum_{Movies\ Theresa\ has\ seen}(Correlation\ of\ movie\ to\ Amour) * (Theresa's\ rating\ for\ movie\ - Theresa's\ average\ rating)}{\sum_{Movies\ Theresa\ has\ seen}|Correlation\ of\ movie\ to\ Amour|}$$

Analogously to Equation 1, Equation 2 gives more weight to the ratings on movies Theresa has seen that are more similar (in the sense of absolute correlation) to *Amour*. For movies whose ratings are positively correlated to *Amour*'s rating, increase your estimate if Theresa rated the movie above her average. For movies whose ratings are negatively correlated to *Amour*'s rating, decrease your estimate if Theresa rated the movie above her average. The worksheet `Correlation sim` in the file `finalitembasednew.xlsx` contains calculations of an estimate of Theresa's rating for *Amour*. The calculations proceed as follows:

1. In C16 and C17 use the drop down box to enter any two movies.

2. Copy the following formula from D16 to D16:I17 to extract each person's rating for the two selected movies Note that if a person did not rate a movie a – is entered.

    ```
    =IF(INDEX($D$8:$I$14,D$15,MATCH($C16,$D$7:$I$7,0))=0,"-",INDEX($D$8:$I$14,D$15,MATCH($C16,$D$7:$I$7,0)))
    ```

3. Copy the formula `=IF(OR(D$16="-",D$17="-"),"-",D16)` from D18 to D18:I19 to extract only the ratings from users who rated both movies.

4. In D22 use the formula `=CORREL(D18:J18,D19:J19)` to compute the correlation between the selected movies. In this case *Amour* and my all-time favorite comedy, *Dodge Ball* (by the way if you like *Dodge Ball* you will love *We're the Millers*), have a –0.49 correlation.

5. As shown in Figure 24-4, use a two-way data table (row input cell of C16 and column input cell of C17) to compute in the cell range N22:T27 the correlation between each pair of movies.

	N	O	P	Q	R	S	T
20							
21	-0.485661864	Sixth Sense	Flight	Amour	Superman	Dodge Ball	The Others
22 Sixth Sense		1	0.763762616	-0.944911183	0.487950036	0.333333	-1
23 Flight		0.76376262	1	-0.333333333	0.158776837	-0.06804	-0.63386569
24 Amour		-0.9449112	-0.333333333	1	-0.422890032	-0.48566	0.94491118
25 Superman		0.48795004	0.158776837	-0.422890032	1	0.979167	-0.29646353
26 Dodge Ball		0.33333333	-0.068041382	-0.485661864	0.979166667	1	-0.33333333
27 The Others		-1	-0.633865691	0.944911183	-0.296463531	-0.33333	1

Figure 24-4: Item correlations

6. In C26 and C27 use the drop down boxes to select the person (Theresa) and the movie (*Amour*) for which you want to predict an estimated rating. The range C28:H37 shown in Figure 24-5 contains the final calculations used to generate your item-based prediction for Theresa's rating of *Amour*.

	C	D	E	F	G	H	I	J
7		Sixth Sense	Flight	Amour	Superman	Dodge Ball	The Others	Mean
8 Lana		2.5	3.5	3		3.5	2.5	3
9 George		3	3.5	1.5	5	3.5	3	3.25
10 Manuel		2.5	3		3.5		4	3.25
11 Charles			3.5	3	4	2.5	4.5	3.5
12 Noel		3	4	2	3	2	3	2.833
13 James		3	4		5	3.5	3	3.7
14 Theresa			4.5		4	1		3.167
15		1	2	3	4	5	6	
16 Amour		3	1.5 -		3	2 -		
17 Dodge Ball		2.5	3.5 -		2.5	2	3.5	
18 Amour		3	1.5 -		3	2 -		
19 Dodge Ball		2.5	3.5 -		2.5	2 -		
20								
21		correlation between selected items						
22		-0.485661864						
25		Person Mean						
26 Theresa		3.166666667						
27 Amour								
28			Rating	Similarity	Movie Rating-Mean	Abs Similarity		
29	1	Sixth Sense	0	0	0	0		
30	2	Flight	4.5	-0.3333333	1.333333333	0.333333333		
31	3	Amour	0	0	0	0		
32	4	Superman	4	-0.42289	0.833333333	0.422890032		
33	5	Dodge Ball	1	-0.4856619	-2.166666667	0.485661864		
34	6	The Others	0	0	0	0		
35								
36 Adjustment		0.205666806						
37 Final rating estimate		3.372333473						

Figure 24-5: Using item-based filtering to estimate Theresa's rating for *Amour*

7. Copy the formula =INDEX($D$8:$I$14,MATCH($C$26,$C$8:$C$14,0),MATCH($D29,$D$7:$I$7,0)) from E29 to E30:E34 to extract Theresa's rating for each movie. (A 0 indicates an unrated movie.) For example, the formula in cell E30 extracts Theresa's rating of 4.5 for *Flight* while E29 contains a 0 because Theresa did not see *Sixth Sense*.

8. Copy the formula =IF(E29=0,0,INDEX($O$22:$T$27,MATCH($C$27,$O$21:$T$21,0),MATCH(D29,$O$21:$T$21,0))) from F29 to F30:F34 to extract for each movie Theresa has seen the correlation of the movie's ratings with *Amour*'s ratings. For example, cell F30 contains the correlation between *Flight* and *Amour* (-0.33) while F29 contains a 0 because Theresa did not see *Sixth Sense*.

9. Copy the formula =IF(E29=0,0,E29-$D$26) from G29 to G30:G34 to compute for each movie Theresa has seen the amount by which Theresa's rating for a movie exceeds her average rating. For example, Theresa's rating of 4.5 for *Flight* exceeded her average rating of 3.17 by 1.33, which is the result shown in G30.

10. Copy the formula =ABS(F29) from H29 to H30:H34 to compute the absolute value of the correlation of each movie's rating with *Amour*'s ratings.

11. In cell D36 use the formula =SUMPRODUCT(G29:G34,F29:F34)/SUM(H29:H34) to compute the second term "adjustment" from Equation 2 to generate Theresa's estimated rating for *Amour*. You should increase Theresa's average rating of 3.167 by 0.21.

12. In cell D37 use Equation 2 to compute the final estimate (3.37) of Theresa's rating (3.37) for *Amour* with the formula =D26+D36. If you select a different movie and a different person in C26 and C27, then cell D37 will contain your estimate of that person's rating for the movie.

Comparing Item- and User-Based Collaborative Filtering

In the past, user-based collaborative filtering was often used because it was easy to program (Sarwar et al., 2001). User-based collaborative filtering also tends to be more attractive in situations where users are personally familiar with each other. A good example would be if Facebook was trying to provide you with music recommendations based on the preferences of your Facebook friends. With user-based filtering Facebook could provide you with a list of your friends whose musical preferences were most similar to yours.

Companies with many customers who aren't necessarily familiar with one another, such as Amazon.com, prefer the item-based approach to the user-based approach because the item-based matrix of correlations is more stable over time than the user-based matrix of correlations and therefore needs to be updated less frequently. Also, when user-based collaborative filtering is applied to a situation in which there are many customers and products, the calculations do become increasingly more burdensome than the calculations associated with the item-based approach.

The Netflix Competition

Perhaps the best-known example of collaborative filtering was the Netflix Prize Competition, which began in October 2006. Netflix made public more than 100 million movie ratings (the training set) and withheld 1.4 million ratings (the test set) from the competitors. Accuracy of a forecasting algorithm was measured by *Root Mean Squared Error* (RMSE). Letting N = Number of ratings in the test set, RMSE is defined as the following:

$$RMSE = \sqrt{\sum all\ ratings\ in\ Test\ Set\ \frac{(actual\ rating - predicted\ rating)^2}{N}}$$

Netflix's algorithm had an RMSE of 0.9514. Netflix offered a $1 million prize to the first entry that beat this RMSE by at least 10 percent. In June 2009 the BellKor Pragmatic Chaos team became the first team to improve RMSE by 10 percent. BellKor won by submitting its entry only 20 minutes before the second place team! The prize-winning recommendation system was actually a combination of more than 100 algorithms. You might enjoy the excellent discussion of the Netflix prize in Chapter 4 of Mung Chiang's book, *A Networked Life* (Cambridge University Press, 2012).

Summary

In this chapter you learned the following:
- User-based collaborative filtering estimates a person's rating for a product by weighting most heavily the opinions of similar users.
- Item-based collaborative filtering estimates a person's rating for a product by weighting most heavily a person's ratings for products most similar to the product in question.

Exercises

The following table shows ratings for six people and six movies.

	Movie 1	Movie 2	Movie 3	Movie 4	Movie 5	Movie 6
Jane		5		4		
Jill	4		3		3	
Britney	5	5	4	5	4	4
Phil					1	2
Gloria	3		7		5	
Mitchell		2	4		4	3

1. Use user-based filtering to predict each missing rating in the table.
2. Use item-based filtering to predict each missing rating in the table.
3. How could the concept of a Training set be used to improve the quality of the estimated ratings defined by Equations 1 and 2?

25

Using Classification Trees for Segmentation

In Chapter 23, "Cluster Analysis," you learned how cluster analysis can be used to determine market segments. Often the marketing analyst wants to develop a simple rule for predicting whether a consumer will buy a product. You can use *decision trees* to determine simple classification rules that can be understood by people with little statistical training. For example, Market Facts of Canada Limited (see `http://www.quirks.com/articles/a1993/19930206.aspx?searchID=30466011`) wanted to determine a simple rule that could be used to predict whether a family was likely to purchase a Canadian savings bond. It used a decision tree to show that the best predictor of bond ownership was annual household income in excess of $50,000, with the second best predictor being the region in which the family resided.

This chapter discusses decision trees and how you can use them to develop simple rules that can be used to predict the value of a binary dependent variable from several independent variables.

Introducing Decision Trees

Decision trees are used to predict a categorical (usually binary) dependent variable such as:

- Will a family purchase a riding mower during the next year?
- Will a person suffer a heart attack in the next year?
- Will a voter vote Republican or Democratic in the next presidential election?

NOTE   See *Victory Lab* (by Sasha Issenberg, Random House, 2012) for a discussion of how decision trees were used in Obama's successful 2012 reelection campaign.

Similar to logistic regression (see Chapter 17, "Logistic Regression"), you can try and determine the independent variables or attributes that are most effective in predicting the binary dependent variable. You begin the tree with a root node that includes all combinations of attribute values, and then use an independent variable to "split" the root node to create the most improvement in *class separation*.

To understand the basic idea of class separation, suppose you want to predict whether a family will buy a riding mower. If every family owning a lot of at least 2 acres in size bought a riding mower and no family owning a lot less than 2 acres in size bought a riding mower, then you could split the root node into two child nodes: one with Lot Size <2 acres and another with Lot Size ≥2 acres, and you would have a simple, perfectly performing classification rule: if Lot Size ≥2 acres, predict a family will buy a riding mower, and if Lot Size <2 acres, predict a family will not buy a riding mower. If the first split does not result in a satisfactory classification performance, then you split the two child nodes, possibly on another independent variable. Eventually a satisfactory but simple to understand classification rule is obtained.

You can see this concept more clearly using a simple example to illustrate the construction of a decision tree.

Constructing a Decision Tree

Suppose that you want to come up with a simple rule to determine whether a person will buy Greek yogurt. Figure 25-1 contains data on a sample of 10 adults (see the Greekyogurt.xlsx file). For example, Person 1 is a single, high-income woman who did not buy Greek yogurt. In this example the dependent variable for each person is whether or not the person purchased Greek yogurt.

	B	C	D	E	F
1					
2	Person	Gender	Marital Status	Income Level	Bought?
3	1	Female	Single	High	No
4	2	Male	Married	Average	No
5	3	Male	Single	Low	No
6	4	Female	Married	High	No
7	5	Male	Divorced	Average	Yes
8	6	Male	Married	Low	No
9	7	Female	Divorced	High	No
10	8	Male	Single	Average	Yes
11	9	Male	Married	Low	No
12	10	Male	Single	Average	Yes

Figure 25-1: Data on Greek yogurt purchasers

A node of a decision tree is considered *pure* if all data points associated with the node have the same value of the dependent variable. You should branch only on impure nodes. In this example, because the root node contains three purchasers of yogurt and seven nonpurchasers, branch on the root node. The goal in branching is to create a pair of child nodes with the least impurity.

There are several metrics used to measure the impurity of a node. Then the impurity of a split is computed as a weighted average of the impurities for the nodes involved in the split, with the weight for a child node being proportional to the number of observations in the child node. In this section you use the concept of *entropy* to measure the impurity of a node. In Exercises 1 and 2 you explore two additional measures of node impurity: the *Gini Index* and *classification error*.

To define the entropy of a node, suppose there are c possible values (0, 1, 2, c-1) for the dependent variable. Assume the child node is defined by independent variable X being equal to a. Then the entropy of the child node is computed as the following equation:

$$(1) \text{ Entropy} = \sum_{i=0}^{i=c-1} P(i|X = a)Log_2(P(i|X = a).$$

In Equation 1 the following is true:

- $P(i|X = a)$ is the fraction of observations in class i given that $X = a$.
- $Log_2(0)$ is defined to equal 0.

Entropy always yields a number between 0 and 1 and is a concept that has its roots in Information Theory. (See David Luenberger's *Information Science*, Oxford University Press, 2006 for an excellent introduction to Information Theory.) With two classes, a pure node has an entropy of 0 ($-0*Log_2 0 + 1*Log_2 1$) = 0). A split of a node can yield a maximum entropy value of 1 when one-half the observations associated with a node have $c = 0$ and $c = 1$ (see Exercise 5). This shows that intuitively picking a split based on entropy can yield pure nodes. It can also be shown that with two nodes the entropy decreases as the fraction of nodes having $c = 1$ or $c = 0$ moves away from 0.5. This means that choosing splits with lower entropy will have the desired effect of decreasing impurity.

Suppose there are S possible values ($s = 1, 2, ..., S$) for the attribute generating the split and there are n_i observations having the independent variable = i. Also assume the parent node has N total observations. Then the impurity associated with the split is defined by the following equation:

$$(2) \text{ Impurity} = \sum_{i=1}^{i=S} \frac{Entropy(i)n_i}{N}$$

For this example suppose that you split the root node based on gender. From Equation 1 you can find that:

$$\text{Entropy (Female)} = -[(3/3) * (\text{Log}_2(3/3) + (0/3) * \text{Log}_2(0/3)] = 0$$
$$\text{Entropy (Male)} = -[(4/7) * \text{Log}_2(4/7) + (3/7) * \text{Log}_2(3/7)] = 0.985$$

Because the data set contains three women and seven men Equation 2 shows you that the impurity of the split is $(3/10) * 0 + (7/10) * (0.985) = 0.69$.

You should split on the independent variable whose child nodes yield the lowest level of impurity. Using the Excel COUNTIFS function, it is easy to compute the level of impurity resulting from a split on each independent variable (see Figure 25-2 and the file Greekyogurt.xlsx). Then you split the root node using the independent variable that results in the lowest impurity level.

	B	C	D	E	F	G	H	I	J	K
1										
2	Person	Gender	Marital Status	Income Level	Bought?					
3		1 Female	Single	High	No					
4		2 Male	Married	Average	No					
5		3 Male	Single	Low	No					
6		4 Female	Married	High	No					
7		5 Male	Divorced	Average	Yes					
8		6 Male	Married	Low	No					
9		7 Female	Divorced	High	No					
10		8 Male	Single	Average	Yes					
11		9 Male	Married	Low	No					
12		10 Male	Single	Average	Yes					
13			Buy							
14			Yes	No	Total	Fraction			Entropy	Impurity
15	Gender	Female	0	3	3	0.3	0	0	0	0.68966
16		Male	3	4	7	0.7	-0.524	-0.461	-0.98523	
17			Buy							
18			Yes	No						
19	Income Level	High	0	3	3	0.3	0	0	0	0.324511
20		Average	3	1	4	0.4	-0.311	-0.5	-0.81128	
21		Low	0	3	3	0.3	0	0	0	
22			Buy							
23			Yes	No						
24	Marital Status	Single	2	2	4	0.4	-0.5	-0.5	-1	0.6
25		Married	0	4	4	0.4	0	0	0	
26		Divorced	1	1	2	0.2	-0.5	-0.5	-1	

Figure 25-2: Impurity calculations from each split

Proceed as follows:

1. Copy the formula =COUNTIFS($C$3:$C$12,$C15,$F$3:$F$12,D$14) from D15 to D15:E16 to compute the number of females and males who buy and do not buy Greek yogurt. For example, you find four males do not buy Greek yogurt.

2. Copy the formula =COUNTIFS($E$3:$E$12,$C19,$F$3:$F$12,D$14) from D19 to D19:E21 to count the number of people for each income level that buy and do not buy Greek yogurt. For example, three average income people bought Greek yogurt.

3. Copy the formula =COUNTIFS($D$3:$D$12,$C24,$F$3:$F$12,D$14) from D24 to the range D24:E26 to count how many people for each marital status buy or do not buy Greek yogurt. For example, two single people buy Greek yogurt.

4. Copy the formula =SUM(D15:E15) from F15 to the range F15:F26 to compute the number of people for the given attribute value. For example, cell F25 tells you there are four married people in the population.

5. Copy the formula =F15/SUM($F$15:$F$16) from G15 to G15:G26, to compute the fraction of observations having each possible attribute value. For example, from G16 you can find that 70 percent of the observations involve males.

6. Copy the formula =IFERROR((D15/$F15)*LOG(D15/$F15,2),0) from H15 to H15:I26 to compute for each attribute value category level combination the term $P(i|X=a)*Log_2(P(i|X=a))$. You need IFERROR to ensure that when P(i|X=a)=0 Log2(0) the undefined value is replaced by 0. In general entering IFERROR(formula, anything) will enter the value computed by the formula as long as the formula does not return an error. If the formula does return an error, IFERROR returns whatever is entered after the comma (in this case 0.)

7. Copy the formula =SUM(H15:I15) from J15 to J15:J26 to compute via Equation 1 the entropy for each possible node split.

8. Copy the formula =-SUMPRODUCT(G15:G16,J15:J16) from K15 to K16:K24 to compute via Equation 2 the impurity for each split.

9. The impurity for income of 0.325 is smaller than the impurities for gender (0.69) and marital status (0.60), so begin the tree by splitting the parent node on income. This yields the three nodes shown in Figure 25-3. Note that this figure was drawn and was not created by Excel.

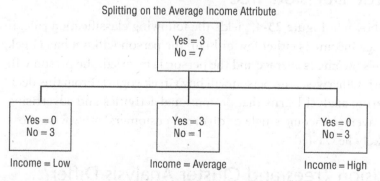

Figure 25-3: Splitting root node with Income variable

10. The Income = Low and Income = High nodes are pure, so no further splitting is necessary. The Income = Average is not pure, so you need to consider splitting this node on either gender or marital status. Splitting on gender yields an impurity of 0.811, whereas splitting on marital status yields an impurity of 0. Therefore, split the Income = Average node on marital status. Because all terminal nodes are pure (that is, each respondent for a terminal node is in the same class), no further splitting is needed, and you obtain the decision tree, as shown in Figure 25.4.

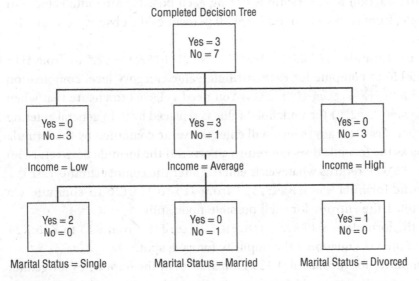

Figure 25-4: Tree after marital status and income splits

Interpreting the Decision Tree

The decision tree, shown in Figure 25-4, yields the following classification rule: If the customer's average income is either low or high, the person will not buy Greek yogurt. If the person's income is average and the person is married, the person will not buy Greek yogurt. Otherwise, the person will buy Greek yogurt. From this decision tree the marketing analyst learns that promotional activities and advertising should be aimed at average income single or divorced customers, otherwise those investments will likely be wasted.

How Do Decision Trees and Cluster Analysis Differ?

The astute reader might ask how cluster analysis (discussed in Chapter 23) and decision trees differ. Recall in Chapter 23 you divided U.S. cities into four clusters.

Suppose you want to determine the cities in which a new product is likely to sell best. The clustering in Chapter 23 does not help you make predictions about sales in each city. The decision tree approach enables you to use demographic information to determine if a person is likely to buy your product. If a decision tree analysis showed you, for example, that older, high income Asian-Americans were likely to buy the product, then your Chapter 23 cluster analysis would tell you that your product is likely to sell well in Seattle, San Francisco, and Honolulu.

Pruning Trees and CART

Extensive calculation is required to create decision trees. Fortunately, widely used statistical packages such as SAS, STATISTICA, R, SPSS, and XLMINER can quickly churn out decision trees. SPSS, for example, uses Leo Breiman's (*Classification and Regression Trees*, Chapman and Hall, 1984) CART algorithm to generate decision trees. A key issue in creating a decision tree is the size of the tree. By adding enough nodes you can always create a tree for which the terminal nodes are all pure. Unfortunately, this usually results in overfitting, which means the tree would do poorly in classifying out of sample observations. CART "prunes" a tree by trading off a cost for each node against the benefit generated by the tree. The benefit derived from a tree is usually measured by the misclassification rate. To compute the misclassification rate for a tree, assume at each terminal node all observations are assigned to the class that occurs most frequently. All other observations associated with a node are assumed to be misclassified. Then the misclassification rate is the fraction of all misclassified observations. To illustrate the calculation of the misclassification rate, compute the misclassification rate for the tree, as shown in Figure 25-5.

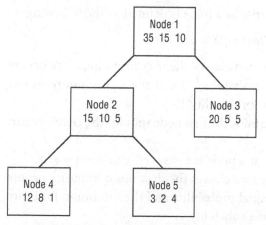

Figure 25-5: Tree for illustrating misclassification rate

For each terminal node the number of misclassified observations is computed as follows:

- For Node 3, 20 observations are classified in Class 1, 5 in Class 2, and 5 in Class 3. For misclassification purposes you should assume that all Node 3 observations should be classified as Class 1. Therefore 10 observations (those classified as Class 2 or 3) are assumed to be misclassified.
- Node 4 observations are classified as Class 1, so the 9 observations classified as Class 2 or 3 are misclassified.
- Node 5 observations are classified as Class 3, so the 5 observations classified as Class 1 or 2 are misclassified.
- In total 24/60 = 40 percent of all observations are misclassified.

Summary

In this chapter you learned the following:

- You can use decision trees to determine simple classification rules that can be understood by people with little statistical training.
- To create a decision tree, split a parent node using a division of attribute values that creates the greatest reduction in overall impurity value.
- The widely used CART algorithm uses pruning of a decision tree to avoid overfitting and creates effective parsimonious classification rules.

Exercises

1. The Gini Index measure of impurity at a node is defined as the following:

$$\sum_{i=0}^{i=c-1} P(Class = i | X = a)^2$$

   a. Show that when there are two classes the maximum impurity occurs when both classes have probability .5 and the minimum impurity occurs when one class has probability 1.
   b. Use the Gini Index to determine the first node split for the Greek yogurt example.
2. The classification error measure at a node is `1-maxi(P(Class=i|X=a))`.
   a. Show that when there are two classes the maximum impurity occurs when both classes have equal probability and the minimum impurity occurs when one class has probability 1.

    b. Use the classification error measure to determine the first node split for the Greek yogurt example.

3. Show that when there are two classes the maximum entropy occurs when both classes have equal probability and the minimum entropy occurs when one class has probability 1.

4. How could L.L. Bean use classification trees?

5. Suppose you want to use age and tobacco use statistics to develop a decision tree to predict whether a person will have a heart attack during the next year. What problem would arise? How would you resolve this problem?

6. For the Greek yogurt example verify that if the parent node is Income = Average then splitting on gender yields an impurity of 0.811, whereas splitting on marital status yields an impurity of 0.

7. Explain how the Obama campaign could have used decision trees.

VII Forecasting New Product Sales

Chapter 26: Using S Curves to Forecast Sales of a New Product

Chapter 27: The Bass Diffusion Model

Chapter 28: Using the Copernican Principle to Predict Duration of Future Sales

26

Using S Curves to Forecast Sales of a New Product

In many industries for which new products require large research and development investments (particularly high tech and pharmaceuticals) it is important to forecast future sales after a product has been on the market for several years. Often a graph of new product sales on the y-axis against time on the x-axis looks like the letter S and is often referred to as an *S curve*. If a product's sales follows an S curve, then up to a certain point (called an *inflection point*) sales increase at an increasing rate, and beyond the inflection point the growth of sales slows. This chapter shows how S curves can be estimated from early product sales. The S curve equation enables you to know how large sales will eventually become and whether sales have passed the inflection point.

Examining S Curves

In his classic book *Diffusion of Innovations* (5th ed., Free Press, 2003), sociologist Everett Rogers first came up with the idea that the percentage of a market adopting a product, cumulative sales per capita of a product, or even sales per capita often follow an S-shaped curve (see Figure 26-1). Some examples include the following (see Theodore Modis, *Predictions*, Simon and Schuster, 1992):

- Sales of VAX minicomputers in the 1980s
- Registered cars in Italy: 1950s–1990s
- Thousands of miles of railroad tracks in the United States: 1850s–1930s
- Cumulative number of supertankers built: 1970–1985

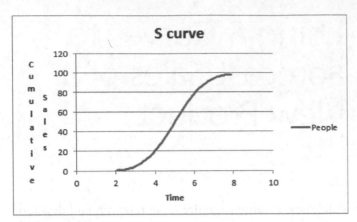

Figure 26-1: Example of S curve

If an S curve is estimated from a few early data points, the marketing analyst can glean two important pieces of information:

- **The upper limit of sales:** Refer to Figure 26-1 and you can see this upper limit is 100.
- **The inflection point:** Defined as the time t when the rate at which sales increase begins to decrease. The inflection point occurs around time 5 because the curve changes from convex (slope increasing) to concave (slope decreasing) (refer to Figure 26-1).

In assessing future profitability of a product, you must know if sales have passed the inflection point. After all, a product whose sales have passed the inflection point has limited possibilities for future growth. For example, 3M incorporates this idea into its corporate strategy by striving to have at least 30 percent of its product revenues come from new products that are less than 5 years old (http://money.cnn.com/2010/09/23/news/companies/3m_innovation_revival.fortune/index.htm). This ensures that a major portion of 3M's product portfolio comes from products whose sales are fast growing because their sales have not yet passed their inflection point.

To see how an S curve may arise, suppose there are 100 possible adopters of a new product and the time for each person to adopt the product is normally distributed with a mean of 5 years and a standard deviation of 1.25 years (see Figure 26-2.) You can graph as a function of time t the total number of people who have adopted the product by time t. This graph will look like the S curve referred to in Figure 26-1. To create this graph, follow these steps in the workbook Scurvenormal.xlsx:

	G	H	I	J	K
4		mean	5		
5		sigma	1.25		
6					
7					
8	Person	Time			
9	1	2.092065			
10	2	2.432814		Time	People
11	3	2.649008		2	0
12	4	2.811642		2.1	1
13	5	2.943933		2.2	1
14	6	3.056533		2.3	1
15	7	3.155261		2.4	1
16	8	3.243661		2.5	2
17	9	3.324056		2.6	2
18	10	3.398061		2.7	3
19	11	3.46684		2.8	3
20	12	3.531267		2.9	4
21	13	3.592011		3	5
22	14	3.649601		3.1	6
23	15	3.704458		3.2	7
24	16	3.756928		3.3	8
25	17	3.807293		3.4	10
26	18	3.855794		3.5	11
27	19	3.90263		3.6	13
28	20	3.947973		3.7	14
29	21	3.991973		3.8	16
30	22	4.034758		3.9	18
31	23	4.076441		4	21

Figure 26-2: Why S curves occur

1. In H9 through H10:H107 compute an "average" time at which the nth person adopts the product. For example, in H18 compute the 10th percentile of the time to adoption and assume that the 10th person will adopt at this time.

2. Copy the formula =NORMINV(G9/100,$I$4,$I$5) from H9 to H10:H107 to compute your estimate of the average time that each person adopts the product. For example, in H18 this computes the 10th percentile of the time to adoption.

3. Copy the formula =COUNTIF($H$9:$H$107,"<="&J11) from K11 to K12:K70 to count the number of people that adopted the product by time t. For example, the formula in cell K21 computes the number of people (five) that have adopted the product by time 3.

4. Graph the range J10:K70 with a scatter chart to create the chart shown in Figure 26-1. Note the graph's inflection point appears to occur near $t = 5$.

Fitting the Pearl or Logistic Curve

The *Logistic curve* is often used to model the path of product diffusion. The Logistic curve is also known as the Pearl curve (named after the 20th century U.S. demographer Raymond Pearl). To find the Logistic curve, let $x(t)$ = sales per capita at time t, cumulative sales by time t, or percentage of population having used the product by time t. If $x(t)$ follows a Logistic curve then Equation 1 is true:

$$(1)\ x(t) = \frac{L}{1 + ae^{-bt}}$$

Given several periods of data, you can use the Excel GRG MultiStart Solver (see Chapter 23, "Cluster Analysis," where the GRG MultiStart Solver was used in your discussion of cluster analysis) to find the values of L, a, and b that best fit Equation 1. As t grows large the term ae^{-bt} approaches 0 and the right side of Equation 1 approaches L. This implies the following:

- If you model cumulative sales, then cumulative sales per capita approach an upper limit of L.
- If you model actual sales per capita, then actual sales per capita approach L.
- If you model percentage of population to have tried a product, then the final percentage of people to have tried a product will approach L.

Together a and b determine the slope of the S curve at all points in time. For a Logistic curve it can be shown that the inflection point occurs when $t = \operatorname{Ln} a/b$.

NOTE In Exercise 10 you can show the inflection point of a Pearl curve occurs when $x(t)$ reaches one-half its maximum value.

To try this out on your own, you can use Excel to fit an S curve to the number of worldwide cell phone subscribers per 100 people. The work is in file `worldcell-pearl.xlxs` (see Figure 26-3).

To estimate L, a, and b, create in Column F an estimate for each year's cell phones per 100 people based on Equation 1. Then in Column G compute the squared error for each estimate. Finally, you can use Solver to find the values of L, a, and b that minimize the sum of the squared estimation errors. Proceed as follows:

1. In F2:H2 enter trial values of L, a, and b.
2. Copy the formula `=L/(1+a*EXP(-b*C5))` from F5 to F6:F15 and use Equation 1 to generate an estimate of cell phones per 100 people for the given parameters.

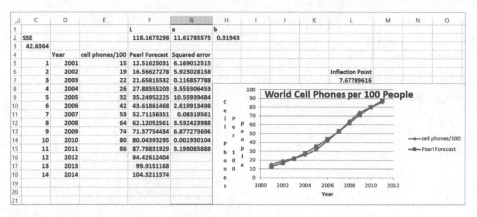

Figure 26-3: World cell phones Pearl curve

3. Copy the formula =(E5-F5)^2 from G5 to G6:G15 to compute the squared error for each observation.
4. In cell C3 compute the Sum of Squared Errors with the formula =SUM(G5:G15).
5. Using the Solver window in Figure 26-4, use the GRG MultiStart Engine to find your estimated Logistic curve to be the following:

$$\text{Cell phones per 100 people during year } t = \frac{118.17}{1 + 11.618e^{-.319t}}$$

Recall from Chapter 23 that before you use the GRG MultiStart Engine, you need lower and upper bounds on changing cells. Setting relatively tight bounds speeds the solution process. You can set lower bounds of 0 for L, a, and b. It seems unlikely that the world will ever see 200 cell phones per person so you can also set $L \leq 200$. Because you know little about a and b, you can set a large upper bound of 1,000 for a and b. If the Solver pushes the value of a changing cell against the bound for the changing cell, then you must relax the bound because Solver is telling you it wants to move beyond the bound.

Therefore, if you estimate cell phones per 100 people will level off at 118.17, then the inflection point for cell phones to occur for $t = \frac{-Ln(11.618)}{.319t} = 7.67$ years. Because $t = 1$ was in 2001, your model implies that the inflection point for cell phone usage that occurred during 2008 and world cell phone usage is well past the inflection point.

Copying the estimation formula in F15 to F16:F18 creates your forecasts (refer to Figure 26-2) for cell phones per 100 people during the years 2012–2014.

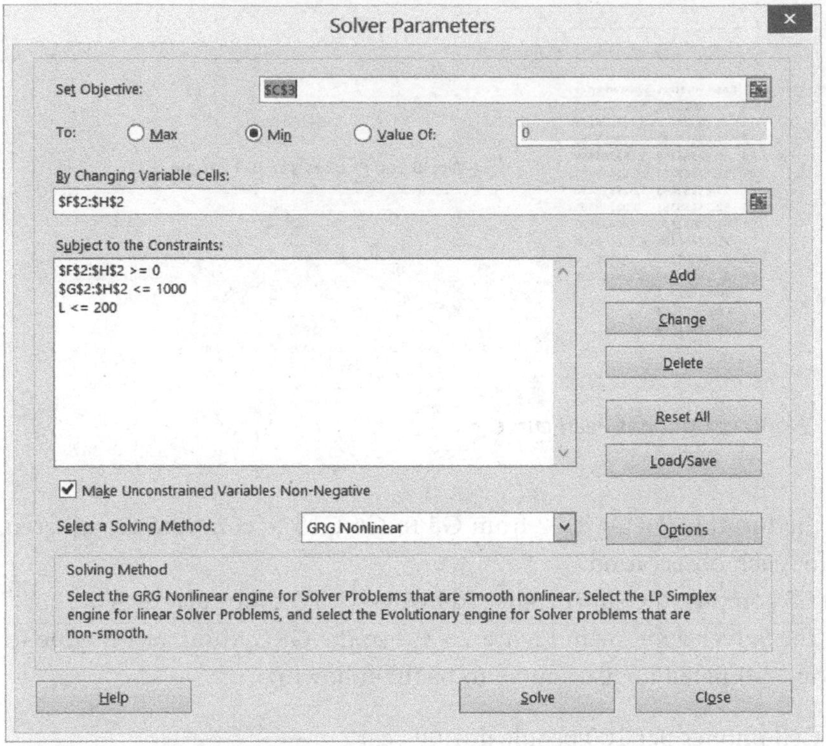

Figure 26-4: Solver window for world cell phone Pearl curve

Fitting an S Curve with Seasonality

If a Logistic curve is fitted to quarterly or monthly data, then the seasonality (see Chapters 12–14 for a discussion of sales seasonality) of sales must be incorporated in the estimation process. To illustrate the idea, try and fit a Logistic curve with seasonality to quarterly iPod sales for the years 2002–2006. The work is in file iPodsseasonal.xls (see Figure 26-5).

To fit an S curve to quarterly data, multiply the forecast from the S curve in Equation 1 by the appropriate seasonal index. After adding the seasonal indices as changing cells, again choose the forecast parameters to minimize the sum of squared forecast errors.

To obtain forecasts proceed as follows:

1. Copy the formula =100*D5/E5 from F5 to F6:F19 to compute for each quarter the sales per 100 people.

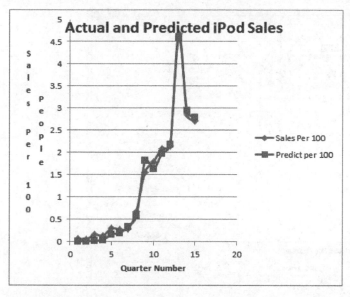

Figure 26-5: Actual and predicted iPod sales

2. Copy the formula `=(L/(1+a*EXP(-b*A5)))*HLOOKUP(C5,seaslook,2)` from G5 to G6:G19 to compute the forecast for each quarter's sales/100 by multiplying the S curve value from Equation 1 (which represents the level of sales in the absence of seasonality) by the appropriate seasonal index. This is analogous to the forecasting formula you developed in your discussion of Winter's Method in Chapter 14.

3. Copy the formula `=(F5-G5)^2` from H5 to H6:H19 to compute the squared error for each prediction.

4. In cell H3 compute the Sum of Squared Errors with the formula `=SUM(H5:H19)`.

5. The constraint `$N$2=1` was added to ensure that the seasonal indices average to 1. Using the Solver window in Figure 26-6 and the GRG MultiStart Engine, obtain a solution in which $a = 1{,}000$. Therefore, you can raise the upper bound on a to 10,000 and obtain the solution shown in Figure 26-7.

You can find an upper quarterly limit of 3.37 iPods per 100 people. As shown in Figure 26-7 the seasonal indices tell you first quarter sales are 10 percent less than average, second quarter sales are 17 percent less than average, third quarter sales are 23 percent less than average, and fourth quarter sales are 49 percent above average.

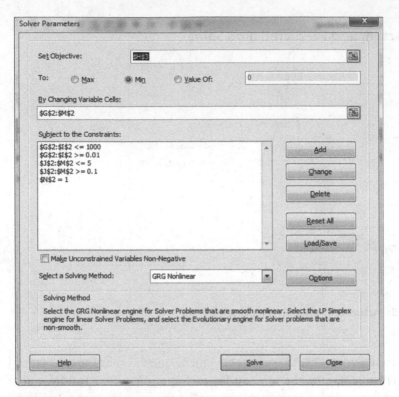

Figure 26-6: Solver window for iPod sales

	A	B	C	D	E	F	G	H	I	J	K	L	M	N
1							L	a	b	1	2	3	4	
2			mill		mill		3.369847063	1516.33	0.74771	0.9049	0.83445	0.772	1.4887	1
3							SSE	0.1963						
4	Quarter#	Year	Quarter	Sales	Pop	Sales Per 100	Predict per 100	sq err						
5	1	2002	4	0.216	290	0.074482759	0.006978377	0.00456						
6	2	2003	1	0.16	290.8	0.055030095	0.008945104	0.00212						
7	3	2003	2	0.467	291.5	0.160205832	0.017366014	0.0204						
8	4	2003	3	0.4	292.3	0.136869119	0.033700384	0.01064						
9	5	2003	4	0.88	293	0.300341297	0.135327094	0.02723						
10	6	2004	1	0.807	293.8	0.274723404	0.16867465	0.01125						
11	7	2004	2	0.86	294.5	0.292020374	0.309493344	0.00031						
12	8	2004	3	2	295.3	0.677392041	0.538775934	0.01921						
13	9	2004	4	4.6	296	1.554054054	1.783787894	0.05278						
14	10	2005	1	5.3	296.8	1.786015164	1.641097551	0.021						
15	11	2005	2	6.2	297.5	2.084033613	1.999583864	0.00713						
16	12	2005	3	6.4	298.3	2.145850796	2.181659436	0.00128						
17	13	2005	4	14	299	4.682274247	4.598072165	0.00709						
18	14	2006	1	8.5	299.8	2.835696414	2.92328865	0.00767						
19	15	2006	2	8.1	300.5	2.695507488	2.755700948	0.00362						

Figure 26-7: Fitting seasonal Pearl curve to iPod sales

Fitting the Gompertz Curve

Another functional form that is often used to fit an S curve to data is the *Gompertz curve*, named after Benjamin Gompertz, a 19th century English actuary and mathematician. To define the Gompertz curve, let $x(t)$ = sales per capita at time t, cumulative sales by time t, or percentage of population having used the product by time t. If $x(t)$ follows a Gompertz curve then you model $x(t)$ by Equation 2:

$$(2)\ x(t) = ae^{-ce^{-bt}}$$

As with the Pearl curve, you can use the GRG MultiStart Engine to find the values of a, b, and c that best fit a set of data. As t grows large, $x(t)$ approaches a, and the inflection points of the Gompertz curve occurs for $t = \text{Ln } c/b$ and $x(t) = a/e$.

In the file `worldcellgompertz.xlsx` (See Figures 26-8 and 26-9) you can see a Gompertz curve fit to the world cell phone data.

	C	D	E	F	G	H
1				a	b	c
2	SSE			207.6169718	0.12099848	3.213029
3	68.99799					
4		Year	cell phones/100	Gompertz Forecast	Squared error	
5	1	2001	15	12.04726328	8.718654124	
6	2	2002	19	16.66446736	5.454712723	
7	3	2003	22	22.21449787	0.046009338	
8	4	2004	26	28.6585119	7.067685518	
9	5	2005	32	35.91404501	15.31974834	
10	6	2006	42	43.86369888	3.473373529	
11	7	2007	53	52.36599749	0.401959178	
12	8	2008	64	61.26671509	7.470846397	
13	9	2009	74	70.40933509	12.89287449	
14	10	2010	80	79.64376449	0.126903737	
15	11	2011	86	88.83288164	8.025218392	

Figure 26-8: Fitting Gompertz curve for world cell phone sales

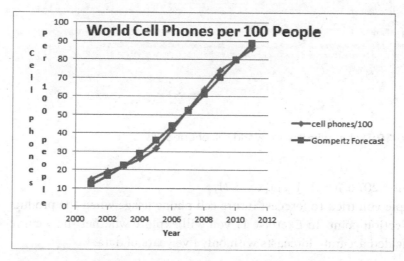

Figure 26-9: Gompertz curve for world cell phone sales

To fit the Gompertz curve to your cell phone data, proceed as follows:

1. Copy the formula =a*EXP(-c_*EXP(-b*C5)) from F5 to F6:F15 that uses Equation 2 to estimate the Gompertz forecast for each year's cell phones per 100 people.

2. Copy the formula =(E5-F5)^2 from G5 to G6:G15 to compute the squared error for each year.

3. In cell C3 compute the Sum of Squared Errors with the formula =SUM(G5:G15).

4. As shown in Figure 26-10, use the Solver window to find the least-squares estimate of the Gompertz curve parameters *a*, *b*, and *c*.

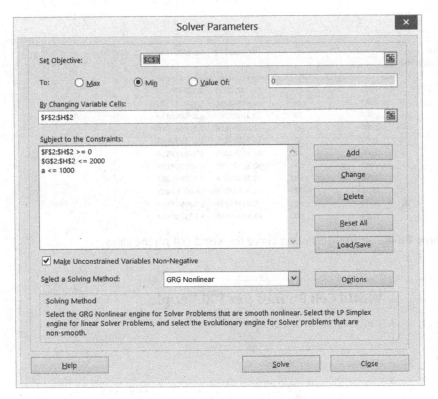

Figure 26-10: Solver window for world cell phone sales

You can find *a* = 207.6, *b* = .121, and *c* = 3.21.

In this example you tried to forecast future cell phone usage when the product was past its inflection point. In Exercise 11 you will explore whether the S curve methodology yielded accurate forecasts with only five years of data.

Pearl Curve versus Gompertz Curve

If you fit both a Pearl curve and a Gompertz curve to sales data, which curve should be used to predict future sales? You would probably think the curve yielding the smaller Sum of Squared Errors would yield the better forecasts. This is not the case. Joseph Martino (*Technological Forecasting for Decision-Making*, McGraw-Hill, 1993) states that if future sales benefit from previous product sales, the Pearl curve should be used to generate forecasts, whereas if future sales do not benefit from previous sales, the Gompertz curve should be used. For example, in predicting cable TV adoptions for the years 1979–1989 from adoptions during 1952–1978 Martino points out that the many customers adopting cable in 1952–1978 helped generate additional, higher quality cable programming, which would make cable more attractive to later adopters. Therefore, Martino used the Pearl curve to forecast future cable TV adoptions. The same reasoning would apply to your world cell phone example. It seems obvious that the more people that have cell phones, the more apps are developed. Also, when more people have cell phones, it becomes easier to reach people, so a phone becomes more useful to nonadopters.

Summary

In this chapter you learned the following:

- Cumulative sales per capita, percentage of population adopting a product, and actual sales per capita often follow an S curve.
- Usually the analyst uses the GRG MultiStart Engine with a target cell of minimizing the Sum of Squared Errors to fit either a Pearl or Gompertz curve.
- If the likelihood of future adoptions increases with the number of prior adoptions, use the Pearl curve to generate future forecasts. Otherwise, use the Gompertz curve to generate future forecasts.

Exercises

Exercises 1–4 use the data in the file `Copyofcellphonedata.xls`, which contains U.S. cell phone subscribers for the years 1985–2002.

1. Fit a Pearl curve to this data, and estimate the inflection point and upper limit for cell phones per capita.
2. Fit a Gompertz curve to this data, and estimate the inflection point and upper limit for cell phones per capita.

3. Forecast U.S. cell phones per capita for the years 2003–2005.

4. In 2002 were U.S. cell phones per capita past the inflection point?

Exercises 5–9 use the data in the file `Internet2000_2011.xls`. This file contains the percentage of people with Internet access for the years 2000–2011. Use this data to answer the following questions:

5. Estimate the percentage of people in Nigeria who will eventually be on the Internet. Is Internet usage in Nigeria past the inflection point?

6. Estimate the percentage of people in the United States who will eventually be on the Internet. Is Internet usage in the United States past the inflection point?

7. Estimate the percentage of people in India who will eventually be on the Internet. Is Internet usage in India past the inflection point?

8. Estimate the percentage of people in Sweden who will eventually be on the Internet. Is Internet usage in Sweden past the inflection point?

9. Estimate the percentage of people in Brazil who will eventually be on the Internet. Is Internet usage in Brazil past the inflection point?

10. Show that for a Logistic curve the inflection point occurs when $x(t) = L/2$.

11. Suppose it is now the end of 2004. Using the data in the file `worldcellpearl.xlsx`, develop predictions for world cell phone usage. How accurate are your predictions?

12. The file `Facebook.xlsx` gives the number of users of Facebook (in millions) during the years 2004–2012. Use this data to predict the future growth of Facebook.

13. The file `Wikipedia.xlsx` gives the number of Wikipedia articles (in English) for the years 2003–2012. Use this data to predict the future growth of Wikipedia.

27

The Bass Diffusion Model

Businesses regularly invest large sums of money in new product development. If the product does not sell well, these investments can reduce the company's value or share price. It is therefore of critical importance to predict future sales of a product before a product comes to market. The *Bass model* and its variants meet this challenge. Unlike the Pearl and Gompertz curves you learned about in Chapter 26, "Using S Curves to Forecast Sales of a New Product," the Bass model has been successfully used to forecast product sales before the product comes to market. The Bass model also gives the analyst an explanation of how knowledge of new products spreads throughout the market place.

Introducing the Bass Model

The Bass model asserts that diffusion of a new product is driven by two types of people:

- **Innovators:** Innovators are people who seek new products without caring if other people have adopted the new product.
- **Imitators:** Imitators are people who wait to try a product until other people have successfully used the product.

The Bass model helps the marketing analysts determine the relative importance of innovators and imitators in driving the spread of the product. To understand the Bass model, you need to carefully develop some notation, defined as follows:

- $n(t)$ = Product sales during period t.
- $N(t)$ = Cumulative product sales through period t.

- $\overline{N}$ = Total number of customers in market; assume that all of them eventually adopt the product.
- P = Coefficient of innovation or external influence.
- Q = Coefficient of imitation or internal influence.

The Bass Model asserts the following equation:

$$(1)\, n(t) = P(\overline{N} - N(t - 1) + \frac{(\overline{N} - N(t - 1))(N(t - 1)}{\overline{N}}$$

Equation 1 decomposes the sales of a product during period t into two parts:

- A component tied to the number of people $(\overline{N} - N(t - 1))$ who have not yet adopted the product. This component is independent of the number of people $(N(t - 1))$ who have already adopted the product. This explains why P is called the *coefficient of innovation* or external influence.
- A component tied to the number of interactions between previous adopters $(N(t - 1))$ and people who have yet to adopt $(\overline{N} - N(t - 1))$. This term represents the *diffusion* of the product through the market. This *imitation* or internal influence component reflects that previous adopters tell nonadopters about the product and thereby generate new adoptions. The imitation factor is often referred to as a network effect.

NOTE The imitation factor is 0 (because $N(0) = 0$) at time 0 and increases until $N(t) = \overline{N}/2$. P and Q are assumed to be between 0 and 1.

Estimating the Bass Model

To fit the Bass model, you must find values of P, Q, and $\overline{N}$, which accurately predict each period's actual sales ($n(t)$). To estimate P, Q, and $\overline{N}$, use the Solver. To illustrate the estimation of the Bass model, use U.S. sales of color TVs; the file ColorTV.xls contains 16 years of color TV sales (1964–1979). Solver is used to determine the values of the Bass model parameters that best fit (in the sense of minimizing the Sum of Squared Errors) the 1964–1979 data. The work is shown in Figure 27-1.

For example when $t = 1$ (in 1964), 4.9 million color TVs were sold. Through 1965, 9.2 million color TVs were sold. To estimate P, Q, and $\overline{N}$, proceed as follows:

1. Put trial values of P, Q, and $\overline{N}$ in E2:G2 and create range names for these cells.

2. Using the trial values of P, Q, and $\overline{N}$, create predictions for 16 years of sales by copying the formula =p*(Nbar-C5)+(q/Nbar)*C5*(Nbar-C5) from D6 to D7:D21.

3. In E6:E21 compute the squared error (SSE) for each year by copying the formula =(B6-D6)^2 from E6 to E7:E21.

4. Compute the Sum of Squared Errors (SSE) for your predictions in cell E3 with the formula =SUM(E6:E21).

5. Use Solver's GRG Multistart Engine (see Figure 27-2) to determine values of P, Q, and $\overline{N}$ that minimize SSE. P and Q are constrained to be between 0 and 1. Minimize SSE (E3) by changing P, Q, and $\overline{N}$. All changing cells should be non-negative. Solver found $P = .056$, $Q = .147$, and $\overline{N} = 98.21$. Because Q is greater than P, this indicates that the word of mouth component was more important to the spread of color TV than the external component.

	A	B	C	D	E	F	G
1					p	q	Nbar
2					0.055874576	0.146583098	98.21177083
3		Color TV		SSE	74.22797114		
4	t	n(t)	N(t)	Predicted	Sq Err		
5		0		0			
6		1	4.9	4.9	5.487541028	0.345204459	
7		2	4.3	9.2	5.896177365	2.54778218	
8		3	5.3	14.5	6.195732482	0.802336679	
9		4	10.9	25.4	6.489012128	19.45681401	
10		5	9.2	34.6	6.828622855	5.623429562	
11		6	2.5	37.1	6.83926985	18.82926283	
12		7	4.2	41.3	6.798506825	6.752237721	
13		8	8.3	49.6	6.688025413	2.598462071	
14		9	9.3	58.9	6.314844077	8.911155882	
15		10	6.2	65.1	5.652405353	0.299859898	
16		11	4.3	69.4	5.0673483	0.588823413	
17		12	2.8	72.2	4.594195616	3.219137909	
18		13	3.2	75.4	4.256424883	1.116033534	
19		14	3.5	78.9	3.841744792	0.116789503	
20		15	3.7	82.6	3.353188832	0.120277986	
21		16	4.5	87.1	2.796954639	2.900363503	

Figure 27-1: Fitting Bass model to color TV data

Fareena Sultan, John Farley, and Donald Lehmann summarized the estimated Bass model parameters for 213 products in their work "A Meta-Analysis of Applications of Diffusion Models," (*Journal of Marketing Research*, 1990, pp. 70–77) and found an average value of 0.03 for P and 0.30 for Q. This indicates that imitation is much more important than innovation in facilitating product diffusion.

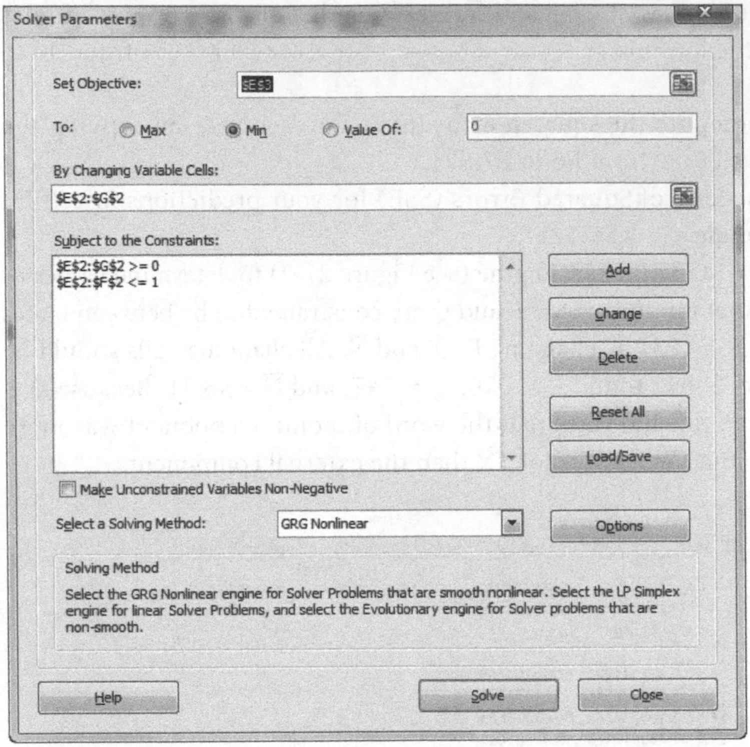

Figure 27-2: Solver window for fitting Bass model

TIME AND VALUE OF PEAK SALES

If a product's sales are defined by Equation 1, then it follows that the time of peak sales is given by the following:

$$\text{Time of peak Sales} = \frac{Ln\ Q - Ln\ P}{P + Q}$$

The value of peak sales is given by this equation:

$$\text{Value of Peak Sales} = \frac{\overline{N}\ (P + Q)^2}{4Q}$$

Using the Bass Model to Forecast New Product Sales

It is difficult to predict the sales of a new product before it comes to market, but an approach that has proven useful in the past is to look for a similar product or industry that has already reached market maturity (for example, a color TV might be an analog for DIRECTV). Similar products or industries are often referred to as *adjacent industries/categories*. You can use the values of P and Q for the analogous product and an estimated value of $\overline{N}$ for the new product to forecast sales. Table 27-1 lists values of P and Q for several products.

Table 27-1: Estimates of P and Q for Bass model

Product	P	Q
CD Player	0.02836	0.368
Dishwasher	0.0128	0.18450
Mammography	0.00494	0.70393
Cell Phone	0.00471	0.50600
Tractor	0.00720	0.11795

To illustrate how you can use the Bass model to model sales of a new product, consider Frank Bass, Kent Gordon, Teresa Ferguson, and Mary Lou Githens' study "DIRECTV: Forecasting Diffusion of a New Technology Prior to a Product Launch (*Interfaces*, May–June 2001, pp. S82–S93), which describes how the Bass model was used to forecast the subscriber growth for DIRECTV. The discussion of this model is in file DIRECTV.xls (see Figure 27-3).

Before DIRECTV was launched in 1994, the Hughes Corporation wanted to predict the sales of DIRECTV for its first four years. This estimate was needed to raise venture capital to finance the huge capital expense needed for DIRECTV to begin operations. The estimate proceeded as follows:

- Hughes surveyed a representative sample of TV households and found 32 percent intended to purchase DIRECTV.
- 13 percent of those sampled said they could afford DIRECTV.

	A	B	C	D	E	F	G
1	afford	0.13					
2	avail	0.65					
3	int prob	0.32					
4					Nbar	21.54786	
5	actual purchase/intended purchase						
6	0.04337				t	actual	cumulative
7					0	0	0
8	fraction buying in year				0.083333	0.105944	0.105944
9	0.0138784				0.166667	0.106708	0.212652
10	tvhomes				0.25	0.107465	0.320117
11	9.50E+07		p	q	0.333333	0.108215	0.428331
12	predicted number buying first year		0.059	0.1463	0.416667	0.108956	0.537287
13	1.32E+06				0.5	0.109689	0.646976
14					0.583333	0.110414	0.75739
15					0.666667	0.111129	0.868519
16					0.75	0.111835	0.980354
17					0.833333	0.112532	1.092886
18	simp*(simNbar-I7)+simq*I7*(simNbar-I7)/simNbar				0.916667	0.113219	1.206105
19					1	0.113895	1.32
20					1.083333	0.114561	1.434561
21					1.166667	0.115216	1.549777
22					1.25	0.115859	1.665636
23					1.333333	0.116491	1.782127
24					1.416667	0.117112	1.899239
25					1.5	0.11772	2.016959
26					1.583333	0.118315	2.135274
27					1.666667	0.118898	2.254172
28					1.75	0.119468	2.37364
29					1.833333	0.120024	2.493664
30					1.916667	0.120567	2.614231
31					2	0.121095	2.735326
53					3.833333	0.128698	5.501728
54					3.916667	0.128843	5.63057
55					4	0.128968	5.759539

Figure 27-3: Predicting DIRECTV subscribers

Research has shown that intentions data greatly overstates actual purchases. A study of consumer electronics products by Linda Jamieson and Frank Bass ("Adjusting Stated Intentions Measures to Predict Trial Purchases of New Products," *Journal of Marketing Research*, August 1989, pp. 336–345) showed that the best estimate of the actual proportion that will buy a product in a year is a fraction k of the fraction in the sample who say they will buy the product, where k can be estimated from the following equation:

$$(2)\ k = -0.899 + (Afford\%age) * (1.234) + (Available\%age) * (1.203)$$

In Equation 2 *Available%age* is the estimated fraction of consumers who will have access to product within a year. Hughes estimated *Available%age* = 65%. At the time DIRECTV was introduced, there were 95 million TV households. Therefore Hughes' forecast for DIRECTV subscribers 1 year after launch is computed in cell A13 as 0.32 * 95 * (−0.899 + (1.234)(0.13) + (1.203)(0.65)) = 1.32 million.

Now assume subscriptions to DIRECTV will follow the Bass model. You can generate the forecasts using color TV as the analogous product. Bass et. al. use slightly different parameters (P = .059 and Q = .1463) than the ones in the following example. You do not know *Nbar*, but for any given value of *Nbar*, you can use Equation 1 to predict cumulative monthly DIRECTV subscriptions for the next 4 years. Then using Excel's Goal Seek command, you can reverse engineer a value of *Nbar*, which ensures that your 1-year subscription estimate for DIRECTV is 1.32 million. Then the Bass model can give you a forecast for the number of subscribers in four years. The work proceeded as follows:

1. Because at time 0 DIRECTV has 0 subscribers, enter 0 in cells F7 and G7.
2. Copy the formula =(1/12)*(p*(Nbar-G7)+q*G7*(Nbar-G7)/Nbar) from F8 to F9:F55 and use Equation 1 to generate estimates for the number of new subscribers during each month. The (1/12) adjusts the annual *P* and *Q* values to monthly values.
3. Copy the formula =G7+F8 from G8 to G9:G55 to compute the cumulative number of subscribers as previous cumulative subscribers + new subscribers during the current month.
4. Use the Excel Goal Seek command to determine the value of *Nbar* that makes your 1-year estimate (in cell G19) of DIRECTV subscribers equal to 1.32 million. From the What-If portion of the Data tab, select Goal Seek... and fill in the dialog box, as shown in Figure 27-4.

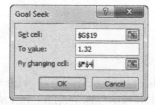

Figure 27-4: Using Goal Seek to estimate *Nbar*

The Goal Seek window tells Excel to find the value for cell $F$4 (which is *Nbar*) that makes your 1-year subscriber estimate (cell $G$19) equal to 1.32 million. In the blink of an eye, Excel plugs different numbers into cell $F$4 until $G$19 equals 1.32. *Nbar* = 21.55 million to make your 1-year Bass forecast match your previous 1-year forecast of 1.32 million subscribers.

Cell G55 contains your 4-year forecast (5.75 million) for the number of DIRECTV subscribers. The forecast was that after four years approximately 6 percent of the 95 million homes would have DIRECTV. In reality after four years, DIRECTV ended up with 7.5 percent of the 95 million homes.

When you use the Bass model to forecast product sales based on an analogous product like this, you are applying the concept of *empirical generalization*. As defined by Frank Bass in "Empirical Generalizations and Marketing Science: A Personal View" (*Marketing Science*, 1995, pp. G6–G19.), an empirical generalization is "a pattern or regularity that repeats over different circumstances and that can be described simply by mathematical, graphical, or symbolic methods." In this case, you have successfully forecasted DIRECTV sales before launch by assuming the pattern of new product sales, defined by the Bass model for an adjacent product (color TV), will be useful in predicting early sales for DIRECTV.

Deflating Intentions Data

The approach to estimating the rollout of DIRECTV subscribers was highly dependent on having an estimate of subscribers 1 year from now. Often such an estimate is based on intentions data derived from a survey in which consumers are asked to rank their likelihood of purchasing a product within 1 year as follows:

- Definitely buy product
- Probably buy product
- Might or might not buy product
- Probably not buy product
- Definitely not buy product

Jamieson and Bass (1989) conducted meta-analysis of intentions surveys for many products that enabled the marketing analyst to "deflate" intentions data and obtain a realistic estimate of a new product's market share after 1 year. The results are summarized in the file Marketsharedeflator.xlsx (see Figure 27-5).

	C	D	E	F	G	H	I	J
8								
9		Definitely will not buy	Probably will not buy	Might or might not buy	Probably will buy	Definitely will buy		
10	Non-durable	0.12	0.14	0.25	0.35	0.41		
11	Durable	0.04	0.05	0.05	0.09	0.12		check
12	results	0	0.1	0.2	0.4	0.3		1
13	Product type	Predicted Share						
14	Non-durable	0.327						

Figure 27-5: Deflating intentions data

To use this market share deflator, you must first identify in cell C14 the product as a durable good (such as a car or TV) or a nondurable good (such as a frozen food dinner or new cosmetic). Note that for a durable good only 12 percent of those who say they will definitely buy actually buy, and for a nondurable good 41 percent of those who say they will definitely buy will actually buy. This is probably because durable goods are generally more expensive. Then the analyst enters the fraction of consumers who chose each option (in this case 30 percent said they will definitely buy, 40 percent said they will probably buy, 20 percent said they might or might not buy, and 10 percent said they probably will not buy). Then cell D14 tells you that your predicted market share in 1 year is 32.7 percent. Even though 70 percent of consumers gave a positive response, you can predict only a 32.7 percent share after 1 year.

Using the Bass Model to Simulate Sales of a New Product

In reality the sales of a new product are highly uncertain, but you can combine the Bass model with your knowledge of Monte Carlo simulation (see Chapter 21, "Customer Value, Monte Carlo Simulation and Marketing Decision Making") to generate a range of outcomes for sales of a new product. Recall that Monte Carlo simulation can be used to model uncertain quantities and then generate a range of outcomes for the uncertain situation. In the Bass model the uncertain quantities are *Nbar* (which you model as a normal random variable) and *P* and *Q*. You will assume the values of *P* and *Q* are equally likely to be drawn from a set of analogous products. For example, if you were a brand manager for Lean Cuisine, you could model the uncertain values of *P* and *Q* as equally likely to be drawn from the parameter values for Lean Cuisine meals that have been on the market for a number of years.

The work for the following example is in the file `Basssim.xls` (see Figure 27-6). In C6:D17 you are given 12 potential scenarios for Bass parameters, and you can assume potential market size is normal with mean = 100,000 and sigma = 20,000. Then proceed as follows:

1. In cell C4 simulate potential market size with the formula `=ROUND(NORMINV(RAND(),C2,C3),0)`.
2. In cell H1 choose a scenario that chooses your Bass parameters from one of the 12 analogous products with the formula `=RANDBETWEEN(1,12)`.
3. In cell H2 find the simulated value of *P* for your chosen Bass scenario with the formula `=VLOOKUP(scenario,B6:D17,2)`.
4. Change the 2 to a 3 in cell H3 to find the simulated value of *Q* for your chosen Bass scenario.

5. Copy the formula =SUM($H$6:H7) from I7 to I8:I118 to compute cumulative product sales for each year. Of course, you need to enter a 0 in cell I6.

6. Copy the formula =simp*(simNbar-I6)+simq*I6*(simNbar-I6)/simNbar from H7 to H8:H18 to compute simulated sales for each year.

7. Following the technique introduced in Chapter 21, use a one-way data table to trick Excel into simulating 1,000 times your 1-year, 5-year, and 10-year cumulative sales.

8. In cells F22, G22, and H22, refer to the 1-year (I7), 5-year (I11), and 10-year (I16) sales.

9. After selecting the table range E22:H1022, choose Data Table. . . from the What-If section on the Data tab.

10. Now select any blank cell as the Column Input cell to simulate 1,000 times the 1-year, 5-year, and 10-year cumulative sales.

11. Copy the formula =AVERAGE(F23:F1022) from F20 to G20:H20 to compute an estimate of the average sales through years 1, 5, and 10.

12. Copy the formula =STDEV(F23:F1022) from F21 to G21:H21 to compute and estimate the average sales through years 1, 5, and 10.

	A	B	C	D	E	F	G	H	I
1		Nbar					scenario	11	
2		mean	100000				simp	0.01	
3		sigma	20000				simq	0.19	
4		simNbar	81227						
5		Product	p	q			Year	n(t)	N(t)
6		1	0.05	0.13			0		0
7		2	0.01	0.13			1	812.27	812.27
8		3	0.02	0.26			2	956.9353	1769.205
9		4	0.01	0.6			3	1123.405	2892.611
10		5	0.05	0.35			4	1313.368	4205.979
11		6	0.001	0.73			5	1527.966	5733.945
12		7	0.001	0.8			6	1767.474	7501.419
13		8	0.06	0.4			7	2030.9	9532.319
14		9	0.06	0			8	2315.543	11847.86
15		10	0.14	0			9	2616.538	14464.4
16		11	0.01	0.19			10	2926.473	17390.87
17		12	0.001	0.26			11	3235.177	20626.05
18							12	3529.816	24155.87
19						1 year	5 year	10 year	
20					mean	3502.988	20635.78	49320.58	
21					sigma	4096.903	18757.59	30577.95	
22						812.27	5733.945	17390.87	
23					1	5544.24	45019.91	86813.34	
24					2	87.084	1713.533	23899.57	
25					3	1743.18	13503.99	41383.26	
26					4	1011.16	6368.066	16810.95	
27					5	5391.6	43780.45	84423.26	
28					6	96.093	2127.796	33959.53	
29					7	4913.65	27651.58	57188.12	
30					8	1212.87	8561.845	25967.8	
31					9	7957.44	64615.39	124599.9	
32					10	6987.6	30989.54	53732.88	
33					11	995.81	14621.3	77999.05	
34					12	99.488	1957.604	27303.75	

Figure 27-6: Bass model simulation

Estimates of new product sales are an important input into capital budgeting analyses, which determine if a new product should be scrapped or brought to market. You can estimate, for example, that after 5 years an average of 20,636 units will have been sold.

Modifications of the Bass Model

Since the Bass model was first introduced in 1969, the model has been modified and improved in several ways. The following list provides some important modifications of the Bass model.

- Due to population growth, the size of the market may grow over time. To account for growth in market size, you may assume that $\overline{N}$ is growing over time. For example, if market size is growing 5 percent a year, you can assume that $\overline{N}(t) = N(0)*1.05^t$ in Year t forecast and have Solver solve for $N(0)$.
- Clearly changing a product's price or level of advertising will have an impact on product sales. The Bass model has been generalized to incorporate the effects of price and advertising on sales by making P and Q dependent on the current level of price and advertising.
- For many products (such as automobiles, refrigerators, etc.), customers may return to the market and purchase a product again. To incorporate this reality, the Bass model has been modified by adjusting $\overline{N}$. For example, if people tend to buy a product every five years, you can adjust $\overline{N}(t)$ to include people who bought a product 5 years ago.
- For quarterly or monthly sales data, Equation 1 can be adjusted for seasonality. See Exercise 5.
- If a new-generation product (like an improved smartphone) is introduced, then an analog of Equation 1 is needed for both the improved and old product.
- You can make P and or Q depend on time. For example, you could allow $q(t) = q(1+kt)^{\frac{\mu-k}{\mu}}$ where k and μ are parameters that can be used to

allow the word of mouth factor to either increase, decrease, or remain constant over time. This model is known as the *flexible logistic model*.

If you want to learn more about these modifications and improvements to the Bass model, refer to *New-Product Diffusion Models* by Vijay Mahajan, Eitan Muller, and Yoram Wind (Springer, 2001).

Summary

In this chapter you learned the following:

- The Bass model breaks down product sales into an innovation (P) and imitation (Q) factor.
- The GRG Multistart Solver Engine can be used to estimate P, Q, and $\overline{N}$.
- By using an analogous product to estimate P and Q and intentions data to estimate $\overline{N}$, you can use the Bass model to estimate new product sales before the product is launched.
- By randomly drawing values of P and Q from a set of analogous products and modeling $\overline{N}$ as a normal random variable, you can simulate the range of possible product sales.

Exercises

1. The file Dishwasher.xlsx contains product sales for dishwashers in the United States. Fit the Bass model to this data.
2. Fit the Bass model to the data in the file Worldcell.xslx.

Exercises 3–5 use the Chapter 26 file Internet2000_2011.xls.

3. Fit the Bass model to the Nigeria Internet data in Chapter 26.
4. Fit the Bass model to the Sweden Internet data in Chapter 26.
5. Explain the differences in the P and Q values you found in Exercises 2–4.
6. For the iPodseasonal.xls data file in Chapter 26, incorporate seasonality and fit a Bass model to the quarterly IPOD sales.
7. Suppose you work for a company that produces frozen food dinners and have found that for "traditional" dinners (mac and cheese, fried chicken, and so on) the Bass model has P near 1 and Q near 0, and for "new wave" dinners (tofu, seaweed, and such), the Bass model has P near 0 and Q near 1. How would this information affect your marketing strategy?
8. Suppose you wanted to determine whether products diffuse more quickly in developed or developing countries. Outline how you would conduct such a study.
9. Determine if the following statement is True or False: As Q/P increases, the trajectory of product diffusion becomes more S-shaped.

28

Using the Copernican Principle to Predict Duration of Future Sales

If you want to determine the future value of a new product, you must have some idea of how long the product will sell. For example, if you want to value the future profits generated by Britney Spears' songs, you need to have some idea of the length of time for which Britney Spears' music will be popular. In this chapter you learn how to use the *Copernican Principle* to model the length of time that a product will sell well. Because the Copernican Principle sheds light on how long a product is likely to sell, it can also aid in the calculations of a customer's lifetime value, discussed in Chapters 19–22.

Using the Copernican Principle

The Copernican Principle attempts to estimate the length of time that a product or event remains in existence, for example:

- How long will people listen to Britney Spears' music?
- How long will people listen to Bach's music?
- How long will Stonehenge exist?

To explain the Copernican Principle, you need the following notation:

- *NOW* = Today
- *MIN* = First date a thing came into existence
- *F* = Future lifetime
- *P* = Past lifetime
- *MAX* = Last date a thing is in existence

Nicolaus Copernicus (1473–1543) was a famous Polish Renaissance astronomer. Copernicus contributed greatly to society when he discovered that the Earth was not the center of the universe. Before Copernicus, egotistical earthlings felt that the Earth was the center of the universe and everything revolved around the Earth.

Copernicus showed that Earth did not occupy a special place in the universe. In the spirit of Copernicus, assume that the present time (like the Earth in Copernicus's view of the solar system) has no special quality. Therefore assume that *NOW* is equally likely to be anywhere between *MIN* and *MAX*. This implies that (*NOW-MIN*)/(*MAX-MIN*) is equally likely to be any number between 0 and 1.

Thus, for example, there is a probability of 38/40 or .95 that Equation 1 is true:

$$(1) \quad \frac{1}{40} \le \frac{NOW - MIN}{MAX - MIN} \le \frac{39}{40}$$

Equation 1 may be rewritten as Equation 2:

$$(2) \quad \frac{1}{40} \le \frac{P}{F + P} \le \frac{39}{40}$$

Equation 2 is satisfied if and only if $F > P/39$ and $F < 39P$. Therefore, there is a 95 percent chance that:

$$\frac{P}{39} \le F \le 39P$$

In general there is probability $1 - (1/N)$ that Equation 3 is true:

$$(3) \quad \frac{1}{2N - 1} \le \frac{F}{P} \le 2N - 1$$

In Equations 1 and 2 you used $N = 20$ to get a 95 percent confidence interval for F/P. Letting $N = 2$ shows you are 50 percent sure that:

$$(4) \quad \frac{1}{3} \le \frac{F}{P} \le 3$$

For example, in 2007 Britney Spears' songs had been listened to for seven years. Therefore when $P = 7$ from Equation 4, you are 50 percent sure that:

$$(5) \quad \frac{1}{3} \le \frac{F}{7} \le 3$$

After rearranging Equation 5, you can find that in 2007 there was a 50 percent chance that Britney Spears' music will be listened to for between 7/3 and 21 more years. In a similar fashion you are 95 percent sure that Britney Spears' songs will be listened to for between 7/39 and 273 more years.

Simulating Remaining Life of Product

You can use the Copernican Principle to simulate the remaining lifetime of a product. The Copernican Principle tells you that (*NOW – MIN*) / (*MAX – MIN*) is equally likely to be any number between 0 and 1. The Excel =RAND() function is equally likely to assume any value between 0 and 1, and therefore in Excel you may model the following equation:

$$(6)\ (NOW{-}MIN)\ /\ (MAX{-}MIN) = \text{RAND}()$$

Now you can solve for *MAX* in Equation 6 and find that *MAX* can be modeled as

$$(7)\ MAX = MIN + (NOW{-}MIN)\ /\ \text{RAND}()$$

For example, suppose in 2007 you wanted to model the last year (highly uncertain) in which Britney Spears' music would be selling. Then *MIN* = 2000 and *NOW* = 2007, so from Equation 7 you would model the latest year during which Britney Spears' music would be popular as $2000 + \dfrac{7}{rand()}$. This modeling of the remaining time for which Britney Spears' music will be popular would be useful in modeling the future value of the royalties earned from Britney Spears' songs.

Summary

In this chapter you learned the following:

- You can use the Copernican Principle to model a product's remaining lifetime.
- Underlying the Copernican Principle is the assumption that the current time is equally likely to be any time between the first time the product was introduced and the last time the product will be sold.
- If F = Future lifetime of a product and P = Past lifetime of a product, then there is probability $1 - (1/N)$ that:

$$(3)\ \frac{1}{2N-1} \le \frac{F}{P} \le 2N-1$$

- The latest date (*MAX*) at which a product will be sold can be modeled as

$$(7)\ MAX = MIN + (NOW{-}MIN)\ /\ \text{RAND}()$$

Exercises

1. Beatles' music was first played in the United States in 1964. By the Copernican Principle, on average for how many more years will Beatles' music be played in the United States?
2. Give a 90 percent confidence interval for the number of future years for which Beatles' music will be played in the United States.
3. *The Simpsons* first aired on TV in the United States in 1989. Give a 95 percent confidence interval for the last year in which *The Simpsons* will air.

VIII Retailing

Chapter 29: Market Basket Analysis and Lift

Chapter 30: RFM Analysis and Optimizing Direct Mail Campaigns

Chapter 31: Using the SCANPRO Model and Its Variants

Chapter 32: Allocating Retail Space and Sales Resources

Chapter 33: Forecasting Sales from Few Data Points

29

Market Basket Analysis and Lift

Many retailers use scanners to create data that lists (among other things) the items purchased by each customer on a given transaction. This data often can be mined for useful information that can lead to increased profits. For example, Bloomingdale's found that women who purchased cosmetics often bought handbags, which led to their decision to place handbags and cosmetics together in an attempt to increase total store sales. In this chapter, you study how to use *market basket analysis* to identify pairs or sets of products that customers tend to purchase together and how this knowledge can help the retailer increase profits. You'll then learn how to use the Evolutionary Solver to both ease the computational burden of finding products that tend to be purchased together and to lay out a store so that products with high lifts are located near each other to optimize sales.

Computing Lift for Two Products

On a given visit to a store, a consumer's *market basket* is simply the list of products purchased by the customer. *Market basket analysis* is therefore concerned with extracting information from consumers' market baskets that can be used to increase a retailer's profit. Most of the time, market basket analysis draws actionable insights after looking at the association between products bought during a given transaction. For example, for most supermarket customers there is a positive association between the purchases of cereal and bananas because a shopper who purchases cereal is more likely than a typical shopper to purchase bananas.

Lift is probably the most commonly used tool in market basket analysis. The concept of lift enables the analyst to easily identify combinations of items (like handbags and makeup or cereal and bananas) that tend to be purchased together. The lift for a combination of purchase items and/or day of week is defined by Equation 1:

$$(1) \quad \frac{\text{(Actual number of times combination occurs)}}{\text{(Predicted number of times combination occurs if items in combination were independent)}}$$

A *two-way product lift* therefore is simply a lift involving two products and can easily be computed in Excel. It can be generalized to situations involving the computation of lifts involving more than two items or other transaction attributes (such as day of week).

To practice computing lift, you'll use the superstore transaction data in the file marketbasket.xls. Figure 29-1 shows a subset of the data. The day of the week is denoted by 1 = Monday, 2 = Tuesday … 7 = Sunday. For example, the first transaction represents a person who bought vegetables, meat, and milk on a Friday.

	A	B	C	D	E	F	G	H
		day week	vegetables	baby	fruit	milk	dvds	meat
8	transaction #							
9	1	5	1	0	0	1	0	1
10	2	4	1	1	1	1	0	0
11	3	5	1	0	0	0	0	0
12	4	5	1	0	1	0	0	0
13	5	7	1	1	0	1	0	1
14	6	2	1	0	1	0	0	1
15	7	3	0	0	0	1	1	0
16	8	3	1	0	0	1	0	1
17	9	6	1	0	1	0	0	0
18	10	6	1	0	0	0	0	0
19	11	1	1	0	0	0	0	0
20	12	4	0	0	0	0	1	0
21	13	1	1	0	0	0	0	0

Figure 29-1: Market basket data

For the superstore data, the lift for meat and vegetables would equal:

$$\frac{(Actual\ number\ of\ transactions\ where\ meat\ and\ vegetables\ were\ purchased)}{(Total\ number\ of\ transactions) * (Fraction\ of\ times\ meat\ was\ purchased) * (Fraction\ of\ time\ vegetables\ were\ purchased)}$$

To be more specific, suppose that in 1,000 transactions, 300 involved a meat purchase, 400 involved a vegetable purchase, and 200 involved a purchase of meat and vegetables. Independence of meat and vegetable purchases implies that the likelihood of a transaction involving meat is 0.30 irrespective of a transaction involving a vegetable purchase. Thus independence implies that 1,000 (0.40) (0.30) = 120 transactions should involve purchase of meat and vegetables. Because 200 transactions involved a purchase of meat and vegetables, knowing that a transaction involves meat makes it 1.67 times (200/120) more likely that a transaction involves vegetables. This is consistent with Equation 1, which tells you that the lift for vegetables and meat is

$$\frac{200}{1,000(0.40)(0.30)} = 1.67$$

Product combinations with lifts much greater than 1 indicate items tend to be purchased together. This is valuable information for the retailer because placing products with large lifts near each other in a store display can increase sales based on the assumption that the sales of one product will stimulate sales of the other product. Because handbags and makeup have a large lift, this explains why Bloomingdale's placed handbags and makeup together.

Promoting cross-selling of products with high lifts can also stimulate profits. Therefore, in the Bloomingdale's example, giving a customer who purchases at least $50 of makeup a coupon for 20 percent off a handbag would likely yield increased profits.

Creating Named Ranges

Returning to the superstore data, you can now try to find the lift for all two-product combinations. Before you begin computing all these lifts, though, it is convenient to create a few named ranges. You can use the Name box to assign the name **data** to the range B9:H2936, which contains all the transactions. Simply select the range B8:H296 and choose INSERT NAME CREATE to name each column of data by its heading. For example, you can call Column B **day_week**, Column C **vegetables**, and so on (refer to `marketbasket.xls` file for the rest of the heading names).

Now perform the following steps to determine the fraction of all transactions involving each type of product and the fraction of transactions taking place on each day of the week. This information is needed to compute the denominator of 1.

1. In cell L7 compute the total number of transactions with the formula `=COUNT(B:B)`. This formula counts how many numbers occur in Column B, which gives you the number of transactions.

2. Copy the formula `=COUNTIF(INDIRECT(K9),1)/$L$7` from L9 to cells L10:L14 to compute the fraction of transactions involving each product. Recall that `COUNTIF` counts the number of entries in a range matching a given number or text string (in this case 1). Any cell reference within an `INDIRECT` function is evaluated as the contents of the cell. Thus `INDIRECT(K9)` becomes vegetables. This enables you to copy your `COUNTIF` statement and pick off the range names. A neat trick! Thus 60.7 percent of all transactions involve vegetables, and so on.

3. Copy the formula `=COUNTIF(day_week,K17)/COUNT(day_week)` from L17 to L18:L23 to determine the fraction of all transactions occurring on each day of the week. For example, 13.9 percent of all transactions occur on Monday, and so on. These calculations will be used in the next section when you compute three-way lifts.

Calculating Lifts for Multiple Two-way Product Combinations Simultaneously

Now you can use a two-way data table to compute the lift for any combination of two products.

1. Enter the range names for any two products in the range N9:O9. To ease the selection of products you can use the drop-down list in cells N9 and O9.

2. In cell Q10 use the formula =IF(N9<>O9,VLOOKUP(N9,K9:L14,2,FALSE)*L7*VLOOKUP(O9,K9:L14,2,FALSE),0) to compute the predicted number of transactions involving the two products assuming independence. This formula computes the denominator of Equation 1. If you choose the same product twice, enter a 0.

3. In cell P10 use the array formula =SUM((INDIRECT(N9)=1)*(INDIRECT(O9)=1)) to compute the number of times the combination of vegetables and fruit occur together. After typing in the formula, press Control+Shift+Enter instead of just Enter. This formula creates two arrays:

   ■ An array containing 1 whenever the entry in the vegetable column is 1 and 0 otherwise.

   ■ An array containing 1 whenever the entry in the fruit column is 1 and 0 otherwise.

   This formula causes the arrays to be pairwise multiplied and then the entries in the resulting array are added together. The pairwise multiplication yields the number of transactions involving both fruits and vegetables (520).

4. In cell R10 compute the total lift for these categories with the formula =IF(Q10=0,1,P10/Q10). If you chose the same item twice, simply set the lift to equal 1. Otherwise, divide actual occurrence of fruits and vegetables together by the predicted number of occurrences (assuming fruits and vegetables are purchased independently.)

The lift for fruits and vegetables does not indicate a lack of independence (.99 is near 1).

Taking this one step further, you can use a two-way data table to compute the lift for all two-product combinations simultaneously.

1. In cell O17 place the formula for lift (=R10) that you want to recalculate. R10 contains the lift for a generic two-product combination.

2. Select the table range O17:U23.
3. Select What-If Analysis from the Data Tools Group on the Data tab and choose Data Table....
4. From the Data Table dialog box enter N9 as the row input cell and O9 as the column input cell.

After clicking, you now have the lift for each two-product combination (see Figure 29-2.) For example, DVDs and baby goods have a relatively large lift of 1.4.

	K	L	M	N	O	P	Q	R	S	T	U
6											
7	total	2928									
8				two-way lift							
9	vegetables	60.7%		vegetables	fruit	actual total	predicted	lift			
10	baby	27.1%		1	1	520	527.098361	0.986533			
11	fruit	29.7%									
12	milk	30.4%									
13	DVDs	21.1%									
14	meat	24.9%									
15											
16	days of week		number		All two-way lifts						
17	1	13.9%	407		0.986533	vegetables	baby	fruit	milk	DVDs	meat
18	2	14.0%	410		vegetables	1.00	0.96	0.99	1.00	0.96	1.01
19	3	13.4%	393		baby	0.96	1.00	1.05	1.00	1.40	1.01
20	4	14.6%	428		fruit	0.99	1.05	1.00	1.00	1.03	0.90
21	5	14.3%	420		milk	1.00	1.00	1.00	1.00	0.98	1.06
22	6	15.3%	448		DVDs	0.96	1.40	1.03	0.98	1.00	0.96
23	7	14.4%	422		meat	1.01	1.01	0.90	1.06	0.96	1.00

Figure 29-2: Computing lifts for market basket example

NOTE The lift matrix is symmetric; that is, the entry in row I and Column J of the lift matrix equals the entry in row J and Column I.

Computing Three-Way Lifts

To illustrate how the concept of lift applies to three or more attributes associated with a transaction, consider calculating the lift for the purchase of baby goods and DVDs on Thursday. This lift would be computed as follows:

$$\frac{\text{(Actual number of Thursday transactions where baby goods and DVDs were purchased)}}{\text{(Total number of transactions)} * \text{(Fraction of transactions on Thursday)} * \text{(Fraction of transactions with baby goods)} * \text{(Fraction of transactions with DVDs)}}$$

You can use the same concept to compute for the superstore data the lift of an arbitrary combination of two products and a day of the week. See Figure 29-3 and the `Initial` worksheet in the `marketbasketoptimize.xls` file.

	J	K	L	M	N	O	P	Q	R	S
5										
6										
7		total	2928							
8	Index				two-way lift					
9	1	vegetables	60.7%		vegetables	fruit	actual total	predicted	lift	
10	2	baby	27.1%		1	1	520	527.098361	0.986533	
11	3	fruit	29.7%		three-way lift					
12	4	milk	30.4%		1	2				
13	5	DVDs	21.1%		vegetables	baby	day_week	actual total	predicted	lift
14	6	meat	24.9%		1	1	5	59	69.08291	0.854046
15										
16		days of week		number						
17		1	13.9%	407						
18		2	14.0%	410						
19		3	13.4%	393						
20		4	14.6%	428						
21		5	14.3%	420						
22		6	15.3%	448						
23		7	14.4%	422						

Figure 29-3: Finding three-way lifts

Complete the following steps:

1. In cell Q14 use the array formula =SUM((INDIRECT(P13)=$P$14)*(INDIRECT (N13)=1)*(INDIRECT(O13)=1)) to compute the actual number of transactions involving vegetables and baby goods on Friday. This formula computes three arrays:

   - An array containing a 1 if the day of the week matches the number in P14 (here a 5) and a 0 otherwise.
   - An array containing a 1 if the vegetables column contains a 1 and 0 otherwise.
   - An array containing a 1 if the baby column contains a 1 and 0 otherwise.

2. For each row of data the array formula in Q14 creates a new array. Create the new array element in any row by multiplying the three listed arrays. A 1 is obtained in a row of the product array if and only if baby goods and vegetables were bought on Friday.

3. Sum up the entries in the product array to yield the actual number of Friday transactions where baby goods and vegetables were purchased.

4. In cell R14 compute the predicted number of transactions involving baby goods and vegetables purchased on Friday with the following formula:

```
IF(N13<>O13,VLOOKUP(N13,K9:L14,2,FALSE)*L7*VLOOKUP(O13,K9:L14,2,
FALSE)*VLOOKUP(P14,K17:L23,2),0)
```

5. If you enter the same product class twice, this formula yields a 0. Otherwise, multiply (total number of transactions) * (fraction of baby transactions) * (fraction of vegetable transactions) * (fraction of Friday transactions). This gives a predicted number of Monday meat and vegetable transactions (assuming independence).

6. Finally, in cell S14, compute the lift with the formula =IF(R14=0,1,Q14/R14).

The lift for vegetables and baby goods on Friday is .85. This means that on Fridays vegetables and baby goods are bought together less frequently than expected.

Optimizing the Three-Way Lift

In an actual situation with many products, there would be a huge number of three-way lifts. For example, with 1,000 products, you can expect $1,000^3 = 1$ billion three-way lifts! Despite this, a retailer is often interested in finding the largest three-way lifts. Intelligent use of the Evolutionary Solver can ease this task. To illustrate the basic idea, you can use the Evolutionary Solver to determine the combination of products and day of the week with maximum lift.

1. Use Evolutionary Solver with the changing cells being the day of the week (cell P14) and an index reflecting the product classes (cells N12 and O12). Cells N12 and O12 are linked with lookup tables to cells N13:O13. For instance, a 1 in cell N12 makes N13 be vegetables. Figure 29-4 shows the Evolutionary Solver window.

2. Maximize lift (S14), and then choose N12 and O12 (product classes) to be integers between 1 and 6. P14 is an integer between 1 and 7.

3. Add a constraint that Q14 >= 20 to ensure you count only combinations that occur a reasonable number of times.

4. Set the Mutation Rate to .5.

You can find the maximum lift combination, as shown in Figure 29-5.

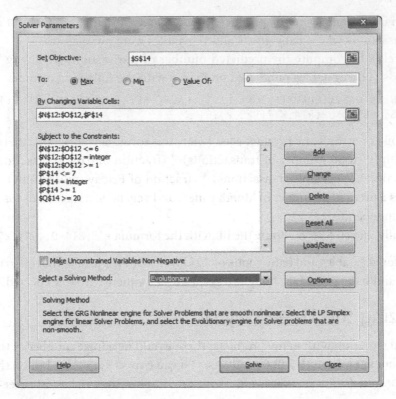

Figure 29-4: Solver window for maximizing three-way lift

	J	K	L	M	N	O	P	Q	R	S
6										
7		total	2928							
8	Index				two-way lift					
9	1	vegetables	60.7%		vegetables	fruit	actual total	predicted	lift	
10	2	baby	27.1%		1	1	520	527.098361	0.986533	
11	3	fruit	29.7%		three-way lift					
12	4	milk	30.4%		5	2				
13	5	DVDs	21.1%		DVDs	baby	day_week	actual total	predicted	lift
14	6	meat	24.9%		1	1	4	155	24.49687	6.327339
15										
16		days of week		number						
17		1	13.9%	407						
18		2	14.0%	410						
19		3	13.4%	393						
20		4	14.6%	428						
21		5	14.3%	420						
22		6	15.3%	448						
23		7	14.4%	422						

Figure 29-5: Maximum three-way lift

The three-way lift, as shown in Figure 29-5, indicates that roughly 6.32 times more people, as expected under an independence assumption, buy DVDs and baby goods on Thursday. This indicates that on Thursdays placing DVDs (often an impulse purchase) in the baby sections will increase profits.

A Data Mining Legend Debunked!

Most of you are probably familiar with one or more "urban legends" that are untrue but are widely believed. Two popular (and untrue) urban legends are:

■ There are alligators in the New York City sewers.
■ Walt Disney had his body frozen so that in the future medical science can bring him back to life.

For years a popular "data mining legend" (certainly believed by the author!) stated that Wal-Mart found that DVDs, beer, and baby goods on Friday had an incredibly large lift. The rationale for this result is that young families often "stock up for a weekend at home with their babies." The legend then states that Wal-Mart increased profits on Fridays by placing DVDs in the baby and alcoholic beverage sections of the store. As pointed out at `http://www.dssresources.com/newsletters/66.php`, this story is untrue.

However, one true data mining legend appears at one of Wal-Mart's well-known competitors: As detailed at `http://www.forbes.com/sites/kashmirhill/2012/02/16/how-target-figured-out-a-teen-girl-was-pregnant-before-her-father-did/`, Target uses market basket analysis to spot pregnant mothers. This information is then used to send coupons for baby products to the prospective mothers. Target looks for large lifts involving women who were signed up for its baby registry. Whenever a customer uses a credit card, fills out a coupon or survey, redeems a coupon, or uses a customer help line, Target assigns the customer a Target Guest ID. Once a customer has a Guest ID Target has a record of the customer's purchases and demographic information. For women in their baby registry who have Guest IDs, Target can combine information from the two databases. Target found large lifts (during the second trimester of pregnancy) involving the purchases of unscented lotions and supplements such as calcium, magnesium, and zinc. Therefore, women who buy these product combinations are sent coupons for other products that pregnant women often purchase.

Using Lift to Optimize Store Layout

As you learned at the beginning of this chapter, handbags and makeup are often purchased together. This information led Bloomingdale's to stimulate impulse buying by placing handbags next to makeup. This suggests that to maximize revenues a store should be laid out so products with high lift are placed near each other. Given a lift matrix for different product categories, you can use the Evolutionary Solver to locate product categories to maximize the total lift of proximate product categories. To illustrate the idea, consider a grocery store that stocks the six product categories shown in Figure 29-6. In rows 8 through 13, the two-way lifts are shown. The work is in the file marketlayout.xlsx.

	E	F	G	H	I	J	K	L	M
7			Produce	Dairy	Meat	Soft Drink	Frozen Food	Bread and Cookies	
8		1 Produce	1	1.2	0.8	0.9	1	0.95	
9		2 Dairy	1.2	1	1.2	1.1	1.3	0.8	
10		3 Meat	0.8	1.2	1	1.3	1.2	0.85	
11		4 Soft Drinks	0.9	1.1	1.3	1	1.2	1.4	
12		5 Frozen Food	1	1.3	1.2	1.2	1	0.8	
13		6 Bread and Cookies	0.95	0.8	0.85	1.4	0.8	1	
14									1
15			1	2	3				
16		B	6	4	3				
17		A	1	2	5				
18									
19			Lift of adjacent products				Bread and Cookies	Soft Drinks	Meat
20							Produce	Dairy	Frozen Food
21		A1	2.15						
22		A2	3.6						
23		A3	2.5						
24		B1	2.35						
25		B2	3.8						
26		B3	2.5						

Figure 29-6: Optimizing store layout

1. In the cell range G16:I17, determine the locations of the product categories that maximize the lifts of adjacent product categories. Assume that customers can travel only in a north-south or east-west direction. This assumption is reasonable because any two store aisles are either parallel or perpendicular to each other. This implies, for example, that location A1 is adjacent to A2 and B1, whereas location A2 is adjacent to B2, A1, and A3.

2. Enter a trial assignment of product categories to locations in cell range G16:I17.

3. In cell range G21:G26, compute the lift for adjacent products for each location. For example, in cell G21 the formula =INDEX(lifts,G17,G16)+INDEX(lifts,G17,H17) adds (Lift for products assigned to A1 and B1) + (Lift

for products assigned to A1 and A2). This gives the total lift for products adjacent to A1. In cell G27 the formula =SUM(G21:G26) calculates the total lift generated by adjacent product categories.

4. Use the Solver window, as shown in Figure 29-7, to find the store layout that maximizes the total lift for adjacent product categories.

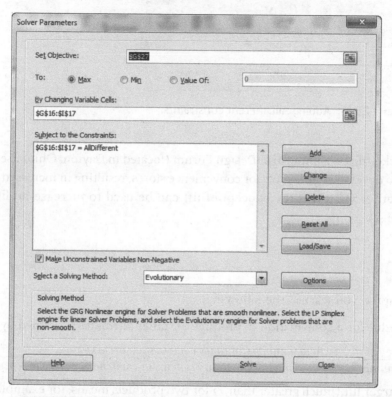

Figure 29-7: Optimizing store layout

The target cell is to maximize the total lift for adjacent products (cell G27). The changing cells are the range G16:I17, which describe the location for each product category. The only entered constraint is G16:I17 AllDifferent. When a range of n changing cells is selected as AllDifferent, Excel knows to assign the changing cells the integers 1, 2, ..., n with each value assigned exactly once. In the example, exactly one cell in the range G16:I17 is assigned one of the integers 1, 2, 3, 4, 5, and 6. This is equivalent to having Excel try out all 6! = 720 permutations of the integers 1–6. Each permutation corresponds to a store layout. You can find the maximum sum of lifts for adjacent categories equals 16.9 and the optimal store layout is summarized in the cell range K19:M20.

4. To make a range of changing cells `AllDifferent`, select Add from the right side of the Solver window, and fill in the Add Constraint dialog box, as shown in Figure 29-8.

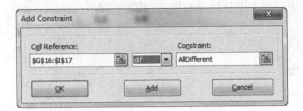

Figure 29-8: Adding AllDifferent constraints

The marketing consulting firm Design Forum (located in Dayton, Ohio) used this approach to develop store layouts for convenience stores, resulting in increased sales.

To see other ways that the concept of lift can be used to increase profits see Exercises 4–8.

Summary

In this chapter, you learned the following:

- The lift for a combination of products or other attributes is defined by:

$$\frac{(Actual\ number\ of\ times\ combination\ occurs)}{(Predicted\ number\ of\ times\ combination\ occurs\ if\ items\ in\ combination\ were\ independent)}$$

- A larger lift (much greater than 1) for two products means, for example, that the two products are often bought together, so they should be located near each other and provide opportunities for cross-selling.

- Using the `AllDifferent` option for changing cells, you can use the Evolutionary Solver to determine a store layout that maximizes the lift associated with adjacent product categories.

Exercises

1. The file `marketbasketdata.xls` contains sales transactions at ITZIs, an upscale grocery store.

   a. Determine all two-product lifts and list the five largest lifts.
   b. Determine the largest three-product lifts.

2. For the file `marketbasket.xls`, find the second-largest two-product and day-of-week lifts.

3. How could Amazon.com use the concept of lift to make book or music recommendations?

4. A virtual lift includes a nonproduct element such as a demographic attribute (age, gender, income, and so on). How could a retailer use knowledge of virtual lifts to increase profits?

5. An intertemporal two-product lift looks at sales of two products at different points in time (say Product 1 at time x and Product 2 at time $x + 6$ months). How could an insurance company use intertemporal lifts to increase profits?

6. True Value hardware stores are considering dropping 3M's higher quality, higher priced painter's tape for the cheaper FROGTAPE. How could a 3M salesperson use market basket analysis to keep True Value from dropping 3M's painter's tape?

7. Research the reasons why Netflix created the (great!!) *House of Cards* TV series starring Kevin Spacey and Robin Wright. How did the concept of lift factor into Neflix's decision to make the show?

30

RFM Analysis and Optimizing Direct Mail Campaigns

When a catalog company such as J.Crew mails catalogs it wants its mailings to generate profits that outweigh its mailing costs. This chapter discusses how mail order companies can use information about a potential customer's recency (date of last purchase), frequency (average number of transactions per year), and monetary value (average amount purchased per year) to optimize the profitability of a mailing campaign. You will walk through all the steps involved in an RFM analysis and see how the Excel functions discussed in Chapter 3, "Using Excel Functions to Summarize Marketing Data," make it easy to perform the analysis.

RFM Analysis

Many direct mail merchants use RFM analysis to predict the response rate and profitability generated by mailing a catalog to a customer. The basic idea is that customers who have bought more recently (R = recency), more often (F = frequency), and spent more dollars (M = monetary value) on the products previously are more likely to order in the future. In an RFM analysis each customer is given a 1–5 rating (5 = likely to purchase, 1 = less likely to purchase) on R, F, and M. A score of 5, for example, is given on recency if a customer ranks in the top 20 percent on recency, and a score of 1 is given if the customer ranks in the bottom 20 percent on recency. Then the combinations of R, F, and M that appear to be profitable based on the customer's recent history receive the next mailing.

Unfortunately, by coding each customer on a 1–5 scale with R, F, and M, you lose valuable information on each customer. For example, Customer 1 and Customer 50 might both score a 5 on monetary value but Customer 1 might have spent $10,000 and Customer 50 only $500. To make up for this shortcoming, you can utilize exact values of R, F, and M to guide the customers who receive a catalog. This type of analysis (call it an *Exact RFM analysis*) is more complex than the traditional RFM analysis but can often yield much larger profits than RFM analysis.

To demonstrate RFM analysis, suppose J.Crew is ready to do a mailing on January 1, 2014 to a subset of 5,000 customers. You are given data on 100,000 sales transactions involving these customers. Use the file RFMexample.xlsx to retrieve the data for this example and to illustrate how RFM analysis works. A subset of the data is shown in Figure 30-1. The first transaction, for example, involves Customer 4184 purchasing $30.00 of items on 9/30/2011.

	Transaction	Customer	Date	Amount
6	Transaction	Customer	Date	Amount
7	1	4184	9/30/11	$30.00
8	2	3657	10/31/13	$34.00
9	3	1011	10/15/11	$47.00
10	4	106	7/4/10	$94.00
11	5	739	7/8/12	$73.00
12	6	4428	11/11/12	$76.00
13	7	1613	9/24/10	$88.00
14	8	4791	9/17/13	$84.00
15	9	4929	8/27/11	$71.00
16	10	2691	4/7/12	$70.00
17	11	2383	2/18/12	$89.00

Figure 30-1: RFM data

Computing R, F, and M

To begin, compute for each customer the following quantities:

- The most recent transaction
- The number of transactions per year for each customer
- The average amount purchased each year by each customer

To accurately perform the calculation of these quantities, proceed as follows (see Figure 30-2):

1. Name each column with its row 6 heading by selecting Create from Selection from the Formulas tab.
2. In the Q7 array enter (see Chapter 3 for details) the formula =MAX(IF(Customer=O7,Date," ")). This creates an array that contains the transaction date if the transaction involves Customer 1 and a blank otherwise. Then the MAX function finds the last date for a transaction involving Customer 1 (9/1/2013). Copy this formula to Q8:Q5006 to compute for each customer the date of the most recent transaction.

	O	P	Q	R	S	T	U	V	W	X	Y	Z	AA
1													
2													
3			Present										
4			1/1/2014										
5													
6	Customer	Total Transactions	Most recent	Start Date	Years with Us	Monetary Value	Frequency	Rank R	Rank F	Rank M	R	F	M
7	1	15	9/1/2013	1/31/2010	3.92	$239.00	3.83	2117	497	442	3	1	1
8	2	20	9/27/2013	1/12/2010	3.97	$349.90	5.03	2995	2204	2807	3	3	3
9	3	19	9/30/2013	3/1/2010	3.84	$348.08	4.95	3127	2025	2764	4	3	3
10	4	22	10/21/2013	3/28/2010	3.77	$411.19	5.84	4199	3568	4105	5	4	5
11	5	13	4/12/2013	2/12/2010	3.89	$203.72	3.34	278	211	165	1	1	1
12	6	17	2/17/2013	1/5/2010	3.99	$275.57	4.26	120	956	1031	1	1	2
13	7	15	10/30/2013	1/3/2010	4.00	$234.16	3.75	4779	419	379	5	1	1
14	8	15	10/21/2013	10/16/2010	3.21	$336.99	4.67	4199	1609	2456	5	2	3
15	9	24	10/22/2013	1/11/2010	3.98	$391.66	6.04	4264	3817	3743	5	4	4
16	10	26	9/21/2013	1/15/2010	3.96	$351.63	6.56	2746	4359	2855	3	5	3
17	11	16	9/20/2013	3/6/2010	3.83	$281.13	4.18	2716	866	1165	3	1	2
18	12	19	7/15/2013	1/11/2010	3.98	$310.92	4.78	1079	1764	1827	2	2	2
19	13	18	8/20/2013	2/12/2010	3.89	$266.74	4.63	1756	1555	828	2	2	1
20	14	12	10/7/2013	6/26/2010	3.52	$234.34	3.41	3446	240	385	4	1	1
21	15	19	5/6/2013	3/1/2010	3.84	$278.57	4.95	385	2025	1100	1	3	2

Figure 30-2: Calculation of R, F, and M

3. Similarly, in the R7 array enter the formula =MIN(IF(Customer=O7,Date," ")). This creates an array that contains the transaction date if the transaction involves Customer 1 and a blank otherwise. Then the MIN function finds the first date for a transaction involving Customer 1 (1/31/2010). Copy this formula to R8:R5006 to compute for each customer the date of the first transaction.

4. Copy the formula =($Q$4-R7)/365 from S7 to S8:S5006 to compute the number of years the customer has been with you as of the date of the mailing. For example, as of 1/1/2014 Customer 1 has been with you 3.92 years.

5. Copy the formula =SUMIF(Customer,O7,Amount)/S7 from T7 to T8:T5006 to compute the average amount purchased per year by each customer. For example, Customer 1 purchased an average of $239.00 per year.

6. Copy the formula =P7/S7 from U7 to U8:U5006 to compute for each customer the average number of transactions per year. For example, Customer 1 was involved in an average of 3.83 transactions per year.

Now determine how each customer ranks on R, F, and M:

1. Copy the formula =RANK(Q7,Most_recent,1) from V7 to V8:V5006 to compute each customer's rank on recency. The last argument of 0 ensures that the customer with the most recent purchase gets a rank of 5,000, and so on. For example, Customer 1 is ranked as the 2,117th lowest on recency.

2. Copy the formula =RANK(U7,Frequency,1) from W7 to W8:W5006 to compute each customer's rank on frequency. For example, Customer 1 is ranked as the 497th lowest on frequency.

3. Copy the formula =RANK(T7,Monetary_Value,1) from X7 to X8:X5006 to compute each customer's rank on monetary value. For example, Customer 1 ranks 442nd lowest on monetary value.

4. Use VLOOKUP formulas to convert a customer's ranks on R, F, and M to the wanted 1–5 rating by copying the formula =VLOOKUP(V7,rfmlookup,2) from Y7 to Y7:AA5006. This converts ranks of 1–1,000 to 1, 1,001–2,000 to 2, 2,001–3,000 to 3, 3,001–4,000 to 4, and 4,001–5,000 to 5. The range AB5:AC10 (see Figure 30-3) is named rfmlookup. For example, Customer 1's R rank of 2,217 converts to 3, her F rank of 497 converts to 1, and her M rank of 442 converts to 1.

	AB	AC	AD	AE	AF	AG	AH
	AX2				fx		
2		Profit=20					
3		Mail cost=50 cents					
4		0.025					
5							
6	1	1					
7	1001	2					
8	2001	3					
9	3001	4					
10	4001	5					
11							
12						5000	
13		R	F	M	Response rate	How Man	Response
14	1	1	1	1	0.092	260	24
15	2	1	2	1	0.045	44	2
16	3	1	3	1	0.000	1	0
17	4	1	4	1	0.000	0	0
18	5	1	5	1	0.000	0	0
19	6	2	1	1	0.093	162	15
20	7	2	2	1	0.105	38	4
126	113	3	3	5	0.000	0	0
127	114	3	4	5	0.170	47	8
128	115	3	5	5	0.128	172	22
129	116	4	1	5	0.000	0	0
130	117	4	2	5	0.000	0	0
131	118	4	3	5	0.000	2	0
132	119	4	4	5	0.121	33	4
133	120	4	5	5	0.114	184	21

Figure 30-3: Calculation of R, F, and M response rates

To Which R, F, and M Values Should You Mail?

The next step in an RFM analysis is to identify the RFM combinations (there are 5^3 = 125 combinations) that appear (based on customer data) likely to yield a profit.

First perform a break even analysis to determine a response rate that would enable J.Crew to break even. Define Profit = Expected profit per order, Response_Rate = chance a customer will respond to a mailing, and Mailcost = cost of mailing the catalog to a customer. J.Crew will break even if the expected profit received per customer equals the mailing cost or both of the following are true:

$$\text{Response\_Rate} * \text{Profit} = \text{Mailcost}$$
$$\text{Response\_Rate} = \text{Mailcost/Profit}$$

Therefore J.Crew should mail to segments for which Response_Rate is likely to exceed Mailcost/Profit. Assume J.Crew expects to earn a profit of $20 per order and mailing a catalog costs $0.50. Then J.Crew should mail to RFM combinations for which it expects a response rate exceeding 0.50/20 = 2.5 percent. To be on the safe side, assume J.Crew will mail to RFM combinations that have at least double the break-even response rate (or 5 percent). Column N (see Figure 30-4) tells you whether a given customer responded to the last mailing (1 = response and 0 = no response). For example, Customers 2 and 5 responded to the last mailing.

	N	O
4		
5		
6	Response	Customer
7	0	1
8	1	2
9	0	3
10	0	4
11	1	5
12	0	6
13	0	7
14	0	8
15	0	9
16	0	10
17	0	11
18	0	12
19	0	13
20	0	14
126	0	120
127	0	121
128	0	122
129	0	123
130	0	124
131	0	125

Figure 30-4: Response by customer

Now you are ready to determine the profitable R, F, and M combinations. To begin, list in the range AC14:AE138 the 125 possible RFM combinations that range from 1 1 1 through 5 5 5. Then proceed as follows:

1. Copy the formula =COUNTIFS(R_,AC14,F,AD14,M,AE14) from AG14 to AG15:AG138 to count the number of customers falling into each RFM category. For example, 260 customers fell into the 1 1 1 category.

2. Copy the formula =COUNTIFS(R_,AC14,F,AD14,M,AE14,actualrresponse,1) from AH14 to AH15:AH138 to calculate the number of customers in each RFM combination that responded to the last mailing. For example, 24 customers in 1 1 1 responded to the last mailing.

3. Copy the formula =IFERROR(AH14/AG14,0) from AF14 to AF15:AF138 to compute the response rate for each RFM combination. For example, the response rate for 1 1 1 is 9.2 percent. The IFERROR function is needed to prevent a #DIV/0! from appearing in R F M cells containing no observations.

4. Use Excel's Conditional Formatting Formula option to highlight all RFM combinations yielding a response rate of at least 5 percent. To do so first put the cursor in the upper-left corner (AC14) of the range you want formatted (AC14:AF138) and select the wanted range.

5. From the Home tab, select Conditional Formatting, choose New Rule, . . . and then select Use a Formula to determine which cells to format. This brings up the dialog box shown in Figure 30-5.

6. In this dialog box first enter a formula that when copied down and across the selected range will evaluate to TRUE for each cell you want formatted. You can use the formula =$AF14>=0.05 for this example.

7. Dollar sign Column AF to ensure that each selected cell will be highlighted if the entry in Column AF of the cell's row is at least .05.

8. To finish filling in the Select Rule Type dialog box, select Format and from Fill tab, select a color (orange in this example). All RFM combinations with response rates of at least 5 percent are now highlighted (refer to Figure 30-3).

NOTE If the database is small in size, the marketing analyst might want you to create terciles (only three categories) for R, F, and M to ensure that sufficient observations exist in each R, F, and M cell to accurately estimate an average response rate.

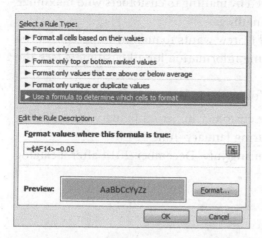

Figure 30-5: Using conditional formatting to highlight profitable R F M combinations

An RFM Success Story

On his website (http://www.dbmarketing.com/articles/Art149.htm) Arthur Hughes, author of the bestselling *Strategic Database Marketing* (McGraw-Hill, 2011), describes a successful application of RFM analysis. A Southern educational products company annually mailed a promotion for a video offer to its entire 2 million customer database and earned little profit on a 1.3 percent response rate. The company then mailed to a sample of 30,000 customers and classified each customer into the 125 RFM cells and recorded the response rate for each cell. This exploratory mailing lost money but led to a mailing to the 34 RFM cells that were profitable in the test mailing. The final mailing to 334,000 customers yielded a 2.76 percent response rate and a profit of $307,000.

Using the Evolutionary Solver to Optimize a Direct Mail Campaign

The 5 percent rate chosen as the mailing cutoff for the J.Crew example was arbitrarily chosen to be double the break-even response rate. In this section you will learn that mailing decisions can actually be optimized by mailing to customers who maximize the expected revenue or profit from the mailings.

Now suppose it is January 1, 2015 and J.Crew wants to mail to 10 percent of the customers. Suppose you have the following information for all customers (see the RFMtop10%.xls file and Figure 30-6).

The RFMtop10%.xls file contains the following information for each customer:

- Number of purchases made by the customer in period January–June 2014
- Amount spent by the customer during January–June 2014
- Amount spent by the customer during July–December 2014 after a catalog was mailed

	B	C	D	E	F	G
1						
2						
3						
4						
5						
6						
7						top 10%
8						1480.02769
9						total revenue
10	weights	7.923820514	0.131723847			449451.5941
11		Number of purchases Jan–June 2014	Amt bought Jan–June 2014	Amt spent July-Dec 2014	Score	buy?
12		9	$ 333.00	$ 285.16	$ 115.18	0.00
13		67	$ 2,814.00	$ 881.26	$ 901.57	0.00
14		30	$ 1,200.00	$ 497.86	$ 395.78	0.00
15		46	$ 828.00	$ 556.66	$ 473.56	0.00
16		70	$ 2,240.00	$ 841.86	$ 849.73	0.00
17		54	$ 4,104.00	$ 932.26	$ 968.48	0.00
18		44	$ 3,080.00	$ 769.86	$ 754.36	0.00
19		74	$ 5,032.00	$ 1,145.06	$1,249.20	0.00
20		62	$ 5,518.00	$ 1,121.66	$1,218.13	0.00
21		91	$ 4,732.00	$ 1,217.06	$1,344.38	0.00
22		31	$ 1,426.00	$ 526.46	$ 433.48	0.00
23		17	$ 714.00	$ 371.26	$ 228.76	0.00
24		84	$ 6,300.00	$ 1,331.86	$1,495.46	1.00
25		36	$ 3,600.00	$ 773.86	$ 759.46	0.00
26		29	$ 1,363.00	$ 508.16	$ 409.33	0.00
27		62	$ 2,976.00	$ 867.46	$ 883.29	0.00
28		70	$ 3,780.00	$ 995.86	$1,052.58	0.00
29		67	$ 1,742.00	$ 774.06	$ 760.36	0.00
30		77	$ 1,617.00	$ 821.56	$ 823.13	0.00
31		9	$ 369.00	$ 288.76	$ 119.92	0.00
32		25	$ 2,400.00	$ 587.86	$ 514.23	0.00
33		9	$ 603.00	$ 312.16	$ 150.74	0.00
34		50	$ 1,250.00	$ 622.86	$ 560.85	0.00
35		37	$ 1,850.00	$ 604.86	$ 536.87	0.00
36		95	$ 6,270.00	$ 1,394.86	$1,578.67	1.00

Figure 30-6: Mailing to 10 percent of customers

You can create a scoring rule of the following form:

```
(frequency weight) * (purchases made in the first 6 months of 2014) +
(amount spent weight) * (amount spent in the first 6 months of 2014)
```

Assume you will mail a J.Crew catalog to the prospective customers that score in the top 10 percent by this formula. You can use the Evolutionary Solver to choose weights that maximize the amount of revenue earned during the last six months of 2014 from the selected customers. The recommended mailing strategy is to mail to anyone in a prospective database whose score exceeds the top 10 percent of scores from the database. The work proceeds as follows:

1. Enter trial weights in cells C10 and D10.
2. Copy the formula =$C$10*C12+$D$10*D12 from F12 to cell F13:F3045 to generate the score for each customer.
3. The formula =PERCENTILE(F12:F3045,0.9) in G8 determines the 90th percentile of the scores.
4. Copy the formula =IF(F12>$G$8,1,0) from G12 to G13:G3045 to determine whether each customer's score is in the top 10 percent.
5. Enter in cell G10 the formula =SUMPRODUCT(G12:G3045,E12:E3045) to compute the total revenue earned from the top 10 percent of the scores by counting only the purchases for each customer whose scores rank in the top 10 percent.
6. Use the Evolutionary Solver to find the weights that maximize the July–December 2012 revenue obtained from mailing to the top 10 percent of the scores. The Solver window is shown in Figure 30-7; constrain your weights to be between .01 and 10.

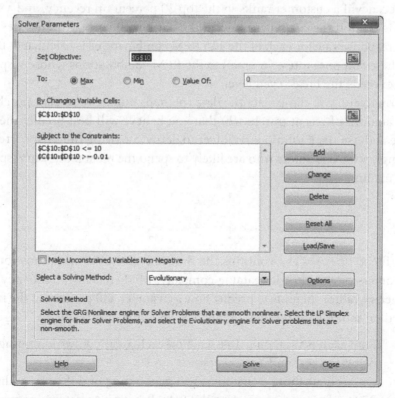

Figure 30-7: Solver window for mailing to best 10 percent of customers

The Solver finds that the best scoring rule is 7.92 * Frequency + .13 * (amount spent in the last six months). If this score is at least 1,480, you should mail to a customer. The weights imply that a 7.92/.13 = $61 increase in the amount spent has the same effect on the score as an increase of 1 in frequency. Note that if you wanted to mail to the top 20 percent or 30 percent, you might get a different set of weights. The advantage of the current approach over RFM is that the current approach does not throw away any information. Also, the weights are chosen to meet your goal of maximizing revenue (or if you want, profit) from the mailing, whereas RFM analysis just chooses the combinations that yield a response rate that exceeds the break-even level. In Exercise 2 you will find a rule that mails to 20 percent of all customers.

Summary

In this chapter you learned the following:

- To conduct an RFM analysis, each customer is classified on a 1–5 scale on recency, frequency, and monetary value. A score of 5, for example, is given on recency if a customer ranks in the top 20 percent on recency, and a score of 1 is given if the customer ranks in the bottom 20 percent on recency.
- The response rate for each of the 125 RFM combinations is calculated. Based on these response rates, you mail to the RFM combinations whose response rate exceeds the break-even level.
- Alternatively, you can isolate the data (perhaps number of recent purchases and amount of recent purchases) that you believe will best predict the revenue and use the Evolutionary Solver to derive a scoring rule that correlates strongly with customers who are likely to spend the most money in response to a mailing.

Exercises

1. The file RFMdata.xlsx contains the date and size of transactions for 256 customers of a mail order catalog company. RFM (recency, frequency, and monetary value) attempts to predict how a customer will perform in the future based on ranking for recency, frequency, and monetary value.

   a. Rate each person on a 1–4 scale on each attribute, with a rating of 4 being the best and 1 the worst.

   b. On each attribute a customer will get a rating of 4 if he is in the top 25 percent, and so on. Use the RANK function to determine where a customer ranks on each attribute. Thus if you rank customers so that the largest value of an attribute gets a 256, then anyone with a rank of 193–256 gets a 4 rating; a rank of 129–192 gets a 3 rating; 65–128 gets a 2 rating; and a rank of 1–64 gets a 1 rating. Assume that each customer has received 80 mailings and a mailing costs $0.50.

   c. In E8:E71 use conditional formatting to highlight in yellow each profitable RFM combination.

2. For the file `RFMtop10%.xls` develop a strategy to maximize revenue generated by mailing to 20 percent of the customers.

31

Using the SCAN*PRO Model and Its Variants

Retailers have many available strategies that can be used to increase profits, including price adjustments, product placement on display, advertising, and so on. The difficulty in determining the profit-maximizing mix of marketing strategies is that factors such as seasonality and just plain random variation can make it difficult to isolate how changes in the marketing mix affect unit sales. In this chapter, you learn how to use the GRG (Generalized Reduced Gradient) multistart Solver Engine to develop forecasting models estimate variants of the SCAN*PRO model that tell the retailer how each portion of the marketing mix affects sales. Once firms understand how all these factors influence sales, they can more efficiently allocate resources to the factors that they control. Firms can also understand how external factors that they cannot control (such as competitor's price, seasonality, competitor's product on display, and so on) hinder the firm's effectiveness.

Introducing the SCAN*PRO Model

Suppose you want to predict weekly sales of Snickers (the world's best-selling candy bar) at your local supermarket. Factors that might influence sales of Snickers include:

- Price charged for Snickers bars
- Prices charged for competitors (Three Musketeers, Hershey's Chocolate, and so on)
- Was the Snickers bar on display?
- Was there a national ad campaign for Snickers?
- Was there an ad for Snickers in the local Sunday paper?
- Seasonality: Perhaps Snickers sell better in the winter than the summer.

Untangling how these factors affect unit sales of Snickers is difficult. In his paper "A Model to Improve the Baseline Estimation of Retail Sales," (1988, see `http://centrum.pucp.edu.pe/adjunto/upload/publicacion/archivo/lamodelto improvetheestimationofbaselineretailsales.pdf`) Dirk Wittink et al. developed the widely used SCAN*PRO model to isolate the effect of these (and other factors) on sales of retail goods. The SCAN*PRO model and its variants (see Dirk Wittink et al. *Building Models for Marketing Decisions*, Kluwer Publishing, 2000) have been widely used by A.C. Nielsen and other organizations to analyze retail sales.

Modeling Sales of Snickers Bars

The SCAN*PRO model is often used to model the impact of various portions of the marketing mix. To predict sales you can model the effect of each part of the marketing mix as described in this section's example and create a final prediction for sales. You do this by multiplying together the terms for each part of the marketing mix and throwing in a constant to correctly scale your final prediction.

To create this model you can use the data from the `Snickers.xlsx` file that shows the weekly sales of Snickers bars at a local supermarket as well as the Snickers price, the price of the major competitor, and whether Snickers is on display. A subset of the data is shown in Figure 31-1. For example, in Week 1, 986 Snickers bars were sold; the price of Snickers was $1.04; the price of the main competitor was $0.81; and Snickers was on display (1 = Snickers on display, 0 = Snickers not on display). To simplify matters assume that Snickers sales do not exhibit seasonality. As you will see later in the chapter, the assumption that seasonality is not present can easily be relaxed.

	A	B	C	D	E	F	G	H	I	J
1									SSE	753677
2									rsq	0.92189
3	displayeffect	1.19815	Week	Our price	Comp price	Display?	Sales	Prediction	Sq Error	
4	ownelas	-3.19015	1	1.04	0.81	1	986	868.4543	13817	
5	compelas	0.4005	2	1.09	1.17	1	788	866.2629	6125.08	
6	constant	893.77	3	1.16	1.04	1	580	677.53	9512.1	
7			4	1.07	1.02	0	660	725.9908	4354.78	
8			5	0.9	0.94	0	1263	1220.216	1830.47	
9			6	0.8	0.89	0	1972	1738.258	54635.4	
10			7	0.84	0.83	0	1522	1446.696	5670.75	
11			8	1.06	1.02	0	755	748.0666	48.0715	
12			9	1.06	0.96	1	904	874.7977	852.773	
13			10	0.86	1.14	1	1751	1825.947	5616.98	
14			11	0.97	1.14	1	1104	1243.736	19526.1	
15			12	1.09	1.13	0	739	712.996	676.206	
16			13	1.16	0.88	1	707	633.6829	5375.39	

Figure 31-1: Snickers sales data

To create a model to predict weekly sales, complete the following steps:

1. Raise the price to an unknown power. (Call this power *OWNELAS*.) This creates a term of the form (Our Price)^{OWNELAS}. The value of *OWNELAS* can estimate the price elasticity. You would expect *OWNELAS* to be negative. For example, if *OWNELAS* = –3, you can estimate that for any price you charge, a 1 percent price increase reduces demand 3 percent.

2. Raise the competitor's price to an unknown power (*COMPELAS*). This creates a term of the form (*Comp Price*)^{COMPELAS}. The value of *COMPELAS* estimates a cross-elasticity of demand. You would expect *COMPELAS* to be positive and smaller in magnitude than *OWNELAS*. For example, if *COMPELAS* = 0.4, then a 1 percent increase in the competitor's price increases demand for Snickers (for any set of prices) by 0.4 percent.

3. Model the effect of a display by a term that raises an unknown parameter (Call it *DISPLAYEFFECT*.) to the power $^{DISPLAY\#}$ (which is 1 if there is a display and 0 if there is no display). This term is of the form (*DISPLAYEFFECT?*)$^{DISPLAY\#}$. When there is a display, this term equals *DISPLAYEFFECT*, and when there is no display, this term equals 1. Therefore, a value of, say, *DISPLAYEFFECT*=1.2 indicates that after adjusting for prices, a display increases weekly sales by 20 percent.

NOTE In Chapter 34, "Measuring the Effectiveness of Advertising," you learn how to model the effect of advertising on sales.

Putting it all together, the final prediction for weekly sales is shown in Equation 1:

$$(1) \text{ Constant} * (\text{Our Price})^{OWNELAS} * (\text{Comp Price})^{COMPELAS} *$$
$$(\text{DISPLAYEFFECT?})^{DISPLAY\#}$$

You can now use the GRG multistart Solver Engine to determine values of *CONSTANT*, *OWNELAS*, *COMPELAS*, and *DISPLAYEFFECT* that minimize the sum of the squared weekly prediction errors. Proceed as follows:

1. Copy the formula `=constant*(D4^ownelas)*(E4^compelas)*(displayeffect^F4)` from H4 to H5:H45 to use Equation 1 to create a forecast for each week's demand.

2. Copy the formula `=(G4-H4)^2` from I4 to I5:I45 to compute the squared error for each week's forecast.

3. In cell J1 compute the sum of the weekly squared errors with the formula `=SUM(I4:I45)`.

4. In cell J2 compute the R-squared value between your predictions and actual sales with the formula =RSQ(G4:G45,H4:H45).

5. Using the Solver window shown in Figure 31-2, find the parameter estimates that minimize the sum of the squared forecast errors. Check Use Automatic Scaling from Options. This improves the performance of the Solver on sales forecasting models.

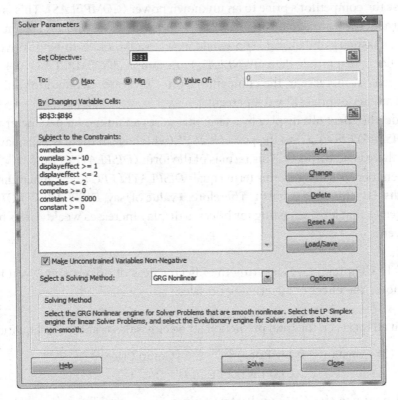

Figure 31-2: Snickers sales Solver window

The GRG Multistart Engine requires bounds on the changing cells. Choosing "tight" bounds improves the performance of the Solver. You can assume the display effect would be between 1 and 2, the competitor's price elasticity is assumed to be between 0 and 2, the Snicker's price elasticity is assumed to be between 0 and –10, and the constant is assumed to be between 0 and 5,000. If the Solver finds a value for a changing cell near its bound, the bound should be relaxed because Solver tells you that violating the bound can probably improve your target cell.

Solver finds that the following parameters make Equation 1 a best fit for your sales data:

- The display effect = 1.198. This implied that after adjusting for prices, a Snickers display increases weekly sales by 19.8 percent.
- The price elasticity for Snickers is –3.19, so a 1 percent increase in the price of Snickers can reduce Snicker's sales by 3.19 percent.
- The cross-price elasticity for Snickers is 0.40, so a 1 percent increase in the competitor's price can raise the demand for Snickers by 0.40 percent.

Substituting your parameter values into Equation 1, you can find your prediction for weekly sales is given by:

$$893.77 * (\text{Snickers Price})^{-3.19} * (\text{Comp Price})^{0.40} * (1.198)^{\text{Display?}}$$

From cell J2 you find that your model explains 92 percent of the variation in weekly sales.

Forecasting Software Sales

Intelligent modification of the SCAN*PRO approach can enable you to build insightful and accurate sales forecasting models that include factors other than price and product displays. To illustrate the idea, suppose you are given quarterly software sales that depend on quarterly PC shipments. Sales are seasonal and increase after a launch and drop off prior to a launch. How can you build a model to forecast sales? The work for this example is in the file `softwaresales.xlsx` (see Figure 31-3). Data is given for 48 quarters of software sales. For example, 700,000 units were sold in Quarter 11. During this quarter there was a software launch, the quarter was the third quarter of the year, and 4.8 million PCs were shipped.

The equation to forecast sales involves the following parameters:

- A seasonal index for each quarter. These seasonal indexes should average to 1. A seasonal index of, say, 1.3 for Quarter 4 means that after adjusting for other factors, sales in the fourth quarter average 30 percent more than an average quarter
- Factors (similar to the effect of the display in the Snickers example) that measure the bump up in sales the quarter of a launch (*LAUNCH1*) and the quarter after the launch (*LAUNCH2*)

- A factor (*LAUNCH*-1) that measures the decline in sales the quarter before a launch
- Because it seems reasonable to assume that an increase in PC shipments will increase sales of your product, you can include a term of the form *BASE*PCSALES* in your forecast. Here (*BASE*) is a changing cell that scales your forecast to minimize MAPE.

	B	C	D	E	F	G	H	I	J	K	L	M	N
1		Season											
2			1	0.7189		base	0.097935						
3			2	0.8427	1	launch1	1.149932						
4			3	1.1508	2	launch2	1.099207						
5			4	1.2876	-1	launch-1	0.779384						
6		mean	1		0	nolaunch	1						
7									stdev			MAPE	sign changes
8							Ignoring launch and seasonalit	0.05855			0.05	20	
9				millions		millions	we sell .098 units per PC sale.						
10				Quarter	PC shipments	Sales	Quarter of year	Launch	Code	Forecast	PE	APE	Sign Change
11				1	4.4	0.31934	1		0	0.30979	0.0299	0.03	
12				2	7	0.60165	2		0	0.57768	0.0398	0.04	0
13				3	5.5	0.68591	3		0	0.61988	0.0963	0.1	0
14				4	6.6	0.77916	4		0	0.83227	-0.068	0.07	1
15				5	4.2	0.31413	1		0	0.29571	0.0587	0.06	1
16				6	5.8	0.51673	2		0	0.47865	0.0737	0.07	0
17				7	6	0.64891	3		0	0.67623	-0.042	0.04	1
18				8	4.1	0.5083	4		0	0.51702	-0.017	0.02	0
19				9	4.8	0.33795	1		0	0.33795	4E-07	0	1
20				10	5.9	0.37343	2		-1	0.37948	-0.016	0.02	1
21				11	4.8	0.7	3	yes	1	0.6221	0.1113	0.11	1
22				12	4	0.58286	4		2	0.55445	0.0487	0.05	0
23				13	7.5	0.53559	1		0	0.52805	0.0141	0.01	0

Figure 31-3: Software sales data

NOTE   Recall from Chapter 14, "Winter's Method," that MAPE is the average of absolute percentage errors.

Putting it all together, your model for predicting quarterly sales (in millions) is given by Equation 2.

(2) BASE * PCSALES * (SEASONAL INDEX) * (LAUNCH EFFECT)

In Equation 2, *BASE* is analogous to the constant term in Equation 1.

When building your sales forecasting model, you can assume that in lieu of minimizing the sum of squared errors you can minimize the average absolute percentage error (MAPE). Minimizing SSE emphasizes avoiding large outliers, and minimizing MAPE emphasizes minimizing the magnitude of the typical prediction error. Also, many practitioners prefer MAPE over SSE as a measure of forecast accuracy. This is probably because MAPE is measured as a percentage of the dependent variable, whereas it is difficult to interpret the units of SSE (in this case units^2). Before using the GRG multistart Solver Engine, proceed as follows:

1. Copy the formula `=base*E11*VLOOKUP(G11,lookup,2)*VLOOKUP(I11,launch,3,FALSE)` from J11 to J12:J58 to compute your forecasts for all 48 quarters of data.

2. Copy the formula `=(F11-J11)/F11` from K11 to K12:K58 to compute the percentage error for each quarter. For example, in Quarter 1 actual software sales were 3.0 percent higher than your prediction.

3. Copy the formula `=ABS(K11)` from L11 to L12:L58 to compute each week's absolute percentage error.

4. Compute the MAPE in cell L8 with the formula `=AVERAGE(L11:L58)`.

The Solver window shown in Figure 31-4 finds the values of base, seasonal indexes, and launch effects that yield the best forecasts. The Target cell minimizes MAPE (cell L8) by changing the following parameters:

- Seasonal indices in cells D2:D5 (which must average to 1)
- A Base (in cell G2) which in effect scales PC Sales into sales of our software
- *LAUNCH*-1 (in cell G5) which represents the drop in sales in the quarter before a launch
- *LAUNCH*1 (in cell G3) which represents the increase in sales during a launch quarter
- *LAUNCH*2 (in cell G4) which represents the increases in sales the quarter after a launch
- The lower bound on each changing cell is 0 and the upper bound 2. The upper bound of 2 was used because it seems unlikely that sales would more than double in a quarter due to a launch and it seems unlikely that one PC sale would lead to more than two sales of the software.

Model Interpretation

You can combine the Solver solution with Equation 2 to yield the following marketing insights:

- Quarter 4 has the highest sales with sales 29 percent better than average, and Quarter 1 has the lowest sales (28 percent below average).
- All other things being equal (*ceteris paribus*) the quarter of a launch, sales increase by 15 percent.
- The quarter after a launch, sales increase (ceteris paribus) by 10 percent.
- The quarter before a launch, sales decrease (ceteris paribus) by 22 percent.

- During an average quarter, an increase in PC shipments of 100 PCs leads to 9.8 more units sold.
- In cell J8 you can compute the standard deviation of percentage errors with the formula =STDEV(K11:K58). The standard deviation of 5 percent tells you that approximately 68 percent of your forecasts should be accurate within 5 percent, and approximately 95 percent of your forecasts should be accurate within 10 percent.
- Any quarter in which your forecast is off by 10 percent or more is an outlier. As shown in Figure 31-5, Quarter 44 is an outlier because your forecast was off by 12 percent.

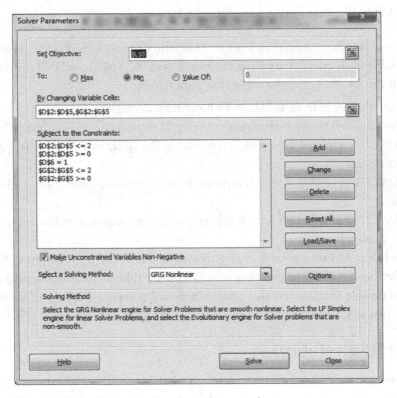

Figure 31-4: Solver window for software sales

Predicting Future Sales

Assuming 6 million PC shipments in Quarter 50, suppose you are asked to forecast Quarter 50 sales and there is no launch planned in quarters 48–51. To predict

Quarter 50 sales, you simply copy the forecast formula in cell J58 to J59. Your forecast for Quarter 50 sales is .495153 million or 495,153 units.

	B	C	D	E	F	G	H	I	J	K	L	M	N
1		Season											
2			1	0.7189		base	0.097935						
3			2	0.8427	1	launch1	1.149932						
4			3	1.1508	2	launch2	1.099207						
5			4	1.2876	-1	launch-1	0.779384						
6		mean	1		0	nolaunch	1						
7										stdev		MAPE	sign changes
8						Ignoring launch and seasonality	0.05855					0.05	20
9				millions		millions	we sell .098 units per PC sale.						
10				Quarter	PC shipments	Sales	Quarter of year	Launch	Code	Forecast	PE	APE	Sign Change
54				44	7.2	1.02933	4		0	0.90793	0.1179	0.12	1
55				45	5.6	0.39001	1		0	0.39428	-0.011	0.01	1
56				46	7.8	0.60663	2		0	0.6437	-0.061	0.06	0
57				47	4.1	0.49677	3		0	0.46209	0.0698	0.07	1
58				48	5.6	0.70625	4		0	0.70617	0.0001	0	0
59				50	6		2			0.49515			
60										Quarter 50 forecast			
61										495,131 units			

Figure 31-5: Software outlier and Quarter 40 forecast

Checking for Autocorrelation

Recall from Chapter 10, "Using Multiple Regression to Forecast Sales," that a good forecasting method should see the sign of forecast change approximately one half the time. Copying the formula =IF(K12*K11<0,1,0) from M12 to M13:M58 yields a 1 each time there is a sign change in the errors. There were 20 sign changes in the errors. The cutoff for "too few" sign changes in errors is given by $\frac{48-1}{2} - \sqrt{48-1} = 16.6$. Because 20>16.6 the forecasts exhibit random changes in sign, and no correction for autocorrelation is needed.

Modeling a Trend in Sales

If you felt there was a possible trend in software sales, you could generalize Equation 2 to account for that trend. To model a trend change, change the forecast equation in J11 to Equation 3:

$$(3) \text{ Predicted Sales} = \text{base} * (\text{TREND}^{\wedge}\text{D11}) * \text{E11} * \text{VLOOKUP(G11,lookup,2)} * \\ \text{VLOOKUP(I11,launch,3,FALSE)}$$

In Equation 3, *TREND* is added as a changing cell. A value of *TREND* = 1.07 means that sales were increasing 7 percent per quarter (after adjusting for all other variables), while if *TREND* = 0.91 this would indicate sales were decreasing 9 percent per quarter.

Summary

In this chapter you learned the following:

- You can use the GRG multistart Solver Engine to determine how aspects of the marketing mix impact retail sales.
- The effect of your product's price can be modeled by a term of the form (Your Price)^{OWNELAS}. The value of *OWNELAS* can estimate your price elasticity.
- The effect of a competitor's price can be modeled by a term of the form (Comp Price)^{COMPELAS}. The value of *COMPELAS* estimates a cross-elasticity of a demand set of prices by 0.4 percent.
- The effect of a display can be modeled by a term of the form (*DISPLAYEFFECT?*)$^{DISPLAY\#}$.
- Seasonality can be incorporated into forecasts by multiplying the seasonal index by the terms involving the marketing mix.
- Other factors such as a trend and the effect of a product launch can also be incorporated in forecast models.

Exercises

1. The file Cranberries.xlsx includes quarterly sales in pounds of cranberries at a supermarket, price per pound charge, and the average price charged by competition.

    a. Use this data to determine how seasonality, trend, and price affect quarterly sales.

    b. Use a Multiplicative Model for seasonality. (The average of seasonal indexes should equal 1.)

    c. Introduce a trend and set up the model so that you can estimate price elasticity.

    d. If you charge $5 a pound in Q1 2012 and the competitor charges $5 per pound, predict the Q1 2012 sales.

    e. Fill in the blank: You are 95 percent sure the Q1 2012 sales are between _____ and ___.

    Problems 2–4 use the workbook Snickers.xlsx.

2. If Snickers had more than one major competitor, how would you modify the forecast model?

3. If Snickers knew whether the competitor's product was on display, how could the model be modified?

4. Suppose you believe that if Snickers had cut its price at any time in the last four weeks, the consumer would become more price-sensitive. How would you incorporate this idea into your forecast?

5. The file POSTITDATA.xlsx contains daily information on sales of Post-it Notes. A sample of this data is shown in Figure 31-6.

	F	G	H	I	J	K
5	Month	Day#	Day	Price	Display?	actualsales
6	1	1	01/01/11	7.52	1	390
7	1	2	01/02/11	7.52	0	344
8	1	3	01/03/11	5.95	0	636
9	1	4	01/04/11	6.2	0	483
10	1	5	01/05/11	6.1	0	486
11	1	6	01/06/11	6.2	0	490
12	1	7	01/07/11	6.98	1	524
13	1	8	01/08/11	5.95	0	620
14	1	9	01/09/11	7.12	1	416
15	1	10	01/10/11	6.98	0	464
16	1	11	01/11/11	5.95	1	709
17	1	12	01/12/11	7.32	0	370
18	1	13	01/13/11	5.95	0	630
19	1	14	01/14/11	7.32	0	362
20	1	15	01/15/11	5.95	1	686
21	1	16	01/16/11	6.1	0	501
22	1	17	01/17/11	7.32	1	396
23	1	18	01/18/11	5.95	0	619
24	1	19	01/19/11	7.32	1	392
25	1	20	01/20/11	6.98	1	521
26	1	21	01/21/11	7.12	0	375

Figure 31-6: Post-it sales data forecast

The following factors influence daily sales:

- Month of the year
- Trend
- Price (Seven different prices were charged.)
- Whether product is on display (1 = display, 0 = no display)

a. Build a model to forecast daily sales. Hint: Look at the values of price that are charged. Why is a model including terms of the form (Price)^{elasticity} inappropriate?

b. Examine your outliers and determine a modification to your model that improves your forecasts. Then describe how price, trend, display, and seasonality affect daily sales.

6. Fill in the blank: In Exercise 5 you would expect 95 percent of your daily forecasts to be accurate within _____.

7. For many products the effect of a price change on sales is actually linked to the change in the product price relative to a *reference price*, which represents the price customers feel they typically pay for the product. For example, the sales of Cheerios may be based on how the price of a box of Cheerios differs from a reference price of $3.50. How would you modify the SCAN*PRO model to include the idea of a reference price?

8. The neighborhood price effect states that brands priced closer together exhibit a greater cross-elasticity than brands priced farther apart. How would you use the SCAN*PRO model to test this hypothesis?

9. How would you use the SCAN*PRO model to determine which is larger:

   - The effect of a 1 percent price cut for a national brand on sales of a generic brand.
   - The effect of a 1 percent price cut for a generic brand on sales of a national brand.

10. When a company promotes their product with a short-term price cut, their sales will increase for two reasons: customers switch from another brand and the product category exhibits temporary sales growth. How could you use the SCAN*PRO model to decompose these two components of increased product sales?

32

Allocating Retail Space and Sales Resources

Often marketing managers must determine the profit-maximizing allocation of scarce resources such as advertising dollars, shelf space in a grocery store, or a drug company's sales force. The key to optimal allocation of marketing resources is to develop an understanding of how a change in the resources allocated to a product affects product sales. To achieve this understanding, you must have the ability to model the relationship between the level of the scarce allocated resource and the achieved response. These relationships are typically modeled using nonlinear functions.

This chapter begins by identifying the relevant types of marketing efforts and responses, and then discusses the curves that are commonly used to model the relationship of sales to marketing effort. You then see how the marketing analyst can determine the curve that best describes the effort response relationship. Finally, you see an example of how the Solver can be used to determine a profit-maximizing allocation of a drug company's sales force.

Identifying the Sales to Marketing Effort Relationship

In many situations the marketing manager must determine how to allocate scarce resources. Here are some examples:

- Eli Lilly must determine the number of salespeople needed and how many calls to doctors should be made for each drug. For example, would more profit be generated by shifting calls from oncology drugs to endocrine drugs?
- Time Warner must determine how to allocate an advertising budget between its many magazines. For example, should more money be spent on ads for *Sports Illustrated* or *People*?

- Target must determine how much shelf space is allocated to each product category. For example, should Target increase the limited space it devotes to jewelry?
- A supermarket must determine how much space to allocate to each pain reliever. For example, should Extra Strength Tylenol or a generic pain reliever be allocated more space?

In each situation you encounter a need to identify the relationship between the amount of resources used and the desired result. Table 35-1 shows the relationships for the first three examples.

Table 35-1: Examples of Situations where Marketing Effort Must Be Allocated

Situation	X = Resource Level Allocated	Y = Response
Eli Lilly	Sales calls per year pitching drug	Annual sales of drug
AOL Time Warner	$ spent advertising in magazine	New subscriptions to magazine
Target	Shelf space allocated to product line	Profit generated by product line

These types of relationships between marketing effort and the response to that effort can be modeled visually with three different types of curves: the Power curve, ADBUDG curve, and the Gompertz curve. These are discussed in the following section.

Modeling the Marketing Response to Sales Force Effort

Three curves are often used to model resource-response relationships:

- **The Power curve:** $y = ax^b$. Values of a and b that best fit the Power curve to data may be found with the Excel Trend Curve. Assuming $0<b<1$, the Power curve exhibits diminishing returns; that is, each additional ad yields fewer extra sales.
- **The ADBUDG curve:** $Y = a + \frac{(b-a)x^c}{(d+x^c)}$. The ADBUDG curve was developed by legendary MIT Professor John Little in his "Models and Managers: The Concept of a Decision Calculus" (*Management Science*, 1970, pp. B466–B485).

This curve can be easily fit using the GRG Multistart Engine. In particular this curve has been used to model response to sales effort or advertising. Although the Power curve always exhibits diminishing returns, the ADBUDG curve can exhibit diminishing returns or look like an S-shaped curve (see Chapter 26, "Using S Curves to Forecast Sales of a New Product"). Note that if the ADBUDG curve is S-shaped, then the S shape of the curve implies that for a small amount of marketing effort little sales response is generated, and for an intermediate amount of marketing effort, increasing returns to marketing effort are observed. Finally, beyond a certain point, decreasing returns to marketing effort are observed.

■ **The Gompertz curve:** $y = a * exp(-c * exp(-bx))$. This curve is often used to model the change in profit resulting from additional shelf space allocation. Like the ADBUDG curve, the Gompertz curve is an S-shaped curve. Estimation of the Gompertz curve is described in Chapter 26.

The following sections detail how data on marketing effort and response to marketing effort can be used to find the curve that best explains the relationship between marketing effort and the response to effort.

Fitting the Power Curve

Suppose a company feels the number of units of a product sold (in thousands) in a month and the number of ads placed are related, as shown in Figure 32-1 (see Powercurve.xlsx file).

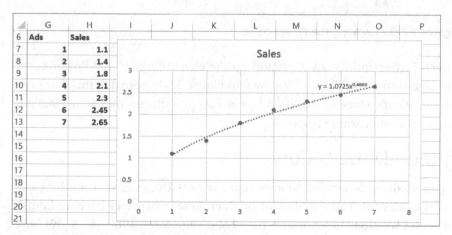

Figure 32-1: Fitting a Power curve to ad response data

To fit a Power curve to this data, complete the following steps:

1. Plot the points by selecting the range G6:H13, and from the Insert tab, select Scatter. (Choose the first option: Scatter with only markers.)

2. Right-click any point and select Add Trendline.... The Format Trendline dialog (as shown in Figure 32-2) appears.

Figure 32-2: Creating the Power curve

3. Check Power and Create Equation on the chart to obtain the Power curve and equation $y = 1.0725x^{-0.4663}$ shown in Figure 32-1. Note that this data (and the decreasing slope of the fitted Power curve) indicates that additional ads generate a diminishing response.

Fitting the ADBUDG Curve

Suppose you want to determine a curve that predicts the sales of a product as a function of the sales effort allocated to the product. Researchers (see Leonard Lodish et al. "Decision Calculus Modeling at Syntex Labs," *Interfaces*, 1988, pp. 5–20) have found that the response to a sales force effort can often be well described by the ADBUDG function of the following form.

Sales of drug i when x calls are made for drug i $= a + \dfrac{(b-a)x^c}{(d+x^c)}$

Figure 32-3 shows an example of a fitted ADBUDG curve.

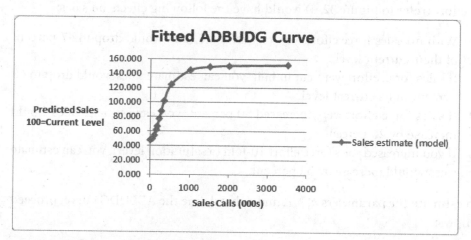

Figure 32-3: Fitted ADBUDG curve

An S curve starts out flat, gets steep, and then again becomes flat. This would be the correct form of the sales as a function of effort relationship if effort needs to exceed some critical value to generate a favorable response.

To illustrate how an ADBUDG response curve can be fit to a product, try and determine an ADBUDG curve that shows how unit sales of a drug depend on the number of sales calls made on behalf of the drug. The work for this example is in the syntexgene.xls file (see Figure 32-4).

To estimate an ADBUDG curve, use the following five points as inputs:

- Estimated sales when there is no sales effort assigned to the drug
- Estimated sales when sales effort assigned to a drug is cut in half
- Sales at current level of sales-force effort (assumed to equal a base of 100)
- Estimated sales if the sales-force effort were increased by 50 percent
- Estimated sales if the sales force "saturated" the market

	A	B	C	D
1	**Estimating the Sales Response Function at Syntex Labs**			
2				
3	**Estimates from management**			
4	Sales calls (1000s)	Sales level	Sales estimate (model)	Squared error
5	0	47	47.584	0.341
6	175	68	66.573	2.037
7	350	100	102.056	4.228
8	525	126	124.464	2.358
9	3500	152	152.350	0.122
10			Sum of squared errors	9.087
11	**Model parameters**			
12		a	b	c	d
13	47.584	152.857	2.285	605287.848
14				

Figure 32-4: ADBUDG curve estimation

Currently 350,000 calls are being made. Syntex Labs estimated that changing sales effort (refer to Figure 32-4) would have the following effects on sales:

- With no sales force effort, you can estimate sales would drop to 47 percent of their current level.
- If sales force effort were cut in half, you can estimate sales would drop to 68 percent of its current level.
- If sales force effort were increased 50 percent, you can estimate sales would increase by 26 percent.
- If you increased sales force effort 10-fold (a saturation level), you can estimate sales would increase by 52 percent.

To estimate the parameters a, b, c, and d that define the ADBUDG curve, proceed as follows:

1. Enter trial values of a, b, c, and d in A13:D13, and name these cells a, b, c, and d, respectively.
2. In cells C5:C9 compute the prediction from the ADBUDG curve by copying the formula =a+((b-a)*A5^c_)/(d+A5^c_) from C5 to C6:C9.
3. In cells D5:D9 compute the squared error for each prediction by copying the formula =(B5-C5)^2 from D5 to D6:D9.
4. In cell D10 compute the sum of the squared errors with the formula =SUM(D5:D9).

NOTE With different starting solutions the GRG Solver (without multistart) will find different final solutions. For example, if you start Solver with $a = 10$, $b = 50$, $c = 5$, and $d = 1,000$, the GRG Solver can obtain only an SSE of 3,875. With a starting solution of $a = 1$, $b = 2$, $c = 3$, and $d = 4$, you will obtain an error message! Selecting the GRG Multistart Engine ensures that your starting values of a, b, c, and d will not affect the answer found by Solver. Because a equals your predicted sales for no sales effort, a should be close to 47. (You can constrain a to be between 0 and 50.) Because b is the predicted sales with infinite sales effort, b should be close to 150. (You can constrain b to be between 0 and 200.) There are no obvious values for c and d. A large value of c, however, can cause your function to involve large numbers that may crash the GRG Multistart Engine, so constrain c to be between 0 and 5. Finally, there are no obvious limits on d, so constrain d to be between 0 and 1,000,000. The GRG multistart Solver Engine window is shown in Figure 32-5.

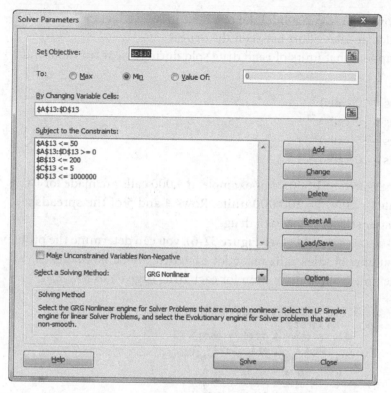

Figure 32-5: Solver window for ADBUDG curve estimation

5. Minimize the sum of squared errors (cell D10) by changing values of a, b, c, and d (cells A13:D13). Bind a, b, c, and d as discussed previously.

The GRG Multistart Engine found the solution shown in Figure 32-4. Observe that none of the "predictions" are off by more than 2 percent. After fitting this curve to each drug, the resulting response curves can be used as an input to a Solver model (see the next section for an example) that can determine a profit maximizing allocation of the sales force effort.

Optimizing Allocation of Sales Effort

Now that you have learned to use different types of curves to model the association between the level of marketing effort and the response, you can use this information to optimize the allocation of marketing resources. To illustrate this process, suppose you know that a Power curve can model the response to sales effort for four drugs. How would you allocate sales effort between the drugs?

In particular, suppose that units of each drug sold during a year (in thousands) are as follows:

- Drug 1 sales = $50(\text{calls})^{.5}$
- Drug 2 sales = $10(\text{calls})^{.75}$
- Drug 3 sales = $15(\text{calls})^{.6}$
- Drug 4 sales = $20(\text{calls})^{.3}$

Calls are also measured in 1,000s. For example, if 4,000 calls are made for Drug 1, then Drug 1 sales = $50(4)^{.5} = 100,000$ units. Rows 4 and 5 of the spreadsheet summarize the response curves for each drug.

In the `salesallocation.xls` file (see Figure 32-6), you can determine the profit, maximizing the number of sales calls made for each drug. Assume that each call costs $200 and the unit profit contribution for each drug is given in row 2.

	A	B	C	D	E
1		cost per call	$ 200.00		
2	unit proft	$ 10.00	$ 15.00	$ 20.00	$ 25.00
3		Drug 1	Drug 2	Drug 3	Drug 4
4	a	50	10	15	20
5	b	0.5	0.75	0.6	0.3
6	sales calls	1.563498784	0.100112	0.768433	0.663003
7	units sold	62519.9725	1779.778	12807.22	17680.1
8					
9					
10	drug profit	1350043.338			
11	call cost	$ 619,009.55			
12	net profit	$ 731,033.78			

Figure 32-6: Sales-force allocation model

Set up the spreadsheet as follows:

1. Enter a trial number of calls for each drug in B6:E6.
2. Compute the unit sales for each drug by copying the formula =1000*B4*(B6^B5) from B7 to C7:E7.
3. In cell B10 compute the profit (excluding sales call costs) with the formula =SUMPRODUCT(B7:E7,B2:E2).
4. In cell B11 compute the annual sales call cost with the formula =1000*C1*SUM(B6:E6).
5. In cell B12 compute the net annual profit with formula =B10-B11.

The Solver window shown in Figure 32-7 enables you to compute the profit, maximizing sales call allocation.

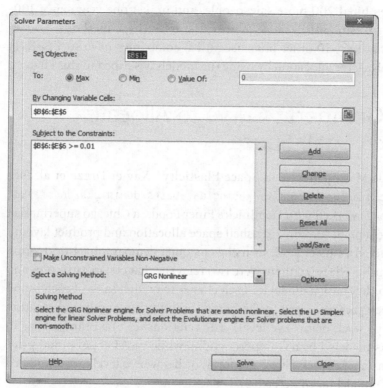

Figure 32-7: Solver window for sales call allocation

NOTE   Each number of calls is constrained to be >=.01 instead of 0. This prevents the Solver from trying a negative number of sales calls. If Solver tried a negative value for the calls made on behalf of a drug, then the unit sales would be undefined and would result in an error message.

A maximum profit of $731,033 is obtained with 1,562 calls for Drug 1, 100 calls for Drug 2, 769 calls for Drug 3, and 663 calls for Drug 4. As shown in Exercise 2, the Solver simply allocates the calls to each drug so that the change in the marginal profit generated by changing a drug's number of calls by a small amount (say .01) equals the cost of .01 calls. In short, the Solver finds the optimal sales force allocation by invoking the old economic adage that marginal revenue = marginal cost.

Lodish et al. (*Interfaces*, 1988) used the methodology of this chapter to analyze sales force allocation at Syntex Laboratories. Following their recommendations, Syntex Laboratories hired 200 more salespeople, and in just one year saw a 100-percent return on investment! Because Syntex first used these methods, Lodish et al. reported that at least 10 other pharmaceutical companies have successfully determined their sales force allocation by using the models described in this chapter.

Using the Gompertz Curve to Allocate Supermarket Shelf Space

In his paper, "Shelf Management and Space Elasticity," Xavier Dreze et al. (see `http://research.chicagobooth.edu/marketing/databases/dominicks/docs/1994-ShelfManagement.pdf`) worked with Dominick's Finer Foods, a Chicago supermarket chain, to determine a profit maximizing shelf space allocation and product layout.

They first conducted a cluster analysis using customer demographic information on 60 stores. The authors decided there were two relevant clusters: urban stores and suburban stores, so they built a model for each cluster to predict sales of each brand as a function of the space allocated to the brand, brand price, and brand location (eye level, above eye level, below eye level). The relationship of a brand's sales to allocated space was modeled by a Gompertz curve, while the effect of brand price and brand location (at eye level, above eye level, or below eye level) was modeled via the SCAN*PRO model (see Exercise 6).

The authors then used Solver for a particular product category to allocate available space between brands and determine the profit-maximizing space allocation and location for each brand. The authors reported a 5 to 6 percent increase in store profits.

Summary

In this chapter you learned the following:

- The key to optimizing the allocation of marketing effort is modeling the functional relationship between the amount of effort and unit sales.
- The Power curve, ADBUDG curve, and Gompertz curve are often used to model the relationship between effort and unit sales.
- When the functional relationship between effort and unit sales is determined, a Solver model, with profit as the target cell and changing cells being the amount of effort assigned to each product, can be used to determine the allocation of marketing effort.

Exercises

1. You want to allocate 2,000 square feet of space in CVS between seasonal and nonseasonal items. You must allocate at least 400 square feet to each type of item. Estimated profit as a function of floor space is given here.

Space	Seasonal Profit	Nonseasonal Profit
500	357,770.9	1,056,381.404
750	438,178	1,217,454.357
1,000	505,964.4	1,346,422.145
1,250	565,685.4	1,455,793.415
1,500	619,677.3	1,551,719.389

    How much space should be allocated to each type of item?

2. Show in the `salesallocation.xlsx` file that Solver's optimal resource allocation has the property that the marginal profit generated by a small change in a drug's calls equals the sales call cost associated with the change in calls.

3. How could the ADBUDG curve be used to determine the optimal allocation of advertising dollars for GM's car models?

4. In 2009 Target began to devote a much larger portion of its stores to groceries. Why would the methods of this chapter understate the benefit Target would obtain by allocating more space to groceries?

5. Paris Lohan is a marketing analyst for Time Warner. She has fit an ADBUDG curve for each magazine that describes how the number of new subscriptions changes when the money spent on advertising the magazine changes. Paris now wants to determine a profit maximizing allocation of the ad budget for each magazine. In Paris' target cell she has multiplied the number of new subscriptions by the annual profit per subscriber to the magazine. Can you find an error in Paris' logic?

6. In Excel, set up a formula that combines the Gompertz curve and SCAN*PRO model to estimate sales of a brand as a function of brand price, brand location (eye level, above eye level, below eye level), and price of competitor's brand.

33

Forecasting Sales from Few Data Points

There are many situations in which a business wants to estimate total sales of a product based on sales during the early portion of the product life cycle. This need brings forth the question, "How many months of sales are needed to make an accurate forecast of product sales during the product's lifetime?" Chapter 26, "Using S Curves to Forecast Sales of a New Product," and Chapter 27, "The Bass Diffusion Model," show how S curves and the Bass model can be used to predict total sales early in the product life cycle. Both the S curve and Bass model require at least five data points, however, to obtain reasonable estimates of future sales. This chapter describes a simpler method that can estimate total product sales from as few as two data points.

Predicting Movie Revenues

When a new movie comes out, how many weeks of revenue are needed to predict total movie revenue? One might guess 5 or 6, however, it is actually possible to predict a movie's total revenues from as few as 2 weeks of revenues.

The 2weeks MAD worksheet of the finalresultmovie.xls file (see Figure 33-1) contains total revenues for 76 movies and revenues for each of the first 3 weeks of the movie's release. Using this data, the goal is to develop a simple model that can accurately predict total revenues from either the first 2 or 3 weeks of revenues. In many industries (such as video games) analysts begin with a simple rule such as the following equation:

(1) (Estimated Total Revenue) = (Some multiple of first two weeks of revenue)

	Movie	Week 1	Week 2	Week 3	Total	Legs	1st 2 weeks	Forecast	Abs Err	Error	
	a	alpha		Total=a*1st 2 wks*Legs^alpha					MAD		stdeverrors
	1.782544587	0.304181							5558530.99		9676525
1	Monster's Ball	2321246	3217185	2097738	19964720	1.385973	6538431	10903007	9061712.718	9061712.718	
2	Beauty & The Beast - SE	2073437	2443280	1470492	8527183	1.178372	4516717	8463423	63760.15565	63760.15565	
3	About A Boy	8557630	9821030	4126600	29370520	1.147634	18378660	34162162	4791642.125	-4791642.125	
4	Gosford Park	3684621	4151226	2782555	27265504	1.126636	7835847	14483647	12781857.12	12781857.12	
5	Jimmy Neutron: Boy Genius	13832786	15035649	9015854	50699555	1.086957	28868435	52781145	2081589.943	-2081589.943	
6	Brotherhood of the Wolf	1533927	1608920	1904085	6219382	1.04889	3142847	5684199	535183.4213	535183.4213	
7	In the Bedroom	2853430	2859733	1941677	21949644	1.002209	6713183	10190805	11758838.74	11758838.74	
8	Big Fat Liar	11554015	11428335	6324015	39453765	0.989122	22982350	40830997	1377232.199	-1377232.199	
9	The Lord of the Rings	47211490	38695582	23006447	1.85E+08	0.819622	85907072	1.44E+08	41287432.6	41287432.6	
10	I Am Sam	8315581	6303148	4619148	28593343	0.767992	14618729	23952252	4641090.77	4641090.77	
11	The Royal Tenenbaums	8514122	6408153	5368838	27476757	0.75265	14922275	24397053	3079704.231	3079704.231	
12	Star Wars Episode II	80027814	60003949	21002876	1.99E+08	0.749789	140031763	2.29E+08	29850222.85	-29850222.85	
13	The Rookie	16021684	11703657	8076763	56652477	0.730489	27725341	44919103	11733373.52	11733373.52	
14	A Walk to Remember	12177488	8836201	5542525	32043262	0.725618	21013689	33976033	1932771.116	-1932771.116	
15	Clockstoppers	10108333	7284214	4652393	27816421	0.720615	17392547	28062062	245640.8396	-245640.8396	

Figure 33-1: Movie revenue data

For example, you may try to estimate total revenue for a movie by simply doubling the revenues earned by the movie during its first 2 weeks. To see the weakness of this type of rule though, consider the revenues (in millions of dollars) for the two movies shown in Table 33-1.

Table 33-1: Weakness of Equation 1

Movie	Week 1 Revenue	Week 2 Revenue
1	80	40
2	60	60

Because each movie made $120 million during the first 2 weeks, any prediction for total revenue generated from Equation 1 will be the same for each movie. Looking at the data tells you, however, that revenue for Movie 1 is dropping fast, but revenue for Movie 2 is holding up well. This would lead you to believe future revenue for Movie 2 will exceed Movie 1. Predicting total movie revenue with Equation 2 will create higher forecasts (after adjusting for total revenue during the first 2 weeks) for Movie 2, as wanted.

(2) Predicted Total Movie Revenue = a * (1st 2 weeks of revenue) * (Legs)^{alpha}

In Equation 2, *Legs* = Week 2 Revenue / Week 1 Revenue. If *Legs* = 1 (which is the case for Movie 2 in Table 33-1), for example, the movie has excellent staying power because Week 2 revenue = Week 1 revenue. The average value of *Legs* for the movies in this data set was 0.63, indicating that Week 2 revenues average 37 percent lower than Week 1 revenues. If you hold a movie's first two weeks of revenue constant, then the forecasted total revenue from Equation 2 is an increasing function of *Legs*, which means a movie's forecasted revenue is an increasing function of the movie's staying power.

NOTE The term "legs" is being used as a synonym for the movie's staying power at the box office.

The worksheet 2weeks MAD uses the GRG Multistart Solver engine to determine the values of *a* and *alpha* that minimize average absolute error. Note that some movies (such as *Lord of the Rings*) make a lot of money relative to other movies (such as *Orange County*). If you minimize MAPE (Mean Absolute Percent Error), then movies that have low revenue can exert an inordinate influence on the target cell. For example, if you predicted $6 million revenue for *Orange County*, you were fairly close in absolute terms to the actual revenue (near $4 million) but your percentage error is nearly 50 percent.

In general, choosing SSE (Sum of Squared Error) as a goodness of fit criteria for a model causes the outliers to have a large effect on the model's estimated parameters. In contrast, if MAD (Mean Absolute Deviation) or MAPE is used as a goodness of fit criteria, then the influence of outliers on the model's estimated parameters is less and Solver concentrates on making the model fit "typical" values of the dependent variable.

To find the values of *a* and *alpha* that minimize MAD, proceed as follows:

1. Copy the formula =a*SUM(D4:E4)*(H4^alpha) from J4 to J5:J79 to generate the forecast for each movie's total revenue implied by Equation 2.
2. Copy the formula =ABS(G4-J4) from K4 to K5:K79 to compute the absolute error for each movie's prediction.
3. In cell K2 compute the average absolute error (the target cell) with the formula =AVERAGE(K4:K79).
4. Using the Solver window in Figure 33-2, find values of *alpha* and *a* that minimize MAD.

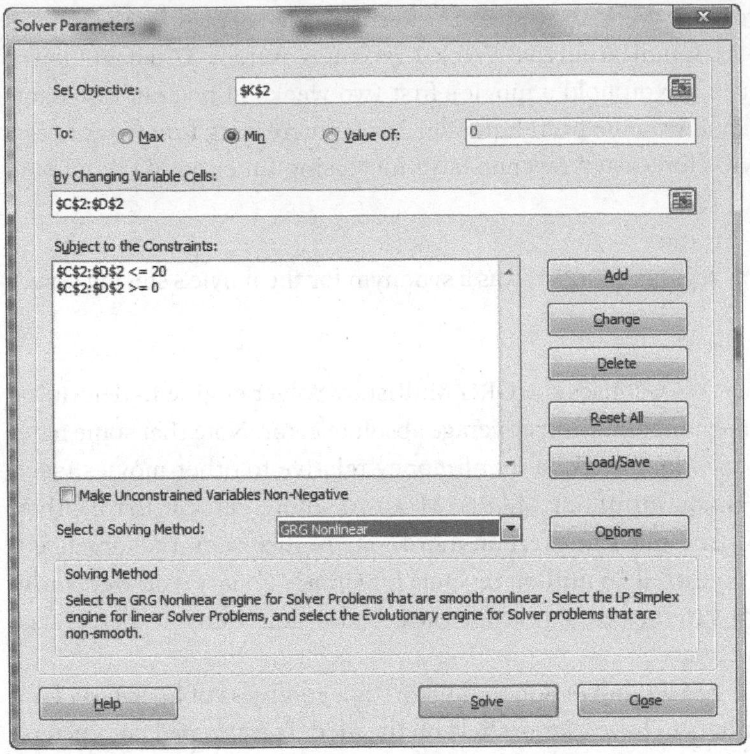

Figure 33-2: Solver window for two-week movie revenue data

The resulting prediction equation is as follows:

Predicted Total Movie Revenue = 1.79 * (First 2 week Total) ^ 0.30

The average error was $5.7 million. The average revenue of the listed movies is $50 million, so using 2 weeks of revenues you conclude that the forecasts are off by approximately 11 percent.

Modifying the Model to Improve Forecast Accuracy

There are a few additional measures you can take to ensure for the most accurate predictions possible. This section covers some of the most common ways you can increase the accuracy of the relatively simple model defined by Equation 2.

Finding Outliers

Recall a forecasted observation is an outlier if the absolute value of the forecast error exceeds 2 * (Standard deviation of the forecast errors). Copying the formula =G4-J4 from L4 to L5:L79 computes the forecast error for each observation. In cell M2 you can compute the standard deviation ($9.7 million) of the forecast errors with the formula =STDEV(L4:L79). Column K highlights the movie outliers, which are all movies whose forecast errors exceed 2 * 9.68 = $19.36 million. The outliers are *The Lord of the Rings*, *Star Wars Episode II*, *Ocean's Eleven*, *Spider-Man* and *Monsters, Inc.* If you could figure out a common thread that explained the model's lack of accuracy in predicting the revenue from these outliers, incorporating this common thread into the forecast equation would greatly improve the model's forecasting accuracy.

Minimizing Squared Errors

The 2 weeks sq error worksheet of the finalresultmovie.xls file estimates the model using the criteria of minimizing squared errors. And *a* = 1.84 and *alpha* = 0.29, which are virtually identical to the previous estimates of *a* and *alpha*. If outliers were having a large effect on the model's estimated parameters, then SSE and MAD would yield substantially different parameter estimates. The similarity of the parameter estimates for the MAD and SSE criteria shows that outliers are not having an outlandish effect on the estimates of the model's parameters.

Ignoring Staying Power

To demonstrate the improvement in forecast accuracy gained by including *LEGS* in the forecast model, set *alpha* = 0 and have Solver find the value of *a* that minimizes MAD (see the Simple model worksheet). The best forecast is obtained by multiplying the total revenue for the first 2 weeks by 1.53. The MAD = $6.57 million, which is 20 percent larger than the MAD obtained by including staying power in the forecast model. This calculation demonstrates the size of the benefit gained from including *LEGS* in the model.

Using 3 Weeks of Revenue to Forecast Movie Revenues

The preceding methods are great ways to help minimize error when you are limited to two weeks of data from which to forecast. Using three weeks of revenues, however, will clearly result in a more accurate forecast. The question is whether the additional week of data results in a substantial enough improvement in forecast accuracy. To see if it does, in the Use 3 weeks worksheet you will develop a model that forecasts total movie revenue from the first three weeks of revenue. The key issue here is how to define a movie's "staying power." Given the first 3 weeks of a movie's revenues, you can define the following equation:

(3) Legs = wt * (Week 2 Legs) + (1–wt) * (Week 3 Legs)

In Equation 3 *Week 2 Legs = Week 2 Revenue / Week 1 Revenue, Week 3 Legs = Week 3 revenue / Week 2 revenue*, and *wt* is a weight that defines the weighted average of Week 2 and Week 3 Legs that minimize MAD. The rationale behind Equation 3 is that (Week 2 Revenue / Week 1 Revenue) and (Week 3 Revenue / Week 2 Revenue) are two different estimates of a movie's staying power, so when averaged, you get a single estimate of a movie's staying power. The prediction equation is the following:

(4) Predicted Total Revenue = a * (1st three weeks revenue) * Legs^{alpha}.

To find the values of *a*, *alpha*, and *wt* that minimize MAD, proceed as follows:

1. Copy the formula =wt*(E4/D4)+(1-wt)*(F4/E4) from H4 to H5:H79 to compute the weighted estimate of Legs for each movie.
2. Copy the formula =a*I4*(H4^alpha) from J4 to J5:J79 to compute the forecast for each movie. The absolute error and MAD formulas are as before, and the new Solver window (reflecting the fact that *wt* is a changing cell) is shown in Figure 33-3.
3. Use the following equation to predict Total Revenue:

Total Revenue = 1.63 * (0.54 * Week 2 Legs + 0.46 * Week 3 Legs) ^ 0.49

The MAD has been reduced to $3.7 million.

Because most movies make most of their revenue within three weeks, it appears that including the third week in the model does not result in a substantial enough improvement in forecast accuracy to make it worth your while.

Having the ability to quickly predict future sales of a product is important in industries where demand for a new product is highly uncertain. For example, for stores that specialize in selling clothing to teens (such as PacSun and Hot Topic), ability to quickly predict future sales is vital. This is because before a new apparel item is introduced, there is great uncertainty about future product sales so a retailer can lose a lot of money if they order too much or too little. If a few weeks of data narrows the "cone of uncertainty" on future sales, then a retailer can begin with a small order and use information from a few data points to derive a reorder quantity that reduces the costs associated with overstocking or understocking the product.

Figure 33-3: Solver window for three-week movie revenue model data

Summary

In this chapter you learned the following:

- To forecast total sales of a product from the first n periods of sales, take $a *$ (first n periods of sales) $*$ (Legs^{alpha}) where Solver is used to find the values of a, *alpha*, and (if necessary) the parameters needed to compute Legs.
- The Target Cell can be to minimize MAD or SSE.

Exercises

1. The `Newmoviedata.xlsx` file contains weekly and total revenues for several movies. Develop a model to predict total movie revenues from 2 weeks of revenues.
2. For your model in Exercise 1, find all forecast outliers.

3. Think of some additional factors that could be added to the movie forecasting model that might improve forecast accuracy.

4. Suppose Microsoft asks you to determine how many weeks of sales for an Xbox game are needed to give a satisfactory forecast for total units sold. How would you proceed?

5. Why is predicting total sales of an Xbox game from several weeks of sales a more difficult problem than predicting total movie revenue from several weeks of movie revenues?

Advertising

Chapter 34: Measuring the Effectiveness of
Advertising
Chapter 35: Media Selection Models
Chapter 36: Pay Per Click (PPC) Online Advertising

34 Measuring the Effectiveness of Advertising

Companies have trouble measuring the effectiveness of advertising. This is due primarily to the lag between exposure to an ad and the consumer response to an ad. Simply put: past ads can (and usually do) affect present and future sales.

For example, the author taught army analysts at Fort Knox who analyzed the disposition of the Army recruiting budget. They found that many visits to Army recruiting offices could be traced to an ad that was shown on TV up to six months before.

John Wanamaker, a 19th-century Philadelphia department store merchant, summarized how difficult it is to measure the benefits of advertising when he said, "Half the money I spend on advertising is wasted; the trouble is I don't know which half." This chapter develops several models that you can use to determine if a firm's advertising is worthwhile. You learn how to incorporate the lagged effect of advertising into your forecast of product sales. You also learn that the optimal allocation of the ad budget over time may involve either *pulsing* (quick bursts of intensive advertising followed by a period of no ads) or *continuous spending* (advertising all the time at a fairly constant rate).

The Adstock Model

Chapter 31, "Using the SCAN*PRO Model and Its Variants," developed models that you can use to determine how price and display affect sales. These models are not too difficult to set up because you can assume that past prices and displays have no effect on current sales. However, this is not the case when it comes to advertising.

To account for the lag between exposure to an ad and the consumer response to an ad, Simon Broadbent developed the *Adstock Model*, detailed in his article "One Way TV Advertisements Work" (*Journal of Marketing Research*, 1979.) This model essentially provides a simple yet powerful way to model the fact that ads do affect present and future sales. The Adstock Model also has the virtue of being easily combined with the versions of the SCAN*PRO model discussed in Chapter 31.

The key idea behind the Adstock Model is the assumption that each given sales period or quarter you retain a fraction (*lambda*) of your previous stock of advertising. For example, if *lambda* = 0.8, then an ad from one period ago has 80 percent of the effect of an ad during the current period; an ad two periods ago has $(0.80)^2$ = 51.2 percent as much effect as an ad during the current period; and so on. *Lambda* will therefore be a changing cell that is determined with Solver. In a sense the Adstock Model assumes that the effect of advertising "depreciates" or wears out in a manner similar to the way a machine wears out.

To try out an analysis using the Adstock Model, suppose you want to model sales of a seasonal price-sensitive product for which sales are trending upward. You can see in the Adstock.xlsx file that for each quarter, you are given the product price, amount of advertising, and units sold (in thousands). For example, during the first quarter of data (which was also the first quarter of the year), the price was $44.00, 44 ads were placed, and 2,639 units were sold.

Coming into the first period, you do not know the current Adstock level, so you can make the period 1 level of Adstock a changing cell (call it **INITIAL ADSTOCK**). Then each period's Adstock value can be computed using Equations 1 and 2:

(1) Quarter 1 ADSTOCK = *LAMBDA* * INITIALADSTOCK + QUARTER 1 ADS
(2) Quarter *T* ADSTOCK = *LAMBDA* * QUARTER *T-1* ADSTOCK + QUARTER *T* ADS

Of course, you need a mechanism by which the Adstock level influences sales. You can assume that the Adstock level in a quarter has a linear effect on sales through a parameter *ADEFFECT*. Use the following model to forecast each quarter's sales:

(3) Predicted Sales = (CONST * (TREND$^{Quarter\#}$ + ADEFFECT * ADSTOCK) * (PRICE)$^{-elasticity}$ * (Seasonal Index)

In Equation 3 CONST * (TREND$^{Quarter\#}$ + ADEFFECT * ADSTOCK) "locates" a base level for sales in the absence of seasonality and advertising and adjusts this base level based on the current Adstock level. Multiplying this base level by (PRICE)$^{-elasticity}$ * (Seasonal Index) adjusts the base level based on the current price and quarter of the year.

In your analysis, find the parameter values that minimize the MAPE associated with Equation 3. You could also, if desired, find the parameters that minimize SSE. The following steps describe how to use Solver to minimize MAPE.

1. In cell F6 compute quarter 1's Adstock level with the formula =E6+intialadstock*lambda using Equation 1.

2. Copy the formula =E7+lambda*F6 from F7 to F8:F29 to use Equation 2 to compute the Adstock level for the remaining quarters.

3. Copy the formula =(const*(trend)^D6+adeffect*F6)*VLOOKUP(C6,season,2)*(G6)^(-elasticity) from H6 to H7:H29 to use Equation 3 to compute a forecast for each quarter's sales.

4. Copy the formula =ABS(I6-H6)/I6 from J6 to J7:J29 to compute each quarter's absolute percentage error.

5. In cell I4 compute the MAPE with the formula =AVERAGE(J6:J29).

6. Use the Solver window in Figure 32-1 with the GRG (Generalized Reduced Gradient) Multistart engine to find the parameter values that minimize the MAPE associated with Equation 3. Most of the upper bounds on the changing cells are "intelligent guesses." Of course, if the Solver set a changing cell value near its upper bound, you need to relax the bound. The constraint $M$11 = 1 ensures that the seasonal indices average to 1. The solution found by Solver is shown in Figure 34-2.

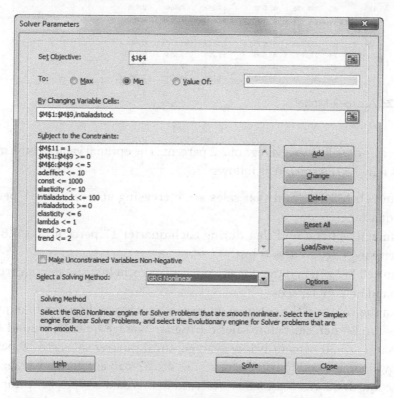

Figure 34-1: Solver window for Adstock Model

	C	D	E	F	G	H	I	J	K	L	M
1						intialadstock	35.295			adeffect	4.996
2										elasticity	1.488
3								MAPE		trend	1.097
4								0.022		lambda	0.831
5	Quarter of Year	Quarter#	Ads	Adstock	Price	forecast	actual	APE		const	502.993
6	1	1	44	73.336	44.000	2.633	2.639	0.002		1	0.798
7	2	2	78	138.953	42.000	3.510	3.486	0.007		2	0.702
8	3	3	59	174.492	35.000	6.425	6.156	0.044		3	0.828
9	4	4	72	217.030	40.000	12.547	12.561	0.001		4	1.672
10	1	5	47	227.385	37.000	7.185	7.263	0.011			
11	2	6	45	233.992	37.000	6.676	6.354	0.051		mean	1.000
12	3	7	34	228.484	37.000	8.107	8.030	0.010			
13	4	8	31	220.905	43.000	13.431	13.892	0.033			
14	1	9	80	263.607	43.000	7.354	7.566	0.028			
15	2	10	49	268.098	44.000	6.586	6.761	0.026			
16	3	11	57	279.831	39.000	9.956	9.074	0.097			
17	4	12	65	297.583	45.000	17.546	16.655	0.054			
18	1	13	54	301.337	40.000	10.541	10.517	0.002			
19	2	14	40	290.458	43.000	8.604	8.647	0.005			
20	3	15	58	299.415	42.000	11.239	11.271	0.003			
21	4	16	23	271.860	36.000	29.014	29.031	0.001			
22	1	17	25	250.958	43.000	10.973	10.929	0.004			
23	2	18	40	248.585	43.000	10.232	9.856	0.038			
24	3	19	26	232.613	43.000	12.641	12.661	0.002			
25	4	20	30	223.337	43.000	27.006	26.056	0.036			
26	1	21	69	254.628	43.000	14.297	13.730	0.041			
27	2	22	28	239.635	43.000	13.268	13.513	0.018			
28	3	23	55	254.174	43.000	17.058	17.161	0.006			
29	4	24	54	265.258	39.000	43.195	43.227	0.001			

Figure 34-2: Adstock Model

The forecasts are off by an average of 2.2 percent. The optimal values of the model parameters may be interpreted as follows:

- From cell M3 you find that sales are increasing at a rate of 9.7 percent per quarter.
- From cell M4 you find that during each quarter 17 percent (1 – 0.83) of advertising effectiveness is lost.
- From cell M2 you find that for any price a 1 percent increase in price reduces demand by 1.49 percent.
- From the values of the seasonal indices in M6:M9 you find that first quarter sales are 20 percent below sales during an average quarter; second quarter sales are 30 percent below average; third quarter sales are 18 percent below average; and fourth quarter sales are 67 percent above average. The large fourth quarter seasonality observed in this data is typical of companies (Mattel and Amazon, for example) whose sales increase greatly during the holiday season.

Another Model for Estimating Ad Effectiveness

Another model used to measure advertising effectiveness is suggested by Gary Lilien, Phillip Kotler, and Sridhar Moorthy in their book *Marketing Decision Models* (Prentice-Hall, 1992). The model is described by Equation 4:

$$(4)\ Q_t = a + \lambda Q_{t-1} + bLN\ (A_t) + c\ \max\ (0, \Delta A_t)_t$$

In Equation 4 the following parameters are true:

- Q_t = Period t sales
- A_t = Period t advertising
- ΔA_t = Percentage increase in advertising for period t compared to period $t-1$
- b, c, a, and λ are parameters that must be estimated.

The LN (A_t) term incorporates the fact that the effectiveness of advertising diminishes as more advertising is done. The last term in the equation gives you an opportunity to model the effect of a change in advertising on sales. The λ represents the fraction of past sales used to predict current sales. Because past sales have been built up by past advertising, this term incorporates the fact that past loyalty built up through advertising affects current sales.

In the next section you will see that the model for sales described by Equation 4 incorporates enough flexibility to enable two very different but interesting advertising strategies (pulsing and continuous spending) to be optimal in different situations.

NOTE In contrast to the multiplicative SCAN*PRO model discussed in Chapter 31, the model defined by Equation 4 is an additive model.

You can now use this new model to measure the effectiveness of advertising based on data in the file addata.xls. This file contains 36 months of sales (in thousands of dollars) and advertising (in hundreds of dollars) for a dietary product. For variety, find the parameters defined by Equation 4 that minimize SSE instead of MAPE. The following steps enable you to fit Equation 4 to this data (see Figure 34-3):

1. For each month compute ΔA_t by copying from F8 to F9:F42 the formula =(D8-D7)/D7.
2. Copy the formula =a+lambda*E8+b*LN(D8)+c_*MAX(0,F8) from G8 to G9:G42 to generate the forecast for sales during months 2–36.

		a	2.372373			
		lambda	0.555179	Sales=a+lambda*lastsales+bLn (A(t))+cmax(0,deltaA(t))		
		b	2.948116	delta A(t)		
		c	-0.42623	SSE	Rsq	stderr
				362.1587	0.693846	3.263698

Month	Sales	Advertising	Lagged Sales	delta A(t)	Forecast	Sq Err	error
1	12	15					
2	20.5	16	12	0.066667	17.18002	11.0223	3.319985
3	21	18	20.5	0.125	22.22141	1.49184	-1.22141
4	15.5	27	21	0.5	23.53452	64.55352	-8.03452
5	21	21	15.5	-0.22222	19.95325	21.65272	-4.65325
6	23.5	49	15.3	1.333333	21.77184	2.986545	1.728162
7	24.5	21	23.5	-0.57143	24.39468	0.011093	0.105322
8	21.3	22	24.5	0.047619	25.06671	14.18808	-3.76671
9	23.5	28	21.3	0.272727	23.90516	0.164155	-0.40516
10	28	36	23.5	0.285714	25.86192	4.571376	2.138078
11	24	40	28	0.111111	28.74526	22.51752	-4.74526
12	15.5	3	24	-0.925	18.9355	11.80265	-3.4355
13	17.3	21	15.5	6	17.39586	0.00919	-0.09586
14	25.3	29	17.3	0.380952	21.74177	12.661	3.55823
15	25	62	25.3	1.137931	28.10064	9.613996	-3.10064
16	36.5	65	25	0.048387	28.5378	63.39671	7.962205
17	36.5	46	36.5	-0.29231	33.92368	6.637448	2.576325
18	29.6	44	36.5	-0.04348	33.79263	17.57812	-4.19263
19	30.5	33	29.6	-0.25	29.11377	1.921625	1.386227
20	28	62	30.5	0.878788	31.09803	9.597781	-3.09803
21	26	22	28	-0.64516	27.03013	1.061166	-1.03013
22	21.5	12	26	-0.45455	24.13281	6.931703	-2.63281
23	19.7	24	21.5	1	23.25176	12.61497	-3.55176
24	19	3	19.7	-0.875	16.54823	6.011175	2.45177
25	16	5	19	0.666667	17.38142	1.908334	-1.38142
26	20.7	14	16	1.8	18.26826	5.913338	2.431736
27	26.5	36	20.7	1.571429	23.75941	7.510828	2.740589

Figure 34-3: Diet product ad data

3. Copy the formula `=(G8-C8)^2` from H8 to H9:H42 to compute the squared error for months 2–36.
4. In H5 compute SSE with the formula `=SUM(H8:H42)`.
5. Copy the formula `=C8-G8` from I8 to I9:I42 to compute the error for each month.
6. Use the Solver window in Figure 34-4 to estimate the parameter values.

You can find the fitted version of Equation 4 to be as follows:

$$Q_t = 2.37 + .56Q_{t-1} + 2.95LN\ (A_t) - .43\max\ (0,\ \Delta A_t)$$

The formula `=RSQ(G8:G42,C8:C42)` in cell I5 shows that the model explains 69 percent of sales variation. The formula `=STDEV(I8:I42)` in cell J5 shows that 68 percent of the forecasts should be accurate within \$3,264 and 95 percent accurate within \$6,528. Of course, if data were seasonal you would have to modify the model to account for the effects of seasonality as you did in the "Forecasting Software Sales" section of Chapter 31.

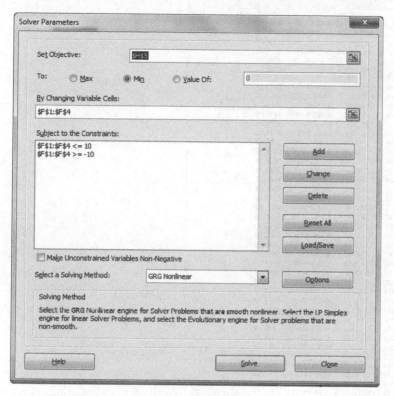

Figure 34-4: Solver window for ad data

Optimizing Advertising: Pulsing versus Continuous Spending

Now that you have modeled the relationship between advertising and monthly sales, you may use Solver to calculate a profit-maximizing advertising strategy. The work for this example is in the `optimize diet` worksheet of the `addata.xls` file (see Figure 34-5).

The following assumptions are made:

- 30 percent profit margin on sales
- Unit product price of $1,000
- Cost of $100 per ad
- Month 1 sales = 12 units
- Month 1 ads = 9

	A	B	C	D	E	F	G	H
1					a	2.37237	price	1000
2					lambda	0.55518		
3					b	2.94812		
4			No pulse		c	-0.42623		
5					profit margin	0.3		
6					total profit	189763		
7		Month	Sales	Advertisin	deltaa	profit		
8		1	12	9				
9		2	17.0704	17.502916	0.944768446	3370.83		
10		3	20.5543	19.47104	0.112445483	4219.19		
11		4	22.5591	19.647133	0.009043861	4803.03		
12		5	23.6846	19.713817	0.003394081	5133.98		
13		6	24.3115	19.719574	0.000292033	5321.51		
14		7	24.6604	19.724865	0.000268274	5425.65		
15		8	24.855	19.730855	0.00030368	5483.42		
16		9	24.9693	19.778669	0.002423319	5512.92		
17		10	25.0334	19.776452	-0.000112084	5532.38		
18		11	25.0687	19.774043	-0.000121802	5543.19		
19		12	25.089	19.780402	0.000321604	5548.67		
20		13	25.1007	19.781844	7.28918E-05	5552.02		
21		14	25.1078	19.787047	0.000263021	5553.64		
22		15	25.1115	19.784109	-0.00014849	5555.03		
23		16	25.1127	19.778488	-0.000284139	5555.95		
24		17	25.1156	19.796015	0.00088616	5555.06		
25		18	25.1185	19.803305	0.000368263	5555.21		
26		19	25.1199	19.801118	-0.000110439	5555.86		
27		20	25.117	19.776389	-0.001248834	5557.47		
28		21	25.1146	19.770563	-0.000294592	5557.31		
29		22	25.1144	19.78006	0.000480329	5556.32		
30		23	25.1108	19.755301	-0.001251679	5557.72		
31		24	25.1074	19.745435	-0.00049944	5557.67		
32		25	25.105	19.74224	-0.000161813	5557.27		
33		26	25.1034	19.740819	-7.19753E-05	5556.95		
34		27	25.0978	19.709174	-0.001602993	5558.44		
35		28	25.0945	19.707543	-8.27835E-05	5557.6		
36		29	25.0809	19.628881	-0.003991473	5561.37		
37		30	25.064	19.567388	-0.003132781	5562.47		
38		31	25.0137	19.297484	-0.013793543	5574.37		
39		32	24.9084	18.797399	-0.025914547	5592.78		
40		33	24.7432	18.129316	-0.035541238	5610.04		
41		34	24.3586	16.41465	-0.094579724	5666.13		
42		35	23.6239	13.754554	-0.162056214	5711.71		
43		36	21.9255	8.8787605	-0.354485756	5689.78		

Figure 34-5: Continuous spending example

The goal is to use the GRG Multistart Solver engine to determine the number of ads during months 2–36 to maximize the total profit earned during months 2–36. Proceed as follows:

1. Determine the profit for months 2–36 by copying the formula `=price*C9*profit_margin-100*D9` from F9 to F10:F43.

2. Generate sales in Column C during months 2–36 by copying the forecasting formula `=a+lambda*C8+b*LN(D9)+c_*MAX(0,E9)` from C9 to C10:C43.

The Solver window shown in Figure 34-6 determines a profit-maximizing advertising strategy:

You can constrain each month's advertising to be at least .10 because an advertising level of 0 causes the LN function to be undefined, and for some reason, if you constrain a changing cell to be non-negative, Solver may try negative values for the changing cell. A relatively constant amount should be spent on advertising each month. This is known as a *continuous spending* strategy. During later months advertising drops because you have less of "a future" to benefit from the advertising. This is similar to the drop in retention and acquisition spending near the end of the planning horizon that was observed in Chapter 22, "Allocating Marketing Resources between Customer Acquisition and Retention."

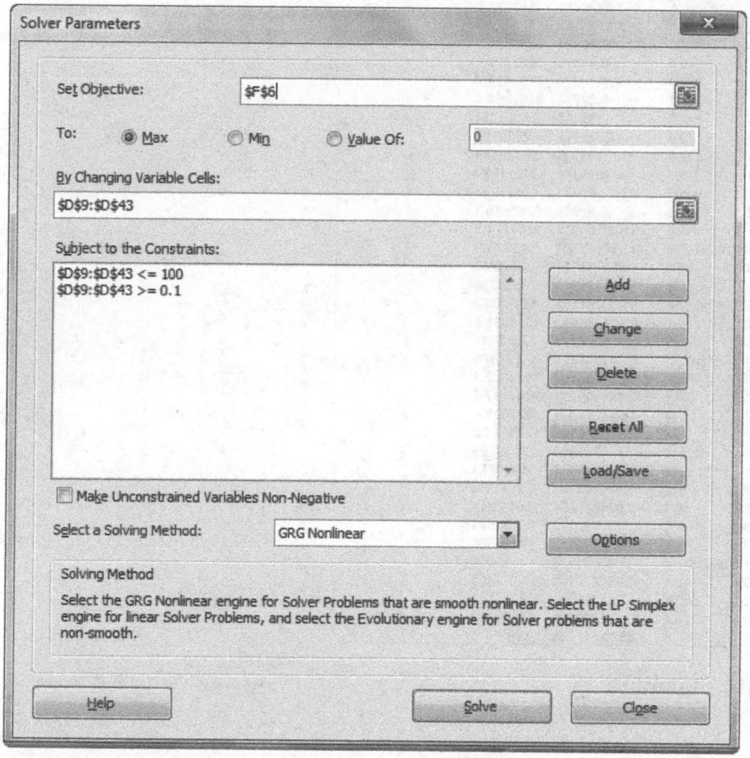

Figure 34-6: Solver window for continuous spending example

The pulse worksheet shows an example where several of the problem parameters are changed, and in doing so, Solver found the optimal advertising policy shown in Figure 34-7.

In Figure 34-7 you can observe a *pulsing* strategy in which you can alternate between a high and low level of advertising. Vijay Mahajan and Eitan Muller ("Advertising Pulsing Policies for Generating Awareness for New Products," *Marketing Science*, 1986, pp. 89–106) discuss in more detail the conditions under which a continuous spending strategy is optimal. Prasad Naik Murali Mantrala and Alan Sawyer ("Planning Media Schedules in the Presence of Dynamic Advertising Quality," *Marketing Science*, 1998, pp. 214–35) discuss conditions under which pulsing is optimal. The general consensus is that in actual situations a continuous spending strategy is much more likely to be optimal than a pulsing strategy.

				a	2.3723729	price	1000
				lambda	0.4		
				b	2.9481161		
		pulse		c	0.3		
				profit margin	0.25		
				total profit	372839285		
	Month	Sales	Advertisin	deltaa	profit		
	1	12	9				
	2	71.4861	1303.9906	143.8878448	-112527.5		
	3	24.1785	0.1	-0.999923312	6034.6319		
	4	30038.9	10000	99999.00021	6509724.2		
	5	12011.1	0.1	-0.99999	3002775.7		
	6	34833.7	10000	99999.00021	7708420.7		
	7	13929.1	0.1	-0.99999	3482254.3		
	8	125605	40000	399999	27401234		
	9	50237.6	0.1	-0.9999975	12559380		
	10	140128	40000	399999	31032084		
	11	56046.9	0.1	-0.9999975	14011720		
	12	52448	10000	99999.00021	12111998		
	13	20974.8	0.1	-0.99999	5243685.3		
	14	38419.1	10000	99999.00021	8604784.5		
	15	15378.7	18.904035	-0.998109597	3842782.9		
	16	6147.06	0.1	-0.994710124	1536755.3		
	17	122492	40000	399999	26623034		
	18	49026.5	10429.54	-0.739261509	11213672		
	19	19606.2	0.1	-0.999990412	4901536.5		
	20	127876	40000	399999	27968947		
	21	51179.4	8676.8676	-0.783078311	11927169		
	22	20482.6	17.718681	-0.99795794	5118882.1		
	23	8188.63	0.1	-0.994356239	2047147.6		
	24	17122.7	4606.7744	46066.74446	3820001.6		
	25	6844.67	0.1	-0.999978293	1711157.6		
	26	122771	40000	399999	26692795		
	27	49135.8	4822.1236	-0.87944691	11801750		
	28	19665.4	19.27025	-0.996003783	4914431.4		
	29	7861.76	0.1	-0.994810654	1965429.4		
	30	123178	40000	399999	26794504		
	31	49266.8	0.1	-0.9999975	12316688		
	32	31731.1	3999.3016	39992.01578	7532856		
	33	12688	0.1	-0.999974996	3172000.5		
	34	125109	40000	399999	27277132		
	35	50039	0.1	-0.9999975	12509739		
	36	22714.1	892.12734	8920.273389	5589307.5		

Figure 34-7: Example of pulsing

Summary

In this chapter you learned the following:

- The following Adstock Model (specified by Equations 1 and 2) enables the marketing analyst to model the fact that the effect of advertising decays over time.

  (1) Quarter 1 ADSTOCK = LAMBDA * INITIALADSTOCK + QUARTER 1 ADS.
  (2) Quarter t ADSTOCK = LAMBDA * QUARTER T-1 ADSTOCK + QUARTER T ADS.

■ Fitting the model shown in Equation 3 allows the marketing analyst to determine how seasonality, price, trend, and advertising affect sales.

(3) Predicted Sales = (CONST * (TREND$^{Quarter\#}$ + ADEFFECT * ADSTOCK) * (PRICE)$^{-elasticity}$ * (Seasonal Index)

■ If sales are modeled by Equation 4, then either a continuous spending or pulsing strategy can be optimal.

(4) $Q_t = a + \lambda Q_{t-1} + bLN(A_t) + c \max(0, \Delta A_t)_t$

Exercises

1. If the Adstock Model is fitted to monthly data and yields *lambda* = 0.7, then what would be the "half life" of advertising?
2. How could the effect of a product display on sales be incorporated into Equation 3?
3. Suppose you model daily sales of 3M painter's tape at Lowe's. 3M runs a national ad campaign for painter's tape on the Home and Garden Channel, whereas Lowe's sometimes runs ads in the local Sunday paper. How can you determine which type of advertising is more effective?

35

Media Selection Models

All companies that advertise must choose an allocation of their ad budgets from a large number of possible choices. These choices include allocating how much money should be spent in different ad channels such as radio, print, TV and the Internet, as well as deciding on which channels, networks, or publications each product should be advertised, and for daily shows, such as the *NBC Evening News*, on what days of the week the ads should be placed. To put the importance of advertising in the U.S. economy in perspective, consider that in 2013 U.S. companies spent $512 billion on advertising. The breakdown of these expenditures is as follows:

- **Newspapers:** $91 billion
- **Magazines:** $42 billion
- **TV:** $206 billion
- **Radio:** $35 billion
- **Movies:** $3 billion
- **Outdoor:** $33 billion
- **Internet:** $101 billion

A method used to allocate ad spending among available media vehicles that maximizes the effectiveness of the advertising is known as a *media selection model*. In this chapter you will learn about several widely used media selection models that can help U.S. companies allocate this $512 billion dollars more effectively.

A Linear Media Allocation Model

A.M. Lee, A.J. Burkart, Frank Bass and Robert Lonsdale were among the first researchers to use linear optimization models for media selection. Using the concepts outlined in their respective articles, "Some Optimization Problems in Advertising Media," (*Journal of the Operational Research Society*, 1960) and "An Explanation of Linear Programming in Media Selection," (*Journal of Marketing*

Research, 1966) you can develop a linear Solver model that can be used to allocate a TV advertising budget among network TV shows to ensure that a company's ads are seen enough times by each demographic group.

Assume Honda has decided it wants its June 2014 TV ads to be seen at least this many times by the following demographic groups:

- 100 million women 18–30
- 90 million women 31–40
- 80 million women 41–50
- 70 million women more than 50
- 100 million men 18–30
- 90 million men 31–40
- 80 million men 41–50
- 70 million men more than 50

Honda can advertise on *Oprah, Jeopardy!*, the *Late Show with David Letterman, Notre Dame Football, Saturday Night Live, The Simpsons, Seinfeld, ER*, and *Monday Night Football (MNF)*. The costs and demographic information for each show are shown in Figure 35-1, and the file `Media data.xls` (see the `basic solver` worksheet). For example, a 30-second ad on *Oprah* costs $32,630 and reaches 6 percent of all women 18–30, and such. There are 20 million women 18–30, and so on.

	A	B	C	D	E	F	G	H	I	J	K
1											
2	Media Data										
3											
4			Total (millions)	20	23	22	40	20	23	21	36
5	Show	Ads	Cost/ 30 Seconds	W 18-30	W 31-40	W 41-50	W>50	M 18-30	M 31-40	M 41-50	M >50
6	Oprah	6	$ 32.63	0.06	0.06	0.06	0.05	0.02	0.01	0.01	0.02
7	Jeopardy!	0	$ 33.00	0.03	0.05	0.06	0.04	0.04	0.04	0.04	0.03
8	Letterman	0	$ 47.50	0.05	0.06	0.06	0.05	0.04	0.04	0.04	0.04
9	ND Football	0	$ 27.50	0.01	0.02	0.01	0.01	0.04	0.04	0.04	0.05
10	SNL	0	$ 31.50	0.03	0.03	0.04	0.05	0.04	0.02	0.03	0.04
11	Simpsons	0	$ 56.00	0.05	0.07	0.08	0.08	0.08	0.09	0.09	0.09
12	Seinfield	0	$ 233.75	0.27	0.25	0.26	0.22	0.2	0.18	0.19	0.3
13	ER	14	$ 199.00	0.28	0.35	0.29	0.27	0.22	0.19	0.19	0.2
14	MNF	12	$ 85.00	0.06	0.07	0.07	0.08	0.15	0.14	0.15	0.14
15			Exposures	100	140.3	115.72	201.6	100	101.2	94.92	165.6
16				>=	>=	>=	>=	>=	>=	>=	>=
17			Goals	100	90	80	70	100	90	80	70
18		Cost									
19			4001.75								

Figure 35-1: Honda's media allocation

An exposure to a group occurs when a member of the group sees an ad. Honda's exposure goal for each age and gender group is given in Row 17. For example, one goal is to have your ads seen by at least 100 million women 18–30, and so on. These numbers are usually determined by either the firm's prior ad experiences or for a new product using the ad agency's prior experience.

Assuming Honda can place at most 20 ads on a given show, try and determine the cheapest way to meet its exposure goal. The following key assumptions will greatly simplify your analysis. The validity of these assumptions is discussed later in this section:

- **Assumption 1:** The cost of placing n ads on a show is n times the cost of placing a single ad. For example, the cost of five ads on *Jeopardy!* is 5 * $33,000 = $165,000.
- **Assumption 2:** If one ad on a show generates e exposures to a group, then n ads generates $n * e$ exposures to a group. For example, one ad on *Jeopardy!* will be seen by 20 * (0.03) = 0.60 million 18–30-year-old women. This assumption implies that 10 ads on *Jeopardy!* would generate 10 * (0.60) = 6 million exposures to 18–30-year-old women.
- **Assumption 3:** The number of ads placed on each show must be an integer.

To find the cost-minimizing number of ads, proceed as follows:

1. Enter a trial number of ads on each show in range B6:B14.
2. In cell B19 compute the total cost of ads with the formula =SUMPRODUCT (B6:B14,C6:C14). This formula follows from Assumption 1.
3. Compute the total number in each demographic group seeing the ads by copying the formula =D4*SUMPRODUCT($B$6:$B$14,D6:D14) from D15 to D15:K15. This formula follows from Assumption 2.
4. The Solver window used to minimize the total cost of meeting exposure goals is shown in Figure 35-2.

The target cell (cell B19) equals the cost of placing the ads. The changing cells (B6:B14) are the number of ads on each show. The number of ads on each show must be an integer between 0 and 20. To ensure that the ads generate the wanted number of exposures for each group, add the constraints D15:K15 >= D17:K17.

Solver finds the minimum cost is $4,001,750 and is obtained with 6 *Oprah* ads, 14 *ER* ads and 12 *MNF* ads.

NOTE The assumption that the number of purchased ads must be an integer can be dropped in many cases. For example, suppose you allow the number of ads placed on a show to be fractional and Solver tells Honda to place 14.5 ads on *ER*. Then Honda could place 14 ads one month on *ER* and 15 the next month, or perhaps place 14 ads in one-half of the United States and 15 ads in the other half of the United States. If the number of ads is allowed to be a fraction then you can simply delete the integer constraints and the model will easily find a solution with possibly fractional changing cell values.

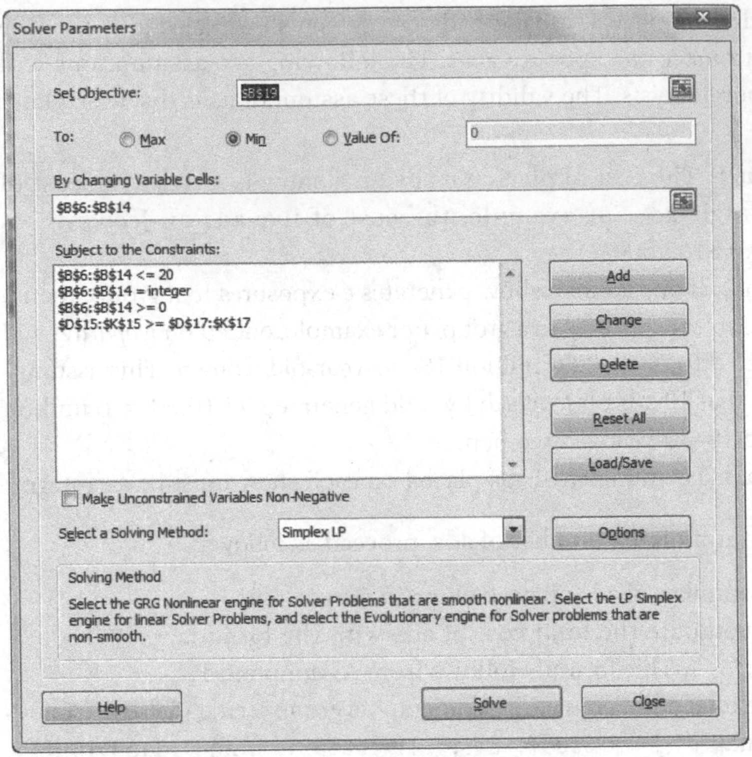

Figure 35-2: Solver window for Honda's media allocation

Quantity Discounts

There is a common advertising incentive that the preceding analysis doesn't take into account, however; Honda will probably receive a *quantity discount* if it places many ads on a given show. For example, Honda might receive a 10-percent reduction on the price of a *Jeopardy!* ad if it places five or more ads on *Jeopardy!* The presence of such quantity discounts causes the previous Solver model to be nonlinear and requires the use of Evolutionary Solver. To illustrate this, suppose that you are given the quantity discount schedule shown in Figure 35-3 (see also the QD worksheet).

For example, 1 ad on *Oprah* costs $32,000, but 10 ads cost $170,000 (much less than 10 times the cost of a single ad). The goal is still to obtain the wanted number of exposures at a minimum cost. You can assume a maximum of 10 ads can be placed on each show. Recall from the discussion of the Evolutionary Solver in Chapters 5 and 6 that constraints other than bounds on changing cells (such as exposures created by *ads ≥ exposures* needed) should be handled using penalties. You will see that incorporating this idea is an important aspect of the model. You can proceed by using a lookup table to "look up" the ad costs and then use `IF` statements to evaluate the amount by which you fail to meet each goal. The target cell then minimizes the sum of costs and penalties. The work proceeds as follows:

1. Copy the formula =`IF(B6=0,0,VLOOKUP(A6,lookup,B6+1,FALSE))` from C6 to C7:C14 to compute the cost of the ads on each show.

2. Copy the formula =`IF(D15>D17,0,D17-D15)` from D18 to E18:K18 to compute the amount by which you fall short of each exposure goal.

3. Assign a cost of 1,000 units (equivalent to $1,000,000) for each 1 million exposures by which you fail to meet a goal. Recall from Chapter 5 that the Evolutionary Solver does not handle non-linear constraints well, so you incorporate non-linear constraints by including in the target cell a large penalty for violation of a constraint.

4. In cell C19 compute the total penalties with the formula =`1000*SUM(D18:K18)`.

5. In cell C21 add together the ad costs and constraint penalties to obtain the target cell =`B19+C19`.

	A	B	C	D	E	F	G	H	I	J	K	L
2	Media Data											
3												
4			Total (millions)	20	23	22	40	20	23	21	36	
5	Show	Ads	Cost	W 18-30	W 31-40	W 41-50	W>50	M 18-30	M 31-40	M 41-50	M >50	
6	Oprah	10 $	170.00	0.06	0.06	0.06	0.05	0.02	0.01	0.01	0.02	
7	Jeopardy!	10 $	190.00	0.03	0.05	0.06	0.04	0.04	0.04	0.04	0.03	
8	Letterman	10 $	250.00	0.05	0.06	0.06	0.05	0.04	0.04	0.04	0.04	
9	ND Football	0 $	-	0.01	0.02	0.01	0.01	0.04	0.04	0.04	0.05	
10	SNL	8 $	181.00	0.03	0.03	0.04	0.05	0.04	0.02	0.03	0.04	
11	Simpsons	0 $	-	0.05	0.07	0.08	0.08	0.08	0.09	0.09	0.09	
12	Seinfield	0 $	-	0.27	0.25	0.26	0.22	0.2	0.18	0.19	0.3	
13	ER	10 $	1,683.33	0.28	0.35	0.29	0.27	0.22	0.19	0.19	0.2	
14	MNF	10 $	595.00	0.06	0.07	0.07	0.08	0.15	0.14	0.15	0.14	
15			Exposures	100.8	141.22	125.84	212	100.4	100.28	95.34	166.32	
16				>=	>=	>=	>=	>=	>=	>=	>=	
17			Goals	100	90	80	70	100	90	60	70	
18		Cost	Penalty	0	0	0	0	0	0	0	0	
19		$ 3,069.33	0									
20		Target										
21		$ 3,069.33	1	2	3	4	5	6	7	8	9	10
22		Oprah	$ 32.00	60	85	110	120	130	140	150	160	170
23		Jeopardy!	$ 33.00	60	80	100	115	130	145	160	175	190
24		Letterman	$ 47.00	85	110	130	150	170	190	210	230	250
25		ND Football	$ 28.00	50	70	90	110	130	150	170	190	210
26		SNL	$ 32.00	58	80	101	121	141	161	181	201	221
27		Simpsons	$ 56.00	106	151	191	231	271	311	351	391	431
28		Seinfield	$ 233.00	440	620	790	950	1116.667	1281.667	1446.667	1611.667	1776.667
29		ER	$ 199.00	380	560	730	880	1043.333	1203.333	1363.333	1523.333	1683.333
30		MNF	$ 85.00	150	210	265	320	375	430	485	540	595

Figure 35-3: Honda Quantity Discount model

The Solver window shown in Figure 35-4 can find the ads Honda should purchase to minimize the cost of obtaining the wanted number of exposures. The Evolutionary Solver is needed due to the use of `IF` statements.

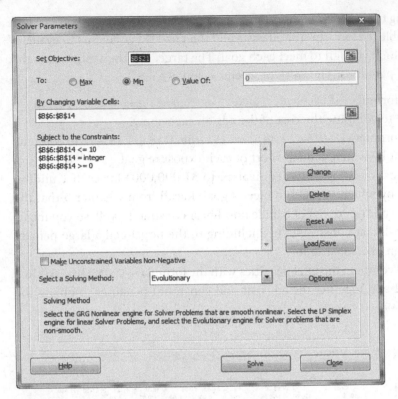

Figure 35-4: Solver window for quantity discounts

As explained in Chapters 5 and 6, the Evolutionary Solver performs better if the mutation rate is increased to 0.5. To increase the mutation rate to 0.5, select Options from the main Solver window and then choose Evolutionary Solver. Now you can adjust the mutation rate to the desired value of 0.5. A larger mutation rate reduces the change that the Solver will get stuck in a "bad" portion of the feasible region.

After setting the Solver mutation rate to 0.5, you find that the minimum cost of $3,069,000 is obtained by placing 10 ads on *Oprah, Jeopardy, Letterman, ER,* and *MNF,* and 8 ads on *SNL.*

A Monte Carlo Media Allocation Simulation

There are two other issues that the linear formulation model doesn't account for:

- First, Honda's goal of a wanted number of exposures for each demographic group is in all likelihood a surrogate for the wanted number of people in each group that Honda would like to see its ads. The problem with this idea is that the same person may see both an *Oprah* and *ER* ad (probably a woman) or an *ER* and *MNF* ad (probably a man). Without knowledge of the overlap or duplication between viewers of different shows, it is difficult to convert exposures into the number of people seeing a Honda ad.

■ Additionally, for any product there is a benefit-response curve that gives the benefit obtained from a person seeing any number of ads for the product. For example, in his book *Marketing Analytics*, (Admiral Press, 2013) Stephen Sorger states that for many products, marketers assume no benefit is obtained unless a person sees a product's ad at least three times, and additional ads do not generate any benefit to the advertiser. If this is the case, the benefit response curve for the product would look like Figure 35-5. (Chapter 32, "Allocating Retail Space and Sales Resources" discusses one method that can be used to estimate the benefit response curve.) Therefore, if Honda gains no benefit when a person sees its ad less than three times, the linear formulation does not enable Honda to determine a media allocation that minimizes the cost of obtaining a wanted benefit from the ads.

To combat these issues, you can use Palisade's RISKOptimizer package (a 15-day trial version can be downloaded at `www.Palisade.com`) to perform a Monte Carlo simulation that will enable Honda to minimize the cost of obtaining the desired benefit from ads. In doing so, assume your goal is to have at least one-half of all people see your ads at least three times. The work for this analysis is shown in Figure 35-6 (see the `ro model` worksheet.)

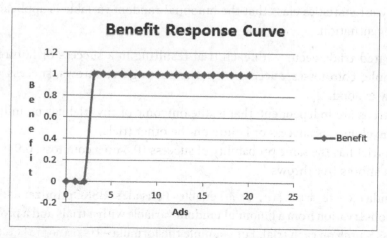

Figure 35-5: Ad response curve

	Type	1		2	3	4	5	6	7	8
	Total (millions)	20		23	22	40	20	23	21	36
Show	Loyalty	Ads	Cost/30 Seconds	W 18-30	W 31-40	W 41-50	W>50	M 18-30	M 31-40	M 41-50	M >50
Oprah	0.3	1	$ 32.63	0.2		0.2	0.2	0.16667	0.06667	0.03333	0.03333	0.06667
Jeopardy!	0.6	5	$ 33.00	0.05	0.083333333	0.1	0.06667	0.06667	0.06667	0.06667	0.05
Letterman	0.2	0	$ 47.50	0.25		0.3	0.3	0.25	0.2	0.2	0.2
ND Football	0.5	5	$ 27.50	0.02		0.04	0.02	0.02	0.08	0.08	0.08
SNL	0.3	0	$ 31.50	0.1		0.1	0.13333	0.16667	0.13333	0.06667	0.1	0.13333
Simpsons	0.6	5	$ 56.00	0.083333	0.116666667	0.13333	0.13333	0.13333	0.15	0.15	0.15
Seinfeld	0.8	1	$ 233.75	0.3375	0.3125	0.325	0.275	0.25	0.225	0.2375	0.375
ER	0.75	5	$ 199.00	0.373333	0.466666667	0.38667	0.36	0.29333	0.25333	0.25333	0.26667
MNF	0.5	5	$ 85.00	0.12		0.14	0.14	0.16	0.3	0.28	0.3	0.28

Customer Type	8			
	Watch Show?	Ads	Number Ads Seen	Cost
4 Oprah	0	1	0	2268.88
5 Jeopardy!	0	5	0	
6 Letterman	0	0	0	
7 ND Football	1	5	3	2268.875
8 SNL	0	0	0	
9 Simpsons	0	5	0	
10 Seinfeld	0	1	0	
11 ER	0	5	0	
12 MNF	0	5	0	
	Total Ads	3		
	>=3	1		

Figure 35-6: RiskOptimizer model for media selection

To develop this model you need to look at the demographics of each show in a different way. Referring to Figure 35-6, you can see that you are given the fraction of each group that views each show as well as the fraction of the time a viewer of a show tunes in (called *loyalty*). For example, 20 percent of women 18–30 are *Oprah* viewers, but on average an *Oprah* viewer watches only 30 percent of all *Oprah* shows. This implies, of course, that on a typical day only 6 percent of all women 18–30 watch *Oprah*, and this matches your previous assumption. Using this model you can randomly generate a customer and generate the number of ads seen by said customer. This approach requires some knowledge of the *binomial random variable*. You may recall from your statistics class that the binomial random variable is applicable in the following situation:

- Repeated trials occur with each trial resulting in a success or failure (for example, coin tosses, success = heads; shooting free throws, success = free throw is good.
- The trials are independent; that is, the outcome of any trial has no influence on the chance of success or failure on the other trials.
- Each trial has the same probability of success (0.5 on a coin toss, 0.9 if Steve Nash shoots free throws.)

The formula =RiskBinomial(n, prob) enables Palisade's RISKOptimizer add-in to generate an observation from a binomial random variable with *n* trials and a probability of success = *prob* on each trial. For example the formula =RiskBinomial(100,.5) generates the number of heads that would occur if a coin is tossed 100 times.

For any set of ads placed by Honda, you can now use RISKOptimizer to generate, say, 1,000 randomly chosen customers, and for each customer simulate the number of times the customer sees the ads. RISKOptimizer can determine if for that set of ads at least one-half of the customers see the ads at least three times. Then Evolutionary algorithms are used to adjust the number of ads to minimize the cost of the ads, subject to the constraint that at least one-half of the people see the ad at least three times. The following steps generate a random customer and her viewing patterns.

1. To begin, generate the customer type. This can be generated as a discrete random variable. For example, because there are 205 million total people, there is a 20 / 205 = 0.098 chance that a generated customer is a woman between 18 and 30.

2. For each show, determine if the generated customer sees the show by using a binomial random variable with one trial and probability of success equal to the chance that a person of the given customer type sees the show. For example, if the generated customer is a woman between 18 and 30 there is a 20-percent chance she watches Oprah.

3. Assuming the generated customer watches a show, again use a binomial random variable to determine the number of times the customer sees the ads. For example, if you placed three ads on *Oprah* and the generated customer was an 18–30-year-old woman, the number of times the woman sees the *Oprah* ads follows a binomial random variable with three trials and 0.3 chance of success.

4. In cell E16 compute a person's randomly chosen customer type with the formula =RiskDiscrete(F3:M3,F4:M4). This formula assigns a customer type from the values in the range F4:M4 with the probability of each customer type occurring being proportional to the frequencies given in the range F4:M4. Note the "probabilities" do not add up to 1, but RiskOptimizer will normalize the weights so they become probabilities. Therefore, there is a 20/205 chance the generated customer is an 18–30-year-old-woman, a 23/205 chance the generated customer is a 31–40-year-old woman, and so on.

5. Copy the formula =RiskBinomial(1,HLOOKUP($E$16,showproblook,C18, FALSE)) from E18 to E19:E26 to determine for each show if the customer is a loyal viewer. Note the customer type keys the column where you look up the probability that the customer watches the show. For the iteration shown in Figure 35-6, the simulated customer was a male >50 , so in E20 RiskOptimizer would use a 0.20 chance to determine if this customer was a *Late Show* viewer.

6. Copy the formula =IF(OR(E18=0,F18=0),0,RiskBinomial(F18,VLOOKUP(D1 8,$B$6:$C$14,2,FALSE))) from G18 to G19:G26 to simulate for each show the number of ads the viewer sees. F18 is the number of ads Honda has placed on the show. If the viewer does not view the show or 0 ads are placed, then, of course, she does not see any ads from that show. Otherwise, the lookup function in Row 18 looks up the probability that the viewer sees a particular episode of *Oprah* and uses the binomial random variable (number of trials = number of ads, probability of success = probability that a loyal viewer sees an ad on a show) to simulate the number of *Oprah* show ads seen by the viewer. For example, if E19 equals 1, the selected customer would be a male >50 *Jeopardy!* viewer and RiskOptimizer would use a binomial random variable with $n = 5$ and *prob* = 0.05 to simulate the number of times the simulated customer saw *Jeopardy!* ads.

7. In cell G29 compute the total number of ads seen by the customer with the formula =SUM(G18:G26).

8. In cell G32 give a reward of 1 if and only if a viewer saw at least three ads with the formula =IF(G29>=3,1,0).

9. In cell I18 compute the total cost of ads with the formula =SUMPRODUCT(E6:E14,D6:D14).

You can now use the RISKOptimizer to determine the minimum cost ad strategy that ensures that at least 50 percent of all people see at least three of the ads. The RISKOptimizer window is shown in Figure 35-7.

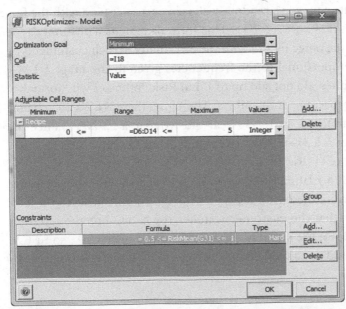

Figure 35-7: RiskOptimizer settings for media selection

The goal is to minimize the value of the total cost (computed in I18). Assume at most five ads could be placed on each show, and you constrain the mean of G31 to be at least 0.5. This ensures that at least one-half of all people see the ads >= 3 times.

RISKOptimizer runs through different ad plans a given number of times (the example uses 1,000 iterations) and stops when it has minimized the cost of a schedule for which at least 0.5 * (1000) = 500 of the generated customers see at least three Honda ads. A minimum cost of $2,268,000 is obtained by placing the following ads:

- Five ads on *Jeopardy!*, *Notre Dame Football*, *MNF*, *ER*, and *The Simpsons*
- One ad on *Seinfeld* and *Oprah*

The key to the Monte Carlo media allocation approach is the fact that you can obtain for any number of *n* exposures the probability that a person will see your ads *n* times. If you know the benefit the product receives from a person seeing the ads *n* times you then can develop an accurate estimate of the benefit created by a product's advertising. This enables the firm or ad agency to make better media allocation decisions.

Summary

In this chapter you learned the following:

- If you assume the cost of placing *n* ads on a given media outlet is *n* times the cost of placing a single ad and *n* ads generates *n* * *e* exposures to a group (where *e* = exposures generated by one ad), then a linear Solver model can be used to generate an optimal media allocation.
- If you assume that for each customer the benefit gained from an ad depends on how many times the customer sees the ad, then the Monte Carlo simulation is needed to determine an optimal media allocation.

Exercises

1. Suppose Honda believes it obtains equal benefit from an exposure to each group. What media allocation minimizes the cost of obtaining at least 100 million exposures?
2. Suppose Honda believes the benefit from an exposure to a woman is twice the benefit from an exposure to a man. Given a budget of $5 million, where should Honda advertise?

3. Drugco is trying to determine how to advertise in the leading medical journals. The Medicaldata.xlsx file (see Figure 35-8) contains the number of annual exposures to each kind of doctor Drugco wants to generate. Drugco knows the cost of a one-page ad in each journal and how many doctors of each type subscribe to each journal. For example, a one-page ad in *American Family Physician (AFP)* costs $19,699, and there are 80,601 family practitioners who subscribe to *AFP*. Assume that each journal is published 12 times a year and Drugco can place at most two ads in each issue of a journal. How can Drugco minimize the cost of obtaining the wanted number of exposures?

	C	D	E	F	G	H	I
1		cost/ad	$ 6,630	$ 19,699	$ 9,505	$ 6,029	$ 9,048
2	exposure goals		American Academy Ortho Surg	Am Family Physician	Am Journal of Anesthesiol ogy	American Journal of Orthopedics	Anesthesiol ogy
3	9362038.156	FPs	-	80,601	-	-	-
4	1746192	GPs	-	13,430	-	-	-
5	8813580	IMs	-	47,811	-	-	-
6	196908	DO's	-	-	1,390	-	-
7	881664	Orthoped	-	-	-	22,830	-
8	1392794.772	Oncol	-	-	-	-	-
9	1241076	Anesthes	-	102	23,351	-	38,000
10	270111.6523	Neuros	-	-	-	-	-
11	164819.0684	Geriatrics	-	100	-	-	-
12	131310	Rheum	-	-	-	2,862	-
13	0	PT's	-	-	-	-	-
14	38400	NP/PA	-	-	-	-	-
15	143654.3272	Residents	-	-	3,380	-	-
16	1030778.773	Cards	-	31	-	-	-
17	7573939.285	Others	26,000	35,395	16,433	2,297	211

Figure 35-8: Medical journal data

4. Suppose Honda believes that for each demographic group the benefit obtained from any customer who sees n ads is n^5. Given an ad budget of $5 million, what media allocation maximizes the benefits from Honda's ads?

5. How might you estimate the monetary value of the benefits Honda would gain from a TV campaign advertising a summer clearance sale?

36

Pay per Click (PPC) Online Advertising

Online advertising is big business. In fact, in 2012 Google alone generated $44 billion in revenue from online advertising. The vast majority of online ad revenue comes from Pay per Click (PPC) advertising in which advertisers pay only when an Internet user clicks through to the advertisers' website. Online advertising revenues are still growing quickly (around 20 percent per year), so it is important to understand how analytics can help advertisers optimize their profits from PPC advertising. The chapter begins by showing how an advertiser can determine if PPC advertising is likely to be profitable. Then it explains how Google runs an auction for ad slots based on a keyword search. Finally, this chapter discusses how advertisers can use Google's Bid Simulator tool to optimize their bid on a keyword.

Defining Pay per Click Advertising

Internet users who want to purchase a product often search the Internet for information on the product. In addition to showing search results, search engines also show paid ads relevant to the users' search. Companies such as Yahoo and Google can, of course, charge advertisers to have their ads appear when users conduct a search. For example, Figure 36-1 shows the results when the author searched for swim goggles. You can see ads appear in both the top search results and on the right side of the page. Following are some common questions pertaining to these ads that a marketing analyst would benefit from asking:

- How does Google determine which ads for goggles appear and who gets each spot on the page?
- How much should advertisers pay for each spot on the results page?
- Advertisers can purchase certain keywords, and their ads appear when a user searches for those keywords. On which keywords should advertisers bid?

- How can Google provide a good experience for both searchers and advertisers and still maximize its profits from search-related ads?

Figure 36-1: Search results for swim goggles

Before 2002, most Internet advertisers paid search engine providers such as Google or Yahoo based on the number of impressions. An impression occurs whenever a company's ad is displayed after a search. When advertisers pay based on the number of impressions, they may find after paying Google that nobody clicked through to their webpage! For obvious reasons, advertisers did not like this method of charging for ads. The website `Basketball-reference.com` provides a great example of impression advertising. There is a webpage for each NBA player (past and present) containing the player's career statistics. On each webpage is a price for which an advertiser can sponsor the page and post ads on the page. For example, the price of sponsoring the LeBron James page is $1,915, whereas the price of sponsoring the Carmelo Anthony webpage is $415. In this situation the price difference probably reflects the fact that the LeBron James webpage is viewed 1,915 / 415 = 4.6 times as often the Carmelo Anthony webpage. In a different situation the relative price of sponsoring a webpage might depend on the attractiveness to the advertiser of the demographics of the webpage viewers as well as the number of times the webpage is viewed.

When a search engine provider charges based on PPC, the advertisers know that they are charged only when a searcher clicks through to their website. Because click-throughs should lead to sales, advertisers know they are getting some value for their payments. The first instance of PPC advertising was developed in 1996 by a division of Packard Bell NEC Corporation. Beginning in 2002, the AdWords system was used for PPC advertising. From that point on PPC advertising took off.

Profitability Model for PPC Advertising

To estimate monthly profitability of PPC advertising, estimates of the following quantities are needed:

- **Estimated Cost per Click:** This is the cost the advertiser must pay for each click. Assume a $1 cost per click.
- **Estimated Clicks per Day:** This is simply the daily number of clicks to their site expected by the advertiser. Assume your ads will generate 10 clicks per day. If you sign up for Google AdWords, Google's Bid Simulator feature (discussed in the "Using Bid Simulator to Optimize Your Bid" section of this chapter) gives you an estimate of the number of clicks per day that can be obtained for a given cost per click.
- **Conversion Rate:** This is the fraction of clicks that results in a sale. The conversion rate can easily be estimated from historical data. Assume a conversion rate of 5 percent.
- **Average Profit per Sale:** This can easily be estimated from historical data. Assume an average profit per sale of $10.00. Assume a 30-day month.

You can see these calculations in action with the following example. The Simple Model worksheet in the Costperclickoptimization.xlsx workbook (see Figure 36-2) shows the calculations needed to determine if PPC advertising can help your company's bottom line.

	D	E
9	Cost per Click	1
10	Clicks per Day	10
11	Conversion Rate	0.05
12	Profit per Sale	$10.00
13	Days per Month	30
14		
15	Conversions per Month	15
16	Profit	$150.00
17	Click Costs	$300.00
18	Total Monthly Profit	-$150.00

Figure 36-2: Profitability analysis for PPC advertising

In the cell range E15:E18, you can use some simple calculations to compute the estimated profit per month from PPC advertising.

1. In E15 compute conversions per month by multiplying the conversion rate by the number of clicks per month. The exact formula is `=Conversion_Rate*Clicks_per_day*Days_per_Month`.

> **NOTE** Multiplying the units of these three quantities yields units of (conversions / click) * (clicks / day) * (days / month) = (conversions / month), as desired.

2. In cell E16 compute the monthly profit by multiplying the expected profit per conversion times the monthly number of conversions. The exact formula is `=Conversions_per_Month*Profit_per_sale`.

3. In cell E17 compute the monthly click costs by multiplying the cost per click times the number of monthly clicks. The exact formula is `=Clicks_per_day*Days_per_Month*Cost_per_click`.

4. In cell E18 compute the monthly profit with the formula `=Profit-Click_Costs`.

Given the assumptions, monthly profit for PPC advertising is -$150.00, so it does not appear that PPC ads would be profitable. A click-through to your webpage might, however, create a new customer who may repeatedly purchase your product. In this case the profit per sale should be replaced by a larger number: the lifetime value of the customer. (See Chapters 19–22 for a discussion of customer value.) Therefore incorporation of the concept of customer value might justify the use of advertising.

An advertiser can use a few simple calculations to determine whether PPC advertising will be profitable. Because you break even if profit per click equals 0, clicks per month do not impact a break-even calculation. Equation 1 provides the key to break-even analysis.

(1) Profit Per Click = (Conversion Rate) * (Profit Per Sale) - (Cost Per Click)
Rearranging Equation 1 you can find you will break even if:
(2) Conversion Rate = (Cost per Click) / (Profit Per Sale)
(3) Cost Per Click = (Profit per sale) * (Conversion Rate)

Substituting your assumptions into Equation 2, you can find the break-even conversion rate to be 1 / 10 = 10%. From Equation 3 you can find the break-even Cost Per Click = ($100) * (0.05) = $0.50. Therefore, you can break even by either doubling the conversion rate or cutting the cost per click in half.

Google AdWords Auction

Google uses the bids and quality scores of advertisers to rank advertisers through their popular tool, Google AdWords. Google's AdWords auction matches up online advertising slots with online advertisers.

Considering the discussion of online ad auctions from well-known economics professor turned Google's chief economist, Hal Varian's, elegant paper "Online Ad Auctions," (*American Economic Review*, 2009, pp.1-6), suppose that N advertisers bid on the same keyword, and advertiser i bids an amount bi as the maximum per click price he is willing to pay. Also assume there are S ad slots available for the keyword. At first glance you would think that Google would rank bidders simply on their bids with the highest bidder getting the top slot, the second highest bidder the second slot, and so on. The problem with this approach is that the top slot might go to a company bidding a lot, but that company could have a terrible ad that nobody clicks on. This would upset searchers who wasted their time reading the poor ad, and because nobody clicked through, Google would earn no money for the valuable top slot. Therefore, Google assigns each bidder a quality score (q_i = quality score for bidder i). A bidder's quality score (a value between 1 and 10, with 10 indicating the highest quality and 1 the lowest quality) is mostly determined by Google's estimate of the ad's click-through rate. *Click-through rate = clicks through to webpage / (total times an ad appears)*. The quality score also includes factors such as Google's evaluation of the quality of the ad, relevance of the ad to the keyword, quality of the advertiser's webpage (often referred to as the landing page), and relevance of the landing page to the keyword. The bidders are now ranked by the product of their bid and quality score ($b_i q_i$). With this information Google can rank-order bidders, for instance, if there are say five slots, and you rank sixth, your ad does not appear!

Determining what an Advertiser Pays Per Click

You might intuitively believe that an advertiser's Cost per Click would be determined by that same advertiser's bid and quality score. Surprisingly, the amount Google charges an advertiser per click is actually determined by the bid and quality score of the advertiser in the ad position immediately below said advertiser. The intuition behind this result will be discussed later in this section.

The following discussion ignores the possibility of ties. Assume that M advertisers bid on S slots. After ranking the bidders based on $b_i q_i$, an advertiser pays the minimum amount needed to maintain her position. If there are fewer bidders than slots, the last bidder pays a reserve price or minimum bid r that is set by Google. If you define p_i = price paid by the ith ranked bidder, then for $i < M$ $p_i q_i = b_{i+1} q_{i+1}$. Rearranging this equation, the price paid by the ith ranked bidder is:

$$(4)\ p_i = b_{i+1} q_{i+1} / q_i$$

If $M < S$ the last advertiser pays the minimum bid, whereas if $M = S$, the bid for the last advertiser is calculated from the bid of the first omitted advertiser.

NOTE   In Equation 4 the advertiser's Cost per Click does depend on the bid and quality score of the next lower ranked advertiser.

This type of auction is known as a *Generalized Second Price Auction* (*GSP*). To see why, note that if all ads have the same quality score, the GSP reduces to each bidder paying the amount bid by the next highest bidder.

From Google's point of view two problems arise with an auction in which all bidders pay the amount they bid for each click (called a first price auction):

- There is no incentive for a bid to equal the advertiser's view of the true value of a click. For example, if Bidder 1 believes a click is worth $1.00 and Bidder 2 believes a click is worth $0.80, and the bidders know this, then Bidder 1 could bid $0.81 and Bidder 2 could bid the minimum acceptable amount. Then Bidder 1 wins the first position by not bidding her true value.

- If bids can be adjusted frequently, then in a first price auction over time, bidding will be unstable. For example, Suppose Bidder 1 values a click at $0.80 and Bidder 2 values a click at $1.00. Suppose Bidder 1 bids her true value of $0.80. Then Bidder 2 would bid $0.81 and win the top spot. Then the first bidder would lower his bid to the reservation bid (say $0.05.) This keeps Bidder 1 in the second spot. Now Bidder 2 will lower his bid to $0.06 and maintain the spot. This unstable behavior would not be satisfactory to Google!

In practice the GSP auction resolves these problems for Google, although the resolution of these problems is accomplished at the expense of the bidders.

Auction Examples

To illustrate how AdWords auctions work, look at the two concrete examples of auctions shown in Figure 36-3. In the first example, there are three bidders for three slots. Each bidder placed a $4 bid, so the bidders will be ranked by their Quality scores. Therefore, Bidder 1 gets the first slot, Bidder 2 gets the second slot, and Bidder 3 gets the third slot. Bidder 1 will pay the minimum amount needed to maintain her position. Because the second bidder has quality * bid = 24 and Bidder 1 has a Quality of 8, a bid by Bidder 1 of 24 / 8 = $3 would maintain her position and she is charged $3.00. Similarly for Bidder 2 to maintain her position, she needs 6 * Bidder 2 cost = $12, so Bidder 2 is charged $2.00. Bidder 3 pays the minimum bid.

	G	H	I	J	K	L	M
1							
2							
3							
4		3 slots					
5							
6	Bidder	Bid	Quality Score	Bid*Quality score	Actual Payment per Click	Slot won	
7	1	$4.00	8	32.00	$3.00	1	
8	2	$4.00	6	24.00	$2.00	2	
9	3	$4.00	3	12.00	Minimum Bid	3	
10							
11		3 slots					
12	Bidder	Bid	Quality Score	Bid*Quality score	Actual Payment per Click	Slot won	
13	1	$4.00	1	4		none	
14	2	$3.00	3	9	$2.67	2	
15	3	$2.00	6	12	$1.50	1	
16	4	$1.00	8	8	$0.50	3	

Figure 36-3: AdWords auction examples

In the second example four bidders compete for three slots. Bidder 3 placed the third highest bid, but Bidder 3's high-quality score enables her to win the top spot. Because the second place in the auction goes to Bidder 2 (with bid * quality = 9), Bidder 3 must pay 9 / 6 = $1.50 per click. In a similar fashion Bidder 2 pays 8 / 3 = $2.67 per click, and Bidder 4 pays 4 / 8 = $0.50 per click. Bidder 1 bid the most per click, but her low-quality score causes her to rank fourth in the auction. Because there are only three slots, Bidder 1 is shut out and wins no ad placement.

Using Bid Simulator to Optimize Your Bid

After you sign up for Google AdWords you gain access to the Bid Simulator feature. If you input a keyword and a given bid per click, the Bid Simulator feature can estimate for bids near (and lower than) your bid how many clicks you will receive for lower bids. This can help the advertiser determine a profit maximizing bid. To illustrate the idea, suppose you sell digital cameras and earn a profit of $100 per camera sale and you expect a 5-percent conversion rate on click-throughs. This implies that you can expect an average profit of 0.05 * (100) = $5 per click, and the most you should ever bid is $5. Suppose you input this information into Google's Bid Simulator tool and receive the information shown in Figure 36-4. (See worksheet BIDSIM of workbook Costperclickoptimization.xlsx; the data comes from Hal Varian's excellent video on AdWords at www.youtube.com/watch?v=jRx7AMb6rZO.)

	D	E	F	G	H	I
1	Click through rate	0.05				
2	Profit per sale	$100.00				
3	Max Bid	Clicks	Cost per click	Profit from Sales	Click Costs	Profit
4	$5.00	208	$3.36	$1,040.00	$698.88	$341.12
5	$4.50	190	$3.13	$950.00	$594.70	$355.30
6	$4.00	154	$2.64	$770.00	$406.56	$363.44
7	$3.50	133	$2.33	$665.00	$309.89	$355.11
8	$3.00	113	$2.04	$565.00	$230.52	$334.48

Figure 36-4: Bid Simulator example

You can find, for example, that reducing your max bid from $5 to $4.50 is estimated to cost you 18 clicks, and the expected cost per click would be $3.13. For each bid you can compute the expected profit as:

(Profit per Sale) * (Click-through rate) * (Clicks) – (Cost per click) * (Clicks)

- For example, for a $4 bid, expect to earn: ($100) * (0.05) * 154 – ($2.64) * 154 = $363.44.

From Figure 36-4, you can find that for the listed bids, a bid of $4 would maximize your expected profit.

Summary

In this chapter you learned the following:

- Profit per click may be computed by:

  (1) Profit Per Click = (Conversion Rate) * (Profit Per Sale) – (Cost Per Click)

- You will break even on each click if:

  (2) Conversion Rate = (Cost per Click) / (Profit Per Sale)

  or

  (3) Cost Per Click = (Profit per sale) * (Conversion Rate)

- Essentially, Google AdWords ranks ads based on (Amount Bid) * (Quality Score). A bidder pays just enough to retain his current ranking.
- Using Google's Bid Simulator tool an advertiser can estimate a profit maximizing bid.

Exercises

1. Suppose you are considering purchasing placement on search results for the keywords swim goggles. You earn a $2 profit per sale of swim goggles. Give several combinations of conversion rates and bid per clicks that enable you to break even.
2. Describe the results of an auction with three slots for the following data. Assume a minimum bid of $0.10.

Bidder	Maximum Bid	Quality Score
1	$2	2
2	$1.5	4
3	$1	5

3. Describe the results of an auction with three slots for the following data. Assume a minimum bid of $0.10.

Bidder	Maximum Bid	Quality Score
1	$2	2
2	$1.5	4
3	$1	5
4	$1	2

X Marketing Research Tools

Chapter 37: Principal Component Analysis (PCA)

Chapter 38: Multidimensional Scaling (MDS)

Chapter 39: Classification Algorithms: Naive Bayes
Classifier and Discriminant Analysis

Chapter 40: Analysis of Variance: One-way ANOVA

Chapter 41: Analysis of Variance: Two-way ANOVA

37

Principal Components Analysis (PCA)

Often the marketing analyst has a data set involving many variables. For example, people might be asked to rate on a 1–5 scale the importance of 50 car characteristics, such as color, fuel economy, type of engine, and so on. *Principle components analysis* (PCA) is used to find a few easily interpreted variables that summarize most of the variation in the original data. As an example, this chapter describes how to use the Excel Solver to perform principal components analysis using the U.S. city demographic data that you studied in Chapter 23, "Cluster Analysis." You'll first learn how to compute the variance of a linear combination of variables and the covariance between two linear combinations of variables, and then learn how PCA works.

Defining PCA

When you come across data sets with large amounts of variables, it can get overwhelming quickly. For instance, consider the following data sets:

- Daily returns for the last 20 years on all 30 stocks in the Dow Jones Index
- 100 measures of intelligence for a sample of 1,000 high school students
- Each athlete's score in each of the 10 events for competitors in the 2012 Olympic decathlon

These data sets contain a lot of variables, making the data difficult to understand! However, you can construct a few easily interpreted factors to help you understand the nature of the variability inherent in the original data set. For example:

- Daily stock returns might be summarized by a component reflecting the overall stock index, a component reflecting movement in the financial sector, and a component reflecting movement in the manufacturing sector.

■ Intelligence might be summarized by a verbal and mathematical component.
■ Ability in the decathlon might be summarized by a speed factor, a distance running factor, and a strength factor.

These factors are usually referred to as principal components; therefore an analysis of these factors is a principal component analysis, or PCA.

Linear Combinations, Variances, and Covariances

Before you can fully understand PCA, you should review some basic statistical concepts. In your review use the data in the `Varcov.xlsx` file (see Figure 37-1). In this file 20 people were asked to rate on a 1–5 scale (5 = highly important and 1 = not important) the role that fuel economy, engine horsepower, and price played in their purchase decision. In what follows you can assume that if you have n data points involving two variables X and Y, the data points are labeled (x_1, y_1), $(x2, y_2), \ldots (x_n, y_n)$.

	J	K	L
9	Fuel Economy	Horsepower	Price
10	5	1	3
11	5	2	1
12	3	3	2
13	3	3	4
14	1	5	5
15	1	5	2
16	4	3	4
17	2	4	3
18	1	4	4

Figure 37-1: Auto attribute data

Sample Variance and Standard Deviation

The *sample variance* for X S_X^2 is defined by Equation 1:

$$(1)\ S_X^2 = \frac{1}{n-1}\sum_{i=1}^{i=n}(x_i - \bar{x})^2$$

Here $\bar{x}$ is the sample mean or average of the x values.

The sample standard deviation of X (S_X) is simply the square root of the sample variance. Both the sample variance and sample standard deviation measure the spread of the variable X about its mean.

Create From Selection is used to name Columns J:L. In cell G4 (see Figure 37-2) the formula =VAR(Fuel_Economy) computes the variance (2.16) of the fuel economy ratings. Analogous formulas in G5 and G6 compute the variance for the horse-power and price ratings. In cell H4 the formula =STDEV(Fuel_Economy) computes the standard deviation (1.47) of the fuel economy ratings. Analogous formulas in H5 and H6 compute the standard deviation of the horsepower and price ratings. Of course, the standard deviation of any variable can be computed as the square root of the variance.

	F	G	H	I	J	K
2						
3		Sample Variances	Sample Standard Deviations		Sample Covariance	Correlations
4	FE	2.155263158	1.46808145	FE HP	-1.784210526	-0.939418666
5	HP	1.673684211	1.29370948	FE PR	-0.315789474	-0.144677052
6	PR	2.210526316	1.48678388	HP PR	0.210526316	0.109451517
7						
8						
9		correl FE HP	-0.93941867		Fuel Economy	Horsepower

Figure 37-2: Sample variances and standard deviations

Sample Covariance

Given two variables X and Y, the *sample covariance* between X and Y, written (S_{xy}), is a unit-dependent measure of the linear association of X and Y. The sample covariance is computed by Equation 2:

$$(2) \quad S_{XY} = \frac{\frac{1}{n-1}\sum_{i=1}^{i=n}(x_i - \bar{x})^2(y_i - \bar{y})}{S_X S_Y}$$

If when X is larger (or smaller) than average Y tends to be larger (or smaller) than average, then X and Y will have a positive covariance. If when X is larger (or smaller) than average Y tends to be smaller (or smaller) than average, then X and Y will have a negative covariance. In short, the sign of the covariance between X and Y will match the sign of the best-fitting line used to predict Y from X (or X from Y.) In cell J4 we computed the sample covariance (–1.78) between the FE and HP ratings with the formula =COVARIANCE.S(Fuel_Economy,Horse_Power). The .S after the word COVARIANCE ensures that you divide by $(n-1)$ and not n when computing the covariance. Analogous formulas in J5 and J6 compute the covariance between FE and PR and HP and PR.

Sample Correlations

The sample covariance is difficult to interpret because it is unit-dependent. For example, suppose that when X and Y are measured in dollars the sample covariance is \$5,000^2. If X and Y are measured in cents, then the sample covariance would equal 50,000,000¢^{2}. The sample correlation (r_0) is a unit-free measure of the linear association between X and Y. The sample correlation is computed via Equation 3:

(3) $r_{XY} = \bar{x}$

The sample correlation may be interpreted as follows:

- A sample correlation near $+1$ means there is a strong positive linear relationship between X and Y; that is, X and Y tend to go up or down together.
- A sample correlation near -1 means there is a strong negative linear relationship between X and Y; that is, when X is larger than average, Y tends to be smaller than average, and when X is smaller than average, Y tends to be larger than average.
- A sample correlation near 0 means there is a weak linear relationship between X and Y; that is, knowledge that X is larger or smaller than average tells you little about the value of Y.

Cells K4:K6 computed the relevant sample correlations for the data. In cell K4 the formula =CORREL(Fuel_Economy,Horse_Power) computes the correlation between FE and HP (-0.94). This correlation indicates that there is a strong negative linear relationship between the importance of FE and HP in evaluating a car. In other words, a person who thinks fuel economy is important is likely not to think horsepower is important. Analogous formulas in H5 and H6 show that there is virtually no linear relationship between HP and PR or FE and PR. In short, how a person feels about the importance of price tells little about how the person feels about the importance of fuel economy and horsepower.

Standardization, Covariance, and Correlation

In the study of PCA you will be standardizing the data. Recall from Chapter 23 that a *standardized value* of x for the ith observation (call it z_i) is defined by Equation 4.

(4) $Z_i = \dfrac{x_i - \bar{x}}{S_X}$

After computing the mean for each of the variables in the cell range P5:P7, you can standardize each of the variables (see Figure 37-3). For example, copying the formula =(J10-$P$5)/$H$4 from O10 to the range O11:O29 standardizes the FE ratings. You find that the first person's FE rating was 1.4 standard deviations above average. Because any standardized variable has a mean of 0 and a standard deviation of 1, standardization makes the units or magnitude of the data irrelevant.

	O	P	Q	R
4				
5	mean FE	2.95		
6	mean HP	3.1		
7	mean PR	3	covar z FE z FP	-0.93942
8				
9	z FE	z HP	z PR	
10	1.396380285	-1.62324	0	
11	1.396380285	-0.85027	-1.345185418	
12	0.034058056	-0.0773	-0.672592709	
13	0.034058056	-0.0773	0.672592709	
14	-1.328264173	1.468645	1.345185418	
15	-1.328264173	1.468645	-0.672592709	
16	0.71521917	-0.0773	0.672592709	
17	-0.647103059	0.695674	0	
18	-1.328264173	0.695674	0.672592709	

Figure 37-3: Standardized importance ratings

For the study of PCA, you need to know that after the data is standardized the sample covariance between any pair of standardized variables is the same as the correlation between the original variables. To illustrate this idea, use in cell R7 the formula =COVARIANCE.S(O10:O29,P10:P29) to compute the covariance between the standardized FE and HP variables. You should obtain −0.9394, which equals the correlation between FE and HP.

Matrices, Matrix Multiplication, and Matrix Transposes

A matrix is simply an array of numbers. An *mxn* matrix contains *m* rows and *n* columns of numbers. For example:

$\begin{bmatrix} 2 & 3 \\ 3 & 4 \\ 5 & 6 \end{bmatrix}$ is a 2x3 matrix, [1 2] is a 1x2 matrix, and $\begin{bmatrix} 3 \\ 1 \end{bmatrix}$ is a 2x1 matrix.

An *mxr* matrix A can be multiplied by an *rxn* matrix B yielding an *mxn* matrix whose *i–j* entry is obtained by multiplying the *i*th row of A (entry by entry) times the *j*th column of B. For example, if A = [1 2 3] and B = $\begin{bmatrix} 2 & 3 & 0 \\ 0 & 1 & 2 \\ 3 & 0 & 1 \end{bmatrix}$ then AB = [11 5 7]. For example, the second entry in AB is computed as 1 * 3 + 2 * 1 + 3 * 0 = 5.

The transpose of an *mxn* matrix A is written as A^T. The i–j entry in A^T is the entry in row j and column i of A. For example, if A = $\begin{bmatrix} 1 & 2 \\ 3 & 4 \\ 5 & 6 \end{bmatrix}$ then $A^T = \begin{bmatrix} 1 & 2 & 5 \\ 2 & 4 & 6 \end{bmatrix}$

Matrix Multiplication and Transpose in Excel

The workbook `Matrixmult.xlsx` shows how to multiply and transpose matrices in Excel. Matrices are multiplied in Excel using the `MMULT` function. `MMULT` is an array formula (see Chapter 3, "Using Excel Functions to Summarize Marketing Data"), so before using `MMULT` to multiply matrices A and B, you must select a range of cells having the same size as the product matrix AB. As shown in Figure 37-4, to compute AB complete the following steps:

1. Select the range F15:H15.
2. Array enter in cell F15 (by selecting Control+Shift+Enter) the formula `=MMULT(B7:D7,G6:I8)`.
3. To compute A^T select the range E18:E20 and array enter in cell E18 the formula `=TRANSPOSE(B7:D7)`.

	A	B	C	D	E	F	G	H	I	J
1										
2										
3										
4										
5										
6							2	3	0	
7	A	1	2	3		B	0	1	2	
8							3	0	1	
9										
10										
11										
12										
13										
14										
15					AB	11	5	7		
16										
17										
18					1					
19				A^T	2					
20					3					

Figure 37-4: Matrix multiplication and transpose

Computing Variances and Covariances of Linear Combinations of Variables

A linear combination of n variables $X_1, X_2, ..., X_n$ is simply $c_1X_1 + c_2X_2 + ..., c_nX_n$, where $c_1, c_2, ..., c_n$ are arbitrary constants. Figure 37-5 shows the linear combinations 2FE - HP and PR + 2HP. For example, for the first observation 2FE - HP = $2(5) - 1 = 9$ and PR + 2HP = $3 + (2)(1) = 5$.

	J	K	L	M	N
2					
3	Sample Covariance	Correlations		Direct	Check
4	-1.784210526	-0.939418666	var(2FE-HP)	17.4316	17.4316
5	-0.315789474	-0.144677052	cov (2FE-HP,PR+2HP)	-11.3263	-11.3263
6	0.210526316	0.109451517			
7			stdev (2FE-HP)	4.17511	
8			stdev(PR+2HP)	3.12208	
9	Fuel Economy	Horsepower	Price	2FE-HP	PR+2HP
10	5	1	3	9	5
11	5	2	1	8	5
12	3	3	2	3	8
13	3	3	4	3	10

Figure 37-5: Computing 2FE – HP and PR + 2HP

Assuming you have n variables, you can define two linear combinations by the vectors (a vector is a matrix with one row or one column) C_1 and C_2.

$$C_1 = [c_{11}, c_{12}, ..., c_{1n}]$$
$$C_2 = [c_{21}, c_{22}, ..., c_{2n}]$$

In the study of PCA you need to calculate the variance of a linear combination of the form $LC_1 = c_{11}X_1 + c_{12}X_2 + ..., c_{1n}X_n$. If you define the sample covariance matrix S for the variables $X_1, X_2, ..., X_n$ to be the $n \times n$ matrix whose ith diagonal entry is the sample variance of X_i and for i not equal to j, the i–jth entry of S is the sample covariance of X_i and X_j. It can be shown that the sample variance of LC_1 is given by Equation 5.

(5) Sample Variance of $LC_1 = C_1 S\ C_1^T$.

Here C_1^T is the transpose of C1. To illustrate the use of Equation 5, compute the sample variance for 2FE-HP. In the following situation, C1 = [2 -1 0] and

$$C_1^T = \begin{bmatrix} 2 \\ -1 \\ 0 \end{bmatrix}$$

$$S = \begin{bmatrix} 2.155 & -1.784 & -.316 \\ -1.784 & 1.674 & .211 \\ -.316 & .211 & 2.210 \end{bmatrix}$$

Cell N4 uses Equation 4 to compute the variance of 2FE-HP (17.43). If you array enter into cell N4 the formula =MMULT(_c1,MMULT(covar,TRANSPOSE(_c1))) you compute the variance of 2FE-HP. In cell M4 the variance of 2FE-HP is directly computed with the formula =VAR(M10:M29). Of course, the direct approach also yields a variance of 17.43.

NOTE The range _c1 corresponds to the matrix [2 –1 0] and the range _c2 corresponds to the matrix [0 2 1].

In the study of PCA you also need to find the sample covariance between two linear combinations of variables: $LC_1 = c_{11}X_1 + c_{12}X_2 + \dots c_{1n}X_n$ and $LC_2 = c_{21}X_1 + c_{22}X_2 + \dots c_{2n}X_n$. It can be shown that the following equation is true:

(6) Sample covariance of LC_1 and $LC_2 = C_1 S\ C_2^T$.

You can illustrate the use of Equation 6 by following these steps:

1. Compute the sample covariance between 2FE - HP and PR + 2HP. Here C_1 = [2 – 1 0] and C_2 = [0 2 1].

2. In cell N5 compute the sample covariance between 2FE – HP and PR + 2HP (–11.236) by array entering the formula =MMULT(_c1,MMULT(covar,TRANSPOSE(_c2))).

3. In cell M5 the same result (-11.236) is obtained with the formula =COVARIANCE.S(M10:M29,N10:N29).

Diving into Principal Components Analysis

Suppose you have data involving n variables $X_1, X_2, \dots X_n$. Let S denote the sample covariance matrix for these variables and R denote the sample correlation matrix for these variables. Recall that R is simply the sample covariance matrix for the standardized variables. In the analysis you can determine principal components based on R, not S. This ensures that the principal components remain unchanged when the units of measurement are changed. For more detail on PCA based on the sample covariance matrix, refer to the outstanding multivariate statistics text by Richard Johnson and Dean Wichern *Applied Multivariate Statistical Analysis* (Prentice-Hall, 2007.)

The basic idea behind PCA is to find n linear combinations (or principal components) of the n variables that have the following properties:

- The length of each principal component (sum of the squared coefficients) is normalized to 1.
- Each pair of principal components has 0 sample covariance. Two linear combinations of variables that have 0 sample covariance are referred to as *orthogonal*. The orthogonality of the principal components ensures that the principal components will represent different aspects of the variability in the data.
- The sum of the variances of the principal components equals n, the number of variables. Because each of the standardized variables has a variance of 1, this means the principal components decompose the total variance of the n standardized variables. If principal components are created from a sample covariance matrix, then the sum of the variances of the principal components will equal the sum of the sample variances of the n variables.
- Given the previous restrictions, the first principal component is chosen to have the maximum possible variance. After determining the first principal component, you choose the second principal component to be the maximum variance linear combination of unit length that is orthogonal to the first principle component. You continue choosing for $i = 3, \ldots . 4, n$ the ith principal component to be the maximum variance linear combination that is orthogonal to the first $i{-}1$ principal components.

You can use the cluster analysis data from Chapter 23 (the `clusterfactors.xlsx` file) to illustrate the computation of principal components. Recall that for each of 49 U.S. cities we had the following six pieces of demographic information:

- Percentage of blacks
- Percentage of Hispanics
- Percentage of Asians
- Median age
- Unemployment rate
- Median per capita income (000s)

The actual data is in the `cluster` worksheet of workbook `clusterfactors.xlsx`. The sample correlations between the demographic measures will be used to perform a PCA. To obtain the sample correlations you need the Data Analysis add-in. (See Chapter 9, "Simple Linear Regression and Correlation," for instructions on how to install the Data Analysis add-in.) To obtain the sample correlations, select Data Analysis from the Data tab, and after choosing Correlation from the Analysis dialog, fill in the dialog box, as shown in Figure 37-6.

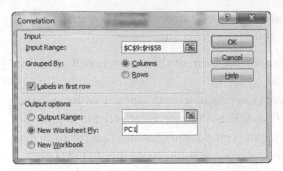

Figure 37-6: Correlation settings for demographic data for PCA

After obtaining the partial correlation matrix shown in cell range A1:G7 of Figure 37–7, select A1:G7, choose Paste Special Transpose and paste the results to the cell range A10:G16. Copy A10:G16. From the Paste Special menu, select Skip Blanks and paste back to B2:G7 to completely fill in the correlation matrix.

	A	B	C	D	E	F	G	H
1		z Black	z Hispanic	z Asian	z Age	z Unemp	z income	
2	z Black	1						
3	z Hispanic	-0.40387	1					
4	z Asian	-0.31675	0.00032	1				
5	z Age	0.01042	-0.22078	0.37294	1			
6	z Unemp	0.307912	0.341241	-0.00072	-0.00729	1		
7	z income	0.125713	-0.298	0.374026	0.480487	0.014133	1	
8	**Then Paste Special Skip Blanks back to B2:G7 to obtain complete correlation matrix**							
9	**Paste Special Transpose to A10:G16**							
10		z Black	z Hispanic	z Asian	z Age	z Unemp	z income	
11	z Black	1	-0.40387	-0.31675	0.01042	0.307912	0.125713	
12	z Hispanic		1	0.00032	-0.22078	0.341241	-0.298	
13	z Asian			1	0.37294	-0.00072	0.374026	
14	z Age				1	-0.00729	0.480487	
15	z Unemp					1	0.014133	
16	z income						1	

Figure 37-7: Filling in Correlation Matrix

Finding the First Principal Component

In the PC 1 worksheet (see Figure 37-8) you can find the first principal component. To do so, complete the following steps:

1. In the cell range B1:G1, enter trial values for the first principal component's weights.

2. In cell B11 compute the length of the first principal component with the formula =SUMPRODUCT(B1:G1,B1:G1).

3. Using Equation 5, the variance of the first principal component is computed in cell B10 with the array entered formula =MMULT(B1:G1,MMULT(B3:G8,TRANSPOSE(B1:G1))).

4. Use the Solver window, as shown in Figure 37-9, to determine the first principal component.

5. Maximize the variance of PC1 subject to the constraint that the length of PC1 equals 1. Use the GRG Multistart Engine, so bounds on the changing cells are required. Because the length of PC1 equals 1, each coefficient in PC must be less than 1 in absolute value, so that provides the needed bounds.

	A	B	C	D	E	F	G
1	PC1	0.06767	-0.38495424	0.429365811	0.557219731	-0.113526417	0.582663759
2		%age Black	%age Hispanic	%age Asian	Median Age	Unemployment rate	r capita income(000's
3	%age Black	1	-0.40387146	-0.31674911	0.01042016	0.307911604	0.12571318
4	%age Hispanic	-0.40387	1	0.00031961	-0.22077588	0.341240839	-0.297997244
5	%age Asian	-0.31675	0.00031961	1	0.372940122	-0.000723651	0.374025581
6	Median Age	0.01042	-0.22077588	0.372940122	1	-0.007288223	0.480486669
7	Unemployment rate	0.30791	0.341240839	-0.00072365	-0.007288223	1	0.014132872
8	Per capita income(000's)	0.12571	-0.29799724	0.374025581	0.480486669	0.014132872	1
9							
10	var	1.94344					
11	length	1					

Figure 37-8: Computing first principal component

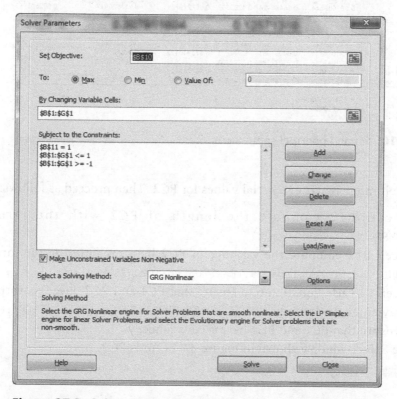

Figure 37-9: Solver window for first principal component

The goal is to pick a unit length linear combination of maximum variance. The first principal component is listed in the range B1:G1 of worksheet PC1. You find that:

$$PC1 = 0.07z_{Black} - 0.38z_{Hispanic} + 0.43z_{Asian} + 0.56z_{Median\ Age} - 0.11z_{UnRate} + 0.58z_{Income}$$

The coefficient of a variable on a principal component is often referred to as the *loading* of the variable on the principal component. Median Age, Income, and Asian load most heavily on PC1.

PC1 explains 1.93/6 = 32 percent of the total variance in the standardized data. To interpret PC1 look at the coefficients of the standardized variables that are largest in absolute value. This shows you that PC1 can be interpreted as an older, Asian, high-income component (similar to the SF cluster from Chapter 23).

Finding the Second Principal Component

In the PC 2 worksheet you can find the second principal component (see Figure 37-10.)

	A	B	C	D	E	F	G
1	PC 1	0.067669844	-0.38495424	0.4293658	0.557219731	-0.113526417	0.582663759
2	PC 2	0.729964737	-0.475718433	-0.4666851	-0.078588497	0.122252451	0.043898661
3		%age Black	%age Hispanic	%age Asian	Median Age	Unemployment rate	Per capita income(000's)
4	%age Black	1	-0.403871459	-0.3167491	0.01042016	0.307911604	0.12571318
5	%age Hispanic	-0.40387146	1	0.0003196	-0.22077588	0.341240839	-0.297997244
6	%age Asian	-0.31674911	0.00031961	1	0.372940122	-0.000723651	0.374025581
7	Median Age	0.01042016	-0.22077588	0.3729401	1	-0.007288223	0.480486669
8	Unemployment rate	0.307911604	0.341240839	-0.0007237	-0.007288223	1	0.014132872
9	Per capita income(000's)	0.12571318	-0.297997244	0.3740256	0.480486669	0.014132872	1
10							
11	var	1.523601193					
12	length	1.00000					
13	cov PC 1 PC 2	1.4386E-12					

Figure 37-10: Second principal component

In the cell range B2:G2 enter trial values for PC2. Then proceed as follows:

1. In cell B12 compute the length of PC2 with the formula =SUMPRODUCT(B2:G2,B2:G2).

2. In cell B11 compute the variance of PC2 by array entering the formula =MMULT(B2:G2,MMULT(B4:G9,TRANSPOSE(B2:G2))).

3. In cell B13 use Equation 6 to ensure that PC1 and PC2 have 0 covariance. Array enter the formula =MMULT(B2:G2,MMULT(B4:G9,TRANSPOSE(B1:G1))) to ensure that PC1 and PC2 have 0 covariance.

4. The Solver window shown in Figure 37-11 finds PC2.

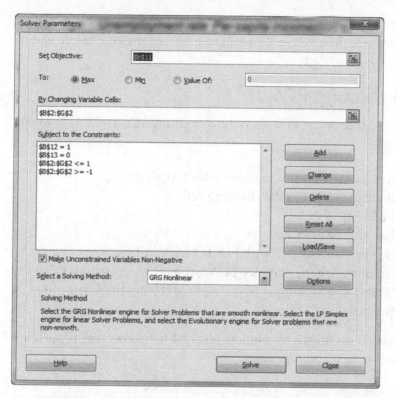

Figure 37-11: Solver window for second principal component

5. Maximize the variance of PC2 subject to the constraint that the length of PC2 = 1 and PC2 has 0 covariance with PC1. Solver tells you that PC2 is given by the following:

$$PC2 = 0.73z_{Black} - 0.48z_{Hispanic} - 0.47z_{Asian} - 0.08z_{Median\ Age} - 0.12z_{UnRate} + 0.04_{Income}$$

The first three coefficients of PC2 are large in magnitude, and the last three are small in magnitude. Ignoring the last three coefficients, you can interpret PC2 as a highly black, non-Hispanic, non-Asian factor. This corresponds to the Memphis cluster in Chapter 23. PC2 explains 1.52/6 = 25% of the variance in the data. Together PC1 and PC2 explain 32% + 25% = 57% of the variation in our data.

Each principal component will explain a lower percentage of variance than the preceding principal components. To see why this must be true, suppose the statement were not true and a principal component (say PC2 = the second principal component) explained more variation than a prior principal component (say

PC1 = the first principal component). This cannot be the case because if PC2 explained more variance than PC1, Solver would have chosen PC2 before choosing PC1!

Finding PC3 through PC6

Worksheets `PC 3-PC 6` compute PC3–PC6. In computing PCi (i = 3, 4, 5, 6) you can proceed as follows:

1. Copy the worksheet `PCi-1` to a new worksheet. (Call it `PCi`.)
2. Set the coefficients for PCi as the changing cells.
3. Compute the length of PCi.
4. Compute the variance of PCi.
5. Compute the covariance of PCi with PCi-1, PCi-2, … PC1.
6. Use Solver to minimize the variance of PCi subject to a constraint that the length of PCi = 1 and all sample covariances involving the first i principal components equal 0.

Figure 37-12 lists all six principal components, and the percentage of variance is explained by each principal component.

	A	B	C	D	E	F	G	H
1		Blacks	Hispanics	Asians	Median Age	Unemployment rate	Per capita income	variance
2	PC 1	0.068	-0.385	0.429	0.557	-0.114	0.583	32.4%
3	PC 2	0.730	-0.476	-0.467	-0.079	0.122	0.044	25.4%
4	PC 3	0.237	0.420	0.151	0.145	0.835	0.162	21.0%
5	PC 4	-0.127	-0.033	-0.326	0.785	0.073	-0.504	9.2%
6	PC 5	-0.175	0.365	-0.639	0.073	-0.154	0.632	8.1%
7	PC 6	0.608	0.561	0.224	0.105	-0.501	-0.063	4.1%

Figure 37-12: Final principal components

How Many Principal Components Should Be Retained?

If you have n variables, then n principal components explain all the variance in the data. The goal in performing the PCA was to explain the data with fewer than n variables. To determine the number of PCs to retain, plot the variance explained by each factor, as shown in Figure 37-13.

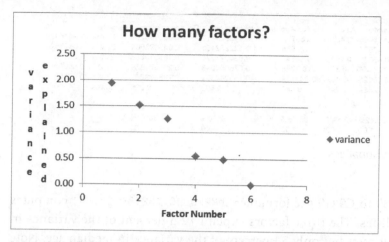

Figure 37-13: Variance explained by each Principal Component

From Figure 37-13 it is clear there is a break point or elbow in the curve at the fourth PC. This indicates that after the third PC the PCs have little explanatory power, so you should keep only three factors. Note that the first three principal components explain 78 percent of the variance in the data.

In some cases there is no obvious break point. In short, the "explained variance" on the Y-axis is also referred to as an *eigenvalue*, and typically eigenvalues smaller than 1 indicate a principal component that explains less variance than an average principal component. For example, with six principal components the average principal component will explain a variance equaling $(1/6) * 6 = 1$.

Communalities

Given that you use $p<n$ principal components (in this case p = 3), the marketing analyst would like to know what percentage of the variance in each variable is explained by the p factors. The portion of the variance of the ith variable explained by the principal components is called the ith *communality*. The ith communality is simply the sum of the squares of the loading of variable i on each of the first p components. In the Communalities worksheet (see Figure 37-14) calculate the communalities for three principal components. For example, the Communality for Percentage of Blacks if you keep the first three principal components = $(0.067)^2$ + $(0.730)2 + (0.237)2 = 59.34\%$.

	A	B	C	D	E	F	G	H	I
1		Blacks	Hispanics	Asians	Median Age	Unemployment rate	Per capita income	variance	
2	PC 1	0.06767	-0.38495	0.4294	0.55722	-0.113526417	0.582663759	32.4%	1.94344
3	PC 2	0.72996	-0.47572	-0.467	-0.078588	0.122252451	0.043898661	25.4%	1.5236
4	PC 3	0.2365	0.42033	0.1509	0.14549	0.834977224	0.162019856	21.0%	1.26022
5	PC 4	-0.0997	0.21346	-0.543	0.7756	-0.076064046	-0.204571659	9.2%	0.55038
6	PC 5	-0.1541	0.30123	-0.469	-0.241779	-0.130284904	0.768063867	7.9%	0.47566
7	PC 6	0.611	0.559	0.245	0.042	-0.502	-0.020	0.0%	0
8									
9	Communality 3 Factors	59.34%	55.12%	42.49%	33.78%	72.50%	36.77%		
10	Totals	1.00	1.00	1.00	1.00	1.00	1.00		

Figure 37-14: Communalities

Copying from B9 to C9:G9 the formula =SUMPRODUCT(B2:B4,B2:B4) computes the six communalities. The three factors explain 72.5 percent of the variance in city unemployment rates but only 34 percent of the variance in median age. Note that most of the variance in median age is explained by PC4.

Other Applications of PCA

Donald Lehman, Sunil Gupta, and Joel Steckel (*Marketing Research*, Prenctice-Hall, 1997) provide an excellent application of PCA. Consumers were asked to rate on a 1–5 scale each of 10 car models on the following 15 attributes:

- Appeals to others
- Expensive looking
- Exciting
- Very reliable
- Well engineered
- Trend setting
- Has latest features
- Luxurious
- Distinctive looking
- Brand you can trust
- Conservative looking
- Family car
- Basic transportation
- High quality

Each row of data contains a consumer's 15 ratings on a given car. After using this data to compute a sample correlation matrix, a PCA was performed and the first three components explained 60 percent of the total variance. The first three factors were interpreted as the following:

- Trendy factor
- Quality and reliability factor
- Basic transportation and family friendly factor

Here you can see that PCA enables you to make sense of 15 diverse variables.

An additional application of PCA can be found in a 1988 study by A. Flood et al. from the *American Journal of Clinical Nutrition* that examined the eating habits of nearly 500,000 American adults. Using PCA they found three primary dietary factors:

- A fruit and vegetable factor
- A dietary food factor
- A red meat and potato factor

The authors found that people who scored high on the fruit and vegetable and dietary food factors and low on the red meat and potato factor were much less likely to get colon cancer than people who scored high on the red meat and potato factor and low on the fruit and vegetable and dietary food factors.

Summary

In this chapter you learned the following:

- You can use principal components to find a few easily interpreted variables that summarize the variation in many variables.
- This chapter assumed that all variables are standardized before the principal components are determined.
- The length of each principal component (sum of the squared coefficients) is normalized to 1.
- Each pair of principal components has 0 sample covariance. The sum of the variances of the principal components equals n, the number of variables. Because each of the standardized variables has a variance of 1, this means the principal components decompose the total variance of the n standardized variables.

■ Given the previous restrictions, the first principal component is chosen to have the maximum possible variance. After determining the first principal component, you chose the second principal component to be the maximum variance linear combination of unit length that is orthogonal to the first principle component. You continued choosing for $i = 3, \ldots 4, n$ the ith principal component to be the maximum variance linear combination that is orthogonal to the first $i-1$ principal component.

■ Each principal component is interpreted by looking at the component's largest loadings.

■ A plot of the variance explained by the principal components usually shows a break or elbow that indicates which principal components should be dropped.

■ The communality of the ith variable is the percentage of the ith variable's variability explained by the retained principal components.

Exercises

1. The file 2012 Summer Olympics.xlsx contains for 2012 Olympic decathletes their scores on all 10 events. Use this data to determine and interpret the first three principal components.

2. The correlations between weekly returns on JPMorgan, Citibank, Wells Fargo, Royal Dutch Shell, and ExxonMobil are given in file PCstocks.xlsx. Use this data to determine and interpret the first two principal components.

3. Interpret the fourth and fifth principal components in the U.S. cities example.

4. The file cereal.xls from Chapter 23 contains calories, protein, fat, sugar, sodium, fiber, carbs, sugar, and potassium content per ounce for 43 breakfast cereals. Determine the needed principal components and interpret them.

5. The file NewMBAdata.xlsx from Chapter 23 contains average undergrad GPA, average GMAT score, percentage acceptance rate, average starting salary, and out of state tuition and fees for 54 top MBA programs. Determine the needed principal components and interpret them.

38 Multidimensional Scaling (MDS)

Often a company wants to determine which industry brands are most similar and dissimilar to its own brand. To obtain this information a marketing analyst might ask potential customers to rate the similarity between different brands. *Multidimensional scaling (MDS)* enables you to transform similarity data into a one-, two-, or three-dimensional map, which preserves the ranking of the product similarities. From such a map a marketing analyst might find that, for example, Porsche and BMW are often rated as similar brands, whereas Porsche and Dodge are often rated as highly dissimilar brands. A chart generated by MDS in one or two dimensions can often be easily interpreted to tell you the one or two qualities that drive consumer preferences.

In this chapter you will learn how to collect similarity data and use multidimensional scaling to summarize product similarities in a one- or two-dimensional chart.

Similarity Data

Similarity data is simply data indicating how similar one item is to another item or how dissimilar one item is to another. This type of data is important in market research when introducing new products to ensure that the new item isn't too similar to something that already exists.

Suppose you work for a cereal company that wants to determine whether to introduce a new breakfast product. You don't know what product attributes drive consumer preferences. You might begin by asking potential customers to rank n existing breakfast products from most similar to least similar. For example, Post Bran Flakes and All Bran would be more similar than All Bran and Corn Pops. Because there are $n(n-1)/2$ ways to choose 2 products out of n, the product similarity rankings can range from 1 to $n(n-1)/2$. For example, if there are 10 products, the similarity rankings can range between 1 and 45 with a similarity ranking of 1 for the most similar products and a similarity ranking of 45 for the least similar products.

Similarity data is *ordinal data* and not *interval data*. Ordinal data is numerical data where the only use of the data is to provide a ranking. You have no way of knowing from similarities whether there is more difference between the products ranked 1 and 2 on similarity than the products ranked second and third, and so on. If the similarities are measured as interval data, the number associated with a pair of products reflects not only the ranking of the similarities, but also the magnitude of the differences in similarities. The discussion of MDS in this chapter will be limited to ordinal data. MDS based on ordinal data is known as nonmetric MDS.

MDS Analysis of U.S. City Distances

The idea behind MDS is to place products in a low (usually two) dimensional space so that products that are close together in this low-dimensional space correspond to the most similar products, and products that are furthest apart in the low-dimensional space correspond to the least similar products. MDS uses the Evolutionary Solver to locate the products under consideration in two dimensions in a way that is consistent with the product's similarity rankings. To exemplify this, you can apply MDS data to a data set based on the distances between 29 U.S. cities.

In the `matrixnba` worksheet of the `distancemds.xls` workbook you are given the distances between 29 U.S. cities based on the location of their NBA arenas (as shown in Figure 38-1). For reasons that will soon become clear the distance between a city and itself is set to be larger than any of the actual distances (for example, 100,000 miles). After ranking the distances between the cities (Brooklyn to New York is the shortest distance and Portland to Miami is the largest distance) you can locate each city in a two-dimensional space in a manner such that when the distances between each pair of cities in the two-dimensional space are ranked from smallest to largest, the ranks match, as closely as possible, to the rankings of the actual distances. Thus you would hope that in the two-dimensional space Brooklyn and New York would also be the closest pair of cities and Portland and Miami would be further apart than any other pair of cities. Before describing the process used to obtain the two-dimensional representation of the 29 cities, consider the OFFSET function, which is used in the approach to MDS.

OFFSET Function

The syntax of the OFFSET function is OFFSET(cellreference, rowsmoved, columnsmoved, height, width). Then the OFFSET function begins in the cell reference and moves the current location up or down based on rows moved. (*rowsmoved* = –2, for example, means move up 2 rows and *rowsmoved* = +3 means move down three rows.) Then, based on columns moved, the current location moves left or right (for example, *columnsmoved* = –2 means move 2 columns to the left and *rowsmoved* =+3 means move 3 columns to the right). The current cell location is now considered to be the upper-left corner of an array with number of rows = height and number of columns = width.

		Boston	Brooklyn	New York	Philadelphia	Washington	Toronto	Miami	Charlotte	Orlando
1	Boston	100000	190.5691	188.4525	273.4812	394.0321	430.2788	1255.3796	721.0678	1114.4964
2	Brooklyn	190.5691	100000	4.7776	82.9309	203.5415	344.4808	1087.3724	530.919	936.0813
3	New York	188.4525	4.7776	100000	85.3069	205.5803	340.8489	1091.3969	533.4217	939.7157
4	Philadelphia	273.4812	82.9309	85.3069	100000	120.9091	337.3232	1015.5591	448.1201	859.1819
5	Washington	394.0321	203.5415	205.5803	120.9091	100000	349.6821	922.4356	329.6312	756.0181
6	Toronto	430.2788	344.4808	340.8489	337.3232	349.6821	100000	1232.1383	585.9562	1046.7
7	Miami	1255.3796	1087.3724	1091.3969	1015.5591	922.4356	1232.1383	100000	651.7075	204.3463
8	Charlotte	721.0678	530.919	533.4217	448.1201	329.6312	585.9562	651.7075	100000	461.1162
9	Orlando	1114.4964	936.0813	939.7157	859.1819	756.0181	1046.7	204.3463	461.1162	100000
10	Cleveland	550.5289	406.4285	404.6595	359.3322	305.0689	189.287	1086.5083	434.9977	892.7242
11	Detroit	621.8399	498.9949	496.5655	462.0264	418.4346	205.971	1178.8073	531.3802	980.9449
12	Atlanta	936.7503	746.279	748.3021	663.5231	542.7399	733.4887	604.6091	226.7323	400.6274
13	Indiana	807.3053	646.7755	645.9692	583.9627	492.7929	440.7895	1023.5996	427.9271	819.5244
14	Chicago	852.8458	717.1072	715.2775	668.1119	598.0248	438.8869	1188.9912	589.2651	984.7548
15	Milwaukee	857.8858	736.5542	734.2535	695.286	636.9575	431.971	1267.7279	659.3097	1063.643
16	Memphis	1136.9348	956.1289	956.709	879.5221	764.8446	817.5461	871.8088	521.1129	681.9176

Figure 38-1: Distances between U.S. cities

Figure 38-2 (see the `Offsetexample.xls` file) illustrates the use of the `OFFSET` function. For example, the formula =SUM(OFFSET(B7,-1,1,2,1)) begins in B7 and moves the cell location B7 one row up to B6. From B6 the cell location moves one column to the right to cell C6. Cell C6 now becomes the upper-left corner of a cell range with 2 rows and 1 column. The cells in this range (C6:C7) add up to 8. You should verify that the formulas in B18 and H10 yield the results 24 and 39, respectively.

	A	B	C	D	E	F	G	H	I	J	K
3		Offset examples									
6		1	2	3	4			1	2	3	4
7		5	6	7	8			5	6	7	8
8		9	10	11	12			9	10	11	12
10	=SUM(OFFSET(B7,-1,1,2,1))	8					=SUM(OFFSET(H6,0,1,3,2))	39			
14		1	2	3	4						
15		5	6	7	8						
16		9	10	11	12						
18	=SUM(OFFSET(E16,-2,-3,2,3))	24									

Figure 38-2: Examples of OFFSET function

Setting up the MDS for Distances Data

The goal of MDS in the distances example is to determine the location of the cities in the two-dimensional space that best replicates the "similarities" of the cities. You begin by transforming the distances between the cities into similarity rankings so small similarity rankings correspond to close cities and large similarity rankings correspond to distant cities. Then the Evolutionary Solver is used to locate each city in two-dimensional space so that the rankings of the city distances in two dimensional space closely match the similarity rankings.

To perform the MDS on the distances data, proceed as follows:

1. In the range G3:H31 enter trial values for the x and y coordinates of each city in two-dimensional space. Arbitrarily restrict each city's x and y coordinate to be between 0 and 10.

2. Copy the formula =RANK(K3,distances,1) from K34 to the range K34:AM62 to compute the ranking of the distances between each pair of cities (see Figure 38-3). The last argument of 1 in this formula ensures that the smallest distance (New York to Brooklyn) receives a rank of 1, and so on. All diagonal entries in the RANK matrix contain 813 because you assigned a large distance to diagonal entries.

	J	K	L	M	N	O	P	Q	R	S	T	U
33		Boston	Brooklyn	New York	Philadelphia	Washington	Toronto	Miami	Charlotte	Orlando	Cleveland	Detroit
34	Boston	813	25	19	51	91	115	511	261	457	171	199
35	Brooklyn	25	813	1	7	27	73	439	157	357	97	143
36	New York	19	1	813	9	31	71	443	163	365	95	141
37	Philadelphia	51	7	9	813	13	67	407	127	313	83	131
38	Washington	91	27	31	13	813	75	347	61	277	55	101
39	Toronto	115	73	71	67	75	813	499	185	421	23	33
40	Miami	511	439	443	407	347	499	813	223	29	435	477
41	Charlotte	261	157	163	127	61	185	223	813	129	119	159
42	Orlando	457	357	365	313	277	421	29	129	813	335	385
43	Cleveland	171	97	95	83	55	23	435	119	335	813	11
44	Detroit	199	143	141	131	101	33	477	159	385	11	813

Figure 38-3: Ranking of distances between U.S. cities

3. Copy the formula =IF($I66=K$64,10000000,(OFFSET($G$2,$I66,0,1,1)-OFFSET($G$2,K$64,0,1,1))^2+(OFFSET($H$2,$I66,0,1,1)-OFFSET($H$2,K$64,0,1,1))^2) from K66 to the range K66:AM94 to compute for each pair of different cities the square of the two-dimensional distances between each pair of cities. The term OFFSET($G$2,$I66,0,1,1) in the formula pulls the x coordinate of the city in the current row; the term OFFSET($G$2,K$64,0,1,1) pulls the x coordinate of the city in the current column; the term OFFSET($G$2,$I66,0,1,1) in the formula pulls the y coordinate of the city in the current row; and the term OFFSET($H$2,K$64,0,1,1)

pulls the y coordinate of the city in the current column. For distances corresponding to the same city twice, assign a huge distance (say 10 million miles). A subset of the distances in two-dimensional space is shown in Figure 38-4.

		1	2	3	4	5	6	7	8	9	10	11
64	Two dim distances											
65		Boston	Brooklyn	New York	Philadelphia	Washington	Toronto	Miami	Charlotte	Orlando	Cleveland	Detroit
66	1 Boston	10000000.00	0.36	0.29	0.64	1.12	1.09	13.16	3.83	8.96	2.06	2.53
67	2 Brooklyn	0.36	10000000.00	0.00	0.04	0.24	0.70	9.29	1.86	5.77	0.99	1.55
68	3 New York	0.29	0.00	10000000.00	0.08	0.31	0.75	9.59	2.03	6.03	1.11	1.68
69	4 Philadelphia	0.64	0.04	0.08	10000000.00	0.08	0.64	8.21	1.33	4.88	0.70	1.26
70	5 Washington	1.12	0.24	0.31	0.08	10000000.00	0.56	7.23	0.83	4.03	0.37	0.86
71	6 Toronto	1.09	0.70	0.75	0.64	0.56	10000000.00	11.08	2.15	6.83	0.33	0.33
72	7 Miami	13.16	9.29	9.59	8.21	7.23	11.08	10000000.00	3.48	0.54	7.95	9.51
73	8 Charlotte	3.83	1.86	2.03	1.33	0.83	2.15	3.48	10000000.00	1.31	0.92	1.57
74	9 Orlando	8.96	5.77	6.03	4.88	4.03	6.83	0.54	1.31	10000000.00	4.38	5.53
75	10 Cleveland	2.06	0.99	1.11	0.70	0.37	0.33	7.95	0.92	4.38	10000000.00	0.12
76	11 Detroit	2.53	1.55	1.68	1.26	0.86	0.33	9.51	1.57	5.53	0.12	10000000.00

Figure 38-4: Two-dimensional distance between U.S. cities

4. Your strategy is to have Solver choose the two-dimensional locations of the cities so that the ranking of the distances in the two-dimensional space closely matches the actual rankings of the distances. To accomplish this goal compute the ranking of the distances in two-dimensional space. Copy the formula (see Figure 38-5) =RANK(K66,twoddistances,1) from K98 to K98:AM126 to compute the rankings of the distances in two-dimensional space. For example, for the two-dimensional locations in G3:H31, Brooklyn and New York are the closest pair of cities.

		Boston	Brooklyn	New York	Philadelphia	Washington	Toronto	Miami	Charlotte	Orlando	Cleveland	Detroit
95												
96	Two dim Ranks											
98	1 Boston	813	35	23	61	109	105	541	275	453	175	201
99	2 Brooklyn	35	813	1	3	19	65	459	161	349	99	139
.00	3 New York	23	1	813	7	25	69	469	171	357	107	151
.01	4 Philadelphia	61	3	7	813	9	59	435	123	313	67	117
.02	5 Washington	109	19	25	9	813	57	419	77	283	37	81
.03	6 Toronto	105	65	69	59	57	813	507	183	397	27	29
.04	7 Miami	541	459	469	435	419	507	813	249	55	431	467
.05	8 Charlotte	275	161	171	123	77	183	249	813	121	95	143
.06	9 Orlando	453	349	357	313	283	397	55	121	813	295	337
.07	10 Cleveland	175	99	107	67	37	27	431	95	295	813	11
.08	11 Detroit	201	139	151	117	81	29	467	143	337	11	813

Figure 38-5: Ranking of two-dimensional distance between U.S. cities

5. In cell C3 compute the correlation between the original similarity ranks and the two-dimensional ranks with the formula =CORREL(originalranks,twodranks). The range K34:AM62 is named originalranks and the range K98:AM126 is named twodranks.

6. Use the Evolutionary Solver to locate each city in two-dimensional space to maximize the correlation between the original ranks and the ranks in two dimensions. This should ensure that cities that are actually close together

will be close in two-dimensional space. Your Solver window is shown in Figure 38-6.

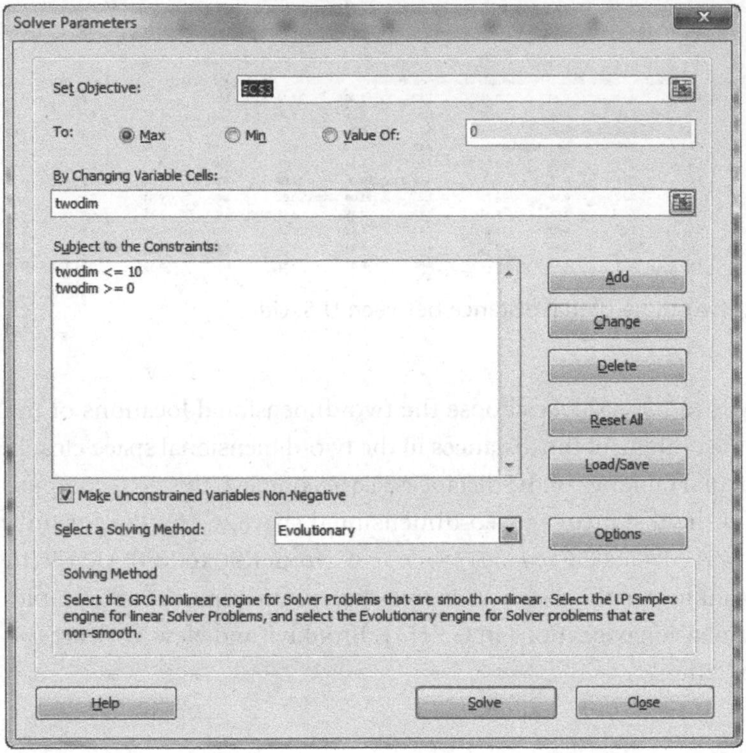

Figure 38-6: MDS Solver window cities

The Solver chooses for each city an *x* and *y* coordinate (changing cell range into two dimensions is the range G3:H31) to maximize the correlation between the original similarities and the two-dimensional distance ranks. You can arbitrarily constrain the *x* and *y* coordinates for each city to be between 0 and 10. The locations of each city in two-dimensional space are shown in Figure 38-7.

Referring to cell C3 of Figure 38-7, you can see that the correlation between the original similarity ranks and the two-dimensional ranks is an amazingly large 0.9964. Figure 38-8 shows a plot of the city locations in two-dimensional space.

	C	D	E	F	G	H
1						
2	correlation				x	y
3	0.99642503			BO	3.02156	6.06834
4				BR	3.42992	5.63438
5				NY	3.37078	5.65782
6				PH	3.61082	5.52417
7				WA	3.88457	5.45415
8				TOR	4.06012	6.18356
9				MIA	4.89088	2.95989
10				CHA	4.49651	4.78239
11				ORL	4.83969	3.68956
12				CLE	4.41958	5.74069
13				DET	4.61183	6.03101
14				ATL	5.09447	4.57926
15				IND	5.12666	5.6031
16				CHI	5.20529	6.02497
17				MIL	5.19449	6.26493
18				MEM	5.91683	5.06224
19				NOH	6.21345	4.21237
20				MIN	5.67844	6.789
21				HOU	7.04241	4.50546
22				DAL	6.99154	5.01395
23				OKC	7.00367	5.46442
24				SAN	7.59632	4.72501
25				DEN	7.52406	6.70751
26				UTA	7.8262	7.84002
27				PHO	8.77209	6.96438
28				LAL	9.22797	7.82297
29				SAC	8.73713	8.87982
30				GSW	9.08242	8.74384
31				POR	8.13335	9.22375

Figure 38-7: MDS Solver window cities

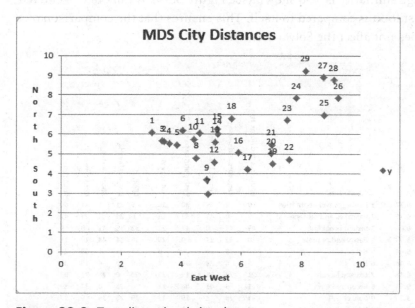

Figure 38-8: Two-dimensional city plot

The cities on the right side of the chart are West Coast cities and the cities on the left side of the chart are East Coast cities. Therefore, the horizontal axis can be interpreted as an East West factor. The cities on the top of the chart are northern cities, and the cities on the bottom of the chart are southern cities. Therefore, the vertical axis can be interpreted as a North South factor. This example shows how MDS can visually demonstrate the factors that determine the similarities and differences between cities or products. In the current example distances are replicated via the two obvious factors of east-west (longitude) and north-south (latitude) distances. In the next section you will identify the two factors that explain consumer preferences for breakfast foods. Unlike the distances example, the two key factors that distinguish breakfast foods will not be obvious, and MDS will help you derive the two factors that distinguish breakfast foods.

MDS Analysis of Breakfast Foods

Paul Green and Vithala Rao (*Applied Multidimensional Scaling*, Holt, Rinehart and Winston, 1972) wanted to determine the attributes that drive consumer's preferences for breakfast foods. Green and Rao chose the 10 breakfast foods shown on the MDS worksheet in the `breakfast.xls` workbook and asked 17 subjects to rate the similarities between each pair of breakfast foods with 1 = most similar and 45 = least similar. (There are 45 different ways to choose 2 foods out of 10.) The ranking of the average similarity is also shown (see Figure 38-9). A rank of 0 is entered when a breakfast food is compared to itself. This ensures that the comparison of a food to itself does not affect the Solver solution.

	B	C	D	E	F	G	H	I	J	K	L	M	N	O	P
1															
2	correlation														
3	0.9881479					1	2	3	4	5	6	7	8	9	10
4		x	y		Similarities	Ham eggs and home frie	Pancakes and sausage	Instant breakfast	Pastry and or toast	Hot cereal	Eggs	Lox and bagels	Bacon and eggs	Cold cereal	Fruit dish
5		6.71	9.77		1 Ham eggs and home fries	0	2	45	30	16	5	21	1	31	40
6		6.85	9.71		2 Pancakes and sausage	2	0	43	32	18	6	24	3	28	42
7		5.41	0.09		3 Instant breakfast	45	43	0	17	22	33	35	41	8	9
8		1.46	3.33		4 Pastry and or toast	30	32	17	0	25	38	14	44	10	15
9		7.14	5.84		5 Hot cereal	16	18	22	25	0	7	29	11	13	27
10		6.73	8.46		6 Eggs	5	6	33	38	7	0	20	4	19	36
11		1.00	8.38		7 Lox and bagels	21	24	35	14	29	20	0	26	23	37
12		7.37	9.51		8 Bacon and eggs	1	3	41	44	11	4	26	0	34	39
13		4.26	3.34		9 Cold cereal	31	28	8	10	13	19	23	34	0	12
14		4.00	0.44		10 Fruit dish	40	42	9	15	27	36	37	39	12	0

Figure 38-9: Breakfast food data

For example, the subjects on average deemed ham, eggs, and home fries and bacon and eggs as most similar and instant breakfast and ham, eggs, and home fries as least similar.

USING CARD SORTING TO COLLECT SIMILARITY DATA

Because of the vast range of the ranking scale in this scenario, many subjects would have difficulty ranking the similarities of pairs of 10 foods between 1 and 45. To ease the process the marketing analyst can put each pair of foods on 1 of 45 cards and then create four piles: highly similar, somewhat similar, somewhat dissimilar, and highly dissimilar. Then the subject is instructed to place each card into one of the four piles. Because there will be 11 or 12 cards in each pile, it is now easy to sort the cards in each pile from least similar to most similar. Then the sorted cards in the highly similar pile are placed on top, followed by the somewhat similar, somewhat dissimilar, and highly dissimilar piles. Of course, the card-sorting method could be easily programmed on a computer.

To reduce the breakfast food similarities to a two-dimensional representation, repeat the process used in the city distance example.

1. In the range C5:D14 (named location), enter trial values for the location of each food in two-dimensional space. As in the city distances example, constrain each location's *x* and *y* coordinate to be between 0 and 10.

2. Copy the formula `=(INDEX(location,$E18,1)-INDEX(location,G$16,1))^2+(INDEX(location,$E18,2)-INDEX(location,G$16,2))^2` from G18 to G18:P27 (see Figure 38-10) to determine (given the trial *x* and *y* locations) the squared distance in two-dimensional space between each pair of foods. You could have used the `OFFSET` function to compute the squared distances, but here you choose to use the `INDEX` function. When copied down through row 27, the term `INDEX(location,$E18,1)`, for example, pulls the *x* coordinate for the current row's breakfast food.

3. Copy the formula `=IF(G$29=$E31,0,RANK(G18,$G$18:$P$27,1))` from G31 to G31:P40 to compute the rank (see Figure 38-11) in two-dimensional space of the distances between each pair of breakfast foods. For diagonal entries enter a 0 to match the diagonal entries in rows 5–14.

Distances	Ham eggs and home fries	Pancakes and sausage	Instant breakfast	Pastry and or toast	Hot cereal	Eggs	Lox and bagels	Bacon and eggs	Cold cereal	Fruit dish
	1	2	3	4	5	6	7	8	9	10
1 Ham eggs and home fries	0	0.02	95.2	69	15.62	1.697	35	0.5	47	94.3
2 Pancakes and sausage	0.024	0	94.5	69.8	15.06	1.565	36	0.3	47	94.1
3 Instant breakfast	95.22	94.5	0	26.09	35.97	71.77	88	93	12	2.12
4 Pastry and or toast	69	69.8	26.1	0	38.58	54.13	26	73	7.8	14.8
5 Hot cereal	15.62	15.1	36	38.58	0	7.064	44	14	15	39
6 Eggs	1.697	1.57	71.8	54.13	7.064	0	33	1.5	32	71.8
7 Lox and bagels	34.56	36.1	88.1	25.71	44.21	32.86	0	42	36	72
8 Bacon and eggs	0.507	0.31	92.6	73.24	13.56	1.519	42	0	48	93.7
9 Cold cereal	47.32	47.3	11.8	7.849	14.55	32.37	36	48	0	8.46
10 Fruit dish	94.32	94.1	2.12	14.79	39.02	71.83	72	94	8.5	0

Figure 38-10: Squared distances for breakfast foods example

Ranks	Ham eggs and home fries	Pancakes and sausage	Instant breakfast	Pastry and or toast	Hot cereal	Eggs	Lox and bagels	Bacon and eggs	Cold cereal	Fruit dish
	1	2	3	4	5	6	7	8	9	10
1 Ham eggs and home fries	0	11	99	75	41	21	51	15	69	95
2 Pancakes and sausage	11	0	97	77	39	19	57	13	67	93
3 Instant breakfast	99	97	0	45	53	79	87	89	31	23
4 Pastry and or toast	75	77	45	0	59	73	43	85	27	37
5 Hot cereal	41	39	53	59	0	25	65	33	35	61
6 Eggs	21	19	79	73	25	0	49	17	47	81
7 Lox and bagels	51	57	87	43	65	49	0	63	55	83
8 Bacon and eggs	15	13	89	85	33	17	63	0	71	91
9 Cold cereal	69	67	31	27	35	47	55	71	0	29
10 Fruit dish	95	93	23	37	61	81	83	91	29	0

Figure 38-11: Two-dimensional distance ranks for breakfast food example

4. In cell B3 the formula =CORREL(similarities,ranks) computes the correlation between the average subject similarities and the two-dimensional distance ranks.

5. You can now use the Solver window shown in Figure 38-12 to locate the breakfast foods in two-dimensional space. The Solver chooses an x and y coordinate for each food that maximizes the correlation (computed in cell B3) between the subjects' average similarity rankings and the ranked distances in two-dimensional space. The Solver located the breakfast foods (refer to Figure 38-9). The maximum correlation was found to be 0.988.

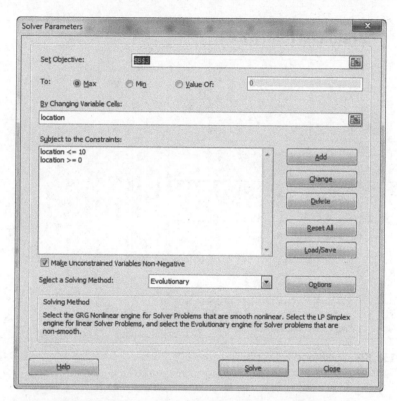

Figure 38-12: Solver window for breakfast food MDS

Unlike the previous MDS example pertaining to city distances, the labeling of the axis for the breakfast foods example is not as straightforward. This task requires taking a holistic view of the two-dimensional MDS map when labeling the axis. In this case, it appears that the breakfast foods on the right side of the chart tend to be hot foods and the foods on the left side of the chart tend to be cold foods (see the plot of the two-dimensional breakfast food locations in Figure 38-13). This suggests that the horizontal axis represents a hot versus cold factor that influences consumer preferences. The foods on the right also appear to have more nutrients than the foods on the left, so the horizontal axis could also be viewed as a nutritional value factor. The breakfast foods near the top of the chart require more preparation time than the foods near the bottom of the chart, so the vertical axis represents a preparation factor. The MDS analysis has greatly clarified the nature of the factors that impact consumer preferences.

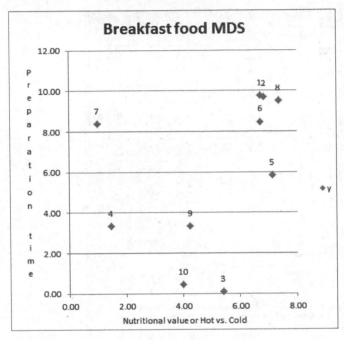

Figure 38-13: Breakfast food MDS plot

Finding a Consumer's Ideal Point

A chart that visually displays (usually in two dimensions) consumer preferences is called a perceptual map. A *perceptual map* enables the marketing analyst to determine how a product compares to the competition. For example, the perceptual map of automobile brands, as shown in Figure 38-14, is based on a sportiness versus conservative factor and a classy versus affordable factor. The perceptual map locates Porsche (accept no substitute!) in the upper-right corner (high on sportiness and high on classy) and the now defunct Plymouth brand in the lower-left corner (high on conservative and high on affordable).

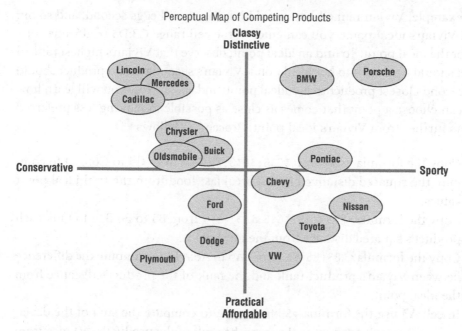

Figure 38-14: Automobile brand perceptual map

When a perceptual map of products or brands is available, the marketing analyst can use an individual's ranking of products to find the individual's ideal point or most-wanted location on the perceptual map. To illustrate the idea I asked my lovely and talented wife Vivian to rank her preferences for the 10 breakfast foods (see `Ideal Point` worksheet of the `breakfast.xls` workbook and Figure 38-15). Vivian's product ranks are entered in the range D5:D14.

	A	B	C	D	E	F	G	H	I
1			ideal	point					
2	Total Penalties		x	y					
3	10		6.052321	6.442101349					
4	Penalty	Distance Rank	Distance	Vivian' s Rank		x	y		Similarities
5	2	5	11.47581	3	3	6.70891	9.765459	1	Ham eggs and home fries
6	1	4	11.30716	5	5	6.853417	9.707895	2	Pancakes and sausage
7	0	10	40.7099	10	10	5.41282	0.093799	3	Instant breakfast
8	1	8	30.79182	9	9	1.459466	3.328022	4	Pastry and or toast
9	0	1	1.551521	1	1	7.141222	5.837274	5	Hot cereal
10	2	2	4.54127	4	4	6.728649	8.462956	6	Eggs
11	1	7	29.30308	8	8	0.996765	8.377155	7	Lox and bagels
12	1	3	11.17555	2	2	7.374804	9.512376	8	Bacon and eggs
13	0	6	12.85278	6	6	4.261007	3.336627	9	Cold cereal
14	2	9	40.25209	7	7	3.998366	0.439322	10	Fruit dish

Figure 38-15: Finding the ideal point

For example, Vivian ranked hot cereal first, bacon and eggs second, and so on. To find Vivian's ideal point, you can enter in the cell range C3:D3 trial values of x and y for the ideal point. To find an ideal point, observe that Vivian's highest ranked product should be closest to her ideal point; Vivian's second ranked product should be the second closest product to her ideal point; and so on. Now you will learn how Solver can choose a point that comes as close as possible to making less preferred products further from Vivian's ideal point. Proceed as follows:

1. Copy the formula =SUMXMY2($C$3:$D$3,F5:G5) from C5 to C6:C14 to compute the squared distance of each breakfast food from the trial ideal point values.

2. Copy the formula =RANK(C5,$C$5:$C$14,1) from B5 to B6:B14 to rank each product's squared distance from the ideal point.

3. Copy the formula =ABS(B5-D5) from A5 to A6:A14 to compute the difference between Vivian's product rank and the rank of the product's distance from the ideal point.

4. In cell A3 use the formula =SUM(A5:A14) to compute the sum of the deviations of Vivian's product ranks from the rank of the product's distance from the ideal point. Your goal should be to minimize this sum.

5. The Solver window, as shown in Figure 38-16, can find an ideal point (not necessarily unique) by selecting x and y values between 0 and 10 that minimize A3.

As shown in Figure 38-17, Vivian's ideal point is $x = 6.06$ and $y = 6.44$, which is located between her two favorite foods: hot cereal and bacon and eggs. The sum of the deviation of the rankings of the product distances from the ideal point and the product rank was 10.

You can use ideal points to determine an opportunity for a new product. After plotting the ideal points for, say, 100 potential customers, you can use the techniques in Chapter 23, "Cluster Analysis," to cluster customer preferences based on the location of their ideal points on the perceptual map. Then if there is a cluster of ideal points with no product close by, a new product opportunity exists. For example, suppose that there were no Diet 7UP or Diet Sprite in the market and an analysis of soft drink similarities found the perceptual map shown in Figure 38-18.

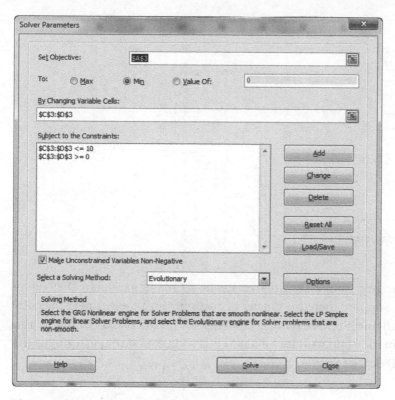

Figure 38-16: Solver window for finding the ideal point

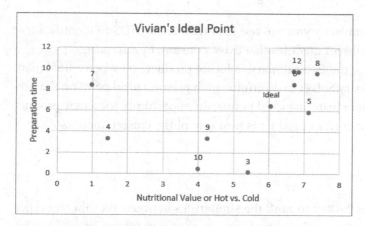

Figure 38-17: Vivian's ideal point

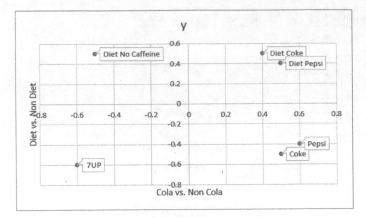

Figure 38-18: Soda perceptual map

You can see the two factors are Cola versus non-Cola (x axis) and Diet versus non-Diet (y axis). Suppose there is a cluster of customer ideal points near the point labeled Diet no caffeine. Because there is currently no product near that point, this would indicate a market opportunity for a new diet soda containing no caffeine (for example Diet 7UP or Diet Sprite).

Summary

In this chapter you learned the following:

■ Given product similarity you can use data nonmetric MDS to identify a few (usually at most three) qualities that drive consumer preferences.
■ You can easily use the Evolutionary to locate products on a perceptual map.
■ Use the Evolutionary Solver to determine each person's ideal point on the perceptual map. After clustering ideal points, an opportunity for a new product may emerge if no current product is near one of the cluster anchors.

Exercises

1. Forty people were asked to rank the similarities between six different types of sodas. The average similarity rankings are shown in Figure 38-19. Use this data to create a two-dimensional perceptual map for sodas.

	F	G	H	I	J	K	L
25		Coke	Pepsi	Diet Coke	Diet Pepsi	7UP	Sprite
26	Coke	-	3	11	7	19	15
27	Pepsi	3	-	11	7	19	15
28	Diet Coke	11	11	-	3	25	27
29	Diet Pepsi	7	7	3	-	23	27
30	7UP	19	19	25	23	-	1
31	Sprite	15	15	27	27	1	-

Figure 38-19: Soda perceptual map

2. The ranking for the sodas in Exercise 1 is Diet Pepsi, Pepsi, Coke, 7UP, Sprite, and Diet Coke. Determine the ideal point.

3. The file `countries.xls` (see Figure 38-20) gives the average ratings 18 students gave when asked to rank the similarity of 11 countries on a 9-point scale (9 = highly similar and 1 = highly dissimilar). For example, the United States was viewed as most similar to Japan and least similar to the Congo. Develop a two-dimensional perceptual map and interpret the two dimensions.

	A	B	C	D	E	F	G	H	I	J	K	L	M
1		Brazil	Congo	Cuba	Egypt	France	India	Israel	Japan	China	USSR	USA	Yugoslavia
2	Brazil	0.00	4.83	5.28	3.44	4.72	4.50	3.83	3.50	2.39	3.06	5.39	3.17
3	Congo	4.83	0.00	4.56	5.00	4.00	4.83	3.33	3.39	4.00	3.39	2.39	3.50
4	Cuba	5.28	4.56	0.00	5.17	4.11	4.00	3.61	2.94	5.50	5.44	3.17	5.11
5	Egypt	3.44	5.00	5.17	0.00	4.78	5.83	4.67	3.83	4.39	4.39	3.33	4.28
6	France	4.72	4.00	4.11	4.78	0.00	3.44	4.00	4.22	3.67	5.06	5.94	4.72
7	India	4.50	4.83	4.00	5.83	3.44	0.00	4.11	4.50	4.11	4.50	4.28	4.00
8	Israel	3.83	3.33	3.61	4.67	4.00	4.11	0.00	4.83	3.00	4.17	5.94	4.44
9	Japan	3.50	3.39	2.94	3.83	4.22	4.50	4.83	0.00	4.17	4.61	6.06	4.28
10	China	2.39	4.00	5.50	4.39	3.67	4.11	3.00	4.17	0.00	5.72	2.56	5.06
11	USSR	3.06	3.39	5.44	4.39	5.06	4.50	4.17	4.61	5.72	0.00	5.00	6.67
12	USA	5.39	2.39	3.17	3.33	5.94	4.28	5.94	6.06	2.56	5.00	0.00	3.56
13	Yugoslavia	3.17	3.50	5.11	4.28	4.72	4.00	4.44	4.28	5.06	6.67	3.56	0.00

Figure 38-20: Exercise 3 data

4. Explain the similarities and differences between using cluster analysis and MDS to summarize multidimensional data.

5. Explain the similarity and differences between using principal components and MDS to summarize multidimensional data.

39

Classification Algorithms: Naive Bayes Classifier and Discriminant Analysis

In marketing and other areas, analysts often want to classify an object into one of several (most often two) groups based on knowledge of several independent variables, for example:

- Based on gender, age, income, and residential location, can you classify a consumer as a user or nonuser of a new breakfast cereal?
- Based on income, type of residence, credit card debts, and other information, can you classify a consumer as a good or bad credit risk?
- Based on financial ratios, can you classify a company as a likely or unlikely candidate for bankruptcy?
- Based on cholesterol levels, blood pressure, smoking, and so on, is a person at high risk for a heart attack?
- Based on GMAT score and undergraduate GPA, is an applicant a likely admit or reject to an MBA program?
- Based on demographic information, can you predict which car model a person will prefer?

In each of these situations, you want to use independent variables (often referred to as attributes) to classify an individual. In this chapter you learn two methods used for classification: *Naive Bayes classifier* and *linear discriminant analysis.*

You begin this chapter by studying some topics in basic probability theory (conditional probability and Bayes' Theorem) that are needed to understand the Naive Bayes classifier. Then you learn how to easily use the Naive Bayes classifier to classify observations based on any set of independent variables. Finally you learn how to use the Evolutionary Solver (first discussed in Chapter 5, "Price Bundling") to develop a linear discriminant classification rule that minimizes the number of misclassified observations.

Conditional Probability

The concept of *conditional probability* essentially allows you to adjust the probability of an event (A) based on the occurrence of another event (B.) Therefore, given two events A and B, you write P(A|B) to denote the conditional probability that event A occurs, given you know that event B occurs. P(A|B) may be written as the following equation:

(1) $P(A|B) = \dfrac{P(A \cap B)}{P(B)}$

Equation 1 can be rearranged to yield Equation 2:

(2) $P(A \cap B) = P(B)P(A|B)$

In Equation 1, $P(A \cap B)$ denotes the probability that A and B occur. To illustrate the idea of conditional probability, suppose that 10 percent of all adults watch the TV show *The Bachelor*. Assume that 80 percent of *The Bachelor* viewers are women and that one-half of U.S. adults are men. Define the following as:

- ■ B = Event adult watches *The Bachelor*
- ■ M = Event adult is a man
- ■ W = Event adult is a woman
- ■ NB = Event adult does not watch *The Bachelor*

To illustrate the concept of conditional probability you will compute the probability that a given woman or man is a *Bachelor* viewer. Assume one-half of all adults are men. All adults fall into one of four categories: women *Bachelor* viewers, men *Bachelor* viewers, men non-*Bachelor* viewers, and women non-*Bachelor* viewers. Now calculate the fraction of all adults falling into each of these categories. Note that from Equation 2 you can deduce the following:

$P(B \cap \text{Woman}) = P(B)P(W|B) = (0.10)(0.8) = 0.08$

Because the first row of the Table 39-1 must add up to 0.10 and each column must add up to 0.5, you can readily compute all probabilities.

Table 39-1: Bachelor Probabilities

	W	M
B	0.08	0.02
NB	0.42	0.48

To cement your understanding of conditional probability, compute P(B|W) and P(B|M). Referring to Table 39-1 and Equation 1, you can find that:

P(B|W) = 0.08 / 0.50 = 0.16 and P(B|M) = 0.02 / 0.50 = 0.04

In other words, 16 percent of all women and 4 percent of all men are *Bachelor* viewers. In the next section you learn how an extension of conditional probability known as Bayes' Theorem enables you to update conditional probabilities based on new information about the world.

Bayes' Theorem

Bayes' Theorem was developed during the 18th century by the English minister Thomas Bayes.

NOTE   If you are interested in exploring the fascinating history of Bayes' Theorem, read Sharon McGrayne's marvelous book *The Theory That Would Not Die* (Yale University Press, 2011).

To introduce Bayes' Theorem you can use a nonmarketing example commonly taught to future doctors in medical school. Women are often given mammograms to detect breast cancer. Now look at the health of a 40-year-old woman with no risk factors for breast cancer. Before receiving a mammogram, the woman's health may be classified into one of two states:

- C = Woman has breast cancer.
- NC = Woman does not have breast cancer.

Refer to C and NC as *states of the world*. A priori, or before receiving any information, it is known that $P(C) = 0.004$ and $P(NC) = 0.996$. These probabilities are known as *prior probabilities*. Now the woman undergoes a mammogram and one of two outcomes occurs:

- + = Positive test result
- – = Negative test result

Because many healthy 40-year-old women receive mammograms, the likelihood of a positive test result for a healthy 40-year-old woman or a 40-year-old woman with breast cancer is well known and is given by $P(+|C) = 0.80$ and $P(+|NC) = 0.10$.

The goal of Bayes' Theorem is to factor in observed information (in this case mammogram results) and update the prior probabilities to determine posterior probabilities that incorporate the mammogram test results. In this example, you need to determine $P(C|+)$ and $P(C|-)$.

Essentially, Bayes' Theorem enables you to use Equation 1 to factor in likelihoods and prior probabilities to compute posterior probabilities. For example, to compute $P(C|+)$ use Equation 1 to find that:

(3) $P(C|+) = \dfrac{P(C \cap +)}{P(+)}$

To compute the denominator of Equation 3, observe that a + test result can be observed from women with cancer and women without cancer. This implies that $P(+)$ = $P(+\cap C) + P(+\cap NC)$. Then by Equation 2 you find $P(+) = P(+|C) * P(C) + P(+|NC) *$ $P(NC)$. Substituting this result in the denominator of Equation 3 yields the following:

$$P(C|+) = \dfrac{P(+|C)P(C)}{P(+|C) * P(C) + P(+|NC) * P(NC)} = \dfrac{.80 * 004}{.80 * .004 + .996(.10)} = 0.031$$

Thus even after observing a positive mammogram result, there is a small chance that a healthy 40-year-old woman has cancer. When doctors are asked to determine $P(C|+)$ for the given data, only 15 percent of the doctors get the right answer (see W. Casscells, A. Schoenberger, and T.B. Graboys, "Interpretation by physicians of clinical laboratory results," *New England Journal of Medicine*, 1978, pp. 999–1001)!

Here is a more intuitive way to see that $P(C|+) = 0.031$: Look at 10,000 women and determine how many of them fall into each possible category (Cancer and +, Cancer and –, No Cancer and +, No Cancer and –).

- 10,000(0.004) = 40 women have cancer.
- Because $P(+|C) = 0.8$, 80 percent of the 10,000 women, or 32 women, will have cancer and test positive.
- 10,000(0.996) = 9,960 women do not have cancer.
- Since $P(+|NC) = 0.10$, 9,960 * (0.10) = 996 women without cancer test positive!
- Combining your knowledge that 32 women with cancer test positive and 996 women without cancer test positive with the fact that the first row of Table 39-2 must total to 40 and the second row totals to 9,960, you may complete Table 39-2.

Table 39-2: Another Way to Understand Bayes' Theorem

	+ Test Result	– Test Result
Cancer	32	8
No Cancer	996	8,964

Now it is clear that $P(C|+) = \dfrac{32}{(996 + 32)} = 0.031$.

This argument makes it apparent that the large number of false positives is the reason that the posterior probability of cancer after a positive test result is surprisingly small. In the next section you use your knowledge of Bayes' Theorem to develop a simple yet powerful classification algorithm.

Naive Bayes Classifier

The general classification problem may be stated as follows: Each observation is in one of k classes: $C_1, C, \ldots C_k$, but for each observation you do not know to which class the observation belongs. For each observation you know the values of n attributes X_1, $X_2, \ldots, X_n$. In this discussion of Naive Bayes, assume each attribute is a qualitative variable (such as a person is male or female) and not quantitative (such as a person's height or weight). Given knowledge of the attributes, to which class should you assign an observation? To explain how the Naive Bayes classifier works, assume $n = k = 2$. Then it seems reasonable to compute $P(C_1|X_1, X_2)$ and $P(C_2|X_1, X_2)$ and classify the object in the class with the larger posterior probability. Before showing how Naive Bayes is used to compute these probabilities, you need to develop Equation 4 to compute joint probabilities involving attributes and categories.

(4) $P(C_1 \cap X_1 \cap X_2) = P(X_2 | X_1 \cap C_1) * P(X_1 | C_1) * P(C_1)$

Applying Equation 1 twice to the right side of Equation 4 transforms the right side of Equation 4 to $\frac{P(X_2 \cap X_1 \cap C_1)}{P(X_1 \cap C_1)} * \frac{P(X_1 \cap C_1)}{P(C_1)} P(C_1) = P(C_1 \cap X_1 \cap X_2)$, which is the left side of Equation 3. This proves the validity of Equation 4. Now applying Equation 1 and Equation 4 you can show that

(5) $P(C_1 | X_1, X_2) = \dfrac{P(C_1 \cap X_1 \cap X_2)}{P(X_1 \cap X_2)} = \dfrac{P(X_2 | X_1 \cap C_1) * P(X_1 | C_1) * P(C_1)}{P(X_1 \cap X_2)}$

NOTE The key to Naive Bayes is to assume that in computing $P(X_2|X_1 \cap C_1)$ you may assume that this probability is conditionally independent of (does not depend on) X_1. In other words, $P(X_2|X_1 \cap C_1)$ may be estimated as $P(X_2|C_1)$. Because this assumption ignores the dependence between attributes, it is a bit naive; hence the name Naive Bayes.

Then, using Equation 5, the posterior probability for each class may be estimated with Equations 6 and 7.

(6) $P(C_1|X_1, X_2) = \dfrac{P(X_2 | C_1) * P(X_1 | C_1) * P(C_1)}{P(X_1 \cap X_2)}$

(7) $P(C_2 | X_1, X_2) = \dfrac{P(X_2 | C_2) * P(X_1 | C_2) * P(C_2)}{P(X_1 \cap X_2)}$

Because the posterior probabilities of all the classes should add to 1, you can compute the numerators in Equations 6 and 7 and normalize them so they add to 1. This means that you can ignore the denominators of Equation 6 and 7 in computing the posterior probabilities. Then an observation is assigned to the class having the largest posterior probability.

More generally, if you have knowledge of n attributes, Naive Bayes estimates the posterior probability of class C_i by using Equation 8:

$$(8)\ P(C_i\ |X_1, X_2\,, \ldots X_n) = \frac{P\,(X_n\ |C_i)\,^*\,(P\,(X_{n-1}\,|C_i)\,^*\,\ldots,P\,(X_1\ |C_i)\,^*\,P\,(C_i)}{P\,(X_1 \cap X_2, \ldots, \cap X_n)}$$

The numerator of Equation 8 can easily be computed for each class from sample data using COUNTIFS functions. Then each observation is assigned to the class having the largest posterior probability. You might ask why not just use COUNTIFS functions to exactly compute the numerator of Equation 8 by estimating $P(X_1 \cap X_2, \ldots, \cap X_n \cap C_i)$ as the fraction of all observations that are in class C_i and have the wanted attribute values. The problem with this approach is that if there are many attributes there may be few or no observations in the relevant class with the given attribute values. Because each $P(X_k|C_i)$ is likely to be based on many observations, the Naive Bayes classifier avoids this issue.

You are now ready to apply the Naive Bayes classifier to an actual example. The file ESPNBayes.xlsx (see Figure 39-1) contains the following information for a random sample of U.S. adults:

- **Age:** Young Adult, Gen X, Boomer, or Old
- **Gender:** Male (M) or Female (F)
- **Income:** Low, Middle, or Upper
- **Location:** Rural, Suburban, or Urban
- Whether the person is a subscriber (1) or a nonsubscriber (0)

Your goal is to compute the posterior probability that a person is a subscriber or nonsubscriber given the person's age, gender, income, and location. As shown in Figure 39-2, you need to compute the following quantities:

- For each attribute the likelihood of the attribute is conditioned on whether the person is a subscriber or nonsubscriber. For example, for gender you need to compute P(M|S), P(F|S), P(M|NS), and P(M|NS).
- For a subscriber and nonsubscriber, compute (given the person's value for each attribute) the numerator of Equation 8 by multiplying the class (either N or NS) prior probability times the conditional probability of each attribute value based on the class value.
- Normalize the numerator of Equation 8 for each class, so the posterior probabilities add to 1.

	A	B	C	D	E
1					
2					
3					
4	Age	Gender	Income	Location	Subscriber
5	old	m	low	rural	1
6	young adult	m	low	suburban	0
7	genx	f	low	suburban	0
8	young adult	f	low	suburban	0
9	genx	m	upper	urban	1
10	genx	m	low	urban	1
11	young adult	f	low	rural	0
12	young adult	f	low	urban	1
13	genx	f	low	urban	0
14	young adult	f	middle	urban	1
15	young adult	f	low	suburban	0
16	genx	f	middle	urban	0
17	young adult	f	low	rural	0
18	young adult	m	middle	suburban	1
19	young adult	f	middle	rural	0
20	boomer	f	low	suburban	0
21	young adult	f	low	urban	0
22	young adult	m	low	urban	0

Figure 39-1: ESPN Naive Bayes classifier data

	F	G	H	I	J
4		young adult	genx	boomer	old
5	S	0.417582418	0.467032967	0.082418	0.032967
6	NS	0.443939394	0.396969697	0.09697	0.062121
7		m	f		
8	S	0.67032967	0.32967033		
9	NS	0.436363636	0.563636364		
10		low	middle	upper	
11	S	0.392857143	0.57967033	0.027473	
12	NS	0.453030303	0.515151515	0.031818	
13		rural	suburban	urban	
14	S	0.123626374	0.458791209	0.417582	
15	NS	0.157575758	0.456060606	0.386364	
16					
17					
18					
19					
20	total	1024			
21	Subscribers	364			
22	Non Subscribers	660			
23		Naive Bayes Estimate	0.547964323	0.452036	
24		Numerator	0.026937711	0.022222	
25			S	NS	
26	Age	genx	0.467032967	0.39697	
27	Gender	m	0.67032967	0.436364	
28	Income	middle	0.57967033	0.515152	
29	Location	urban	0.417582418	0.386364	

Figure 39-2: GenX, middle income, urban, male is classified as subscriber.

These calculations proceed as follows:

1. In cell G21 compute the number of subscribers (364) with the formula =COUNTIF(E5:E1030,1).

2. In cell G22 compute the number of nonsubscribers (660) with the formula =COUNTIF(E5:E1030,0).

3. In cell G20 compute the total number of subscribers (1,024) with the formula =SUM(G21:G22).

4. Copy the formula =COUNTIFS($A$5:$A$1030,G$4,$E$5:$E$1030,1)/$G21 from G5 to G5:J6 to compute for each class age combination the conditional probability of the age given the class. For example, cell H5 tells you that P(GenX|S) = 0.467.

5. Copy from G8 to G8:H9 the formula =COUNTIFS($B$5:$B$1030,G$7,$E$5:$E$1030,1)/$G21 to compute for each class gender combination the conditional probability of the gender given the class. For example, the formula in cell H9 tells you that P(F|NS) = 0.564.

6. Copy the formula =COUNTIFS($C$5:$C$1030,G$10,$E$5:$E$1030,1)/$G21 from G11 to G11:I12 to compute for each class income combination the conditional probability of the income given the class. For example, the formula in cell I11 tells you P(Middle|S) = 0.580.

7. Copy the formula =COUNTIFS($D$5:$D$1030,G$13,$E$5:$E$1030,1)/$G21 from G14 to G14:I15 to compute for each class location combination the conditional probability of the location given the class. For example, the formula in cell G14 tells you P(Rural|S) = 0.124.

8. In the cell range G26:G29, use a drop-down box to select the level of each attribute. For example, with the cursor in cell G26, the drop-down box was created by selecting Data Validation from the Data tab and filling in the dialog box, as shown in Figure 39-3.

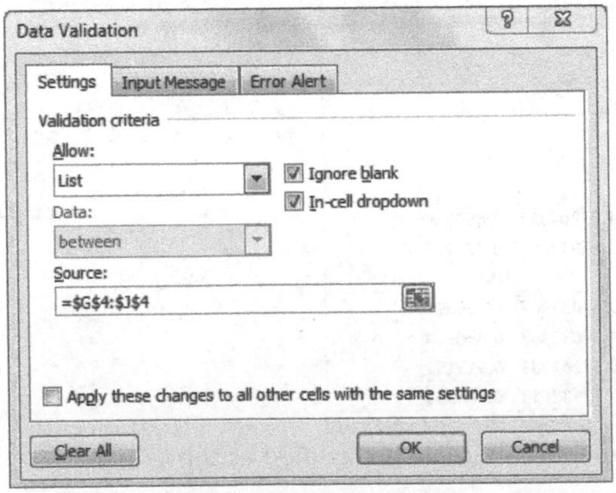

Figure 39-3: Creating a drop-down list for age

9. Copy the formula =HLOOKUP($G26,INDIRECT($F26),2,FALSE) from H26 to H26:H29 to look up the conditional probability of each of the person's attributes given that the person is a subscriber. For example, in H27 you can find that 67 percent of all subscribers are male. Note the lookup ranges for each attribute are named as age, gender, income, and location, respectively. Combining these range name definitions with the INDIRECT function enables you to easily reference the lookup range for each attribute based on the attribute's name!

10. Copy the formula =HLOOKUP($G26,INDIRECT($F26),3,FALSE) from I26 to I26:I29 to look up the conditional probability of each of the person's attributes given that the person is not a subscriber. For example, in I27 you can find that 44 percent of the nonsubscribers are male.

11. In H24 the formula =PRODUCT(H26:H29) * Non Subscribers/total computes the numerator of Equation 8 for the classification of the person as a subscriber. The PRODUCT term in this formula multiplies the conditional likelihood of each attribute based on the assumption that the person is a subscriber, and the Subscribers/Total portion of the formula estimates the probability that a person is a subscriber.

12. In I24 formula =PRODUCT(I26:I29)*Subscribers/total computes the numerator of Equation 8 for the classification of the person as a nonsubscriber.

13. Copy the formula =H24/SUM($H24:$I24) from H23 to I23 to normalize the numerators for Equation 8 so the sum of the posterior probabilities add to 1. You can find that for a middle income, urban, Gen X male Naive Bayes estimates a 54.8 percent chance the person is a subscriber and a 45.2 percent chance that the person is not a subscriber. Because Naive Bayes gives a higher probability that the person is a subscriber than a nonsubscriber, you would classify the person as a subscriber. As shown in Figure 39-4, a low income, rural, young adult male would be estimated to have only a 35.2 percent chance of being a subscriber and would be classified as a nonsubscriber.

The Naive Bayes classifier has been successfully applied to many classification problems including:

- Classifying e-mails as spam or nonspam based on words contained in the email
- Classifying a person as likely to develop Alzheimer's disease based on the genome makeup
- Classifying an airline flight as likely to be on time or delayed based on the airline, airport, weather conditions, time of day, and day of week
- Classifying customers as likely or unlikely to return purchases based on demographic information

	F	G	H	I	J
4		young adult	genx	boomer	old
5	S	0.417582418	0.467032967	0.082418	0.032967
6	NS	0.443939394	0.396969697	0.09697	0.062121
7		m	f		
8	S	0.67032967	0.32967033		
9	NS	0.436363636	0.563636364		
10		low	middle	upper	
11	S	0.392857143	0.57967033	0.027473	
12	NS	0.453030303	0.515151515	0.031818	
13		rural	suburban	urban	
14	S	0.123626374	0.458791209	0.417582	
15	NS	0.157575758	0.456060606	0.386364	
16					
17					
18					
19					
20	total	1024			
21	Subscribers	364			
22	Non Subscribers	660			
23		Naive Bayes Estimate	0.351568045	0.648432	
24		Numerator	0.004832567	0.008913	
25			S	NS	
26	Age	young adult	0.417582418	0.443939	
27	Gender	m	0.67032967	0.436364	
28	Income	low	0.392857143	0.45303	
29	Location	rural	0.123626374	0.157576	

Figure 39-4: Young adult, low income, rural male is classified as nonsubscriber.

Similarly, for a more in-depth example, Naive Bayes can be used to efficiently allocate marketing resources. Suppose *ESPN The Magazine* is trying to determine how to allocate its TV advertising budget. For each TV show Nielson can provide ESPN with the demographic makeup of the show's viewing population. Then Naive Bayes can be used to estimate the number of subscribers among the show's viewers. Finally, the attractiveness of the shows to ESPN could be ranked by Estimated Subscribers in Viewing Population/Cost per Ad.

Linear Discriminant Analysis

Similar to Naive Bayes classification, linear discriminant analysis can be used in marketing to classify an object into a group based on certain features. However, whereas Naive Bayes classifies objects based on any given independent variable, linear discriminant analysis uses a weighted, linear combination of variables as the basis for classification of each observation.

In the discussion of *linear discriminant analysis* you can assume that n continuous valued attributes X_1, X_2, ..., X_n are used to classify an observation into 1 of 2 groups. A linear classification rule is defined by a set of weights W_1, W_2, ... W_n

for each attribute and a cutoff point *Cut*. Each observation is classified in Group 1 if the following is true:

W1(value of attribute 1) + W2(value of attribute 2) + ...Wn(value of attribute n) ≥ Cut

The observation is classified in Group 2 if the following is true:

W_1(value of attribute 1) + W_2(value of attribute 2) + ...W_n(value of attribute n) < Cut

You can call W1(value of variable 1) + W2(value of variable 2) + ...Wn(value of variable n) the individual's *discriminant score*.

The goal is to choose the weights and cutoff to minimize the number of incorrectly classified observations. The following examples show how easy it is to use the Evolutionary Solver to find an optimal linear classification rule.

Finding the Optimal Linear Classification Rule

The file WSJ.xlsx (see Figure 39-5) contains the annual income and size of investment portfolio (both in thousands of dollars) for 84 people. A "0" indicates the person does not subscribe to *The Wall Street Journal*, whereas a "1" indicates the person is a subscriber.

	A	B	C	D	E	F	G	H	I
1					Standardized	0.00774	0.049886565		
2	Discriminant analysis: two groups and two explanatory variables					Income	Invest	Cut	
3						0.11598	0.813589559	45.529	
4	Person	WSJSubscriber?	Income	Invest	Actual	Score	Classified As	Wrong?	Errors
5	1	No	66.4	26.9	0	29.5863	0	0	6
6	2	No	68	7.1	0	13.6628	0	0	
7	3	No	54.9	21.5	0	23.8592	0	0	
8	4	No	50.6	19.3	0	21.5706	0	0	
9	5	No	54.1	16.7	0	19.8612	0	0	
10	6	No	78.2	31.9	0	35.0228	0	0	
11	7	No	66.2	23.8	0	27.041	0	0	Actual
12	8	No	43.9	12.4	0	15.1798	0	0	
13	9	No	41.9	5	0	8.92731	0	0	
14	10	No	61.1	25.2	0	27.5885	0	0	
15	11	No	64.5	11.8	0	17.0808	0	0	
16	12	No	59.4	27.3	0	29.0999	0	0	
17	13	No	45.9	16.8	0	18.9916	0	0	
18	14	No	59.7	14.9	0	19.0462	0	0	
19	15	No	76	41.9	0	42.9035	0	0	
20	16	No	89.9	46.2	0	48.014	1	1	
21	17	No	32.7	16.9	0	17.5421	0	0	
22	18	No	57.8	23.4	0	25.7414	0	0	
23	19	No	66.9	34.4	0	35.7462	0	0	
24	20	No	87.2	51	0	51.6061	1	1	
57	53	No	60.9	25.8	0	28.0535	0	0	
58	54	No	88.9	28.6	0	33.5788	0	0	
59	55	No	68.2	12.3	0	17.9167	0	0	
60	56	No	88.4	34.5	0	38.321	0	0	
61	57	No	66.6	32.2	0	33.9215	0	0	
62	58	Yes	77.8	48.5	1	48.482	1	0	
63	59	Yes	86.6	66.6	1	64.2285	1	0	
64	60	Yes	72.9	39.4	1	40.51	0	1	
65	61	Yes	90.9	63.8	1	62.4492	1	0	
66	62	Yes	64.3	50.1	1	48.218	1	0	
67	63	Yes	53.9	36.4	1	35.8657	0	1	

Figure 39-5: *Wall Street Journal* subscriber data

Using income and size of investment portfolio, you can determine a linear classification rule that minimizes the number of people incorrectly classified as subscribers or nonsubscribers by following these steps:

1. In F3:G3 enter trial values for the income and investment weights. In H3 enter a trial value for the cutoff.

2. In F5:F88 compute each individual's "score" by copying from F5 to F6:F88 the formula =SUMPRODUCT($F$3:$G$3,C5:D5).

3. In G5:G88 compare each person's score to the cutoff. If the score is at least equal to the cutoff, classify the person as a subscriber. Otherwise, classify the person as a nonsubscriber. To accomplish this goal copy the formula =IF(F5>$H$3,1,0) from G5 to G6:G88.

4. In H5:H88 determine if you correctly or incorrectly classified the individual. A "0" indicates a correct classification, whereas a "1" indicates an incorrect classification. Simply copy the formula =IF(G5-E5=0,0,1) from H5 to H6:H88.

5. In I5 use the formula =SUM(H5:H88) to compute the total number of misclassifications by adding up the numbers in Column H.

6. Because your spreadsheet involves many non-smooth functions (IF statements) use the Evolutionary Solver to devise a classification rule that minimizes the number of errors. The Solver window, as shown in Figure 39-6, chooses the weights and cutoffs to minimize the number of errors.

You want to minimize the total number of misclassifications (cell I5) by adjusting weights (F3 and G3) and the cutoff (H3). Recall that to use the Evolutionary Solver weights are needed on the changing cells. It is not clear what bounds to place on the changing cells. Because the cutoff may be set to any number, the keys to the classification are the ratios of the attribute weights. Without loss of generality you can assume an upper bound of 1 on each weight and a lower bound of –1). For example, if Solver found that a person should be classified as a subscriber if 2 * (Income) + 5(Investment Portfolio) >= 200, then you could simply divide the rule by 5 and rewrite the rule as 0.4 * (Income) + Investment Portfolio >= 40.

This equivalent classification rule has weights that are between –1 and +1. After noting that the maximum income is 100.7 and the maximum investment portfolio is 66.6, you can see that the maximum score for an individual would be 1 * (100.7) + 1 * (66.6) = 167.3. To be conservative, the upper bound on the cutoff was set to 200. The Evolutionary Solver was used because the model has many IF statements. After setting the Mutation rate to 0.5, the Solver found the following classification rule: If 0.116 * (Income in 000's) + 0.814 * (Investment amount in 000's) ≥ 45.529, then classify the individual as a subscriber; otherwise classify the individual as a nonsubscriber. Only 6 or 7.1 percent of the individuals are incorrectly classified. There are many different classification rules that yield six errors, so the optimal classification rule is not unique.

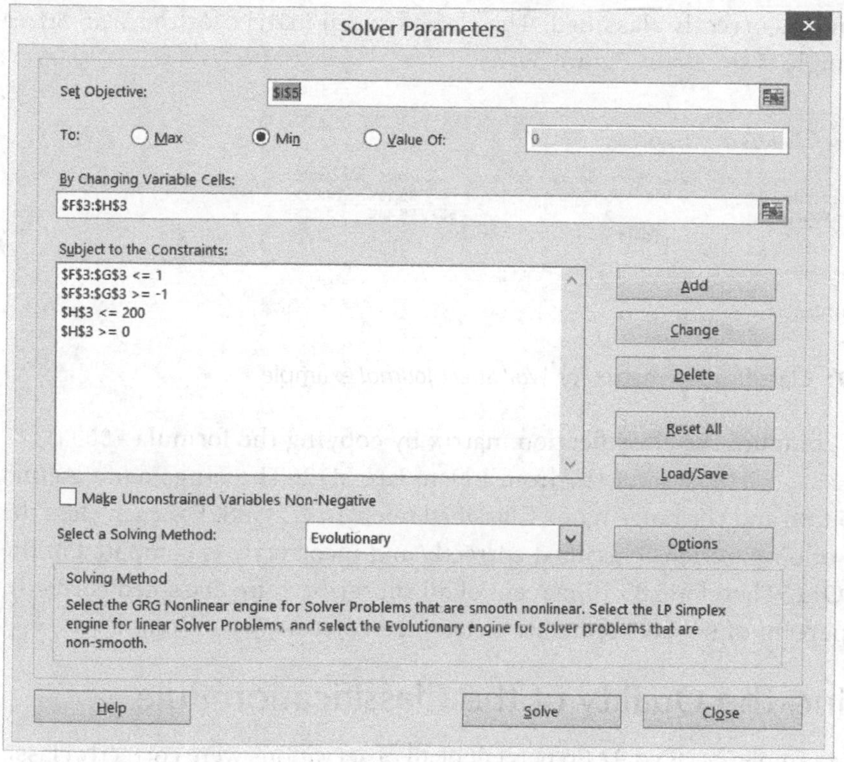

Figure 39-6: Solver window for *Wall Street Journal* example

Finding the Most Important Attributes

You might think that the attribute with the largest weight would be most important for classification. The problem with this idea is that the weights are unit dependent. For example, if the investment portfolio were measured in dollars, the weight for the Investment Portfolio would be 0.814/1,000, which would be much smaller than the income weight. The attributes may be ranked, however, if the weight for each attribute is standardized by dividing by the standard deviation of the attribute values. These standardized weights are computed in the cell range F1:G1 by copying from F1 to G1 the formula =F3/STDEV(C5:C88). Because the standardized investment portfolio weight is much larger than the standardized income weight, you can conclude, if you want to classify a person as a subscriber or nonsubscriber to the *Wall Street Journal*, that an individual's investment portfolio is more useful than the individual's annual income.

Classification Matrix

The results of a linear discriminant analysis are often summarized with a *classification matrix*, which gives for each class the number of observations that are correctly and incorrectly classified. The classification matrix for the *Wall Street Journal* example is shown in Figure 39-7.

	J	K	L	M	N	O
8		Classification Matrix	Classified as			
9			1	0		
10			Subscriber	Non -subscriber	Correct	Incorrect
11		1 Subscriber	23	4	85.19%	14.81%
12		0 Non-Subscriber	2	55	96.49%	3.51%
13			29.76%	70.24%		
14						
15		Benchmark				
16		58.19%				
17		Total Correct				
18		92.86%				

Figure 39-7: Classification matrix for *Wall Street Journal* example

You can compute the classification matrix by copying the formula =COUNTIFS (Actual,$J11,Classified,L$9) from L11 to L11:M12. The range name Actual refers to E5:E88 and the range name Classified refers to G5:G88. For each class the percentage of observations classified correctly and incorrectly is computed in the range N11:O12. Therefore, 85.19 percent of all subscribers are classified correctly, and 96.49 percent of nonsubscribers are classified correctly.

Evaluating the Quality of the Classification Rule

In the WSJ example 79 / 85 = 92.86 percent of all observations were correctly classified. To evaluate the performance of the linear classification rule, you can develop a benchmark classification rate. Suppose fraction P_i of the observations are members of class i. Then a simple classification procedure (known as *proportional classification*) would be to randomly classify each observation in class 1 with probability P_1 and randomly classify each observation in class 2 with probability P_2. Using proportional classification, the fraction of observations correctly classified can be computed as

P_1* (Probability observation is classified in class 1) + P_2 (Probability observation is classified in class 2) = $(P_1)^2 + (P_2)^2$

In the *Wall Street Journal* example proportional classification would classify $(0.2976)^2 + (0.7024)^2 = 58.19$ percent.

The 92.86 percent correct classification rate looks good when compared to the 58.19 percent benchmark as set via proportional classification.

Linear Classification with More Than Two Groups

You can easily use the Evolutionary Solver to determine an optimal linear classification rule when there are more than two groups. To illustrate the idea suppose you want to classify MBA applicants as likely admits, likely rejects, or marginal admits based on the applicants' GMAT scores and undergraduate GPAs. As changing cells you can use W_1 and W_2 as weights and use two cutoffs: C_1 and C_2. Then the classification rule works as follows:

- Classify applicant as likely admit if $W_1 * GMAT + W_2 * GPA >= C_1$
- Classify applicant as marginal admit if $C_1 > W_1 * GMAT + W_2 * GPA > C_2$
- Classify applicant as likely reject if $W_1 * GMAT + W_2 * GPA <= C_2$

You can use the Evolutionary Solver to choose the values of W_1, W_2, C_1, and C_2 that minimize the number of classification errors.

Classification Rules Involving Nonlinearities and Interactions

A classification rule involving nonlinearities and interactions could significantly improve classification performance. The *Wall Street Journal* example illustrates how you can evaluate a classification rule involving nonlinearities. Following the discussion of nonlinearities and interactions in Chapter 10, "Using Multiple Regression to Forecast Sales," you would choose C, W_1, W_2, W_3, W_4, and W_5 so that the following classification rule minimizes classification errors.

If $W_1*(Income) + W_2(Investment\ Portfolio) + W_3(Income^2) + W_4*(Investment\ Portfolio^2) + W_5*(Income*Investment\ Portfolio) >= C$, then classify the person as a subscriber; otherwise classify the person as a nonsubscriber. This classification rule (see Exercise 4) improves the number of errors from 6 to 5. This small improvement indicates that you are justified in using the simpler linear classification rule instead of the more complex rule involving nonlinearities and interactions.

Model Validation

In practice, classification models such as Naive Bayes and linear discriminant analysis are deployed using a "calibration" and "validation" stage. The model is calibrated using approximately 80 percent of the data and then validated using the remaining 20 percent of the data. This process enables the analyst to determine how well the model will perform on unseen data. For example, in the *Wall Street Journal* example suppose in the testing phase 95 percent of observations were correctly classified but in the validation phase only 75 percent of the observations were correctly classified. The relatively poor performance of the classification rule in the validation phase would make you hesitant to use the rule to classify new observations.

The Surprising Virtues of Naive Bayes

In addition to linear discriminant analysis, logistic regression (see Chapter 17, "Logistic Regression") and neural networks (see Chapter 15, "Using Neural Networks to Forecast Sales") can be used for classification. All these methods utilize sophisticated optimization techniques. On the other hand, Naive Bayes uses only high school probability and simple arithmetic for classification. Despite this fact, Naive Bayes often outperforms the other sophisticated classification algorithms (see D.J. Hand and K. Yu, "Idiot's Bayes — not so stupid after all?" *International Statistical Review*, 2001, pp. 385–99.) The surprising performance of Naive Bayes may be because dependencies between attributes are often distributed evenly between classes or dependencies between attributes can cancel each other out when used for classification. Finally, note the following two advantages of Naive Bayes:

- If you have made your data an Excel table, then when new data is added, your Naive Bayes analysis automatically updates while other classification rules require you to rerun a neural network, logistic regression, or linear discriminant analysis.
- If an important attribute is missing from the analysis this can greatly reduce the performance of a classification analysis based on a neural network, logistic regression, or linear discriminant analysis. The absence of an important attribute will often have little effect on the performance of a Naive Bayes classification rule.

Summary

In this chapter you learned the following:

- In the general classification problem, you classify an observation into 1 of k classes based on knowledge of n attributes.
- Given values $X_1, X_2, ..., X_n$ for the attributes, the Naive Bayes classifier classifies the observation in the class that maximizes

  $$P(X_n \mid C_i) * P(X_{n-1} \mid C_i) * ...., P(X_1 \mid C_i) * P(C_i)$$

- A linear classification rule for two classes is defined by weights for each attribute and a classification cutoff. Each observation is classified in class 1 if the following is true:

  $$W_1 \text{ (value of attribute 1)} + W_2 \text{ (value of attribute 2)} + ... W_n \text{ (value of attribute } n) \geq \text{Cut}$$

It is classified in class 2 otherwise.

- You can use the Evolutionary Solver to determine the weights and cutoffs that minimize classification errors.

Exercises

1. For 49 U.S. cities, the file `Incomediscriminant.xlsx` contains the following data:

   - Income level: low, medium, or high
   - Percentage of blacks, Hispanics, and Asians

   a. Use this data to build a linear classification rule for classifying a city as low, medium, or high income.
   b. Determine the classification matrix.
   c. Compare the performance of your classification rule to the proportional classification rule.

2. For a number of flights, the file `Flighttimedata.xlsx` contains the following information:

   - Was the flight on time or delayed?
   - Day of week: 1 = Monday, 2 = Tuesday, ..., 7 = Sunday
   - Time of day : 1 = 6–9 AM, 2 = 9 AM–3 PM, 3 = 3–6 PM, 4 = After 6 PM
   - Was the weather good or bad?

   a. Using this data develops a Naive Bayes classifier that can classify a given flight as on-time or delayed.
   b. Compare the percentage of the flights correctly classified by Naive Bayes to the fraction correctly classified by the proportional classification rule.

3. Develop a linear classification rule for the `Flighttimedata.xlsx` data. Does your rule outperform the Naive Bayes classifier?

4. Using the *Wall Street Journal* data, incorporate nonlinearities and interactions into a classification rule.

40

Analysis of Variance: One-way ANOVA

Often the marketing analyst wants to determine if varying a single factor has a significant effect on a marketing outcome such as sales or click-through rates. For example, take the following situations:

- Does a Valentine's Day card sell better on the top, middle, or bottom shelf?
- Does the number of click-throughs generated by an online ad depend on whether the background color is red, green, or blue?
- Do cookies sell more if they are placed on display in the candy aisle, cookie aisle, or cereal aisle?
- Does the sale of a computer book depend on whether the book is placed in the front, back, or middle of the computer section?

The factors being analyzed here include the shelf position, background color, display aisle, or placement. One-way Analysis of Variance (ANOVA) provides an easy way to help with this analysis. In this chapter you use the ANOVA: Single Factor option from the Data Analysis add-in to determine if varying a single factor such as these has a significant effect on the mean value of a marketing outcome.

Testing Whether Group Means Are Different

In one-way or single-factor ANOVA, the analyst measures the level of a response variable for G different levels of a single factor. The different levels of the single factor are often referred to as *groups* or *treatments*. For example, in the Valentine's Day example, $G = 3$ and the groups are the top, bottom, and middle shelf. The analyst wants to choose between the following hypotheses:

- **Null Hypothesis:** The means of all groups are identical. For example, in the Valentine's Day card situation, the Null Hypothesis states that mean card sales in all three shelf positions are identical.
- **Alternative Hypothesis:** There is a statistically significant difference between the groups' means. For example, in the Valentine's Day card situation, the Alternative Hypothesis states that there is a statistically significant difference between card sales for different shelf placement of the card.

To test these hypotheses in Microsoft Office Excel, you can use the ANOVA: Single Factor option in the Data Analysis dialog box. If the p-value computed by Excel is small (usually less than or equal to 0.05), you can conclude that the Alternative Hypothesis is true. (The means are significantly different.) If the p-value is greater than 0.05, you can conclude that the Null Hypothesis is true, that is, the group means are identical.

Example of One-way ANOVA

Suppose Wiley Publishing wants to know whether its books sell better when a display is set up in the front, back, or middle of the computer book section. Weekly sales (in hundreds) were monitored at 12 different stores. At 5 stores the books were placed in the front; at 4 stores in the back; and at 3 stores in the middle. Resulting sales are contained in the Signif worksheet in the file OnewayANOVA.xlsx, which is shown in Figure 40-1. Does the data indicate that the location of the books has a significant effect on sales?

	A	B	C	D
1	One-Way ANOVA			
2				
3		Front	Back	Middle
4		7	12	10
5		10	13	11
6		8	15	12
7		9	16	
8		11		

Figure 40-1: Bookstore data where null hypothesis is rejected

The analysis requires the assumption that the 12 stores have similar sales patterns and are approximately the same size. This assumption enables you to use one-way ANOVA because you believe that, at most, one factor (the position of the display in the computer book section) is affecting sales. (If the stores were different sizes, you would need to analyze your data with two-way ANOVA, which is discussed in Chapter 41, "Analysis of Variance: Two-way ANOVA.")

To analyze the data, on the Data tab, click Data Analysis, and then select ANOVA: Single Factor. Fill in the dialog box, as shown in Figure 40-2.

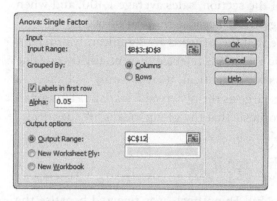

Figure 40-2: Dialog box for bookstore example

Use the following settings (The data for your input range, including labels, is in cells B3:D8.):

1. Select the Labels option because the first row of your input range contains labels.
2. Select the Columns option because the data is organized in columns.
3. Select C12 as the upper-left cell of the output range.
4. The selected Alpha value is not important. Just use the default value.
5. Click OK, and you obtain the results, as shown in Figure 40-3.

	C	D	E	F	G	H	I
12	Anova: Single Factor						
13							
14	SUMMARY						
15	Groups	Count	Sum	Average	Variance		
16	Front	5	45	9	2.5		
17	Back	4	56	14	3.333333		
18	Middle	3	33	11	1		
19							
20							
21	ANOVA						
22	Source of Variation	SS	df	MS	F	P-value	F crit
23	Between Groups	55.66667	2	27.83333	11.38636	0.00343	4.25649
24	Within Groups	22	9	2.444444			
25							
26	Total	77.66667	11				
27							
28	est std error	1.563472					

Figure 40-3: ANOVA results for bookstore example where Null Hypothesis is rejected

In cells F16:F18, you can see average sales depending on the location of the display. When the display is at the front of the computer book section, average sales are 900; when the display is at the back of the section, sales average 1,400; and when the display is in the middle, sales average 1,100. Because the p-value of 0.003 (in cell H23) is less than 0.05, you can conclude that these means are significantly different, so the Null Hypothesis of identical group means is rejected. Essentially the p-value of 0.003 means that if the group means were identical, there are only 3 chances in 1,000 of getting an F statistic at least as large as the observed F statistic. This small probability leads you to reject the hypothesis that the group means are identical.

The Role of Variance in ANOVA

In the Wiley bookstore example, the Null Hypothesis was rejected because the means differed significantly, but ANOVA stands for One-way Analysis of Variance, not One-way Analysis of Means. Therefore, the bookstore example result changes if you add variation in sales to your data.

Take a look instead at the data on a book sales study from the Insig worksheet of the file OnewayANOVA.xlsx, as shown in Figure 40-4. If you run a one-way ANOVA on this data, you can obtain the results shown in Figure 40-5.

	E	F	G	H	I
9					
10					
11					
12	Anova: Single Factor		Overall mean		
13			11.1666667		
14	SUMMARY				
15	Groups	Count	Sum	Average	Variance
16	Front	5	45	9	44
17	Back	4	56	14	90
18	Middle	3	33	11	64
19					

Figure 40-4: Bookstore data where Null Hypothesis is accepted

	E	F	G	H	I	J	K	L
21	ANOVA							
22	Source of Variation	SS	df	MS	F	P-value	F crit	
23	Between Groups	55.66667	2	27.83333	0.436411	0.659334	4.25649	
24	Within Groups	574	9	63.77778				
25								
26	Total	629.6667	11					
27								
28	est std err	7.986099						

Figure 40-5: ANOVA results where Null Hypothesis is accepted

The mean sales for each part of the store are exactly as before, yet the *p*-value of .66 indicates that you should accept the Null Hypothesis and conclude that the position of the display in the computer book section doesn't affect sales. The reason for this strange result is that in the second data set, you have much more variation in sales when the display is at each position in the computer book section. In the first data set, for example, the variation in sales when the display is at the front is between 700 and 1,100, whereas in the second data set, the variation in sales is between 200 and 2,000. The variation of sales within each store (called the Within Groups Sum of Squares on the printout but more commonly the Sum of Squared Errors) is measured by the sum of the squares of all the observations about their group means. For example, in the first data set, the Within Groups Sum of Squares is computed as the following:

$$(7-9)^2+(10-9)^2+(8-9)^2+(9-9)^2+(11-9)^2+(12-14)^2+(13-14)^2+$$
$$(15-14)^2+(16-14)^2+(10-11)^2+(11-11)^2+(12-11)^2=22$$

This measure is shown in cell D24 in the first data set and in cell F24 in the second. In the first data set, the sum of squares of data within groups is only 22, whereas in the second data set, the sum of squares within groups is 574! The large variation within the data points at each store for the second data set masks the variation between the groups (store positions) and makes it impossible to conclude for the second data set that the difference between sales in different store positions is significant. Because the variation within a group plays a critical role in determining the acceptance or rejection of the Null Hypothesis, statistics call the technique Analysis of Variance instead of Analysis of Means.

> **NOTE**   If you simply wanted to determine the actual difference in group means (and not test for statistical significance), then you could utilize PivotTables (Chapter 1, "Slicing and Dicing Marketing Data with PivotTables") or Excel's AVERAGEIF or AVERAGEIFS functions (Chapter 3, "Using Excel Functions to Summarize Marketing Data").

Forecasting with One-way ANOVA

If there is a significant difference between group means, the best forecast for each group is simply the group's mean. Therefore, in the `Signif` worksheet in the file `OnewayANOVA.xlsx`, you can predict the following:

- Sales when the display is at the front of the computer book section will be 900 books per week.

- Sales when the display is at the back will be 1,400 books per week.
- Sales when the display is in the middle will be 1,100 books per week.

If there is no significant difference between the group means, the best forecast for each observation is simply the overall mean. Thus, in the second data set, you can predict weekly sales of 1,117, independent of where the books are placed.

You can also estimate the accuracy of the forecasts. The square root of the Within Groups MS (Mean Square) is the standard deviation of the forecasts from a one-way ANOVA. As shown in Figure 40-6, the standard deviation of forecasts for the first data set is 156. Two assumptions needed for a one-way ANOVA to be valid are:

- The residuals or forecast errors for each observation (residual = actual sales – predicted sales) are normally distributed.
- The variance of the residuals for each group is identical. (This is analogous to the homoscedasticity assumption for multiple regression discussed in Chapter 10.)

	C	D	E	F	G	H	I
11							
12	Anova: Single Factor						
13							
14	SUMMARY						
15	Groups	Count	Sum	Average	Variance		
16	Front	5	45	9	2.5		
17	Back	4	56	14	3.333333		
18	Middle	3	33	11	1		
19							
20							
21	ANOVA						
22	Source of Variation	SS	df	MS	F	P-value	F crit
23	Between Groups	55.66667	2	27.83333	11.38636	0.00343	4.25649
24	Within Groups	22	9	2.444444			
25							
26	Total	77.66667	11				
27							
28	est std error	1.563472					
29							

Figure 40-6: Computing standard deviation of forecasts

Assume that in the current example these assumptions are met. Recall that for a normal random variable, the rule of thumb tells you that for 68 percent of all observations the absolute value of the residual should be less than one standard deviation, and for 95 percent of all observations, the absolute value of the residual should be less than two standard deviations. It now follows that:

- During 68 percent of all the weeks in which books are placed at the front of the computer section, sales will be between 900-156=744 and 900+156=1056 books.

- During 95 percent of all weeks in which books are placed at the front of the computer book section, sales will be between `900-2(156)=588` books and `900+2(156)=1212` books.

Contrasts

The ANOVA output provided by Excel tells whether there is a significant difference between the group means. If a significant difference between the group means exists, then the marketing analyst often wants to dig deeper and determine which group means result in the rejection of the Null Hypothesis. The study of *contrasts* can help you better understand the difference between group means.

Suppose there are G groups in a one-way ANOVA and group g has an unknown mean of μg. Marketing analysts often want to analyze a quantity of the form $c_1\,\mu_1 + c_2\,\mu_2 + \ldots, c_G\mu_G$, where the c_is is added to 0. Such a linear combination of the group means is called a *contrast*. As an example of why analyzing contrasts is important, suppose Barnes & Noble wants to determine if computer books sell at a different rate in East Coast and West Coast bookstores. During the month of June, daily sales of computer books were tracked in eight stores (see Figure 40-7 and worksheet `final` of workbook `CityANOVA.xlsx`) in each of six cities: San Francisco, Seattle, Los Angeles, New York City, Philadelphia, and Boston. Assume that all the stores are of similar size and have had similar sales patterns of books in the past. The hypothesis that East Coast and West Coast sales are the same is equivalent to Equation 1:

$$(1)\quad \frac{\mu_1 + \mu_2 + \mu_3}{3} - \frac{\mu_4 + \mu_5 + \mu_6}{3} = 0$$

The left side of Equation 1 is a contrast with $c_1 = c_2 = c_3 = 1/3$ and $c_4 = c_5 = c_6 = -1/3$.

	E	F	G	H	I	J	K	L	M	N
1	Ci^2/Ni	0.01388889		0.013888889	0.013889	0.013889	0.013889	0.013889			
2	Ci^2	0.1111111		0.1111111	0.1111111	0.1111111	0.1111111	0.1111111			
3	Ci	0.3333		0.3333	0.3333	-0.333333	-0.333333	-0.333333		∑CiMeani	-0.31458
4	Ni	8		8	8	8	8	8		∑Ci^2/Ni	0.083333
5	means	51.66		51.335	51.24	51.6225	51.69875	51.8575			
6		SF	Seattle		LA	NYC	PHIL	BOS		Test Statistic	-3.30112
7		51.28		51.46	51.07	51.7	51.82	52.12		df	42
8		51.63		51.15	51.44	51.69	51.7	52.29		Critical Value	2.018082
9		51.06		51.21	50.91	52.12	51.25	51.42			
10		51.66		51.07	51.11	51.23	51.68	51.88		pvalue	0.001971
11		52.2		51.84	50.77	51.51	51.76	52			
12		51.27		51.46	51.86	52.02	51.63	51.84			
13		52.31		51.5	51.22	51.36	51.61	51.57			
14		51.87		50.99	51.54	51.35	52.14	51.74			

Figure 40-7: Computer book sales

Once you have determined the contrast, you can test whether a given contrast is statistically significant from 0. For this example the following hypotheses are of interest:

- **Null Hypothesis:** A given contrast = 0. In this example the Null Hypothesis corresponds to average West Coast sales = average East Coast sales
- **Alternative Hypothesis:** The given contrast is not equal to 0. In this example the Alternative Hypothesis corresponds to average West Coast sales are not equal to average East Coast sales.

To test these hypotheses you need to compute the following test statistic:

$$(2) \quad \frac{\sum_{i=1}^{i=G} (Group\ i\ sample\ mean) * c_i}{s * \sqrt{\sum_{i=1}^{i=G} c_i^2 / n_i}}$$

In Equation 2, n_i = number of observations taken in Group i and $s = \sqrt{MSE}$.

The p-value for the hypothesis is that the contrast =0 can be computed in Excel via the formula =T.DIST.2T(ABS(Test Statistic), N-G), where N = total number of observations. In this example $N = 48$ and $G = 6$.

After running a one-way ANOVA on the data (refer to Figure 40-7), you obtain the results shown in Figure 40-8. Cell J35 gives the MSE = 0.108976, and you find in cell I18 that $s = \sqrt{0.108976} = 0.330115$. The calculations to compute the test statistic are shown in Figure 40-7. Complete the following steps to test whether or not the contrast of interest is significantly different from 0.

1. In the range F3:K3 enter each C_i. The first three C_i's = 1/3 and the last three = –1/3.
2. In F4:K4 enter each N_i = 8.
3. Copy the formula =F3^2 from F2 to G2:K2 to compute each C_i^2.
4. Copy the formula =F2/F4 from F1 to G1:K1 to compute each C_i^2/N_i.
5. In cell N3 use the formula =SUMPRODUCT(F3:K3,F5:K5) to compute $\sum C_i$*(Sample Mean Group i).
6. In cell N4 use the formula =SUM(F1:K1) to compute $\sum C_i$^2/N_i.
7. In cell N6 compute the test statistic (which is known to follow a t-distribution with $N - G$ degrees of freedom) with the formula =N3/(I18*SQRT(N4)).
8. In cell N10 compute the p-value for your hypothesis test with the formula =T.DIST.2T(ABS(N6),42). The p-value of 0.00197 indicates that according to the data, there are roughly 2 chances in 1,000 that the mean sales in East Coast and West Coast cities are identical. Therefore, you can reject the Null Hypotheses and conclude that West Coast sales of computer books are significantly higher than sales of East Coast computer books.

9. For alpha = 0.05 compute the cutoff or *critical value* for rejecting the Null Hypothesis in Excel with the formula =TINV(.05,N-G). In this case a test statistic exceeding 2.02 in absolute value would result in rejection of the Null Hypothesis.

	G	H	I	J	K	L	M
16					West Coast Mean=East Coast Mean		
17					Is rejected		
18		s	0.330115		for alpha = .05		
19							
20	Anova: Single Factor						
21							
22	SUMMARY						
23	*Groups*	*Count*	*Sum*	*Average*	*Variance*		
24	SF	8	413.28	51.66	0.202229		
25	Seattle	8	410.68	51.335	0.078943		
26	LA	8	409.92	51.24	0.1272		
27	NYC	8	412.98	51.6225	0.103707		
28	PHIL	8	413.59	51.69875	0.06107		
29	BOS	8	414.86	51.8575	0.080707		
30							
31							
32	ANOVA						
33	*Source of Variation*	*SS*	*df*	*MS*	*F*	*P-value*	*F crit*
34	Between Groups	2.19366	5	0.438732	4.025955	0.004489	2.43769264
35	Within Groups	4.576988	42	0.108976			
36							
37	Total	6.770648	47				
38							

Figure 40-8: ANOVA output for computer book sales

Exercise 3 will give you more practice in testing hypotheses involving contrasts.

Summary

In this chapter you learned how to analyze if a single factor has a significant effect on a measured variable.

- After running the ANOVA: Single Factor choice from Data Analysis on the Analysis group on the Data tab, you can conclude that the factor has a significant effect on the mean of the measured variable if the p-value is less than 0.05.
- If the ANOVA p-value is > 0.05, the predicted mean for each group equals the overall mean, whereas if the ANOVA p-value is < 0.05, the predicted mean for each group equals the group mean.

To test whether a contrast of the form $c_1\mu_1 + c_2\mu_2 + \ldots, c_g\mu_g = 0$, compute the test statistic using Equation 2:

$$(2) \quad \frac{\sum_{i=1}^{i=g}(\text{Group } i \text{ sample mean}) * c_i}{s * \sqrt{\sum_{i=1}^{i=g} c_i^2 / n_i}}$$

You can compute the p-value for the Null Hypothesis in Excel with the formula =T.DIST.2T(ABS(Test Statistic), N-G). If this p-value is < 0.05, the Null Hypothesis is rejected, and you conclude that the contrast is significantly different from 0. Otherwise, the Null Hypothesis is accepted.

Exercises

1. In the file Usedcars.xlsx you are given daily sales of used cars sold by four used-car salespeople.

   - Is there evidence that the salespeople exhibit a significant difference in performance?
   - Fill in the blank. You are 95 percent sure that the number of cars sold in a day by Salesperson 1 is between ___ and ___.
   - If the first two people are men and the last two are women, is there significant evidence that the male salespeople perform differently than the female salespeople?

2. A cake can be produced by using a 400-degree, 300-degree, or 200-degree oven. In the file cakes.xlsx you are given the quality level of cakes produced when the cakes are baked at different temperatures.

   - Does temperature appear to influence cake quality?
   - What is the range of cake quality that you are 95 percent sure will be produced with a 200-degree oven?
   - If you believe that the size of the oven used influences cake quality, does this analysis remain valid?

3. The file Salt.xlsx gives weekly sales of salt (in pounds) when one, two, and three package facings were used at Kroger's supermarkets of similar size.

   - Does the number of facings impact sales of salt?
   - Does adding the third facing result in a significantly different sales improvement than when adding the second facing?

4. In Exercise 3 suppose you thought there was seasonality in salt sales and the data points were from different months of the year. Could one-way ANOVA still be used to analyze the data?

41

Analysis of Variance: Two-way ANOVA

In Chapter 40, "Analysis of Variance: One-way ANOVA," you studied one-way ANOVA where only one factor influenced a dependent variable. When two factors might influence a dependent variable, you can use two-way analysis of variance (ANOVA) to determine which, if any, of the factors have a significant influence on the dependent variable. In this chapter you learn about how two-way ANOVA can be used to analyze situations in which two factors may possibly affect a dependent variable.

Introducing Two-way ANOVA

In many marketing situations the marketing analyst believes that two factors may affect a dependent variable of interest. Here are some examples:

- How can the salespeople and their territory affect sales?
- How can price and advertising affect sales?
- How can the type of button and shape of a banner ad affect the number of click-throughs?

When two factors might influence a dependent variable you can use two-way analysis of variance (ANOVA) to easily determine which, if any, of the two factors influence the dependent variable. In two-way ANOVA the dependent variable must be observed the same number of times (call it k) for each combination of the two factors. If $k = 1$, the situation is called two-way ANOVA without replication. If $k>1$ the situation is called two-way ANOVA with replication. When $k > 1$ you can determine whether two factors exhibit a significant *interaction* (discussed in more detail in the section, "Two-way ANOVA with Interactions"). For example, suppose you want to predict sales by using product price and advertising budget. Price and advertising interact significantly if the effect of advertising depends on the product price. Interaction was discussed in the study of multiple regression in Chapter 10, "Using Multiple Regression to Forecast Sales." In a two-way ANOVA without replication there is no way to examine the significance of interactions.

Two-way ANOVA without Replication

In a *two-way ANOVA without replication* you can observe each possible combination of factors exactly once. Unfortunately, there is never enough data to test for the significance of interactions. A two-way ANOVA without replication can, however, be used to determine which (if any) of two factors have a significant effect on a dependent variable.

Suppose you want to determine how a sales representative and the sales district to which the representative is assigned influence product sales. To answer the question in this example, you can have each of four sales reps spend 1 month selling in each of five sales districts. The resulting sales are given in the `Randomized Blocks` worksheet in the `Twowayanova.xlsx` file, as shown in Figure 41-1. For example, Rep 1 sold 20 units during the month she was assigned to District 4.

	C	D	E	F	G
4					
5		Rep 1	Rep 2	Rep 3	Rep 4
6	Dist 1	1	3	10	12
7	Dist 2	17	12	16	14
8	Dist 3	17	21	22	25
9	Dist 4	20	10	17	23
10	Dist 5	22	21	37	32

Figure 41-1: Randomized blocks data

This model is called a two-way ANOVA without replication because two factors (district and sales representative) can potentially influence sales, and you have only a single instance pairing each representative with each district. This model is also referred to as a *randomized block* design because you can randomize (chronologically) the assignment of representatives to districts. In other words, you can ensure that the month in which Rep 1 is assigned to District 1 is equally likely to be the first, second, third, fourth, or fifth month. This randomization hopefully lessens the effect of time (a representative presumably becomes better over time) on the analysis. In a sense, you "block" the effect of districts when you try to compare sales representatives and use randomization to account for the possible impact of time on sales.

To analyze this data in Microsoft Office Excel, click Data Analysis on the Data tab, and then select the Anova: Two-Factor Without Replication option. Fill in the dialog box as shown in Figure 41-2. Use the following information to set up your analysis (the input range data is in cells C5:G10):

1. Check Labels because the first row of the input range contains labels.
2. Enter B12 as the upper-left cell of the output range.
3. The alpha value is not important, so just use the default value.

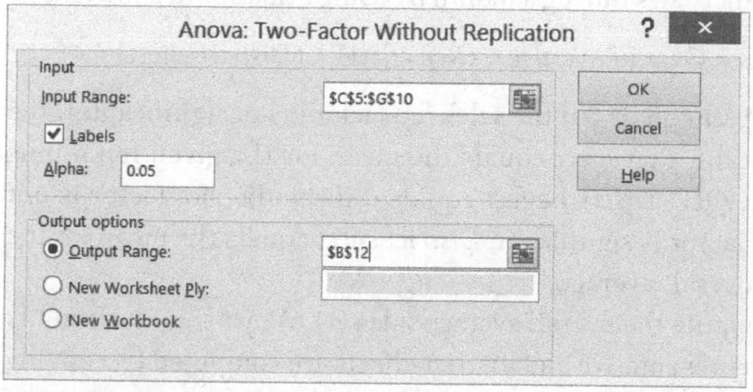

Figure 41-2: Randomized blocks dialog box settings

The output obtained is shown in Figure 41-3. (The results in cells G12:G24 were not created by the Excel Data Analysis feature. Instead, formulas are entered in these cells, as explained later in this section.)

	B	C	D	E	F	G	H
12	Anova: Two-Factor Without Replication					17.6	
13							
14	SUMMARY	Count	Sum	Average	Variance		
15	Dist 1	4	26	6.5	28.33333	-11.1	
16	Dist 2	4	59	14.75	4.916667	-2.85	
17	Dist 3	4	85	21.25	10.91667	3.65	
18	Dist 4	4	70	17.5	31	-0.1	
19	Dist 5	4	112	28	60.66667	10.4	
20						-17.6	
21	Rep 1	5	77	15.4	69.3	-2.2	
22	Rep 2	5	67	13.4	59.3	-4.2	
23	Rep 3	5	102	20.4	104.3	2.8	
24	Rep 4	5	106	21.2	67.7	3.6	
25							
26							
27	ANOVA						
28	Source of Variation	SS	df	MS	F	P-value	F crit
29	Rows	1011.3	4	252.825	15.87598	9.74E-05	3.25917
30	Columns	216.4	3	72.13333	4.529566	0.024095	3.49029
31	Error	191.1	12	15.925			
32			stdev	3.990614			
33	Total	1418.8	19				

Figure 41-3 Randomized Block output

To determine whether the row factor (districts) or column factor (sales representatives) has a significant effect on sales, just look at the p-value. If the p-value for a factor is low (less than 0.05) the factor has a significant effect on sales. The row p-value (0.0000974) and column p-value (0.024) are both less than 0.05, so both the district and the representative have a significant effect on sales.

Given that the representative and the district both have significant effects on product sales, you can predict sales during a month by using Equation 1, shown here:

(1) *Predicted sales = Overall average + (Rep effect) + (District effect)*

In this equation, *Rep effect* equals 0 if the sales rep factor is not significant. If the sales rep factor is significant, *Rep effect* equals the mean for the given rep minus |the overall average. Likewise, *District effect* equals 0 if the district factor is not significant. If the district factor is significant, *District effect* equals the mean for the given district minus the overall average.

In cell G12 you can compute the overall average sales (17.6) by using the formula =AVERAGE(D6:G10). The representative and district effects are computed by copying from cell G15 to G16:G24 the formula =E15-$G$12. For example, you can compute predicted sales by Rep 4 in District 2 as 17.6 – 2.85 + 3.6 = 18.35. This value is computed in cell D38 (see Figure 41-4) with the formula =G12+G16+G24. If the district effect was significant and the sales representative effect was not, the predicted sales for Rep 4 in District 2 would be 17.6 – 2.85 = 14.75. If the district was not significant and the sales rep effect was significant then the predicted sales for Rep 4 in District 2 would be 17.6 + 3.6 = 21.2.

	C	D
34		
35		
36	District 2	
37	Rep 4 Forecast	
38	Mean	18.35
39	Lower	10.3688
40	Upper	26.3312

Figure 41-4: Estimating sales by Representative 4 in District 2

As in one-way ANOVA, the standard deviation (3.99) of the forecast errors is the square root of the mean square error shown in cell E31. This standard deviation is computed in cell E32 with the formula =SQRT(E31). Thus, you are 95 percent sure that if Rep 4 is assigned to District 2, monthly sales will be between 18.35 – 2 * (3.99) = 10.37 and 18.35 + 2 * (3.99) = 26.33. These limits are computed in cell D39 and D40 with the formulas =$D$38-2*$E$32 and =$D$38+2*$E$32, respectively.

Two-way ANOVA with Replication

When you have more than one observation for each combination of the row and column factors, you have a two-factor ANOVA *with* replication. To perform this sort of analysis, Excel requires that you have the same number of observations for each row-and-column combination.

In addition to testing for the significance of the row and column factors, you can also test for significant interaction between them. For example, if you want to understand how price and advertising affect sales, an interaction between price and advertising would indicate that the effect of an advertising change would depend on the price level. (Or equivalently, the effect of a price change would depend on the advertising level.) A lack of interaction between price and advertising would mean that the effect of a price change would not depend on the level of advertising.

As an example of two-factor ANOVA with replication, suppose you want to determine how the price and advertising level affects the monthly sales of a video game. In the Two Way ANOVA no interaction worksheet in the file Twowayanova.xlsx, you have the data shown in Figure 41-5. During the three months with low advertising and a medium price, for example, 21, 20, and 16 units were sold. In this example there are three replications for each price-advertising combination. The replications represent the three months during which each price-advertising combination was observed.

	B	C	D	E	F	G
1		Average	25.04			
2			Price			
3			Low	Medium	High	Effect
4		Low	41	21	10	-5.5926
5	Adv		25	20	11	
6			23	16	8	
7		Medium	28	28	11	-1.8148
8			30	22	22	
9			32	18	18	
10		High	35	26	21	7.4074
11			45	40	26	
12			47	32	20	
13		Effect	8.963	-0.2593	-8.7	

Figure 41-5: Data for two-way ANOVA with no interaction

Cell D1 shows the computation for the overall average (25.037) of all observations with the formula =AVERAGE(D4:F12). Cells G4, G7, and G10, show the computation for the effect for each level of advertising. For example, the effect of having a low level of advertising equals the average for low advertising minus the overall average. Cell G4 shows the computation for the low advertising effect of –5.59 with the formula =AVERAGE(D4:F6)-$D$1. In a similar fashion, you can see the effect of each price level by copying from D13 to E13:F13 the formula =AVERAGE(D4:D12)-$D$1.

To analyze this data, click Data Analysis on the Data tab, and then select Anova: Two-Factor With Replication in the Data Analysis dialog box. Fill in the dialog box as shown in Figure 41-6.

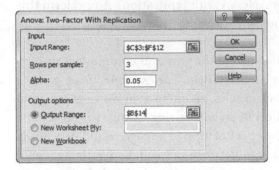

Figure 41-6: ANOVA: Two-Factor with Replication dialog box for running a two-factor ANOVA with replication

You can use the following information to set up your analysis (The input range data, including labels, is in C3:F12):

1. In two-way ANOVA with replication, Excel requires a label for each level of the column effect in the first row of each column in the input range. Thus, enter low, medium, and high in cells D3:F3 to indicate the possible price levels.

2. Excel also requires a label for each level of the row effect in the first column of the input range. These labels must appear in the row that marks the beginning of the data for each level. Thus place labels corresponding to low, medium, and high levels of advertising in cells C4, C7, and C10.

3. In the Rows Per Sample box, enter 3 because you have three replications for each combination of price and advertising level.

4. Enter B14 in the upper-left cell of the output range.

The only important portion of the output is the ANOVA table, which is shown in Figure 41-7.

As with randomized blocks, an effect (including interactions) is significant if it has a p-value that's less than 0.05. Sample (this is the row for advertising effect) and Price (shown in the row labeled Columns) are highly significant and there is no significant interaction. (The interaction p-value is 0.79!) Therefore, you can conclude that price and advertising influence sales and that the effect of advertising on sales does not depend on the price level. Figure 41-8 graphically demonstrates that price and advertising do not exhibit a significant interaction. To create this chart, complete the following steps:

1. In the cell range I20:K22 compute the average sales for each price and advertising combination.
2. Select the range I19:K22 and select the first line chart option.
3. From the Design tab choose Switch Row/Column to place advertising categories on the x-axis.

	B	C	D	E	F	G	H	I
42	ANOVA							
43	Source of Variation	SS	df	MS	F	P-value	F crit	F crit
44	Sample	804.962963	2	402.481	13.52	0.0003	3.5546	3.55456109
45	Columns	1405.407407	2	702.704	23.6	9E-06	3.5546	3.55456109
46	Interaction	50.59259259	4	12.6481	0.425	0.7888	2.9277	2.92774871
47	Within	536	18	29.7778				
48								
49	Total	2796.962963	26					

Figure 41-7: Two-way ANOVA with replication output; no interaction

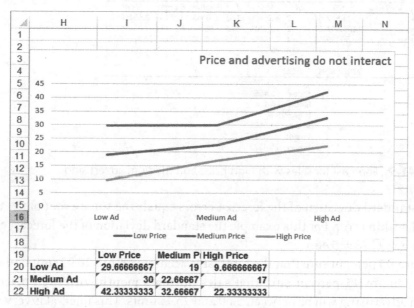

Figure 41-8: Price and advertising do not interact in this data set

Notice that as advertising increases, sales increase at roughly the same rate, whether the price level is low, medium, or high. This fact is indicated by the near parallelism of the three curves shown in the graph.

Forecasting Sales if Interaction is Absent

In the absence of a significant interaction, you can forecast sales in a two-factor ANOVA with replication in the same way that you do in a two-factor ANOVA without replication. Use Equation 2 to do so:

(2) Predicted sales = Overall average + [Row or advertising effect
(if significant)] + [Column or price effect(if significant)]

The analysis assumes that price and advertising are the only factors that affect sales. If sales are highly seasonal, seasonality would need to be incorporated into the analysis. (Seasonality was discussed in Chapters 10 and 12–14.) For example, when price is high and advertising is medium, the predicted sales are given by $25.037 + (-1.814) + (-8.704) = 14.52$. (See cell E54 in Figure 41-9.) Referring to Figure 41-5, you can see that the overall average is equal to 25.037, the medium advertising effect equals –1.814, and the high price effect equals –8.704.

	B	C	D	E	F	G	H	I
42	ANOVA							
43	Source of Variation	SS	df	MS	F	P-value	F crit	F crit
44	Sample	804.962963	2	402.481	13.52	0.0003	3.5546	3.55456109
45	Columns	1405.407407	2	702.704	23.6	9E-06	3.5546	3.55456109
46	Interaction	50.59259259	4	12.6481	0.425	0.7888	2.9277	2.92774871
47	Within	536	18	29.7778				
48								
49	Total	2796.962963	26					
50								
51				Stdev	5.4569			
52				Medium Ad				
53				High Price				
54				Mean	14.5185			
55				Lower	3.60471			
56				Upper	25.4323			

Figure 41-9: Forecast for sales with high price and medium advertising

The standard deviation of the forecast errors equals the square root of the mean squared within error. For this example the standard deviation of the forecast errors is given by $\sqrt{29.78} = 5.46$.

You are 95 percent sure that the forecast is accurate within 10.92 units. In other words, you are 95-percent sure that sales during a month with high price and medium advertising will be between 3.60 and 25.43 units. This interval is very wide, suggesting that even after knowing the price and advertising level, a great deal of uncertainty remains about the level of sales.

Two-way ANOVA with Interactions

The Two WAY ANOVA with Interaction worksheet contains data from the previous example changed to the data shown in Figure 41-10. After running the analysis for a two-factor ANOVA with replication, you can obtain the results shown in Figure 41-11.

	C	D	E	F	G
1					
2				Price	
3					
4			Low	Mediur	High
5		Low	41	21	15
6	Adv		25	20	14
7			23	16	13
8		Medium	28	28	14
9			30	22	13
10			32	18	12
11		High	50	34	13
12			51	40	13
13			52	32	13

Figure 41-10: Sales data with interaction between price and advertising

	C	D	E	F	G	H	I
43	ANOVA						
44	*Source of Variation*	*SS*	*df*	*MS*	*F*	*P-value*	*F crit*
45	Sample	828.963	2	414.48	24.22	7.86E-06	3.55456
46	Columns	2498.74	2	1249.4	73.02	2.31E-09	3.55456
47	Interaction	509.926	4	127.48	7.45	0.001006	2.92775
48	Within	308	18	17.111			
49							
50	Total	4145.63	26				
51		Std dev	4.137				
52							

Figure 41-11: Output for the two-way ANOVA with Interaction

In this data set, you can find the *p*-value for interaction is 0.001. When you see a low *p*-value (less than 0.05) for interaction, *do not even check p-values for row and column factors!* You simply forecast sales for any price and advertising combination to equal the mean of the three observations involving that price and advertising combination. For example, the best forecast for sales during a month with high advertising and medium price is:

$$\frac{30+40+32}{3} \ 35.333 \text{ units}$$

The standard deviation of the forecast errors is again the square root of the mean square within $\sqrt{17.11} = 4.137 =$ units.

Thus you are 95-percent sure that the sales forecast is accurate within 8.27 units.

Figure 41-12 illustrates why this data exhibits a significant interaction between price and advertising. For a low and medium price, increased advertising increases sales, but if price is high, increased advertising has no effect on sales. This explains why you cannot use Equation 2 to forecast sales when a significant interaction is present. After all, how can you talk about an advertising effect when the effect of advertising depends on the price? Figure 41-12 is in sharp contrast to Figure 41-8 in which the near parallelism of the three curves indicates that for any level of price a change in advertising has a similar effect.

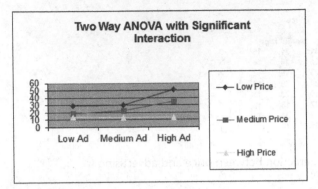

Figure 41-12: Price and advertising exhibit significant interactions in this set of data

Summary

In this chapter you learned the following:

- For two-way ANOVA without replication a factor is significant if its p-value is less than 0.05.
- For two-way ANOVA without replication the predicted value of the response variable is computed from Equation 1:

  (1) Predicted sales = Overall average + (Factor 1 effect) + (Factor 2 effect).

- In Equation 1 a factor effect is assumed to equal 0 if the factor is not significant.
- For two-way ANOVA with replication, first check if the Interaction effect is significant. This occurs if the p-value is less than 0.05. If the interaction effect is significant, then predict the value of the response variable for any combination of factor values to equal the mean of all observations having that combination of factor levels.
- If the interaction effect is not significant, then the analysis proceeds as in the two-way ANOVA without replication case.

Exercises

1. Assume that pressure (high, medium, or low) and temperature (high, medium, or low) influence the yield of a production process. Given this theory, use the data in the file `Yield.xlsx` to determine the answers to the following:
   a. Use the data in file `Yield.xlsx` to determine how temperature and/or pressure influence the yield of the process.
   b. With high pressure and low temperature, you are 95-percent sure that the process yield will be in what range?

2. Determine how the particular sales representative and the number of sales calls (one, three, or five) made to a doctor influence the amount (in thousands of dollars) that each doctor prescribes of a drug. Use the data in the `Doctors.xlsx` file to determine the answers to the following problems:
   a. How can the representative and number of sales calls influence the sales volume?
   b. If Rep 3 makes five sales calls to a doctor, you are 95-percent sure she will generate prescriptions within what range of dollars?

3. Answer the questions in Exercise 2 using the data in the `Doctors2.xlsx` workbook.

4. The `Coupondata.xlsx` file contains information on sales of peanut butter for weeks when a coupon was given out (or not) and when advertising was done (or not) in the Sunday paper. Describe how the coupon and advertising influence peanut butter sales.

XI Internet and Social Marketing

Chapter 42: Networks

Chapter 43: The Mathematics Behind *The Tipping Point*

Chapter 44: Viral Marketing

Chapter 45: Text Mining

42

Networks

You may be familiar with the movie *The Social Network* that describes the early days of Facebook. In general, a network consists of points (usually called *nodes*) that are connected by *links* (sometimes called arcs). You can easily associate (a huge!) network with Facebook in which the nodes are the members of Facebook and a link exists between two nodes if the people represented by the two nodes are friends. In this chapter you learn how marketing analysts describe networks and gain insight into how networks such as Facebook evolve. Applications of network theory to the spread of new products are also discussed. The chapter closes with a brief discussion of the well-known Klout score, which purports to measure an individual's online influence.

Measuring the Importance of a Node

It is important to have a way to measure the importance of a node or link. For example, on the Internet, Google, Bing, and Amazon.com are clearly more important nodes than the author's blog (www.waynewinston.com). Marketers would love to have a measure of influence so that they can reach the most influential people and have these people spread the word about their products. This section discusses three metrics (assuming that each link in the network is bidirectional) that you can use to measure the importance of a node:

- Degree centrality
- Closeness centrality
- Betweenness centrality

Degree Centrality

For any node its *degree centrality* is simply the number of nodes connected to the given node by a link. Take a look at the network shown in Figure 42-1.

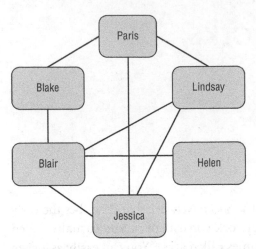

Figure 42-1: Example of a simple network

Table 42-1 shows the degree centrality of each node:

Table 42-1: Degree Centrality

Node	Degree Centrality
Paris	3
Blake	2
Blair	4
Jessica	3
Helen	1
Lindsay	3

For example, Lindsay's degree centrality is 3 because there are links connecting Lindsay to Paris, Blair, and Jessica. Also Helen's degree centrality is 1 because the only link to Helen is Blair. Degree centrality indicates that Blair is most influential and is only slightly more important than Jessica and Lindsay. Referring to Figure 42-1, however, it appears that Blair is much more influential than say Lindsay. For example, removing Blair from the network would result in there being no path to Helen. You can soon see that betweenness centrality (see the section "Betweenness Centrality") illuminates Blair's importance to the network. Therefore, the shortcoming of degree centrality is that it does not measure the extent to which a node's links help connect pairs of nodes.

Closeness Centrality

One way to look at the importance of a node is to assume a node is more important if the node is close to other nodes. To implement this idea, pick a given node (say Paris) and find the shortest path from Paris to each other node. Averaging those path lengths gives you an idea of how far Paris is from the rest of the network. Taking the reciprocal of the average path length (that is 1 / average path length) yields your measure of *closeness centrality*. This measure of closeness centrality is larger for nodes that tend to be closer to the other nodes in the network. Referring to the network in Figure 42-1, you can determine Paris' closeness centrality as follows:

- Shortest path from Paris to Blake has length 1.
- Shortest path from Paris to Blair (Paris-Blake-Blair) has length 2.
- Shortest path from Paris to Jessica has length 1.
- Shortest path from Paris to Helen has length 3 (Paris-Lindsay-Blair-Helen).
- Shortest path from Paris to Lindsay is length 1.
- The average of the length of these shortest paths is:

$\frac{1+2+1+3+1}{5}$ = 1.6 so Paris' closeness centrality is 1 / 1.6 = 5 / 8.

In a similar fashion you can find the closeness centrality of all nodes in Figure 42-1, as shown in Table 42-2.

Table 42-2: Closeness Centralities for Figure 42-1

Node	Closeness Centrality
Paris	5 / 8 = 0.625
Blake	5 / 8 = 0.625
Blair	5 / 6 = 0.833
Jessica	5 / 8 = 0.625
Helen	5 / 10 = 0.50
Lindsay	5 / 8 = 0.625

Closeness centrality indicates that Lindsay and Blake are almost as important as Blair. Note, however, the closeness centrality values of the nodes are close in value. This is typical, and changing even a large network by adding or deleting a few links can result in a large change in how the nodes rank for closeness centrality. Because a node with a large closeness centrality is close to the other nodes, a node with large closeness centrality is a good position to view what happens in the network. Closeness centrality does not measure the power of a node to influence how information flows through the network. To measure the power of a node to influence the flow of information through the network, you need the measure of betweenness centrality.

Betweenness Centrality

Suppose a marketer wants to spread knowledge of a new product throughout a network. She would then want to know which nodes have the most impact on the spread of information through the network. To illustrate how the concept of *betweenness centrality* measures a node's impact of information spread, focus on Blair. To compute Blair's betweenness centrality, follow these steps:

1. For each pair of nodes excluding Blair, find all shortest paths between the pair of nodes. For example, for the Blake-Lindsay pair, two shortest paths exist (Blake-Paris-Lindsay and Blake-Blair-Lindsay).

2. Determine the fraction of these shortest paths that include Blair. In this case ½ = 0.5 of the shortest paths that include Blair. Blair now earns 0.5 points toward betweenness centrality.

3. Summing Blair's points over the 10 pairs of nodes which exclude Blair yields Blair's betweenness centrality.

All the computations needed to compute Blair's and Paris' betweenness centrality are summarized in Table 42-3 and Table 42-4.

Table 42-3: Blair's Betweenness Centrality

Pair of Nodes	Shortest Paths	Points for Blair
Paris Blake	Paris-Blake	0 / 1 = 0
Paris Jessica	Paris-Jessica	0 / 1 = 0
Paris Helen	Paris-Blake-Blair-Helen and Paris-Lindsay-Blair-Helen	2 / 2 = 1
Paris Lindsay	Paris-Lindsay	0 / 1 = 0
Blake Jessica	Blake-Blair-Jessica	1 / 1 = 1
Blake Helen	Blake-Blair-Helen	1 / 1 = 1
Blake Lindsay	Blake-Paris-Lindsay and Blake-Blair-Lindsay	1 / 2 = 0.5
Jessica Helen	Jessica-Blair-Helen	1 / 1 = 1
Jessica Lindsay	Jessica-Lindsay	0 / 1 = 0
Helen Lindsay	Helen-Blair-Lindsay	1 / 1 = 1

Adding up the last column of this table, you can find that Blair's betweenness centrality is 5.5.

Table 42-4 shows the calculations needed to compute Paris' betweenness centrality.

Table 42-4 Paris' Betweenness Centrality

Pair of Nodes	Shortest Paths	Points for Paris
Blake Blair	Blake-Blair	0 / 1 = 0
Blake Jessica	Blake-Blair-Jessica	0 / 1 = 0
Blake Helen	Blake-Blair-Helen	0 / 1 = 0
Blake Lindsay	Blake-Paris-Lindsay and Blake-Blair-Lindsay	1 / 2 = 0.5
Blair Jessica	Blair-Jessica	0 / 1 = 0
Blair Helen	Blair-Helen	0 / 1 = 0
Blair Lindsay	Blair-Lindsay	0 / 1 = 0
Jessica Helen	Jessica-Blair-Helen	0 / 1 = 0
Jessica Lindsay	Jessica-Lindsay	0 / 1 = 0
Helen Lindsay	Helen-Blair-Lindsay	0 / 1 = 0

Adding up the last column of this table, you can see that Paris' betweenness centrality measure is 0.5. This indicates that Paris is not important in passing information through the network. This is good because while in South Africa, Paris Hilton said, "I love Africa in general. South Africa and West Africa they are both great countries." (http://www.foxnews.com/story/2008/03/25/paris-hilton-west-africa-is-great-country/)

Table 42-5 summarizes the betweenness centrality for each node referred to in Figure 42-1.

Table 42-5: Betweenness Centrality for Figure 42-1

Node	Betweenness Centrality
Paris	0.5
Blake	2 / 3 = 0.67
Blair	5.5
Lindsay	2 / 3 = 0.67
Helen	0
Jessica	2 / 3 = 0.67

Table 42-5 makes it clear that Blair is the key to spreading information through the network.

Measuring the Importance of a Link

Analogous to betweenness centrality for a node, you can define *link betweenness* as a measure of a link's importance in the network. To illustrate the concept, determine (see Table 42-6) the link betweenness for the Blake-Blair link.

1. For each pair of nodes, find all shortest paths between the pair of nodes. For example, for the Blake-Lindsay pair of nodes, two shortest paths of length 2 exist (Blake-Paris-Lindsay and Blake-Blair-Lindsay).

2. Determine the fraction of these shortest paths that include the Blake-Blair link. In this case ½ = 0.5 of the shortest paths includes Blair. The Blake-Lindsay pair of nodes now earns 0.5 points toward link betweenness for the Blake-Blair link.

3. Summing these points over all pairs of nodes yields the Blake-Blair link's link betweenness.

Table 42-6: Link Betweenness for Blake-Blair Link

Node Pair	Number of Shortest Paths Between Node Pair	Number of Shortest Paths Between Node Pair Including the Blake-Blair Link	Points Contributed to Link Betweenness
Blake-Blair	1	1	1 / 1 = 1
Blake-Jessica	1	1	1 / 1 = 1
Blake-Helen	1	1	1 / 1 = 1
Blake-Lindsay	2	1	1 / 2 = 0.5
Blake-Paris	1	0	0 / 1 = 0
Blair-Jessica	1	0	0 / 1 = 0
Blair-Helen	1	0	0 / 1 = 0
Blair-Lindsay	1	0	0 / 1 = 0
Blair-Paris	2	1	1 / 2 = 0.5
Jessica-Helen	1	0	0 / 1 = 0
Jessica-Lindsay	1	0	0 / 1 = 0
Jessica-Paris	1	0	0 / 1 = 0

continues

Table 42-6: Link Betweenness for Blake-Blair Link *(continued)*

Node Pair	Number of Shortest Paths Between Node Pair	Number of Shortest Paths Between Node Pair Including the Blake-Blair Link	Points Contributed to Link Betweenness
Helen-Lindsay	1	0	0 / 1 = 0
Helen-Paris	2	1	1 / 2 = 0.5
Lindsay-Paris	1	0	0 / 1 = 0

Adding up the third column of Table 42-6 shows the link betweenness for the Blake-Blair link is 4.5.

Table 42-7 shows the computation of the link betweenness for the Jessica-Blair link.

Table 42-7: Computation of Link Betweenness for Jessica-Blair link

Node Pair	Number of Shortest Paths Between Node Pair	Number of Shortest Paths Between Node Pair Including the Jessica-Blair Link	Points Contributed to Link Betweenness
Blake-Blair	1	0	0 / 1 = 0
Blake-Jessica	1	1	1 / 1 = 1
Blake-Helen	1	0	0 / 1 = 0
Blake-Lindsay	2	0	0 / 2 = 0
Blake-Paris	1	0	0 / 1 = 0
Blair-Jessica	1	1	1 / 1 = 1
Blair-Helen	1	0	0 / 1 = 0
Blair-Lindsay	1	0	0 / 1 = 0
Blair-Paris	2	0	0 / 2 = 0
Jessica-Helen	1	1	1 / 1 = 1
Jessica-Lindsay	1	0	0 / 1 = 1
Jessica-Paris	1	0	0 / 1 = 0
Helen-Lindsay	1	0	0 / 1 = 0
Helen-Paris	2	0	0 / 2 = 0
Lindsay-Paris	1	0	0 / 1 = 0

Adding up the numbers in the third column, you find that the Jessica-Blair link has a link betweenness of 3.

Summarizing Network Structure

Because large networks are complex, you need simple metrics that can be used to summarize a network's structure. In Chapter 3, "Using Excel Functions to Summarize Marketing Data," you learned how a large data set could be summarized by two numbers: the mean or median as a measure of typical value and the standard deviation as a measure of spread about the mean. In this section you learn how the structure of a large complex network can be summarized by two numbers:

- L = a measure of the average distance between network nodes.
- C = a local cluster coefficient, which measures the extent to which your friends are friends of one another.

Six Degrees of Separation

In 1967, Harvard sociology professor Stanly Milgram performed an interesting experiment. He gave 296 residents of Omaha, Nebraska, a letter and the name and address of a stockbroker living in a Boston suburb. The goal was to get the letter to the stockbroker with the minimum number of mailings, but the rule of the game was each time the letter was mailed the letter had to be mailed to a friend of the person mailing the letter. Two hundred and seventeen of the Omaha residents mailed the letter, and 64 made it to the stockbroker. Each time the letter mailed was referred to as a "hop." On average it took 5.2 hops to get the letter to the stockbroker (never more than 10 hops!) and the median number of hops was 6, hence the phrase "six degrees of separation."

Another example of six degrees of separation is the famous six degrees of the actor Kevin Bacon. Define a network in which the nodes are movie actors and actresses, and there is a link between two actors and/or actresses if they appeared in the same movie. Most actors can be linked to Kevin Bacon in six links or less. The website http://oracleofbacon.org/ enables you to find the path linking an actor or actress to Bacon. For example, as shown in Figure 42-2, Cate Blanchett can be linked to Kevin Bacon through John Goodman. You can then say Cate Blanchett's Bacon number is 2.

Definition and Computation of L

For any network define L = average over all pairs of nodes of the length of the shortest between the pairs of nodes. Essentially a small value for L means that for a randomly chosen pair of nodes it is likely that there exists a fairly short path connecting the nodes. On the other hand, a large value of L indicates that many pairs of nodes are not connected by short paths.

Cate Blanchett has a Bacon number of 2.

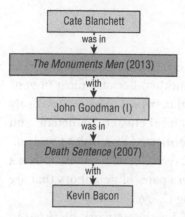

Figure 42-2: Cate Blanchett's Bacon number

For the network in Figure 42-1, the computations for L are shown in Table 42-8.

Table 42-8: Computation of L for Figure 42-1

Node Pair	Length of Shortest Path Between Node Pair
Blake-Blair	1
Blake-Jessica	2
Blake-Helen	2
Blake-Lindsay	2
Blake-Paris	1
Blair-Jessica	1
Blair-Helen	1
Blair-Lindsay	1
Blair-Paris	2
Jessica-Helen	2
Jessica-Lindsay	2
Jessica-Paris	1
Helen-Lindsay	2
Helen-Paris	3
Lindsay-Paris	1

Adding the second column you get 24, so $L = 24 / 15 = 1.6$. For such a small network, the small value of L is not surprising. The film actor network amazingly has $L = 3.65$. Amazingly the Facebook friends network has $L = 4.7$ and for just U.S Facebook users $L = 4.3$!

The Local Cluster Coefficient

A network's local cluster coefficient is a number between 0 and 1 that measures the tendency of a person's friends to be friends of one another. Because most of your friends know each other, you would expect most social networks to have a relatively large cluster coefficient. Before defining a network's local cluster coefficient, you need a definition: A *neighbor* of node n is any node connected by a link to node n.

To define a network's local clustering coefficient C, you define for each node n a cluster coefficient C_n, which is the fraction of node n's pairs of neighbors that are linked to each other. Then C is obtained by averaging C_n over all nodes.

The following illustrates the determination of C for the network pictured in Figure 42-1:

- Paris has three pairs of friends (Blake and Lindsay, Blake and Jessica, and Lindsay and Jessica) and one of these pairs (Lindsay and Jessica) is linked, so $C_{Paris} = \dfrac{1}{3}$.
- Blake has one pair of friends (Paris and Blair) and they are not linked, so $C_{Blake} = 0$.
- Blair has four friends (Blake, Jessica, Helen, and Lindsay), which results in six pairs of friends (Blake and Jessica, Blake and Helen, Blake and Lindsay, Jessica and Helen, Jessica and Lindsay, and Helen and Lindsay.) Of the six pairs of friends, only Jessica and Lindsay are linked, so $C_{Blair} = \dfrac{1}{6}$.
- Jessica has three pairs of friends (Blair and Lindsay, Blair and Paris, and Lindsay and Paris). Blair and Lindsay and Lindsay and Paris are linked, so $C_{Jessica} = \dfrac{2}{3}$.
- Helen has no pair of friends, so you can omit her when computing the average of the cluster coefficients for each node.
- Lindsay has three pairs of friends (Blair and Jessica, Blair and Paris, and Paris and Jessica). Paris and Jessica and Blair and Jessica are linked, so $C_{Lindsay} = \dfrac{2}{3}$.

You now find that the following is true:

$$C = \frac{\frac{1}{3}+0+\frac{1}{6}+\frac{2}{3}+\frac{2}{3}}{5} = \frac{11}{30} = 0.37$$

The film actor/actress network has $C = 0.79$.

The next two sections use your understanding of L and C to demonstrate how various real-life networks were created.

Random and Regular Networks

This section looks at random and regular networks and then discusses the seminal work of Steven Strogatz and Duncan Watts (then of Cornell) on small world networks (see "Collective Dynamics of 'small-world' networks," *Nature*, June 4, 1998).

Random Networks

Consider a network with n nodes. Then there are $n * (n - 1) / 2$ possible links in this network. You can form a *random network* by choosing a probability p for each possible link to be included in the network. For example, choose $n = 10$ and $p = 0.25$. Then you might obtain the network shown in Figure 42-3.

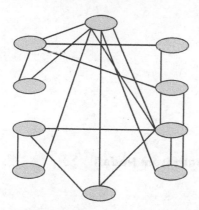

Figure 42-3: Example of random graph

In general a random network has a low C and low L. For example recall that for the film actor network $L = 3.65$ and $C = 0.79$. Strogatz and Watts used simulation to repeatedly generate a random network with the same number of nodes and links as the film actor network. They found $L = 2.99$ and $C = 0.08$. As this example illustrates, randomly generated networks typically have a small L and a small C. Because most social networks (like the film actor network) have low L and high C, it is not likely that a social network was generated by successive random generation of links.

Regular Networks

Another type of network often studied is a *regular network*. A network is regular if every node is linked to the same number of nodes. Figure 42-4 shows an example of a regular network on a circle in which each node is linked to four neighboring nodes.

It is easy to compute L and C for the network in Figure 42-4 because the network looks the same when viewed from any node. Therefore, you can choose node 1 and compute L for the network by computing (as shown in Table 42-9) the average length of the shortest paths from node 1 to nodes 2–12. You can view the top node in the middle as node 1 and then the nodes are numbered clockwise.

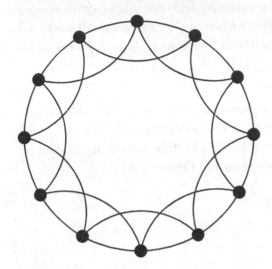

Figure 42-4: Regular network

Table 42-9: Lengths of Shortest Paths from Node 1

Node	Length of shortest path from Node 1
2	1 (1-2)
3	1 (1-3)
4	2 (1-3-4)
5	2 (1-3-5)
6	3 (1-3-5-6)
7	3 (1-3-5-7)
8	3 (1-11-10-8)
9	2 (1-11-9)
10	2 (1-11-10)
11	1 (1-11)
12	1 (1-12)

Averaging the lengths of the paths in the second column, you can find $L = 21 / 11$. By the symmetry of the network, you can compute C as the fraction of pairs of node 1's friends that have links between them. Node 1 has six pairs of friends: 11-12, 11-2, 11-3, 12-2, 12-3, and 2-3. Of these pairs 11-12, 12-2, and 2-3 are linked, so $C = 3 / 6 = 0.5$. If you drew a regular network with more nodes (say 1,000) in which each node has four neighbors, then it is straightforward to show (see Problem 9) that C remains at $\frac{1}{2}$ and $L = 125.4$. In general for a large regular graph both L and C are large. This implies that social networks such as the movie star network cannot be represented by a regular graph. Thirty-one years after Milgram coined six degrees of separation, Strogatz and Watts figured out a reasonable explanation for the prevalence of social networks having a small L and large C.

It's a Small World After All!

Strogatz and Watts began with a regular network like the network shown in Figure 42-5. This network has 10 nodes and each node is linked to two neighboring nodes.

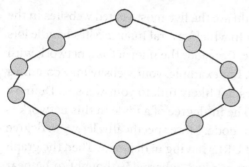

Figure 42-5: Regular network 10 nodes

Strogatz and Watt's brilliant insight was to define for each link a probability (call it *PROB*) that the link is deleted. Then the deleted link is replaced by a link joining a randomly chosen pair of nodes. Figure 42-6 shows an example of how the regular network might look after two links are deleted and then replaced.

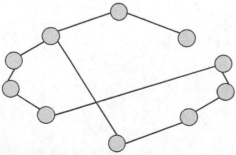

Figure 42-6: New network after two links are replaced

In the original network node 10 was four links away from node 6. In Figure 42-6 the new link has reduced the distance from node 10 to node 6 to one link. Strogatz and Watts showed that even a small value of *PROB* can create a network with a much smaller *L* than the regular network and virtually the same *C* value as the regular network. Strogatz and Watts referred to the new arcs as *weak ties*. For most people the great majority of their friends live in their city of residence, but most have several "weaker" acquaintances in different cities. These weak ties provide a possible explanation for the creation of networks (like the movie star network) having a small *L* and large *C*.

In their wonderful book *Networks Illustrated* (Edwiser Scholastic Press, 2013) Princeton graduate student Chris Brinton and Princeton professor Mung Chiang report simulations that start with a 600-node network having six links per node. Even if *PROB* is relatively small (say 0.1) *L* is reduced by 70 percent and *C* hardly changes.

The Rich Get Richer

Google, Facebook YouTube, Yahoo, and Baidu are the five most-visited websites in the world. The Internet has evolved to the point in which several Internet sites handle lots of traffic, and many sites handle little traffic. Consider the Internet as a network with unidirectional links defined by hyperlinks. For example, your website may contain a link to Amazon.com but Amazon.com does not likely link to your website. Define a node for the Internet to simply be a URL. The in-degree of a node in this network is the number of websites linking to the given node. More specifically, let x = in degree of a network URL and $y(x)$ = the number of URLs having in degree x. Then the graph of $y(x)$ versus x follows a Power Law where $y = cx^{-a}$, where a is thought to be near 2. Amazingly if you graph the relationship between x and $y(x)$, you get a graph like Figure 42-7, which follows the Power Law (so called because x is raised to a power).

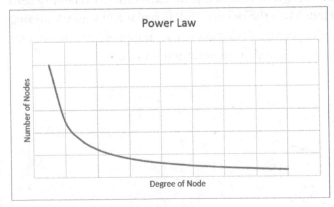

Figure 42-7: Power Law for networks

Figure 42-7 illustrates the Power Law for the Internet viewed as a network. The many URLs with small *x* represent the many URLs with few URLs pointing to them. The URLs with large *x* represent the few URL's with many nodes pointing toward them.

The Power Law with *a* = 2 implies, for example:

- $\frac{1}{4}$ as many sites have 1,000,000 nodes pointing to them as have 500,000 nodes pointing to them.
- $\frac{1}{4}$ as many sites have 2,000,000 nodes pointing to them as have 1,000,000 nodes pointing to them.

Consider for any integers *k* > 0 and x > 0 the following ratio:

$$\frac{\textit{Number of nodes with in degree kx}}{\textit{Number of nodes with in degree x}}$$

If a network follows a Power Law then this ratio is independent of *x* (see Exercise 11). Therefore, networks following the Power Law are also known as *scale-free networks*.

Neither random networks, regular networks, nor small world networks yield a Power Law. In 1976, D.J. Price of Yale University provided an elegant explanation of network evolution that is consistent with Power Laws in his article "A general theory of bibliometric and other cumulative advantage processes" (*Journal of American Society of Information* Sciences). The following steps detail this explanation:

1. Begin with a network (see Figure 42-8) having two nodes and one link.

Figure 42-8: Rich Get Richer step 1

2. At each step create a new node. The new node will be linked to an existing node and the probability that an existing node is selected is proportional to the number of links possessed by the existing node. In Figure 42-9, node 3 is added. Because nodes 1 and 2 each have one link, there is a 50-percent chance that node 3 will be linked to either node 1 or 2. As shown in Figure 42-9, you can assume that the new link connects node 3 to node 2.

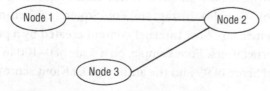

Figure 42-9: Rich Get Richer step 2

3. Now add another node (node 4.) Because node 2 has two links and nodes 1 and 3 have one link, there is a 50 percent chance that node 4 will link to node 2, a 25 percent chance node 4 will link to node 1, and a 25 percent chance node 4 will link to node 3. Now suppose that node 4 links to node 2. The resulting network is shown in Figure 42-10.

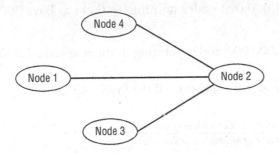

Figure 42-10: Step 3: Rich Get Richer

If you now add node 5, there would still be a 3 / 6 = 50 percent chance that node 5 links to node 2.

Because nodes with more links are more likely to get the newest link, this view of network formulation is called the Rich Get Richer or the method of preferential attachment. Price showed that networks formed by the Rich Get Richer mechanism follow the Power Law.

The Rich Get Richer mechanism also provides a possible explanation for why high-tech product markets are sometimes dominated by a single player (such as Microsoft Office or the Google Search engine.) The more people who use Office, the more attractive Office becomes to prospective customers seeking a productivity suite. Similarly, more people using a search engine leads to better performance, making it more likely that people will use the dominant search engine.

Klout Score

Anyone who uses social media, and especially a marketing analyst, could benefit from knowing how their posts, tweets and other contributions to the Internet move the opinions of others. The website Klout.com aids in this task by creating Klout scores based on Twitter, Facebook, Google+, Instagram, FourSquare, LinkedIn, and even YouTube which purport to measure how Internet content created by a person moves the opinions of other Internet users. For example, on a scale of 0–100 in April 2013, Barack Obama had a Klout Score of 99 and the author had a Klout score of 43.

While nobody outside of Klout knows how an individual's Klout score is computed the following are believed to be true:

- Increasing the number of followers you have on Twitter, Facebook, or Instagram will (all other things equal) increase your Klout score.
- A key to your Klout scores is the likelihood that your activity will be acted upon. For example, increasing your Likes on Facebook or Instagram will increase your Klout score, and being retweeted more often will also increase your Klout score.
- The influence of your engaged audience affects your Klout score. For example, being retweeted by one person with a Klout score of 95 might be more important than being retweeted by 40 people each having a Klout score of 2.
- Sean Golliher (see `www.seangolliher.com/2011/uncategorized/how-i-reversed-engineered-klout-score-to-an-r2-094/`) cleverly attempted to "reverse engineer" the computation of Klout score. For 99 people Golliher attempted to predict their Klout scores using only each person's number of Twitter followers and each person's number of retweets. Golliher found the following simple equation explained 94 percent of the variation in Klout scores:

  Klout Score = 23,474- 0.109 * Log (TwitterFollowers) + 4.838 * Log(Retweets)

Summary

In this chapter you learned the following:

- A network consists of nodes and links connecting the nodes.
- The importance of a node can be evaluated by degree centrality, closeness centrality, or betweenness centrality.
- The importance of a link can be evaluated by link betweenness.
- The structure of a network can be characterized by L, a measure of the average distance between nodes and C, the local clustering coefficient that measures the tendency of a person's friends to be friends of one another.
- Random networks have a small L and small C.
- Regular networks have a large L and large C.
- Most social networks have a small value of L (probably caused by weak ties that are the essence of the Strogatz-Watts model) and a large value of C.
- The Rich Get Richer theory explains how few nodes with lots of traffic came about on the Internet.

- If you let x = in degree of a network URL and $y(x)$ = the number of URLs having in degree x, then the graph of $y(x)$ versus x follows a Power Law where $y = cx^a$, where a is thought to be near 2.
- Klout score measures a person's online influence across a variety of channels.

Exercises

For Exercises 1–3 use the network shown in Figure 42-11.

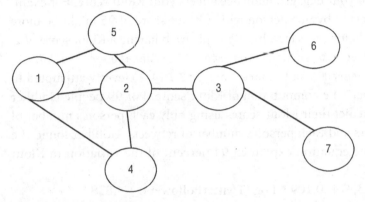

Figure 42-11: Network for exercises 1–3

1. For each node in the network, compute all three centrality measures.
2. Compute the link betweenness measure for nodes 1 and 2.
3. Compute L and C for the network in Figure 42-11.
4. Compute L and C for a regular network on a circle consisting of 12 nodes and 2 links per node. That is, node 1 links to nodes 12 and 2, and so on.
5. Consider the U.S. power grid network where nodes are generators, substations, and transformers and two nodes are linked if there is a transmission line joining them. Explain why you would expect this network to have a large L and small C.
6. The tributaries of the Mississippi River follow a Power Law. Can you explain which variable should go on each axis?
7. Zipf's Law states that the number of times a word appears in the English language follows a Power Law. Can you explain which variable should go on each axis?
8. How is the Pareto principle (80-20 rule discussed in Chapter 1, "Slicing and Dicing Marketing Data with PivotTables") related to the Power Law?

9. Consider a regular network on a circle with 1,000 nodes in which each node has links to its four neighbors. Show that $L = 125.4$

10. Explain why Twitter is a unidirectional network and Facebook is not.

11. Show that for any network following a Power Law $\dfrac{\textit{Number of nodes with in degree kx}}{\textit{Number of nodes with in degree x}}$ is independent of x.

43

The Mathematics Behind *The Tipping Point*

Malcolm Gladwell's book *The Tipping Point* (Back Bay Books, 2000) has sold nearly 3 million copies. In his book Gladwell explains how little things can have a large effect on determining whether a new product succeeds or fails in the marketplace. This chapter builds on the discussion of networks in Chapter 42, "Networks," and examines two mathematical models that illuminate some of Gladwell's key ideas.

- You begin with an explanation of the classical theory of *network contagion*, which enables you to determine whether all nodes in a network eventually get turned on. The contagion model enables you to see how little things do indeed make a difference in the spread of a new product.
- You then modify the Bass model of product diffusion discussed in Chapter 27, "The Bass Diffusion Model," to further illustrate some of Gladwell's main ideas.

Network Contagion

Marketing analysts want to know how knowledge of networks can help spread knowledge of their product. Consider the metaphor that each person who might buy a product is a node in a network. When the product first comes out, all nodes are in the "off" position corresponding to nobody having knowledge of the product. If you define the "on" position for a node as denoting that a person has knowledge of the product, then the marketer's goal is to turn all nodes on as quickly as possible.

Now reconsider the 10-node ring network with two links per node discussed in Chapter 42. Figure 43-1 shows this network.

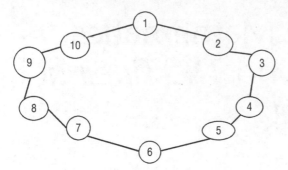

Figure 43-1: 10-Node Network with two nodes per link

Suppose at present only Person 1 knows about your product. Call a person who knows about the product an *on node* and a person who does not know about the product an *off node*. To model the spread of a product (or disease!) the contagion model assumes there is a Threshold level (call it *T*) between 0 and 1 such that an off node can switch to on if at least a fraction *T* of a node's neighbors are on. Assume *T* = 0.5. Then the following sequence of events can ensue:

- Round 1: Nodes 2 and 10 turn on.
- Round 2: Nodes 3 and 9 turn on.
- Round 3: Nodes 4 and 8 turn on.
- Round 4: Nodes 5 and 7 turn on.
- Round 5: Node 6 turns on.

Even though you began with only one person knowing about the product, quickly everyone learned about it.

Now assume instead that *T* = 0.51. In Round 1 Nodes 2 and 10 are the only candidates to turn on. Node 2 has only 50 percent of its neighbors on, so Node 2 does not turn on. The same is true of Node 10. Therefore none of the other nine nodes will ever turn on. This example shows how a small increase in the threshold can make a big difference in who knows about the product. As Gladwell says, "Little things can make a big difference."

Now try and figure out who eventually will know about the product for the network in Figure 43-2 if *T* = 0.50 and originally only Node 2 is on. On nodes are shaded in subsequent figures.

- **Round 1:** 50 percent of Node 1 neighbors are on (Node 2 is on and Node 6 is off), so Node 1 turns on. Also 50 percent of Node 5 neighbors (Node 2 is on and Node 6 is off) are on, so Node 5 turns on. Node 3 does not turn on because only one of five neighbors is on. Node 7 has one of five neighbors on, so it does not turn on. None of Node 4's, Node 6's, or Node 8's neighbors are on, so none turn on. After Round 1 the network looks like Figure 43-3. (On nodes are shaded.)

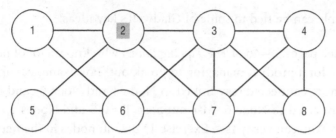

Figure 43-2: Node 2 is initially on

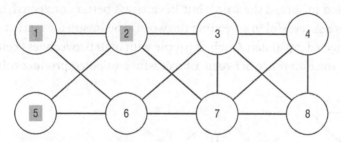

Figure 43-3: Round 1: Nodes 1, 2, and 5 are on

- **Round 2:** Two out of four neighbors of Node 6 are on, so Node 6 turns on. Node 3 has one of five neighbors on, so Node 3 does not turn on. Nodes 4 and 8 do not have neighbors on, so neither turns on. Node 7 has one of five neighbors turned on, so Node 7 remains off. The network now looks like Figure 43-4.

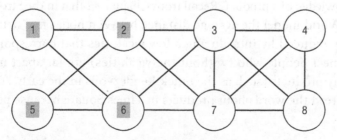

Figure 43-4: Round 2: Nodes 1, 2, 5, and 6 are on

■ **Round 3:** Node 3 has two of five neighbors on, so Node 3 stays off. Nodes 4 and 8 have no neighbors on, so they remain off. For Node 7, two out of five neighbors (or 40 percent) are on, so Node 7 stays off. At this point Nodes 3, 4, 7, and 8 never turn on.

This simple example can be tied to some of Gladwell's key ideas:

■ Connectors (see pages 38–46 of *The Tipping Point*) who know a lot of people can be the key for a product managing to break out. For example, suppose Node 1 was more connected (say linked to Node 3 and Node 5) and Node 2 was also connected to Node 6. Also suppose $T = 0.5$ and Nodes 1 and 2 are initially on. You can verify (see Exercise 1) that all nodes in the network shown in Figure 43-5 eventually turn on due to the increased influence of the connectors: Nodes 1 and 2. Gladwell's classic example of a connector was Paul Revere spreading the word that "The British are coming." William Dawes also tried to spread the word, but Revere was better connected, so he was much more successful in spreading the word. The lesson for marketers is that well-connected customers (such as people with high betweenness centrality) can make the difference between a successful and failed product rollout.

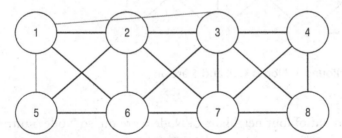

Figure 43-5: All nodes turn on

■ Gladwell also discusses the importance (see pages 54–55) of *weak ties* in spreading knowledge of a product. Recall from Chapter 42 that in the Strogatz-Watts Small World model the average distance between nodes in a network can be greatly reduced by introducing a few weak ties that correspond to arcs that connect people who (without the weak ties) are far apart in the network. Many products (such as the Buick Rendezvous in the early 2000s) try hard to spread the word about products in Times Square because people in Times Square are often connectors who are not from New York City and have weak ties to people from far-flung areas of the United States and the rest of the world.

■ *Mavens* (see pages 59–68) are people who are knowledgeable and highly persuasive about a product. In effect mavens reduce the threshold T. You can see (Exercise 2) that all nodes in the network of Figure 43–2 would turn on eventually if you could lower T to 0.4.

■ Great salespeople (see pages 78–87) can make the difference between a successful and failed product rollout. A great salesperson reduces T because she makes the potential customer less resistant to trying a new product.

For an arbitrary 8-node network, the Contagion.xlsx file enables you to vary T, the links in the network, and the nodes that begin on and trace the path of nodes turning on. Define a node that is initially on as a *seeded node*. As shown in Figure 43-6, you enter a 1 in the range D5:K12 for each arc in the network. Also enter T in cell K2 and the initial on nodes are indicated by a 1 in the range D15:K15. As shown in K24 of the Initial Seeding worksheet, only four nodes eventually turn on. In the Seed 2 nodes worksheet (see Figure 43-7) you can see that if the firm seeded Node 7 as well as Node 2, you could eventually turn the whole market on. This example shows it might pay to give away your product to members of difficult-to-reach market segments.

	C	D	E	F	G	H	I	J	K	L
1										
2								threshold	0.5	
3	Links									
4		1	2	3	4	5	6	7	8	Neighbors
5	1		1				1			2
6	2	1		1		1		1		4
7	3		1		1		1	1	1	5
8	4			1				1	1	3
9	5		1				1			2
10	6	1		1		1		1		4
11	7		1	1	1		1		1	5
12	8			1	1			1		3
13										
14	Round	1	2	3	4	5	6	7	8	Round
15	1	0	1	0	0	0	0	0	0	1
16	2	1	1	0	0	1	0	0	0	2
17	3	1	1	0	0	1	1	0	0	3
18	4	1	1	0	0	1	1	0	0	4
19	5	1	1	0	0	1	1	0	0	5
20	6	1	1	0	0	1	1	0	0	6
21	7	1	1	0	0	1	1	0	0	7
22	8	1	1	0	0	1	1	0	0	8
23									Total on	
24				4					4	

Figure 43-6: Only four nodes turn on when you start with Node 2

							threshold	0.5	
Links									
	1	2	3	4	5	6	7	8	Neighbors
1		1					1		2
2	1		1		1		1		4
3		1			1	1	1	1	5
4			1				1	1	3
5		1					1		2
6	1		1		1		1		4
7		1	1	1			1	1	5
8			1	1			1		3

Round	1	2	3	4	5	6	7	8	Round
1	0	1	0	0	0	0	1	0	1
2	1	1	0	0	1	0	1	0	2
3	1	1	0	0	1	1	1	0	3
4	1	1	1	0	1	1	1	0	4
5	1	1	1	1	1	1	1	1	5
6	1	1	1	1	1	1	1	1	6
7	1	1	1	1	1	1	1	1	7
8	1	1	1	1	1	1	1	1	8
							Total on		
								8	

Figure 43-7: Nodes 2 and 7 on cause all nodes to turn on

A Bass Version of the Tipping Point

On pages 12 and 13 of his book Gladwell gives several examples of the tipping point concept, including the following:

- When the fraction of African-Americans in a neighborhood exceeds 20 percent, most remaining whites suddenly leave the neighborhood.
- Teenage pregnancy rates in neighborhoods with between 5 and 40 percent professional workers are relatively constant, but in neighborhoods with 3.2 percent professionals, pregnancy rates double.

Essentially the central thesis of *The Tipping Point* is that in many situations involving social decision making there exists a threshold value (call the threshold p^*) for a key parameter (call the parameter p) such that small movements of the parameter around p^* can elicit a huge response. In the first example p = the fraction of African-Americans and when $p > p^* = 0.20$ a huge social response (more whites moving out) is elicited. In the second example p = fraction of professional workers in the neighborhood and for $p < p^* = 0.05$ a huge social response (more teenage pregnancies) is elicited.

The idea of a threshold is easily understood if you consider every individual in a population to be either sick or healthy. Let p = probability that a contact between a sick person and a healthy person infects the healthy person. In this context the tipping point corresponds to the existence of a threshold value p^* such that a small increase of p above p^* elicits a large increase in the number of people who eventually become sick. You can use your knowledge of the Bass diffusion model (see Chapter 27) to analyze this situation. This model demonstrates that a small change in p can result in a large change in the number of people who eventually get infected. The model is in the `basstippoint.xlsx` file (see Figure 43-8). The evolution of the number of infected and healthy people at time t = 0, 1, 2, ..., 100 is described here:

	A	B	C	D	E	F	G
1				infect	0.0013		
2				get better	0.2		
3				total	1000		
4							
5		Time	Sick	Got Better	Contacts	Get it	Never Had it
6		0	0	0	0	0	1000
7		1	1	0.2	1000	1.3	998.7
8		2	2.1	0.42	2097.27	2.72645	995.974
9		3	4.40645	0.88129	4388.71	5.70532	990.268
10		4	9.23048	1.8461	9140.65	11.8828	978.385
11		5	19.2672	3.85345	18850.8	24.506	953.879
12		6	39.9198	7.98396	38078.7	49.5023	904.377
13		7	81.4381	16.2876	73650.8	95.746	808.631
14		8	160.896	32.1793	130106	169.138	639.493

Figure 43-8: Bass Tipping Point model

1. Assume there is a total of 1,000 people (enter this in E3), and at Time 0 nobody has been sick.
2. In cell E1 enter the probability (0.0013) that a contact between a sick and healthy person will infect the healthy person.
3. In cell E2 enter the probability (0.2) that a sick person gets better during a period. This implies that a person is sick for an average of 5 days. When a sick person gets better, he cannot ever infect anyone. This corresponds in the

marketing context to a person "forgetting" about a product and not spreading the word about the product.

4. At Time 1 assume 1 person is sick. In cell D7 compute the number of people who will get better at Time 1 with the formula =C7*get_better.

5. Copy this formula to the range D8:D106 to compute the number of people who get better during each of the remaining periods.

6. In cell E7 use the formula =C7*G6 to compute the number of contacts for $t = 1$ between sick people and people who have never been sick. This formula is analogous to the Bass model formula that models the word-of-mouth term by multiplying those people who have purchased the product times those who have not.

7. Copy this formula to the range E8:E106 to compute the number of contacts between sick people and people who are never sick during the remaining periods.

8. In cell F7 use the formula =infect*E7 to compute the number of contacts for $t = 1$ that result in infection.

9. Copy this formula to the range F8:F106 to determine the number of new infections during the remaining periods.

10. In cell G7 use the formula =MAX(G6-F7,0) to reduce the number of people who have never been sick by the number of infections at $t = 1$. This yields the number of people who have not been sick by the end of period 1.

11. Copy this formula to the range G8:G106 to compute for $t = 2, 3, …, 100$ the number of people who are not sick by the end of period t. Using the max function ensures that the number of people who are not sick will stop at 0 when everyone has become sick.

Figure 43-9 shows a two-way data table with row input cell = probability of getting better; column input cell = probability of infection; and output cell =Total-G107, which measures the number of people who have become sick by $t =100$.

As expected, an increase in the chance of getting better decreases the number of people who eventually get sick. This is because an increase in the chance of getting better means a sick person has less time to infect healthy people. An increase in the chance of infection increases the number of people who eventually get sick. Also the infection probability needed to infect everyone increases as the chance of getting better increases. This is reasonable because if people are "carriers" for less time, you need a more virulent disease to ensure that everyone is infected. Figure 43-10 summarizes the data table by graphing for each probability of getting better the dependence of the number of people who eventually fall ill on the chance of infection. For each curve there is a steep portion that indicates the tipping point for the infection probability. For example, if there is a 50-percent chance of a healthy person getting better, the tipping point appears to occur when the probability of a contact between a healthy and sick person resulting in a new sick person reaches a number between 0.005 and 0.006.

	J	K	L	M	N	O	P	Q	R	S	T	U
5				chance of getting better								
6		999.9485	0.05	0.1	0.15	0.2	0.25	0.3	0.35	0.4	0.45	0.5
7		0.0001	192.97	9.79	1.98	1.00	0.67	0.50	0.40	0.33	0.29	0.25
8		0.0002	973.86	757.52	243.72	18.63	3.94	1.99	1.33	1.00	0.80	0.67
9		0.0003	997.85	946.18	804.30	577.81	232.38	25.96	5.85	2.98	1.99	1.50
10		0.0004	999.81	984.63	922.30	809.10	652.71	458.29	207.34	31.62	7.70	3.96
11	infection	0.0005	999.99	995.67	967.92	906.35	812.26	690.05	544.39	378.30	183.20	35.76
12	probability	0.0006	1000.00	998.86	986.91	953.44	895.79	815.43	715.08	597.63	465.91	322.09
13		0.0007	1000.00	999.73	994.88	977.13	941.95	888.74	818.68	733.56	635.31	525.85
14		0.0008	1000.00	999.94	998.13	989.13	968.09	933.09	884.10	822.02	748.11	663.74
15		0.0009	1000.00	999.99	999.38	995.11	982.97	960.35	926.36	881.16	825.44	760.13
16		0.001	1000.00	1000.00	999.82	997.97	991.33	977.16	953.97	921.35	879.49	828.95
17		0.0011	1000.00	1000.00	999.96	999.25	995.88	987.40	972.01	948.85	917.71	878.80
18		0.0012	1000.00	1000.00	999.99	999.77	998.24	993.48	983.68	967.66	944.86	915.20
19		0.0013	1000.00	1000.00	1000.00	999.95	999.36	996.94	991.06	980.38	964.10	941.85
20		0.0014	1000.00	1000.00	1000.00	1000.00	999.83	998.78	995.55	988.82	977.59	961.30
21		0.0015	1000.00	1000.00	1000.00	1000.00	999.98	999.64	998.11	994.22	986.87	975.34
22		0.0016	1000.00	1000.00	1000.00	1000.00	1000.00	999.98	999.44	997.46	993.04	985.29
23		0.0017	1000.00	1000.00	1000.00	1000.00	1000.00	1000.00	999.98	999.28	996.96	992.13
24		0.0018	1000.00	1000.00	1000.00	1000.00	1000.00	1000.00	1000.00	999.92	999.08	996.56
25		0.0019	1000.00	1000.00	1000.00	1000.00	1000.00	1000.00	1000.00	1000.00	1000.00	999.09
26		0.002	1000.00	1000.00	1000.00	1000.00	1000.00	1000.00	1000.00	1000.00	1000.00	1000.00

Figure 43-9: Data table summarizing number of people who eventually get sick

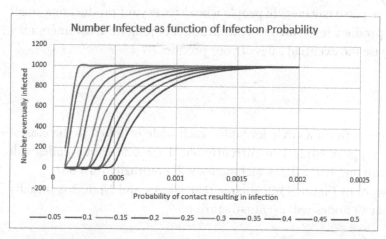

Figure 43-10: Number infected as a function of infection probability

The marketing analog of the epidemic model is clear: to be infected is to know about a product and to become healthy means you are no longer discussing the product. After recognizing that the marketer's goal is to "infect" everyone, this model provides two important marketing insights:

- Lengthening the amount of time that people talk about your product (decreasing chance of becoming healthy) can enhance the spread of your product.
- Sometimes, a small increase in the persuasiveness of people who discuss your product or a small decrease in product resistance to your product among noncustomers can greatly increase the eventual sales of your product.

Summary

In this chapter you learned the following:

- The contagion model assumes that a node will turn on if at least a fraction T of a node's neighbors is already on.
- A small difference in T or the number of initial on nodes can make a huge difference in the eventual number of on nodes.
- Connectors, mavens, and salespeople can provide the extra energy needed for a product to achieve 100-percent market penetration.
- The Bass version of Gladwell's tipping point model implies that lengthening the amount of time that people talk about your product (decreasing chance of becoming healthy) can enhance the spread of your product. Also a small increase in the persuasiveness of people who discuss your product or a small decrease in product resistance to your product among noncustomers may greatly increase the eventual sales of your product.

Exercises

1. Consider a network on a circle for which each node is linked to the closest four nodes. Suppose Node 1 in currently on. If $T = 0.5$, which nodes will eventually turn on? If $T = 0.3$, which nodes will eventually turn on?
2. For the network in Figure 43-2, assume that $T = 0.4$ and Node 2 is initially on. Show that all nodes will eventually turn on.

3. Modify the network in Figure 43-2 so that Node 1 is now also linked to Node 3 and Node 5; and Node 2 is now also linked to Node 6. Assume that $T = 0.5$ and Nodes 1 and 2 are initially on. Verify that if Node 2 is initially on and $T = 0.5$ that all nodes will eventually turn on.

44   Viral Marketing

On July 14, 2010, Old Spice launched a viral video campaign (see `www.you-tube.com/watch?v=owGykVbfgUE`) involving ex-San Francisco linebacker Isaiah Mustafa. This video received 6.7 million views after 24 hours and 23 million views after 36 hours. Likewise, the famous "Gangnam Style" (`www.youtube.com/watch?v=9bZkp7q19f0`) video has now received nearly 2 billion views! Because views of these videos spread quickly like an epidemic, the study of such successes is often referred to as *viral marketing*. Of course, many videos are posted to YouTube (like the author's video on Monte Carlo simulation) and receive few views. This chapter discusses two mathematical models of viral marketing that attempt to model the dynamics that cause a video to either go viral or die a quick death.

For simplicity this chapter assumes that the viral campaign is a video and you want to describe the viewing history of the video. The two mathematical models attempt to explain how the number of people viewing a video grows over time. Assume at the beginning of the first period ($t = 1$), N people view the video.

- The first model (Watts' Model) is based on Duncan Watts' 2007 article "The Accidental Influentials" (*Harvard Business Review*, Vol. 85, No. 2, 2007, pp. 22–23). This model provides a simple explanation for the spread of a video, but as you will see, Watts ignores the fact that several people may send the video on to the same person. Watts' Model predicts the total views of a video based on two parameters: N = initial number of people who view the video and R = the expected number of new viewers generated by a person who has just seen the video.
- The second model improves on Watts' Model by including the fact that some of the videos sent on at a given time will be sent to the same person.

Watts' Model

Watts assumes that at the beginning of the first period ($t = 1$) the maker of the video "seeds" the video by getting N people to view it. Then during each time period, each new viewer is assumed to pass the video on to R new viewers. This implies that at $t = 2$, NR new viewers are generated; at time $t = 3$, $NR(NR) = NR^2$ new viewers are generated; at $t = 4$, $(NR^2) * NR = NR^3$ new viewers are generated; and so on. This implies that there will be a total of S distinct viewers of the video where Equation 1 is true:

$$(1)\ S = N + NR + NR^2 + NR^3 + \ldots$$

If $R >= 1$, S will be infinite, indicating a "viral" video. Of course, R cannot stay greater than 1 forever, so in all likelihood R will drop after a while.

Assuming that R stays constant at a value less than 1, you may evaluate S by using an old trick from high school algebra. Simply multiply Equation 1 by R, obtaining Equation 2:

$$(2)\ RS = NR + NR^2 + NR^3 + \ldots$$

Subtracting Equation 2 from Equation 1 yields $S - RS = N$. Solving for S you find Equation 3:

$$(3)\ S = N/(1-R).$$

In many situations you know S and N, so you may use Equation 3 to solve for R and find $R = (S-N)/S$.

Watts' Model can be used with many examples of viral marketing campaigns. Listed here are a few for which Watts listed the relevant model parameters:

- Tom's Petition was a 2004 petition for gun control. This petition had $R = 0.58$ and $N = 22,582$.
- Proctor and Gamble started a campaign to promote Tide Coldwater as an energy-efficient detergent. This campaign began with N near 900,000 and $R = 0.041$.
- The Oxygen Network ran a campaign to raise money for Hurricane Katrina, which had $N = 7,064$, $S = 30,608$, and an amazingly large $R = 0.769$.

Watts' Model shows that the initial seeding (N) and the number of new viewers (R) are both critical to determining the final number of video views. Watts'

Model assumes, however, that each person reached at, say, time t has never been reached before. This is unreasonable. For example, suppose there is a population of 1,000,000 people, and at the beginning of time t 800,000 people have seen the video. Then it seems highly unlikely that the NR^{t-1} new viewers the Watts Model generates at Time t are all people who have not already seen the video. Also if $R >= 1$, Watts predicts an infinite number of people will see the video, and this does not make sense. In the next section you modify, the Watts Model in an attempt to resolve these issues.

A More Complex Viral Marketing Model

A revised version of Watts' Model is in the worksheet basic of the workbook viral. xlsx (see Figure 44-1). The model requires the following inputs:

- The population size N (named as *pop* and entered in C2). Assume that a maximum of 10 million people might see the video. Note that $1.00 + E + 07$ is scientific notation and is equivalent to $1*10^7 = 10,000,000$.
- The probability (given range name *prob* entered in C3) that a person who sees the video will send the video on to at least one person. Assume this probability is 0.1. Assume that everyone who is sent the video views the video. In Exercise 6, you modify this assumption.
- If the video is sent on, the average number of people (given the range name of people entered in C4) to whom a person will send the video. Assume that on average a person will send the video to 20 people. Note that Watts' $R = prob *$ people. In this case $R = (0.1) * 20 = 2$. In this case Watts' Model would predict an infinite number of people to see the video. As you will see the model predicts that 7,965,382 of the 10,000,000 potential viewers will eventually see the video.
- In cell E5 enter the number of people who are "seeded" as video viewers at the beginning of Period 1. Assume 10,000 viewers are seeded.

During each period t, the model tracks the following quantities:

- At the start of period t, the number of people who have seen the video
- The number of people who were newly introduced to the video during period $t - 1$ and are potential spreaders of the video during period t

- The probability that a given person will receive the video during period *t*. Estimating this probability requires some discussion of the *binomial* and *Poisson random variables*.
- The number of new viewers of the video who are created during period *t*
- The number of people who have viewed the video by the end of period *t*
- Assume 400 time periods

B	C	D	E Start	F Peoplespreading	G Prob person gets it	H How many new	I Final Total
2 pop	1.00E+07						
3 prob	0.1						
4 people	20 Period						
5		1	10000	1000	0.002	19960	29960
6		2	29960	19960	0.00398	39721.1	69681.2
7		3	69681.2	39721.1	0.00791	78576.2	148257
8		4	148257	78576.2	0.01559	153612	301870
9		5	301870	153612	0.03026	293420	595290
10		6	595290	293420	0.057	536024	1131314
11		7	1131314	536024	0.10166	901576	2032890
12		8	2032890	901576	0.16499	1314518	3347407
13		9	3347407	1314518	0.23118	1537973	4885380
14		10	4885380	1537973	0.26479	1354283	6239663
15		11	6239663	1354283	0.23727	892231	7131894
16		12	7131894	892231	0.16343	468737	7600631
17		13	7600631	468737	0.08949	214713	7815344

Figure 44-1: Improved viral marketing model

Before explaining the formulas that underlie the model, you need to briefly consider the binomial and Poisson random variables.

The Binomial and Poisson Random Variables

The *binomial random variable* is used to compute probabilities in the following situation:

- *N* repeated trials occur in which each trial results in success or failure.
- The probability of success on each trial is *P*.
- The trials are independent, that is, whether a given trial results in a success or failure has no effect on the result of the other *N*-1 trials.

■ The Excel `BINOMDIST` function can be used to compute binomial probabilities in the following situations:

■ Entering the formula `=BINOMDIST(x, N, P, 1)` in a cell computes the probability of <=x successes in N trials.

■ Entering the formula `=BINOMDIST(x, N, P, 0)` in a cell computes the probability of exactly x successes in N trials.

■ The mean of a binomial random variable is simply $N*P$.

The file `BinomialandPoisson.xlsx` (see Figure 44-2) illustrates the computation of binomial probabilities. Assume that 60 percent of all people are Coke drinkers and 40 percent are Pepsi drinkers. Define a success such that a person is a Coke drinker. In cell D4 you can use the formula `=BINOMDIST(60,100,0.6,1)` to compute the probability (53.8 percent) that <= 60 people in a group of 100 are Coke drinkers. In cell D5 you can use the formula `=BINOMDIST(60,100,0.6,0)` to compute the probability (8.1 percent) that exactly 60 people are Coke drinkers.

	C	D	E
1	**Binomial and Poisson**		
2			
3			
4	Probability <=60 people are Coke drinkers	0.537924659	=BINOMDIST(60,100,0.6,1)
5	Probability exactly 60 people are Coke drinkers	0.081219145	=BINOMDIST(60,100,0.6,0)
6			
7		1 chance in a 1000 of an accident per day	
8		Probability 0 accidents in a year	
9	binomial	0.694069887	=BINOMDIST(0,365,0.001,0)
10	Poisson	0.694196651	=POISSON(0,365*0.001,0)

Figure 44-2: Illustration of binomial and Poisson probabilities

The Poisson random variable is a discrete random variable that can assume the values 0, 1, 2, …. To determine the probability that a Poisson random variable assumes a given value, all you need is the mean (call it M) of the Poisson random variable. Then the following Excel formulas can be used to compute Poisson probabilities:

■ `POISSON(x, M, 1)` gives the probability that the value of a Poisson random variable with mean M is $\leq x$.

■ `POISSON(x, M, 0)` gives the probability that the value of a Poisson random variable with mean $M = x$.

The Poisson random variable is relevant in many interesting situations (particularly in queuing or waiting line models), but for your purposes, use the fact that when N is large and P is small, binomial probabilities can be well approximated by Poisson probabilities where $M = NP$. To illustrate this idea, assume that a teen driver has a 0.001 chance of having an accident each day. What is the chance the teen will have 0 accidents in a year? Here define a "success" on a day to be an accident. You have $N = 365$ and $P = 0.001$. In cell D9 the formula `=BINOMDIST(0,365,0.001,0)` computes the chance of 0 accidents (69.41 percent) in a year. Now the mean number of accidents in a year is 0.001(365) = 0.365, so using the Poisson approximation to the binomial, you can estimate the probability of 0 accidents in a year with the formula `= POISSON(0,365*0.001,0)`. You obtain 69.42 percent, which is an accurate approximation.

Building the Model of Viral Marketing

Armed with your knowledge of the binomial and Poisson random variables, you are now ready to explain how your model estimates the ultimate penetration level for a viral video.

In Period 1, 10 percent of the 10,000 people will spread the product. This number is computed in cell F5 with the formula `=prob*E5`.

Now comes the hard part! Of the 10,000 people who have seen the video in Period 1, (.10)*10,000 = 1,000 of them will pass it on. Each of these 1,000 people sends the video to an average of 20 people, so 20,000 e-mails or text messages describing the video will be sent during Period 1. This does *not* mean (as Watts assumes) that 20,000 new people see the video. This is because it is possible that a single person will receive e-mails or texts about the video from several different people.

Now estimate the probability that a person will receive a video during Period 1. For a given person there is a chance 1/*pop* that each of the 20,000 e-mails or texts sent out during Period 1 will go to the person. Thus on average a person receives 20,000/*pop* e-mails during Period 1, and the chance that the person receives *0 e-mails* can be approximated by `= POISSON(0,F5people/pop,TRUE)`, and the probability that a person will receive at least 1 e-mail during Period 1 is in cell G5 with the formula `=1-POISSON(0,F5people/pop,TRUE)`.

The following steps allow you to trace the evolution of the number of people who have seen the video:

1. Multiply the number of people who have not yet seen the video (*pop* – G5) times 0.0002 to compute the number of new Period 1 video viewers. The formula =(pop-E5)*G5 computes the number (1,997.8) of new viewers of the video during Period 1.

2. In cell I5 use the formula =E5+H5 to add the 1,997.8 new viewers to the original 10,000 viewers to obtain the number of total viewers of the video (11,997.8) by the end of Period 1.

3. Copy the formula =I5 from E6 to E7:E404 to compute the number of total viewers at the beginning of the period by simply copying the ending viewers from the previous period.

4. Copy the formula =H5 from F6 to F7:F404 to list the number of people available to spread the video during each period. This number is simply the number of new viewers during the previous period.

5. Copy the formula =1-POISSON(0,F6*prob*people/pop,TRUE) from G6 to G7:G404 to apply the Poisson approximation to the binomial to compute the probability that a person who has not already seen the video will be sent the video during the current period.

6. Copy the formula =(pop-E5)*G5 from H5 to H6:H404 to compute for each period the number of new viewers of the video by multiplying the number of people who have not seen the video times the chance that each person sees the video.

7. Copy the formula =E5+H5 from I5 to I6:I404 to compute the total number of viewers to date of the video by adding previous viewers to the new viewers created during the current period.

It is estimated that 7,971,541 people will eventually see the video.

Using a Data Table to Vary *R*

In your new viral marketing model, *prob* and *People* impact the predicted spread of the video only through their product *prob * People*, which is the expected number of people to whom each new video viewer passes the video. Watts set *prob * People* = *R*. The worksheet data table of the workbook viral.xlsx varied *R*. Figure 44-3 shows the dependence of the final viewers on R. Note that until R exceeds 1 the video does not go viral. For example, when $R = 0.8$, only 49,413 people eventually see the video while if $R = 2$ nearly 8 million people see the video.

	U	V	W
4	R	Final Viewers	New Viewers
5	0.2	12496.4859	2496.485896
6	0.4	16651.8728	6651.872804
7	0.6	24934.66174	14934.66174
8	0.8	49412.59724	39412.59724
9	1	440680.4574	430680.4574
10	1.2	3175292.136	3165292.136
11	1.4	5125545.164	5115545.164
12	1.6	6428175.642	6418175.642
13	1.8	7329454.377	7319454.377
14	2	7971540.996	7961540.996
15	2.2	8439765.376	8429765.376
16	2.4	8787670.573	8777670.573
17	2.6	9050154.044	9040154.044
18	2.8	9250695.795	9240695.795
19	3	9405522.317	9395522.317
20	3.2	9526104.724	9516104.724
21	3.4	9620711.138	9610711.138
22	3.6	9695401.221	9685401.221
23	3.8	9754680.544	9744680.544
24	4	9801941.321	9791941.321
25	4.2	9839765.501	9829765.501
26	4.4	9870137.063	9860137.063
27	4.6	9894593.217	9884593.217
28	4.8	9914333.684	9904333.684
29	5	9930300.754	9920300.754

Figure 44-3: Dependence of video spread on R

Summary

In this chapter you learned the following:

- Let N = initial viewers of a video and R = new viewers generated per person by a video. Then for $R>1$, the Watts' Model predicts the eventual number of viewers will be infinite, and for $R<1$, the Watts' Model predicts the video will eventually reach $N/(1-R)$ viewers.
- Because an infinite number of viewers is impossible, the Watts' Model is flawed. The major flaw is that many people may send the video to the same person. The more complex model (which utilizes the Poisson approximation to the binomial random variable) resolves this problem.

Exercises

1. Verify that for the Oxygen Network the values of $N = 7{,}064$ and $S = 30{,}608$ imply that $R = 0.769$.
2. Using the Watts' Model estimate the number of new viewers generated by the Coldwater Tide campaign. Use $N = 900{,}000$ and $R = 0.041$.
3. Apply your new viral marketing model to the Tide Coldwater campaign.
4. Determine the dependence of the spread of the video on the population size as the population size varies between 10 and 100 million.
5. For the Watts' Model estimate the final number of viewers for Tom's Petition. This petition had $R = 0.58$ and $N = 22{,}582$.
6. Suppose a fraction $F<1$ of people receiving your video view it, but a fraction $1-F$ do not look at the video. How does this modify the Watts' Model?

45 Text Mining

Every day Twitter handles more than 400 million tweets. Miley Cyrus' 2013 VMA fiasco generated more than 17 million tweets! Many of these tweets comment on products, TV shows, or ads. These tweets contain a great deal of information that is valuable to marketers. For example, if you read every tweet on a Super Bowl ad, you could determine if the United States liked or hated the ad. Of course, it is impractical to read every tweet that discusses a Super Bowl ad. What is needed is a method to find all tweets and then derive some marketing insights from the tweets. *Text mining* refers to the process of using statistical methods to glean useful information from unstructured text. In addition to analyzing tweets, you can use text mining to analyze Facebook and blog posts, movies, TV, and restaurant reviews, and newspaper articles. The data sets from which text mining can glean meaningful insights are virtually endless. In this chapter you gain some basic insights into the methods you can use to glean meaning from unstructured text. You also learn about some amazing applications of text mining.

In all of the book's previous analysis of data, each data set was organized so that each row represented an observation (such as data on sales, price, and advertising during a month) and each column represented a variable of interest (sales each month, price each month, or advertising each month). One of the big challenges in text mining is to take an unstructured piece of text such as a tweet, newspaper article, or blog post and transform its contents into a spreadsheet-like format. This chapter begins by exploring some simple ways to transform text into a spreadsheet-like format. After the text has been given some structure, you may apply many techniques discussed earlier (such as Naive Bayes, neural networks, logistic regression, multiple regression, discriminant analysis, principal components, and cluster analysis) to analyze the text. The chapter concludes with a discussion of several important and interesting applications of text mining including the following:

- Using text content of a review to predict whether a movie review was positive or negative
- Using tweets to determine whether customers are happy with airline service
- Using tweets to predict movie revenues
- Using tweets to predict if the stock market will go up or down
- Using tweets to evaluate viewer reaction to Super Bowl ads

Text Mining Definitions

Before you can understand any text mining studies, you need to master a few simple definitions:

- A *corpus* is the relevant collection of documents. For example, if you want to evaluate the effectiveness of a Sofia Vergara Diet Pepsi ad, the corpus might consist of all tweets containing references to Sofia Vergara and Diet Pepsi.
- A *document* consists of a list of individual words known as *tokens*. For example, for the tweet "Love Sofia in that Diet Pepsi ad," it would contain seven tokens.
- In a tweet about advertising, the words "ad" and "ads" should be treated as the same token. *Stemming* is the process of combining related tokens into a single token. Therefore "ad" and "ads" might be grouped together as one token: "ad."
- Words such as "the," appear often in text. These common words are referred to as *stopwords*. Stopwords give little insight into the meaning of a piece of text and slow down the processing time. Therefore, stopwords are removed. This process is known as *stopping*. In the Sofia Vergara tweet, stopping would remove the words "in" and "that."
- *Sentiment analysis* is an attempt to develop algorithms that can automatically classify the attitude of the text as pro or con with respect to a topic. For example, sentiment analysis has been used in attempts to mechanically classify movie and restaurant reviews as favorable or unfavorable.

Giving Structure to Unstructured Text

To illustrate how you can give structure to unstructured text, again consider the problem of analyzing tweets concerning Sofia Vergara in Diet Pepsi ads. To begin you need to use a statistical package with text mining capabilities (such as R, SAS,

SPSS, or STATISTICA) that can interface with Twitter and retrieve all tweets that are relevant. Pulling relevant tweets is not as easy as you might think. You might pull all tweets containing the tokens Sofia, Vergara, Diet, and Pepsi, but then you would be missing tweets such as those shown in Figure 45-1, which contain the token Sofia and not Vergara.

Figure 45-1: Tweets on Sofia Vergara Diet Pepsi ad

As you can see, extracting the relevant text documents is not a trivial matter. To illustrate how text mining can give structure to text, you can use the following guidelines to set the stage for an example:

- Assume the corpus consists of N documents.
- After all documents undergo stemming and stopping, assume a total of W words occur in the corpus.
- After stemming and stopping is concluded for $i = 1, 2, ..., W$ and $j = 1, 2, ..., N$, let F_{ij} = number of times word i is included in document j.
- For $j = 1, 2, ..., W$ define D_j = number of documents containing word j.

After the corpus of relevant tweets has undergone stemming and stopping, you must create a vector representation for each document that associates a value with each of the W words occurring in the corpus. The three most common vector codings are *binary coding, frequency coding,* and the *term frequency/inverse document frequency score (tf-idf* for short). The three forms of coding are defined as follows:

> **NOTE** Before coding each document, infrequently occurring words are often deleted.

- The binary coding simply records whether a word is present in a document. Therefore, the binary representation for the ith word in the jth document is 1 if the ith word occurs in the jth document and is 0 if the ith word does not occur in the jth document.
- The frequency coding simply counts for the ith word in the jth document the number of times (F_{ij}) the ith word occurs in the jth document.
- To motivate the term frequency/inverse document frequency score, suppose the words cat and dog each appear 10 times in a document. Assume the corpus consists of 100 documents, and 50 documents contain the word cat and only 10 documents contain the word dog. Despite each appearing 10 times in a document, the occurrences of dog in the document should be given more weight than the occurrences of cat because dog appears less frequently in the corpus. This is because the relative rarity of dog in the corpus makes each occurrence of dog more important than an occurrence of cat. After defining T_j = number of tokens in document j, you can define the following equation:

$$(1)\ tf - idf = (F_{ij} / T_j) * \log(N / D_j).$$

The term F_{ij} / T_j is the relative frequency of word i in document j, whereas the term $log(N / D_j)$ is a decreasing function of the number of documents in which the word i occurs.

These definitions can be illustrated by considering a corpus consisting of the following three statements about Peyton Manning (see Figure 45-2 and the `Text mining coding.xlsx`) file.

- Document 1: Peyton Manning is a great quarterback.
- Document 2: Peyton is a great passer and has a great offensive line.
- Document 3: Peyton is the most overrated of all quarterbacks.

After stemming and stopping is performed, the documents are transformed into the text shown in rows 10–12. Now you can work through the three vector codings of the text.

	C	D	E	F	G	H	I	J	K	L	M	N
2	Original Text											
3		1	Peyton Manning is a great QB									
4		2	Peyton is a great passer and has a great offensive line									
5		3	Peyton is the most overrated of all QBs									
6												
7	After Stemming and Stopping											
8												
9	Document											
10		1	Peyton		Manning	great	QB					
11		2	Peyton		great	passer	great	offensive	line			
12		3	Peyton		most	overrated	all	QB				
13	Binary Coding											
14	Document	Peyton		Manning	great	most	passer	overrated	QB	all	offensive	line	Total
15	1	1		1	1	0	0	0	1	0	0	0	4
16	2	1		0	1	0	1	0	0	0	1	1	5
17	3	1		0	0	1	0	1	1	1	0	0	5
18	How Many Documents	3		1	2	1	1	1	2	1	1	1	
19	Frequency Coding											
20	Document	Peyton		Manning	great	most	passer	overrated	QB	all	offensive	line	Total Words
21	1	1		1	1	0	0	0	1	0	0	0	4
22	2	1		0	2	0	1	0	0	0	1	1	6
23	3	1		0	0	1	0	1	1	1	0	0	5
24	tf-idf Coding											
25	Document	Peyton		Manning	great	most	passer	overrated	QB	all	offensive	line	
26	1	0.0000		0.1193	0.0440	0.0000	0.0000	0.0000	0.0440	0.0000	0.0000	0.0000	
27	2	0.0000		0.0000	0.0587	0.0000	0.0795	0.0000	0.0000	0.0000	0.0795	0.0795	
28	3	0.0000		0.0000	0.0000	0.0954	0.0000	0.0954	0.0352	0.0954	0.0000	0.0000	

Figure 45-2: Examples of text mining coding

Binary Coding

Rows 15–17 show the binary coding of the three documents. You simply assign a 1 if a word occurs in a document and a 0 if a word does not appear in a document. For example, cell F16 contains a 1 because Document 2 contains the word great, and cell G16 contains a 0 because Document 2 does not contain the word most.

Frequency Coding

Rows 21–23 show the frequency coding of the three documents. You simply count the number of times the word appears in the document. For example, the word great appears twice in Document 2, so you can enter a 2 in cell F22. Because the word "most" does not occur in Document 2, you enter a 0 in cell G22.

Frequency/Inverse Document Frequency Score Coding

Copying the formula =(D21/$N21)*LOG(3/D$18) from D26 to the range D26:M28 implements Equation 1. In this formula D21 represents F_{ij}; $N21 represents the number of words in the document; 3 is the number of documents in the corpus; and D$18 is the number of documents containing the relevant word. Note that the use of dollar signs ensures that when the formula is copied the number of words in each document and the number of documents containing the relevant word are pulled from the correct cell. The tf-idf coding attaches more significance to "overrated" and "all" in Document 3 than to "great" in Document 2 because "great" appears in more documents than "overrated" and "all."

Applying Text Mining in Real Life Scenarios

Now that you know how to give structure to a text document, you are ready to learn how to apply many tools developed earlier in the book to some exciting text mining applications. This section provides several examples of how text mining can be used to analyze documents and make predictions in a variety of situations.

Text Mining and Movie Reviews

In their article "Thumbs up? Sentiment Classification using Machine Learning Techniques" (Proceedings of EMNNP, 2002, pp. 79–86) Pang, Lee, and Vaithyanathan of Cornell and IBM applied Naive Bayes (see Chapter 39, "Classification Algorithms: Naive Bayes Classifier and Discriminant Analysis") and other techniques to 2,053 movie reviews in an attempt to use text content of a review as the input into mechanical classification of a review as positive or negative.

The authors went about this process by first converting the number of stars a reviewer gave the movie to a positive, negative, or neutral rating. They then applied frequency and binary coding to each review. You would expect that reviews containing words such as brilliant, dazzling, and excellent would be favorable, whereas reviews that contained words such as bad, stupid, and boring would be negative.

They also used Naive Bayes (see Chapter 39) based on binary coding in an attempt to classify each review, in terms of the Chapter 39 notation C_1 = Positive Review, C_2 = Negative Review, and C_3 = Neutral review. The n attributes $X_1, X_2, ..., X_n$ correspond to whether a given word is present in the review. For example, if X_1 represents the word brilliant, then you would expect $P(C_1 \mid X_1 = 1)$ to be large and $P(C_2 \mid X_1 = 1)$ to be small.

The authors then used *machine learning* (a generalization of the neural networks used in Chapter 15, "Using Neural Networks to Forecast Sales") to classify each review using the frequency coding.

Surprisingly, the authors found that the simple Naive Bayes approach correctly classified 81 percent of all reviews, whereas the more sophisticated machine learning approach did only marginally better than Naive Bayes with an 82-percent correct classification rate.

Sentiment Analysis of Airline Tweets

Jeffrey Breen of Cambridge Aviation Research (see pages 133–150 of *Practical Text Mining*, by Elder et. al, 2012, Academic Press) collected thousands of tweets that commented on airline service. Breen simply classified a tweet as positive or negative by counting the number of words associated with a positive sentiment and number of words associated with negative sentiments (for a sample list of positive and negative words, see `http://www.wjh.harvard.edu/~inquirer/Positiv.html` and `http://www.wjh.harvard.edu/~inquirer/Negativ.html`.

A tweet was classified as positive if the following was true:

```
Number of Positive Words - Number of Negative Words >= 2
```

The tweet was classified as negative if the following was true:

```
Number of Positive Words - Number of Negative Words <= -2
```

Breen found that that JetBlue (84-percent positive tweets) and Southwest (74-percent positive tweets) performed best. When Breen correlated each airline's score with the national survey evaluation of airline service conducted by the American Consumer Satisfaction Index (ACSI) he found an amazing 0.90 correlation between the percentage of positive tweets for each airline and the airline's ACSI score. Because tweets can easily be monitored in real time, an airline can track over time the percentage of positive tweets and quickly see whether its service quality improves or declines.

Using Twitter to Predict Movie Revenues

Asu and Huberman of HP Labs used tweets to create accurate predictions of movie revenues in their article, "Predicting the Future with Social Media" submitted in 2010 (see the PDF at `www.hpl.hp.com/research/scl/papers/socialmedia/socialmedia.pdf`).

For 24 movies the authors used the number of tweets each day in the 7 days before release and the number of theaters in which the movie opened to predict each movie's opening weekend revenues. They simply ran a multiple regression (see Chapter 10, "Using Multiple Regression to Forecast Sales") to predict opening weekend revenue from the aforementioned independent variables. Their regression yielded an adjusted R^2 value of 97.3 percent. Adjusted R^2 adjusts the R^2 value discussed in Chapter 10 for the number of independent variables used in the regression. If a relatively unimportant independent variable is added to a regression, then R^2 never decreases, but adjusted R^2 decreases. Formally adjusted R^2 may be computed as:

$$1 - (1 - R^2)*(n - 1) / (n - k - 1),$$

where n = number of observations and k = number of independent variables.

The authors compared their predictions to predictions from the Hollywood Stock Exchange (www.hsx.com/). HSX is a prediction market in which buyers and sellers trade based on predictions for a movie's total and opening weekend revenues. Using the HSX prediction and number of theaters as independent variables, a multiple regression yielded an adjusted R2 value of 96.5 percent of the variation in opening weekend revenues. Therefore, the author's use of tweets to predict opening weekend movie revenues outperformed the highly regarded HSX predictions.

In trying to predict a movie's revenue during the second weekend, the authors applied sentiment analysis. They classified each tweet as positive, negative, or neutral. (See the paper for details of their methodology.) Then they defined the PNratio (Positive to Negative) as *Number of Positive Tweets / Number of Negative Tweets*. Using the tweet rates for the preceding seven days to predict second weekend revenues yielded an adjusted R^2 of 0.84, whereas adding a PNratio as an independent variable increased the adjusted R^2 to 0.94. As an example of how a large PNratio reflects favorable word of mouth, consider the movie *The Blind Side*, for which Sandra Bullock won a Best Actress Oscar. In the week before its release, this movie had a PNratio of 5.02, but after 1 week the movie's PNratio soared to 9.65. Amazingly, *The Blind Side*'s second week revenues of $40 million greatly exceeded the movie's week 1 revenues of $34 million. Most movies experience a sharp drop-off in revenue during the second week, so *The Blind Side* illustrates the powerful effect that favorable word of mouth can have on future movie revenues.

Using Twitter to Predict the Stock Market

Bollen, Mao, and Zheng of Indiana University and the University of Manchester used the collective "mood" expressed by recent tweets to predict whether the Dow Jones Index would decrease or increase in their article, "Twitter Mood Predicts the stock market," (*Journal of Computational Science*, Volume 2, 2011, pp. 1–8). They first used sentiment analysis to classify 9.8 million tweets as expressing a positive or negative mood about the economy. For Day t they defined PNt = ratio of positive to negative tweets and Dt = Dow Jones Index at end of day t – Dow Jones Index at end of day $t - 1$.

The authors tried to predict D_t using PN_{t-1}, PN_{t-2}, PN_{t-2}, D_{t-1}, D_{t-2}, and D_{t-3}. Predictions from a neural network (See Chapter 15, "Using Neural Networks to

Forecast Sales") correctly predicted the direction of change in the Dow 84 percent of the time. This is truly amazing because the widely believed Efficient Market Hypothesis implies that the daily directional movement of a market index cannot be predicted with more than 50-percent accuracy.

Using Tweets to Evaluate Super Bowl Ads

In 2013 companies paid approximately $3 million dollars for a 30-second Super Bowl ad. Naturally, advertisers want to know if their ads are worthwhile. Professor Piyush Kumar of the University of Georgia analyzed more than one-million tweets that commented on Super Bowl 2011 ads. By performing sentiment analysis on the ads, Kumar found that the 2011 Bud Light ad (`www.youtube.com/watch?v=I2AufnGmZ_U`) was viewed as hilarious. Unfortunately for car manufacturers, only the Volkswagen ad `http://www.youtube.com/watch?v= 9HOxPWAtaa8` received a lot of tweets. The lack of tweets concerning other auto ads indicates that these ads made little impact on Super Bowl viewers.

Summary

In this chapter you learned the following:

- To glean impact from the text, the text must be given structure through a vector representation that implements a coding based on the words present in the text.
- Binary coding simply records whether a word is present in a document.
- Frequency coding counts the number of times a word is present in a document.
- The term-frequency/inverse document frequency score adjusts frequency coding of a word to reduce the significance of a word that appears in many documents.
- After text is coded many techniques, such as Naive Bayes, neural networks, logistic regression, multiple regression, discriminant analysis, principal components, and cluster analysis, can be used to gain useful insights.

Exercises

1. Consider the following three snippets of text:

- The rain in Spain falls mainly in the plain.
- The Spanish World Cup team is awesome.
- Spanish food is beyond awesome.

After stemming and stopping these snippets, complete the following tasks:

   a. Create binary coding for each snippet.
   b. Create frequency coding for each snippet.
   c. Create `tf-idf` coding for each snippet.

2. Use your favorite search engine to find the definition of "Amazon mechanical Turk." If you were conducting a text mining study, how would you use Amazon mechanical Turks?

3. Describe how text mining could be used to mechanically classify restaurant reviews as favorable or unfavorable.

4. Describe how text mining could be used to determine from a member of Congress' tweets whether she is conservative or liberal.

5. Describe how text mining could be used to classify *The New York Times* stories as international news, political news, celebrity news, financial news, science and technology news, entertainment news, obituary, and sports news.

6. Alexander Hamilton, John Jay, and James Madison wrote *The Federalist Papers*, a series of 85 essays that provide reasons for ratifying the U.S. Constitution. The authorship of 73 of the papers is beyond dispute, but for the other 12 papers, the author is unknown. How can you use text mining in an attempt to determine the authorship of the 12 disputed *Federalist Papers*?

7. Suppose you are a brand manager for Lean Cuisine. How can use text mining of tweets on new products to predict the future success of new products?

8. Suppose that on the same day the Sofia Vergara Diet Pepsi ad with David Beckham aired on two different shows. How would you make a decision about future placement of the ad on the same two TV shows?

9. Two word phrases are known as *bigrams*. How can coding text with bigrams improve insights derived from text mining? What problems might arise in using bigrams?

Index

Symbols

& (concatenate sign), 42
3M example (inflection points), 416

A

The Accidental Influentials (Harvard Business Review), 653
acquisition rate (customers), 366–367
adaptive methods, 241
adaptive/hybrid conjoint analysis, 280
ADBUDG curves
  basics of, 484–485
  fitting (Syntex Labs), 486–489
additive model for estimating trends/seasonality, 228–231
Adelman, Sydney, 267
adjacent industries/categories, 431
Adstock Model (advertising), 505–508
advertising. *See also* media selection models; Pay per Click (PPC) advertising
  Adstock Model, 505–508

Advertising Pulsing Policies for Generating Awareness for New Products (Marketing Science), 513
Equation 4 model for measuring effectiveness of, 509–511
One Way TV Advertisements Work (Journal of Marketing Research), 505
Online Ad Auctions (American Economic Review), 533
Planning Media Schedules in the Presence of Dynamic Advertising Quality (Marketing Science), 513
pulsing vs. continuous spending, 511–514
Some Optimization Problems in Advertising Media (Journal of the Operational Research Society), 517
Super Bowl ads, evaluating with tweets, 671
Volkswagen ad, 671
AdWords auctions (Google), 533–536
After Tax Profits equation, 345

ages of subscribers, analyzing (ESPN magazine), 21–22, 25
airline miles
  forecasting with neural networks, 258–259
  Winter's Method, 243–247
airlines, overbooking, 151–153
Albright, Chris, 99
algorithms, Evolutionary, 113
AllDifferent option (Solver), 276
alternative hypothesis
  contrasts (ANOVA), 602
  linear regression, 182
  testing group means, 596
Altman's Z-statistic method, 251
ALVINN (Automated Land Vehicle in a Neural Network), 250
American Consumer Satisfaction Index (ACSI), 669
Ameritech study (customer value model), 336
Amour movie ratings, 396, 398–400
Analysis of Variance, 599
Analysis Toolpak, 172–174
ANOVA (Analysis of Variance), One-way contrasts, 601–603

forecasting one-way ANOVA,
599–601
one-way ANOVA example,
596–598
overview, 595
role of variance in, 598–599
testing group means,
595–596
ANOVA, Two-way. *See* two-
way ANOVA
*Applied Multidimensional
Scaling* (Holt Rinehart
and Winston), 566
*Applied Multivariate Statistical
Analysis* (Prentice-Hall),
548
array formulas for ESPN
subscriber demographics,
78–79
array functions (Excel), 59–60
array LINEST function
(Excel), 388–390
attributes, product, 264–265
auctions (Google AdWords),
533–535
auto sales (regressions),
186–191
autocorrelation (linear
regressions)
checking for (software sales),
479
non-independence of errors,
198–204
positive, 199
AVCO Financial (neural
networks), 252
AVERAGE function (Excel),
65
AVERAGEIF/AVERAGEIFS
functions (Excel), 72–74,
599

B

bankruptcies, predicting with
neural networks, 251–252
Barnes and Noble (contrasts),
601–603
Bass, Frank, 517

Bass diffusion model
basics of, 427–428
deflating intentions data,
434–435
estimating, 428–430
forecasting new product
sales with, 431–434
modifications of, 437
simulating sales of new
products with, 435–437
Bass version of *The Tipping
Point*, 646–650
Bates Motel (revenue
management)
determining booking limits,
150–151
determining single profit-
maximizing price,
146–147
estimating demand curve,
144–146
segmenting customers with
capacity constraints,
150
segmenting customers with
two prices, 147–149
Bayes Theorem, 579–581
Before Tax Profits formula,
345
betweenness centrality
(network nodes),
624–626
Bid Simulator feature
(AdWords), 536
bigrams, 672
bin ranges, 61
binary coding (text mining),
666–667
binary dependent variables,
285–286, 288–289
BINOMDIST function (Excel),
657
Binomial random variables,
524, 656–658
Blattberg, Robert, 365, 394
The Blind Side (film revenues),
670
brand equity (discrete choice
analysis), 313–314

breakfast foods (MDS
analysis), 566–570,
571–574
breast cancer test results
(Bayes Theorem),
579–581
Breen, Jeffrey, 669
Brinton, Chris, 634
Broadbent, Simon, 505
Bud Light ad, 671
*Building Models for Marketing
Decisions* (Kluwer
Publishing), 472
bundling, price. *See* price
bundling
Burkart, A.J., 517
businesses, valuation of. *See*
valuation (customer
value)

C

C (local cluster coefficient)
(networks), 631
cable TV subscribers
(customer value), 331,
333–334
cake sales (statistical
functions), 71–74
capacity constraints,
segmenting customers
with (Bates Motel), 150
car brands (perceptual maps),
570–571
car models (PCA), 556–557
card sorting (similarity data),
567
carpet cleaner (full profile
conjoint analysis),
265–271
cars, driving with neural
networks, 251
CART algorithm (decision
trees), 408–410
cash flows (health club
business), 339–340, 345
catsup market (neural
networks), 252
causal forecasting, 177

ceilingAcq parameter, 366
ceilingRet parameter, 366
cell phone sales (S curves),
    418–420, 423–424
centered moving averages,
    236–237
ceteris paribus,
    190, 217
Change Data Source option
    (PivotTables), 8
ChapStick pricing (demand
    curves), 96–99
charts, Excel. *See* Excel charts
Chase Bank (neural networks),
    252
check boxes for controlling
    chart data, 45–47
Chi Square Test, 319
Chiang, Mung, 634
chocolate preferences (discrete
    choice analysis),
    305–309
choice-based conjoint analysis,
    280
churn rate, 328
class separation, 404
Classic PivotTable
    Wizard, 28
classification
    *Classification and Regression
        Trees* (Chapman and
        Hall), 409
    error, 405, 410
    matrix (linear discriminant
        analysis), 589–590
    proportional (linear
        discriminant analysis),
        590
classification algorithms
    linear discriminant analysis.
        See linear discriminant
        analysis
    Naive Bayes classifier,
        581–586, 592
    overview, 577
click-through rate (PPC
    advertising), 533
closeness centrality (network
    nodes), 623–624

cluster analysis. *See also*
        clustering U.S. cities
    vs. decision trees, 408–409
    segmenting customers with,
        271
clustering U.S. cities
    cluster analysis, 378–379
    determining correct number
        of clusters, 386
    finding optimal clusters with
        Solver, 380–382
    identifying clusters, 379–380
    interpretation of clusters,
        384–386
    overview, 378–379
    setting up Solver model for,
        382–384
    standardizing demographic
        attributes, 379–380
coefficients
    coefficient of innovation, 428
    logistic regression, 293
    multiple linear regressions,
        182
    regression, 185
collaborative filtering
    item-based, 398–400
    item-based vs. user-based,
        400–401
    Netflix Prize Competition,
        401
    user-based, 393–397
*Collective Dynamics of 'small-
    world' networks* (Nature),
    631
column graphs
    adding product images to,
        32–34
    creating, 30
Column Labels zone
    (PivotTables), 6
Column Sparklines, 51
combination charts (Excel)
    adding labels/tables to charts,
        34–36
    adding product images to
        column graphs, 32–34
    basics of, 29–32

communalities (PCA),
    555–556
competition (pricing), 136
complementary products,
    pricing (Solver), 94–96
computer hardware (price
    bundling), 109–110
Conditional Formatting
    Formula option (Excel),
    464
Conditional Formatting icon
    sets (Excel), 43
conditional probability,
    578–579
conjoint analysis
    adaptive/hybrid, 280
    choice-based, 280
    *On the Creation of Acceptable
        Conjoint Analysis
        Experimental Designs*
        (Decision Sciences),
        273
    developing conjoint
        simulators, 277–279
    full profile. *See* full profile
        conjoint analysis
    generating product profiles
        with Solver, 272–276
    overview, 263
    product sets/attributes/levels,
        263–265
    segmenting markets with,
        271, 386–391
    value-based pricing with,
        271–272
connectors (*The Tipping
    Point*), 644
constraints on changing cells
    (Solver model), 91
consumer surplus
    bundling products to extract,
        108
    defined, 107–108
contagion model (networks),
    641–646
continuous spending
    (advertising)
    defined, 505
    vs. pulsing, 511–514

contrasts (one-way ANOVA),
601–603
Conversion Rate (PPC
advertising), 531–533
Copernican Principle
basics of, 439–440
simulating remaining life of
products with, 440–441
corpus (text mining), 664
CORREL function (Excel),
174, 395
correlations, sample, 544–548
correlations between variables
finding with Data Analysis
Add-in, 172–174
"regression toward the
mean" and, 174
summarizing linear
relationships with,
170–172
Cost per Click (PPC
advertising), 532–534
cost plus pricing, 271
count format (data), 298–299
COUNT function (Excel), 71
COUNTBLANK function
(Excel), 71
COUNTIF function (Excel),
69–72
COUNTIFS functions (Excel),
72–74, 406, 582
Counting Your Customers:
Who Are They and What
Will They Do Next?
(Management Science),
334
country clubs (two-part
tariffs), 129
Courtyard by Marriott:
Designing a Hotel
Facility with Consumer-
Based Marketing Models
(Interfaces), 264
covariances
of linear combinations of
variables, 547–548
sample covariance, 543–544

Create PivotTable
dialog box, 4
credit card transactions
(neural networks), 252
Credit Union (forecasting).
See forecasting based on
special events
critical values formula
(ANOVA), 603
cross-sectional data, 179
crosstabs analysis (ESPN
magazine), 25–27
currentretentionrate
parameter, 366
currentspendpercustomer
parameter, 366
curves for modeling resource-
response relationships,
484–489
customer lifetime value
Customer Lifetime Value:
Foundations and Trends
in Marketing (Now
Publishing), 335
customer value multiplier,
328, 331
estimating active customers,
334–335
Friday Night Lights (FNL),
333–334
ideas to enhance customer
value model, 335–336
multiplier formula, 331
overview, 327
sensitivity analysis,
measuring with two-
way data tables, 330
template, 328–330
varying customer margins,
331–333
customers
customer-centric approach to
valuation. See valuation
(customer value)
finding ideal points on
perceptual maps,
570–574

life cycles of, 347
Manage Marketing by the
Customer Equity Test
(Harvard Business
Review), 365
Managing Customers as
Investments (Pearson
Prentice-Hall), 328
optimizing acquisition/
retention spending on,
368–373
relationship between
spending and
acquisition/retention of,
365–367

D
data
controlling chart data with
check boxes, 45–47
Data Analysis Add-in,
172–174, 179–181
Data Analysis and Business
Modeling with Excel
2010, 42
Data Analysis dialog box,
596
data mining legends, 453
Data Set Manager, 254–255
Data Validation drop-down
box, 328–329
rule for summarizing data
sets, 68
rule of thumb for
summarizing data sets,
68, 70–71
slicing/dicing sales data. See
PivotTables (Excel)
Strategic Database Marketing
(McGraw-Hill), 465
summarizing marketing data.
See Excel charts
summarizing with statistical
functions. See statistical
functions (Excel)

summarizing with Subtotals
    feature, 74–77
typical values for data sets,
    64–67
data points. *See also* outliers
    (data points)
forecasting sales from,
    495–501
Data Tables
measuring sensitivity
    analysis with, 330
recalculation tip, 351
Database Marketing (Springer),
    335, 394
day of the week effect on sales
    (La Petit Bakery), 15–16
*Decision Calculus Modeling at
    Syntex Labs* (Interfaces),
    486
decision trees
vs. cluster analysis, 408–409
CART algorithm, 409–411
constructing, 404–408
interpreting, 408
overview, 403–404
pruning, 409–410
deflating intentions data (Bass
    model), 434–435
degree centrality (network
    nodes), 621–622
Deighton, John, 365
demand curves
for all products, finding with
    SolverTable, 101–103
estimating (revenue
    management), 144–146
estimating linear and power,
    85–90
forms of, 86–90
pricing using subjectively
    estimated, 96–99
willingness to pay and
    (nonlinear pricing),
    124–125
demographics
analyzing effect on sales (La
    Petit Bakery), 21–25

clustering by attributes,
    378–379
standardizing demographic
    attributes (clustering),
    379–380
dependent variables
in neural networks, 249
nonlinear relationships with
    independent variables,
    192
relationships to independent
    variables, 161–162
Dhoakia, Utpal, 353–357
Diffusion of Innovations (Free
    Press), 415
direct mail
optimizing campaigns with
    Solver, 465–468
targeting with neural
    networks, 251
DIRECTV. *See also* cable TV
    subscribers (customer
    value)
Base model, 431–434
discount rate, per period, 328
discount sales, 138–141
discrete choice analysis
chocolate preferences,
    305–309
*Discrete Choice Methods with
    Simulation* (Cambridge
    University Press), 304
Discrete Choice *Modeling
    and Air Travel Demand*
    (Ashgate Publishing),
    317–319
discrete choice theory, 280
dynamic discrete choice,
    315–316
evaluating brand equity,
    313–314
incorporating price/brand
    equity into, 309–311
Independence of Irrelevant
    Alternatives (IIA)
    assumption, 316–317
overview, 303

price elasticity and, 317–318
pricing optimization,
    311–313
random utility theory,
    303–305
testing for significance in,
    314–315
discriminant analysis
    (regression), 251
discriminant score (linear
    discriminant analysis),
    587
Disney World (bundling
    products), 108
documents (text mining)
defined, 664
term frequency/inverse
    document frequency
    score (tf-idf), 666–668
Dominick's Finer Foods (shelf
    space allocation), 492
Dreze, Xavier, 492
dummy variables, 187–188,
    268–270
dynamic discrete choice,
    315–316

E

eating habits (PCA), 557
*Economic Prediction Using
    Neural Networks: The
    Case of IBM Daily Stock
    Returns*, 250
Efficient Market Hypothesis,
    671
eigenvalues, 555
elasticity, price
demand curves, 86–90
discrete choice analysis,
    317–318
property of uniform cross
    elasticity, 318
elevators, directing with
    neural networks, 252
empirical generalization, 433

Empirical Generalizations and Marketing Science: A Personal View (Marketing Science), 433
ending credits (customers), 371
entropy, 405
epidemic model (*The Tipping Point*), 647–650
Equation 4 model (advertising), 509–511
error terms (linear regressions)
  basics of, 178
  nonconstant variance (heteroscedasticity), 197–198
  nonindependent, 198–199
  normally distributed, 196–197
errors/residuals, 167–168
ESPN magazine advertising budget (Naive Bayes), 586
ESPN magazine subscribers (demographics)
  analyzing ages of, 21–22
  analyzing gender of, 22–23
  array formulas for summarizing, 78–79
  constructing crosstabs analysis of age /income, 25
  describing income distribution of, 23–24
  describing location of, 24
  overview, 21
estimating Bass model, 428–430
evaluating user similarity, 394
Evolutionary algorithms, 113
Evolutionary engine, 92
Evolutionary Solver
  basics of, 112–115
  finding optimal bundle prices with, 111–118
  finding optimal linear classification rules with, 587–591

generating product profiles with, 272–276
maximizing lift of product categories, 454–456
maximizing quantity discounts with, 520–522
MDS analysis of U.S. city distances, 560–566
nonlinear pricing strategies and, 123–124, 126
optimizing direct mail campaigns with, 465–468
optimizing three-way lift with, 451–453
running model multiple times, 391
setting Mutation rate with, 384, 522
Excel
Analysis ToolPak, 293
array functions, 59–60
AVERAGE function, 65
AVERAGEIF/AVERAGEIFS functions, 72–74, 599
BINOMDIST function, 657–658
calculating best-fitting trend lines with, 167
Conditional Formatting Formula option, 464
Conditional Formatting icon sets, 43
CORREL function, 174, 395
COUNT function, 71
COUNTBLANK function, 71
COUNTIF/COUNTIFS functions, 69–74, 406, 582
Excel 2010 Data Analysis and Business Modeling (Microsoft Press), 65
Excel Solver. *See* Excel Solver
FREQUENCY function, 61–62
GETPIVOTDATA function, 25–27, 52–54
GOAL SEEK command, 433

HLOOKUP function, 99
IFERROR function, 42
INDIRECT function, 273, 275
INTERCEPT function, 162–166, 170
KURT function, 196
LARGE function, 69
MATCH function, 41, 112, 396–397
matrix multiplication and transpose in, 545–546
MEDIAN function, 65
MMULT function, 546
MODE function, 65
OFFSET function, 560–561
outlines, 77
PERCENTILE.EXC/ PERCENTRANK.EXC functions, 68–69
RAND() function, 349–350
RANDBETWEEN function, 356–358
Report Filter, 11–14
RSQ function, 162–166, 170
SKEW function, 64
Slicers feature, 11–14
SLOPE function, 170
SMALL function, 69
statistical functions. *See* statistical functions (Excel)
STDEV function, 67
STEYX function, 169
SUMIF/SUMIFS functions, 69–74
TABLE feature, 39, 52–53
TEXT function, 42
TRANSPOSE function, 59–60
TREND function, 207–208
Trendline feature, 96
VAR function, 67
VLOOKUP function, 15
VLOOKUP function/ formulas, 462
XNPV and XIRR functions, 339–340, 345

Excel charts
combination charts. *See*
    combination charts
    (Excel)
controlling data with check
    boxes, 45–47
dynamically updating labels,
    40–43
GETPIVOTDATA for end-
    of-week sales reports,
    52–54
overview, 29
PivotCharts, 36–38
sparklines for multiple data
    series, 48–51
summarizing monthly sales-
    force rankings, 43–45
updating automatically,
    39–40
Excel Solver
activating, 90
building special forecasting
    models with. *See*
    forecasting based on
    special events
defining Solver model, 90–91
finding optimal clusters with,
    380–382
generating product profiles
    with (conjoint analysis),
    272–276
modeling trends/seasonality
    with, 228–231
optimizing acquisition/
    retention spending, 367,
    370, 372–373
pricing multiple products
    with SolverTable,
    99–103
pricing razors, 92–94
pricing razors with
    complementary
    products, 94–96
Select a Solving Method
    drop-down menu,
    91–92
setting up model for cluster
    analysis of U.S cities,
    382–384

Solver Parameters dialog
    box, 97–98
Two-Way SolverTable, 101
*An Explanation of Linear
    Programming in Media
    Selection* (Journal of
    Marketing Research),
    517
eyeball approach, 339
E-ZPass example (conjoint
    simulator), 278

F

Farley, John, 429
feasible solutions (Solver
    model), 92
Fidelity Corporation (neural
    networks), 250
Field List (PivotTables), 5–8,
    17, 28
filtering, collaborative. *See*
    collaborative filtering
forecasting
accuracy of regression
    forecasts, 183
airline miles with neural
    networks, 258–259
causal, 177
future months (Winter's
    Method), 246
improving accuracy of
    (movie revenues),
    498–499
movie revenues,
    495–498
movie revenues with 3 weeks
    of revenue, 499–501
movie revenues with Twitter,
    669–670
new product sales with Bass
    model, 431–434
one-way ANOVA, 599–601
sales for future quarters,
    237–238
sales from few data points,
    495–501
sales with Bass model,
    431–434

sales with no interactions
    (two-way ANOVA),
    614
sales with Ratio to Moving
    Average Forecasting
    Method, 235–238
software sales with
    SCAN*PRO model,
    475–479
stock markets with Twitter,
    670–671
*Technological Forecasting
    for Decision-Making*
    (McGraw-Hill), 425
forecasting based on special
    events
building basic model,
    213–217
checking randomness of
    forecast errors,
    221–222
evaluating forecast accuracy,
    217–218
refining base model,
    218–221
Format Data Series,
    32–33
Format Trendline
    dialog box, 97
frequency coding (text
    mining), 666–668
FREQUENCY function
    (Excel), 61–62
Friday Night Lights (FNL) TV
    show, 333–334
*Frontiers of Econometric
    Behavior* (Academic
    Press), 317–318
full profile conjoint
    analysis
determining product profiles,
    266–267
overview, 265
ranking attributes/levels,
    270–271
running regression with
    dummy variables,
    268–270
shortcomings of, 279

G

Gangnam style video, 653
gender of subscribers,
    analyzing (ESPN
    magazine), 22–23
*A general theory of bibliometric
    and other cumulative
    advantage processes*
    (Journal of American
    Society of Information
    Sciences), 635
Generalized Second Price
    Auction (GSP), 534
genetic algorithms, 113
GETPIVOTDATA function
    (Excel)
    for end-of-week sales
        reports, 52–54
    pulling data from
        PivotTables with,
        25–27
Gini Index, 405, 410
Gladwell, Malcolm, 641–642,
    644
Global Seek command, 89
Goal Seek, 89, 433
Goldberg, David, 113
Golliher, Sean, 637
Gompertz curves
    vs. Pearl curves, 425
    allocating supermarket shelf
        space with, 492
    defined, 485
    fitting S curves to data with,
        422–424
Google AdWords auctions,
    533–536
great salespeople (*The Tipping
    Point*), 645
Greek Yogurt (decision trees),
    404–408
Green, Paul, 566
GRG Multistart engine
    determining values in Bass
        model, 429
    finding values fitting sets of
        data, 423

in SCAN*PRO model, 423
setting bounds on changing
    cells, 419, 474
GRG Nonlinear engine, 92
GRG Nonlinear option, 101
group means, testing
    (ANOVA),
    595–596
Groupon offers
    analyzing with Monte Carlo
        simulation, 357–359
    lifetime customer value and,
        327
    pizza parlor example,
        353–357
    using one-way data tables to
        simulate, 357–359
Grucca, Thomas, 252

H

HAL Computer (linear
    multiple regressions),
    178–186
health club business valuation.
    See valuation (customer
    value)
Henderson, Bruce, 136
heteroscedasticity, 197
histograms
    summarizing data with,
        59–64
    summarizing Monte Carlo
        simulation results with,
        359
HLOOKUP function (Excel),
    99
Hollywood Stock Exchange
    (HSX), 670
Honda TV advertising,
    518–527
Housing Starts (Ratio
    to Moving Average
    Forecasting), 238
Hughes, Arthur, 465
Hypothesis of No Linear
    Regression, 182

I

ideal points on perceptual
    maps, 570–574
*Idiot's Bayes - not so stupid
    after all?* (International
    Statistical Review), 592
IFERROR function (Excel), 42
imitators (Bass model), 427
impressions (online
    advertising), 530
income of subscribers,
    analyzing (ESPN
    magazine), 23–25
Independence of Irrelevant
    Alternatives (IIA)
    assumption, 316–317
independent variables
    dealing with insignificant
        (regressions),
        184–185
    determining significant
        (regressions), 183
    logistic regression with
        multiple, 296–298
    in neural networks, 249
    nonlinear relationships with
        dependent variables,
        192
    relationships with dependent
        variables, 161–162
INDIRECT function (Excel),
    273, 275
inflection points (S curves),
    415–416
Information Science (Oxford
    University Press), 405
innovators (Bass model), 427
input cells (neural networks),
    249
intentions data, deflating (Bass
    model), 434–435
interactions
    two-way ANOVA with,
        614–616
    of variables (linear
        regressions), 193–195
intercept (constant term), 178

INTERCEPT function (Excel), 162–166, 170
Interfaces (1988), 492
Interpretation by physicians of clinical laboratory results (New England Journal of Medicine), 580
interval data, 560
Interviews with Real Traders (Ward Systems Group), 250
inverse rankings (product profiles), 268
iPod sales (S curves), 420–422
IRR (internal rate of return), 339–340, 343
Issenberg, Sasha, 403
item-based collaborative filtering, 398–401

J

J.Crew (RFM analysis), 460–468

K

keywords (online advertising), 529
Klemz, Bruce, 252
Klout scores (networks), 636–637
kRet parameter, 366
Kumar, Piyush, 671
KURT function (Excel), 196
kurtosis, 196–197

L

L value, definition/ computation of (network nodes), 628–630
La Petit Bakery sales
analyzing effect of promotions on, 20–21
analyzing product seasonality, 16–18
analyzing yearly trends, 19–20
day of the week effect on, 15–16
overview, 14–15
labels
adding to charts, 34–36
dynamically updating in charts, 40–43
LARGE function (Excel), 69
learning curves (pricing), 135–136
least squares estimates (coefficients), 182
least-squares lines (Excel), 167
Lee, A.M., 517
Legs value (staying power), 496–497, 499–500
Lehmann, Donald, 331, 429
levels of product attributes, 264–265
lifts
calculating for multiple two-way product combinations, 448–449
computing for two products, 445–449
computing three-way product, 449–453
optimizing store layouts with, 454–456
linear combinations of variables, 547–548
linear demand curves, 86–88
linear discriminant analysis
classification matrix, 589–590
classification rules involving nonlinearities/ interactions, 591
evaluating classification rule quality, 590
finding most important attributes, 589
finding optimal linear classification rule, 587–589
linear classification with more than two groups, 590–591
model validation, 591
overview, 586–587
linear forecasting models, 230
linear media allocation, 517–520
linear pricing, 107
linear regression. *See* simple linear regression
linear relationships, summarizing with correlations, 170–172
LINEST function (Excel), 388–390
links, measuring importance of (networks), 626–628
Little, John, 484
loading of variables on principal components, 552
loans, determining with neural networks, 252
local cluster coefficient (C) (networks), 630
location of subscribers, analyzing (ESPN magazine), 24
Lodish, Leonard, 486, 492
Log Likelihoods, 309–311
log odds ratio, 289
Logistic curves
vs. Gompertz curves, 425
basics of, 418–420
logistic regression
dialog box, 294
estimating model with maximum likelihood method, 290–293
estimating probabilities with, 292–293
interpreting coefficients, 293
model, 289–290
with multiple independent variables, 296–298
necessity of, 286–289

overview, 285–286
performing with count data, 298–299
StatTools. *See* StatTools
logit regression model, 289
logit transformation, 289
Lohan, Paris, 493
Lonsdale, Robert, 517
Loyalty Effect (Reichfeld and Teal), 330
Luenberger, David, 405

M

machine learning, 668
MAD (Mean Absolute Deviation), 259, 497–498
magazine subscribers (logistic regression), 286–299
Manage Marketing by the Customer Equity Test (Harvard Business Review), 365
Managing Customers as Investments (Pearson Prentice-Hall), 328
Mao's Palace restaurant (linear regression), 162–168
MAPE (Mean Absolute Percent Error), 247, 476–477, 497
margins, varying customer, 331–333
markdown pricing (revenue management), 153–155
market basket analysis
computing lift for two products, 445–449
computing three-way product lifts, 449–453
data mining legends, 453
optimizing store layouts with lift, 454–456
market values, using customer value to estimate, 344
marketing
Market Facts of Canada, 403
Marketing Analytics (Admiral Press), 523

Marketing Decision Models (Prentice-Hall), 509
Marketing Research (Prenctice-Hall), 556
viral. *See* viral marketing
Markov Chains, 347–349
Martino, Joseph, 425
MATCH function (Excel), 41, 112, 396–397
matrix multiplication/matrix transposes (Excel), 545–546
mavens (*The Tipping Point*), 645
maximum likelihood method, 290–293, 307–310
MBA applicants (linear discriminant analysis), 590–591
McGrayne, Sharon, 579
media selection models
linear media allocation, 517–520
Monte Carlo media allocation simulation, 522–527
overview, 517
quantity discounts and, 520–522
MEDIAN function (Excel), 65
Mellon Bank (neural networks), 252
A Meta-Analysis of Applications of Diffusion Models (Journal of Marketing Research), 429
Milgram, Stanley, 628
misclassification rate (decision trees), 409
mixed bundling (prices), 110
MMULT function (Excel), 546
MODE function (Excel), 65
A Model to Improve the Baseline Estimation of Retail Sales, 472
Models and Managers: The Concept of a Decision Calculus (Management Science), 484

Monte Carlo simulation
analyzing Groupon offers with, 357–359
basics of, 347–348
media allocation simulation, 522–527
modeling customer values using, 347–353
predicting market initiative successes using, 353–357
summarizing results with histograms, 359
movie revenues
forecasting with 3 weeks of revenue, 499–501
predicting, 495–498
predicting with Twitter, 669–670
movie reviews (text mining), 668
moving averages
eliminating seasonality with, 225–228
Ratio to Moving Average Forecasting Method, 235–238
multicollinearity (linear regressions), 204–207
multidimensional scaling (MDS)
analysis of breakfast foods, 566–570
analysis of U.S. city distances, 560–566
finding ideal points on perceptual maps, 570–574
similarity data and, 559–560
multinomial logit model, 304
multinomial logit version of discrete choice, 319
multiple linear regression
autocorrelation, 198–204
basics of, 178–179
heteroscedasticity, 197
interactions of variables, 193
interpreting output of, 182–186

multicollinearity, 204–207
nonlinear relationships
  between variables, 192
normally distributed error
  terms, 196–197
overview, 177
predicting potential
  customer value with,
  335
qualitative independent
  variables in, 186–191
R^2 and, 168
running with Data Analysis
  Add-in, 179–181
testing for nonlinearities/
  interactions, 193–195
testing validity of regression
  assumptions, 195–196
validation of, 207–209
multiplicative model for
  estimating trends/
  seasonality, 231–233
multiplier formula (customer
  value), 331
Multistart option (Solver), 232
Mutation rate (Evolutionary
  Solver), 114, 385
mxn matrix, 545–546

N

Naive Bayes classifier
  basics of, 581–586
  *Idiot's Bayes - not so stupid
    after all*? (International
    Statistical Review), 592
  virtues of, 592
named ranges (two product
  lifts), 447
Nash equilibrium, 315–316
negative autocorrelation, 200
negatively skewed histograms,
  63
neighbor nodes (networks),
  630
Netflix Prize Competition
  (collaborative filtering),
  401

networks. *See also* neural
  networks
  defining/computing L value,
  628–630
  Klout scores, 636–637
  local cluster coefficient (C),
  630
  measuring importance of
  links, 626–628
  network contagion,
  641–646
  A Networked Life (Cambridge
  University Press), 401
  Networks Illustrated
  (Edwiser Scholastic
  Press), 634
  nodes. *See* nodes (networks)
  Power Law for, 634–636
  random, 631
  regular, 631–633
  Rich Get Richer theory,
  634–636
  scale-free, 635
  six degrees of separation,
  628
  Strogatz and Watts network,
  633–634
Neumann, James von, 348
neural networks
  analyzing scanner data with,
  252
  credit card and loan
  applications, 252
  direct mail targeting with,
  251
  directing elevators with,
  252
  driving cars with, 251
  *Economic Prediction Using
  Neural Networks: The
  Case of IBM Daily Stock
  Returns*, 250
  forecasting airline miles
  with, 258–259
  overview, 249
  predicting bankruptcies
  with, 251–252
  predicting sales with,
  253–258

predicting stock markets
  with, 250
  regression and, 249–250
  NeuralTools (Excel add-in),
  249
  *New Way to Measure
  Consumers' Judgments*
  (Harvard Business
  Review), 265
  New-Product Diffusion Models
  (Springer), 433
nodes (networks)
  betweenness centrality,
  624–626
  closeness centrality,
  623–624
  degree centrality, 621–622
  entropy of (decision trees),
  405–407
  measuring importance of,
  621
  seeded, 645
nonlinear pricing
  defined, 107
  demand curves and
  willingness to pay,
  124–125
  optimizing nonstandard
  quantity discounts,
  127–128
  optimizing standard quantity
  discounts, 125–127
  optimizing two-part tariffs,
  129–131
  overview, 123–124
  profit maximizing with,
  125–131
nonlinear relationships
  between variables, 192
nonmetric MDS, 560
nonstandard quantity
  discounts (nonlinear
  pricing), 127–128
NPV (Net Present Value) of
  cash flows,
  339–340, 343
Null Hypothesis
  ANOVA, 596, 602
  linear regressions, 182

O

objective (target) cells (Solver model), 90
OFFSET function (Excel), 560–561
Old Spice video, 653
On the Creation of Acceptable Conjoint Analysis Experimental Designs (Decision Sciences), 273
One Way TV Advertisements Work (Journal of Marketing Research), 505
One-way Analysis of Variance (ANOVA). *See* ANOVA (Analysis of Variance), One-way
one-way data tables
  measuring sensitivity analysis with, 343–344
  One-Way SolverTable, 101
  using to simulate Groupon offers, 357–359
Online Ad Auctions (American Economic Review), 533
ordinal data, 560
orthogonal designs (product profiles), 266–267
Orthogonal Main-Effect Plans for Asymmetrical Factorial Experiments (Technometric), 266–267
orthogonality (covariance), 549
Otis Elevator (neural networks), 252
outliers (data points)
  defined, 68
  finding (movie revenues), 499
  in regressions, 183–184
  spotting omitted special forecasting factors, 220
  spotting omitted special forecasting factors with, 217–218

outlines, Excel, 77
output cells (neural networks), 249
overbooking models, 151–153

P

Pareto 80–20 Principle, 10–11
Pay per Click (PPC) advertising
  basics of, 529–530
  Bid Simulator feature (AdWords), 536
  Google AdWords auctions, 533–535
  profitability model for, 531–532
peak sales, time/value of, 430
Pearl curves
  basics of, 418–420
  vs. Gompertz curves, 425
per period discount rate, 328
per period retention rate, 328
PERCENTILE.EXC/ PERCENTRANK.EXC functions (Excel), 68–69
perceptual maps (product comparisons), 570–574
periods parameter (customer margin values), 332
Peterson, Ann Furr, 252
PivotCharts (Excel), 36–38
PivotTables (Excel)
  analyzing demographics effect on sales, 21–25
  analyzing La Petit Bakery sales. *See* La Petit Bakery sales
  analyzing True Colors Hardware sales. *See* True Color Hardware sales
  Create PivotTable dialog box, 4

pulling data with GETPIVOTDATA function, 25–27
pizza parlor
  customer acquisition/ retention spending, 368–370
  Groupon offers, 353–357
Planning Media Schedules in the Presence of Dynamic Advertising Quality (Marketing Science), 513
Poisson random variables, 656–658
positive autocorrelation, 199
positively skewed histograms, 63
power company (nonlinear pricing), 125–128
power curves, 484–486
power demand curves, 86–87, 88–90
Power Law for networks, 634–636
Power Pricing (Dolan), 96
Practical Text Mining (Academic Press), 669
Predicting the Future with Social Media, 669
Predictions (Simon and Schuster), 415
Price, D. J., 635
price bundling
  extracting consumer surplus with, 107–108
  finding optimal bundle prices with Evolutionary Solver, 111–118
  mixed bundling, 110
  overview, 107–108
  pure bundling, 109–110
pricing
  cost plus, 271
  determining single profit- maximizing price (Bates Motel), 146–147

dropping prices over time, 135–138

markdown (revenue management), 153–155

multiple products with SolverTable, 99–103

optimization of (discrete choice analysis), 311–313

optimizing with Excel Solver, 90–96

Power Pricing (Dolan), 96

price elasticity (demand curves), 86–90

price elasticity (discrete choice analysis), 317–318

price reversals, 116–117

price skimming, 136–138

(price–unit cost)*demand formula, 96, 102

razors, 92–94

razors with complementary products, 94–96

reservation prices, 124

using subjectively estimated demand curves, 96–99

value-based (conjoint analysis), 271–272

principle components analysis (PCA)

applications of, 556–557

basics of, 548–550

communalities, 555–556

determining number of PCs to retain, 554–555

finding first principal component, 550–552

finding PC3 through PC6, 554

finding second principal component, 552–554

overview, 541–542

prior probabilities, 579

probability, conditional, 578–579

probit regression, 304–305

product profiles. *See also* conjoint analysis

defined, 263

generating with Evolutionary Solver, 272–276

ranking, 266–267

products

New-Product Diffusion Models (Springer), 433

product sets/attributes/levels (conjoint analysis), 263–265

Profit per Click (PPC advertising), 532

profitability model for PPC, 531–532

promotions, analyzing effect on sales (La Petit Bakery), 20–21

property of uniform cross elasticity, 318

proportional classification (linear discriminant analysis), 590

pruning decision trees, 409–410

pulsing (advertising)

vs. continuous spending, 511–514

defined, 505

pure bundling (prices), 109–110

Q

qualitative independent variables in regression analysis, 186–191

quantitative independent variables in regression analysis, 186

quantity discounts

defined, 123

in media selection, 520–522

standard/nonstandard, 125–128

R

R2 value, defining, 168–169

RAND() function (Excel), 349–350

RANDBETWEEN function (Excel), 356–358

random forecast errors, 221–222

random networks, 631

random utility theory, 303–305

random variables

Binomial/Poisson, 656–658

defined, 356

randomized block designs (two-way ANOVA), 608

ranking product attributes/levels (conjoint analysis), 270–271

Rao, Vithala, 566

Ratio to Moving Average Forecasting Method

applying to monthly data, 238

calculating moving averages /centered moving averages, 236

computing seasonal indexes, 237

fitting trend lines to centered moving averages, 237

forecasting sales for future quarters, 237–238

overview, 235–236

Red Bus/Blue Bus Problem, 316–317

regression

discriminant analysis version of, 251

logistic. *See* logistic regression

model to predict sales, 253–254

multiple linear. *See* multiple linear regression

neural networks and,
    249–250
regression coefficients, 178,
    185
"regression toward the
    mean" (correlations),
    174
running with dummy
    variables (product
    attributes), 268–270
regressions
  accuracy of predictions from
    trend lines. *See also*
    simple linear regression
regular networks, 631–633
Reichfeld, Frederic, 330
Report Filter (Excel), 11–14
Report Filter zone
    (PivotTables), 6
reservation prices, 124
residuals/errors, 167–168
resources
  allocating scarce, 483–484
  curves for modeling
    resource-response
    relationships, 484–489
retention rate
  per period, 328
  retentionrate parameter,
    366–367
revenue management
  Bates Motel. *See* Bates Motel
    (revenue management)
  markdown pricing, 153–155
  overbooking models,
    151–153
  overview, 143–144
RFM (Recency/Frequency/
    Monetary Value) analysis
  computing R, F, and M,
    460–462
  direct mail campaign, 251
  identifying profit-yielding
    combinations, 462–465
  overview, 459–460
  success story, 465
Rich Get Richer theory
    (networks), 634–636
RISKOptimizer, 523–526

Rogers, Everett, 415
Root Mean Squared Error
    (RMSE), 401
Row Labels zone
    (PivotTables), 5
RSQ function (Excel),
    162–166, 170
rule of thumb for summarizing
    data sets, 68,
    70–71
rxn matrix, 545

S

S curves
  basics of, 415–417
  fitting with seasonality,
    420–422
  Gompertz curves and,
    422–424
  Logistic curves and,
    418–420
sales
  analyzing at Mao's Palace
    restaurant, 162–166
  Copernican Principle to
    predict future of,
    439–441
  discount, 138–141
  forecasting from few data
    points, 495–501
  forecasting with Bass model,
    431–434
  forecasting with no
    interactions (two-way
    ANOVA), 614
  forecasting with Ratio
    to Moving Average
    Forecasting Method,
    235–238
  forecasting with SCAN*PRO
    model, 475–479
  great salespeople (*The
    Tipping Point*), 645
  identifying relationship
    to marketing effort,
    483–484
  La Petit Bakery. *See* La Petit
    Bakery sales

*A Model to Improve the
    Baseline Estimation of
    Retail Sales*, 472
modeling marketing
    response to sales force
    effort, 484–489
modeling trends and
    seasonality of, 225–233
modeling trends in
    (software), 479–480
modeling with SCAN*PRO
    model, 472–475
optimizing allocation of sales
    effort, 489–492
predicting with neural
    networks, 253–258
setting quotas, 186
simulating with Bass model,
    435–437
summarizing monthly sales-
    force rankings, 43–45
True Color Hardware. *See*
    True Color Hardware
    sales
using multiple linear
    regressions to forecast.
    See multiple linear
    regressions
salvage values (customers),
    371
sample correlations, 544–548
sample covariance, 543–544
sample standard deviation(s),
    67, 543
sample variance of data sets,
    67
scale-free networks, 635
SCAN*PRO model
  forecasting software sales
    with, 475–479
  modeling Snickers sales
    with, 472–475
  overview, 471–472
scanner data, analyzing with
    neural networks, 252
seasonal indexes, 228, 231,
    237
seasonality. *See also* Winter's
    Method

additive Solver model for
estimating, 228–231
eliminating with moving
averages, 225–228
fitting S curves with,
420–422
multiplicative Solver model
for estimating, 231–233
of products, analyzing (La
Petit Bakery), 16–18
seeded nodes, 645
segmenting customers (Bates
Motel)
with capacity constraints,
150
with two prices, 147–149
segmenting markets with
conjoint analysis, 271,
386–391
sensitivity analysis
measuring with one-way data
tables, 343–344
measuring with two-way
data tables, 330
sentiment analysis (text
mining)
of airline tweets, 669
defined, 664
predicting movie revenues
with, 670
sets, product, 264–265
Sharda, Ramesh, 252
*Shelf Management and Space
Elasticity*, 492
Significance F values (multiple
linear regressions), 182,
195
similarity data (MDS), 559–
560, 567
simple linear regression
accuracy of predictions from
trend lines, 169–170
analyzing sales at Mao's
Palace restaurant,
162–166
calculating best-fitting trend
lines with Excel, 167
computing errors/residuals,
167–168

defining R2 values, 168–169
independent/dependent
variable relationships,
161–162
SLOPE/INTERCEPT/RSQ
functions, 170
Simplex LP engine (Solver),
91–92
simulating
conjoint simulators, 277–279
new product sales with Bass
model, 435–437
remaining product life with
Copernican Principle,
440–441
Single Factor option (Data
Analysis dialog box), 596
six degrees of separation
(networks), 628
SKEW function (Excel), 64
skimming, price, 136–138
Slicers feature (Excel),
11–14
slicing/dicing sales data. *See*
PivotTables (Excel)
SLOPE function (Excel), 170
SMALL function (Excel), 69
smoothing methods, 241
smoothing parameters/
constants (Winter's
Method), 242, 244–245
Snickers bars (SCAN*PRO
model), 471–475
Solver, Evolutionary. *See*
Evolutionary Solver
Solver, Excel. *See* Excel Solver
SolverTable
finding demand curves with,
101–103
pricing multiple products
with, 99–103
*Some Optimization Problems
in Advertising Media*
(Journal of the
Operational Research
Society), 517
Sorger, Stephen, 523
sparklines for multiple data
series, 48–51

spending
modeling relationship
between customer
acquisition/retention
and, 365–367
optimizing acquisition/
retention, 368–373
spentpercustomer parameter,
366
spread about typical data
values, 64
spread of typical value, 64
squared errors, minimizing,
499
standard deviation, sample,
543
standard error of regression
(SER), 169
standard quantity discounts
(nonlinear pricing)
defined, 123
optimizing, 125–127
standardized values, 544–545
standardizing demographic
attributes (clustering),
379–380
states of the world (Bayes
Theorem), 579
statistical functions (Excel)
array formulas for
ESPN subscriber
demographics, 78–79
computing typical values
with, 64–67
COUNTIFS/SUMIFS/
AVERAGEIF/
AVERAGEIFS, 72–74
COUNTIF/SUMIF, 69–72
LARGE/SMALL, 69
overview, 64
PERCENTILE.EXC/
PERCENTRANK.EXC,
68–69
rule for summarizing data
sets, 68
summarizing data with
subtotals, 74–77
summarizing variation with
VAR/STDEV, 67

StatTools
interpreting logistic regression output, 295
logistic regression with multiple independent variables, 296–298
running logistic regression with, 293–295
STDEV function (Excel), 67
steady state margin per customer parameter (customer values), 332
stemming (text mining), 664
STEYX function (Excel), 169
stock markets
predicting with neural networks, 250
predicting with Twitter, 670–671
stopwords (text mining), 664
store layouts, optimizing with lifts, 454–456
Strategic Database Marketing (McGraw-Hill), 465
Strogatz, Steven, 631
Strogatz and Watts network, 633–634
Strogatz-Watts Small World model, 644
structuring unstructured text (text mining), 664–668
Subtotals feature (Excel), 74–77
Sultan, Fareena, 429
Sum of Squared Errors, 599
SUMIF function (Excel), 69–72
SUMIFS function (Excel), 72–74
Super Bowl ads, evaluating with tweets, 671
supermarket shelf space (Gompertz curves), 492
symmetric histograms, 63
Syntex Labs (ADBUG curves), 486–489, 492

T

tables (Excel)
adding to charts, 34–36
summarizing weekly sales data with, 52–53
updating sales data with, 39
Target store (market basket analysis), 453
Technological Forecasting for Decision-Making (McGraw-Hill), 425
term frequency/inverse document frequency score (tf-idf), 666–668
testing
logistic regression hypotheses, 293
for nonlinearities/ interactions (linear regressions), 193–195
for significance in discrete choice analysis, 314–315
validity of regression assumptions, 195–196
TEXT function (Excel), 42
text mining
definitions, 664
evaluating Super Bowl ads with tweets, 671
movie reviews and, 668
overview, 663–664
Practical Text Mining (Academic Press), 669
predicting movie revenues with Twitter, 669–670
predicting stock markets with Twitter, 670–671
sentiment analysis of airline tweets, 669
structuring unstructured text, 664–668
The Theory That Would Not Die (Yale University Press), 579

three-way product lifts, 449–453
Thumbs up? Sentiment Classification using Machine Learning Techniques (Proceedings of EMNNP), 668
time series data, 179
The Tipping Point (Back Bay Books)
Bass version of, 646–650
central thesis of, 646–647
overview, 641
tokens (text mining), 664
Train, Kenneth, 304–305
TRANSPOSE function (Excel), 59–60
trend lines
accuracy of predictions from, 169–170
calculating best-fitting with Excel, 167
fitting quadratic demand curve with, 96–98
Format Trendline dialog box, 97
overlaying 12-month moving average with, 227
trends. *See also* Winter's Method
additive Solver model for estimating, 228–231
fitting trend lines to centered moving averages, 237
multiplicative Solver model for estimating, 231–233
in software sales, modeling, 479–480
TREND function (Excel), 207–208
True Color Hardware sales
calculating revenue for each product, 9–10
calculating sales percentage per store, 4–8
overview, 3–4

Pareto 80–20 Principle, 10–11
Report Filter/Slicers features, 11–14
summarizing revenue by month, 8–9
Twitter
  evaluating Super Bowl ads with, 671
  predicting movie revenues with, 669–670
  predicting stock markets with, 670–671
two-part tariffs (nonlinear pricing)
  defined, 123
  optimizing, 129–131
two-way ANOVA
  basics of, 607–608
  forecasting sales with no interactions, 614
  with interactions, 614–616
  with replication, 611–614
  without replication, 608–610
two-way data tables
  calculating lifts with, 448–449
  measuring sensitivity analysis with, 330
  performing Monte Carlo simulation with, 351–353
two-way product lifts, 446–449
Two-Way SolverTable, 101
typical values for data sets, 64–67

U

Ulam, Stanislaw, 348
updating charts automatically, 39–40
U.S. city distances (MDS analysis), 560–566

user similarity, evaluating, 394
user-based collaborative filtering, 393–397, 400–401

V

validation of multiple linear regressions, 207–209
validity of regression assumptions, testing, 195–196
valuation (customer value)
  analysis of health club business, 340–343
  computing cash flows, 339–340
  estimating business market value using, 344
  Markov Chain model of, 347–353
  measuring sensitivity analysis with one-way tables, 343–344
  modeling with Monte Carlo simulation, 347–353
Values zone (PivotTables), 6
VAR function (Excel), 67
variables. *See also* dependent variables; independent variables
  Binomial random, 524
  Binomial/Poisson random variables, 656–658
  correlations between, 170–174
  nonlinear relationships between, 192
  variable cells, changing (Solver model), 91
Varian, Hal, 533
variance
  of linear combinations of variables, 547–548
  role in ANOVA, 598–599

sample variance, 542–543
Variance Inflation Factor (VIF), 206
Verizon cell phones (price bundling), 111–113
Victory Lab (Random House), 403
viral marketing
  overview, 653
  Watts model. *See* Watts model
VLOOKUP function/formulas (Excel), 15, 462
Volkswagen ad, 671

W

The Wall Street Journal (linear discriminant analysis), 587–591
Wanamaker, John, 505
Ward Systems Group (neural networks), 250
Watts, Duncan, 631, 633–634, 653
Watts model
  basics of, 654–655
  Binomial/Poisson random variables, 656–658
  building viral marketing model, 658–660
  complex version of, 655–656
weak ties (networks), 634, 644
websites for downloading
  NeuralTools Excel add-in, 249
  Predicting the Future with Social Media, 669
  RISKOptimizer package, 523
  SolverTable, 99
websites for further information
  AdWords, 536
  Bud Light ad, 671
  computer driven cars, 250

customer value concept for
banks, 335
*Economic Prediction Using
Neural Networks: The
Case of IBM Daily Stock
Returns*, 250
Gangnam style video, 653
Hollywood Stock Exchange
(HSX) predictions, 670
impression advertising, 530
Interviews with Real Traders,
250
Klout scores, 635
logistic regression for
predicting churn rate,
335
Market Facts of Canada, 403
*A Model to Improve the
Baseline Estimation of
Retail Sales*, 472
neural networks for
predicting market share,
252
*New Way to Measure
Consumers' Judgments*,
265

Old Spice video, 653
positive/negative tweet
words, 669
Sean Golliher, 637
*Shelf Management and Space
Elasticity*, 492
SSRN direct mailing article,
251
Volkswagen ad, 671
White, Halbert, 250
Wiley Publishing (one-way
ANOVA), 596–601
Wilson, Rick, 252
Wingdings 3 font, 43
Win-Loss Sparklines, 51
Winter's Method
estimating smoothing
constants, 244–245
forecasting future months,
246
initializing, 243–244
Mean of Absolute Percentage
Error (MAPE), 247
overview, 241
parameter definitions for,
241–242

Within Groups Sum of
Squares, 599
Wittink, Dirk, 472
Working Capital equation, 345

X

Xbox/PlayStation/Wii (discrete
analysis), 309–316, 318
XNPV/XIRR functions (Excel),
339–340, 345
X-Y Scatter Chart, 42

Y

yearly trends, analyzing (La
Petit Bakery), 19–20
yield management. *See*
revenue management

Z

z scores (clusters), 384–385
Zipf's Law, 638
zones (PivotTables), 5–6